Recommendations of the National Knowledge Commission

Recommendations of the National Knowledge Commission

NATIONAL KNOWLEDGE COMMISSION
GOVERNMENT OF INDIA
NEW DELHI

ACADEMIC FOUNDATION

NEW DELHI

First published in 2009 by

Academic Foundation
4772-73 / 23 Bharat Ram Road, (23 Ansari Road), Darya Ganj, New Delhi - 110 002 (India).
Phones : 23245001 / 02 / 03 / 04. Fax : +91-11-23245005. E-mail : academic@vsnl.com
www : academicfoundation.com

Published in association with :
National Knowledge Commission
Government of India, New Delhi

Recommendations of the National Knowledge Commission

ISBN 13: 978-81-7188-767-5
ISBN 10: 81-7188-767-8

Typeset by Italics India, New Delhi.
Printed and bound in India.

Contents

III Creation

IV Applications

V Services

VI Consultations

Foreword

The National Knowledge Commission (NKC) was set up by the Prime Minister Dr. Manmohan Singh to prepare a blueprint to tap into the enormous reservoir of our knowledge base so that our people can confidently face the challenges of the 21st century. We were conscious that this was a daunting task, which requires not only resources and time but also a bold vision and a long-term focus on speedy implementation.

At the heart of NKC's mandate are five key areas related to ACCESS, CONCEPTS, CREATION, APPLICATIONS and SERVICES. We have addressed the question of how to build a knowledge society from these perspectives, with particular focus on access to knowledge. Under these five focus areas we have covered various subjects related to right to education, languages, translation, libraries, national knowledge network, portals, health information network, school education, vocational education and training, higher education, more students in science and mathematics, professional education, more quality Ph.Ds, open and distance education, open education resources, intellectual property rights, legal framework for public funded research, national science and social science foundation, innovation, entrepreneurship, traditional health systems, agriculture, enhancing quality of life and E-governance.

In most of these areas we organised Working Groups consisting of domain experts from the government, academia, industry, civil society, media and others to make the entire process democratic, transparent and participative. The Working Groups were requested to have various consultations and prepare a white paper for discussion and debate at the Commission. Based on this methodology, a final set of recommendations was agreed upon by the majority of the members of the Commission. As a result, we believe that these recommendations reflect and incorporate the concerns and aspirations of domain experts and other concerned stakeholders.

In the last three years, NKC has submitted around 300 recommendations on 27 subjects in the form of letters to the Prime Minister. These have been widely disseminated in our Reports to the Nation, seminars, conferences, discussions and covered by national and regional media. These recommendations are also accessible through the NKC website in 10 languages. As part of our outreach programme we have organised various conferences and workshops in collaboration with universities, colleges, schools, CII, FICCI, AIMA and others. We have also been reaching out to various state governments to discuss recommendations and associated implementation at the state level. The response from most of the states has been very good.

The UPA's commitment to NKC's vision is reflected in the 11th Five Year Plan adopted by the National Development Council. The Plan places high priority on education as a central instrument for achieving rapid and inclusive growth with specific emphasis on expansion, excellence and equity. This is reflected in the proposed allocation of Rs. 3 trillion, a four-fold increase over the Tenth Plan. The share of education in the total Plan will accordingly increase, from 7.7 to 20 per cent, representing a credible progress towards the target of 6 per cent of GDP. The vision of the Prime Minister and support of our leadership from across the political spectrum is indeed laudable. This is a landmark initiative in the history of government planning. We believe that the education agenda outlined in the 11th Plan is a critical step towards realising the objective of an equitable society. It is also fundamental to our continuing growth, employment generation, infrastructure development and other developmental priorities.

While releasing the first NKC Report to the Nation in January 12, 2007, the PM emphasised that the Commission "must be involved in ensuring the implementation of their innovative ideas". The focus of our work has been on ensuring that while the Central government designs appropriate strategies supported by financial allocations to implement our recommendations, we engage simultaneously with diverse stakeholders to build a groundswell of favourable opinion and assist preparation of implementation strategies at the grassroots. Continuing dialogue with a wide and diverse set of stakeholders has been a critical part of our process, both in the formulation of the recommendations and in the subsequent dissemination.

Regarding implementation, we find that there is indeed a great deal of enthusiasm and emphasis on education as a means of achieving personal growth and development. The growing aspirations of children and parents across the cross-section of society are reflected in an increasing demand for education, which has far exceeded the supply. There is still resistance at various levels in the government to new ideas, experimentation, process re-engineering, external interventions, transparency and accountability, due to rigid organisational structures with territorial mindsets. As a result, the real challenge lies in organisational innovation with new regulatory frameworks, new delivery systems and new processes. In their absence, increasing resources could well result in more of the same things being replicated. Our country is too large, too complex and too diverse for 'one size fits all' solutions. Decentralisation and community participation at the local level would be the key to devising effective programmes for implementation.

We hope that our recommendations find enthusiasm and support at various levels at state and Central government for speedy implementation. We believe that implementation is the key going forward to address three fundamental challenges related to demography, disparity and development. Knowledge, education and innovations are critical to provide opportunities for the poor and underprivileged to reduce disparities in our society. These are equally important to expedite the process of development and to improve productivity, efficiency and reduce cost. To get the real demographic dividends, we need to empower and educate the 550 million young below the age of 25 through proper education to build future growth and prosperity. The destiny of India is in their hands.

While making the recommendations we have been guided by how knowledge will impact the lives of ordinary people of India. We are conscious that knowledge is about farmers having access to accurate information about water, land, weather and fertilisers; students having access to quality education and jobs; scientists having access to laboratories; industry having access to skilled workforce; and people feeling empowered with good governance in a vibrant democracy.

Finally, I want to thank all the members and our young associates for their exceptional hard work, dedication and ongoing support. I would also like to thank the members of various Working Groups and workshops, the Planning Commission, the Prime Minister's Office, and various other individuals and organisations in the government and industry for the their contribution and support.

As we have said in the past, the recommendations of the National Knowledge Commission are really a call to action. It is time to act and implement these recommendations now.

Sam Pitroda
Chairman
National Knowledge Commission

Terms of Reference and Organisation

The National Knowledge Commission (NKC) was constituted on 13th June 2005 as a high level advisory body to the Prime Minister of India. The vision for NKC was articulated by Dr. Manmohan Singh, Prime Minister of India, in the following words:

"The time has come to create a second wave of institution building, and of excellence in the fields of education, research and capability building."

The Terms of Reference of NKC are:

- Build excellence in the educational system to meet the knowledge challenges of the 21st century and increase India's competitive advantage in fields of knowledge.
- Promote creation of knowledge in science and technology laboratories.
- Improve the management of institutions engaged in intellectual property rights.
- Promote knowledge applications in agriculture and industry.
- Promote the use of knowledge capabilities in making government an effective, transparent and accountable service provider to the citizen and promote widespread sharing of knowledge to maximise public benefit.

National Knowledge Commission had a designated timeframe of three years from 2nd October 2005 to 2nd October 2008, which was extended to 31st March 2009.

Organisation

NKC consists of eight members, including the Chairman. All members perform their duties on a part-time basis and do not claim any remuneration.

The members are assisted in their duties by a small technical support staff. The Commission is also free to co-opt experts to assist in the management of its tasks.

The Planning Commission is the nodal agency for the NKC for planning and budgeting purposes as well as for handling Parliament submissions or responses.

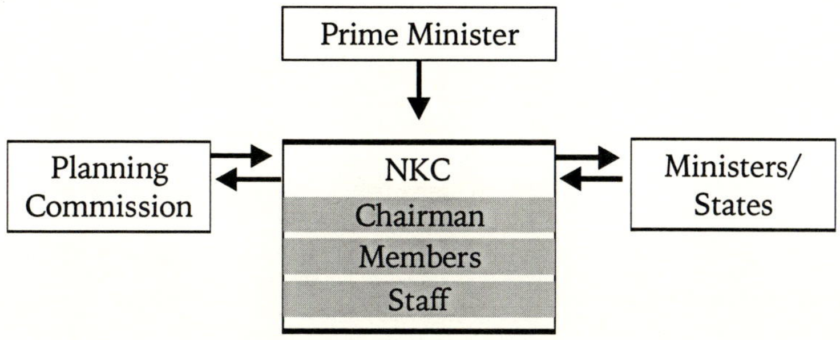

Members

Sam Pitroda (Chairman) has spent four decades in the world of telecommunications, having pioneered its use as a means to expedite the process of development and nation building, and in bridging the global communications divide. His professional career has been divided between the three continents of North America, Asia and Europe, and he has received international acclaim for using telecommunications as a tool for national development. Sam Pitroda is also a recipient of the Padma Bhushan.

As Adviser to Prime Minister Rajiv Gandhi, Mr. Pitroda helped to build India's telecommunications and information technology infrastructure. He was the founding Chairman of the Telecom Commission in India and headed the National Technology Missions on Drinking Water, Literacy, Immunisation, Oilseeds and Dairy. In these roles, he made a notable contribution to India's developmental planning and policy approaches. Mr. Pitroda has owned and run several companies in the United States and Europe; as an inventor he owns more than 75 patents worldwide.

Ashok Ganguly is the Chairman of Firstsource Ltd. and ABP Pvt. Ltd., and a Director on the Central Board of the Reserve Bank of India, since November 2000. He heads his own consulting company, Technology Network India Pvt. Ltd. He also currently serves as a non-executive director of Mahindra & Mahindra, Wipro Ltd., Tata AIG Life Insurance Co Ltd. and ICICI Knowledge Park.

He is a member of the Prime Minister's Council on Trade and Industry as well as the Investment Commission. Dr. Ganguly's professional career spanned 35 years with Unilever Plc/N.V. He was the Chairman of Hindustan Lever Ltd. from 1980 to 1990 and a member of the Unilever Board from 1990 to 1997, with responsibility for worldwide research and technology.

He was a member of the Science Advisory Council to the Prime Minister of India (1985-1989) and the UK Advisory Board of Research Councils (1991-1994). A recipient of the Padma Vibhushan and an Honorary Professor at the Chinese Academy of Science, Dr. Ganguly has authored three books – *Industry and Liberalisation, Strategic Manufacturing for Competitive Advantage* and *Business Driven R&D—Managing Knowledge to Create Wealth.*

P. Balaram is a Professor of Molecular Biophysics and currently the Director of the Indian Institute of Science, Bangalore. Prior to this, he was Lecturer (1973-1977), Assistant Professor (1977-1982), Associate Professor (1982-1985), Chairman, Molecular Biophysics Unit (1995-2000) and Chairman, Division of Biological Sciences (2002-2005) at the Institute. His main research interests are in bio-organic chemistry and molecular biophysics. He is the author of over 370 research papers. He received his M.Sc from IIT Kanpur (1969) and Ph.D in Chemistry from Carnegie-Mellon, Pittsburgh, USA (1972).

Professor Balaram is a Fellow of the Indian Academy of Sciences, Indian National Science Academy and the Third World Academy of Sciences, Trieste, Italy. Professor Balaram has received many awards and honours in recognition of his work, including the Shanti Swarup Bhatnagar Prize, CSIR (1986), Alumni Award for Excellence in Research, IISc (1991), TWAS Award in Chemistry (1994), G.D. Birla Award for Scientific Research (1994) and the Padma Shri awarded by the Government of India (2002).

Professor Balaram currently serves on many committees of the Government of India, and is a Member, Science Advisory Committee to the Union Cabinet, Board of Research in Nuclear Science of DAE, Advisory Board of CSIR and Scientific Advisory Council to the Prime Minister. He has been the editor of *Current Science* for over 10 years.

Jayati Ghosh is a Professor of Economics and Chairperson of the Centre for Economic Studies and Planning, School of Social Sciences, Jawaharlal Nehru University and is an alumnus of Delhi University, Jawaharlal Nehru University and the University of Cambridge. Her research interests include globalisation, international trade and finance, employment patterns in developing countries, macroeconomic policy and issues related to gender and development.

Her published works include *Crisis as a Conquest: Learning from East Asia, The Market that Failed: A Decade of Neoliberal Economic Reforms in India* and *Work and Well-being in the Age of Finance* (co-authored with Prof. C.P. Chandrashekhar). She was the principal author of the *West Bengal Human Development Report 2004* which received the UNDP Award for excellence in analysis, and numerous academic papers. She is a regular columnist for leading journals and periodicals. Dr. Ghosh is involved in managing several public information websites, a founder of the Economic Research Foundation and is the Executive Secretary of International Development Economics Associates (IDEAS), an international network of heterodox development economists. She chaired the Andhra Pradesh Commission on Farmers' Welfare in 2004, and continues to be closely involved in working with progressive organisations and social movements.

Deepak Nayyar is Professor of Economics at Jawaharlal Nehru University, New Delhi. Earlier, he has taught at the University of Oxford, the University of Sussex and the Indian Institute of Management, Calcutta. Professor Nayyar was Vice Chancellor of the University of Delhi from 2000 to 2005. He also served as Chief Economic Adviser to the Government of India and Secretary in the Ministry of Finance.

He was educated at St. Stephen's College, University of Delhi. Thereafter, as a Rhodes Scholar, he went on to study at Balliol College, University of Oxford, where he obtained a B. Phil and a D. Phil in Economics. He has received the V.K.R.V. Rao Award for his contribution to research in Economics. He is an Honorary Fellow of Balliol College, Oxford.

He has published more than 50 papers in academic journals and is the author of 12 books, which include *India's Exports and Export Policies Migration, Remittances and Capital Flows, The Intelligent Person's Guide to Liberalisation, Governing Globalisation: Issues and Institutions, Stability with Growth: Macroeconomics, Liberalisation and Development, Trade and Globalisation* and *Liberalisation and Development*.

Dr. Nayyar is Chairman of the Board of Governors of the UNU World Institute for Development Economics Research, Helsinki. He is Vice President of the International Association of Universities, Paris. He has also served as a Member of the Board of Directors of the Social Science Research Council in the United States, and Chairman of the Advisory Council for the Department of International Development, Queen Elizabeth House, University of Oxford. He was a Member of the World Commission on the Social Dimension of Globalisation.

Nandan Nilekani, one of the founders of Infosys Technologies Ltd., he is also the Co-Chairman of the Board of Directors. He has formerly held the post of Managing Director, President and Chief Operating Officer at Infosys. Mr. Nilekani co-founded India's National Association of Software and Service Companies (NASSCOM). He is Vice-Chairman of The Conference Board, Inc., an international research and business membership organisation and Member of the London Business School's Asia-Pacific Regional Advisory Board. He has served as Chairman of the Government of India's IT Task Force for the power sector. He was a member of the insider trading sub-committee of the Securities and Exchange Board of India (SEBI), and of the Reserve Bank of India's Advisory Group on corporate governance. He is also a member of the review committee of the Jawaharlal Nehru National Urban Renewal Mission and serves on the Board of Reuters as a non-executive member.

His many honours include *Fortune* magazine's 'Asia's Businessmen of the Year 2003' award (along with Infosys Chairman Mr. N.R. Narayana Murthy), the Corporate Citizen of the Year Award at the Asia Business Leader Awards (2004) and Padma Bhushan (2006). In 2002 and 2003, he was named among the 'World's Most Respected Business Leaders' in a global survey by *Financial Times* and PricewaterhouseCoopers.

Mr. Nilekani became one of the youngest entrepreneurs to join 20 global leaders on the prestigious World Economic Forum (WEF) Foundation Board in January 2006.

Sujatha Ramdorai is a Professor at the School of Mathematics, Tata Institute of Fundamental Research (TIFR). She has held visiting positions in several universities and research institutions around the world. Currently, she is a visiting Professor at the Chennai Mathematical Institute.

Dr. Ramdorai is a recipient of the Shanti Swarup Bhatnagar Award and the ICTP Srinivasa Ramanujan Medal awarded by the Norwegian Academy of Science and Letters for her research in algebraic number theory. She has been involved with issues related to education and research, especially research in the pure sciences in India. She has authored several research papers in internationally reputed journals and has collaborated widely in her research work. She is the co-author (with Prof. J. Coates) of *Cyclotomic Fields and Zeta Values.*

Amitabh Mattoo is a Doctorate in International Relations from the University of Oxford, United Kingdom. He is the former Vice-Chancellor of the University of Jammu. He was also Professor of International Relations at Jawaharlal Nehru University and concurrently Director of the Core Group for the Study of National Security. Professor Mattoo is on the Governing Council of the Pugwash Conference on Science and World Affairs, on the Board of the India-Afghanistan Foundation and the President of the Jammu and Kashmir chapter of SPICMACAY.

Professor Mattoo has been on the Governing Council of the Nuclear Science Centre, a member of the Standing Committee of the Association of Indian Universities and on the Executive Council of several Universities. He has been the recipient of several national and international awards and was, till recently, a member of India's National Security Council's Advisory Board. In 2008, he was conferred the Padma Shri by the Government of India.

Methodology

The methodology followed by the National Knowledge Commission involves identification of focus areas in the first instance. This selection arises from wide consultation, within and outside the government. After the identification of focus areas, Working Groups of specialists and practitioners are constituted. Working Groups typically consist of five to ten experts, and meet periodically over three to four months in order to prepare a report. Working Group reports are one of the inputs used by the NKC during deliberations to frame its recommendations. In addition, workshops and seminars are held periodically along with informal consultations with concerned experts and stakeholders to get as broad-based a point of view as possible.

Following this, NKC members discuss the issues raised during Consultations and in the Working Group Reports to finalise recommendations. After several rounds of deliberations, a letter is sent to the Prime Minister containing key recommendations. Widespread dissemination of NKC recommendations to state governments, civil society and other stakeholders takes place after the recommendations have been received by the Prime Minister and the relevant ministries. The implementation of the recommendations under the aegis of the Prime Minister's Office is then initiated, along with coordination and follow up with various implementing agencies. Key steps include:

- Identification of key focus areas.
- Identification of diverse stakeholders and understanding major issues in the area.
- Constitution of Working Groups and organising of workshops/seminars, extensive formal and informal consultations with concerned experts and stakeholders.
- Consultation with administrative ministries and the Planning Commission.
- Discussion in NKC to finalise recommendations in the form of letter to the PM from the Chairman.
- Letter to PM containing key recommendations, first steps, financial implications etc., supported by the relevant explanatory documents by NKC.
- Dissemination of recommendations to State Governments, civil society and other stakeholders.
- Initiating the implementation of the recommendations under the aegis of the Prime Minister's Office.

Working Groups

Libraries, Language, Knowledge Applications in Agriculture, Health Information Network, Higher Education, Medical Education, Legal Education, Management Education, Engineering Education, Traditional Health Systems, More Students in Maths and Science, Open and Distance Education, Using Knowledge for Enhancing Quality of Life.

Workshops/Seminars

Literacy, Translation, Networks, School Education, Muslim Education, Vocational Education, Open and Distance Education, Intellectual Property Rights, Science and Technology, Agriculture, Open Education Resources, Portals, Quality of Life, More Quality Ph.Ds.

Surveys

Innovation, Health Information Network, Traditional Health Systems, Entrepreneurship, More Quality Ph.Ds.

I

Access

1 Right to Education

National Knowledge Commission (NKC) believes that providing universal access to quality school education is a cornerstone of development and a minimum necessary condition for any progress towards making India a knowledge society. NKC is in the process of extensive consultations and will make detailed recommendations on various issues relating to school education at a later date.

However, at this point NKC would like to respond specifically to the recent initiative of the Central Government of sending a model Right to Education Bill to the Secretaries of State Education Departments, with incentives for the State Governments to enact this bill. NKC has perused the bill and consulted with a wide range of experts and educationists. It feels that the model bill is flawed for a number of reasons, and most importantly that such legislation must be enforced by the Central Government following upon the commitment made in the Constitutional Amendment Article 21A.

NKC recognises that there may be concerns about federalism, since school education is dominantly the responsibility of the State Governments at present. However, it feels that this matter can be resolved through an appropriate central legislation which takes into account the following proposals:

1. Central Legislation

Legislation at the national level is required to affirm the Right to Education, which is a fundamental right mandated by Article 21A. Since it cannot be dependent upon which state a citizen lives in, a model bill sent to be enacted individually by State Governments is not adequate to meet the constitutional responsibilities of the Government of India. Therefore, a central legislation should be enacted along the lines of the Panchayati Raj (Amendment) Act, requiring the States to enact Right to Education Bills within a specified time period, and with the primary financial responsibility for this resting with the Central Government.

2. Financial Commitment

The Central Government must provide the bulk of the additional funds required to ensure the Right to Education. Therefore there must be financial provision in the central legislation, requiring the Central Government to share the revenues of the Prarambhik Shiksha Kosh with State Governments and to provide additional resources as required to meet the requirement of ensuring the right to all children. Estimates for the additional resources required to achieve the goal of universal elementary education currently range from 0.8 per cent to 2.5 per cent of the GDP, depending on the criteria used. However, the required financial resources are likely to be at the lower end of these estimates, since there is already close to universal provision in several states and there has been recent progress in providing more access through the Sarva Shiksha Abhiyan in other states.

3. Time Frame

The state-level legislation should specify the period within which universal education of reasonable quality is sought to be achieved, preferably within three years. The model bill does not provide any time frame for adoption and implementation of the provisions.

4. Schedule of Norms and Standards

To ensure a minimum quality of education, it is important to have a schedule of norms for all schools to follow. The model bill does not have such a schedule of norms, and there is no specification of the minimum quality of education that schools should provide. There is only a reference to 'equitable quality' without defining the parameters of quality. While ensuring quality is a complex matter, certain norms regarding infrastructure, number of teachers per school and per student, teaching methods and other facilities, must be adhered to as necessary conditions.

5. Specification for Teachers

Since teachers are critical to ensuring the quality of education, it is particularly important to lay down well-defined but flexible norms for the minimum qualifications of teachers. The model bill has no specification of a teacher, or the qualifications and in-service training needed for the position. A teacher is only defined as a person who teaches in the classroom. It is necessary to specify norms for teacher qualification and training.

6. Justiciability

Any right, including the Right to Education, is only meaningful if it is justiciable. However, in the model bill sent to State Governments, the onus is placed on parents or guardians of the child. The responsibility of the Government, at different levels, must be recognised and made justiciable. The example of the National Rural Employment Guarantee Act (NREGA) could be used in this context.

7. Redressal Mechanism

To ensure justiciability, a redressal mechanism should be outlined and an appropriate procedure must be set in place for students or parents in case the right is not upheld.

8. Universal Schooling

School education must be provided to all. This necessarily also requires that children of the disadvantaged, landless and minority communities must also be integrated, along with children with disabilities or special needs. There should be no distinction made in terms of the type of schooling provided within the government system for children from different social, economic and cultural backgrounds. The model bill has the potential of creating a parallel and discriminatory system of schooling which can result in stratification of the education system for children from disadvantaged communities and backgrounds, because it requires only provision of non-formal education in such cases, rather than mandating the provision of regular schooling.

Obviously, in all cases, the school system should be flexible enough to cater to particular needs of students.

NKC can offer detailed explanations on these points. Continuing to consult with stakeholders and examine other issues in relation to school education, it is focussing in particular on the questions of how to ensure better quality across the board; the institutional structures and forms of control by local communities that could contribute to improved quality of schooling; issues related to common schooling and neighbourhood schools; ensuring adequate quantity and quality of school teachers, especially in specified areas.

NKC will make a broader set of recommendations on school education in the near future.

In a subsequent letter to Prime Minister, NKC reiterated that the proposed central legislation on RTE must include a financial commitment on the part of the Central Government. NKC believes that the potential expenditure on this is probably less than has been estimated earlier. The Kapil Sibal Committee that had prepared the CABE draft had estimated an expenditure of Rs.2,20,643 crore for the period 2008-2012. However, this was based on population projections for the future that have since been revised downwards by the Census of India. For example, current population projections suggest that there will be at least 6 million less children in 2011-12 than the earlier projections used by the Sibal Committee had indicated. This in turn means a significant reduction in the estimated costs for universal schooling. Using the same per capita spending with the new population projections gives a total cost for the five year period 2008-2012 of Rs. 1,51,273 crore, based on 50:50 division of SSA. This amounts to an average of just above Rs. 30,000 crore per annum, which is much less than 1 per cent of the GDP and also less than 8 per cent of total Central Government spending.[1]

In this connection, NKC would also like to express its concern about the recent decision of the Central Government to reduce the central funding for the Sarva Shiksha Abhiyan from 75 per cent to 50 per cent. There is a fear that this may lead to a sharp curtailment of progress towards universal school education, especially in the more backward states where the gap is greater. It is worth noting that State Governments are already incurring the bulk of school education expenditure.[2] NKC strongly recommends that, in addition to 50 per cent of SSA, the Centre should provide all the necessary funding to ensure the Right to Education in those states where the State Government is already spending at least 15 per cent of its total budget on school education.

1. If the Centre provides 75 per cent of the spending for SSA, the additional cost would be Rs. 37,000 crore over the 11th Plan period, that is around Rs. 7,000 crore per annum.

2. Currently, the ratio of Central Government to State Government spending for school education, including SSA, is 12:88. If mid-day meals are included, it is 20:80.

2 Language

The National Knowledge Commission (NKC) has emphasised the importance of an inclusive society as the foundation for a knowledge society. NKC has also recognised the significance of language, not only as a medium of instruction or a means of communication but also as a determinant of access. An understanding and command over the English language is a most important determinant of access to higher education, employment possibilities and social opportunities. School-leavers who are not adequately trained in English as a language are always at a handicap in the world of higher education. More often than not, teaching is in English. Even if it is not, in most subjects, books and journals are available only in English. And those who do not know English well enough find it exceedingly difficult to compete for a place in our premier educational institutions. This disadvantage is accentuated further in the world of work, not only in professional occupations but also in white-collar occupations overall.

This reality is not lost on our people, who recognise that the English language is a critical determinant of access to, and opportunities for a better life. Available information suggests that middle-income or lower-income households spend a large proportion of their modest income on sending their children to relatively expensive English medium schools. Such educational opportunities for children are a priority that is almost at par with health care for the family. But there are a very large number of people who simply do not have the resources for such investment. The outcome is exclusion. We believe that inclusion is possible through public provision.

There is an irony in the situation. English has been part of our education system for more than a century. Yet English is beyond the reach of most of our young people, which makes for highly unequal access. Indeed, even now, no more than one per cent of our people use it as a second language, let alone a first language.

These realities cannot be changed overnight. But NKC believes that the time has come for us to teach our people, ordinary people, English as a language in schools. Early action in this sphere would help us build an inclusive society and transform India into a knowledge society. In just 12 years, it would provide the country's school-leavers with far more equal access to higher education and, three to five years thereafter, much more equal access to employment opportunities.

The Commission engaged in informal consultations on this subject with a wide range of people in government, academia, media and industry. It consulted some Chief Ministers in the states. It consulted Members of Parliament. It consulted people in professions such as medicine and law as well as civil society organisations. There was unanimity that this can and should be done. A Working Group was constituted to work out the modalities in terms of first steps. The report submitted by this group was used as an input in NKC's deliberations.

NKC recommends that the teaching of English as a language should be introduced, along with the first language (either the mother tongue or the regional language) of the child, starting from Class I in school. This phase of language learning should focus on using both languages to create meaningful learning experiences for the child without disproportionate emphasis on grammar and rules.

NKC recognises that nine States (of which six are in the northeast) and three Union Territories have already introduced English as a compulsory subject from Class I onwards. In addition, as many as 12 States and 3 Union Territories have made English a compulsory subject, at different stages in primary school, by Class V at the latest. However, the implementation is slow and the quality of English language teaching is simply not good enough. The support systems, such as the number of teachers or materials for teaching, are neither adequate nor appropriate. NKC is recommending a fundamental change that seeks to introduce, nationwide, the teaching of English as a language from Class I onwards. This is not meant to be a stand alone, add-on subject but is meant to be integrated into the school curriculum.

Language learning cannot be separated from, and must be integrated with, content learning. Therefore, English should also be used to teach some non-language, content subjects, starting from Class III in school. The choice of subjects for this purpose can be left to schools depending on the proficiency of teachers and availability of materials. This would, in effect, create multi-medium schools. It would also help reduce the divide between English medium schools and regional language medium schools.

The pedagogy of language learning as well as teaching should be suitably contextualised, to lend meaning to real situations and daily lives. Moreover, assessment should be based on proficiency rather than specifying achievement targets that reward mastery of single texts acquired through rote learning. To this end, a National Testing Service (NTS) for certification of language competence as well as recruitment of language teachers should be set up.

In order to meet the requirement for a large pool of English language teachers, graduates with high proficiency in English and good communication skills should be inducted without formal teacher-training qualifications. They could be selected through an appropriate procedure developed by the National Testing Service and then given a short-term orientation. The nearly four million school teachers all over the country, regardless of their subject expertise, especially teachers at the primary level, should be trained to improve their proficiency in English through vacation training programmes or other short-term courses. Most teacher training programmes are not based on a real assessment of the needs of teachers. Thus, the entire teacher training system catering to pre-service and in-service training that exists today, including training for language teaching, needs to be thoroughly reviewed, recognising the centrality of language in the curriculum.

A multiplicity of English textbooks should be made available to address the diversity of English language environments in the country. However, to ensure that certain standards are maintained, benchmarks may be laid down for the content of textbooks at each stage. For this purpose, an expert group should be set up to develop pedagogically sound English textbooks for every level, from Class I to XII. These should be used as models by states and made freely available on the web to allow easy access. While the State Council for Educational Research and Training (SCERT) may continue to be a nodal agency for textbook development for state board schools, the writing of textbooks needs to be further decentralised. To make the exercise more collaborative, civil society organisations with expertise in the domain should be involved in developing textbooks.

Since language learning takes place not only through direct instruction but also through assimilation from the environment, the classroom needs to be equipped with appropriate supplementary audio-visual and print material. Resource libraries could be set up in every classroom, comprising of a collection of books, magazines, newspapers, audio-visual material and posters, appropriate to the age of the students, on a variety of subjects. Language learning opportunities should also be created outside the classroom through specific bi-lingual radio and TV channels, which could be introduced for formal and informal teaching and learning of English. Knowledge clubs could be formed to discuss and disseminate knowledge as well as extend the use of English outside the classroom. Given that language learning requires extensive resources, a centrally sponsored scheme of financial assistance for developing English language resources (teachers and materials) should be instituted to address this requirement.

State governments would need to be equal partners in the implementation of this idea. NKC therefore proposes that the Prime Minister discuss this matter with all Chief Ministers at the National Development Council, to formulate a national plan for the teaching of English as a language, in addition to the regional language, starting in Class I. This would also ensure that at the end of 12 years of schooling, every student is proficient in at least two languages.

3 Translation

There is an urgent need to expand the quantity and improve the quality of translation of different types (human, machine-aided or instant) and in different domains (literary, scientific, technical, business) that would provide greater access to knowledge across the country. The current facilities available are inadequate and less than what is socially required. There is latent unrecognised demand which is not being met because of incomplete and asymmetric information. Inadequacy of information, compounded by the lack of coordination between potential users, also leads to market failures. There is inadequate dissemination of good quality translations which would provide a benchmark and create incentives for more private activity in this area. This therefore, requires some amount of public intervention, not as a permanent feature but as a set of measures to kick-start a process of encouraging private initiative so that the large commercially viable provision of high quality translation in different areas becomes feasible. The direct and indirect employment generation potential of translation activities is very high, and could absorb a substantial part of educated unemployed youth.

Based on these insights, NKC formed a Working Group led by Dr. Jayati Ghosh to bring together people and agencies involved in translation, publishing and dissemination activities. They included representatives of some of the relevant government bodies, academics, language experts, publishers, teachers and others associated with translation activities in India. They met several times for workshops and consultations.

As a result of their work and discussions, NKC recommends the following:

1. Provide impetus for developing translation as an industry in the country. Going by the experiences of other countries, in a country like India with its many languages, as well as the huge potential for foreign language translation, the entire translation industry has the potential eventually to employ between 200,000 and half a million people.

2. Establish a storehouse of information on all aspects of translation involving Indian languages, and make this available by creating, maintaining and constantly updating information on translations published, training programmes, translation tools/instruments and new initiatives and facilities such as a 'National Register for Translators'.

3. Promote printed as well as virtual publication of works on translation studies; provide a clearing house for all translation activities, both in theoretical and applied subjects, in as many Indian languages as possible.

4. Create and maintain various tools for translation, including digital tools like thesauri, bilingual dictionaries and software for translation. In addition, promote machine translation, leveraging emerging technologies to provide a rapid and large volume of translation at a relatively low cost.

5. Provide quality training and education for translators. This could be done through short-term training programmes, course packages for translators that could be incorporated in language teaching programmes and fellowship programmes and research projects to encourage quality. There is also need for guidance in the methodology of translation and for action to enrich teaching and training activities in translation studies.

6. Translate pedagogic materials at all levels (including primary onwards to tertiary education), specifically in natural and social sciences.

7. Project Indian languages and literatures within South Asia and outside through high-quality translation.

8. Set up a national web portal on translation as a one-stop shop for all information on translation and to provide a forum for dialogue by creating a bulletin board for people to post questions and answers.
9. Organise annual national conferences on translation to take stock of activities and initiatives in the field, for experts, industry and practitioners in the field to confer.
10. Promote book launches, festivals, fellowships and prizes and encourage collaborative translation work, as well as long-term multi-translator projects, and organise workshops for translators to interact and exchange views and experiences.

NKC feels that in order to achieve these goals as rapidly and efficiently as possible, the Government of India may establish a National Translation Mission (NTM), which would take up these tasks in a systematic way. The NTM would be a relatively small body in terms of its own infrastructure and be flexible in organisation but would have a budget sufficient to enable it to carry out targeted funding in identified areas. It would not function in a centralised way but will require involvement of state and local levels, and coordination with many different agencies. Since immediate requirements may be different from future needs not only in terms of translation activities but also the nature of interventions required, the NTM should be flexible and responsive to current and future social realities and market conditions.

It is envisaged that a National Translation Mission performing these activities could be set up during the 11th Plan, with a proposed budget of Rs. 250 crore for the entire Plan period (around Rs. 80 crore for organisational costs, manpower and scholarships, and around Rs. 170 crore for all other activities, which would involve funding other collaborating institutions or parties). Depending upon the experience during the 11th Plan period, the extent of this support could be enhanced subsequently. In addition, the NTM would require some one-time support for creating and developing the necessary infrastructure.

A proposal on these lines was sent to the Planning Commission which made some further suggestions on the organisation and structure of the National Translation Mission.

Translation activities should be seen in tandem with the plan to increase access to English language training across the population and the promotion of English in school education at the primary level. Both are aspects of the goal of increasing access to knowledge.

4 Libraries

Public libraries play a pivotal role in dissemination of knowledge and are an extremely important element of the foundation of a knowledge economy. There is widespread agreement that there is an urgent need for reform in the Libraries and Information Services (LIS) sector. Several initiatives in this regard have already been taken by the Government. NKC has consulted extensively with diverse stakeholders, including a Working Group of experts and professionals. NKC's recommendations for formulating strategies in the LIS sector are as follows:

1. *Set up a National Commission on Libraries:* A permanent, independent and financially autonomous National Commission on Libraries should be set up by the Central Government as a statutory body to address the information and learning needs of the citizens of India. To launch the process in a mission mode, a National Mission on Libraries should be set up immediately, for a period of three years.

2. *Prepare a national census of all libraries:* A national census of all libraries should be prepared by undertaking a nationwide survey. Collection of census data on libraries would provide baseline data for planning. The Task Force that has been set up by the Department of Culture for this purpose should be given financial and administrative support to implement this activity and complete the survey on a priority basis (within one year). User needs and reading habits should be periodically surveyed at the national level as part of the National Sample Survey.

3. *Revamp LIS education, training and research facilities:* The proposed Mission/Commission on Libraries must assess as soon as possible the manpower requirements of the country in the area of LIS management, and take necessary steps to meet the country's requirement through LIS education and training. To keep the LIS sector abreast of latest developments, necessary encouragement should be given to research after evaluating the research status in this field. Establishing a well-equipped institute for advanced training and research in library and information science and services would provide the necessary impetus to this task.

4. *Re-assess staffing of libraries:* In the changed context, it is necessary to assess the manpower requirements for different types of libraries and departments of library and information science, keeping in mind job descriptions, qualifications, designations, pay scale, career advancement and service conditions.

5. *Set up a Central Library Fund:* A specified percentage of the Central and state education budgets must be earmarked for libraries. In addition, a Central Library Fund should be instituted for upgrading existing libraries over a period of 3-5 years. The initial funding from the Government may be Rs. 1,000 crore, which may be matched by the private sector through corporate philanthropy. This fund should be administered by the National Mission/Commission on Libraries.

6. *Modernise library management:* Libraries should be so organised and the staff so trained that they become relevant to user communities (including special groups) in every respect. Also, to optimise resources, efforts should be made to synergise the strengths of different types of libraries through innovative collaboration. NKC proposes the creation of a model library charter, a list of services to be performed by libraries, a library network and a national repository for bibliographic records.

7. *Encourage greater community participation in library management:* It is necessary to involve different stakeholders and user groups in the managerial decision-making process for libraries. Public libraries must be run by local self-government through committees representing users of the library. These committees should ensure local community involvement and should be autonomous enough to take independent decisions to conduct cultural and educational community-based

programmes. Libraries should integrate with all other knowledge-based activities in the local area to develop a community-based information system. In the rural sector, the responsibility for village libraries or Community Knowledge Centres must lie with the *panchayats*. These should be set up in close proximity or on the premises of schools.

8. *Promote Information Communication Technology (ICT) applications in all libraries:* The catalogues of all libraries should be put on local, state and national websites with necessary linkages. This will enable networking of different types of libraries and setting up of a national repository of bibliographic records and a centralised collaborative virtual enquiry-handling system using the latest ICT. To enable equitable and universal access to knowledge resources, libraries should be encouraged to create more digital resources by digitising relevant reading material in different languages, which can be shared at all levels. Peer-reviewed research papers resulting from publicly funded research should also be made available through open access channels, subject to copyright regulations. It is recommended that open standards and free and open source software may be used for the above.

9. *Facilitate donation and maintenance of private collections:* There are numerous rich private and personal collections in India which need to be identified, documented and preserved for posterity. While there is a need to create a decentralised model for identification of personal collections, it is also necessary to sensitise organisations to receive and preserve donations of personal collections through a simplified process. The National Mission/Commission may set up a committee on private and personal collections under the chairpersonship of an eminent scholar. Since special facilities for maintaining private or personal collections are not easily available, it is suggested that 10 regional centres with specific mandates be set up in different parts of the country for this purpose.

10. *Encourage public-private partnerships in LIS development:* Philanthropic organisations, industrial houses and other private agencies should be encouraged through fiscal incentives to support existing libraries or set up new libraries. The ingenuity of civil society may also be utilised to prepare necessary infrastructure to meet the special ICT needs of the LIS sector.

In order to facilitate the coordinated development of libraries across different sectors and to provide the legislative framework, required legal support and financial backing to the library sector, the Government could, in course of time, consider including libraries in the Concurrent List of the Constitution of India. This should be done without, in any way, abrogating the existing responsibilities of the states towards libraries.

Annexure 4.1: National Mission on Library and Information Services (NMLIS)

Library and information services are fundamental to the goals of creating, disseminating, optimally utilising and preserving knowledge. They are instrumental in transforming an unequal society into an egalitarian, progressive knowledge society. Developments in information communication technology (ICT) have enabled libraries to provide access to all, and also bridge the gap between the local, the national and the global.

Yet the library and information services (LIS) sector in India has not kept pace with the paradigmatic changes taking place in society. It is imperative that all libraries (public, academic, research and special) change gear and develop at an accelerated pace. At present, being a State subject and coming under the purview of different apex agencies, there is no common direction or coordination among them.

To give a proper direction to the LIS sector, there is a need to set up a body which will deal with this sector in a more rational manner. The activities which are now being performed as piecemeal and isolated ventures by different agencies may be streamlined for the benefit of a much larger group of stakeholders at all levels. In order to launch this process immediately, a National Mission on LIS must be set up for a period of three years with statutory backing and a regular budget. NMLIS should be converted into a permanent National Commission on LIS in not more than three years, to become an important part of the development process.

1. The Role of the NMLIS

1. Develop libraries and information services.
2. Advise the Government on libraries and information sector.
3. Set standards for collection, services and technical processing.
4. Encourage public-private participation.
5. Interact with state governments.
6. Conserve cultural heritage.
7. Review and assess LIS education and in-service training needs.
8. Support R&D and technological development.
9. Ensure access to all publications including government and institutional public documents.
10. Set up a system for monitoring the working of public libraries

NMLIS and later the National Commission should be headed by a person of eminence and high public credibility with demonstrated interest in and knowledge of libraries.

Annexure 4.2: Indian Institute of Library and Information Science (ILIS)

India has a long tradition of libraries and has contributed to the development of basic concepts in the discipline such as fundamental principles of library services and knowledge organisation tools. However, R&D activities in library and information services (LIS) today are extremely limited. LIS, though concerned with global information resources, need to pay close attention to the local environment. The diversity within the country in terms of socio-economic-cultural factors, the multiplicity of languages, varying levels of literacy and educational achievements and access to information and communication technologies, make it essential that planning for LIS take into account the ground realities. Further, the exponential rate of change and innovation relating to this discipline also warrants intensive R& D initiatives. It is also necessary to provide guidelines and training for the use of tools and technology so that research results are effectively utilised.

Globally, much of the research in the field of LIS is being adopted and utilised in organising the Internet. It is generally accepted that the present search engines lack semantic knowledge of the documents processed. Whether it is a huge collection of information within a library or Internet, the tools and techniques that have long been used by Library and Information Science professionals will be of immense help in making the web a "semantic web".

Keeping the above in view, it is felt that a national institute for advanced training and R&D in LIS (suggested name: Indian Institute of Library and Information Science) needs to be set up. The proposed institute would have two major functions:

a. To offer training programmes in relevant areas and to conduct continuing education programmes (including training of trainers) for the library and information professionals.

b. To identify, sponsor and conduct R&D programmes in the field of Library and Information Science, including newly emerging research areas. Among the areas needing immediate R&D, the following were identified by the Working Group:

   - Cross-Language Information Retrieval with an emphasis on information in Indian languages.
   - Standardisation of Indian names.
   - Vocabulary control over Indian subjects developed in terms of multilingual thesauri and subject heading lists.
   - Development of open source software.
   - Development of digital libraries, both in English and Indian languages.
   - Technical standards for Indian scripts, Optical Character Recognition (OCR) for Indian scripts and search engines which can implement stemming algorithms for Indian languages.
   - User needs and reading habits for different groups.
   - Organisation of community information and development of appropriate standards.

The institute's scientists will carry out research in major areas contributing to Libraries and Information Science. In addition, they can undertake externally funded projects and provide consultancy to other organisations.

The institute will also undertake activities to disseminate the research findings such as printed and online publications, seminars and conferences, web portal, etc.

1. Proposed Organisational Structure for ILIS

ILIS should have an advisory board consisting of experts, a director (administrative head), research groups for different activities and other supporting staff.

2. Aegis

The institute would logically function under Ministry of Culture as major libraries of India, including The National Library are already under its purview.

Annexure 4.3: Proposals on Staffing of Libraries

I. Classification of Libraries

i. National library and other national level subject libraries.

ii. Public libraries which have four tiers *viz.*, State Central Library, District Library, Sub-Divisional/Town Library, Rural Knowledge Centre/Community Information Centre.

iii. Academic libraries which have three tiers *viz.*, university, college and school libraries.

iv. Special libraries including government libraries (special libraries would comprise R&D libraries, industrial libraries and specialised libraries).

II. Skills Required to Fulfil the Changing Role of Libraries

i. Library and information handling skills

ii. Service orientation

iii. ICT knowledge skills

iv. Communication and training skills

v. Marketing and presentation skills

vi. Understanding of cultural diversity

vii. Knowledge mapping skills

III. Staffing Requirement of Various Types of Libraries

1. National Library

The National Library, Kolkata has been categorised as a Category VI library. It is the only library in India which has been mentioned in the Constitution of India as an institution of national importance. Therefore, it must be developed into an institute of excellence with high academic standing. The Department of Culture may review the staffing pattern of the National Library and the Central Reference Library in context of their changing roles and national responsibilities.

2. Public Libraries

a. To ensure that the services match the changing scenario, these libraries will also act as knowledge centres and be expected to perform the following types of activities in addition to the library's routine responsibilities (the lists given below are only indicative and not exhaustive):

   i. State Central Library: Information service, e-learning, knowledge management, knowledge centre activities, content creation and management, subject gateways, content analysis, collaborative publishing, e-governance, training.

   ii. District Library: Information service, e-governance, content development, coordination of rural knowledge centres.

   iii. Sub-Divisional/Town Library: Lending of books, reference services, inter-library loan, web-based services such as e-learning, banking and insurance, community information, content and database creation.

   iv. Rural Knowledge Centre/Community Information Centre: Lending of books, web-based services such as e-learning, banking and insurance, *panchayat*-level information, e-governance, community information, content and database creation.

b. There should be proper coordination of activities between the different levels of libraries, specially in respect of those activities which will be of common interest, e.g., training, sharing of databases and contents, problem solving, transaction analysis, gathering of information towards developing uniform standards and modeling of inspection of need, access and dissemination, and inspection of progress of knowledge-based activities and identifying weaknesses in the system, if any.

c. The following routine jobs may be outsourced: stack management, library binding, stock verification, retro conversion, bar coding, borrowers' registration, digitisation, library security and upkeep, physical infrastructure and maintenance, computer network and maintenance. Work of administrative staff such as night watchman, cleaner, gardener, driver, bookbinder and sweeper may also be outsourced.

d. Keeping in view the above categorisation, the following staff structure is recommended for public libraries.

State Central Library (Category III)

i. Managerial Staff (Group A)
   a. State Librarian
   b. Deputy Library Director
   c. Assistant Library Director (presently designated as Information Officer)

ii. Professional/Technical Staff (Group B)
   a. Information Assistant
   b. Junior Information Assistant
   c. Data Entry Operator

iii. Paraprofessional/Support Staff (Group C)
   a. Library Attendant

iv. Administrative Staff
   a. Administrative Officer
   b. Stenographer
   c. Cashier
   d. Administrative Support Staff
   e. Night Watchman, Cleaner, Gardener, Driver, Bookbinder, Sweeper, etc., to be outsourced.

District Library (Category II)

i. Managerial Staff (Group A)
   a. District Librarian

ii. Professional/Technical Staff (Group B)
   a. Information Assistant
   b. Data Entry Operator

iii. Paraprofessional/Support Staff (Group C)
   a. Library Attendant

iv. Administrative Staff
   a. Night Watchman, Cleaner, Gardener, Driver, Bookbinder, Sweeper, etc., to be outsourced.

Sub-Divisional/Town Library (Category I)

i. Managerial Staff (Group A)
   a. Town Librarian

ii. Professional/Technical Staff (Group B)

   a. Data Entry Operator

iii. Paraprofessional/Support Staff (Group C)

   a. Library Attendant

iv. Administrative Staff

   a. Night Watchman, Cleaner, Gardener, Book Binder, Sweeper, etc., to be outsourced.

Rural Knowledge Centre/Community Information Centre (Block Level)

i. Professional/Technical Staff (Group B)

   a. Information Assistant

ii. Para-professional/ Support Staff (Group C)

   a. Library Attendant

iii. Administrative Staff

   a. Village Level Volunteers

An information officer is needed to look after and coordinate the activities of clusters of four to six district libraries and their knowledge centres.

3. Academic Libraries

Keeping in view the changing scenario and new responsibilities, the existing staffing pattern, duties and qualifications of library staff in schools, colleges and university libraries should be reviewed and altered wherever required to meet the new challenges. The existing designations may also be reviewed by the National Mission/Commission.

4. Special Libraries

Special libraries are parts of parent institutions and unlike public and academic libraries, do not enjoy any individual identity in their staffing structure. In the emerging knowledge society era, special libraries must be reshaped as knowledge management centres that will require linking people, knowledge and technology that would facilitate knowledge flow and transfer to foster knowledge assimilation and knowledge creation. Special libraries should have the same staffing pattern and promotional avenues as available to other staff in the same organisation.

Staffing Pattern of LIS Departments

a. A system should be set up to foster close cooperation between the teaching/research faculty and practicing librarians at all academic and research institutions, by measures such as:

   i. Mobility of staff (in terms of recruitment and in terms of teaching) should be made possible.

   ii. Practicing librarians and experts should be associated with the teaching faculty for offering specialised courses.

   iii. Similarly, teachers could be associated with libraries as consultants, for carrying out projects and for carrying out continuing education programmes to practicing librarians, etc.

b. The minimum staffing pattern for the Bachelor in Library and Information Science (B.L.I.Sc.) course should be as follows:

i. Professor	1	(where possible)
ii. Reader	1	
iii. Lecturers	2	

c. The minimum staffing pattern for the M.L.I.Sc. course should be as follows:

i.	Professor	1
ii.	Readers	2
iii.	Lecturers	4

d. There should be a 1:10 teacher-student ratio.

e. It was felt that the department should have not more than 50 students in one class for B.L.I.Sc.course, 20 students for M.L.I.Sc. course and Ph.D. students according to the University norms.

f. All departments of LIS should set up computer laboratories and well-equipped departmental libraries with appropriate teaching tools.

g. Appropriate physical facilities such as classrooms, must be made available to each LIS department.

h. E-learning materials for upgrading the skills of the existing staff should be provided.

i. Teachers who will teach in areas such as ICT applications in libraries and other modern methods, should have a specialisation in these areas. A system must be set up to allow stringent review of the performance of teachers. A suitable system of rewards, including promotions, should be instituted.

Annexure 4.4 : Modernising Library Management

Appropriate steps must be taken by all institutions/organisations that run their own libraries to ensure that they meet the four objectives of the LIS sector stated below. The Government of India should issue a notification to all institutions/ organisations to take appropriate steps to ensure that libraries working under their aegis meet these objectives.

I. A Library Charter

Individual libraries should be asked to display their objectives as part of a library charter. A sample charter is below:

The Library Charter

Recognising that the library's objectives are to:

- Disseminate knowledge as widely as possible.
- Serve as a major vehicle to facilitate creation of new knowledge.
- Facilitate optimal use of knowledge by all sectors, such as government, industry, rural sector and civil society.
- Ensure that people from all sectors and all parts of the country have easy access to knowledge relevant to their needs, in their own language.

The library undertakes to:

- Serve as the local centre of information and a gateway to national and global knowledge providing fair access to knowledge and information to as many users as possible.
- Offer an inviting and attractive physical space with clean drinking water and toilet facilities.
- Offer proactive services to its user communities.
- Ensure that users are treated with courtesy and respect by library staff.
- Pay attention to the needs of children, women, senior citizens and the physically challenged.
- Optimise its potential to provide access to information and knowledge to all.
- Help users develop information skills to make optimum use of resources.
- Improve its collections and services on a continuing basis in consultation with users.
- To work more effectively and efficiently by undertaking every activity in a professional manner.
- To bridge the gap between the information poor and the information rich.

II. Guidelines for Collection Development

General Guidelines

1. All libraries must maintain a well-rounded core collection, including reference material to satisfy the regular needs of its user community. These may be supplemented through networks, e-resources, etc., to achieve better qualitative and quantitative standards.
2. Library collections are dynamic resources and there should be, therefore, constant renewal of materials to ensure that the collection remains relevant to the user communities.
3. Except in the case of national repositories, weeding out of books should be a regular process. Each library should evolve a weeding out policy, approved by the competent authority.
4. The criteria for categorising libraries in government and public libraries and grading of librarians should be reviewed keeping in mind factors such as size of collection, immediacy index (ratio of current books to total books), users, services and access to electronic resources.

Public Library Collections

1. The size and nature of the collection should reflect the local requirements.
2. Locally relevant language material should be available.
3. Book purchase should be a continuous process and at least 10 per cent of the book collection should be less than five years old.
4. At least 60 per cent of the library's budget should be spent on collection development.

Academic Library Collections

1. In general, the library collection of academic institutions should take into account the number of disciplines offered, the level of the courses, the number of students and faculty and the research activities of the parent organisation.
2. At least 6 – 10 per cent of the total institutional budget should be utilised for collection development on a recurring basis.
3. For a new college/university or a course, a one-time budget may be provided for setting up the basic collection.

Special Library Collections

In the case of special libraries, the collection should be relevant to the specific research needs and thrusts of the institution. Further, depending on their areas of interest, they should acquire materials at the national and international research fronts of their disciplines. The library should acquire books and journals to meet at least 80 per cent of the internal requirements of its user community.

National Library

In the case of the National Library and other national level libraries, the collections should be as comprehensive as possible.

III. Services to be Provided by Libraries

To provide access to knowledge and resources, each library must provide a range of services to meet the needs of a diverse user community.

1. Kinds of services to be provided by all libraries:

    i) Lending of materials for home use; however, this will not apply to special libraries or special collections in libraries. The National Library should distinguish between its statutory functions as a national repository and its historical obligations as a public library. In course of time, it should develop ways and means of segregating these functions.

    ii) Reading facilities on premises need to be attractive, bright and comfortable. Opening hours should be at the convenience of readers. Libraries should be closed only on national holidays.

    iii) Reference service providing qualified and willing staff (knowledge workers) for acting as intermediaries between the users and the collection.

    iv) Providing Internet access to link the local library to national and global information.

    The above four basic services should be free to users at point of use.

    The following services may be made available (against payment wherever appropriate), depending on the size of the library and the needs of the user community:

    v) Inter-library loan.

    vi) Photocopying.

    vii) Document delivery, including Electronic Document Delivery (EDD).

    viii) Extension services in public and academic libraries for women, children, senior citizens and physically challenged persons.

ix) Community information services.

x) OPAC (Online Public Access Catalogue).

xi) Electronic/AV resources, workstations and appropriate infrastructure for use and delivery.

xii) Training users in information literacy.

xiii) Institutional repositories of research articles, reports, institutional publications and Electronic Theses and Dissertations (ETD).

xiv) Websites, portals, subject gateways, etc (especially in case of special libraries).

xv) Digitisation of rare resources (before any digitisation programme, one must consider what is to be digitised and whether any other libraries have undertaken similar exercises).

xvi) Identify non-users and promote the use of libraries among them.

xvii) A periodical review to determine the needs of users and effectiveness of services should be conducted by libraries.

2. Consortia of libraries/institutions with a common membership should be instituted, facilitated and encouraged.
3. Besides offering routine library services, libraries should initiate new and imaginative services in consultation with the local community relevant to their needs.
4. All academic institutions must set up institutional repositories of ETD. This should be made mandatory for accreditation. Such repositories should be made open access.
5. All public academic and research institutes should be encouraged to set up freely accessible institutional repositories of their full-text articles and publications subject to copyright restrictions.

IV. Monitoring and Evaluation of Collection and Services

Statistics should be collected on the following and be used for monitoring and evaluation:

1. Percentage of registered users to total population.
2. Percentage of collection on loan on any given day.
3. Number of books lent during a stated period.
4. Average books issued per user per unit time.
5. Number of books (including journals, documents, etc.) consulted in each house, per member per unit time.
6. Number of reference queries answered per unit time.
7. Number of registered users.
8. Number of recommendations received for purchase of books per year.
9. Number of library publications produced by the library per year.
10. Number of books withdrawn from collection per year.
11. Number of photocopies made per unit time.
12. Number of hours that the reading room is open per week.

V. Networking of Libraries

The key to opening the resources of a library is its access mechanism. In today's context, it is possible to use technology to bring together the resources of small individual libraries into one seamless large library. The ability to retrieve information from this library depends on standardisation of classification, cataloguing, database structuring and exchange formats.

Collection Organisation and Integrated Access

Local Access

i. Access to every document (print and electronic) in a library should be possible through a proper system of cataloguing and classification.

ii. To help all libraries accomplish this task easily and without delay, and to ensure optimal utilisation of expertise and resources, it is essential to develop bibliographic utilities which permit downloading of records (catalogue entries) and uploading of holdings information by all libraries.

iii. Libraries having collections of print and electronic resources should provide integrated access using latest ICT.

National and Global Access

i. Union catalogues (print and electronic) of periodicals should be updated and put online.

ii. Projects should be developed by the National Library and the Central Reference Library, with support of institutions such as National Book Trust, Sahitya Akademi, Central Institute of Indian Languages at Mysore, C-DAC and Departments of Library and Information Science in order to: a. Convert Indian language scripts/dialects to Roman script; and b. Develop convenient authority files for rendering of names of Indian authors and institutions.

iii. Vocabulary control over Indian subjects should be developed in terms of multilingual thesauri and subject heading lists.

Infrastructure Requirements for Cataloguing, Database Creation and Networking:

i. Open source software should be used wherever possible at present and eventually at all levels.

ii. An open source web-enabled library management software should be developed if necessary and provided to all public libraries for facilitating networking. This software should support multiple Indian language scripts/dialects.

Networking of Public Libraries

i. Networking of public libraries should be undertaken in a phased manner. There are approximately 54,000 public libraries in existence.

- PHASE I: 1,000 of these will be networked in Phase I as a pilot project, by DELNET and INFLIBNET, each covering about 500 libraries in 12–18 months.
- PHASE II: Based on the experiences of Phase I, up to 10,000 libraries will be covered in one year.
- PHASE III: The remaining libraries may be networked in the third and final phase in three years.

This project should be completed by 2011.

ii. Raja Rammohan Roy Library Foundation may give the necessary infrastructural support for the above activity and coordinate it.

iii. The networking agencies should ensure state-of-the-art technology with the following features:

a) Open source platform for the software, which also supports multilingual environment with multi-user and multimedia content creation capabilities.

b) Storage, dissemination and replication of the data through mirror sites, gateways, portals and inter-library loan facilities.

c) Capability of conducting exhaustive training programmes.

National Repository of Bibliographic Records

A national repository of bibliographic records should be instituted, according to the following guidelines:

i. The central repository will contain records of bibliographic resources available in the country.

ii. State central libraries and district/municipal/sub-divisional libraries should be provided with a server with dedicated internet connectivity, and should be responsible for creating bibliographic records.

iii. The libraries at block/village level should have broadband connectivity to enable them not only to access Internet but also to create and upload local content to the library next in hierarchy.

iv. For this purpose, the present infrastructural facilities provided by agencies such as BSNL, MTNL, or other ISPs, should be used.

v. In order to operationalise the above, the National Mission/Commission should:

   a) Define the scope and objectives of the proposed national repository of bibliographic records.

   b) Take stock of the existing situation with regard to bibliographic records.

   c) Suggest technical and operational details and necessary linkages to achieve the above.

   d) Assess the strengths and weaknesses of the stakeholders effectively participating in this programme.

   e) Evaluate the adequacy of the existing legal framework for this purpose and suggest suitable measures.

   f) Critically evaluate the capabilities of National Library and Central Reference Library as designated agencies for creation of the national bibliographic repository and suggest suitable measures for strengthening them.

   g) Assess the financial requirements for achieving the said objectives.

Annexure 3.5: Private and Personal Collections

Recognising the importance of private and personal collections in knowledge creation and dissemination process, and the fact that there are several rich and valuable private and personal collections in existence in the country which need to be preserved for posterity, there should be an effort to include them in the LIS sector. For this purpose, the National Mission/Commission may set up a committee under the chairpersonship of an eminent scholar.

Terms of Reference of the Committee

1. Survey and assess the national situation with regard to identification, documentation and preservation of private collections. This would entail surveys at both the national/state and at the micro level to identify the existing institutions and private/personal collections. The survey should be undertaken keeping in mind the categorisation of private collections between heritage and contemporary, historical and cultural and personal and institutional. The survey would also need to classify the material into manuscripts, old and rare printed materials and historical documents, letters and diaries, contemporary documents of historical and cultural relevance, audio-visual material and other materials such as awards, medals, citations, etc.
2. To suggest a decentralised model for identifying, documenting and preserving private collections.
3. To develop institutional networks at the national and state level to make available inventories or catalogues of private collections, with a view to disseminate information regarding the availability of these collections.
4. To evolve effective measures and schemes for conservation, preservation, documentation and sharing of information on private collections.
   a) Conservation and Preservation
      i. A directory of conservation and preservation experts and institutions should be compiled.
      ii. Survey and documentation of existing methodologies of preservation, both indigenous and international, should be carried out and kept updated to include new state-of-the-art technologies.
      iii. New technologies for preservation should be introduced at all levels.
      iv. Standards and benchmarks for conservation of different materials should be prepared.
      v. Archives for digital documents should be established in each state/union territory.
   b) Documentation
      i. Descriptive cataloguing of personal and private collections should be introduced.
      ii. International standards should be maintained in the cataloguing.
      iii. Nodal agencies at the state and national level may be entrusted with the responsibility of conducting the surveys mentioned earlier and cataloguing the private collections. Necessary financial support should be extended to these agencies.
   c) Dissemination
      i. The catalogues of private collections created at the national and state level should be accessible through the web.
      ii. Private records and collections of importance should be digitised into full text form with proper indexing facilities and should be made available to users against payment where appropriate.
      iii. Archives of digital documents should also be made accessible through the web.
5. To outline suitable advocacy and outreach strategies for this purpose.

a) Sensitise individuals and institutions/business houses about the value and significance of private collections as national property, cultural heritage and historical sources.

b) Have information about private collections reach all levels of society including administrators, scholars, students and the general public.

c) Have extension activities organised by the concerned institutions through different media, including audio-visual and electronic media, to generate awareness about the merits, use and importance of private collections.

6. To formulate necessary approaches for human resource development and creation of infrastructure.

   a) Human Resources

      i. A system of training may be established in areas such as cataloguing, conservation and preservation, digitisation, digital archiving, archival management, rare languages and scripts. Suitable training courses could be devised for this purpose by the Indian Institute of Library and Information Science (ILIS).

      ii. Existing institutions which have the capacity to undertake the management, digitisation, documentation, etc., of private collections, should be suitably supported for this purpose.

   b) Infrastructure

      Existing nodal agencies and their network of associated institutions should be provided suitable infrastructural facilities such as computers, printers, Internet access, multilingual software and manpower, in accordance with certain minimum standards as may be specified.

7. To evaluate the adequacy of existing policy and legal framework and suggest suitable measures to ensure that:

   a) Valuable personal collections are not destroyed or sold/smuggled out of India.

   b) Everyone has a right to access the contents of those private and personal collections that are supported by the Government, except those excluded by mutual agreement.

   c) Owners of private and personal collections provide access to their collections by voluntary permission on the basis of mutually agreed terms regarding access/user fee.

   d) Institutions supported by the Government that maintain archival materials be strengthened to archive documents and disseminate these materials for use to the public. These institutions must formulate access guidelines and enabling legal provisions for access (with the help of legal experts), and make these available to all concerned.

8. To develop guidelines for owners of private collections, keeping in view the following:

   a) Copyright issues and the application of Right to Information Act.

   b) Proprietary rights.

   c) Government support for individuals having private collections, especially for conservation and publication.

   d) Training facilities for individuals having private collections.

   e) Terms and conditions for the acquisition, donation or loan of private collections.

   f) Terms of reference under which collections could be digitised for wider dissemination.

   g) Any other issue emanating from local situations.

5 Knowledge Network

NKC strongly feels that to optimally utilise the potential of institutions engaged in generation and dissemination of knowledge in various areas, such as research laboratories, universities and other institutions of higher learning, including professional institutions, it is important to connect them through a high-speed broadband network. In order to explore the feasibility of establishing broadband connectivity among such institutions, NKC spent six months studying various issues and alternatives. Extensive consultations with experts, potential users, telecom service providers, government officials and various educational and research institutions provided insights on the requirements, implementation issues and benefits of creating an integrated national knowledge network.

The purpose of such a knowledge network goes to the very heart of the country's quest to build quality institutions with requisite research facilities and to create a pool of highly trained persons. Considering the magnitude of the challenge, NKC believes an immediate objective of the network will be to share the existing content, coursework, expertise, ideas, innovations, equipment and facilities available in the limited number of centres of excellence, with a wider group of institutions, educators and students.

Globally, research and development activities and innovations are increasingly multi-disciplinary and collaborative, and require substantial computational power. The key to successful research today is live consultations, data sharing and resource sharing. Therefore, it is essential to provide broadband connectivity to our knowledge institutions to improve access, quality and quantity of R&D activities.

The primary objective is to interconnect all our knowledge institutions in various fields and at various locations throughout the country, through an electronic digital broadband network with adequate capabilities and access speed to encourage sharing of resources and collaborative research.

NKC commissioned an expert to examine what it would take to create a national knowledge network. NKC also held detailed discussions with the office of the Principal Scientific Adviser (PSA) to the Government of India. The discussions yielded a consensus on the optimal approach to be adopted for setting up such a network, whether it is for a broad range of institutions as envisaged by NKC or a specific community of Science and Technology (S&T) research institutions. Based on the various discussions, NKC recommends the following:

1. *National Knowledge Network:* Build a national knowledge network with gigabit capabilities to connect all universities, libraries, laboratories, hospitals and agricultural institutions to share data and resources across the country. This will ultimately require provision of connectivity to around 5,000 nodes covering all major institutions. The actual implementation could be in phases targeting 500 to 1,000 nodes in the first phase. However, the design of the network will have to be based on the final network. The prioritisation of the nodes for implementation purposes should be on the basis of the institutions which are most likely to use the network from day one and which would be able to demonstrate the benefits. Based on a detailed analysis of the country's existing optic fibre infrastructure and technologies available, it is estimated that a 500 to 1000-node network can be commissioned within three to six months.

2. *Options:* Wide consultations with experts and technology providers suggest that there are four possible networking options:

    - The first one involves hiring dark fibres that have been extensively laid out by various telecom service providers and lighting them.

- The second involves lit fibres and differs from the first in not requiring transmission equipment procurement and its maintenance.
- The third involves using existing commercial networks, making capital investment in equipment unnecessary. It requires minimum maintenance and operations organisation.
- The fourth is a hybrid approach where the core consists of two layers in which the inner higher-speed layer is wholly owned by the stakeholders while the lower layer is provided by commercial service providers.

  From the viewpoint of cost, the third approach based on the utilisation of the available commercial networks appears to be most attractive to start with. This is because the capital expenditure is negligible if the operator chosen has a well established network which is being used by a large number of existing customers. However, lack of experience of architectural fiexibility and security aspects of virtual private networks (VPN) set up on a commercial basis, do not allow prospective users to be entirely comfortable with this approach. Therefore, NKC recommends that existing commercial networks be utilised. Subsequently, feedback from this exercise could enable a shift to a hybrid network with a central core, preferably of a relatively few nodes, and an outer network constituted by practically each one of the other operators' networks.

3. *Architecture:* The network should consist of a core using Internet Protocol (IP) and Multi-Packet Labeled Services (MPLS) technology, an aggregation or distribution network, and an access or edge network linking the institution's local area network (LAN) to the core. The core network could be a single hierarchy or a two-stage network with a higher speed network at the top to accommodate architecture flexibility and security concerns in a VPN-based commercial Internet Protocol-Multi Protocol Label Switching (IP-MPLS) network. The detailed specification of the network will have to be drawn up with a view to inviting bids for speedy implementation. The network should be implemented in phases. The first phase should cover about 1000 institutions and should be commissioned in three to six months.
4. *Congruence with e-Governance:* The question of whether the network for e-Governance and the knowledge network should be one single network assumes importance and relevance depending upon the approach adopted for the realisation of the network. In the recommended approach in the first phase, namely VPNs on commercial MPLS networks on Dense Wavelength Division Multiplexing (DWDM), this question becomes irrelevant because several VPNs can be created on a commercial network and they could be entirely uncorrelated, as may be the case with these two networks. This question would assume importance only if the country were to implement a purely owned network on lighted fibres. On the other hand, even in the hybrid approach, the e-Governance network with an entirely different geographical spread and much lower bandwidth requirements, can be realised as VPNs and the security and fliexibility could be addressed by the inner core. The issue of congruence of the two networks therefore, no longer remains important and the two aspects can be totally delinked.
5. *Security and Privacy:* Methods will have to be evolved both at the time of commissioning of the network as well as during operations, to ensure security of data along with privacy and confidentiality. Access to data from the data centre of a given institution should be under the control of the institution being addressed. An arrangement for authentication and authorisation, with the participation of the connected institutions is essential to launch the network.
6. *One-time Support for LANs:* The proposed broadband network envisages higher access bandwidth and therefore, almost all user institutions will have to upgrade their networks to be able to cater to these speeds. While several institutions may have the resources for doing this, a large number will need one-time capital support to set up Fast Ethernet LAN (FELAN) which includes expenditure on routers, switches and optic fibre cable on the campus.
7. *Costs:* The knowledge network initially proposed to be launched on existing commercial networks will therefore involve a recurring cost of Rs. 20-40 lakh per institution connected, amounting to Rs. 200-400 crore annually for 1000 institutions in the first phase. In addition, there will be a one-time capital investment in upgrading the LANs of these institutions to a 100 Mbps capability FELAN. Thereafter, based on feedback, the installation of the inner core network of 10 Gbps or higher capability will be taken up. This will involve a capital investment of around Rs. 1,000 crore on a 7 or 8-node inner core network, its gigabit connectivity to the commercial IP-MPLS networks, as also direct connectivity to a few users who are particularly concerned about the security and internetworking experiments. This expenditure will be incurred

over a period of time. There will be an additional recurring expenditure for this inner core on hiring large bandwidths from bandwidth service providers. This amount will depend on the number of nodes and the negotiated or bid-based price.

8. *Organisation:* To ensure day to day coordination, operation and efficient utilisation, NKC recommends establishing a Special Purpose Vehicle (SPV) consisting of major stakeholders. Such an SPV should have professional experts pooled from various stakeholder institutions for coordinating and guiding various private vendors for speedy implementation. The policy, security and overall management should be the responsibility of the SPV and the operational support requirements should be met by the industry. One of the compelling reasons for such a mechanism is to provide assurance that the use of cyber space will in no way compromise the security concerns of the country.

9. *Ownership:* The knowledge network should be owned by the SPV consisting of major stakeholders. Government ownership is not desirable, despite the fact that substantial funding will be from the Government, because:

    - It is the Government's policy to withdraw from direct operations and maintenance activities in the ICT sector.
    - The type of trained manpower needed, though not large, is in great demand in the market, and therefore will require special remuneration and incentives.

10. *Special Group:* NKC recommends the setting up of a special Working Group of experts to finalise specifications, implementation plans, cost estimates and network plans, as well as to carry out the actual task of procurement and commissioning of the network. This group will also establish the SPV needed for running the network on a day to day basis.

NKC believes that a national knowledge network interconnecting our knowledge institutions and infrastructure with access speeds of 100 mbps and more will give a major push to collaborations and sharing needed to enhance the quality of our education, research and applications and at the same time will empower our people to be competitive in the global economy.

6 Health Information Network

The National Knowledge Commission (NKC) is convinced that extensive use of IT in health care will promote the delivery of efficient health care in the country. However, as the use of IT in the management of health care and medical knowledge will increase, the health care establishments will develop and use their own health IT systems. It has been the experience of western countries that these individually developed systems are often not interoperable with other establishments, which makes the health care system inefficient and expensive. NKC believes that India has a unique opportunity to learn from the world experience and adopt only the proven best practices in the field.

In this context, NKC constituted a Working Group, under the chairmanship of Dr. N.K. Ganguly, Chairman Indian Council for Medical Research (ICMR) to study the use of IT in future health care. The Working Group studied the future need, conducted several meetings and deliberations, and held consultations with various national and international experts. NKC believes that the use of IT in health care needs a national direction for its proper implementation and makes the following recommendations for developing a Health Information Network:

1. Initiate Development of Indian Health Information Network

India needs to develop a web-based network, connecting all health care establishments, in both private and public sector. When fully functional, all health care transactions will be recorded electronically and this data will be available in the health data vault to authorised users when they need it and where they need it.

The proposed knowledge network with gigabit capabilities may provide the backbone and network infrastructure on which the health information network may ride. The network will be a 'hub and spoke model'. All health care establishments in a district will connect to a central data repository at the district level. All the district nodal data repositories will connect with a state level data bank, which in turn will connect with a central data bank.

There should be active involvement of private and public health entities to effectively address the creation of this network, portals, electronic health records, health data vault, security, privacy and other related issues in future, which will encourage the participation of the following:

- Citizens,
- Health care providers and payers,
- Education, research institutions and investigators,
- Government departments and institutions,
- Public health agencies and NGOs,
- Pharmaceutical industry and medical device makers,
- Telemedicine institutions, and
- Software and hardware developers.

The ready availability of information will accrue enormous benefits to public health planning, medical education, cost control, medical research, drug development, prevention of fraud, disaster management and improved patient care.

2. Establish National Standards for Clinical Terminology and Health Informatics

For a web-based interoperable national grid, it is imperative to have common clinical nomenclature, or else disparate programmes developed by the industry will not be interoperable. The clinical standards will establish a common lexicon to be used in electronic transactions. This will enable all geographically scattered entities to communicate in one common language and facilitate data transmission and collection. It is important to develop common nomenclature standards for the traditional medical systems, as large numbers of people depend on these systems for their medical needs. Besides the common clinical language, adoption of a common national standard in health informatics will facilitate the messaging, collation and analysis of data.

3. Create a Common Electronic Health Record (EHR)

An electronic health record (EHR) is the record of a person from birth to death where all heath care encounters are recorded. Health transactions are presently recorded in a paper format, like a hospital patient chart, prescriptions, laboratory tests, etc. The technology to capture and store this information electronically already exists and has been developed by many private and public organisations in India. For uniform data capture, storage and subsequent use, it is recommended to create a common national EHR based on common clinical and IT standards. The record should be able to capture data generated by the 'traditional medicine' health providers. To promote the early adoption of the health IT, this EHR may be given free of cost or at subsidised rates to all users. The other IT tools and applications can be developed by the private industry and should be compatible with the national EHR.

4. Frame Policies to Promote Use of IT in Health Care

The use of IT in health care needs an impetus from the Government; otherwise the development and penetration will be slow and arbitrary. These policies should be formed, not to hamper but promote the health IT business in the country and generate employment in this sector. The Central government should declare a time period after which all transactions in health care in the country will be in electronic format. Sufficient time should be given for the health establishments to adopt electronic transaction. NKC feels 7-10 years is an adequate time for all parties to evolve electronic transactions after which all health establishments should be able to comply.

5. Create Appropriate Policy Framework to Protect Health Data of Citizens

The integrity of data at the primary data collection site will determine the usefulness of this enterprise. To ensure that only correct patient and other health data is collected, it is of utmost importance to gain the confidence of the citizens that their health data will not be misused by the health providers, insurance companies, employers and the government. Both technological and legal framework is important to achieve this. While encryption, anonymity and other IT security measures should be in place, it is also important to have rules in place. It is important to maintain confidentiality and security of the personal health data and to govern the access and use of data.

6. Medical Informatics to be Part of Medical and Paramedical Curriculum

Medical education needs to take full advantage of the power of ICT. A well-structured health informatics curriculum needs to be made an integral part of medical education at all levels. Basic ICT facilities, such as good quality access to Internet and e-Journals, need to be made compulsory for all medical colleges in the country. For capacity building, ICT tools should be effectively deployed to train the large number of health workers. Short- and medium-term courses need to be developed and made available on the net to address training needs of all health workers in the field. It should be made affordable, accessible and easily available for small players. There is a need to evolve common formats for data reporting to facilitate IT enablement of medical manpower at all levels. Education-related portals should also be set up for training of medical manpower.

7. Create an Institutional Framework for Implementation

An autonomous body with the Ministry of Health should be responsible for planning and implementing the project in a time bound manner. This body should be autonomous and a non-profit organisation with representation from private, public and voluntary sectors.[1] All stakeholders should be represented in this body and it should have the resources to promote and implement the plan. It should also have the authority to ensure the smooth functioning of the Indian health information network. The objectives for this institutional body will be:

- To formulate an implementation plan,
- To coordinate the participation of all stakeholders,
- To create linkages with E-governance, medical education network,
- To ensure financial viability of the project,
- To set up a comprehensive and interactive national health portal,
- To suggest common national standards,
- To protect confidentiality and security of data,
- To facilitate the ownership, access and flow of data, and
- To maintain and upgrade the system in future.

The next step in the development of the Indian health information network is to formalise the institutional body with appropriate professional people with domain expertise, adequate budget, time tables and measurable milestones to implement these recommendations. The body may consider conducting pilot programmes before scaling at the national level.

1. It may be modeled after the Canadian Health Infoway, which is a non-profit autonomous body funded by the federal and provincial governments in Canada.

7 Portals

Recognising that the Internet constitutes a powerful and democratic source of information and knowledge, the National Knowledge Commission (NKC) deliberated on ways to create a series of web portals. These web portals should become a decisive tool in the popular movements in support of the right to information, decentralisation, transparency, accountability and people's participation.

In order to increase openness and enhance accessibility, NKC recommends the creation of web portals to aggregate, organise and present relevant and useful content in local languages, in a highly uniform, customisable, user-friendly and personalised way for several key areas related to basic human needs.

In this context, the Commission recommends the following:

1. *Create national portals for basic needs:* National web-based portals should be set up on certain key sectors such as water, energy, environment, education, food, health, agriculture, employment, citizen rights, etc. These would serve as a single point of access for consolidated information, applications and resources on the sector and will cater to a wide spectrum of users from citizens, entrepreneurs, small scale industries, students, professionals, researchers, local practitioners, etc.

2. *Management and ownership by consortium:* While the Government will be a key partner in the initial set-up, the portals should be managed by a consortium with adequate representation from a wide range of stakeholders from the sector including NGOs, research and scientific groups, academic institutions, advocacy groups, government agencies/departments, international bodies, other funding agencies, private sector, technology experts, educators, e-learning experts, etc.

This will ensure that:

- The portal remains a dynamic repository of information from multiple sources to aggregate content.
- A collaborative model is adopted so that all stakeholders such as citizens, NGOs, businesses, etc., participate in the creation, collaboration, sharing and discussions in a rich and meaningful way such that information cannot be monopolised by any one group.
- The portal would have greater community ownership in order to ensure its success.
- Experiences, technology, processes, etc., would be shared between various portals.

3. *Establish procedures:* A set of procedures should be followed for setting up portals:

- Agreement on the subject area,
- Identification of champion/lead organisation/s,
- Submission of proposal on architecture of the portal by the champion organisations for consideration of the Commission,
- Identification of stakeholders and partners and setting up of framework for portal management,
- Development of content,
- Launch of portal, and
- Development of rich, useful and relevant content.

The cycle is expected to take between nine months to a year to complete, at the end of which a portal would be put in place which could then continuously be enhanced, populated and promoted.

4. *Provide access to government held data:* There are a host of issues related to data for a portal, such as sourcing, validation, quality and formats. The Government is a major source of extensive data on various sectors. All Government departments should easily make available data sets they have, in a digital format to the portal consortium. Data from different sectors needs to be analysed holistically so that planning becomes more data-driven and reflects the ground situation. This means that data that is traditionally collected and managed separately, unrelated to each other, should now be seen together. There are no platforms or mechanisms currently in place to allow this to be done easily. Clear guidelines should be developed under which this data could be sourced in appropriate formats and regularly updated. The Right to Information may make this easier but it continues to be a long drawn process. These procedures need to be streamlined and made simpler.

5. *Encourage collaborative funding:* The portal effort can escalate quickly as the scale of content, partnerships and the scope is very large. The issue of funding for the effort includes big line items like technology development, map preparation, data gathering, developing applications, content creation, organising and coordinating partnerships. Solutions need to be evolved depending on the sector in question. Several possibilities including public-private partnerships and new business models should be explored. The Government may also look at providing some public money for these efforts through grants.

6. *Reform mapping policy:* The advance in computer-based Geographic Information Systems (GIS) has given mapping and use of maps a huge impetus in various fields. The ability to make sense of large amounts of interrelated data in spatial and attribute form has helped in visual decision-making in various areas such as agriculture, transport, disaster management, etc. An unambiguous mapping policy coupled with clear guidelines for use of spatial data are necessary to share GIS data and thereby maximise the use of cutting edge technology and applications. Under the new mapping policy announced in May 2005, there is still some ambiguity about publishing of GIS maps on the Internet by NGOs, Government and other development-oriented agencies. Rich GIS-based content in various sectors like water, health, education, etc., can be delivered by various organisations and bodies in order to share information, foster an informed debate and allow for more effective planning. The mapping policy needs to allow for such access and provide clear guidelines.

7. *Enhance Internet penetration and access:* At this stage, the use of portals may be limited by the low Internet penetration in the country, where less than five per cent of the population has access to Internet. To address this challenge, it is essential that the portal team should work proactively with NGO and Government networks, use mass distributions channels like radio, television and the print media to ensure this knowledge is leveraged to precipitate change on the ground. There needs to be a firm commitment to support alternate non-web outreach methods that make this knowledge accessible to all sections of society (the digital haves and have-nots).

An alternate IT technology can support those who do not have Internet access. This calls for a locally resident tool that is run on a desktop PC which can provide information and run applications pertaining to specific topics. Since these applications are not relying on the Internet or storing information at a distant server, they can be used locally at the site without network connectivity.

Subsequently, it would be useful to be able to connect to a server to upload local data or download updates and information. These thick client software applications can be the source of bottom-up data, since NGOs and individuals can upload local data over the Internet for analysis at a central server. This provides an alternative bottom-up way of collecting fine grained local data in a continuous manner.

The portal will thus address the needs of a very diverse spectrum of users from researchers and policy makers to local practitioners at the ground level who stand to benefit greatly from the comprehensive availability of information on a sector relevant for them in an open and transparent manner.

8. *Translate into Indian languages:* The portals should be translated into all Indian languages to reach a wider audience. Interactive applications and e-learning content must be made available in local languages for it to be relevant.

II

Concepts

8 School Education

Ensuring quality school education to all is the foundation upon which any further advances towards a knowledge society must be based. Noting the crucial importance of school education, the National Knowledge Commission (NKC) held a series of workshops and consultations around the country involving a very wide range of stakeholders, to discuss issues of quantity, quality and access in school education. NKC recognises that the primary responsibility for school education is borne by the state governments, and therefore, any policy changes must be with the full participation and involvement of the states. Nevertheless, NKC believes that positive changes in systems of schooling will require the active involvement of the Central government as well as state governments, not only in the matter of providing resources but also in promoting organisational and other changes. NKC has a number of suggestions and recommendations covering the different aspects of school education, but the essential thrust can be summarised in terms of more resources, more decentralisation and more flexibility.

1. Central Legislation for the Right to Education, Backed by Financial Commitment

NKC endorses the speedy enactment of a Central legislation that will ensure the right of all children in the country to good quality school education up to Class VIII, supported with financial commitments of the Central and state governments. This obviously requires substantially increased public spending for both elementary and secondary school education, which must be seen as a priority area for spending. Currently school education is highly segmented, even in government-run institutions, as a result of the parallel track of "education centres" in some states. These separate systems must be integrated to give all children access to schools of acceptable quality, which will obviously require additional spending.

2. More Flexibility in Disbursal of Funds

However, there is a strong case for changes in the manner in which such expenditure is incurred. The current norms for the Central government's disbursal of funds to states for (including for Sarva Shiksha Abhiyan (SSA)) the planned SUCCESS programme for secondary education and other central schemes, are too rigid and must be made more flexible. NKC strongly recommends a system of funds transfer and accounting that will allow for regional and other differences as well as changing requirements over time, and thereby allow state governments to use the resources in the most effective way. There should also be greater flexibility in disbursing funds down to the school level and a greater degree of autonomy of local level management in the use of funds. The norms and rules should allow schools to adapt to local conditions and meet particular requirements of their students.

3. Decentralisation and Greater Local Autonomy

Community participation is an important instrument to ensure accountability and improve the day-to-day functioning of schools. This in turn means that the management of schools, including the use and management of funds, should be decentralised to local authorities as far as possible, whether they be *panchayats*, Village Education Committees or municipalities, and to School Boards that have representation of all stakeholders including parents.

4. Expansion of Functional Literacy

NKC would like to stress the continuing importance of a focus on expanding functional literacy among the population. Illiteracy remains a major problem, even among the age group 15-35 years, and therefore, literacy programmes must be expanded rather than reduced, and given a different focus that is directed towards improving life skills and meeting felt needs, especially (but not only) among the youth.

5. Planning for School Infrastructure

It is important to remember that land is an essential requirement of schools, and this requirement is likely to increase in the near future given the expansion implied by demographic changes and need to ensure universal schooling. Therefore, urban master plans and local development plans must explicitly incorporate the physical requirements for schooling, including provisions for playgrounds and other school facilities.

6. Enabling and Regulating Mechanisms for Private Schools

Since private schools play an important role in the provision of education, there is need for both enabling and regulating mechanisms to be developed and strengthened for them. There should be transparent, norm-based and straightforward procedures for the recognition of private schools, to reduce harassment and bureaucratic delay. There should also be transparent criteria as for the disbursement of aid from the Government to some self-financing schools, especially those which cater to underprivileged children, and clear norms with respect to the ability of school managements to raise resources from other sources. The monitoring of private schools, in terms of ensuring a transparent admissions process, regulation of fee structures, as well as meeting minimum set standards for quality of teaching and infrastructure, also requires attention. The possibility of greater exchange between schools, including mentoring of one school by another, should be allowed and encouraged.

7. Database on School Education

Educational planning and monitoring are made much more difficult because of the lack of comprehensive and accurate data on schools, school-age children and actual attendance of both students and teachers. The collection and speedy dissemination of accurate and current data on schooling must be made a priority. It is necessary to create a complete database on schools and school-age children so as to track the actual coverage and quality of schooling at different levels, and to make it widely available in a timely manner. Such data collection may be made an essential part of the fund allocation for school education, with appropriate institutional mechanisms.

8. More Co-ordination between Departments

The multiplicity of management structures and government departments that currently governs schooling creates confusion, unnecessary replication and possibly inconsistent strategies across different schools. There must be greater co-ordination between different departments of government on school education policy, even while ensuring more autonomy to the local management of schools.

9. National Evaluation Body for Monitoring Quality

Educational administration also needs to be more conscious of actual learning outcomes at different levels, which will determine both policy and functioning. NKC, therefore, proposes a national evaluation body to monitor the quality of both government and private schools, using a results-based monitoring framework based on a short list of monitorable criteria that include both process and outcome indicators.

10. Revamping School Inspection

The system of school inspection needs to be revamped and revitalised, with a greater role for local stakeholders and greater transparency in the system. The solution does not lie in simply expanding the system—rather, we need to develop systems to ensure meaningful monitoring, including provision of greater facilities to school inspectors, a separation of inspection of qualitative and administrative aspects, transparency in the criteria of inspection and greater involvement of local stakeholders.

11. Teachers and Teacher Training

Teachers are the single most important element of the school system, and the country is already facing a severe shortage of qualified and motivated school teachers at different levels. It is urgent to restore the dignity of school teaching as a profession and provide more incentives for qualified and committed teachers. Non-teaching official duties such as electoral activities should not be allowed to interfere with the teaching process. Forums that allow and encourage teachers to exchange ideas, information and experiences, including a web-based portal, should be developed.

At the same time, there should be transparent systems for ensuring accountability of school teachers. As far as possible, teachers should be recruited to particular schools.

The training of teachers is a major area of concern at present, since both pre-service and in-service training of school teachers is extremely inadequate and also poorly managed in most states. Pre-service training needs to be improved and differently regulated in both public and private institutions, while systems for in-service training require expansion and major reform that allows for greater flexibility.

12. Reforms in the Curriculum and Examination System

Curriculum reform remains a critically important issue in almost all schools. School education must be made more relevant to the lives of children. There is need to move away from rote-learning to understanding concepts, developing good comprehension and communication skills and learning how to access knowledge independently. This also requires substantial changes in the examination system, especially at Board level but also earlier.

13. Use of Information and Communication Technology

Wherever feasible, ICT should be made more accessible to teachers, students and administration for learning, training, research, administration, management, monitoring, etc. This requires the provision of more facilities such as computers as well as connectivity and broadband facilities. Computer-aided learning also requires training of teachers and other staff in order to make the best use of technology.

14. English Language Teaching

Proficiency in English is widely perceived as an important avenue for employment and upward mobility, which also greatly facilitates the pursuit of higher education. The incorporation of English into the curriculum through the teaching of English as a language in Class I and teaching of one other subject in English medium in later classes requires making pedagogical changes to contextualise language learning, increasing the availability of English language teachers and providing more bilingual and supplementary teaching materials. At the same time, mutlilinguality must be promoted and language issues must be explicitly taken on board in designing school curricula and methods of pedagogy.

15. Interventions to Ensure Access of Educationally Deprived Categories

Special interventions are necessary to ensure greater access to education of educationally deprived categories, and some proposals for this are developed in more detail in the accompanying Note. Obviously, specific measures are required to ensure greater enrolment and retention of girl students. Education of SC children must be a priority, which necessitates both flexibility of approach and avoidance of discrimination. The access of children from scheduled tribes requires more flexible and sensitive schooling strategies. Language issues must be explicitly taken on board in designing school curricula and methods of pedagogy. Special strategies are required to ensure greater access to schools for children in backward regions, remote locations and difficult terrains. Official strategies for ensuring better access of Muslim children to schooling are excessively focused on madrasas which cater to only a tiny minority of such children; the emphasis should be on creating enabling conditions for Muslim children in the general school system. Children of seasonal migrants require special conditions and efforts to ensure continuous access to schooling. Similarly, labouring children require incentives and bridge courses. The needs of physically disadvantaged children, as well as teachers, have to be factored in more thoroughly in provisions for school education.

There is wide diversity across states in terms of progress towards achieving universal elementary education, and also diversity within states with respect to the quality of school education. But NKC believes that these proposals, which require the active involvement of the Central government as well as state governments, will go some way in terms of ensuring universal access to elementary education, wider access to secondary education as well as better quality and greater relevance of all schooling. Given the strong synergies between this and other areas such as libraries, translation, knowledge networks, etc., these suggestions should be seen in conjunction with other recommendations that have already been made in these other areas, as part of a systematic set of knowledge initiatives for the young.

Annexure 8.1: Note on School Education

The Prime Minister has repeatedly emphasised that ensuring quality school education to all is one of the most important priorities of the Government, and the National Knowledge Commission has also recognised the crucial significance of this as the foundation upon which any further advances must be based. NKC has held a series of workshops around the country, addressing issues of quantity, quality and access in school education, and tried to involve a very wide range of stakeholders in the consultations.

NKC recognises that the primary responsibility for school education is borne by the state governments, and therefore, any policy changes must be with the full participation and involvement of the states. Also, there is wide diversity across states in terms of progress towards achieving universal elementary education, and also diversity within states with respect to the quality of school education. Nevertheless, NKC believes that positive changes in systems of schooling that will ensure universal access to elementary education, wider access to secondary education as well as better quality and greater relevance of all schooling, will require the active involvement of the Central government as well as state governments. Such involvement is necessary not only in the matter of providing resources but also in promoting organisational and other changes. NKC has a number of suggestions and recommendations covering the different aspects of school education, but the essential thrust can be summarised in terms of more resources, more decentralisation and more flexibility. Outlined below are the most important areas of possible intervention. NKC is aware that while some proposals are new, other recommendations have found expression in different ways in previous reports and studies. However, NKC has chosen to reiterate them because they are still crucial and relevant.

NKC would also like to emphasise that there are very strong synergies between these recommendations for school education and other proposals of NKC with respect to libraries, translation, networks, language in schools and vocational education. These suggestions should therefore, be seen in conjunction with the other recommendations that have already been made in these areas, as part of a systematic set of knowledge initiatives for the young.

1. Quantity and Resources

1.1 Substantially Increased Public Spending is Required for both Elementary and Secondary Education

NKC strongly endorses the speedy enactment of a Central legislation that will ensure the right of all children in the country to good quality school education up to Class VIII. We also believe that this should be extended to cover universal schooling up to Class X as soon as possible. NKC has emphasised that a vibrant, good quality and universally accessible government school system is the basic foundation upon which the schooling system in the country must rest.

Therefore, this must be supported with a financial commitment of the Central government, in such a way as to ensure that the right to quality school education is provided to all children of the country, regardless of which state they are residing in. This necessarily requires a significant expansion of the resources to be provided to elementary school education. While the Government has increased allocations for school expenditure, the amounts are still far below what is required to achieve universal school education of reasonable quality for all. This is even more true because of the need to upgrade the "Education Centres" that are operating in many states to proper schools that meet all the norms in terms of trained teachers, minimum facilities, etc. Therefore, NKC strongly recommends a substantial increase in the Central government allocation.

NKC has already expressed concern on the recent decision of the Central government to reduce the central funding for the Sarva Shiksha Abhiyan (SSA) from 75 per cent to 50 per cent. This may lead to a sharp curtailment of progress towards universal school education, especially in the more backward states where the gap is greater. It is worth noting that the state governments are already incurring the bulk of school education expenditure. NKC strongly feels that, in addition to 50 per cent of SSA funds, the Centre should provide all the additional funding required to ensure the Right to Education in those states where the state government is already spending at least 15 per cent of its total budget on school education.

At the same time, the importance of increased spending on secondary education is greater than ever before. There is a huge shortage of middle and secondary schools, which is one of the important reasons for the low rates of retention after Class V. Currently, secondary education is massively under funded, which in turn creates not only absolute shortages but also problems of inadequate quality in many government secondary and higher secondary schools. The aim should be to reach universal secondary school education within a maximum of 10 years. Given the demographics, this implies that expenditure on secondary schooling must be increased by several multiples within the next two years, indeed by at least five times the current level if the CABE estimates are used. Currently, many primary schools are being upgraded to secondary school status, without provision of sufficient teachers, rooms and other pedagogical requirements, which severely comprises on the quality of such secondary education. The norms for secondary schools, which include not only provision for specialised subject teachers but also for science labs, counselling etc., must be strictly adhered to when new schools are created and when primary schools are upgraded.

1.2 Urban Planning and Local Planning must Explicitly Incorporate the Physical Requirements for Schooling, Including Provisions for Playgrounds and Other School Facilities

It is important to remember that land is an essential requirement of schools, and this requirement is likely to increase in the near future given the expansion required by demographic changes and the need to ensure universal schooling. In the context of rapid urbanisation, it has been found that urban conglomerations often come up without adequate provision for ensuring the physical space required for schools in the vicinity. This is particularly a problem in new settlements with quickly increasing density of population, not only in large cities but also in smaller towns and fast growing villages. This makes it difficult to establish schools where required, and to ensure that schools are able to provide all the necessary facilities including sports fields, etc. It is essential that the urban land use policies and regulations in all states and municipalities explicitly factor in the physical requirements of schools in areas of a certain population density.

Similarly in rural areas, there must be adequate provision for land for setting up schools in areas that surpass a certain population density. In rural areas with low population density, difficult terrain or extreme climatic conditions, the government may consider setting up residential schools, which could also address the problem of migrant labourers and nomadic populations.

1.3 The Norms for Central Government Disbursal to States of Sarva Shiksha Abhiyan (SSA) Funds and Other Central Schemes for School Education are too Rigid and must be Made More Flexible

The current system of funds transfer and the accounting rules create unnecessary rigidities that often do not allow the state governments to use the money in the most efficient or desirable way, and also lead to less than complete utilisation of the budgetary allocation.

Some of these problems include:

- very rigid norms on unit costs and what is allowed in terms of spending, that do not recognise the diverse requirements of different states or particular regions;
- inadequate financial provisions for infrastructure such as buildings etc., especially for some states and cities, which leads to the creation of poor quality infrastructure;
- an inflexible accounting system that does not allow transferring funds across heads to meet particular or changing requirements, and therefore, inhibits full utilisation and also prevents synergies from developing;
- insufficient allocation for repair and maintenance of infrastructure;
- treating rural and urban schools in the same manner even though the requirements are often very different (for example, urban government schools may require different infrastructure and facilities in order to attract students);
- treating all districts and geographical areas in the same manner regardless of the degree of backwardness, topographical conditions, etc. (This is especially a problem for schools in hilly or heavily forested areas or those with poor physical connectivity, for which per capita allocations are the same as for other more accessible areas); and
- problems in the timing of fund transfer, as well as uncertainties in fund provision created by the insistence on matching funds and the fact that plan ceilings keep changing every year.

NKC strongly recommends a less rigid and more flexible system of funds transfer and accounting that will allow for regional and other differences as well as changing requirements over time, and thereby allow state governments to use the resources in the most effective way. This recommendation is both for the SSA and for the planned SUCCESS programme for secondary education, and also for other centrally sponsored schemes relating to school education.

1.4 There should be Greater Flexibility in Disbursing Funds Down to the School Level and a Greater Degree of Autonomy of Local Level Management in the Use of Funds

Even within the states, the norms for fund disbursal and the requirements are often very time consuming and breed delays and unnecessary rigidities. There should be recognition of differences in per capita resource requirement according to particular criteria, such as geographical and spatial characteristics, the presence of children with special needs, seasonality and other features.

In addition, there is a strong case for providing greater autonomy to local level management of schools, including locally elected bodies, school boards, Village Education Committees, etc., in the use and management of funds, subject to some overall criteria. Within the stipulated norms for expenditure, there should be scope for greater flexibility in the use of funds in response to local needs and local innovation.

1.5 There should be Transparent, Norm-based and Straightforward Procedures for the Recognition of Private Schools, as well as for the Disbursement of Aid from the Government to Self-Financing Schools and the Ability of School Management to Raise Resources from Other Sources

Private schools play a significant role in dispensing school education. It is estimated by NUEPA that around 15 per cent of schools in the country are privately owned and managed, while in some urban areas, private schools cater to a very large proportion of school going children. Their role must be recognised, and those providing quality education should be encouraged, especially when they cater to less privileged children.

However, many private schools have identified the time consuming procedures for renewal of recognition from the government, which have to be undertaken at relatively frequent intervals, as a source of harassment. It is necessary to simplify the rules and reduce the multiplicity of clearances required for private schools, by developing a modality for coordinated point of clearance as far as possible. There is also a case for increasing the time period for which recognition is granted to such schools, especially those with a proven track record. Transparency in dealings between the government and private schools will also be aided if the information on rules and criteria for registration and the results of all school applications for granting of recognition are made public in an accessible form, including by making the relevant information available on websites.

Those charitable schools that provide quality education to children from underprivileged and marginalised sections of society deserve encouragement, and may be considered for receipt of government resources, according to transparent and norm-based procedures. However, all mechanisms of government aid disbursement to privately run schools should be transparently conducted, according to defined norms.

There is a widespread perception that the government rules currently reduce the ability of school managements to raise resources from other sources for the expansion of infrastructure or to provide other facilities. This varies across states, but in general in most states the current system does allow schools to raise funds from donations, resources extended from the *panchayat* and other sources. However, it is important to ensure that the available flexibility for school management to raise resources should be widely known and publicised. In addition, innovative methods of raising additional resources could be allowed and encouraged. For example, schools, particularly in urban areas, could use assets such as buildings during non-school hours to generate additional funds to improve the quality of facilities.

1.6 Illiteracy Remains a Major Problem, and therefore Literacy Programmes Cannot be Ignored or given Less Importance. Expenditure on the National Literacy Mission (NLM) must be Expanded Rather than Reduced, and Given a Different Focus

The shift in policy focus from the National Literacy Mission (NLM) to the Sarva Shiksha Abhiyan has led to a declining emphasis on the need to ensure universal functional literacy. However, according to the 2001 Census, a significant proportion of the population—nearly half of all females and one-quarter of males—remains functionally illiterate. According to the NSSO, a significant proportion of households in 2004-05 (more than a quarter in rural India and nearly 10 per cent in urban India) have no literate member. The lack of functional literacy is much more marked among women, those residing in backward areas and those from marginalised social groups. Also, a significant proportion of young people—around 30 per cent of the age-cohort of 15-35 years – is functionally illiterate, since they were too old to benefit from the SSA and also slipped through the net of the literacy programmes. This is of great concern because such people will continue to be active citizens for the next half century and therefore, must not be denied the capacities and opportunities that come from being literate.

NKC therefore, recommends the following measures for literacy:

- Ensure greater funds for the NLM, including provision for more pedagogical resources including not only ICT but also locally generated teaching material as well as local hiring of temporary staff wherever required.
- Encourage the NLM to shift to creating Continuing Education Centres in both rural and urban areas, to impart functional literacy that is of relevance and interest to those who are currently illiterate or recently literate, as well as provide further learning material and other resources and facilities to the newly literate.
- Orient the post-literacy and continuing education programmes to the emotional, physical and psychological needs of adults rather than children, incorporating issues regarding citizens' rights, human rights, sex education, health and livelihood government programmes, etc.
- Use a variety of methods to ensure functional literacy, which combine more centralised schemes based on ICT and other new technology with continuous work at the local level based on a clear institutional structure. While new technologies such as ICT provide important new methods for imparting literacy in a short time, they necessarily have a limited role. They cannot be seen as stand-alone quick-fix solutions, but must be combined with other methods.
- Move to a sustainable system of literacy generation that does not rely on underpaid "volunteer" labour alone, which therefore, involves budgetary provision for better remuneration for literacy workers.
- Create synergies between NLM and the proposed Skill Development Mission, while taking local needs and field requirements into account. For example, in some primarily agrarian economies, undue emphasis on industrial skills in ITIs may be incongruous while horticultural and animal husbandry skills may be more relevant.

1.7 Early Childhood Education is Extremely Important and must be Universalised

There are two aspects to ensuring the universalisation of early schooling and pre-school education. The first is the systematic extension of *balwadis* with trained staff to handle child pedagogy. The second is the provision for one year of pre-schooling in all institutions of elementary education. Both of these have implications for resource allocation and recruitment of the requisite staff.

1.8 The Collection and Speedy Dissemination of Accurate and Current Data on Schooling must be made a Priority. It is Necessary to Create a Complete Database on Schools and School-age Children so as to Track the Actual Coverage and Quality of Schooling at Different Levels, and to make it Widely Available in a Timely Manner. Such Data Collection may be made an Essential Part of the Fund Allocation for School Education, with Appropriate Institutional Mechanisms

India has an extensive and regular mechanism of data collection for primary education. However, its methodology and use leave much to be desired. For example, at present there is no reliable method for establishing which children are in schools. Data collection is too extensive, time-intensive and done almost entirely by teachers, rather than by independent and specialised personnel. There is minimal cross tabulation, coordination and cross referencing of data. The results are typically revealed to administrators, schools etc., too late to be relevant—often several years after the survey takes place. It is immensely difficult even for stakeholders, as well as other concerned citizens, to access the data lying with official sources, despite repeated requests.

It is necessary to have a system to provide reliable school education statistics which must be transparently formulated and freely available to all. This requires mechanisms that are incorporated into the funding for all school education, at the Central and state government levels. These would ensure data collection and access, provide up to date information as rapidly as possible, make it more relevant for planning and implementation and more accessible for everyone. The following goals are relevant in this context:

- The process of data collection must be streamlined, made less time consuming and more relevant.
- A comprehensive mapping is required of schools and children of school going age, so as to have accurate information on which children in which localities are enrolled, and attending which schools, as well as those not enrolled. This would also map out localities where there are high rates of dropout and/or non-enrolment.
- A tracking mechanism for all school children should be set up, to track their individual school going status, and progress in school. This tracking should cover both government schools and private schools. This would ensure universal access for children in all locations, as well as for girls and specific categories. A tracking mechanism will also facilitate checking for dropouts and related problems, and allow for speedy intervention to address such problems. It should be noted that there are already ongoing initiatives in this regard in some states, which can be replicated and scaled up.
- Data collected for the purposes of planning must provide all the relevant information. This is also important with respect to information on infrastructure provision: for example, the number of rooms should also mention whether these are electrified; where availability of toilets is described, there should also be information on the availability of water in the toilets.
- Safeguards must be instituted against "creative readjustment" of data, which is a common problem given the structure of incentives and the fact that the data are most often provided by the teachers or school management. This requires that data should be collected by independent agencies as far as possible, or necessarily subject to frequent and random cross-checks.
- ICT must be integrated for data collation and management, wherever required. A local area network with digital entry provisions could be set up to make it easier for the teachers and others who provide and use the data.
- The data thus collected must be freely available and easily accessible, provided on dedicated websites in addition to the usual means of publication.
- More specialised micro level surveys and research should be commissioned. There should also be attempts to bring together other relevant research for easy access by practitioners.

2. Quality and Management

2.1 Currently School Education is Highly Segmented, even in Government-run Institutions, as a Result of the Parallel Track of "Education Centres" in some States. These Separate Systems must be Integrated to give All Children Access to Schools of Acceptable Quality. This will Require Additional Spending

In a number of states, funds under various schemes (SSA, EGS and AIE) were used to create "Education Centres" (Shiksha Kendras) rather than proper schools. These typically involve "teachers" who are essentially local women who have just passed Class VIII (or even Class V in some cases) and are paid between Rs. 1000 to Rs. 3000 per month in the different states. They typically receive no training or a two-week training at best, and may have to teach multigrade classes often in single rooms. The proportion of children in such schools varies widely, but the all India average amounts to around 16 per cent of total enrolment in primary education, according to the Planning Commission. All such children are described in the official statistics as enrolled in schools, even though going to an Education Centre cannot be treated as school enrolment on par with the proper schools, and such instructors do not meet the required norms for teachers. Currently, state governments allow these parallel (and deeply unequal) systems of schooling to continue to be run by different departments – "proper schools" by the Education Department, and education centres under the *panchayats* and therefore, by the Panchayat Department.

The need to integrate these two parallel systems must be explicitly recognised. This requires special budgetary allocations for upgradation and quality improvement of the Education Centres through better infrastructure, as well as intensive training of existing teachers and additional employment of adequate numbers of qualified teachers—all of which will have financial implications.

2.2 *At the same time, Planning for School Education must take into Account the Ecology of Education—the need to Adjust School Systems to Agro-Climatic and Other Local Variations*

This requires flexibility with respect to school timings, vacations, teacher recruitment—but without sacrificing quality. Norms for schools must recognise the possibility of regional and local differences as well as the particular requirements of certain communities, such as nomadic groups, tribal communities, short-term migrant households, etc.

2.3 *School Management must be Decentralised as far as Possible*

Decentralisation of the management of schools, combined with community participation, is the most effective instrument for ensuring accountability, improving the day-to-day functioning of schools and allowing for flexible responses to local requirements. Therefore, there should be devolution of authority to local levels, whether to *panchayats*, Village Education Committees or municipalities. School Management Committees that include representatives of all stakeholders, including parents and teachers, should be empowered to make many decisions. Social audits of schools should be supported and encouraged.

2.4 *There is a Multiplicity of Management Structures and Government Departments in the Administration of School Education. This Creates Confusion, Unnecessary Replication and Possibly Inconsistent Strategies Across Different Schools. There must be Greater Coordination between Different Departments of Government on School Education Policy, even While Ensuring more Autonomy to the Local Community in Matters of day-to-day Management of Schools*

Currently schools are run or funded and monitored not only by the Central and state governments, but also by different departments within state governments—the Education Department, the Panchayat Department, the Department for Tribal Welfare, the Department for Minority Welfare, etc. This creates overlapping and conflicting structures of authority, an excess of bureaucratic tangles, unnecessary replication of some activities (and even replication of enrolment in some cases!), different guidelines and differential standards for acceptable quality and other sorts of confusion. For example, in the rural areas of several states, the local Panchayati Raj Institution (PRI) runs parallel to the SSA-run Village Education Committee (VEC). The exact remit of each is not clear and the policy intentions of both become diluted in the process.

It is necessary to make systematic efforts to integrate or at least coordinate the activities of these separate management structures. The precise roles and responsibilities of each local level and state level department should be clearly specified, but even more than that, there should be some sort of pressure for these different bodies to work together as far as possible and provide a common and equal schooling. Education policy must be part of the integrated framework of decentralised planning.

In the day-to-day management of schools, it is also necessary to work towards segregating teachers from managers in the school administration. At the same time, as noted above in point 1.4, the decentralisation of authority is critical in improving and maintaining the quality of education. Therefore, the local level management of schools, including locally elected bodies, school boards, Village Education Committees, must be allowed a significant degree of autonomy in handling matters relating to their schools, including not only the exact allocation of funds, but also other matters relating to school functioning and monitoring of teachers, etc.

2.5 *There is Need for a National Body to Monitor the Quality of Both Government and Private Schools, to Ensure that Minimum Standards are Met in Terms of Learning Outcomes*

Currently there is no systematic and continuous feedback on the actual impact and outcome of various educational schemes and initiatives, or the actual quality of education imparted in schools. There is a strong case for a testing body at the national level for quality assessment of schools. A results-based monitoring framework with due process indicators and outcome indicators needs to be evolved. This should be based on a short list of monitorable criteria. These should include fixed infrastructural requirements, enrolment and attendance, as well as outcome indicators such as learning levels achieved in certain basic areas such as language skills and numeracy, etc. Such a process of assessment needs to be applied to all schools—both public and private. However, the testing of students must not involve topics or questions that provide any incentives for rote-learning. The tracking mechanism should ideally be concerned with the profile of skill attainment of each student.

Since school education is largely a state subject but it is also important to achieve minimum schooling norms at the national level, the institutional framework for this could be at the national level with state subsidiaries. The role of this testing body will simply be to provide information on the results of its assessments, with the state governments free to act upon this information. The results of such regular tests must be made publicly available in a format accessible to all, including websites.

The monitoring of private schools, in terms of ensuring a transparent admissions process, regulation of fee structures, as well as meeting minimum set standards for quality of teaching and infrastructure, also requires attention. There is currently no exact data on the numbers and enrolment of unrecognised private schools in the country, their fee structure or admissions policy, or their standards of infrastructure and quality. Private schools should become the subject of regulation and inspection within a set framework which is universally applicable.

2.6 The System of School Inspection needs to be Revamped and Revitalised in most States, with a Greater Role for Local Stakeholders

The current inspection system is overburdened and inadequate, with a small number of inspectors required to cover a large number of schools, often spread over wide physical areas. The solution does not lie in simply expanding the system—rather, we need to develop systems to ensure meaningful monitoring. NKC recommends that the strategy for the revitalisation of the school inspection system should include the following:

- Local stakeholders should be involved in the monitoring of schools, whether in the form of Village Education Committees, parent associations, or other such bodies.
- The number of inspectors needs to be increased in many states, and they must be provided the facilities to undertake their activities properly, such as transport, communications devices, etc.
- The inspectors themselves must be accountable to the stakeholders of the area, through appropriate checks and balances.
- The criteria for inspection, the dates on which inspection of particular schools has taken place and the results should be made publicly available, including by posting on websites.
- The monitoring and inspection of schools must be separated from school administration, as the two functions require completely different orientations.
- The criteria for inspection should include not only infrastructure, facilities and teacher presence but also minimum standards for quality.

2.7 The Dignity of School Teaching as a Profession must be Restored, and at the Same Time there should be Transparent Systems for Ensuring Accountability of School Teachers

Teachers constitute the basic foundation of the school education system. However, there is a general decline in morale among school teachers, especially those in primary schools, and consequently it is no longer seen as an attractive profession for qualified young people. Two types of public perceptions, also propagated in the media and among officialdom, contribute to the low morale among school teachers: first, that anyone can teach and no particular pedagogical skills or training are required; second, that in any case most teachers do not work much and are frequently absent from school. While the latter may be the case for a relatively small minority of teachers, most school teachers are committed to their profession even if they have to function under very difficult conditions. However, they are also subject to many other pressures such as political pressure and obligations to perform non-teaching duties, which can prevent them from fulfilling their teaching duties adequately.

It is essential to ensure that qualified teachers are hired and provided with the necessary incentives to enable them to work better. The professional status of teachers should not be diluted, and all drives at recruiting untrained teachers must be checked, although it is important to allow for flexibility in recruitment of teaches for specific subjects such as art, craft and livelihood skills. The use of para-teachers must be treated as a strictly transitional measure until proper schools are established.

The imposition of a wide range of non-teaching duties, such as that of manning poll booths and collecting data for surveys etc., cuts into the available teaching time and also undermines the professional status of teachers. These activities should be shared out among a wider range of public employees or even those hired specifically for the purpose, and the burden of such work on teachers must be reduced. Specifically, unemployed local youth and recently retired people may be considered for such activities as far as possible.

The recruitment of teachers from the locality has many advantages, as they can become accountable to the community, and have added stakes in improving the quality of education in their schools. In cases where local language or dialect is different from the state language, teachers familiar with the local language are likely to make better teachers.

NKC proposes that teachers should be recruited to particular schools as far as possible. At the very minimum, school teachers should be appointed to a particular location for a minimum fixed term of at least five years, since a major problem cited by many teachers in the government school system is that of frequent transfers. (The specific case of attracting teachers to remote and backward areas is considered below under access.)

There should be increased attempts to improve public recognition of the contribution of school teachers, through various incentives such as more local, state-level and national awards, etc.

It is necessary to monitor the emoluments and working conditions of teachers in private schools, which vary substantially, and prevent exploitation of teachers by private school employers as far as possible.

However, in addition to improving the working conditions of teachers, it is also necessary to institute measures to provide greater accountability of school teachers not only to their superiors, but to students, parents and the local community. Currently, any mention of increasing teacher accountability is viewed with hostility and suspicion by teachers themselves. Such an outlook needs to be changed. There is clearly a need for greater accountability of teachers to the community and the school, and this will be facilitated by greater decentralisation of school management to local stakeholders as has been suggested above. This should be accompanied by recognition of the concerns of teachers and allowing them more space to be active in school management and school activities. The actual administrative arrangements whereby this is done should be left to be decided at the state and local level. Systems of self-evaluation and peer evaluation of teachers should be encouraged.

2.8 The Training of School Teachers is Extremely Inadequate and also Poorly Managed. Pre-service Training needs to be Improved and Regulated, while Systems for In-service Training Require Expansion and Major Reform in all States

Both pre-service and in-service teacher training programmes face major problems at present, at the national level and in almost all states. With respect to pre-service training, there is a proliferation of private colleges awarding the B.Ed. degree, and these are inadequately monitored or regulated. A significant proportion of those who receive B.Ed. degrees do so through correspondence or distance learning courses, which involve absolutely no practical exposure. In any case, classroom experience is underplayed in standard B.Ed courses. At the same time, the employment of ad hoc teachers and those without even high school diplomas as teachers in the parallel stream perpetuates the notion that it is not necessary for school teachers to have systematic and prolonged pre-service training.

In-service training shows problems of inadequate quantity, uneven quality, outdated syllabi, and poor management. A very large proportion of school teachers in the country have received no in-service training at all. In any case, many DIETs are currently understaffed, demoralised and incapable of giving good quality training to teachers. In part, this is because teacher training positions are often occupied by those who have not themselves been school teachers. In many states the administration of DIETs is left to bureaucrats who view this as a punishment posting and have no pedagogical experience. Further, DIETs typically lack adequate infrastructural facilities. Even when in-service training is regularly held, there is no mechanism which can monitor the impact of in-service teacher training courses on the subsequent teaching-learning process in the classroom. Most SCERTs themselves hire contract teachers since there are very few qualified and regular teachers and lecturers. These therefore, find it difficult to supervise functions at the block level unless their numbers are greatly increased. Funds are needed from the Central government for human resource development at this level.

NKC therefore, suggests the following for teacher training:

- Institutions providing pre-service teacher training and granting B.Ed degrees should be subject to the same regulatory authority, and there should be adequate monitoring of the training provided by private organisations.

- The budgetary allocation for teacher training needs to be enhanced and made explicit, and Central government provisions are required for this.
- There has to be greater flexibility in the modalities of teacher training. Diverse strategies such as greater use of ICT, visiting trainers and empowering local trainers who would visit schools should be encouraged.
- State-level teacher training needs to be revamped in most states. The system of DIETs needs to be restructured. In some smaller states, there is a strong case for one state-level institution for teacher training. In other states, the DIETs need to be strengthened and undergo structural changes. The faculty of SCERTs, SIEs and DIETs must be expanded, and include experienced school teachers. The use of contract teachers must be kept to a minimum. In addition, the link between university departments and school teaching needs to be strengthened.
- The administrative hierarchies within DIET and SCERT have to be restructured, so that there is a clear separation of personnel engaged in administrative and academic activities. (This distinction is currently blurred in most states.)
- The teacher training course should not be seen in terms of a finite period of time, but as a process by which the quality of teaching and learning in the classroom can be regularly improved, in a context that fosters an attitude of lifelong learning. Therefore, there should be a mechanism for feedback and subsequent interaction between teachers and the training institutes, especially for pedagogical techniques that are new or require more continuous innovation from the teacher.
- Currently in-service training is offered through pre-determined themes which trivialise the role of personal meaning while upholding requirements dictated by educational reform agendas. Greater freedom of choice would help to increase personal initiative and absorption of training inputs. NKC therefore, suggests the provision of short term in-service courses (in both contact and distance mode) that teachers can choose from. These could include courses developed outside the DIET/SCERT structure, subject to a thorough review of quality.
- In addition to being made more flexible, in-service teaching courses need to be incentivised, possibly by making attendance at and completion of such courses prerequisites to professional advancement.
- There is need for curricular reform in both pre-service and in-service teacher training. The curriculum should be framed in ways that are directly relevant to teachers and the requirements of particular classroom situations, such as multigrade teaching, special needs of first-generation learners, etc. This means that curricula should be framed with greater inputs from teachers themselves, and their practical requirements in the classroom.
- ICT must be incorporated more fully into teacher training programmes, which in turn leads to ICT being used more freely in the classroom.
- It is necessary to develop content for and access to open educational resources for teacher training.

2.9 It is Important to Develop and Nurture Leadership for Managing Schools

Even talented individuals who could be suitable for the tasks of school management need to be trained for this purpose. Such capacity building would create a pool of potential principals or heads. There are several ways in which this can be done. State governments could assign such training to existing institutions such as SCERTs or SIEs, leveraging the expertise available in Navodaya Vidyalayas, Kendriya Vidyalayas, other government schools and private schools. Such training programmes, as well as re-training programmes for existing principals, could also seek the expertise of specialists in management education. Also, individual mentoring programmes for school leaders could be evolved.

2.10 The Possibility of Greater Exchange between Schools, Including Mentoring of One School by Another should be Allowed and Encouraged.

The current system creates many distinctions and prevents interaction between schools. There is a need to constitute mechanisms of exchange and interaction between students and teachers of different schools. In addition, schools that wish to do so should be allowed to exercise the option of being 'mentored' by another school to improve facilities and teaching methods.

2.11 *Curriculum Reform Remains an Important Issue in Almost all Schools. School Education must be made more Relevant to the Lives of Children. There is need to move Away from Rote Learning to Understanding Concepts, Good Comprehension and Communication Skills and Learning how to Access Knowledge Independently*

Successive Commissions and Committees set up by the government have emphasised the need to make the curriculum more interesting, relevant, creative and useful for students. The National Curriculum Framework 2005 also clearly articulated such an approach. Nevertheless it appears that in a majority of schools across the country, a significant emphasis on rote learning and memorising facts remains the norm. Also, there is evidence of children being overburdened with too much detail and an excess of scholastic requirements at the elementary level.

It is important to orient students towards independent and continuous learning. This makes it essential to make greater efforts to change the attitude to learning and knowledge. It has been noted in several states that learning results have improved considerably upon providing inputs for communication and comprehension in language and basic mathematical skills using activity-based and imaginative pedagogical strategies. The focus of primary schooling in particular must be on good language and communication skills, basic foundation maths and inculcation of self-learning and critical examination through innovative teaching methods. For language teaching in particular, there should be much greater emphasis on communication skills at a practical level.

It is also important to ensure that the curriculum contains locally relevant content that children can relate to their own lives. For example, in certain parts of the country (such as,but not only, the Northeast) the curriculum at both primary and secondary levels could also include training in disaster management, especially for floods, while in other parts of the country responses to earthquakes may be more relevant. In rural areas, horticulture and pisciculture techniques should be included in the syllabus. Co-curricular reading material should be propagated, such as children's books with local stories and histories to strengthen the linkages between school and home.

To make secondary school education more relevant, and also address the problem of dropouts, NKC recommends the setting up of Livelihood Centres in secondary schools that would impart practical employable skills and provide career counselling to students. All school children should be encouraged to be involved in some practical activities that require working with the hands. These activities should *not* be treated as catering to a parallel stream, but should be provided to all students and integrated with the overall syllabus. Once again, links with the Skill Development Mission should be developed wherever possible.

2.12 *Changes in the Examination System are Required, Especially at Board Level but also Earlier, to ensure that the Pressure for Rote Learning is Reduced*

The current overemphasis on details, memorising of facts and similar abilities rather than on understanding and accessing knowledge independently is reflected in the pattern of examinations. Board examinations in which marks are awarded based on the ability to recall lots of details or on rapidity of response or on the ability to do large numbers of sums in a limited period through practice in pattern recognition, are not sufficiently discriminatory and may end up providing misleading results. They also put pressure on schools to ensure that memory and pattern recognition skills are developed at the expense of genuine understanding.

This is also reflected in the pattern of annual examinations which many schools continue to run even in junior classes such as Class III and Class V. Performance in such examinations then becomes the basis for choosing students who will be eligible for scholarships or gain entrance to Navodaya Vidyalayas and similar schools. Forcing children to undergo a large number of examinations in different subjects, with an emphasis on memory rather than comprehension, must be discouraged at the primary level.

For curriculum reform to be successful, it is necessary to make major changes in the examination system. This applies equally to some of the national school boards (such as CBSE) and the state-level boards. It is also crucial to push for such reform in the annual examinations held by schools, where the testing must be focused on language and comprehension, numeric and quantitative skills and ability to use knowledge creatively.

2.13 New Technologies, Especially but not only ICT, should be used as much as Possible to Reduce Costs, Enable more Effective Use of Resources, and Provide Wider Exposure to Students and Teachers

The use of ICT as a teaching and learning device needs to be more firmly incorporated into the classroom. Both teachers and students need to be far more familiar with ICT, and get practical experience of web-based research. Therefore, ICT should be made more accessible to teachers, students and administration for learning, training, research, administration, management, monitoring, etc. This requires the provision of more facilities such as computers as well as connectivity and broadband facilities. Computer aided learning also requires training of teachers and other staff in order to make the best use of the technology.

2.14 There is need for a Web-based Portal for Teachers to Exchange Ideas, Information and Experiences

A forum for teachers needs to be developed where they may interact, share experiences and ideas. This needs to be incorporated into teacher training programmes, and also provided generally for in-service teachers. A web-based teachers' portal can play an important role as such a networking forum.

3. Access

3.1 Special Strategies are Required to Ensure Greater Access to Schools in Backward Regions, Remote Locations and Difficult Terrains

There is a tremendous shortage of teachers and also great difficulty in ensuring minimum schooling infrastructure in some areas that have been historically deprived or have difficult topographical conditions. Distance and difficulty of physical access are important reasons for school dropout, especially in such areas. Sometimes it is also the case that such areas are inhabited by particular communities with their own language or dialect that is different from the state language. In order to ensure access to schools for children in such areas, special measures must be taken.

NKC recommends the following measures for such areas:

- Financial norms for schools in such locations must be different from those in more accessible areas, as they will require additional resource allocation based on particular conditions.
- Special incentives, including a financial incentive (such as a "hardship bonus") need to be provided for teachers to take up jobs in such areas. Two different models may be considered—one based on recruiting local teachers on a permanent basis for a job in a particular school without transfer; and another based on a transfer policy that divides locations into hard/ middle/easy categories and allows teachers to rotate among them at specified intervals. Ideally, there should be at least one local teacher and one non-local teacher to ensure some variation, local acceptability and quality.
- Residential arrangements must be made for teachers in such locations, by providing quarters next to or near the school. The cost of building such quarters should be factored into the costs of the school building.
- There are some geographical zones especially in mountainous regions, that are plagued by unique problems due to vast tracts of land, difficult topography and a sparse and nomadic population. In such areas, well equipped residential schools should be set up instead of insisting on a school in every habitation. These schools must be equipped to look into the needs of very young children living away from their families.

3.2 Measures are Required to Ensure Greater Enrolment and Retention of Girl Students

The high dropout rate of girls especially from Class V onwards is a matter of great concern. One major reason, as noted above, is the sheer lack of secondary schools nearby, as parents are reluctant to send girls to travel long distances to school. However, social conditioning and other constraints also play a role. Some policies to address this include:

- Special incentives for girls in secondary education where these are required (they are not required everywhere), in addition to free textbooks and uniforms, such as bicycles.
- Girls-only schools especially in particular areas.

- An enhanced scholarship scheme especially for girls, with particular emphasis on girls from socially deprived groups.
- The need for separate and functional toilets for girls in all schools, with access to water, is very important, especially but not exclusively in urban areas.

3.3 Language Issues must be Explicitly taken on Board in Designing School Curricula and Methods of Pedagogy

Language has been found to be a highly alienating factor in the education of many school children, particularly amongst minorities, tribal communities with languages without a script, as well as linguistic minorities in most states. Many children resent the imposition of the state language as the medium of instruction, or as second language in school.

More teachers for teaching minority languages must be appointed in government schools to increase the intake of children from minority language communities. Qualified teachers from the local community and therefore, speaking the same language must be recruited on a larger scale, as a means of encouraging retention amongst those who feel marginalised, as well as a means of bringing greater community control in the school. This would also act as a boost to confidence, and provide role models to students from disadvantaged backgrounds.

3.4 The Teaching of English should be Introduced Along with the First Language, Starting from Class I in School

Proficiency in English is widely perceived as an important avenue for employment and upward mobility, which also greatly facilitates the pursuit of higher education. The incorporation of English into the curriculum, through the introduction of English as a language in Class I and the teaching of one other subject in English medium in later classes, requires pedagogical changes to contextualise language learning, increasing the availability of English language teachers and those who can teach at least one subject in English, as well as bilingual and supplementary teaching materials.

At the same time, school education must commit to promoting multilinguality, given the multilingual nature of our country.

3.5 There is need to Re-orient Official Strategies for Ensuring Better Access of Muslim Children to Schooling

Areas with Muslim majority population have tended to be overlooked in the implementation of government educational schemes. In addition, with a few exceptions, there has been less private initiative in this regard. As a consequence, Muslims as a community, have access to fewer government schools, girls schools, and higher educational institutions. It is important to rectify this gap and ensure adequate public expenditure to ensure that the physical and social infrastructure for schooling is made available. This means that the government should have a minority component in all its school development schemes and budget outlays, which should be in proportion to the minority population.

The strategy cannot be based solely on more public resources provided to madrasas for their modernisation, as according to the Sachar Committee Report, 96 per cent of Muslim children do not attend madrasas for schooling. Indeed, if the modernisation of madrasa education is the only policy for increasing access for Muslim school children to modernised education, it will only result in their being further isolated.

It is important to ensure that children from all minorities and socially deprived groups are not discriminated against in the process of attending school. This must be an active and concerted campaign, in which syllabi and curriculum are checked to avoid prejudice, teachers are sensitised and instances of discrimination are punished. This also requires grievance redressal mechanisms at the school level and also at higher levels.

3.6 The Access of Children from Scheduled Tribes Requires more Flexible and Sensitive Schooling Strategies

Tribal children face problems of inadequate geographical access, discrimination at school and issues of language, which have been discussed earlier but are especially relevant in these cases. Tribal students have to compete with SC students, often at a disadvantage to the former. All of these must be addressed at the local level as well as at the district and state level.

Every state should have an education policy for tribal and minority education, with a long term vision of eventual integration into the mainstream.

Rather than setting up separate schools for those who have dropped out because they felt discriminated against, teachers should be better sensitised to the needs of the students from such communities, as well as the particular needs of first generation learners.

The issue of language is particularly important in areas with tribal population, and care must be taken to find and train teachers who can deal with children in their own language, rather than forcing them to adjust to the regional language.

3.7 Education of SC Children must be a Priority, but with the Required Flexibility and Avoidance of Discrimination

The points made earlier with respect to discrimination are especially valid also for SC children, and must be addressed in similar ways.

In addition, scholarships should be increased and provided to much larger numbers of Dalit children, along with other provisions such as free textbooks up to Class X and other incentives.

3.8 Children of Seasonal Migrants Require Special Conditions and Efforts to Ensure Continuous Access to Schooling

Seasonal and short-term migration is a major cause for early dropouts and non-enrolment. In order to ensure that such children have access to a quality and complete education, their economic insecurity has to be taken into account while formulating educational schemes. Tent schools and mobile schools must be made a part of the urban landscape for migrant children, while rural schools also have to be made aware of the need to admit migrant children. This requires a significant change in the way that school admissions and enrolment are carried out, as well as greater sensitivity, flexibility and effort on the part of the school administration, all of which require hard and soft resources. It is necessary to identify good practices in this regard which can serve as a model to be emulated elsewhere.

3.9 Labouring Children Require Incentives and Bridge Courses

Some sort of monetary stipend may have to be paid to labouring children to bring them into schools. In addition, synergies must be created with NREGA to look into school education concerns of labouring children. Pre-school systems like *balwadis* and *anganwadis* must be strengthened, so that a school going habit can be ingrained, as well as providing a space for small children to be cared for, while their elder siblings may go to school. Alternative centres for education must be utilised specifically to provide bridge courses aimed at different age groups and classes for dropouts. However, the use of alternative centres for education must be no more than in a transition capacity. AIE should not become the only option for access to poor school children for a school education.

Study centres must be provided for first generation learners and seasonal migrants as a space which is more conducive to learning than what may be available at home. These may also be used as community centres, libraries, etc.

3.10 The Needs of Physically Disadvantaged Children, as well as Teachers, have to be Factored in more thoroughly in Provisions for School Education

The goal in all schools should be inclusive education, which means that all systems must be oriented to allow the greatest possible access to children with different needs and abilities. This requires substantial changes in both infrastructure and pedagogical methods. School buildings must have provisions for access and navigation for the visually impaired, the physically handicapped, etc. Teachers must be trained, sensitised and empowered to deal with children with different abilities in the classroom situation.

While this is the ultimate goal, it must also be recognised that current schooling patterns are not always conducive to bringing out the full potential of physically disadvantaged children, and therefore, there is still a case for special schools. There is a perception that government mechanisms may not be best suited to provide sustained and sympathetic support for learners with special needs and severely disabled children (such as the blind). In this context, it may be better to identify appropriate and willing institutions outside the government who may become partners.

9 Vocational Education

NKC considers Vocational Education and Training (VET) to be an important element of the nation's education initiative. In order for VET to play its part effectively in the changing national context and for India to enjoy the fruits of the demographic dividend, there is an urgent need to redefine the critical elements of imparting vocational education to make them flexible, contemporary, relevant, inclusive and creative. The Government is well aware of the important role of VET and has already taken a number of important initiatives. Through consultations with industry groups, academics, civil society and practitioners, NKC has deliberated on ways and means to strengthen these initiatives and recommends the following long and short-term strategies.

1. Place Vocational Education Entirely under the Ministry of Human Resource Development (MHRD)

In view of the role of VET in human resource development and importance of its linkages with other streams of education, the Government may consider placing all aspects of VET under MHRD. Currently, VET falls under the purview of MHRD as well as the Ministry of Labour, which leads to fragmented management of the VET framework. MHRD may consider setting up a National Institute for Vocational Education Planning and Development to formulate strategy, advise the Government, and undertake research and development in areas pertaining to technology and workforce development.

2. Increase the Flexibility of VET within the Mainstream Education System through the Following Steps

i. Aspects of general education (such as numeracy skills) should be retained in VET as far as possible, to enable students to return to mainstream education at a later stage.

ii. Courses in training institutes and polytechnics should have distinct tracks for students of different educational attainments.

iii. Entry requirements for certain trades should reflect the requirement of the trade (as appropriate, for instance the entry requirement of Class X could be relaxed to Class VIII in some cases). Students should be permitted multiple entry and exit options in the vocational education stream.

iv. Links should be established between the vocational education stream and school education as well as higher education.

v. Courses devoted to certain skill training at the primary and secondary level should be introduced in all schools.

vi. Vocational training should be made available in various literacy and adult education schemes.

vii. Schemes for lifelong skill upgradation,through short training programmes, should be introduced.

viii. There should be a provision for generating a cadre of multi-skilled persons.

3. Quantify and Monitor the Impact of Vocational Education

Data should be collected periodically and analysed in order to assess the impact of training on employability. Empirical evidence on wage premium or other advantages enjoyed by VET graduates, seat utilisation in training institutes, nature of employment post-training, and the efficacy of various schemes is essential for continuous improvement. A detailed exercise of manpower analysis is a necessary step to understanding the nature and quantum of demand for VET and the mismatch between the skills of VET certificate holders and the requirements of the labour market. This exercise may be undertaken by the proposed National Institute for Vocational Education Planning and Development.

4. Increase Resource Allocation to Vocational Education

In per capita terms, vocational education costs more than general education, however, public expenditure on vocational education has been extremely low, as compared to general secondary education. Given the demand for skilled manpower in manufacturing and services, the Government should aim to spend at least 10-15 per cent of its total public expenditure on education as well as on vocational education. Some options that may be considered for raising additional funds to finance a modernised VET scheme are:

i. Enhancing fees, coupled with student loan schemes. This would also make VET institutions more responsive to market needs.

ii. Raising funds through a cess on employers (for instance two per cent of salaries of all employees, as in Singapore).

iii. Making it obligatory for companies to finance public vocational education and training programmes (as in Korea).

5. Expand Capacity through Innovative Delivery Models

In order to meet the burgeoning requirements of skilled and unskilled labour, a massive increase in quantity of training is needed. The Government could explore new delivery models to increase capacity such as public-private partnerships, decentralised delivery, distance learning and computerised vocational training. At the same time, the Government must introduce certain minimum standards as a measure of quality, and ensure that all public and private VET institutions adhere to these.

6. Enhance the Training Options Available for the Unorganised and Informal Sector

The greatest challenge lies in providing training for potential entrants in the unorganised/informal sector, which accounts for the largest proportion of employment. Systematic efforts need to be made to impart the skills required by the unorganised sector. These should be formally introduced in the curricula and practical training courses. In order to achieve this, the Government should act as a facilitator and provide financial support. This aspect of VET is critical for the success of the system as a whole.

7. Strengthen the Current Institutional Structure

The existing Industrial Training Institutes (ITIs) and Industrial Training Centres (ITCs) are widely recognised to face problems such as poor quality trainers, lack of flexibility, and outdated infrastructure. Measures to improve the existing institutions are as follows:

i. Extent of functional autonomy must be increased, ITIs should be given more power to strengthen and adapt their training programmes to better meet local market needs.

ii. Indicators of internal and external efficiency should be developed (by the proposed National Institute) to incentivise good performance.

iii. Modules on literacy, numeracy, communication skills, entrepreneurship and other general skills relevant to workplace requirements must be introduced in all courses.

iv. Different tracks within courses for different levels of specialisation should be introduced.

v. Students should be offered incentives such as tools, membership of trade associations, etc., as part of their degree or diploma.

vi. Industry and trade involvement should be enhanced not only at the internship stage, but also at the time of examinations and placements.

vii. Curricula should be constantly monitored and updated.

viii. The skills and courses offered should be reviewed periodically. The number of skills currently offered needs to be increased.

ix. Teaching should be conducted in English as well as local languages.

x. Infrastructure should be regularly upgraded.

xi. Quality of teaching should be drastically improved.

8. Ensure a Robust Regulatory and Accreditation Framework

In order to achieve the desired modernisation and expansion, a critical aspect will be to regulate entry of new institutions and accreditation of all institutions. NKC therefore, recommends that an independent regulatory agency for VET be established. This body would license accreditation agencies and prescribe standards for certification. The procedures and methodologies adopted by the body would need to be simple and transparent to ensure unhindered growth in the sector.

9. Ensure Proper Certification

At present, the process of certification is handled by the National Council for Vocational Training (NCVT), in association with State Councils for Vocational Training (SCVTs). Clear demarcation between the roles of the NCVT, the SCVTs and the Directorate General of Employment and Training is essential for the proper functioning of the certification process. In order to ensure recognition of certification by employers, both in India and abroad, an electronic database of certified training providers as well as electronic identification for certified workers should be introduced. Electronic identification should contain information regarding skills and qualifications (and eventually other relevant information as well) about certified individuals and can be used to facilitate mobility of workers, encourage bank linkages and entrepreneurial initiatives.

10. Undertake a Re-branding Exercise

It is widely recognised that a crucial problem with vocational training in India is a negative association with manual labour. In order to match the modern requirement of the skills and competitiveness of the workforce, a massive re-branding exercise is of the highest priority. This could be the prime task of the recently announced National Skills Mission. Initiatives such as replacing the use of terms like 'vocational education' by 'skill development' are a step in the right direction. Training institutes should try to chart out a career path for their students and introduce entrepreneurship training modules.

It is crucial to significantly increase public and private investment in VET. However, a detailed analysis of manpower requirements in terms of numbers, skills and competitiveness is essential before formulating a master plan and deciding the quantum of expenditure in the 11th Plan. A robust framework put in place as a visible and dedicated resource in the MHRD is a prerequisite to ensuring quality and facilitating significant private investment and participation. Most importantly, the quality as well as the image of VET needs to be actively promoted in order for it to be viewed as comparable to general secondary education, and as relevant.

10 Higher Education

Higher education has made a significant contribution to economic development, social progress and political democracy in independent India. But there is serious cause for concern at this juncture. The proportion of our population, in the relevant age group, that enters the world of higher education is about 7 per cent. The opportunities for higher education in terms of the number of places in universities are simply not adequate in relation to our needs. Large segments of our population just do not have access to higher education. What is more, the quality of higher education in most of our universities leaves much to be desired.

Foundations are critical. NKC believes that an emphasis on expansion and reform of our school system is necessary to ensure that every child has an equal opportunity to enter the world of higher education. It is engaged in consultations on school education and will submit recommendations in this crucial area in due course. In this recommendation, it focuses on higher education.

NKC has engaged in formal and informal consultations on the issue with a wide range of people in the world of higher education. In addition, it consulted concerned people in parliament, government, civil society and industry. Concerns about the higher education system are widely shared. There is a clear, almost unanimous, view that higher education needs a systematic overhaul, so that India can educate much larger numbers without diluting academic standards. Indeed, this is essential because the transformation of economy and society in the 21st century would depend, in significant part, on the spread and the quality of education among our people, particularly in the sphere of higher education. It is only an inclusive society that can provide the foundations for a knowledge society.

The objectives of reform and change in our higher education system must be expansion, excellence and inclusion. NKC recognises that meaningful reform of the system, with a long-term perspective, is both complex and difficult. Yet, it is imperative.

1. Expansion

1.1 Create many more Universities

The higher education system needs a massive expansion of opportunities, to around 1500 universities nationwide, that would enable India to attain a gross enrolment ratio of at least 15 per cent by 2015. The focus would have to be on new universities, but some clusters of affiliated colleges could also become universities. Such expansion would require major changes in the structure of regulation.

1.2 Change the System of Regulation for Higher Education

The present regulatory system in higher education is flawed in some important respects. The barriers to entry are too high. The system of authorising entry is cumbersome. There is a multiplicity of regulatory agencies where mandates are both confusing and overlapping. The system, as a whole, is over-regulated but under-governed. NKC perceives a clear need to establish an Independent Regulatory Authority for Higher Education (IRAHE). The IRAHE must be at an arm's length from the Government and independent of all stakeholders including the concerned Ministries of the Government.

- The IRAHE would have to be established by an Act of Parliament, and would be responsible for setting the criteria and deciding on entry.
- It would be the only agency that would be authorised to accord degree-granting power to higher education institutions.
- It would be responsible for monitoring standards and settling disputes.
- It would apply exactly the same norms to public and private institutions, just as it would apply the same norms to domestic and international institutions.
- It would be the authority for licensing accreditation agencies.
- The role of the University Grants Commission (UGC) would be redefined to focus on the disbursement of grants to, and maintenance of, public institutions in higher education. The entry regulatory functions of the All India Council for Technical Education (AICTE), the Medical Council of India (MCI) and the BCI would be performed by the IRAHE, so that their role would be limited to that of professional associations.

1.3 Increase Public Spending and Diversify Sources of Financing

The expansion of our system of higher education is not possible without enhanced levels of financing. This must necessarily come from both public and private sources.

- Since government financing will remain the cornerstone, government support for higher education should increase to at least 1.5 per cent of GDP, out of a total of at least 6 per cent of GDP for education overall.
- Even this would not suffice for the massive expansion in higher education that is an imperative. It is essential to explore other possibilities that can complement the increase in public expenditure.
- Most public universities are sitting on a large reservoir of untapped resources in the form of land. It should be possible to draw up norms and parameters for universities to use their available land as a source of finance.
- It is for universities to decide the level of fees but, as a norm, fees should meet at least 20 per cent of the total expenditure in universities. This should be subject to two conditions: first, needy students should be provided with a fee waiver plus scholarships to meet their costs; second, universities should not be penalised by the UGC for the resources raised from higher fees through matching deductions from their grants-in-aid.
- India should nurture the tradition of philanthropic contributions through changes in incentives for universities and for donors. At present, there is an implicit disincentive in both tax laws and trust laws. These laws should be changed so that universities can invest in financial instruments of their choice and use the income from their endowments to build up a corpus.
- Universities should also seek to tap other sources such as alumni contributions and licensing fees. There is need to create supportive institutional mechanisms that allow universities to engage professional firms for this purpose.
- It is essential to stimulate private investment in education as a means of extending educational opportunities. It may be possible to leverage public resources, especially in the form of land grants, to attract more (not-for-profit) private investment.

1.4 Establish 50 National Universities

NKC recommends the creation of 50 National Universities that can provide education of the highest standard. As exemplars for the rest of the nation, these universities would train students in a variety of disciplines, including humanities, social sciences, basic sciences, commerce and professional subjects, at both the undergraduate and postgraduate levels. The number 50 is a long-term objective. In the short run, it is important to begin with at least 10 such universities in the next three years. National Universities can be established in two ways, by the Government, or by a private sponsoring body that sets up a society, charitable trust or Section 25 company.

Since public finance is an integral constituent of universities worldwide, most of the new universities shall need significant initial financial support from the Government. Each university may be endowed with a substantial allocation of public land, in excess of its spatial requirements. The excess land can be a subsequent source of income generation. Exceptions need to be made in existing income tax laws to encourage large endowments. There should be no restriction on the utilisation of income in any given period or in the use of appropriate financial instruments. These universities should have the autonomy to set student fee levels and tap other sources for generating funds.

The National Universities, NKC proposes, will admit students on an all India basis. They will adopt the principle of needs-blind admissions. This will require an extensive system of scholarships for needy students. Undergraduate degrees in the National Universities, in a three-year programme, should be granted on the basis of completing a requisite number of credits, obtained from different courses. The academic year will therefore, be semester-based and students will be internally evaluated at the end of each course. Transfer of credits from one National University to another would also be possible. An appropriate system of appointments and incentives is required to maximise the productivity of faculty in these National Universities. Strong linkages would be forged between teaching and research, universities and industry, and universities and research laboratories. The National Universities shall be department-based and shall not have any affiliated colleges.

2. Excellence

2.1 Reform Existing Universities

The endeavour to transform higher education must reform existing institutions. Some essential steps are:

- Universities should be required to revise or restructure curricula at least once in three years.
- Annual examinations, which test memory rather than understanding, should be supplemented with continuous internal assessment which could begin with a weight of 25 per cent in the total to be raised to 50 per cent over a stipulated period.
- NKC proposes a transition to a course credit system where degrees are granted on the basis of completing a requisite number of credits from different courses, which provides students with choices.
- Universities must become the hub of research once again to capture synergies between teaching and research that enrich each other. This requires not only policy measures but also changes in resource allocation, reward systems and mindsets.
- There must be a conscious effort to attract and retain talented faculty members through better working conditions combined with incentives for performance.
- The criteria for resource allocation to universities should seek to strike a much better balance between providing for salaries or pensions and providing for maintenance, development or investment. It should also recognise the importance of a critical minimum to ensure standards and strategic preferences to promote excellence.
- The elements of infrastructure that support the teaching-learning process, such as libraries, laboratories and connectivity, need to be monitored and upgraded on a regular basis.
- There is an acute need for reform in the structures of governance of universities that do not preserve autonomy and do not promote accountability. Much needs to be done, but two important points deserve mention. The appointments of Vice-Chancellors must be freed from direct or indirect interventions on the part of governments, for these should be based on search processes and peer judgment alone. The size and composition of University Courts, Academic Councils and Executive Councils, which slow down decision-making processes and sometimes constitute an impediment to change, need to be reconsidered on a priority basis.
- The need is for smaller universities which are resposive to change and easier to manage, and these should be created.

2.2 Restructure Undergraduate Colleges

The system of affiliated colleges for undergraduate education, which may have been appropriate 50 years ago, is no longer adequate or appropriate and needs to be reformed. There is an urgent need to restructure the system of undergraduate colleges affiliated to universities.

- The most obvious solution is to provide autonomy to colleges either as individual colleges or as clusters of colleges, on the basis of criteria that have been stipulated. However, this would provide a solution for a limited proportion, or number, of undergraduate colleges.
- Some of these affiliated colleges could be remodelled as community colleges, which could provide both vocational education and formal education.
- A Central Board of Undergraduate Education should be established, along with State Boards of Undergraduate Education, which would set curricula and conduct examinations for undergraduate colleges that choose to be affiliated with them. These Boards would separate the academic functions from the administrative functions and, at the same time, provide quality benchmarks.
- New undergraduate colleges could be established as community colleges and be affiliated with the Central Board of Undergraduate Education or State Boards of Undergraduate Education, or with some of the new universities that are established.

2.3 Promote Enhanced Quality

The higher education system must provide for accountability to society and create accountability within. An expansion of higher education which provides students with choices and creates competition between institutions is going to be vital in enhancing accountability.

- There should be stringent information disclosure norms for all educational institutions such as their financial situation, physical assets, admissions criteria, faculty positions, academic curricula, as also their source and level of accreditation.
- Evaluation of courses and teachers by students as well as peer evaluation of teachers by teachers should be encouraged.
- There must be a focus on upgrading infrastructure, improving the training of teachers and continuous assessment of syllabi and examination systems.
- It is particularly important to enhance the ICT infrastructure. Websites and web-based services would improve transparency and accountability. A portal on higher education and research would increase interaction and accessibility. A knowledge network would connect all universities and colleges for online open resources.
- It may be necessary to rethink the issue of salary differentials within and between universities along with other means of attracting and retaining talented faculty members. Such salary differentials between and within universities could be effective without being large.
- It is necessary to formulate appropriate policies for the entry of foreign institutions into India and the promotion of Indian institutions abroad, while ensuring a level playing field for foreign and domestic institutions within the country.
- The system of higher education must recognise that there is bound to be diversity and pluralism in any system of higher education, and avoid a uniform 'one size fits all' approach. This sense of pluralism must recognise, rather than ignore or shy away from, such diversity and differentiation.

3. Inclusion

3.1 Ensure Access for all Deserving Students

Education is the fundamental mechanism for social inclusion through the creation of more opportunities. It is therefore, essential to ensure that no student is denied the opportunity to participate in higher education due to financial constraints. NKC proposes the following measures.

- Institutions of higher education should be encouraged to adopt a needs-blind admissions policy. This would make it unlawful for educational institutions to take into account any financial factor while deciding whether or not to admit a student.
- There must be a well-funded and extensive National Scholarship Scheme targeting economically underprivileged students and students from groups that are historically, socially disadvantaged.

3.2 Affirmative Action

A major aim of the higher education system must be to ensure that access to education for economically and historically socially underprivileged students is enhanced in a substantially more effective manner.

- Reservations are essential, but they are only a part, and one form of affirmative action.
- Disparities in educational attainments are related to caste and social groups, but are also strongly related to other indicators such as income, gender, region and place of residence. There is need to develop a meaningful and comprehensive framework that would address the multi-dimensionality of differences that still persist. For example, a deprivation index could be used to provide weighted scores to students and the cumulative score could be used to supplement a student's school examination score.

NKC's recommendations require action at three different levels: reforms within existing systems, changes in policies, and amendments in, or the introduction of, new statutes or legislation. The suggested changes would also be implemented at three different levels: universities, state governments and the Central government. It is important to recognise that there is a quiet crisis in higher education in India which runs deep. The time has come to address this crisis in a systematic and forthright manner. NKC's recommendations constitute an important beginning; the changes suggested would make a real difference. Of course, the process of reform and change is continuous. There is more to be done, and NKC will continue to think about next steps, but it emphasises the urgency of the situation, because India's future depends on it. It is important to act here and now.

Annexure 10.1: Note on Higher Education

1. Introduction

The spread of education in society is at the foundation of success in countries that are latecomers to development. In the quest for development, primary education is absolutely essential because it creates the base. But higher education is just as important, for it provides the cutting edge. And universities are the lifeblood of higher education. Islands of excellence in professional education, such as Indian Institutes of Technology (IITs) and Indian Institutes of Management (IIMs), are valuable complements but cannot be substitutes for universities which provide educational opportunities for people at large.

There can be no doubt that higher education has made a significant contribution to economic development, social progress and political democracy in independent India. It is a source of dynamism for the economy. It has created social opportunities for people. It has fostered the vibrant democracy in our polity. It has provided a beginning for the creation of a knowledge society. But it would be a mistake to focus on its strengths alone. It has weaknesses that are a cause for serious concern.

There is, in fact, a quiet crisis in higher education in India that runs deep. It is not yet discernible simply because there are pockets of excellence, an enormous reservoir of talented young people and an intense competition in the admissions process. And, in some important spheres, we continue to reap the benefits of what was sown in higher education 50 years ago by the founding fathers of the Republic. The reality is that we have miles to go. The proportion of our population, in the age group 18-24, that enters the world of higher education is around 7 per cent, which is only one-half the average for Asia. The opportunities for higher education, in terms of the number of places in universities, are simply not enough in relation to our needs. What is more, the quality of higher education in most of our universities requires substantial improvement.

It is clear that the system of higher education in India faces serious challenges. It needs a systematic overhaul, so that we can educate much larger numbers without diluting academic standards. This is imperative because the transformation of economy and society in the 21st century would depend, in significant part, on the spread and the quality of education among our people, particularly in the sphere of higher education. It is only an inclusive society that can provide the foundations for a knowledge society.

The challenges that confront higher education in India are clear. It needs a massive expansion of opportunities for higher education, to 1500 universities nationwide, that would enable India to attain a gross enrolment ratio of at least 15 per cent by 2015. It is just as important to raise the average quality of higher education in every sphere. At the same time, it is essential to create institutions that are exemplars of excellence at par with the best in the world. In the pursuit of these objectives, providing people with access to higher education in a socially inclusive manner is imperative. The realisation of these objectives, combined with access, would not only develop the skills and capabilities we need for the economy but would also help transform India into a knowledge economy and society.

We recognise that a meaningful reform of the higher education system, with a long-term perspective is both complex and difficult. Yet, it is imperative. And we would suggest the following building blocks in this endeavour. First, it is essential to reform existing public universities and undergraduate colleges. Second, it is necessary to overhaul the entire regulatory structure governing higher education. Third, every possible source of financing investment in higher education needs to be explored. Fourth, it is important to think about proactive strategies for enhancement of quality in higher education. Fifth, the time has come to create new institutions in the form of National Universities that would become role models as centres of academic excellence. Sixth, the higher education system must be so designed that it provides access to marginalised and excluded groups.

2. Universities

Universities perform a critical role in an economy and society. They create knowledge. They impart knowledge. And they disseminate knowledge. Universities must be flexible, innovative and creative. They must be able to attract the best talent whether teachers or students. They must have the ability to compete and the motivation to excel. We cannot even contemplate a transformation of our higher education system without reform in our existing universities.

There is, however, a serious cause for concern about universities in India. The number of places for students at universities is simply inadequate. The quality of education at most universities leaves much to be desired. The gap between our universities and those in the outside world has widened. And none of our universities rank among the best, say the top 50, in the world. The symptoms are clearly visible, even if we do not wish to diagnose what ails our universities. Of course, every problem does not exist everywhere. And there are exceptions. But the following problems are common enough to be a cause for concern. First, curricula, which have remained almost unchanged for decades, have not kept pace with the times, let alone with the extending frontiers of knowledge. Second, learning and creativity are at a discount in a system of assessment that places a premium on memory rather than understanding. Third, the milieu is not conducive to anything beyond the classroom, for it is caught in a 9.30 to 1.30 syndrome. Fourth, the academic calendar is no longer sacrosanct for classes or for examinations, as there are slip pages in schedules so much so that, at several places, classes in the timetable are not held and results are often declared with a time-lag of 6 to 12 months. Fifth, the infrastructure is not only inadequate but also on the verge of collapse. Sixth, the boundaries between disciplines have become dividing walls that constitute barriers to entry for new disciplines or new courses, while knowledge is developing most rapidly at the intersection of disciplines. Seventh, the importance attached to research has eroded steadily over time. Eighth, the volume of research in terms of frequency of publication and the quality of research reflected in the frequency of citation or the place of publication, on balance, is simply not what it used to be. Ninth, as in most public institutions, there is little accountability, because there are no rewards for performance and no penalties for non-performance. Tenth, structures of governance put in place 50 years ago are not responsive to changing times and circumstances but the system is readily subverted by vested interests.

It is difficult enough to provide a complete diagnosis of what ails our universities. It is even more difficult, if not impossible, to outline a set of prescriptions for our universities. Nevertheless, it is clear that a reform of existing institutions must be an integral part of our endeavour to transform higher education. We recognise that this is easier said than done. Even so, we believe that reforms in the following spheres, along the lines suggested by us, are not only possible but would also make a difference.

Number and size: India has about 350 universities. This number is simply not enough with reference to our needs in higher education, or in comparison with China which has authorised the creation of 1250 new universities in the last three years. Yet, some of our universities are much too large, for ensuring academic standards and providing good governance. We need to create more appropriately scaled and more nimble universities. The moral of the story is not only that we need a much larger number of universities, say 1500 nationwide by 2015 but also that we need smaller universities which are responsive to change and easier to manage.

Curriculum: The syllabi of courses in universities, which remain unchanged for decades, need to be upgraded constantly and revised frequently. The laws of inertia reinforced by resistance to change must be overcome. Universities should be required to revise or restructure curricula at least once in three years. These revisions must be subjected to outside peer review before implementation. The process for such revisions should be streamlined and decentralised, with more autonomy for teachers, through a change in statutes wherever necessary. For existing systems often act as major impediments to a timely or speedy revision of curricula. There should be some mode of censure for departments or universities that do not upgrade their courses regularly. It needs to be recognised that it is very difficult to introduce new courses or innovative courses in universities because of departmental divides. Appropriate institutional mechanisms should be put in place to resolve this problem.

Assessment: The nature of annual examinations at universities in India often stifles the teaching-learning process because they reward selective and uncritical learning. There is an acute need to reform this examination system so that it tests understanding rather than memory. Analytical abilities and creative thinking should be at a premium. Learning by rote should be at a discount. Such reform would become more feasible with decentralised examination and smaller universities. But assessment cannot and should not be based on examinations alone. There is a clear need for continuous internal assessment which empowers teachers and students alike, just as it breathes life back into the teaching-learning process. Such internal assessment would also foster the analytical and creative abilities of students which are often a casualty in university-administered annual examinations. To begin with, internal assessment could have a weight of 25 per cent in the total but this should be raised to 50 per cent over time.

Course credits: The present system is characterised by too many rigidities and too few choices for students. Universities that are smaller, or run semester-based systems, are obviously more flexible. Even in large universities, however, it is necessary to introduce greater diversity and more flexibility in course structures. This would be the beginning of a transition to a course credit system, where degrees are granted on the basis of completing a requisite number of credits from different courses. Every student should be required to earn a minimum number of credits in his/her chosen discipline but should have the freedom to earn the rest from courses in other disciplines. It is essential to provide students with choices instead of keeping them captive.

Research: We attempted to create stand-alone research institutions, pampered with resources, in the belief that research should be moved out of universities. In the process, we forgot an essential principle. There are synergies between teaching and research that enrich each other. And it is universities which are the natural home for research. What is more, for universities, research is essential in the pursuit of academic excellence. It is time to reverse what happened in the past and make universities the hub of research once again. This would need changes in resource allocation, reward-systems and mindsets. Substantial grants should be allocated for research. The provisions of these grants should be competitive and the criteria for these grants should be different from the usual criteria for non-plan and plan grants.

Faculty: There must be a conscious effort to attract and retain talented faculty members. This is necessary because talented students who are potential faculty members have choices that are far more attractive in other professions in India or in the academic profession outside India. It is necessary to provide working conditions in the form of office space and research support combined with housing. But it may not be sufficient. This must be combined with some incentives and rewards for performance. There is, however, another dimension to the problem. Universities do not always choose the best in part because of native-son/daughter policies which leave them to select their own former students. This tends to lower quality and foster parochialisation in universities. Therefore, cross-pollination between universities should be encouraged. It may be worth introducing a ceiling, say one-half or even one-third, on the proportion of faculty members than can be hired from within the university. This would almost certainly engender greater competition and more transparency in faculty appointments.

Finances: There is a serious resource crunch in universities which leaves them with little financial flexibility. In general, about 75 per cent of maintenance expenditure is on salaries and pensions. Of the remaining 25 per cent, at least 15 per cent is absorbed by pre-emptive claims such as rents, electricity, telephones and examinations. The balance, less than 10 per cent, is not even enough for maintenance let alone development. Laboratories and libraries languish while buildings crumble. But that is not all. In most universities, plan (investment) expenditure is less than 5 per cent of non-plan (maintenance) expenditure. Such a small proportion of investment in total expenditure can only mortgage the future. It is doing so. The time has come for some strategic thinking on the re-allocation of budgets for universities with some allocation for development grants and on needs other than salaries. The criteria for resource allocation should seek to strike a much better balance between providing for salaries/pensions and providing for maintenance/development/investment.These criteria should recognise the importance of a critical minimum to ensure standards and strategic preferences to promote excellence.

Infrastructure: The elements of infrastructure that support the teaching-learning process, most directly, need to be monitored and upgraded on a regular basis. This means attention, particular attention to libraries and laboratories, in addition to class rooms, sports facilities and auditoriums. It is imperative that universities provide broadband connectivity to all students and teachers in campuses. In parallel, information technology systems should be used for admissions, administration and examinations along with other relevant web services for campus communities. And, as soon as possible, a digital infrastructure for networking universities should be put in place.

Governance: There is an acute need for reform in the structures of governance of universities. The present system is flawed. On the one hand, it does not preserve autonomy. On the other, it does not promote accountability. The autonomy of universities is eroded by interventions from governments and intrusions from political processes. This must be stopped. At the same time, there is not enough transparency and accountability in universities. This must be fostered. It is exceedingly difficult to provide generalised prescriptions. Some steps, which would constitute an important beginning, are clear. First, the appointments of Vice-Chancellors should be based on search processes and peer judgment alone. These must be freed from direct or indirect intervention on the part of the governments. Once appointed, Vice- Chancellors should have a tenure of six years, because the existing tenure of three years in most universities and five years in central universities is not long enough. Second, the size and composition of University Courts, Academic Councils and Executive Councils slows down decision-making processes and sometimes constitutes an impediment to change. University Courts, with a size of 500 plus, which are more a ritual than substance, could be dispensed with. Large Academic Councils do not meet often. Even when they meet, decisions are slow to come. Thus, Standing Committees of Academic Councils, which are representative, should be created for frequent meetings and expeditious decisions. The Vice-Chancellor should, then, function as a Chief Executive Officer who has the authority and the flexibility to govern with the advice and consent of the Executive Council which would provide checks and balances to create accountability. Third, experience suggests that implicit politicisation has made governance of universities exceedingly difficult and much more susceptible to entirely non-academic interventions from outside. This problem needs to be recognised and addressed in a systematic manner not only within universities but also outside, particularly in governments, legislatures and political parties.

3. Undergraduate Colleges

Undergraduate education, which accounts for about 85 per cent of the enrolled students, is the largest component of our higher education system. It is imparted through colleges where students enrol for first degrees in Arts, Science or Commerce. There are a total of about 17,700 undergraduate colleges. Of these, a mere 200 colleges are autonomous. The rest, as many as 17,500 colleges, are affiliated to, or constituent in, 131 universities. On average, each university has more than 100 affiliated colleges, but there are some universities each of which has more than 400 affiliated colleges.

This system of affiliated colleges for undergraduate education, which may have been appropriate 50 years ago, is neither adequate nor appropriate at this juncture, let alone for the future. It is cumbersome to manage. And it is difficult to ensure minimal academic standards across the board. The problem has at least three dimensions. First, it imposes an onerous burden on universities which have to regulate admissions, set curricula and conduct examinations for such a large number of undergraduate colleges. The problem is compounded by uneven standards and geographical dispersion. Second, the undergraduate colleges are constrained by their affiliated status, in terms of autonomy and space, which makes it difficult for them to adapt, to innovate and to evolve. The problem is particularly acute for undergraduate colleges that are good, for both teachers and students are subjected to the 'convoy problem' insofar as they are forced to move at the speed of the slowest. There is also a problem for undergraduate colleges that are not so good, or are poor, because universities cannot address their special needs or unique problems. Third, it is difficult to set curricula and assess performance for such a large number of students where there is such a large dispersion in performance at school before entering college. This reality tends to make courses less demanding and examinations less stringent across the board. In fact the design of courses and examinations needs to be flexible rather than exactly the same for large student communities.

There is an urgent need to restructure the system of undergraduate colleges affiliated to universities. In doing so, it is important to make a distinction between undergraduate colleges that already exist and undergraduate colleges that will be established in the future. It is also important to remember that undergraduate colleges are afflicted by problems which are very similar to those that afflict universities.

The most obvious solution is to provide autonomy to colleges, either as individual colleges or as cluster of colleges.

Individual colleges: Colleges with a proven record of academic excellence and efficient administrative functioning can be granted autonomy in terms of academic self-governance. Existing affiliated or constituent colleges should be granted autonomy in phases after due assessment by professional accreditation bodies. A review of performance of these colleges should be institutionalised and they may be granted university status on the fulfilment of stated criteria of academic and administrative performance. The college authorities should be given financial autonomy with regard to internal allocation of resources. However, existing methods of financing should be retained. In operational terms, the autonomy would then be accorded in setting of curriculum and evaluation of students.

College clusters: Autonomy can be provided to clusters of colleges, selected on the basis of criteria such as similar standards or geographical proximity. These colleges could then form a group, complementing each other, offering different courses between them. In time, these clusters could be upgraded to universities. The course-credit system can be implemented in these autonomous clusters, whereby different colleges offer semester-based courses on a credit system and credits can be transferred across colleges. A mechanism for the administration of courses across colleges and for the resolution of problems should be institutionalised with provision for representation in committees.

Such autonomous colleges, or clusters of colleges, would constitute a part of the 1500 universities we propose nationwide by 2015. It must be recognised, however, that this is, at best, a limited solution. There are two discernible problems.

The first problem with the model of autonomous colleges is the principal-agent problem of providing autonomy as an option. It becomes necessary to distinguish between the motivations and the capabilities of colleges. We need to make a distinction between colleges that wish to become autonomous but do not deserve to, and colleges that have the capabilities to be autonomous but do not wish to opt for autonomy. For colleges that wish to become autonomous but may not be suitable, clear cut criteria should be put in place as a filtering mechanism for colleges wishing to attain autonomous status: critical number of faculty and disciplines, governance, track record in terms of students, faculty and research, administrative competence measured by utilisation of grants, regularity of audits, office resources and account maintenance, contribution to university processes, infrastructural facilities and ratings, if available, by accreditation agencies. For colleges that can be autonomous but do not wish to be, appropriate incentives have to be designed, especially for the teaching staff to encourage a move towards autonomy. Institutional incentives relating to funding and resource generation and professional incentives for staff including positions of professors, research grants and greater mobility should be provided.

The second problem with the model of autonomous colleges is that it would be able to provide a solution for a limited proportion, or number, of undergraduate colleges. There would be a significant number of undergraduate colleges that would remain because they may not have the capabilities to become autonomous or join an autonomous cluster. The obvious solution would be for this latter group to continue as affiliated colleges with their present universities. In that event, problems will persist not only for these undergraduate colleges but also for their affiliating universities. Nevertheless, a proportion of these undergraduate colleges will continue to be affiliated to their present universities on the basis of stipulated criteria. There are two other possibilities that could be explored.

The first possibility is that some of these affiliated colleges could be remodelled as community colleges. These colleges could provide both vocational education through two-year courses and formal education through three-year courses. This would serve the needs of a particular segment of the student population better. They could focus on promoting job-oriented, work-related, skill-based and life-coping education. These community colleges could provide a unique opportunity to provide holistic education and eligibility for employment to the disadvantaged.

The second possibility is that we establish a Central Board of Undergraduate Education along with State Boards of Undergraduate Education which would set curricula and conduct examinations for undergraduate colleges that choose to be affiliated with them. These Boards would separate the academic functions from the administrative functions and at the same time provide quality benchmarks. Governance would become much simpler. It is possible that some of the existing undergraduate colleges, particularly those that are at some geographical distance from their parent university, may wish to affiliate themselves to these Boards.

New undergraduate colleges are bound to be an integral part of the expansion of opportunities in higher education. Where would these be located? It would be difficult for them to become autonomous colleges without a track record. It may be possible for some to join a cluster of autonomous colleges but this would be more the exception than the rule. It would not be possible for them to affiliate with existing universities which are already overloaded. Hence, there are three possible options for new undergraduate colleges to come. First, they could be established as community colleges. Second, they could be affiliated with the Central Board of Undergraduate Education or State Boards of Undergraduate Education. Third, they could be affiliated with new universities that are established.

There are, of course, issues related to governance, curricula, examinations, course credits and access which arise in the context of undergraduate colleges. These have been discussed in the context of universities in the preceding section of this note.

4. Regulation

There is a clear need to establish an Independent Regulatory Authority for Higher Education (IRAHE). Such a regulatory authority is both necessary and desirable.

It is necessary for two important reasons. First, in India, it requires an Act of Legislature of Parliament to set up a University. The deemed university route is much too difficult for new institutions. Entry through legislation alone, as at present, is a formidable barrier. The consequence is a steady increase in the average size of existing universities with a steady deterioration in their quality. The absence of competition only compounds problems. Second, as we seek to expand the higher education system, entry norms will be needed for private institutions and public-private partnerships. The institutional framework for this purpose must be put in place here and now.

It is desirable for four important reasons. First, it would minimise conflicts of interest as it would create an arm's length distance from stakeholders. Second, it would replace the present system which is over-regulated but under-governed, through more appropriate forms of intervention. Third, it would rationalise the existing system where mandates are both confusing and overlapping. Fourth, it would dispense with the multiplicity of regulatory agencies to provide a single-window clearance.

The present regulatory system in higher education is flawed in many respects. The barriers to entry are too high. The system of authorising entry is cumbersome. And there are extensive rules after entry, as the UGC seeks to regulate almost every aspect of an institution from fees to curriculum. The system is also based on patently irrational principles. The UGC Act section 3.1.2(a) suggests that permission for receiving grants will be accorded only if the Commission is satisfied that the existing institutions in the state are not adequate to serve the needs of the state. The other regulators, say in the sphere of professional education, are often inconsistent in their adherence to principles. There are several instances where an engineering college or a business school is approved, promptly, in a small house of a metropolitan suburb without the requisite teachers, infrastructure or facilities, but established universities experience difficulties in obtaining similar approvals. Such examples can be multiplied. These would only confirm that the complexity, the multiplicity and the rigidity of the existing regulatory structure is not conducive to the expansion of higher education opportunities in India.

In sum, the existing regulatory framework constrains the supply of good institutions, excessively regulates existing institutions in the wrong places, and is not conducive to innovation or creativity in higher education. The challenge is, therefore, to design a regulatory system that increases the supply of good institutions and fosters accountability in those institutions. An independent regulator has to be the cornerstone of such a system.

The proposed IRAHE will rationalise the principles on which entry is regulated. There are two aspects to this rationalisation: what is to be regulated and what are the principles used for regulation.

In higher education, regulators perform five functions: (1) Entry: licence to grant degrees. (2) Accreditation: quality benchmarking. (3) Disbursement of public funds. (4) Access: fees or affirmative action. (5) Licence: to practice profession.

India is perhaps the only country in the world where regulation in four of the five functions is carried out by one entity, that is, the UGC. The purpose of creating an IRAHE is to separate these functions. The proposed IRAHE shall be responsible for setting the criteria and deciding on entry. It would, in addition, license agencies to take care of accreditation. The role of the UGC will be limited to disbursing public funds. Issues of access will be governed by state legislation on reservations and other forms of affirmative action. And, professional associations may, in some institutions, set requirements to determine eligibility for conducting a profession. All other regulatory agencies such as the AICTE will need to be abolished while the MCI and the BCI will be limited to their role as professional associations. These professional associations could conduct nationwide examinations to provide licences for those wishing to enter the profession.

The second aspect of regulation is the principle used to regulate. The IRAHE will determine eligibility for setting up a new institution based on transparent criteria rather than discretionary controls. Its main role would be to exercise due diligence at the point it approves a licence to grant degrees. In doing so, it would assess the academic credibility and the financial viability of the proposed institution on the basis of information submitted in accordance with the stipulated criteria. It will apply exactly the same norms to public and private institutions, just as it will apply the same norms to domestic and international institutions.

The IRAHE would be constituted as follows. It would have a Chairperson and six Members. The tenure of the Chairperson would be six years. The tenure of the Members would also be six years. One-third of the Members of the Authority will retire every two years. The Chairperson would be a distinguished academic from any discipline with experience of governance in higher education. The Members would be distinguished academics drawn from the following sets of disciplines: physical sciences, life sciences, social sciences, humanities and professional subjects such as engineering, medicine, law or management. The IRAHE could have some part-time members or standing committees drawn from academia to advise the Authority in each of the aforesaid sets of disciplines. The Chairperson and the Members of the IRAHE would be appointed by the Prime Minister based on the recommendations of a Search Committee.

The IRAHE would have to be established by an Act of Parliament. It would be the only agency that would be authorised to accord degree granting power to higher education institutions. It would also be responsible for monitoring standards and settling disputes. It should also be thought of as the authority for licensing accreditation agencies. The IRAHE must be at an arm's length from the Government and independent of all stakeholders including the concerned Ministries of the Government. The Acts of the UGC, AICTE, MCI and BCI would have to be amended. The role of the UGC would be re-defined to focus on the disbursement of grants to, and maintenance of, public institutions in higher education. The entry regulatory functions of the AICTE, the MCI and the BCI would be performed by the IRAHE, so that their role would be limited to that of professional associations. These professional associations could conduct nationwide examinations to provide licenses for those wishing to enter the profession.

5. Financing

The expansion of our system of higher education, which is both necessary and desirable, is not possible without financing. For an increase in supply of quality education depends upon an increase in investment which, in turn, requires financial resources. There are several sources of such financing.

Government support: There is no system of higher education in the world that is not based upon significant public outlays. And the government financing will remain the cornerstone of any strategy to improve our system of higher education. The present support for higher education at 0.7 per cent of GDP is simply not adequate. In fact, over the past decade, in real terms, there has been a significant decline in the resources allocated for higher education, in the aggregate as also per student. In an ideal world, government support for higher education should be at least 1.5 per cent, if not 2 per cent of GDP, from a total of 6 per cent of GDP for education. This is easier said than done. But the government should endeavour to reach these levels by 2012. Even this magnitude of state financing, however, would not suffice for the massive expansion in higher education that is an imperative. Therefore, it is essential to explore a wide range of possibilities which can be complements to the increase in public expenditure.

Better asset management: Most public universities are sitting on a large reservoir of untapped resources in the form of land. In effect, with some imagination, many of our universities can be converted into institutions that are similar to land grant universities. Each university should thus have an innovative asset management plan. Such plans should be in consonance with objectives of universities. At the moment, however, universities have no strategy in this sphere. And there is considerable room to think in strategic terms about the use of physical assets in the possession of universities. It should be possible to draw up norms and parameters for universities to use their land as a source of finance.

Rationalisation of fees: On an average, fees constitute less than 10 per cent of total expenditure in our universities. And, in most universities, fees have remained unchanged for decades. In theory, universities have the freedom to decide on fees. In practice, however, universities have not exercised this freedom in part because of some genuine concerns about access but in larger part because of the rhetoric and populism in the political process. The problem has been compounded by the UGC method of providing grants-in-aid to bridge the difference between income and expenditure. Consequently, there is no incentive for universities or colleges to raise income through higher fees as that sum would be deducted from their UGC (or State government) grants. The low fees in public universities, without any means test, have meant unquantifiable benefits for unintended beneficiaries. But private players and foreign institutions have not been restrained in charging fees that the market can bear. The time has come to rethink, as we have no choice but to rationalise fees. It is for universities to decide the level of fees but, as a norm, fees should meet at least 20 per cent of the total expenditure in universities. In addition, fees need to be adjusted every two years through price indexation. Such small, continuous, adjustments would be absorbed and accepted far more easily than large, discrete changes after a period of time. This rationalisation of fees should be subject to two conditions: first, needy students should be provided with a fee waiver plus scholarships to meet their costs; second, universities should not be penalised by the UGC for the resources raised from higher fees through matching deductions from their grants-in-aid.

Philanthropic contributions: It is clear that we have not exploited this potential. In fact, the proportion of such contributions in total expenditure on higher education has declined from more than 12 per cent in the 1950s to less than 3 per cent in the 1990s. It should be possible to nurture this tradition of philanthropy through changes in incentives for universities and for donors. In the present system, there is an explicit disincentive. If universities mobilise resources from elsewhere, they are in effect penalised through a matching deduction in their grant-in-aid. What we need to do is exactly the opposite. Universities which mobilise resources through contributions should be rewarded with matching grants-in-aid. At present, there is also an implicit disincentive in both lax laws and trust laws. Endowments of universities can only be placed in specified securities where rates of return are low and barely keep up with rates of inflation. What is more, trusts must spend 85 per cent of the income stream from the endowment in the same year, so that only 15 per cent of the income stream can be used to build up the corpus in the endowment. These laws should be changed so that universities can invest in financial instruments of their choice and use the income from their endowments to build up a corpus.

Other sources: Obviously, universities must not be driven by commercial considerations. But it would be both prudent and wise to tap other sources such as alumni contributions, licensing fees, or user charges (for facilities in universities used by people from outside). We need to create supportive institutional mechanisms that allow universities to engage professional firms for this purpose. Mobilising resources, even from former students, is a task that cannot be performed by academics because it needs specialised talents and experience. Current UGC practice also penalises universities for any resources mobilised with a matching deduction from the grants-in-aid provided to the institution. Rather than penalising universities for raising resources, the UGC should incentivise them. In addition, universities must have the autonomy and flexibility to mobilise resources from elsewhere by creating or using appropriate institutional mechanisms.

Private investment: In three professions—engineering, medicine and management—there has been a *de facto* privatisation of education so that two-thirds to three-fourths of the seats are in private institutions. But private investment in university education, where more than 70 per cent of our students study, is almost negligible. It is essential to stimulate private investment in higher education as a means of extending educational opportunities. We must recognise that, even with the best will in the world, government financing cannot be enough to support the massive expansion in opportunities for higher education on a scale that is now essential.

Public-private partnerships: It might be possible to leverage public funding, especially in the form of land grants, to attract more (not-for-profit) private investment. The present system of allotment of land, where political patronage is implicit, discourages genuine educational entrepreneurs and encourages real estate developers in disguise. In principle, it should be possible to set up new institutions in higher education, not just more IITs and IIMs but also more universities, as public-private partnerships where the government provides the land and the private sector provides the finances. Such public-private partnerships which promote university-industry interface would also strengthen teaching and research.

International students: India is not an attractive destination for international students, not even as much as it used to be 30 years ago. It is time for us to make a conscious attempt to attract foreign students to India for higher education. This would enrich our academic milieu. This would enhance quality. This would be a significant source of finance. Even 50,000 foreign students charged fees at an average rate of US$ 10,000 per annum would yield US$ 0.5 billion: the equivalent of Rs. 2,300 crore per annum in current prices at current exchange rates. The other side of the coin is perhaps even more important. Estimates suggest that there are about 160,000 students from India studying abroad. If their average expenditure on fees and maintenance is US$ 25,000 per student per year, Indian students overseas are spending US$ 4 billion: the equivalent of Rs. 18,400 crore per annum in current prices at current exchange rates. This has an enormous potential as a source of finance for higher education in India, if only we could create more opportunities for students with increased places and enhanced quality in our system.

6. Quality

The introduction of an independent regulator in higher education, the reform of existing public universities and the creation of national universities, taken together, would contribute to enhancement of quality in higher education. But this needs to be supported with some proactive steps that would foster quality in higher education.

Accountability: The quality of higher education depends on a wide range of factors. But accountability, at every level, is a critical determinant. The higher education system must, therefore, provide for accountability *vis-à-vis* the outside world and create accountability within the system. Accountability of universities must not be confused with control of the state. Institutional mechanisms, based on checks and balances, constitute the most effective system for this purpose. The essential objective of accountability to society must be to empower students to take decisions rather than simply increase the power of the state. Stipulated performance criteria or inspections are forms of control. We need to create systems that enable students, or their parents, to choose between and assess universities.

Competition: The supply constraint on higher education is an impediment to accountability. When students have relatively few choices, institutions have greater power over them. An expansion of higher education which provides students with choices and creates competition between institutions is going to be vital in enhancing accountability. Such competition between institutions within India is, of course, essential. But the significance of competition from outside India, more qualitative than quantitative, must not be underestimated. For this purpose, we must formulate appropriate policies for the entry of foreign institutions into India and the promotion of Indian institutions abroad. Such policies must ensure that there is an incentive for good institutions and a disincentive for sub-standard institutions to come to India. The present regime does the opposite: sub-standard players rush in while premier universities stay away as they care more about their autonomy and wish to set benchmarks for themselves. However, a level playing field should be ensured and all rules that apply to domestic institutions should also be applicable to foreign institutions. At the same time, policies must encourage rather than discourage Indian institutions to create campuses abroad not as business opportunities but as competition opportunities in their quest for academic excellence. Of course, expansion abroad should not be at the cost of domestic provision, either at present or in the future.

Accreditation: So far, we have sought to create accountability by increasing the powers of government regulators. Yet, it has done little to improve the quality of higher education. Consider, for example, the National Accreditation and Assessment Council (NAAC). This system has three characteristics which significantly erode its credibility. First, it grants one institution, the NAAC, monopoly power over accreditation. Second, NAAC itself does not have the capacity to rate all the institutions. It has rated just about 10 per cent of the total number so far. Third, the methodology of NAAC is much too discretionary. Instead of vesting one institution created by the state with monopoly power, the IRAHE may be empowered to license a number of accreditation agencies, public and private, to do the ratings. In doing so, the regulator would set standards for them. This will need to be accompanied by stringent information disclosure norms for all educational institutions, including the source and level of their accreditation. The rapid growth in higher education, particularly in the private sector, has created a strong need for empowering students and parents with reliable information from a credible accreditation process. This system can be supplemented with the creation of self-regulatory bodies in the higher education system and the freedom to seek recognition from global accreditation systems.

Internal systems: In most universities, the main stakeholders, students, are minimally part of any mechanism for accountability. Obviously, student evaluations need to be used with care. Even so, they can be part of a baseline set of accountability measures which could at least establish whether classes scheduled in the timetable are held. But that is not all. Evaluation of courses and teachers by students is also needed, just as much as we need peer evaluation of teachers by teachers. Such internal systems of evaluation would strengthen accountability in the teaching-learning process. These must be combined with institutional mechanisms for accountability in other dimensions of university systems.

Information: Almost everywhere, information in the public domain is an important source of accountability. Higher education should be no exception. There should be disclosure norms for universities and institutions imparting higher education. They should be required to place basic information relating to their financial situation, physical assets, accreditation ratings, admissions criteria, faculty positions, academic curricula, and so on, in the public domain. This would empower students and parents and enable them to make informed choices. Information, along with competition, fostered by increased supply, will close the accountability loop.

Incentives: Even if we cannot introduce penalties for non-performance, it is necessary to introduce rewards for performance. We must, of course, recognise that universities are different from the hierarchical worlds in governments and corporate structures. The web of incentives is far more subtle. Even so, the time has come to think of salary differentials within and between universities as a means of attracting and retaining talented faculty members. The salary differentiation among teachers within the same university needs to reflect the opportunity costs for teachers in some departments. This will help retain talent in some disciplines where remuneration in the market is much higher than in other subjects. Salary differentiation may enable some universities to develop centres of excellence in some disciplines. At the same time, it is important to ensure that disciplines which are essential for a good liberal education such as social sciences and humanities, as well as basic sciences which are not necessarily rewarded by the market, are given appropriate incentives to attract both teachers and students. Such salary differentials between and within universities could be effective without being large. Indeed, there is a good reason to stipulate a maximum ratio for differences in salaries between faculty members so as not to threaten the identity of the professoriate. Obviously, universities cannot compete with salaries elsewhere, but they should endeavour to provide a comfortable minimum for all, with some premium for those who perform. It is also important to think of other incentives, such as housing, good facilities for teaching and research and some flexibility for non-teaching professional activities so long as these do not impinge on the primary responsibilities to the institution.

Differentiation: We have to recognise that there is bound to be diversity and pluralism in any system of higher education. Therefore, in a country as large as India, we cannot afford to adopt the principle that one size fits all. We must allow diversity to blossom. This could have many dimensions: curriculum, specialisation, institutional architecture, students' composition, and so on. Similarly, differentiation is inevitable if not natural. Even if we do not wish to recognise it, such differentiation is a reality. Students and parents have clear preferences, possibly implicit rankings, based on their perceptions derived from available information. Our sense of pluralism must recognise, rather than ignore or shy away from, such diversity and differentiation. It is characteristic of every higher education system in the world. For higher education is about a quest for excellence. It is, at least in part, about distinction and not always about levelling. The institutions which excel are the important peaks that raise the average. They are also role models others seek to emulate. And institutions that become such role models could mentor and guide other selected institutions.

7. National Universities

We need to create substantial additional capacity in higher education for achieving a quantum jump in the gross enrolment ratio for a rapidly expanding population of young people. It would be expeditious to do so by simply expanding on our existing educational infrastructure. A fundamental paradigm shift in our understanding of quality and standards in higher education, however, requires creating completely new institutions that operate unconstrained by the current institutional and regulatory framework. We recommend the creation of up to 50 National Universities that can provide education of the highest standard. As exemplars for the rest of the nation, these universities shall train students in a variety of disciplines, including humanities, social sciences, basic sciences, commerce and professional subjects, at both the undergraduate and postgraduate levels. The number 50 is a long term objective. In the short run, it is important to begin with at least 10 such universities in the next three years. It is worth noting that the National Universities need not all be new universities. Some of the existing universities could also be converted into National Universities, on the basis of rigorous selection criteria, to act as exemplars. We recognise that there could be a human resource constraint if faculty members are not available in adequate numbers to establish these universities. But, for such centres of academic excellence, it should be possible to attract talent from among those who choose other professions in India or the academic profession outside India.

National Universities can be established in two ways, by the government, or by a private sponsoring body that sets up a society, charitable trust or section 25 company. Since public finance is an integral constituent of universities worldwide, most of the new universities shall need significant initial financial support from the government. This could be in several forms. Each university may be endowed with a substantial allocation of public land, in excess of its spatial requirements. The excess land can be a subsequent source of income generation, its value rising over time due to the growing stature of the university. In the case of privately executed charitable trusts, exceptions need to be made in existing income tax laws to encourage large endowments. In particular, there should be no restriction on the utilisation of income in any given time period, the trusts should be allowed to invest their funds in financial instruments of their choice, and all proceeds from the sale of capital assets should be exempt from capital gains tax. These universities shall have the autonomy to invest in financial instruments of their choice, by employing private fund managers if required. Appropriate mechanisms also need to be put in place for the optimal management of physical assets, like laboratories, libraries, classrooms and other facilities. Finally, these universities shall have the autonomy to set student fee levels and tap other sources for generating funds such as industry collaborations, overseas operations, as also commercial use of university facilities and alumni networks.

The National Universities we propose shall admit students on an all-India basis. They shall adopt the principle of needs-blind admissions, thereby ensuring that an applicant's ability or inability to pay shall not influence the admission decision made by a university. Further, once admitted, the university should ensure that no student has to forego his/her place due to financial constraints. This will require a host of scholarships, freeships, bursaries and awards for economically disadvantaged students. At the undergraduate level, a nationwide test that objectively measures the verbal, quantitative and analytical abilities of applicants shall be administered by an independent testing body. Admissions shall be based on a combination of Class XII results, scores from the nationwide test, application materials including written work and personal statements, as also interviews. At the postgraduate level, admissions shall be based on a combination of the applicant's academic record, application materials, interviews and academic or professional references that indicate his/her aptitude for further studies in the relevant discipline.

Undergraduate degrees in the National Universities shall have a duration of three years so that these are in conformity with the duration of undergraduate courses elsewhere in India. In the first year, students shall have the opportunity to study foundation, analytical and tools courses before choosing a specific discipline in the second year. They shall also have the option, at the end of the second year, of completing an integrated five-year master's degree. Degrees should be granted on the basis of completing a requisite number of credits, obtained from different courses. Each student shall be required to earn a minimum number of credits in his/her chosen discipline, and shall have the freedom to earn the rest from courses in other disciplines. The academic year shall, therefore, be semester-based and students shall be internally evaluated at the end of each course. Transfer of credits from one National University to another shall also be possible. A wide variety of courses shall be offered, in traditional academic disciplines, employment-oriented specific areas and cross-cutting competencies. Syllabi shall be revised every year to keep up with changes and current developments in various disciplines. Departments that do not update their syllabus for two consecutive years shall be asked to provide justification. Students shall have the option of taking up internships in private companies or research institutions in lieu of a certain number of credits.

An appropriate system of appointments and incentives is required to maximise the productivity of faculty in the National Universities. There shall be scope for salary differentials between National Universities and also between disciplines. Faculty training will be contingent on periodical reviews of research output and student evaluation. The most accomplished faculty members shall be encouraged to teach undergraduate courses. There shall be no career advancement schemes and appointments at every level shall be through open competition. The total number of faculty positions may be specified, but there should be complete flexibility in choosing the level at which faculty appointments are made, so that, for talented faculty members, career paths are not constrained by the number of vacancies. In order to maintain the quality of the National Universities, mechanisms should be in place to monitor and evaluate the performance and progress of teachers including peer reviews. The procedures and results of these evaluations will be open and transparent.

The research outputs of these universities shall be vital contributors to India's socio-economic development and progress in science and technology. Strong linkages shall be forged between teaching and research, universities and industry, and universities and research laboratories.

The National Universities shall be department-based and shall not have any affiliated colleges. Each department will administer undergraduate and postgraduate courses. Non-teaching functions should be outsourced wherever possible, and a maximum ratio of 2:1 should be maintained between non-teaching and teaching staff. Each university should appoint an internal ombudsman for the redressal of faculty, staff, student and public grievances. Administrative processes, wherever possible, should be streamlined and made transparent and accountable by the use of information and communications technology.

8. Access

Education is an essential mechanism for inclusion through the creation of social opportunities. It is, therefore, essential that in addition to ensuring that no student is denied the opportunity to participate in higher education due to financial constraints, access to education for economically and historically socially underprivileged students is enhanced in a substantially more effective manner.

Economic barriers to higher education can be addressed by ensuring financial viability for all students wanting to enter the world of higher education. This can be done through two strategies. One is to adopt a needs blind admissions policy. This would make it unlawful for educational institutions to take into account any financial factor while deciding whether or not to admit a student. Every institution will be free to use a variety of instruments to achieve this aim: scholarships or cross-subsidies. In addition, academic institutions would be able to set a fee of their own choice subject to the provision that there are at least two banks that are willing to finance the entire cost of education at that institution, without any collateral other than the fact of admission. The cost of education includes not just fees but also reasonable living expenses including costs such as hostel and mess fees and any other expenses associated with the course of study. Since commercial banks may be wary of funding economically deprived students, especially in non-professional courses, we need a well-funded and extensive National Scholarship Scheme targeting economically underprivileged students and students from historically socially disadvantaged groups, particularly students from rural and backward areas. The success of this proposal depends on generous government support. For instance, the government should endeavour to make available about 100,000 scholarships for such students. These scholarships should be set at a level where students are empowered to go to any institution of their choice.

We also need to undertake more proactive forms of affirmative action to ensure inclusion of marginal and excluded groups. Reservations are essential but they are a part, and one form of affirmative action. Disparities in educational attainments are related to caste and social groups, but are also strongly related to other indicators such as income, gender, region and place of residence. Access to quality higher education is further limited for students from certain types of schools. Therefore, deprivation of educational opportunities is a multidimensional problem and attention needs to be paid to different salient levels of deprivation faced by students. A meaningful and comprehensive framework would account for the multidimensionality of differences that still persist. Such a deprivation index could provide weighted scores to students and the cumulative score could be used to supplement a student's school examination score. After adding the score from the deprivation index, all students could compete for admissions.

The indicators need to be easily identifiable and verifiable for the system to work effectively. They should cover the different types of disadvantages that a student could face at the school level, and while applying for admissions to higher education. This system serves the dual purpose of considering various disadvantages and ensuring that a reserved category student who has otherwise enjoyed other benefits does not get great preference at the time of admissions.

Illustrative indicators of backwardness that need to be measured by such an index could include social background covering caste (keeping in view regional variations), religion and gender, family education history, family income, type of school distinguishing between government and private schools and between schools from different locations, the medium of instruction, place of residence distinguishing between urban and rural areas and accounting for regional deprivation by sorting districts along an index of infrastructure or access to social benefits and physical disability.

Appointment of Heads of Institutions

The recent measures introduced by the Government leading to a major expansion of the higher education sector are probably among the most important steps in making India globally competitive in the long run. Expansion and inclusiveness, drawing larger sections of Indians into the arena of knowledge creation and utilisation will be the key drivers to a better future.

The National Knowledge Commission would like to draw attention to the central role of governance structures in allowing these new institutions to grow rapidly, efficiently and productively and also, to review procedures in some of our best existing institutions like IITs, IIMs, Central Universities and AIIMS.

It is imperative to separate governance mechanisms from the day-to-day operations of Ministries in order to protect functional autonomy in its fullest sense. NKC would like to draw attention to the following ideas.

1. The appointment of Directors/Vice-Chancellors of the new IITs, IIMs, IISERs, Central Universities, AIIMS must be made by a Search Committee that has an independent Chair, capable of exercising the highest quality of judgment. The direct involvement of administrative ministries can result in unfortunate situations.
2. The procedure for appointment of the Chairperson and members of governing Councils/Boards needs to be carefully crafted in order to ensure that institutions have the benefit of the widest inputs from academia and society.
3. The involvement of the Chair of the Governing Board and at least two independent members in the selection of the Director/Vice-Chancellor will ensure smooth functioning at later stages of an institution's development.
4. Appointments of heads of institutions must be made well in advance of a vacancy arising, so that a smooth transition is effected. In view of fixed tenures, there is no reason that this cannot be done in all institutions.
5. The proposal for an independent regulatory body for higher education was also advanced by the Commission as an expression of its concern at the deteriorating ambience of institutions of learning in many parts of the country.

In summary, NKC believes, that governance issues may be central to any debate on improving the status of higher education in India.

11 Medical Education

The quality, quantity, distribution and availability of human resources for the health sector in India at present, need to be improved substantially to deliver care-driven, rural-oriented and equitable health services. Over the years, health-related education and training has become more urban-oriented, doctor-centric and technology-driven. The environment of medical education needs to be both nationally sensitive and globally competitive. To realise these objectives, our medical education system needs radical reforms.

The National Knowledge Commission therefore, considered it imperative to carry out a comprehensive appraisal of the system. For this purpose, a Working Group was constituted which included some of the most distinguished members of the medical profession in India, chaired by Dr. Sneha Bhargava, former Director, AIIMS. Based on the inputs provided by the Working Group and further consultations with concerned stakeholders, NKC recommended the following:

1. Regulation and Accreditation

Regulation

At present, medical education in India is regulated by the Medical Council of India (MCI). This system of regulation is neither adequate nor appropriate to meet the needs of the profession. Therefore, in conformity with NKC recommendations on Higher Education, a Standing Committee within the structure of the Independent Regulatory Authority for Higher Education (IRAHE) may be constituted. The primary function of the Standing Committee will be to ensure that medical practice and teaching are updated and revised regularly and minimum quality standards are maintained. The members of the Standing Committee would include faculty from recognised universities, practising physicians, members of civil society, students and a director from autonomous institutions representing educators. The Chairman and the members of the Standing Committee would be accountable to IRAHE. The Standing Committee would look into manpower planning and development based on disease-profile, doctor-population ratio and skill-mix ratio.

Professional Councils

The Indian Medical Council Act should be amended such that MCI functions only as a professional association, with powers to conduct nationwide examinations, and to provide licenses for those who wish to join the profession. Similar changes are needed for all the other Councils *viz.,* Nursing Council, Pharmacy Council, Dental Council and Rehabilitation Council.

Accreditation

IRAHE should be empowered to license suitable agencies for accreditation. Accreditation agencies could award different degrees of accreditation, such as "Full", "Provisional" or "On Probation" and have the power to de-recognise. Institutions would have to ensure transparency in their admission processes, able and responsible faculties, a multidisciplinary academic learning environment, transparency in assessment of students and close linkages with regional health care and delivery systems, in order to be accredited.

Admission

Policies of admission and fee structure of private colleges have to be regulated, not only to stop them from becoming sources of political and financial power but also to arrest falling standards. There should be only one All India Common Entrance Test for all students who would like to get admission to self-financing medical colleges. Since the CBSE conducted examination for the 15 per cent all India quota in government medical colleges is taken by a very large number of students, this would appear to be the ideal examination whose ambit can be expanded. All self-financing medical colleges should announce their fees in their prospectus so that students can make their choice for admission. Information technology should be used to increase transparency and efficiency in the admission, examination, administration, teaching, content delivery and other related processes.

2. Quality

Curriculum

All institutions must constitute Curriculum Committees that plan curricula and instructional methods, which are regularly updated. The structure and composition of the curriculum must describe the content, scope and sequencing of the courses, including the balance between core and optional courses. Integration of ICT in the learning process is essential. Incorporating new skills like management, disciplines like health economics and frontier areas like bioinformatics should be considered.

Standards Test

An independent and standardised National Exit Examination at the end of 4½ years of study, is essential to conduct a national level assessment of skills and knowledge. The National Exit Examination could be conducted immediately after the University examination, and would also serve as a postgraduate entrance exam.

Internship Assessment

The internship year must be assessed to ensure skill development. The current practice of students continuing to study in the internship year without going to clinics needs to be addressed. There must be compulsory rotation from the teaching hospital to the community and district hospital during the internship period. Duration of the term in the district hospital should be six months, in the Community Health Centre three months and in the tertiary care hospital the remaining three months. Each intern should be assigned a "mentor" at the district hospital and the credits should be based on the assessment by the mentor. The entrance to postgraduate programmes should be based on a summation of the pre- and post-internship examinations.

Continuing Education

There is a need to revamp Continuing Medical Education (CME) based on distance learning. All professionals should be required to undergo a re-certification process every five years, which can be evaluated by credits earned through CME. ICT can be used extensively to provide CME at the convenience of the learner.

3. Faculty Development

Teaching

Attracting and retaining quality faculty should be accorded top priority. Measures such as opportunities to attend international conferences regularly, sabbaticals, dual appointments, rewarding research, fast-track promotions and dissociating remuneration from government pay scales should be explored. All institutions must clearly lay down exact definitions of what constitutes conflict of interest for faculty members in public medical colleges, who have a private practice in addition to their official duties, and receive a full time teacher's salary. Those who flout these regulations should be penalised.

Research

With a view to encouraging research in medicine, a Mentored Medical Student Research Programme should be set up as a catalyst to introduce medical students to a potential career in patient-oriented/community-oriented research including interdisciplinary research. Two points of entry into Ph.D programmes should be considered: one after MBBS and another after MD depending on the student's interest. The government should facilitate setting up of research centres in medical colleges. Validating Indian Systems of Medicine using bio-sciences' tools should form an integral component of the research effort.

Training

Five Regional Centres for teacher training/faculty development should be set up so that teachers from the outlying regions can be sent to these centres periodically for upgradation of their teaching skills.

4. Post-graduate Education

General Physicians

The medical profession needs to be structured like a pyramid with the base made up of general physicians. At present there is little, if any, space for such doctors in postgraduate courses. Therefore, we suggest that adequate representation should be given to general physicians while carrying out expansion of post-graduate seats such that 50 per cent seats are reserved for general physicians. New streams for postgraduation should be looked at based on needs.

Admissions

Admission to postgraduate courses should be done on the basis of credits received in the National Exit Examination and pre- and post-internship clinically-oriented exams after internship. There is a need to reserve postgraduate seats (up to 20 per cent of total available seats) for graduates who have worked in rural areas for at least three years.

5. Regional Balance

Location Priorities

The number of medical colleges in relation to population in some states is much higher than in other states. The Central government should aid new colleges in these states to address this regional disparity. For instance, northeastern states require urgent attention in this context. The Central government can develop a list of priority sites for establishing new colleges where the impact of new clinical facilities would benefit the surrounding rural population.

Role Models

Further at least one institution should be identified in each state that can serve as a centre of excellence and role model for the other institutions of the state. These institutions should have state-of-the-art infrastructural equipment such as research laboratories, teacher training facilities and libraries, as well as talented faculty of adequate strength to act as a common resource and also to serve as a benchmark of excellence.

Medical education cannot be stand-alone. It requires support in the form of trained nurses, pharmacists, paramedic workers. It must all also serve the essential purpose of delivering health care to the people. Therefore, NKC also set out some recommendations on education for supporting services and public health.

6. Education for Support Services

Nursing

There is a need to create additional capacity for training nursing staff. In addition, every district hospital should have attached to it a nursing school, which offers diploma in nursing specifically to operate primary health centres as nurse practitioners. A career growth pathway should be ensured for nurses after a specific period of primary health care service. For graduate nurses in city hospitals, specialised courses for family nurse practitioners, nurse anesthetists and in areas of tertiary care are recommended.

Pharmacy

Pharmacy education should be popularised and the number of seats for pharmacy education should be increased substantially. Gradual phasing out of untrained pharmacists should be considered.

Paramedics

The role of paramedic workers should be expanded. A Paramedical Council needs to be immediately established, which would prepare training programmes for multi skill and speciality technicians and oversee their delivery and quality. Paramedics, such as compounders, dressers and laboratory technicians can also perform public health functions, such as health education, providing immunisation and first aid. Such a health worker could be trained through vocational training at the higher secondary level followed by a one year diploma. Career paths should be built into their service in order to retain them because international demand is high.

7. Public Health

Education

A three tiered structure consisting of a one year diploma course, a three year B.Sc. course and a three year Master's course may be introduced. These programmes can be attached to departments of Community Medicine in all medical colleges for providing hands on training. All universities, all district hospitals and the Public Health Foundation of India can run them.

ASHA

The role of Accredited Social Health Activists (ASHA) needs to be re-conceptualised within this framework, and ASHA must be viewed as an accessible and effective health worker. The training period of the ASHA needs to be lengthened from its current duration. Steps should be taken to review the system of remuneration and improve the working conditions of the ASHA workers.

12 Legal Education

The National Knowledge Commission, while deliberating on issues related to knowledge concepts, recognises legal education as an important constituent of professional education. The vision of legal education is to provide justice-oriented education essential to the realisation of values enshrined in the Constitution of India. In keeping with this vision, legal education must aim at preparing legal professionals who will play decisive leadership roles, not only as advocates practising in courts, but also as academics, legislators, judges, policy makers, public officials, civil society activists as well as legal counsels in the private sector, maintaining the highest standards of professional ethics and a spirit of public service. Legal education should also prepare professionals equipped to meet the new challenges and dimensions of internationalisation, where the nature and organisation of law and legal practice are undergoing a paradigm shift. Further, there is need for original and path breaking legal research to create new legal knowledge and ideas that will help meet these challenges in a manner responsive to the needs of the country and the ideals and goals of our Constitution. As part of a consultative process, NKC constituted a Working Group of experts, including distinguished members of the Bar, the bench and academia under the chairmanship of Justice M. Jagannadha Rao to suggest necessary measures to improve the quality of legal education in India. Based on further consultations with stakeholders, NKC has proposed the following:

1. Regulatory Reform: A New Standing Committee for Legal Education

A new regulatory mechanism under the Independent Regulatory Authority for Higher Education (IRAHE), vested with powers to deal with all aspects of legal education and whose decisions are binding on the institutions teaching law and on the union and state governments, should be established. The Standing Committee for Legal Education may consist of 25 persons (including eminent lawyers, members of the Bar Council of India/BCI, judges, academics, representatives from trade, commerce and industry, economists, social workers, students and others) and it must aim at revamping legal education to meet the needs and challenges of all sections of society.

At the time of enactment of the Advocates Act, 1961, it was envisaged that legal education would only produce lawyers for the courts and accordingly the BCI had been entrusted with the limited role of "promoting legal education and laying down minimum standards of legal education" required for students who "are entitled to practice". In the last 50 years, and particularly after liberalisation in 1991, the entire concept of legal education has changed considerably. Today, legal education has to meet not only the requirements of the Bar but also the new needs of trade, commerce and industry, in the context of growing internationalisation of the profession. The need for improvement in overall quality to match global standards has become even more salient when viewed from such a perspective. In light of the changed scenario in the last 50 years and the existing gaps and deficiencies in overall quality, it is clear that the BCI has neither the power under the Advocates Act, 1961 nor the expertise to meet the new challenges both domestically and internationally. It is, therefore, necessary to constitute a new regulatory mechanism with a vision both of social and international goals, to deal with all aspects of legal education and to cater to the needs of the present and the future. The BCI would, however, continue to exercise its powers to recommend minimum standards required for practice in the courts. Further, the BCI would continue to enjoy its powers of discipline so far as the members of the Bar are concerned.

2. Prioritise Quality and Develop a Rating System

There is a need to develop an independent rating system based on a set of agreed criteria to assess the standard of all institutions teaching law as a mechanism to ensure consistent academic quality throughout the country. The criteria for rating would be evolved by the Standing Committee for Legal Education while the rating would be done by independent agencies licensed by IRAHE for the purpose. Recognition could be either granted or withdrawn on the basis of such ratings. The rating results should be reviewed annually, regularly updated, monitored and made available in the public domain.

3. Curriculum Development

Curriculum should be made contemporary, integrated with other disciplines ensuring regular feedback from stakeholders. Autonomy may be granted to universities, National Law Schools (NLSUs) and other law schools to decide the core and optional courses to be offered. This is a departure from current practice where the BCI largely determines curricula and syllabi. A committee should be formed that includes faculty and practitioners and seeks student feedback to discuss curricula, syllabi and reading material of all core and optional courses, and devise a 'model' syllabus for all core and optional courses. Law schools and universities would be free to use and depart from the 'model' syllabus.

Law teaching must be interwoven with related contemporary issues, including international and comparative law perspectives. The curricula and syllabi must be based in a multidisciplinary body of social science and scientific knowledge. Curriculum development should include expanding the domain of optional courses, providing deeper understanding of professional ethics, modernising clinic courses, mainstreaming legal aid programmes and developing innovative pedagogic methods. Legal education must also be socially engaged and sensitise students on issues of social justice.

4. Examination System

The prevailing examination systems may be revised and evaluation methods be developed that test critical reasoning by encouraging essential analytical, writing and communication skills. The end-semester examination should be problem-oriented, combining theoretical and problem-oriented approaches rather than merely test memory. Project papers, project and subject viva, along with an end-semester examination to be considered as pedagogic methods imperative for improving quality.

5. Measures to Attract and Retain Talented Faculty

To attract and retain talented faculty, better incentives, including improving remuneration and service conditions may be introduced. It may be necessary to think of salary differentials within and between universities and law schools along with other means of attracting and retaining talented faculty members. Such salary differentials between and within universities and law schools could be effective without being large. This will help retain talent in legal academia where the problem of inadequate remuneration is far more acute than in other disciplines. Salary differentials could be considered as a means to retain quality talent and also promote a culture of excellence.

To foster quality and create better incentives, there is also need to remove fetters on faculty that pertain to opportunities in legal practice (such as consultancy assignments and legal practice in courts). These reforms need to be introduced in a balanced, reasonable and regulated manner to ensure adequate incentivisation for faculty without compromising on the maintenance of consistent academic quality. As a further incentive, it is necessary to create better opportunities for active involvement of academia in the shaping of national legal education policy.

There is also need to reconsider existing promotional schemes and avenues to promote meritorious faculty members. Other incentives for faculty include fully paid sabbaticals; adequate House Rent Allowance (HRA); instituting awards to honour reputed teachers and researchers at national and institutional levels; flexibility to appoint law teachers without having an LL.M degree if the individual has proven academic or professional credentials; faculty exchange programmes with leading universities abroad and upgrading existing infrastructure.

6. Developing a Research Tradition in Law Schools and Universities

Creating a tradition of research in law schools and universities is imperative if India has to transform itself from being only a consumer of available legal knowledge to being a leading producer in the world of new legal knowledge and ideas. The following measures are required to develop such a serious culture of research: emphasising analytical writing skills and research methodology as integral aspects of the LL.B programme; creating excellent infrastructure (including research friendly library facilities, availability of computers and Internet; digitisation of case law; access to latest journals and legal databases available worldwide); rationalising the teaching load to leave faculty members sufficient time for research; granting sabbatical leave to faculty to undertake research; creating incentives if research results in peer reviewed publications, either through additional increments (beyond the UGC scheme) or in any other appropriate manner; institutionalising periodic faculty seminars; establishing quality peer-reviewed journals; prescribing research output as one of the criteria for promotion; creating a database of citations to identify the most cited and influential writings as well as considering such data for promotion purposes; establishing prerequisites such as a mandatory dissertation in the LL.M programme, a pre-registration presentation and a course in methodology for M.Phil and Ph.D programmes respectively; and establishing four new centres for advanced legal research.

7. Centres for Advanced Legal Studies and Research (CALSAR)

There is need to set up four autonomous, well networked Centres for Advanced Legal Studies and Research (CALSAR), one in each region, to carry out cutting edge research on various aspects of law and also serve as a think tank for advising the government in national and international fora. The CALSARs would maintain adequate linkages and institutionalised interaction opportunities with law schools and universities, including continuing legal education for faculty. Some other specific functions and objectives of these centres would include: publishing a peer reviewed journal of international quality; facilitating multidisciplinary approaches to law; institutionalising arrangements for scholars in residence; organising workshops and undertaking in-depth research on new and developing areas of law.

Each CALSAR would require an initial investment of around Rs. 50 crore to build an academic complex, conference facilities, a world-class library and other infrastructure. These institutes would also need to be provided with an annual budget to the tune of Rs. 5 crore for salaries, fellowships, administrative expenses and related expenses. The initial investment and the annual budgets should be borne by the Central and respective state governments (that would host the CALSAR) respectively, but the CALSARs should gradually aim at financial self-sustenance, through innovative financial methods.

8. Financing of Legal Education

It is for law schools and universities to decide the level of fees but as a norm, fees should meet at least 20 per cent of the total expenditure in universities. This should be subject to two conditions: first, needy students should be provided with a fee waiver plus scholarships to meet their costs; second, universities should not be penalised by the UGC for the resources raised from higher fees through matching deductions from their grants-in-aid. The Central and state ministries may also be urged to endow chairs on specialised branches of law. State financing can be complemented with endowments from the private sector, including synergistic arrangements such as appropriate public-private partnerships. Incentives such as tax holidays for donations above a high minimum threshold by the corporate sector may be considered. Institutions should be given the autonomy to evolve their own innovative methods of financing to maximise infrastructure and resource utilisation.

9. Dimensions of Internationalisation

Building world class law schools today will require creatively responding to the growing international dimensions of legal education and of the legal profession, where it is becoming increasingly necessary to incorporate international and comparative perspectives, along with necessary understanding of domestic law. Suggested initiatives to promote such international perspectives include building collaborations and partnerships with noted foreign universities for award of joint/dual degrees; finding ways of evolving transnational curricula to be taught jointly by a global faculty through video conferencing and Internet modes; as well as creating international faculty, international courses and international exchange opportunities among students.

10. Technology for Dissemination of Legal Knowledge

For maximum dissemination of legal knowledge, all information available in the Indian Law Institute ("ILI"), Supreme Court Library, Indian Society for International Law ("ISIL") as well as those of all law schools, universities and public institutions in the country, be networked and digitised. Such networking is in addition to the need for adequate infrastructure such as computers, law journals, legal databases and excellent libraries in the institutions teaching law.

13 Management Education

Management education has seen phenomenal growth in the past six years with the number of institutions providing undergraduate and postgraduate level courses rising to over 1700. Of these, more than 1000 were added after the year 2000. This has been possible largely due to the entrepreneurial initiative of promoters, taking advantage of the ever increasing demand for management graduates, hence management education. Unfortunately, this has also led to an exploitative and commercial environment with quality being compromised. Regulatory focus only on physical infrastructure rather than research, qualified faculty and relevance of courses has created a mismatch between supply and demand.

As a part of its consultative process, NKC constituted a Working Group of experts from academia and industry under the chairmanship of Mr. P.M. Sinha. Based on the Working Group's inputs and consultations with concerned stakeholders, NKC proposed the following set of initiatives:

1. New Regulatory Framework

NKC advocates good governance rather than the prevalent system of a prior control being exercised by AICTE in this sphere. The current regulatory regime focuses on punitive actions rather than on nurturing institutions. NKC proposes that an autonomous Standing Committee for Management Education be set up under the Independent Regulatory Authority for Higher Education. Its main role would be to exercise due diligence at the point it approves a license to grant degrees/ diplomas. In doing so, it would assess the academic credibility and the financial viability of the proposed institution on the basis of information submitted in accordance with the stipulated criteria. It will apply exactly the same norms to public and private institutions, just as it will apply the same norms to domestic and international institutions. It would, in addition, license agencies to take care of accreditation. Other responsibilities of the Standing Committee will be to collate as well as communicate information on Management Educational Entities (MEEs)[1]; set up an information exchange; conduct demand forecasting of managerial manpower and develop and maintain a low cost e-monitoring system.

2. Grading Institutions

The Standing Committee will stipulate grading norms and nominate independent rating agencies to assess and categorise MEEs. Mushrooming private MEEs necessitate a reliable rating system to help the market function better, enabling students and employers to compare different MEEs. Hence, a two stage rating process is recommended. In the first stage, rating covering infrastructure may be mandated before an MEE can admit students. The second stage would consist of rating of quality (admission process, teaching, research and publications) which shall be conducted every three years to ensure accountability. Grading norms for each of these steps should be established in consultation with experts. CRISIL and ICRA were consulted in the process and they have agreed to undertake rating of MEEs. The Standing Committee shall decide on a fair and transparent mechanism to deal with conflicting points of view between a rating agency and an MEE.

---

1. In view of the variety of institutions delivering management education, MEE is used to cover all educational institutions, institutes, departments, affiliated and autonomous colleges, Departments in Deemed Universities, Private Business Schools, etc.

3. Accreditation

For MEEs which wish to go beyond rating, the Standing Committee shall determine the criteria and the processes of accreditation in consultation with experts from academia and industry. Mentoring to help MEEs sustain quality standards should be an integral part of the process. Select international accreditations may also be recognised. Branding of accreditation, similar to international standards such as ISO 9001, may be considered to encourage MEEs to pursue excellence.

4. Improve Access

In addition to the framework of affirmative action already in place, we suggest improving access based on work experience and educational loans. NKC believes that management education can be made available to a much wider student community by adopting a two pronged approach. First, we suggest that more weightage be assigned to work experience in admissions. This would help in overcoming disadvantages faced by prospective students due to lack of proficiency in English. Secondly, steps may be taken to ensure easier access to educational loans through banks. Default concerns can be addressed if the respective MEE and the first employer cooperate with the banks. MEEs must also offer scholarships to socially disadvantaged students.

5. Social Context

It is essential to widen the scope of management studies and enhance its relevance.

- Sensitise management education to our unique socio-cultural situation by including India specific case studies in the curriculum, reflecting our diversity and incorporating traditional wisdom.
- Integrate management with other knowledge sources and increase research funding for management and supporting disciplines. With globalisation, the need for management education to pursue a wider scope and realise a more wholesome impact on society has increased. Management departments in universities should therefore, draw upon knowledge sources in other departments.
- Encourage MEEs to design and offer executive programmes for government officials, NGOs and defence personnel. Short term courses for government officials will help them in their role as economic managers.
- Revamp the existing Bachelor's degree in management, the Bachelor's in Business Administration, to cater to the burgeoning need of management graduates. Compulsory apprenticeship in organisations and study of under managed sector areas should be included as part of the programme. The current bookish nature of the curriculum is not sufficient to prepare students for junior management levels.
- Distance learning has considerable potential in this domain. We therefore, need to fully realise the potential of Online Management Programmes to bridge the demand-supply gap.

6. Faculty Development

Non-availability of adequate proficient faculty is a major constraint for sustainable growth of quality management education in India. An autonomous, financially sound and academically credible institute with active support from the leading management institutes, industry and Government should be set up for faculty development. Standards for curriculum covering the entire spectrum need to be set. Active involvement of MEE faculty in training, conferences, industry engagement and curriculum revision should be encouraged. Given the current demand-supply gap, additional faculty would need to be attracted by appropriate incentives.

7. Mentoring

To achieve excellence in the field of management, NKC recommends that all the leading Management Institutions adopt 3-4 MEEs for mentoring and upgradation of quality. Funding and other modalities can be mutually worked out between the institutions.

8. New Institutions

There is a need for a new wave of management institutions which will focus on entrepreneurship, leadership and innovation. These institutions will enable to launch India into the global arena, without the legacy associated with operating in a protected environment. These institutions should set new standards and become role models for MEEs that have the desire to become leaders in the global market place. Incentives need to be provided to Indian entrepreneurs/corporates to set up institutions of excellence on their own or in collaboration with foreign universities. We could also consider allowing reputed foreign universities to enter this field, regulations for them being at par with private institutions.

9. Autonomy

All existing management institutes excluding management departments in universities should register with the Standing Committee of IRAHE and be accorded independent status. In the case of MEEs set up by Central and State governments, government should be treated as a promoter. Registered institutes will benefit from the Standing Committee's mentoring and better funding opportunities apart from other advantages associated with autonomy.

10. Governance

NKC recommends a board of governors for all MEEs, consisting of 50 per cent independent members as there are independent directors under Company Law. The key focus of the governing board should be to continuously improve quality of education and research. For this purpose, they would have to maximise the resource/fund inflows and allocate/spend them purposively and efficiently. The Board should encourage faculty to publish reputed journals and publications, obtain regular feedback from students on teaching-learning process, obtain recruiter feedback for improving quality, institutionalise faculty evaluation and management system and encourage faculty to write India based case studies. The appointment of Directors of public MEEs should be freed from direct or indirect interventions on part of the governments, for these should be based on search processes and peer judgement alone. Likewise, the appointment of directors of private MEEs should be based on a transparent selection process. This would of course be accompanied by enhanced accountability based on performance indicators and independent external evaluation.

11. Non-traditional Management Education

The need for better management in education, health, local government, cooperatives and civil society organisations and so on has often been felt. However, the experience of graduates of Institute of Rural Management and Institute of Forestry Management shows that a lack of advancement opportunities in the Government acts as a barrier to the success of such programmes. There is a need to establish career opportunities in public management, and systematise recruitment and retention policies. Structure of fees for these courses should be formulated in accordance with earning opportunities. We also need to encourage reputed MEEs to develop specialised courses for agri-business, rural banking, public utilities, regulatory agencies and services sector in the coming years as private players entering this space would create demand for the same. The Standing Committee should undertake a study in this field to institutionalise these programmes.

14 Engineering Education

Engineering education is among the key enablers of growth for transforming India's economy. The quality of teaching and research in this sphere will play a critical role in the emergence of our country as a global knowledge leader. It will also provide vital inputs for enhancing productivity across sectors. In the past two decades, we have seen an eight-fold increase in the number of institutions imparting engineering education at the undergraduate level. Yet, there are some fundamental issues that need to be addressed.

A glaring regional imbalance has emerged in the availability of engineering education. Two-thirds of the engineering institutions are located in four southern states, plus Maharashtra, even though they account for less than one-third of the population. There is much less access for the youth in under-provided states, particularly because only 15 per cent of the total seats are available for those who come from outside the state. It would be worthwhile to study whether there are any cultural or region-specific factors that influence the choice of engineering as a career in some states and not elsewhere. This could help make the spread of such colleges more even nationwide.

Several recent studies have flagged the problem of unemployability of engineering graduates, largely because curriculum and syllabi are not quite compatible with industry requirements. Further, the standards of a very large proportion of institutions at the bottom of the pyramid have also been found to be abysmal. Even good institutions are plagued by deficiency of quality students at post-graduate and research level. The problems are complex and deep rooted. The situation calls for a new paradigm in regulation, accreditation, governance and faculty development.

As part of its consultative process, NKC constituted a Working Group of experts from academia and industry under the chairmanship of Prof. M.S. Ananth, Director, IIT Chennai. The Group has also considered the inputs provided by the earlier committees on this subject chaired by R.A. Mashelkar (1998), U.R. Rao (2003) and P. Rama Rao (2004). The study conducted by Professors Banerjee and Muley of IIT Bombay (2007) has also been taken into account. Based on inputs from the Working Group and consultations with other stakeholders, NKC proposes the following set of initiatives:

1. Reforming the Regulatory Framework

As stated in our earlier recommendations relating to Higher Education, there is a need to establish an Independent Regulatory Authority for Higher Education (IRAHE) to cover all streams. The role of the Standing Committee on Engineering Education under IRAHE would be to exercise due diligence at the point it approves entry for an institution to grant degrees/diplomas. The members of the Committee should comprise eminent educationists, education administrators and management specialists drawn from industry. The Committee would follow transparent and uniform processes, under the overall supervision of IRAHE. The Committee shall also determine the criteria and the processes of accreditation and license multiple agencies for the same. A mechanism for ranking of institutions to enable students to take informed decisions at the time of admissions by stipulating grading norms and nominating independent rating agencies also needs to be established. These initiatives will enable the All India Council for Technical Education (AICTE) to focus on important issues such as curriculum development, pedagogy, faculty development, etc.

2. Improving Governance of Institutions

In order to encourage greater flexibility and autonomy, there is a need to progressively do away with the system of affiliation of engineering institutions/colleges to universities. Where feasible, they should be given full autonomy. To attain greater transparency and accountability, it should be made compulsory for all engineering institutions to display information about their buildings, labs, faculty, intake of students, performance of students, recognition status and placements, on their websites. As emphasised by NKC repeatedly, appointments of Heads of Institutions must be made through the process of a Search Committee that has an independent Chair and is at an arm's length from the government. The direct involvement of administrative ministries in the process can result in unfortunate situations.

3. Attracting and Retaining Faculty

The most serious challenge in engineering education is the dearth of well-qualified faculty. Several measures must be undertaken in this direction:

- Institutions should be encouraged to create adjunct positions and invite professionals from industry and research institutions to participate in the teaching process.
- The criterion of holding a Ph.D for teaching undergraduate students may be relaxed to Master's degrees which are specifically designed with more course work in lieu of thesis. Special efforts should be made at the undergraduate level to identify and motivate those who have the potential as well as the inclination towards teaching.
- Incentives like better salary, modern infrastructure, better living and working environment, possibility of secondment to industry during vacations should be made available.
- Shortage of faculty could also be overcome by innovative use of Information and Communication Technology and Open Educational Resources (OER) by leveraging the content available from the best universities across the world.
- Several initiatives need to be undertaken to improve training and professional development of the faculty. A two-week teacher induction training course should be made compulsory. A one-day regional workshop on teaching/learning processes should be arranged as a part of the academic calendar. Course development should be made an integral part of the training programmes conducted by Academic Staff Colleges. Better opportunities may be created for continuing education using the distance mode.

4. Curriculum Reform

The current curriculum should be modified to provide greater flexibility, interdisciplinary perspective and choice of electives. The focus in the teaching/learning process should be on integrating skills such as problem solving and logical reasoning, process orientation, learning ability, English communication and programming fundamentals. Industry participation to discuss real life case studies should be encouraged. Laboratory courses must be revamped to develop a healthy attitude towards experimental work. Environment must be created to encourage students to participate in co-curricular activities.

5. Integrating Sciences and Engineering Education

We have entered a period in history where the distinction between sciences and engineering has all but disappeared. Sciences are at the heart of engineering. To that extent there is no distinction between the two. In order to reduce the perceived gap between sciences and engineering, we need to create mechanisms that allow mobility between the two streams. One option could be to start four-year undergraduate programmes in sciences, initially in institutes of excellence where facilities for science programmes already exist. This would enable pursuing doctoral programmes in science and technology, without a Master's degree.

6. Encouraging Research

Several initiatives are necessary to promote research in engineering disciplines:

- Vibrant and well funded Ph.D programmes with opportunities for international exposure should be rolled out to attract students who currently go abroad for Ph.Ds.
- The new academic and research institutions being established should be so located that they can optimise mutual collaboration. Likewise, existing academic institutions with active research programmes should be supported to set up high-tech industrial research parks in the vicinity of their campuses.
- Universities must become the hub of research once again to capture synergies between teaching and research. This will require changes in resource allocation, reward systems and mindsets.

7. Industry-Academia Interaction

In order to attain greater alignment of engineering education with employment opportunities, frequent dialogue with industry and government through seminars and workshops is necessary. To enhance employability, summer internships should be made an integral part of the curriculum. Restrictive provisions and the elaborate regulatory framework of the Apprenticeship Act 1961 have inhibited industry from adequately using the apprenticeship scheme for honing the skills of engineering graduates. Clauses need to be incorporated in the Act that will enable training in multiple skills (not just a specific trade) and allow entry to and exit from the scheme at different points in the education and career cycle. Likewise, industry needs to encourage continuing education programmes for their employees by collaborating with appropriate educational institutes. Academia and industry should engage in joint research to encourage innovation and competitiveness in the global economy.

8. Improve Access

While the government would need to establish new institutions in the under-provided states, it must be emphasised that the recent proliferation of engineering institutions in the southern states is largely the result of private initiatives. A framework for public-private partnerships should, therefore, be developed in collaboration with the concerned states to establish new quality institutions.

9. Mentoring

Elite institutions should consider some additional responsibilities such as adopting a few engineering institutions of their choice and helping them raise their standards, creating and making available educational resources in the public domain for use of all students and conducting distance education courses, especially for students at the post-graduate level and working professionals. In particular, the existing IITs could mentor the new ones being established. The latter, in due course, could play a similar role *vis-à-vis* others. Similarly, National Institutes of Technology and Regional Engineering Colleges could play a mentoring role for selected engineering institutions in their respective regions. Mentoring by its definition is a voluntary activity, but if we can create an atmosphere where institutions of distinction feel a sense of calling in the interest of the larger national good, it would transform our education.

The changes and reforms proposed above are necessary to bring about a qualitative transformation in engineering education to meet present and future needs.

15 Open and Distance Education

The National Knowledge Commission (NKC) believes that a radical reform of the system of Open and Distance Education (ODE) is imperative to achieve the objectives of expansion, inclusion and excellence in higher education. The significance is obvious. For one, more than one-fifth of the students enrolled in higher education are in the ODE stream. For another, ODE has an enormous potential to spread higher education opportunities beyond the brick and mortar world. But there are reasons for concern. First, the quality of higher education provided in large segments of ODE, particularly in correspondence courses in universities, leaves much to be desired. Second, it is not sufficiently recognised that ODE provides educational opportunities not only to those who discontinue formal education on account of economic or social compulsions, but also to young school leavers who are simply unable to secure admission in the formal stream at universities. It is time to address these problems. There is a clear need to improve the quality of ODE and to make it more appropriate to the needs of society. It is just as important to expand opportunities in higher education through the use of technology in ODE. It would not be possible to attain a gross enrolment ratio of 15 per cent by 2015 without a massive expansion in ODE. In this endeavour, we must not forget that ODE is seen as inferior to conventional classroom learning. This perception, and the reality, both need change. We must realise that ODE is not simply a mode of educational delivery, but an integrated discipline engaged in the creation of knowledge.

In light of the above, NKC constituted a Working Group composed of distinguished experts in this field, chaired by Prof. Ram Takwale, former Vice-Chancellor, IGNOU. Based on inputs provided by the working group and consultations with stakeholders, NKC recommended the following reforms:

1. Create a National ICT Infrastructure for Networking ODE Institutions

A national Information and Communication Technology (ICT) infrastructure must be set up through government support for networking all ODE institutions. In this regard, we recommend that the digital broadband Knowledge Network proposed by NKC should have provision for interconnecting the major ODE institutions and their study centres in the first phase itself. Eventually, minimum connectivity of 2 Mbps must be extended to the study centres of all ODE institutions. A national ICT backbone would enhance access and e-governance in ODE, and enable the dissemination of knowledge across all modes, that is, print, audio-visual and Internet-based multimedia.

2. Set-up a National Education Foundation to Develop Web-based Common Open Resources

A National Educational Foundation with a one-time infusion of adequate funds must be established to develop a web-based repository of high quality educational resources. Open Educational Resources (OER) must be created online through a collaborative process, pooling in the efforts and expertise of all major institutions of higher education. The OER repository would supply pedagogical software for various programmes run through ODE and be available for utilisation by all ODE institutions. An enabling legal framework that would allow unrestricted access without compromising intellectual authorship must be devised for this purpose.

3. Establish a Credit Bank to Effect Transition to a Course Credit System

Transition to a course credit system must be carried out to enable the learner to undertake programmes across all ODE institutions and disciplines. As a part of this process, an autonomous credit bank must be established for storing and filing credits acquired by every learner. In addition, admission criteria and the system of credits should be as flexible and adaptable as possible. Provisions must be made for multiple entry points and exit points, a flexible timetable and assessment mechanisms for supporting life-long learning.

4. Establish a National Education Testing Service for Assessing ODE Students

An autonomous National Education Testing Service (NETS) must be established through legislation and invested with functional powers and responsibility for assessing all potential graduates in ODE. This unified examination system would test the learners' ability to perform intellectual and practical tasks. All courses, degrees and activities offered through ODE should be certified through this system.

5. Facilitate Convergence with Conventional Universities

The lack of convergence between programmes run by open universities and correspondence courses offered by the distance education wings of conventional educational institutions is a cause of great concern. Rather than function as parallel systems at odds with each other, open universities must forge organisational alignments with conventional universities geared towards common goals and strategies. They must engage each other in the collaborative creation of pedagogical resources via OER and its delivery along shared modes. Programmes and courses offered by each should be subject to the same stringent norms of quality assurance. This implies that the distance education departments operating within conventional universities must be encouraged to put correspondence courses through the NETS for purposes of assessment. At the same time, universities must also ensure that their distance education programmes are not stand-alone, but should benefit from regular interaction with university departments in concerned disciplines. The aim of such convergence is to eventually enable learners to move freely from one system to the other.

6. Set-up a Research Foundation to Support Research Activity in ODE

An autonomous and well-endowed Research Foundation must be established to commission and facilitate multidimensional and multidisciplinary research in ODE. In addition, a favourable environment for research must be created by setting up infrastructure like libraries, digital databases and online journals, holding regular workshops and seminars, granting sabbatical leave for undertaking research, establishing a peer reviewed journal to provide a platform for publication for scholars, and other such measures. A robust research environment is essential to accord ODE value as a discipline, as opposed to it being consigned to a 'mode'.

7. Overhaul Training Programmes for Educators

Training and orientation programmes must be conceptualised to enable educators and administrators to effectively utilise technology to cater to diverse learners' interests. The content of the training modules must promote familiarity with the theories and practices of self-learning. Their delivery should take place through several modes, including web-supported, audio-visual and face-to-face interaction on a regular basis with experts, practitioners and peers. Most importantly, these packages must be updated regularly and administered directly. The B.Ed. curriculum must also be revised, updated and made to emphasise theories and practices of self-learning.

8. Increase Access for Learners with Special Needs

Special Education Committees must be set up in all ODE institutions to address the needs of learners with disabilities as well as senior citizens. These committees must devise mechanisms to ensure their participation and provide effective mechanisms for monitoring, evaluation of policies and collection of feedback. Admission criteria and timetables must be flexible enough to provide diverse options for meeting programme requirements to differently able learners and senior citizens. Pedagogical tools and components from the open educational resources must be adaptable to alternative formats for special learning needs. This could include, for example, Braille, colour-contrast texts and voice recordings for the visually disabled.

9. Create a New Standing Committee for the Regulation of ODE

At present, the Distance Education Council (DEC) under IGNOU arbitrates standards and disburses funds for ODE institutions across the country. NKC believes that this arrangement cannot provide adequate and appropriate regulation. A new regulatory mechanism must be established by appointing a Standing Committee on Open and Distance Education under the Independent Regulatory Authority for Higher Education (IRAHE) proposed by NKC. This statutory body would be responsible for developing broad criteria for accreditation as well as laying down standards for quality assurance. It would be accountable to stakeholders at all levels and to IRAHE, and have representation from public, private and social institutions involved in the education and development sectors. These include the central open university, state open universities, private open universities, conventional education institutes, as well as chairpersons of the specialised bodies to be set up to look into infrastructural requirements of ODE.

In addition, two specialised bodies should be established under the aegis of the Standing Committee:

(i) A Technical Advisory Group with representatives from the IT sector, telecom, space and industry should be constituted to provide guidelines, ensure flexibility and track the latest developments in application. The most important function would be to devise common standards for labelling learning content developed by different agencies in order to support indexing, storage, discovery and retrieval of this content by multiple tools across multiple repositories.

(ii) An Advisory Group on Pedagogical Content Management should be set up to provide guidelines on curricular content and development of repositories, exchange of material, access to students and other such issues.

The Standing Committee on Open and Distance Education would also serve as the nodal agency for the National Educational Foundation on open educational resources, the National Education Testing Service (NETS) and the Credit Bank.

10. Develop a System for Quality Assessment

Reliable external assessment is valued by employers, students and other stakeholders in the given context of a market driven economy. In view of this, a rating system to assess the standard of all institutions imparting ODE must be evolved and made publicly available. The Standing Committee would stipulate grading norms and independent rating agencies would be licensed by IRAHE to carry out this function. In addition, it is recommended that every ODE institution has an internal quality assurance cell to ensure that statutory quality compliances are regularly met.

Establishment of the new organisations proposed above, namely, the National Education Testing Service, the Credit Bank, the National Educational Foundation for developing common open resources, the Technical Advisory Group and the Advisory Group on Pedagogical Content Management would initially require financial support from the government. Additional finances for networking ODE institutions and creating access centres, developing training programmes for educators and administrators and providing scholarships and services for needy students would also be required.

16 Open Educational Resources

Our success in the knowledge economy hinges to a large extent on upgrading the quality of, and enhancing the access to, education. One of the most effective ways of achieving this would be to stimulate the development and dissemination of quality Open Access (OA) materials and Open Educational Resources (OER) through broadband Internet connectivity. This would facilitate easy and widespread access to high quality educational resources and drastically improve the teaching paradigm for all our students. As a part of its consultative process, NKC constituted a Working Group of experts, including distinguished members from the academia, government, private sector and users to suggest necessary measures to improve the quality of Open Access in India. NKC consultations with stakeholders helped identify a few key reform proposals which are elaborated as follows:

1. Support the Production of Quality Content by a Select Set of Indian Institutions

A set of key institutions should be selected and experts representing diverse knowledge areas like agriculture, engineering, medicine, arts, humanities, science, education, etc., should be asked to develop standards-based content, which can be customised to diverse user needs. This should be made available not only to Indian institutions but also for global use. The efforts made through the project of Ministry of Human Resources Development—National Programme on Technology Enhanced Learning (NPTEL) for creation of OER in the areas of Engineering and Technology should be applied in other areas of education also. The content in the repositories should be multimedia, interactive and available in different regional languages. These projects should cover a wide range of subjects mentioned above. To speed up the creation, adaptation and utilisation of OER, it is necessary to launch a 'National E-content and Curriculum Initiative'.

2. Leverage Global Open Educational Resources

Sustainable development of quality content relevant to India is a difficult and expensive proposition, given the diverse needs of various sectors in our emerging knowledge economy. Emerging international and national initiatives are offering quality educational content as open resources. It is vital for India to leverage these initiatives as they are readily available for adoption and adaptation and to serve as a model for further indigenous content production. NKC found that there are already 200-300 free knowledge repositories available across the world. The National Knowledge Commission is separately disseminating this information through its website.

3. Encourage Open Access

Open Access material stimulates research and helps students, teachers and researchers across the world. Therefore, at the policy level, all research articles published by Indian authors receiving substantial government or public funding must be made available under Open Access and should be archived in the standard OA format at least on his/her website. As a next step, a national academic OA portal should be developed. The government should allocate resources to increase the current digitisation efforts of books and periodicals which are outside copyright protection. Separate funding should be allocated to develop a new high quality OCR software package so that new and old fonts in many different Indian languages can be converted into ISCI/ASCI code and OA portals and servers could be upgraded regularly. Appropriate financial resources should be earmarked for these endeavours. This will also facilitate machine translation of these valuable resources.

4. Develop Network-enabled Delivery Infrastructure

Along with the national initiative for content development, we must develop a network-enabled delivery infrastructure with a focus on two primary areas: access and delivery. For access to the network, high bandwidth connections across institutions and a national backbone that provides advanced networking capabilities are major requirements. Additionally, connectivity to global networks is essential. Delivery of the OER content would be done through distributed repositories of educational resources.

5. Create a Faculty and Institutional Development Programme

Faculty development and teacher training is the primary area that needs to be addressed in order to realise the benefits of extended access and improved quality through OER. The training programme must develop domain competencies and teaching skills using new educational technologies. The training will also help developers of new OER and in contextualising existing educational resources. Centres at specific institutions should be identified so that the faculty of these institutions will eventually own, modify and expand OER repositories. These must be integrated into university curricula and organisational structures. The availability of learning management systems and other quizzing, authoring and collaborating tools should be increased. The evaluation system should be based on the use of the content and the pedagogy in OER.

To implement and monitor the above recommendations urgently and efficiently, the Government of India may designate a suitable organisation or establish a new institution with necessary mandate to achieve the above objectives. This institute may serve the following functions:

- Provide leadership and coordination of network-based open education resources
- Select institutional collaborations for developing content
- Develop adoption support strategies
- Recommend and monitor standards for content development and adoption
- Advise on policy implications *vis-à-vis* licencing, intellectual property rights, etc.
- Identify and set benchmarks based on global best practices
- Establish relationships with global OA and OER initiatives.

17 More Talented Students in Maths and Science

A strong foundation in the pure sciences is essential to transform India into a knowledge superpower. Unfortunately, as the economy grows, fewer students are opting for the pure sciences. This has led to a talent crunch, seriously impeding the development of the future generation of scientists and teachers. We are aware that this is a worldwide phenomenon, but countries like China and South Korea, having invested prudently in science education, are now beginning to reap rich dividends.

In this context, NKC carried out wide consultations with experts through a series of workshops and interviews. A working group of eminent persons was also constituted to consider all aspects of the problem. Based on these inputs, NKC has formulated a set of recommendations to attract and retain talented students in basic sciences which are summarised in the following paragraphs. NKC has chosen to reiterate some of the proposals which overlap with the views of other expert groups. NKC would like to stress that this matter is extremely urgent and a rapid implementation is now crucial to effect a paradigm change in the field of science education and research in the country.

1. *Invest in upgrading and expanding the existing infrastructure and promote sharing of available resources:* University departments and leading undergraduate science colleges should be generously funded to upgrade their staff and facilities. To encourage good departments, 'Centres of excellence' should be identified with comprehensive review and evaluation procedures in place. To create a critical mass of scientists in each science stream undergraduate seats should be increased in good institutes and undergraduate programmes should be introduced at institutes where only postgraduate teaching is currently undertaken. Innovative methods for sharing resources and faculty between institutes and universities need to be evolved. At the same time, university management at all levels should be made more professional and sensitive towards working in an academic and research environment to promote optimal utilisation of resources.

2. *Revitalise the teaching profession to attract and retain quality teachers:* The working condition of teachers needs to be drastically improved. Rewards and recognition should be publicised and given at all levels. Teachers at the school and college level should be encouraged to develop innovative teaching methods. Research should be promoted in colleges by building linkages between colleges and research institutions. Academic autonomy and flexibility should be encouraged. Further, a mentoring programme for young faculty members should be started in universities and colleges. Many reserved faculty posts remain vacant in the absence of innovative or flexible appointment modes to fill these posts, creating enormous practical difficulties in teaching. There is a need to start a systematic affirmative campaign to rectify this situation. Young students who can eventually fill these posts could be selected from an early age and nurtured and trained carefully to induct them into a career in teaching.

3. *Revamp teacher training at all levels and promote development of teaching aids to retain student attention in classrooms:* A systemic change in science pedagogy from primary and high school levels is required. There is a need to launch a large scale in-service training programme for all science teachers based on the initiative undertaken by science academies. At the undergraduate level, the present method of faculty training conducted by Staff Training Institutes/Centres should be reviewed and revamped. In addition, there is a need to provide a platform for lifelong skill enhancement of teachers. Teacher organisations like the Indian Association of Physics Teachers should be strengthened and financially supported so that they can become leaders in developing new teaching methodologies and make significant contributions to content and evaluation reforms.

4. *Restructure masters and graduate degrees to promote career flexibility after graduation:* To bring graduate degrees in science at par with other professional streams, a four-year Bachelor in Science (flexible and modular in nature) is proposed. This degree course should be aptly branded and devised so that it is significantly stronger than the regular three-year programme. It should enable students aspiring for a research career to directly enter a Ph.D programme. For others, it should provide them with measurable value additions like interdisciplinary skills, niche skills required in industry, or rigorous training in science education, science communication, etc. To ensure the success and acceptability of such programmes, the course content must be planned in consultation with diverse expert groups, and implemented at institutions with a proven track record of success. Simultaneously, the existing B.Sc. and M.Sc. courses should be reformed. The integrated five-year M.Sc. programme should have the provision to be integrated with the Ph.D programme so that the total effective time spent for a Ph.D is reduced.

5. *Reform the science curriculum content in line with the changing world and increase research component at all levels:* There is an urgent need to reduce information load of curriculum at the higher secondary level. Courses should be made engaging and the amount of hands on work at all levels should be increased. Books should be written by teachers who teach the subject and not by curriculum committees. Pedagogy should be modified to impart creativity and global vision training. Avenues for research should be increased at all levels.

6. *Radical changes are required in the evaluation system to encourage scientific thinking and promote better understanding of basic science concepts:* The system should move from examination-based evaluation to more open assessment mechanisms. Memory, comprehension and creativity should be given equal importance in evaluations. Continuous assessment at the school level will reduce dependence on year-end examinations. To enable the modifications in the evaluation process, teachers need to be trained in new methods of evaluation.

7. *Promote access to quality science educational material at all levels:* There is a need to disseminate high quality science educational material and self-learning aids in local languages to assist students from non-English medium education background. One important factor which has to be kept in mind while translating into local languages is that the technical/scientific terms should be retained in English. This will make it easier to migrate to English medium teaching in sciences at higher level for the students. Special teaching aids need to be developed for tribal children and children from rural backgrounds to attract them towards science. Tribal schools should be equipped with teachers who are trained in pedagogical methods suited to the special needs of tribal children.

8. *Re-brand and promote careers in basic sciences:* Existing careers in sciences, namely teaching and research, should be made more attractive. There is a need to increase salaries in this field to reflect the shortage of skilled manpower and to attract students towards a career in science. Science colleges should collaborate with research institutes and industry for campus placements. More modules/courses could be designed which prepare students for employment in industry. The four-year bachelor's course offered by quality institutes should dispel the myth that science bachelors are in any way less employable than graduates from other professional streams. Research institutes should collaborate with professional streams to pursue and create more opportunities. New institutes will create a demand for quality science Ph.Ds and these career opportunities need to be publicised.

9. *Launch a massive science outreach programme aimed at students and their parents:* A science popularisation programme should be launched to effectively cover children across India. This programme should bring all popular science activities under one umbrella for rapid implementation and replication of successful initiatives. A large chain of science talent cells should be created and each school should be funded to open a science club. The effectiveness of mobile labs in reaching the rural students and teachers is very high. Replication of the Agastya International Foundation's mobile lab programme, with possible public-private partnership mode for implementation, should be considered for various states.

10. *Encourage industry participation in promoting sciences at all levels:* As research-based industries flourish in India, more and more companies will need employees qualified in basic sciences, thus creating other attractive career opportunities in science. Industry should be encouraged to sponsor students for Masters and Ph.Ds in science and also internships of longer duration in industry for postgraduate students. Science undergraduates should be exposed to various applications of science in industry through seminars and popular science lectures by industry leaders. Academic institutions should

develop groups at each institute which specialise in developing novel funding mechanisms involving industry and explore other possible modes of industry participation.

India has a long and rich history attesting to the high talents of Indians in science. To bring back the glory that the pure sciences once held in the minds of the students, an urgent restructuring of the entire system is needed. These recommendations are just the beginning of a systemic overhaul process, requiring great support from the government and committed individuals. The crucial ingredient for ensuring success would be an effective, mission-oriented platform for delivery. Therefore, a National Science and Mathematics Mission is proposed.

Annexure 17.1: Note on Attracting More Talented Students to Maths and Science

Pure sciences form the bedrock of all applied sciences. Advancement in sciences is a necessary condition for future technological revolutions. While innovative science and scientific discoveries have the potential of enabling a quantum leap in human civilisation, pursuit of sciences promotes a culture of open mindedness and rationality. India has a rich heritage in abstract thinking and has contributed to scientific discoveries since ancient times. As India ventures into the 21st century and seeks to establish itself as a knowledge superpower, it is essential that a strong foundation in science is firmly in place. This will help the nation in building excellence in technology, achieving self-reliance and in propelling economic growth and prosperity, consequently raising the living standards of all its citizens. Yet, as the economy progresses, it has become increasingly difficult to ensure a sustained input of fresh young scientists and educationists into the system. This situation has become particularly alarming in the pure sciences. Since developing competence in the basic sciences has a long incubation time, it is important that this problem be addressed with alacrity. Science and mathematics are living subjects which grow rapidly and give rise to new areas which build on other existing areas. Therefore, they need a constant input of fresh and young talent. It is worthwhile to note that developing countries like China and South Korea have invested massively in science education in the past few decades and are reaping enormous benefits today in terms of economic development and global standing in science.

The Prime Minister has repeatedly stressed the importance of making science a preferred discipline of study for students and has also pointed out the need for both a qualitative and quantitative expansion in the pool of science students. The strategy for the promotion of science education in the 11th Plan aims at (a) expanding and strengthening the science and technology base in our universities, and (b) promoting excellence through competitively secured funding at centres for advanced research.

In this context, NKC conducted workshops and expert interviews to analyse the issue and recommend steps to attract and retain talented students in basic sciences. A working group of eminent members representing universities, science colleges, research institutes, industry and NGOs was constituted to look into the ideas in greater detail, and this Note is a result of these deliberations. Broadly, the recommendations can be summarised as better infrastructure and pedagogy, curricular and structural reforms, improved access, re-branding of science careers, massive outreach and greater industry participation. We are glad to note that some recent UGC initiatives are in line with a few of these recommendations. We are aware that while some of the proposals below are new, various expert groups have previously made proposals which overlap in spirit and content with the others. They are reiterated here because it is felt that these proposals need fast-track implementation for effecting a change in science education which is critical and urgent.

Resources

Recommendation 1: Invest in upgrading and expanding the existing infrastructure and promote sharing of available resources

Science is a capital-intensive subject and its pursuit requires good infrastructure, adequate resources and regular maintenance of the same. Further, better infrastructure will play a vital role in attracting students towards sciences.

Issues: The condition of basic infrastructure in most science colleges and universities remain largely unattractive and uninspiring to today's high school student who has an array of other attractive options while choosing his/her career. Basic infrastructure like classrooms and buildings and essential laboratory equipments deteriorate due to lack of proper maintenance. This creates a grim atmosphere for students and teachers who are interested in pursuing pure sciences.

1.1 Basic infrastructure

The number of seats presently available in good institutes for bachelors or integrated masters in science is limited. There is a need to expand seats at entry level in science disciplines to create a critical mass of scientists in each stream. Substantial expansion of capacity of bachelor's programme in all good institutes is required. The starting of IISERs is a step in the right direction and it is crucial that they succeed in setting an example. Care should be taken that while excellence is cultivated in them, it should not lead to their isolation.

A continuum of institutes in quality is needed. While there are IISERs on one the end, and government science colleges on the other end, there is a need to start undergraduate courses at universities and other places which currently offer only postgraduate education in sciences to complete the continuum of institutes for students with varying abilities. Select universities can offer Bachelor's honours (four-year course–detailed later) with an option to directly move to Ph.D. programme after successful completion of honours.

Independent but standardised accreditation of science departments and regular evaluation of accredited institutions is necessary. Accreditation agencies should be sufficiently supported to carry out regular evaluations. This rating information will help students to take informed decisions when they choose their place of study. This will also serve to direct public funding where it is most optimally utilised.

University departments should be generously funded and upgraded with staff and facilities. To begin with, a few departments could be identified, a plan prepared for their conversion to centres of excellence and then continual monitoring of the progress could be undertaken. This task can be accomplished by either UGC or directly by MHRD. Leading undergraduate science colleges should be chosen to provide them with additional assistance and turn them into centres of excellence. Clusters of undergraduate colleges should make a centralised request through university for comprehensive funding.

UGC has a provision to provide grants to the universities for providing financial support to the faculty for travel or to organise seminars. This should be extended to colleges with a proven track record. In fact, a comprehensive funding mechanism needs to be in place which will cover capital as well as maintenance expenses, work related field trips for students, support to publish articles etc.

1.2 Sharing Resources

Many valuable facilities are not optimally shared among research institutes, laboratories and universities. The funding agencies should promote the formation of centres for shared instrumentation, by facilitating a consortium approach. Full-fledged laboratories within the campuses of our universities and other educational institutions can be set up. Greater collaboration should be promoted between research institutes and universities through appropriate incentives. Further, colleges which do not have adequate infrastructure should form clusters with nearby colleges and institutes to share laboratory resources, especially expensive equipments.

1.3 Scholarships

The number of direct scholarships to meritorious students like KVPY (Kishore Vigyanik Protsahan Yojana) should be increased to cover a larger student population. To enlarge the pool of scientific manpower and foster research in the sciences, the Government of India has announced a programme entitled "Innovation in Science Pursuit for Inspired Research" (INSPIRE). The INSPIRE programme should be launched as soon as possible.

1.4 Autonomy and Flexibility

"A university is about learning that molds a lifetime, learning that transmits the heritage of the millennia, learning that shapes the future." While efficient university administration should facilitate this, bureaucratic stranglehold and political interference vitiates the academic environment, creating a war of nerves between academicians and the administrators. Universities have to be financially accountable to the Government, but the academic matters should be under the sole purview of the university bodies. At present, even academic matters like starting new innovative courses have to be approved by the state governments. These proposals do not see the light of the day even after several years. Academic autonomy is essential to contemporise syllabus and make it more relevant. The administration at all levels should be made transparent, professional and sensitised towards working in an academic and research environment.

To facilitate teaching in universities by research scientists, supporting infrastructure should be created in universities for visiting professors. Further, university and research institute faculty members should be given the flexibility of taking sabbaticals for teaching in colleges, doing work in educational field and for popularising science among children, teachers and communities in rural and urban areas. Appropriate checks and balances can be put in place to ensure that the organisations where the faculty members choose to work are indeed benefiting from their participation.

There is a horde of grant disbursing government departments and organisations. Researchers seeking funds for their projects have to manoeuvre across all these administrative hassles to get funds. A web portal which brings all relevant funding information together should be launched. Administrative problems and delays created by funding agencies should be done away with. Competitive process for grants should be established. Principles of e-governance should be incorporated to promote transparency in the system.

Recommendation 2: Revitalise the teaching profession to attract and retain quality teachers

The working conditions for science teachers at all levels should be improved. Massive efforts are needed not only to make teaching an attractive profession for young science trained professionals, but also to revive the desire to teach and inspire students in existing teachers.

Issues: The base salary of teachers is low. Further, reward and recognition mechanisms do not exist. Basic infrastructure is inadequate and poorly maintained. In addition, systematic politicisation of universities has contributed to the deteriorating environment. Overall, the morale of the teachers is severely affected. Teaching is taken up by uninspired practitioners who do not communicate the passion for doing science. Shortage of teachers in colleges results in additional burden of teaching load leaving little room for innovation in teaching. The practice of contractual teaching without appropriate remuneration has created its own problems. Access to good libraries, teaching aids, etc., is not available. College teachers do not get exposure to newest developments in their fields. Academic freedom and flexibility is lacking in the present rigid system.

2.1 Rewards and Recognition

The teaching profession has been severely undermined in recent years and the working conditions of the teachers needs to be drastically improved. It is essential that teachers are given due recognition for their contribution to society. Salaries need to be hiked across the board. Rewards should be instituted for good teaching based on student feedback in colleges. The rewards should be given at all levels and should be organised with sufficient publicity. Innovation in teaching should be encouraged through appropriate incentives. The practice of instituting chairs like National Professors should be extended to school and college teachers too.

2.2 Professional Development

School teachers should be provided with avenues to discuss new pedagogical developments. For instance, they should be encouraged to do projects in laboratories in colleges during vacation time. Colleges can be given separate funds to run such programmes. School teachers should be sufficiently incentivised to develop new experiments and activities to be used at school level.

Teaching load in colleges should be lightened to provide scope for professional development. There should be a provision of research facilities in all colleges or a system wherein interested college teachers can avail of nearby research facilities. Access to journals and Internet-based learning must be provided. New faculty members should be given lighter teaching load and a start up grant for research. This will enable them to establish themselves in their chosen research area. There is a need to increase academic freedom at all levels. Academic autonomy is important in retaining teachers. Teachers should be encouraged and empowered to try new pedagogical tools. Flexibility is important to contemporise classroom learning and make it more engaging.

2.3 Mentoring

A mentoring programme for young faculty members should be started in universities and colleges. Experienced faculty members can mentor junior members on issues related to starting new research projects, grant application writing etc. They can share tips on different aspects of classroom teaching, like syllabus planning, managing the classes, etc. Peer evaluation of teaching and exchange of ideas on pedagogy should be encouraged.

Many reserved faculty posts remain vacant in the absence of innovative or flexible appointment modes to fill these posts. This leads to excess strain and teaching load on the existing teachers. In addition, this has contributed to the gradual decay and death of many departments of pure sciences in colleges and universities around the country, which were once famous for their science teaching. There is a need to start a systematic affirmative campaign to rectify this situation. Young students who can eventually fill these posts should be selected from an early age and nurtured carefully to induct them into a career in teaching. Special mentor programmes with highly individualised attention should be an inbuilt part of this programme.

Recommendation 3: Revamp teacher training at all levels and promote development of teaching aids to retain student attention in classrooms

A systemic change in science pedagogy from primary and high school levels is required. Teaching should be made more inquiry-based. It should raise curiosity, convey the excitement of science and enable understanding of nature through experiments.

Issues: Unimaginative science teaching has promoted rote learning, thereby dousing the very spirit of enquiry that a study of science should nurture in young minds. Teaching is accompanied by a limited number of demonstrations and activities. Science is projected as an abstract difficult subject to its young practitioners. There is no effort on the part of the system to engage students in the process of scientific enquiry. Emphasis is not laid on thorough understanding of fundamental concepts. Instead, students are overloaded with more and more information. This is also encouraged by the current evaluation system and various competitive examination bodies.

3.1 Teacher Training

To help teachers keep pace with recent advances in their subjects and new pedagogic tools, there is a need to launch large scale in-service training programme for all science teachers. Training teachers are necessary because at the middle school level, they are expected to teach general science courses though they might have received training in only one of the disciplines. The delivery medium should be classroom-based, supported by materials based on ICT. Video-conferencing sessions can be very useful. Science academies have launched such a training programme, and this can serve as a model for other institutes.

The in-service training programme for teachers needs to be revamped. The frequency of training should be increased. Teacher training institutes should be measured on their performance based on outcomes. Every training school can be linked to nearby schools for this purpose. The performance of students can be taken as a substitute for measuring the performance of teachers associated with the training school. Apart from fundamental concepts, inquisitiveness, creativity, problem solving and research orientation should be included in teaching. At the undergraduate level, the present method of faculty training conducted by Staff Training Institutes/Centres should be reviewed and the training system with lectures alone should be done away with. There is a need to revamp the Refresher and Orientation courses conducted under the guidance of UGC. The need is to provide a platform for life long skill enhancement of teachers.

Dedicated training centres can be established at research institutes/universities for advanced level courses. A database of good teachers should be created so that they can be tapped for discussion forums, video-conferencing sessions and for live interactions with trainees. Lectures of good teachers should be recorded and made available in CDs/Internet for easy accessibility. Web enabled discussion forums should be promoted. Teachers should be connected with one another so that in time, teacher organisations can become leaders in developing new teaching methodologies and make significant contributions to content and evaluation reforms. Well established associations like Indian Association of Physics Teachers and others like the nascent Indian Association of Teachers in Biological Sciences should be strengthened by appropriate financial and other support.

3.2 Teaching Aids

With the advent of new technology, there is a need to develop better teaching aids to make classrooms livelier. There is an array of open source material and ICT aided tools, which can make classroom transactions in math and science more engaging and participatory. At present, it is felt that neither the teachers nor students are fully familiar with these resources. Multi media should be appropriately used, and easily replicable hands on activities to demonstrate scientific concepts should be made part of regular teaching. The Hoshangabad Science Teaching Programme should be emulated by the training schools to enable teachers to use these concepts in their own schools. Virtual laboratories programme should be encouraged and scaled up so that schools which are in a position to benefit from such experiments have the opportunity to do so.

3.3 Some External Measures to Raise Quality of Science Teaching

- Good teachers can offer common courses in an institute cluster. This will enable access to good teaching for a large number of students and provide them with an option of host of electives.
- Bright young faculty should be attracted with high salaries. This will inject much needed fresh blood in our universities.
- Researchers in India and alumni in research institutes abroad should be encouraged to teach. They are best positioned to convey the excitement of science.
- Schemes that permit utilisation of the skills of talented teachers and scientists, who have reached formal retirement age, will be an important step in maintaining standards in many disciplines, which have been hard hit by declining recruitments over the years.
- Universities should be given financial support to attract good teachers and researchers from institutes in India or abroad (for periods ranging from one semester to an academic year or so) to help introduce teaching in new fields.

Science Education in Schools and Colleges

Recommendation 4: Restructure masters and graduate degrees to promote career flexibility after graduation

Structural reforms in courses are needed to streamline available options and present students with multiple options. Preferences of students who intend to pursue a career in research will be different from those who want to work in industry immediately after graduation. Many students may want to pursue a more generalised science course while others may prefer a highly specialised course focused on a particular stream.

Issues: The present courses of study available at various colleges and universities involve repetition at each level. This affects students' interest adversely. There is a need to integrate course curriculum from senior secondary level to master level in sciences. Most of the B.Sc. courses in the country fail to provide a wider conceptual base in diverse disciplines of science and thus severely limit "inter-disciplinary" capability of the graduating students. In the absence of extensive laboratory work, the graduates do not know how to actually do an experiment and without any self-undertaken exploratory experimental work, they also fail to learn how to ask new questions for research.

4.1 To bring a graduate degree in science at par with other streams, a four-year Bachelors in Science course is proposed. This degree course should be aptly branded so that it gains more significance than the regular three-year programme. To ensure the success and acceptability of this programme, the course content must be planned in consultation with diverse expert groups, and implemented at institutions with a proven track record of success. The first two years of this course would be common for all students. The students may choose their streams based on interest and performance after two years. If the course is offered in an institute/university where engineering courses are also offered there can be a provision of flexibility to move from B.Sc. to B.Tech.. Further, a student could also choose to take a four-year integrated B.Sc. plus B.Ed. course in colleges where such a facility is available. A four-year B.Sc + B.Ed. Programme is a more effective training programme than the current practice of B.Ed. after completing B.Sc.. Funding of this programme should be given special attention. Universities/Science colleges must be encouraged to run such programmes. If the student does not opt for B.Ed. then she can either do a research project in final year or take up employment-friendly modules like clinical research, statistics, etc.

The exact duration of the course need not be fixed but should be based on credits. Thus, if a bright student completes the requirement of all necessary credits a semester before, s/he could do additional advanced courses in the remaining period. Also if the place s/he is studying offers M.Sc. and Ph.D., there should be flexibility to start earning credits for the master's courses such that the total effective time spent in B.Sc. + M.Sc. is reduced, and the student can directly opt for Ph.D. at the end of the course. The government should encourage universities and IITs/ IISERs/ research institutes to start a broad-based undergraduate degree programme in science. Based on the course credits students acquire, the degree can be aptly named like Bachelor in Mathematics and Computer Science, Bachelor in Chemistry and Biology, etc. Highly specialised courses like biotechnology or bioinformatics at undergraduate level should be avoided. Instead the emphasis should be on broad-based knowledge of various science streams.

4.2 The three-year regular B.Sc. course should be reformed. In the first year, the programme should include courses in all major disciplines of science, so that all students learn the basics of "physical", "life" and "earth" sciences. These courses should advance the student's understanding beyond the +2 level where the focus is more on information due to limited evaluation methodology. "Deficiency" courses may need to be planned for those who have not studied mathematics or biology at the +2 level. In the second year, a student may select three main subjects; however, about 15-20 per cent of credits should be earned through courses from other streams (e.g., a student of "Physics/Maths" stream may take some courses in biological/earth sciences and vice versa. In the final year, the student may select one subject (Major subject) out of the three studied in the second year. Again, 15-20 per cent credits should be obtained through courses in other streams. These should also include courses designed to improve "skills" like computer programming, statistics, instrumentation (optical/electronic), etc.

All science courses must include 30 to 40 per cent credits in laboratory and field work (where applicable as in earth sciences and some areas in biological sciences) and the laboratory exercises should be planned in such a manner that students have opportunities for "hands on" training, and a certain proportion of practicals should be "open-ended" so that students can learn to be innovative/exploratory. The "open-ended" exercises may also be in form of "projects", which should include, besides the actual study, preparation of a formal report. Care must be exercised to ensure that the practicals do not become "rituals" or "demonstrations", and project reports do not get replicated from one batch to the next.

It is also desirable that language courses are introduced, at least from the viewpoint of presentation of data etc., in scientific reports/papers. In addition, the students should also be encouraged to take some extra credits in courses in other faculties, like arts, social sciences, etc., to develop a more integrative personality. To encourage communication skills, each student should be required to give at least one seminar on a current topic in the final year of B.Sc.

4.3 The integrated M.Sc. offered by many institutes should be made more flexible. The programme should offer more elective choices for students. The programme should be restructured so that the students have the option to pursue a part of their training outside the mother institute. This is being followed successfully in institutes like BITS Pilani. Further, a student should have the flexibility to major in a science stream and obtain a minor in engineering or technology or another science stream. The programme should have the provision to be integrated with the Ph.D. programme offered by the institute so that the effective time spent in B.Sc. + M.Sc. + Ph.D. reduces. Also the integrated M.Sc. should have a provision of exit for a student after three years with a B.Sc. degree. As an integrated M.Sc. course by its very nature will have a major interdisciplinary component, it should be run in institutes or universities which have the infrastructure to provide such flexibility. Students should have the option to study a wide variety of subjects before choosing their thesis topic. A cluster of institutes in the same locality can come together to present and offer such a bouquet of courses.

4.4 Premier engineering institutes should be encouraged to offer a combined master's degree in technology and sciences to lure some students to sciences. Flexibility to change streams from engineering and medicine to sciences and vice versa should be built in. Masters and doctorates in pure sciences should be open to graduate engineering and medicine students. Remedial courses can be run by premier institutes to bridge the gap in the knowledge of professional degree students. The BITS Pilani model is worth studying in this context. Frequent interactions with students of engineering and medical streams are important to expose and enable students to contribute to interdisciplinary research. Interactions can be planned in the form of research projects, student seminars and conferences on recent advances in each discipline where participation is open to all.

Recommendation 5: Reform the science curriculum content in line with the changing world and increase research component at all levels

There is a need to change the balance of content in favour of hands-on activities and research at all levels. Increase in experimental learning will increase students interest in science. Content development activities also need to be altered to cater to all segments of student population.

Issues: Firstly, the curriculum load at school level has significantly impacted the understanding of fundamental concepts. Inflexibilities in the course curriculum, lack of application-oriented content and poorly designed laboratory courses have made sciences unattractive. Secondly, emerging technology has reshaped and continues to reshape every discipline rapidly. Competitive advantage will rest with those who have lifelong self-learning skills and humanistic grounding and not with those stuffed with most information. Globalisation demands individuals who can cope with exploding and challenging landscapes of the future world. There is a need to modify the current education system to adapt to changing needs of society.

5.1 Reduction of load: There is an urgent need to reduce information load of curriculum at higher secondary level. Courses should be made engaging and not very heavy. Fundamentals should be emphasised by providing more background and application related problems on each concept.

5.2 Content reforms: The amount of hands-on work at all levels should be increased. To make sciences interesting, local environment can be made a part of learning. Students can apply principles of science to solve local problems. This can be coordinated with local science bodies. Group activities, hands-on training, student seminars, project camps in summers should be encouraged at all levels. Laboratory courses should follow a continuum. To aid learning by inquiry, more exploratory methods must be incorporated into the curriculum. A larger number of experiments, kits and multimedia teaching aids should be created using, as far as possible, locally available materials with accompanying do-it-yourself books. Most textbooks at school level do not describe the details of experiments and teachers are often not sure how to do the experiments or why their experiments fail—it should be ensured that practical manuals explaining details should be made available. Details about where the requirements/kit items can be available and expected cost should be provided. Students should be encouraged to experiment in a creative, unfettered fashion. This calls for changes in the curriculum, teaching and attitude of school administrators (not viewing labs or instruments or chemicals as prized possessions, etc).

Books should be written by teachers who teach the subject and not by curriculum committees. A culture of writing books needs to be developed. Mass collaboration for content development should be encouraged. The government should promote Indian edition of latest books in science.

To be ready for the ever changing scientific world, we should develop and impart creativity training that is the ability to synthesise conceptually. Pedagogy should be modified to entail such training. To empower students to face future challenges imposed by globalisation, global vision training should be imparted to students. Student exchange programmes should be increased as international students bring fresh perspective crucial for turning out global citizens.

5.3 Increasing avenues for research: As students advance in their studies, whether undergraduate or graduate, they should be frequently exposed to people who are immersed in solving serious problems in global change, energy and environment, pharmaceuticals, biology and biotechnology, finance, cryptography and communication again without dilution of standards. At the undergrad level, this can be done through popular science lectures. Research institutes and universities should collaborate to launch attractive programmes for students. These specialised courses will help in channelling student interest towards sciences. Scientists should be incentivised for teaching. If the research institutes have adequate teaching infrastructure, some of them can run six months residential courses at their premises and offer research training in the final semester to postgraduate students.

Undergraduate summer fellowships should be popularised and increased in number. The fellowship programme currently run by science academies and other research institutes should be integrated and popularised so that students have uniform access to information and opportunity to do a project at a premier institute.

A "University Innovation Fund" can be constituted to promote projects by college/university researchers showing potential for innovation. The funding system should be intensively peer reviewed. These innovative grants should be closely monitored in terms of performance with a provision for early termination if milestones are not achieved. On the same lines, the College Science Improvement Programme can be promoted. Teachers should come together to design and fabricate new lab experiments.

Recommendation 6: Radical changes are required in the evaluation system to encourage scientific thinking and promote better understanding of basic science concepts

Issues: The present evaluation system tests memory instead of comprehension. It does not promote creative thinking or problem solving. The selection processes discount originality in thought, innovative ability and passion for hands-on science. These elements are far more important for a career in research. The fun of studying science has been forgotten in the current competitive scenario where science students are focussed at solving problems which appear in various entrance examinations in the shortest possible time.

6.1 Alternative evaluation methodologies: The system should move from examination-based evaluation to more open assessment mechanisms. Memory, comprehension and creativity should be given equal importance in evaluations. More weightage should be given to round the year hands-on activities and laboratory work. Continuous assessment at school level will reduce dependence on year end examinations. If we could develop a system where a holistic record of student performance from school to college is maintained, then this can be used as an alternative or additional input to entrance examinations for entry into various institutes after higher secondary level.

At the college level, introduction of semester system will reduce the anxiety related to year end examinations. Internal assessment should be increased and given more weight. Internal assessment should focus on experimental projects which will create demand for laboratories. This in-turn will lead to demand for better laboratory facilities and consequently improved infrastructure in all colleges. Other measures which will encourage students to go beyond rote learning are open ended examinations which test comprehension rather than memory and open book examinations focusing on problem solving and critical thinking. Group testing and field-work-based testing should be used extensively.

6.2 Enablers: To enable the modifications of evaluation process, teachers need to be trained in new methods of evaluation. Academic calendar should be strictly adhered to. There is a need to increase the teacher to student ratio to ensure better interaction and assessment. A ratio of 1:40 should be targeted. One can look at a unified national level testing at mid-school level and after school completion to reduce load of competitive exams on students. Another important application of such testing could be to bring forth areas where teachers need to be trained.

Recommendation 7: Promote access to quality science educational material at all levels

To attract more talented students to maths and science, it is essential to ensure access to quality science education to all students. There is a need to disseminate high quality educational material in local languages to assist students from non English medium education background. Educational materials should be provided to all at subsidised rates.

Issues: The quality of education in sciences across the country varies widely. Many meritorious students have no access to quality education. There is a large section of student population which receives school education in local languages. These students do wonderfully well in the sciences till graduate level where the medium of instruction remains vernacular. But at postgraduate and higher levels because of the monopoly of English language in science education, they face serious problems. They have to put a lot more effort to understand concepts in the English language at a higher level; often making it difficult to cope with the course work.

7.1 Study material: The current study material available at bachelor's and postgraduate courses in science is limited and does not promote or enable self-learning for students. Self-learning aids will increase access to quality education and hence should be promoted. Internationally available courses in different streams can be adapted for local use. Incentives for people to create such material in academia should be provided so that people are encouraged to take up such work willingly. Further, lectures of teachers reputed for their teaching should be recorded and disseminated all over the country, enabling students and teachers to have access to quality education material.

7.2 Translation: Language should not act as a barrier in science teaching. To bring such students to level playing ground, apart from English language lessons, there is a need to arrange speedy and widespread dissemination of basic science education materials in local languages. These courses should be designed to facilitate understanding of fundamental concepts in the local languages and also provide a bridge towards subsequent studies in the English language. Resources should be provided to translate the best science books in local languages. Internet dissemination of these translated books should be carried out. To aid conceptual understanding, science lectures in local languages can be prepared by good science teachers capable of doing so. These lectures can be recorded and distributed to libraries of all science teaching colleges and universities and made freely available on the Internet. As there is an urgent need for this task to be carried, it is important that the right agencies and people be identified and networked to carry out this work in an organised and comprehensive manner. One important factor which has to be kept in mind while translating into local languages is that the technical terms/scientific terms should *be* kept in English. This will make it easier to migrate to English medium teaching in sciences at higher level for students.

7.3 Special needs of tribal children: Early childhood education is very important as the brain develops the fastest up till six years of age. In this context, special teaching aids need to be developed for tribal children as they are not exposed to modern technology like rest of the children. Motivation for learning has to be created by providing exposure to scientific developments. Tribal schools should be equipped with teachers who are trained in pedagogical methods suited to special needs of tribal kids. They should be well versed in local tribal dialect. Science subjects should be taught in local language till mid-school level. However, the teacher should explain fundamental concepts in tribal dialect to ensure sound conceptual understanding. Tribal dialect can be used for evaluation purposes too at lower levels. Nutritional requirements of tribal children should be taken care of. Migration is a major problem which hinders education of tribal children. Hostel facilities should be provided for older students to ensure continuity in learning.

Career Opportunities, Outreach and Industry Participation

Recommendation 8: Re-brand and promote careers in basic sciences

The prime reason that students opt for professional courses is the perception that there are no attractive career opportunities in sciences. There is an urgent need on the part of all science teaching colleges, universities and institutes to better brand the careers in science and to spread awareness of increasing career opportunities in basic sciences.

Issues: Financial unattractiveness at all levels is a major reason for the downfall of interest in science. The two main occupations associated with pure sciences are teaching and research. Both careers no longer carry the respect and recognition in society as they used to. The financial attractiveness of jobs in other streams pulls students away from sciences. Parental and peer pressure de-motivates even interested students.

8.1 Current careers: Existing careers in sciences, namely teaching and research, should be made more attractive by providing better emoluments, security of tenure, academic freedom and facilities. Joint appointments within the country and appointment of eminent scientists in such areas from other countries under long term visiting professorships should be looked into. Ph.D.s need to be restructured to ensure better stipends for longer duration and secured post docs. It is vital that all such recommendations of appointments and salary structures have a visible component of accountability in their implementation.

8.2 Some other suggestions to attract students to careers in sciences:

- Information about job opportunities for individuals with a master or doctorate qualification in pure sciences should be made available on a portal. New opportunities in emerging fields like financial mathematics etc., should be appropriately marketed. Companies working in these fields should be invited to deliver talks in science colleges.
- Science colleges should collaborate with research institutes and industry for campus placements. Career cells need to be established. Close interaction with industry and research institutes is needed to project type, expertise level and amount of manpower.
- Additional training at bachelor's level has already been suggested for increased employability. More modules/courses could be designed which prepare students for employment in industry. Students should have the choice to take such courses while pursuing bachelors. The four-year bachelor's course offered by good institutes will dispel the myth that science bachelors are in any way less employable than graduates from other professional streams. The ability of lifelong learning should be instilled in students. This should be marketed well to attract companies to employ science background students.
- New opportunities in science streams need to be developed. Research institutes should collaborate with professional streams to pursue and create more opportunities. Research in emerging areas should be systematically developed. Research activities in research laboratories and universities needs to be massively increased. Government should provide all possible incentives to encourage research and development in every sector of the economy.
- Large research groups should be developed. These groups should focus on taking an idea from basic research to market ready application. Such groups can be partially funded by industry. These groups should look at problems which affect a large section of society and devise plan to come up with solutions. Young researchers should be recruited in such initiatives. These research groups should be headed by a well-known scientist who is capable of attracting young doctorates.
- New institutes will create a demand for Ph.D.s. A study on shortage of skilled manpower in science should be commissioned by DST. There is a need to increase salaries in this field to reflect the shortage of skilled manpower. More students will be attracted to pursue basic sciences if they realise that the rewards in scientific profession are not controlled by fixed pay scales but show an upward trend as a reflection of the scarcity of talent in the field.

8.3 Trained technicians: Shortage of trained technicians for science laboratories has resulted in poor maintenance of laboratories across universities, colleges and institutes. Appropriate vocational courses may be designed and introduced in areas that can provide direct employment. This may require a good analysis of local industrial and other requirements. Some general examples are: i) Bio-Medical Laboratory Techniques; ii) Bioinformatics; iii) Computer Applications; iv) Laboratory Techniques (for Physics/Chemistry labs), etc. These courses need to be so designed that the students may be ready for gainful employment. These courses can also be offered to students who are still pursuing their B.Sc. as additional courses.

8.4 Mentoring programme: A structured programme for mentoring students in science should be introduced. It was felt that the students in lower classes in different schools across the country are intimidated by their science and math teachers because of the teacher's attitude towards the students or the teacher's gap in knowledge. As a result, students feel inhibited in asking questions. This in turn, leads to the development of a complex, which is detrimental for academic progress. On the other hand, if good students of higher classes, at least four-years older, come forward to assist the younger students, the latter would benefit by peer learning as this is associated with a with a sense of ease and freedom. The Young Instructors programme of Agastya International Foundation is a model which could be replicated in this context at all levels. This programme will instil confidence in senior students and lead to their holistic development too.

The programme can be started at first in schools where a few hours every week are kept aside for close contacts like informal tutorials between groups of seniors and juniors. Such a tutorial programme should be expanded later to cover students' questions on careers. School teachers can be trained to act as career counselors. Students' doubts regarding uncertainty in pursuing a career in science should be effectively dealt with.

Recommendation 9: Launch a massive science outreach programme aimed at students and their parents in particular

The declining interest in sciences is a wider phenomenon and needs to be addressed comprehensively. Large scale science popularisation programmes are needed to re-establish the passion that science once generated. The objectives of science programmes should include:

- To spark curiosity and imbibe scientific way of thinking.
- To spread awareness about latest discoveries and their impact on society.
- To discuss issues related to adverse effects of scientific developments.
- To promote science as a medium of socio-economic development.
- To glorify careers in science - The media, parents and students should be sensitised to the various career options and job situations available to students coming out of science streams. This would encourage more students to science and reverse the alarming trend of lack of interest in basic sciences.

9.1 A large science popularisation programme: A science popularisation programme should be launched to cover 250 + million children effectively across India. This programme should include all the objectives mentioned above. Apart from money, it will require committed people with vision and capacity towards execution. The importance of this programme necessitates consideration of out-of-the box organisation and service delivery alternatives. This programme should bring all popular science activities under one umbrella for effective implementation and replication of successful initiatives.

9.2 Science cells, centres and mobile labs: A large chain of science talent cells should be created. Each school should be funded to open a science club. A network of good teachers, laboratory facilities and reading resources connecting like-minded students in every town/city is needed. The school science clubs can be then networked to the local centres of science. The local science centres should have experimental models to demonstrate basic science concepts. The centres would be equipped with personnel to explain and answer questions of students. Provision should be made to facilitate visits to this science centre by connected science cells. The centre would act as an "anchor" for the rest of the state's science activities and mobile lab programmes, which would be dispersed across rural *taluks*. In general, the various state governments should facilitate building of more engaging and interactive science parks and museums for learning science outdoors.

To tap talent from rural India, special efforts needed. Science programmes for rural children should be started—book grants, computer grants, etc., can be given apart from direct scholarship. The effectiveness of mobile science labs in reaching rural students is very high and the programme should be replicated across India. The Agastya International Foundation's mobile lab programme should be studied in this regard. A suitable public-private partnership mode can be worked out where a company can sponsor the capital cost of the mobile labs in return for some minimal publicity like logo, etc., on the van. The

Government under its Sarva Sikhsha Abhiyaan can sponsor the operating costs of mobile labs to reach rural schools. Such a model is running successfully in many districts of Karnataka. Apart from mobile science labs like in vans, such labs can also be put in coaches of passenger trains run in the interior regions of the country by Indian Railways and in buses of State Transport Corporations.

Mobile science libraries similar to mobile science laboratories can also be promoted. These should have child friendly volumes on interesting topics including science fiction. Alternatively, children's/public libraries should be opened all over the country by the government. These could lend out books to schools and other registered institutions in bulk, say 100 or more books at a time for, say a month—this could be useful since expecting each school to be able to identify and purchase suitable books is unreasonable. Good books could be identified for each state and purchased in bulk for/by the public libraries.

9.3 Local science programmes: While we need to build a very strong machinery to promote sciences, science research institutes, science academies and local science organisations and scientists (role models) in their individual capacity should participate in this task of nation building. Science should be used as a means to engage students in a variety of extra curricular activities. Science exhibitions, science competitions and popular science lectures can be organised by local science organisations/ teachers' association/group of schools to promote application of what students learn in their environment. Different ventures to encourage and popularise science, such as mobile vans, science centres, interactive exhibits, workshops and activity centres for children should be supported financially.

Journals and popular science magazines can play an important role in spreading the scientific temper among citizens must be more aggressively encouraged, especially among college going students. The country needs many more child friendly science magazines, especially in local languages. TV programmes like 'Turning Point' and 'Quest' that were hugely popular and provided a platform (turning point) for asking 'scientific questions' for children and adults alike should be promoted.

Science programmes focused at non-metro students should be launched. Local languages should be used in science dissemination. Scientists should communicate more to masses through the media. A national science portal, promoting science contests etc., can be created. The Government can mandate outreach programmes as part of grant applications.

The Children Science Congress organised by the Department of Science and Technology is a laudable effort. Its scale should be expanded and more schools should be included. Information should be made available, and should be readily accessible at all high schools and junior colleges about careers in science, and this should be publicised among the teachers at these levels. Programmes like Vigyan Manthan Yatra of the Madhya Pradesh government, Science centre proposed by Assam government, Science city concept of Tamil Nadu and Gujarat government etc., are also good efforts and should be replicated across India wherever possible.

Recommendation 10: Encourage industry participation in promoting sciences at all levels

Industry participation is important in making sciences popular. As research-based industries flourish in India, more and more companies will need employees qualified in basic sciences. This will visibly provide more attractive career options.

Issues: The current industry participation in science education is very low. It needs to be increased manifold. Companies need to realise that their investment in science education is a long term investment for their own benefit.

10.1 Select companies, which employ research scientists, can come forward to offer jobs to Ph.D. students post-completion of their doctoral degree. Ideally this commitment should be made at the time when a prospective Ph.D. student is deciding about joining the degree programme. Some industries are already doing this in computer science. Industry can sponsor Ph.D.s for students after setting some certain minimum criteria or it can hire students at master's level and provide scholarships to pursue Ph.D. in chosen fields.

10.2 Industry internships of longer duration for postgraduate students should be encouraged for students who intend to pursue a career in industry. This will enable them to learn work place skills as well as expose them to latest technologies and research methodologies. Industry should also devise methods to optimally utilise the student's stay in their workplace.

10.3 At bachelor's level, employable skills like computer training, communication skills, etc., should be included in the curriculum. Undergraduates should be exposed to industry problems through seminars and popular science lectures by industry leaders. This will engage students in scientific issues and motivate them to solve some of these problems in the future.

10.4 Teaching aids: Industry can participate in creating study material which can be directly used by students. Self-learning should be promoted at all levels. The massive efforts required in translating science study material into local languages can be undertaken by companies which have some expertise in this field.

10.5 Industry sponsorships for science fairs, laboratories, science centres and mobile labs should be sought. A mutually beneficial partnership can be worked out between universities, NGOs and industries to promote science popularisation programmes. Industry should be encouraged to invest in basic infrastructure and maintaining them in universities and also in providing scholarships to deserving students. Universities should interact with industry in terms of needs, employability skills, etc. In India, a few technology companies have started exploring possible symbiotic relationships with universities in recent years. This needs to be structured and massively encouraged. Further, if the academia desires industry cooperation, it has to move away from examination orientation. Interdisciplinary approach is needed to handle partnership projects. This should be facilitated.

10.6 Academic institutions should develop groups at each institute which specialise in developing novel funding mechanisms involving industry. The academia on its part should run courses to train industry personnel. It should take up industry sponsored projects for effective interaction. Academic institutes should invite industry to visit institutes and demonstrate facilities to create confidence in the industry people. Universities can create interface bodies for effective research work. Such collaborative work will generate funds for universities too.

In short, restructuring of the entire system is needed to bring back the glory that the basic sciences once held in the minds of the students. Many of our recommendations on infrastructure, autonomy, access, evaluation and pedagogy have synergies with NKC recommendations on higher education, school education, libraries, translation and open educational resources. We have highlighted the most important things which have to be in place to work the system around. We believe that the implementation of all these recommendations in a coordinated fashion will charge the system to act as a magnet to attract students towards basic sciences.

Annexure 17.2

Concept Note on National Science and Mathematics Mission

1. Background

While all these recommendations are necessary to reform science education in the country, the crucial ingredient for ensuring success is people with vision, ability and commitment to execute, supported by an effective, mission-oriented and formalised organisational platform for implementation and to achieve the goals and objectives of science education and popularsation. Progress in the field of science in India has been on the decline. Countries like China and South Korea which were behind India in scientific standing have marched ahead. Developed countries are also facing similar onslaught due to shortage of skilled manpower in this field.

The rapid progress of science and growth of new scientific areas in recent years has resulted in many of these areas being unrepresented in the country. This has been largely caused by the decrease in the number of people who pursue the sciences, and we have already lost decades of scientific progress. It is high time that we put our act together and launch a nationwide science movement to regain our lost glory. The pressures and challenges we face call for bold, innovative and decisive action. The penalty for not acting is falling back irreversibly, condemning millions of lives to mediocrity, and ceding the potential for the country's transformation and greatness in the 21st century.

Therefore, a National Science and Mathematics Mission is proposed. The Mission will consolidate, streamline and coordinate all the activities which are now being performed as piecemeal and isolated ventures by different agencies. The Mission will be directly responsible for achieving the goals and objectives of reforming science education. It will be an autonomous and unifying body providing leadership, direction and inspiration to all organisations working in the field of science education, research and popularisation. It will launch a nationwide campaign to attain its objective of a paradigm shift in the field of science, which would include both strategic long-term and specific goal-oriented projects.

2. Vision

To promote excellence in the field of science education and research and to popularise science and the scientific spirit in society.

3. Constitution

The choice of the Mission Leader is hypercritical for success. The Mission should be headed by a person (under 50 years, preferably younger) with demonstrated interest in and knowledge of science education, and the management and entrepreneurial skills necessary to build and inspire a nationwide science movement. The Mission head will enjoy the freedom to run and operate the Mission similar to the freedom and responsibilities enjoyed by the CEO of any major organisation. A core group of 40-50 or more young people, of whom the majority will be under 45 years, with knowledge, management skill and deep interest in changing the science education landscape of the country will lead the effort to catalyse and disseminate science education. These Change Leaders of Science will be selected on a nationwide basis with appropriate representation of scientists, school, college and university teachers, science NGOs, innovators, industry leaders and science popularisation organisations. The Mission Leader and the team will then draw up a 10-year master plan for science and mathematics training and research for India.

Above all, the Mission must demonstrate passion, innovation and the capacity to inspire. It should be run as an independent and autonomous organisation with clearly defined goals and milestones, and must have the freedom to act decisively to achieve its goals.

4. Objectives

The proposed Mission will strive to achieve the following objectives:

- To launch and manage a massive science outreach programme and to support and coordinate science popularisation activities of all member organisations.
- To coordinate among various governments/government departments and set up science centres and mobile labs across the country.
- To create and manage a Science Corps of teachers, students, educators, scientists, retirees and others who are interested in working with/reaching out to deprived children and teachers across the country.
- To create a platform where curriculum designers at all levels interact to integrate course curriculum from higher secondary to postgraduate level in science.
- To promote creation and disbursal of quality science educational materials and teaching aids. To facilitate development of courses in line with recent development in science and emerging employment opportunities.
- To promote research opportunities in science and science education for teachers and students in schools and colleges. To ensure access to information related to science education, research and career.
- To ensure and monitor upgradation of infrastructure in universities and colleges. To plan, execute and supervise a nationwide in-service science teacher training programme.
- To organise academia industry meets and discover novel ways of participation in science-related activities by industry.

To ensure the success of this country-wide programme the Mission must operate as a 10-year programme. It can delegate most of its responsibilities to concerned organisations with a systematic process of review after the end of 10 years. NKC could provide anchor support and coordination in the launch of the Mission.

18 More Quality Ph.Ds

It is widely recognised that a nation's transformation to a Knowledge and Skills Economy is critically dependent on the original research and development taking place within the country. If India is to make the transition to a Knowledge economy, it is therefore, vital that research and development within the country be dramatically improved. There is ample evidence that India is not well-placed for this future transformation. For example, in many disciplines, there is already a severe shortage of well-trained young doctorates to fill in existing posts in research institutes and universities. This problem is likely to be even more acute in the envisaged elite new universities. The growth in the number of doctorates has only been 20 per cent in India in the period 1991-2001 compared to 85 per cent in China.[1] Not more than 1 per cent of those completing undergraduate degrees currently opt for doctoral studies in India, and a substantial number of students prefer to go abroad. To address these problems, there is a pressing need for urgent government policy interventions, including high priority initiatives to attract, nurture, and retain the country's best young minds in academia and research.

With this objective, the NKC conducted a widespread investigative survey across the country and abroad. Workshops and consultations were also held with other stakeholders from industry, research institutes and universities. The attached note on 'More Quality Ph.Ds', identifies the critical issues and discusses the remedial steps in detail. NKC recommends the following to improve the quality and quantity of Ph.D. students in the country.

1. Launch a national publicity campaign to attract the best young minds for careers in teaching at all levels, and also academic research: One of the casualties of the expanding market economy has been the devaluation of the academic profession as a whole, and this is now seriously affecting the desirability of this profession. Specific measures for addressing this problem include:

- Enhancing the prestige, social-standing and remuneration of people in the academic profession.
- Systematic and targeted initiatives to unleash the potential of gifted students outside the urban population centres.
- Utilisation of current technology to provide greater access to quality learning at all levels, and bridging the language gap.
- Increased coverage in the media of different facets of teaching, research and academic achievements, both nationally and internationally.

2. Initiate major academic reforms in universities: Throughout the world, universities are the natural home for the interface between teaching and research. But this is far from reality in the vast majority of Indian universities. In fact, the overall current situation in Indian universities is dismal largely due to the lack of quality infrastructure and the inability to recruit good young faculty and gifted students. Some concrete interventions for improving the situation include:

- Urgent Regulatory reforms in Higher Education, reducing regulation while improving governance; the details have been articulated by NKC in its earlier recommendations on Higher Education.
- Greater autonomy for departments within universities to introduce new relevant courses, along with encouragement and rewards for innovation in teaching and research.
- Identifying and supporting university departments as Centres of Excellence.

1. "Measures of Progress of Science in India", Report by NISTADS 2006.

- Greater flexibility and increased funding for university departments to recruit and retain good faculty from across the world.
- Periodic peer reviews of departments in the universities. Encouraging recruitment of capable and talented younger faculty.

3. Implement administrative reforms in universities: It is equally important that reforms in the administration of universities accompany academic reforms. This will ensure professional administration of universities, and help in attracting students and good faculty. These reforms should include the following:

- Ensuring a capable administration headed by an able Vice-Chancellor and Registrar; these appointments should be based on academic and administrative credentials.
- Increasing efficiency and transparency in university administration at all levels. De-politicisation of appointments and more administrative autonomy.
- Better systems for monitoring and maintaining the physical infrastructure, especially buildings.
- Sensitising the administration towards academic freedom and the academic needs for a good research environment.

4. Enable research environments in universities: Academic reforms and better infrastructure should go hand in hand with nurturing and sustaining a research environment. Some key enablers for this are:

- Mechanisms for greater academic cooperation between universities and research institutions; in particular embedding research institutes (granting sufficient autonomy) within university campuses.
- Providing access to digital media in universities, in parallel with funds for better libraries and laboratories.
- Focused engagement towards making universities a natural home for research as well as teaching.

5. Set up more quality undergraduate teaching institutions across disciplines: Dedicated researchers involved in direct training of the students at the undergraduate level create a greater impact. Most of the universities or elite institutions in the country are currently involved in training for the Masters or Ph.D degrees. However, it is now widely recognised that the students emerging from the undergraduate programmes are ill-prepared for a research career. The following steps are proposed to address this:

- Introduction of well-planned four-year courses to enable direct entry into Ph.D programmes.
- Encouragement of various measures to ensure multiple sources of input of talented people into the academic profession.
- Credit portability across a network of institutions.

6. Increase funding for education at all levels and for R&D: Even in the developed countries, it is fully accepted that long-term investment in education and increased spending on R&D is necessary to maintain the lead in cutting-edge research. This is even more relevant in India today. NKC proposes the following measures:

- Strengthening of education at the school level, with particular focus on teacher training.
- Creation of effective monitoring and assessment mechanisms, nimble enough to measure outcomes and adopt new strategies.
- Consulting stakeholders in making policy decisions.

7. Rejuvenate doctoral programmes across disciplines: While the above recommendations are aimed at attracting potential doctoral students and enabling a research environment, it is vital that prospective doctoral students are chosen with sufficient care. The following measures are proposed with this objective in mind:

- A review of the whole selection procedure and monitoring process for graduate students.
- Multiple pathways for entry to a Ph.D programme while maintaining entry standards.
- Support for quality research in arts, humanities and other areas.

- Support and promotion of cross-disciplinary teaching and research programmes.
- Greater exposure of undergraduate and postgraduate students to cutting edge research.

8. Ensure quality of doctoral work and academic research in institutions: At the same time as striving for greater influx of people towards research careers, institutions must ensure that the research undertaken matches global quality in the relevant field. In addition, the graduate programmes should be continually reviewed so as to make them vibrant, challenging and internationally relevant. Here are some steps to be taken in this regard:

- A preliminary vetting of the synopses of the theses followed by rigorous external examination of doctoral theses.
- Broad funding for the organisation of and participation in workshops, seminars and symposia, in India and overseas.
- Encouraging doctoral students to teach, with remuneration provided via Teaching Assistantships.
- Wider dissemination of research work, especially through current digital media in universities and research institutions.

9. Enable vigorous industry-academia interaction: In the modern context, there is a crying need for a healthy and enlightened cooperation between private industry and academia, which replaces the existing feelings of doubt and mistrust. While industry should recognise that support for education is beneficial, universities should take cognizance of the changing needs of private enterprise in planning new courses. This could be achieved by the following measures:

- A policy framework for meaningful public-private partnership in universities, and concerted efforts to nurture industry-academia interactions.
- Encouraging private investment in education, research and innovation, backed by appropriate taxation measures.
- Promoting collaboration between research and development units within industry and universities.

10. Foster a global outlook in research: Research is increasingly becoming a collective global endeavour. It is thus necessary to harness global talent and expertise to develop capacity within the country. This is also essential if the nation is to remain a participant in global cutting edge research. With this in view, the following is recommended:

- Encouraging NRI/PIO Scientists to establish meaningful links with Indian institutions, and participate in the academic development of the nation. Creating joint Ph.D programmes between universities both within and outside of the country.
- Financial and administrative support for international research collaborations.
- Identifying important areas of research where national expertise needs to be developed and initiating steps for funding and capacity building by way of collaborations, guest faculty, proactive hiring, etc.

In conclusion, it must be recognised that investment in education and research produces a broad range of dividends, both tangible and intangible. Our existing base in research needs to be urgently strengthened to arrest any further erosion. While the NKC welcomes the augmented allocation for education in the Eleventh Five Year Plan, it is important that these funds are effectively utilised to make a visible difference in our academic landscape. As a first step, we urge the government to set itself a target of tripling the existing research base within the next dozen years, and meaningfully work towards it. NKC strongly feels that a mission-oriented approach is necessary for creating the required research ecosystem in the country. Hence, a National Research Mission which can be spearheaded by National Science and Engineering Research Board, proposed in the current Five Year Plan is recommended.

Annexure 18.1: Note on More Quality Ph.Ds

Research is an activity based on intellectual investigation and has the purpose of discovering, interpreting, and revising human knowledge and experience on various aspects of life. It is crucial for the overall development of human society. As the economic paradigm undergoes a change in the globalised world, future economic progress will increasingly be a function of the intellectual capital that a nation can create. This in turn depends crucially on the quality of academic research that is done in the nation. Thus, if India is to play a key role in the envisaged knowledge economy of the world, a significant investment in research, accompanied by sustained vision and policy is vital to achieve a long term competitive advantage. While the importance of research and development in science and technology is increasingly recognised, basic research in many other areas like economics, management, social sciences, arts, etc., play an equally important role in the overall development and well-being of a nation.

Historically, India has had an enviable standing in the world of research. However, the current situation is unsatisfactory across multiple dimensions, and the reasons for this are manifold. An important factor which impacts the quality and quantum of research is the scarcity of talented and dedicated manpower engaged in research. We need qualified doctorates for our research laboratories, to teach and engage in research in our universities and to work for research and development in all sectors of the industry. The number of researchers in India was 112 per million inhabitants compared to 633 in China and 4374 in USA in 2002. The growth in the number of doctorates has been only a modest 20 per cent in India from 1991-2001 compared to 85 per cent in China during the same period.[1] The current state of affairs thus requires urgent policy intervention.

Research in any area requires continuous intellectual engagement along with a passion for ideas and creative thinking. We thus need to create a system where these qualities are nurtured and encouraged, thereby providing a pool of students wishing to pursue doctoral studies. Simultaneously, it must be ensured that once they acquire a Ph.D, further employment opportunities are attractive. This is essential to justify the amount of time and effort invested in doctoral research, even more so in today's modern world where there are many other seemingly easier and more lucrative career options. While achieving a critical mass of researchers in the country is important, it is necessary to ensure that quality standards are maintained at the same time.

With this objective, NKC initially conducted a wide spread survey across the country and abroad. A detailed questionnaire was sent to all the universities, academic and research institutions, government agencies and other stakeholders. More than 250 people responded to the survey. A one day workshop was also held where prominent members from diverse industries, academic and research institutions and universities deliberated on these issues. A list of participants is attached in the annexure. This note captures the main suggestions that evolved from these consultations. Some of the recommendations below have systemic linkages to the previous NKC recommendations in the areas of education, entrepreneurship, intellectual property rights, knowledge network and attracting talented students to maths and science.

Part A: Attracting Potential Doctoral Students

In order to sustain research in the long term and for it to flourish, creating a critical mass of researchers and academics is of the foremost importance. Serious policy interventions are required to ensure that this is achieved within a specified time frame in the country.

Recommendation 1: Create greater awareness and acceptance towards pursuing teaching and research as a career, by communicating the opportunities and excitement at a broader level

Issues: The Indian society at large, especially the younger generation is not well-informed of the career opportunities, excitement and freedom that a research career offers. Consequently, the acceptance level for embarking on such careers is rather low.

Societal pressure affects career choices significantly. A multi-pronged approach needs to be adopted to bring about a change in the national mindset towards recognition and acceptance of a career in research. For long term wealth creation, it is important that the nation trains academics, scientists and teachers, rather than bankers.

1 "Measures of Progress of Science in India", Report by NISTADS 2006.

Awareness

Media: The media has an important role to play in bringing about a fundamental change in attitude and in the nation's consciousness on this issue.

- Short and engaging television or radio programmes related to research can be aired at prime time.
- News channels should highlight and publicise various achievements of academics and other scientists.
- Print and electronic media should be encouraged and incentivised towards promotion and engagement of the intellect.

There are various other means to increase the awareness of society at large:

- Annual R&D shows can be held, where leading research institutes and companies interact with the public, thereby providing a wider exposure.
- Museums, exhibitions and popular lectures are other avenues through which public attention can be engaged. These should be encouraged at as many places as possible. For this purpose, the resources and infrastructure of various educational institutions throughout the country should be used.
- Academic societies should be generously funded and members should be encouraged to participate in the outreach programmes.
- In schools and colleges, career awareness workshops and seminars highlighting research careers should be held regularly.
- Important academic events and visits of reputed academics to India should be publicised and shared with the entire educational community through the use of various channels. This will help create enthusiasm in teachers, students and also acquaint society with academia.
- Talent residing in rural areas remains completely untapped because of various reasons. Basic education and learning resource materials should be made available to all. At the same time, it is important that targeted initiatives be undertaken to identify talented students and to provide them with opportunities for greater exposure, learning and bridging language gaps.
- Women and especially their parents must be made aware of the possibilities and flexibilities that a research career offers, and should be encouraged through targeted initiatives towards such a career path.

Acceptance

- Nobel Prize winners, reputed academics and other scientists should communicate and publicise the joy and opportunities in a research career.
- School teachers play a very important role in orienting students as well as their parents. Hence, teachers should be trained and engaged in this endeavour. Parent-Teacher Associations provide a platform where role models can interact with both parents and teachers at the same time and increase their acceptance towards research.
- Open competitions and projects at different levels should be conceptualised, encouraged and widely publicised. Industry can be involved in such activities.
- Recognising good research work is important for two reasons. It gives a sense of pride to the researcher as well as encourages others to do research. Hence, various means of recognition such as awards, felicitations, publicity etc., should be taken up at all levels.
- Higher learning, along with research and innovation, plays an important role in development of knowledge areas. Its impact on society needs to be publicised widely.
- Both the monetary and non-monetary aspects of a research career, especially the accompanying academic freedom and the international nature of research, should be communicated to students.

Recommendation 2: Expose undergraduate and postgraduate students to cutting edge research and engage them in serious research wherever possible

Issues: The major decision points where a student decides to pursue doctoral studies are towards the final year of either an undergraduate or a master's programme. These students are often not well exposed to various research opportunities and hence remain untargeted.

2.1 Undergraduate Research: A good undergraduate teaching programme is vital for grooming prospective students towards research. Currently, our education system remains largely unimaginative and monotonous with a stress on rote learning and with problems handed down to students. Wide-ranging reforms that encompass pedagogy of teaching, curriculum and evaluation are a pre-requisite to nurture and encourage interested students towards a research path.[2]

- Relevance and application play an important role in attracting applied researchers, while general abstraction and challenge attract theoretical researchers. Taking this into account, a judicious mix of projects and courses may be designed, of which one kind offers an exposure to real life problems from the industry, economy etc., and another imparts foundational training in theoretical aspects of the subject.
- Courses that orient students towards research need to be specifically designed and made part of the curriculum. An important component of these courses should impart knowledge on identifying and defining problems, various research methodologies, analytic methods and presentation. Team projects comprising of different disciplines can be introduced as an optional course for students. This could be combined with changes in syllabus that allow one research-based course even at undergraduate level.
- Summer internships, summer schools, workshops, competitions should all be encouraged. Exciting undergraduate research projects that can involve larger number of students should be rolled out. The vacation period should be utilised to provide undergraduate students with a comprehensive training comprising of exposure to problems in rural areas, industrial training, research project in academic or research institutions and an exposure to foreign universities through various means such as exchange programmes. DST, ICSSR and other organisations can fund a programme of small research projects to be undertaken at undergraduate level, which would introduce students to the actual practice of research.
- Teachers need to be trained to promote research and should be incentivised to create innovative projects where undergrads can participate.
- Exposure to and acquaintance with frontier research should be facilitated. Overall, undergraduate education needs to be strengthened in the country. Creativity should be encouraged at all levels. A continuum of quality institutions from the undergraduate level in all disciplines is required. Residential undergraduate programmes should be increased.

2.2 Postgraduate research and training: To encourage research and innovation at postgraduate level, several measures can be undertaken.

- Postgraduate students should be given the opportunity of spending a semester at research labs or other Indian or foreign universities, outside their own university to broaden exposure. The home universities should facilitate such exposure by entering into alliances with other well established places of research. The BITS Pilani programme is an excellent example of such an initiative.
- Research projects which have the potential to be extended as doctoral projects need to be encouraged at the postgraduate level. Projects should be offered in emerging areas to retain student interest. Faculty must regularly update themselves to be in a position to guide students. Group research projects among postgraduate students will create more interest and add enthusiasm towards research.
- Reduction of course load with a corresponding increase in the research component for students who show deep interest and commitment to research would incite potential doctoral students.
- Postgraduate courses in social sciences and humanities should have a component (perhaps a full course or paper) that requires either desk-based or field research, which could be an optional choice.

---

2. See National Knowledge Commission's recommendations on Higher Education, *http://www.knowledgecommission.gov.in/recommendations/higher.asp*

- All postgraduate departments should organise and hold regular research seminars, and students should be encouraged to attend these. Programmes that facilitate establishing links between interested postgraduate students and their prospective guides should be encouraged.

2.3 Integrated doctoral programmes: There should be flexibility of moving from undergraduate degree to a Ph.D degree when substantial interest and aptitude for research has been shown at the undergraduate level by the student. S.N. Bose Centre for Basic Sciences runs such a programme.

An integrated programme covering bachelors, masters and doctorate degrees with various exit points has multiple advantages. It will establish a vital link between students at all levels. Networking among students at different levels will give rise to new ideas. It will bring much needed fresh energy into research by exposure and induction to research at an early stage.

However, many precautions need to be taken while designing the integrated course, for instance

- Curriculum must be planned well and subject to periodic reviews. It should have a provision for multiple exchange semesters which will enable wider exposure, interaction and exchange of ideas.
- Selection procedure should take research aptitude into consideration.
- The programme, however, should have multiple exit and placement opportunities. There should be enough flexibility provided to students so that while opting for an integrated course, a student should not feel that they are bonded by it for seven to eight years.

In view of all these requirements, it is suggested that a restricted pilot be launched at select institutions. This programme is especially directed towards science streams.

2.4 Linking researchers at all levels: Within an institution, relations among different levels of students (e.g., undergraduate, postgraduate and Ph.D) should be fostered. This could be achieved by judiciously mixing students in projects. Apart from facilitating peer learning, it provides a learning platform for potential doctoral students.

A comprehensive National Projects and Research portal is highly recommended. This is essential for connecting students and researchers at all levels, facilitating formation of virtual peer groups, disseminating information related to various projects and schemes, and providing information of various positions for doctorates etc.

Recommendation 3: Restructure incentives for doctoral degree students to attract and retain them in research

Issues: The gamut of opportunities available to graduate and postgraduate students today has made research in India an obvious secondary choice. Apart from financial unattractiveness and substantial investment of the prime years in their lives, there is a perceived lack of challenge as well as future career opportunities.

3.1 Remuneration: It is generally true that interested and talented people choose to pursue doctoral studies. They could have easily opted for better paying career options. Also, there are many more students whom the system fails to attract on account of remuneration issues. Thus it is important that while deciding remunerations, opportunity costs are factored in.

- There should be a regular upgradation of the amount of fellowships offered for Ph.Ds, and in general for the entire academic profession.
- Various forms of additional compensation should be explored.
- Teaching assistantship to bright Ph.D students should be provided to add to their earnings. This would also have the additional benefit of training and preparing them for a career in academics and teaching. This is vital considering the current serious shortage of competent faculty being faced by our institutions of learning.
- Other possible methods could include summer projects, summer internships in industry and involvement in organisational work as part of academics.
- Subsidised health insurance, home loans etc., could be looked at.
- Generous travel grants should be ensured.

A good placement office for Ph.Ds should be given priority in all universities and institutions. They should have tie-ups with various universities, research institutions, industries at the regional, national and international level.

3.2 Entrepreneurship: More students can be attracted to doctoral studies by providing a platform where they can convert their ideas or research into reality. To foster such an environment,

- Incubation centres must be facilitated and promoted in academic institutions.
- Universities can offer courses on Entrepreneurship.
- Mechanisms should be framed to support start-ups.
- While application-oriented research is important, care should, however, be taken to ensure that
  - traditional base of academic research is not eroded,
  - intellectual property of the university is well protected, and
  - core values and requirements of research are not diluted.

3.3 Joint Ph.D programmes with industry: To address the needs of people from industry interested in doing a Ph.D, academic institutes should focus on networking with industry and work out joint programmes with interested companies. This will create a talent pool of researchers in industry. Consequently, research in private sector will get a boost, thereby creating attractive job opportunities for researchers which, in turn, might entice many students to enrol in a doctorate programme. Thus, a virtual circle can be created.

The opportunity cost of pursuing a Ph.D is very significant for this target group. Hence, a favourable proposal needs to be designed which not only allows but also encourages employees to go for a Ph.D. There should be Memorandum of Understanding (MoU) between the partnering institution and the industry. The MoU could include the clause that the company pays their salary during the period of Ph.D. The Reliance Life Sciences (RLS) model is noteworthy in this aspect. RLS has a mechanism whereby its employees may pursue a doctorate degree at Mumbai University. BITS Pilani also runs a doctorate programme for professionals. The programme has inbuilt flexibilities which attracts people from industry and simultaneously has a very strong scrutiny system to ensure quality Ph.Ds.

One important factor that should be kept in mind is that academic freedom is maintained and an enabling environment is created wherein prospective guides and doctoral students from industry can interact.

This will also potentially attract those bright students who chose to work in industry because of attractive financial packages.

Recommendation 4: Create attractive post-doctoral opportunities to provide fresh doctorates with a valuable cross disciplinary research and teaching experience

Issues: Post-doctoral opportunities in India and abroad are limited. The opportunities existing in India right now do not stand any appeal against post-doctoral offers from abroad. The brightest go abroad and tend to prolong their stay as far as possible. Simultaneously, there is a lack of synergy between research and teaching experience.

This is an important stage where effective intervention should be made to broaden our academic and research base. Therefore, it is vital to create

- Dedicated central fund for Post-Doctoral Fellows (PDFs) so that senior researchers can employ post docs for their research projects.
- More flexible positions for researchers with various institutions, centres of excellence, advanced research labs and industry.
- A large pool of post-doctoral fellows. Projects of national importance, faculty for teaching institutions as well as private companies can choose new doctorates for temporary, yet financially very attractive positions from such a pool. Such centralisation of resources will lead to better information dissemination and effective resource sharing.

Longer term offers could be made to PDFs by including teaching as a vital component. In many universities, a purely post-doc research position is not recognised as teaching experience while making faculty appointments.

- Effective utilisation of the PDFs in universities should be facilitated by flexible and innovative appointment modes. This can provide a means of upgrading university departments in general, and also addressing the faculty shortage. Teaching experience will also increase opportunities of employment in universities after post-doctoral work.
- Mobility across organisations should be facilitated during post-doc tenure. A group of five to six universities can be formed with an understanding that a Ph.D of one university can do a post-doc at another. International peer review mechanisms can be established for PDFs. Overall, this calls for greater coordination among universities and research institutes, better sharing of resources, and for convergence of teaching and research experience.

Part B: Quality

A quality degree which is universally recognised as such, and which is acquired after consistent hard work and application of mind both acts as a magnet to attract talented students and inspires awe in the minds of the general public. It is, therefore, essential that doctoral programmes in the country aspire to attain the highest standards of excellence. At present, the quality of research output in the country is completely uneven across institutions. While, it is necessary to maintain the high quality standards in elite institutions, it is simultaneously imperative to encourage the transition to cutting-edge research in others. It is also crucial that quality in the output of academic research is ensured by a variety of metrics like publications in peer-reviewed journals with good impact factor, academic activities like workshops and conferences, patents, technology transfer activities, etc.

Recommendation 5: Rejuvenate the Ph.D programme and adhere to quality standards to attract talented students

Issues: Other than the financial benefits, a key deciding factor in making a career choice in academics is the intellectual satisfaction that one expects. The quality of research undertaken at a majority of institutions in the country is, however, so low that it deters potential students.

5.1 Entry level screening: Usually, an entry level examination is conducted to ensure good quality of the intake of doctoral students. A prospective doctoral student's aptitude and attitude towards research should also be considered along with other qualifications. At all times, adherence to good standards at the entry level is essential.

- Multiple pathways should be used to fill research positions.
  - Flexibility should be given to universities for conducting their own entrance examinations.
  - A demonstrated research potential should be given due consideration. If an applicant has published a good quality research paper, filed a patent etc, his/her application should be accordingly considered.
  - For working professionals, who may find it difficult to pass an entry level test, other flexible methods of assessment should be put in place.
  - Online testing of students should also be worked out. This is particularly important to attract potential students from abroad.
- Examinations
  - Testing aptitude for research should be made an integral part of the selection process. Apart from a written examination, a personal interview will be greatly useful.
  - Syllabus and quality of the current NET examination needs to be massively reformed.
  - Unlimited attempts should be allowed to pass the qualifying examination.
  - As the borders between disciplines are getting increasingly blurred, it is important to examine the entry requirements for lateral entry across disciplines.
- Adequate care should be taken to ensure that screening methods are transparent and objective.

5.2 Pre-Ph.D courses: It is important to identify and bridge the gaps between the present and the required knowledge of a doctoral student.

National pre-Ph.D programme: In order to utilise the limited pool of talented faculty, a national pre-Ph.D programme of suitable duration, run by major national institutions can be launched. The programme would help in broadening the perspective of a future doctoral student and also increase networking within the research community. The necessary infrastructure for such an initiative needs to be created.

- It should involve qualified researchers who should be sufficiently incentivised to teach in the training programmes. Other distinguished speakers can also be invited for delivering lectures.
- Qualified applicants with a pre-Ph.D degree can return to their respective home institutions once their training is over.
- The programme should be tailored to cater to different disciplines and should include a study of latest trends in particular streams. It should also train students in analytical skills, research methodology, instrument use, dissertation writing, etc.

For students registering for a Ph.D directly after a bachelor's degree, the importance of a pre-Ph.D programme increases. It would not only impart students with necessary background training but also examine their research aptitude. In an integrated doctorate programme, pre-Ph.D can serve as one of the exit points. The pre-Ph.D degree could be recognised as a qualification to teach undergraduate courses.

R&D laboratories can prepare teaching material for pre-Ph.D courses. Lecture notes should be made available on the internet, thereby ensuring wider accessibility. This will also contribute towards greater access to quality educational material among students and faculty. At the individual level, the guides must give sufficient self-study coursework to students.

Recommendation 6: Create effective monitoring and assessment mechanisms during the course of doctoral research and encourage broader engagement with research

Issues: Research in India is carried out solely on the basis of internal motivation. Effective external mechanisms which ensure good quality of research largely do not exist. At the same time, there are no sufficient mechanisms to guarantee broader engagement with research.

To ensure effective monitoring and assessment mechanisms

- Students must be continuously monitored and mentored to ensure that the research output is of requisite quality. Regular seminars by students will ensure that the students adhere to their research work plan and show progress. Regular reporting in lab meetings could be used for informal feedback.
- Experimental projects should be monitored through a well maintained log book. The guide should insist and regularly check whether log books are maintained.
- Independent committees can also be set up before which the students make regular presentations. Any such committee should provide feedback and counsel the doctoral students. External co-guides from industry/other institutes could facilitate a way to ensure better monitoring.
- Any mechanism used for monitoring should check for possibilities of plagiarism. Further, to enable an overall healthy research environment, Ph.D students should be taught ethics and standards of academic research as part of curriculum.

Before designing any new monitoring and assessment mechanisms, it is important to identify why the existing ones have failed and the lessons learnt should be taken into account.

To promote broader engagement with research,

- Regular interaction among the researchers should be facilitated through group meetings, research seminars etc. At some places, lab group meetings are held every week in which each student presents and discusses his/her work with the entire group.
- Wider exposure to research in the form of participation in international conferences, workshops, seminars etc., will strengthen the student's research base and should be encouraged.
- Journal clubs where students discuss articles other than those in their own areas of research provide a means to broaden the academic horizon of students.

- Mentoring doctoral students for meaningful participation by means of poster presentations (individually or in groups), group discussions would provide further impetus in helping the students towards gaining confidence about their research. It will also lead to a larger networking among peers and established researchers from around the world.

Recommendation 7: Comprehensive assessment of doctoral thesis and wider dissemination of research work

Issues: Often there is no objective assessment of doctoral thesis, thus leading to theses of poor quality. The evaluation committee does not subject the thesis to a strict scrutiny. There is a huge problem of uneven quality across institutions, and this is particularly marked in the social sciences and humanities, even to the point where Ph.Ds can be "purchased" on the basis of minimal work in some places.

One of the fundamental requirements for running a quality doctoral programme is to have a strong faculty involved in front-line exciting research. It is equally important that reputed examiners are appointed to validate the quality of output of research thesis.

- A combination of internal and external examiners should be used to make the system more robust. The names of members of the respective evaluation committee should be attached to each approved thesis. It is important to bring transparency in the system and attention to quality.
- Open defence of thesis could be mandated. If a student fails to defend his/her work suitably, a second defence can be planned after six months. Honourable exit options should be provided for doctoral students.
- Publications in quality research journals should be encouraged. Open peer review of publications should be aimed at.
- Ph.D thesis should be uploaded on the internet, preferably on the proposed National Research Portal. In any event, open and free access to research output in archives and other digital media resources should be made mandatory.

Alternative systems to grant a Ph.D can be explored. As practised these days in Germany, five published papers in peer reviewed journals should be deemed sufficient to acquire a Ph.D. This does not stipulate registration, time limit or supervision. Such students should publish in reputed and internationally recognised journals, and these papers may be reviewed collectively by a panel of examiners (at least two from developed countries and two from India). If a minimum of three pass the standards test, Ph.D degree may be awarded to the student and should be recognised in the existing system. Such innovative and alternative systems need to be explored and put into practice.

Part C: Nurturing a Research Environment

In order for research to flourish, it is vital that the entire academic system be made more conducive and vibrant. Universities are the natural homes for academic research the world over, and it is vital that research culture be brought back to our universities. Other stakeholders like industry and government can play an important role in this endeavour.

Recommendation 8: Enable university environment to produce quality Ph.Ds

Issues: Various compulsions in early policy-making in the post-Independent era led to a large number of stand-alone research institutes. It is now increasingly being recognised that separation of research and teaching has been at the cost of creating a good research environment in the universities. We have already lost a couple of generations of talent because of the resulting breakdown in the university system. The present academic environment in many universities remains largely unattractive for researchers.

8.1 Facilitating research opportunities in university environment: University reforms are urgently needed and an integral part of this should be aimed at enabling a research culture in universities. A vibrant research atmosphere in the universities will definitely attract more students towards research. The most essential enablers for such an environment include the presence of a facilitating administration, talented faculty and the availability of adequate research facilities.

i. **Conducive administration:** Often university administration itself militates against creating conditions conducive to research. This is largely because of the centralisation of decision-making, restrictions on faculty autonomy and imposition of rigid financial rules that makes "managing" projects very demanding. Administration should be sensitive to academic needs and should aim to encourage and help faculty to deliver better results. In order to enable a favourable administrative environment, it is essential to

- Ensure a capable administration headed by an able Vice Chancellor and Registrar.
- Grant autonomy in making recruitments to achieve higher standards.
- Undertake steps to completely eradicate politics and inbreeding in the system.
- Simplify bureaucratic procedures to make the system more responsive, transparent and efficient.
- Provide technical help or guidance to potential university researchers for writing grant applications.

ii. **Collaboration for sharing resources and expertise:** It is vital to provide researchers with the required infrastructure to carry out their research work. Universities should be given adequate funds for upgrading infrastructure. Often, the lack of funds acts as a hurdle in building and maintaining capital-intensive infrastructure. Hence, sharing of infrastructure with joint responsibility of maintenance among institutes should be greatly encouraged. For better, meaningful sharing of physical as well as intellectual infrastructure among institutions,

- Collaboration should be formalised by entering into alliances, signing MoUs etc.
- New research and academic institutions should be co-located as much as possible.
- Library facilities, access to journals electronically etc., should be provided freely. The upcoming National Knowledge Network should be leveraged for this purpose.
- Top down systemic linkages from elite institutions to universities and to colleges should be established and encouraged to ensure capacity building.
- Joint doctoral research where students are allowed to select guide and co-guides from across academic and research institutions should be undertaken.
- Research institutes can allocate sub-projects to universities to begin with.
- Inter-disciplinary projects involving multiple agencies should be explored.
- UGC should promote conferences with industry and research institutes to enable conversion of ideas into research to be implemented at universities.

iii. **Revamp of Laboratories:** An inseparable part of research and teaching in science and technology is the laboratory. Laboratories play an important role in creating research attitudes, arousing interest and curiosity. They help in gaining experience in scientific methods and learning the process of scientific enquiry. Given the current state of affairs, there is an urgent need to begin an intervention aimed at addressing the quality issue in laboratory training. It is important that even schools are provided with good laboratories and specific attention should be paid to lab training at the undergraduate level.

A major problem with all laboratory experiments is that they do not attempt to challenge the student sufficiently and the whole exercise is conducted at a very rudimentary level. Vital aspects of experiments are not highlighted for the students. The student is typically not involved in important areas of the experiment such as designing or selecting the apparatus, deciding what measurements need to be taken, or what variables need to be controlled. Students are given no opportunity to think for themselves. Laboratory courses thus need a complete revamp.

- There is a need to redefine the objectives with which experiments in a lab are performed, so as to make the laboratory training more concept based rather than 'result based'.
- It should lay emphasis on a student's contribution to planning, execution and analysis of the experiment.
- Error analysis, up to and including calculation of error bars should be essential requirement for each experiment.
- Training should include maintaining lab journals and technical communication skills.

This will help in guiding the talent towards hard-core experimental sciences.

8.2 Changes in the university system to encourage research and good teaching: Both teaching and research should be promoted by creating mechanisms which provide freedom, encourage innovation, and recognise and reward good work. Good teaching plays an important role in encouraging students to pursue an academic career and this aspect is often unrecognised.

- Faculty should have sufficient resources to carry out research as well as teaching activities. Teachers should be especially encouraged to create innovative teaching material and for providing widespread access.
- Good working conditions are absolutely essential in creating a vibrant academic environment.
- Free flow of researchers between industry and academia should be initiated. Sabbaticals to work in industry for academicians and vice versa for industry employees should be instituted. Sufficient provisions should be made for granting sabbaticals to faculty for undertaking research.
- Liberal rules should be looked into for providing faculty members with the flexibility to hold dual appointments between R&D institutions and universities.
- Flexibility in extramurally funded projects to university-based investigators should be given so that they can travel and participate in international meetings/workshops.
- There should be provisions for mentoring of young faculty by established scientists which involves spending brief period at the mentor's laboratory/institute.
- To incentivise research, performance appraisal for promotions should give a higher weightage to research.
- A component of funding should be used for rewarding good teachers and researchers.
- Separate research wing in universities could be developed with as few bureaucratic hurdles as possible. Group recruitment with a specific mandate of developing frontier areas in research should be explored.

Flexibility should be accompanied with a component of accountability, the norms of which should be periodically reviewed.

8.3 Reduction of teaching load: There is a serious shortage of faculty across institutions. Further, with a large number of teaching posts in colleges and universities remaining vacant, there is severe stress on the existing faculty. Also, in the current system, the whole profession of teaching has been severely undermined with contract teaching in colleges becoming more and more acceptable. Teachers have no time or inclination to participate in anything innovative which has led to a lack of involvement and enthusiasm in the whole system, thereby leading to gradual decay and degradation. It is crucial that these issues are addressed and acted upon with the utmost sense of urgency.

Some steps that could be undertaken to reduce teaching load are:

- Duplicity of courses should be avoided. This calls for greater interdepartmental collaboration at the level of individual institution. Inter-institutional collaboration to offer common courses can also be worked out by means of sharing credit.
- Lectures can be delivered to a large class combined with tutorial sessions in smaller batches of students.
- Positions of adjunct faculty must be created and strengthened. People from research institutes, industry, abroad etc., should be invited to teach few courses every semester. Services of retired professors can also be used. This will also bring in much needed fresh inputs from outside into the university.
- PDFs and Ph.D students should be effectively utilised in teaching or teaching assistantships. Specially, bright students should be allowed as well as encouraged to teach junior classes.
- ICT should be used extensively for teaching wherever appropriate. This will give access to quality educational material to a larger section of the student community.
- Issues regarding new recruitment should be sorted out and new appointments should be made as soon as possible. Adequate facilities for research, seed money, housing and incentives for sponsored research should be offered to attract new faculty.

8.4 Data collection, organisation and access: While there are numerous agencies involved in data collection related to different aspects of higher education and research, the organisation of, and access to these data remain largely nebulous and inaccessible.

This should be rectified. It is important to recognise that such data can play a vital role in policy issues, funding, reforms, etc. Data collected should be cogently organised, analysed and made accessible to a wide section of stakeholders. We also emphasise that there should be strong, vibrant and systematic linkages in place between institutions like NISTADS, NUEPA and the actual stakeholders in the system that these institutions are supposed to address. Just as the modern knowledge system necessitates continuous knowledge upgradation of the academic and scientific personnel, it also necessitates that the university administration be continually exposed to best management and administration practices in the university systems around the world. It is thus essential to create a vibrant and proactive platform for the skill and human resource upgradation of the administration personnel.

Recommendation 9: Foster interdisciplinary research, translational research and basic research in social sciences, arts and humanities

Issues: New interdisciplinary areas of research are emerging rapidly in the global context and these are not adequately represented in the country. Almost in all important professional streams like medicine, engineering, management, law etc., actual practice is divorced from research. Despite the tremendous diversity, rich history and cultural heritage, credible basic research in the social sciences is conspicuous by its absence in most universities.

The face of sciences, or for that matter, every discipline today, is changing rapidly. Conventional boundaries between different streams are fast disappearing. Interdisciplinary projects and doctoral programmes in interdisciplinary areas need to be encouraged to propel research in emerging areas. To facilitate this, interdisciplinary faculty options may be created. Interdisciplinary guide and co-guide combinations should be permitted for guidance towards a doctoral thesis. Generous funding should be provided to encourage research in new areas. Appropriate modification of entry barriers to such doctoral programmes should be looked into.

Translational research, especially in the area of medicine and engineering is largely absent in the academic landscape. As a specific example, medical education and research lack in innovation due to the present lacunae in the education system. This field is largely service-oriented with less or no emphasis on research, reasoning and rigour. In order to drive innovation, it is imperative that a medical education straddling programmes from diverse disciplines such as clinical, epidemiological, laboratory, pure sciences (physics, statistics, optics, medical chemistry, organic chemistry, cell biology, biochemistry) be rolled out in front-ranking institutions. An option of having a component of clinical research in Ph.D programmes in the natural sciences should be introduced. This will require co-mentoring of students by faculty drawn both from a surgical/clinical/para-clinical pool and basic biology/physical/engineering sciences. In general, translational research linking practice, field and lab work should be generously funded and encouraged. The existing regulatory structures make this highly difficult and this needs serious intervention.

The training in the humanities has to be reformulated so as to provide a sound, but preliminary, theoretical classical foundation which is in the end solidly geared towards training the student to understand social life as it actually is. It should equip him/her to tackle its vast range of problems in their full magnitude, reinforced by solid and practical training in the field. Integrated courses which allow for a creative and imaginative choice of subjects should be designed. There could also be a component of management education within the humanities stream. Integrated Masters programmes in the humanities that initiate a congruence of many components ranging from communication skills, traditional knowledge systems and practices, disaster management, community life, local government, international diplomacy, governance and conflict, public administration and beyond should be designed. These courses could also be made open to international students, especially from the developing world. The courses should relentlessly focus on the centrality of human living, and represent a thorough amalgam of its constituents, with the first two years devoted to theoretical foundations, the next two years to applied aspects, and the final year to practical field work. Such programmes would also improve the quality of work at the doctoral level.

Industries probably do not have a tangible stake in funding basic research in social sciences. Hence public funding is vital to ensure research and progress in these areas. It should be recognised that knowledge in these areas contributes directly to the well-being of society and also in nurturing a sense of pride about our cultural heritage.

Overall, undergraduate and postgraduate courses should offer a wider bouquet of subjects within a credit and semester system.

Recommendation 10: Promote excellence at research institutes and universities

Issues: Research institutions have maintained a lead in research activities in the country. However, they need to play a larger role in academic activities by means of linkages with universities, etc.

10.1 Research institutes: To promote better managed institutions, it is essential to groom leaders who can take the institutions forward. Governance of the institution should be based on democratic principles. Wider feedback from scientists at all levels should be taken. An independent Board of Governors with respectable members from academia and civil society should be constituted for each institution. Transparency in recruitment of faculty members is necessary and promotions based on appraisals should be encouraged. An efficient administration totally devoid of corruption should be put in place.

The research institute should be nimble and dynamic in developing new areas of research. Industrial consultancy group should be developed in application research-based institutes. This will bring in funds, ideas and much needed efficiency in the system. Better managed institutes should be encouraged to lead and mentor others. Research institutes should be encouraged to work with universities.

The interaction between research laboratories and universities should be institutionalised. It is important to work towards aggregating research institutes and universities rather than creating new stand-alone research institutes. Possible ways of doing this are to convert research institutes into small-sized research universities, aggregating various CSIR research labs under a common university system whose strengths are interdisciplinary teaching and research, co-location of teaching institutions and research institutions, as between IISER and NCL in Pune. Some research institutes which have outlived their utility can be absorbed in regular universities. This will also give much needed access to quality research personnel at universities.

10.2 Periodical reviews: A good periodical review system of departments to support centres of excellence can be undertaken through independent accreditation, out of turn rewards, and conditional grants. Advisory committee of alumni can be constituted for internal review of the departments.

Ph.D thesis, publications, patents, commercialisation of research and peer review can be included as measures of performance review. Quality of faculty should be strictly monitored.

Recommendation 11: Establish more centres of excellence for research and teaching from the undergraduate level for different disciplines across the country

Issues: There is a serious shortage of institutions which provide both good undergraduate training and research environment. Currently, in most of the existing centres of excellence where doctoral studies are undertaken, the focus is largely on the Ph.D and/or Masters programme.

Sound training at the undergraduate level is vital for students wishing to embark on an academic career. Often, students entering a doctoral programme at elite institutions are found to have an inadequate background for research even after having completed a Master's degree. A high quality four year programme should be rolled out in select institutions[3] which will enable direct entry to a Ph.D programme, thereby effectively reducing the total time spent on doctoral study. A new system of research-based universities starting at the undergraduate level focusing both on teaching and research is essential to create the right environment needed to nurture research. Existing universities or research institutes may be transformed into a smaller research-based universities. Smaller universities ease administrative hurdles. Universities without attached colleges have a higher chance of developing a good research culture. Excellent resources and infrastructure should be created. Also, adequate communication channels should be established with existing universities to provide holistic (broad based) education. The Government has taken a step in the right direction by starting Indian Institutions of Science Education and Research (IISERs) in the field of sciences. Corporate houses could be involved in starting some of these new universities. Research universities for thrust areas can be created in public-private partnership mode.

However, some caution needs to be observed while setting up new research universities.

---

3. See NKC's Publication on "Attracting More Talented Students to Maths and Sciene", Pages 9 and 22, *http://www.knowledgecommission.gov.in/downloads/documents/nkc_maths.pdf*

- An able director is essential for developing a new institute.
- These universities should not become isolated islands of excellence.
- Faculty will remain the most serious issue in expansion and appropriate steps should be taken in this direction.
- Serious investigations into the existing system should be undertaken in order to identify the gaps and to ensure that mistakes are not repeated.

Simultaneously, a comprehensive process of repair and reforms within the existing system should be initiated. This can take the initial form of identifying select departments/colleges/universities with a potential for substantial improvement. Funds should be invested in upgrading and monitoring the progress of these. Vital components of this exercise are transparency, academic autonomy and establishment of systematic linkages.

Colleges within universities which are engaged in quality teaching and research projects should be encouraged and supported with free access to funds, investment of infrastructure, more academic and administrative autonomy. A useful metric for evaluation of colleges could be the placement of its students at research and academic institutions within and outside of the country. On the whole, there should be an overall empowerment of colleges providing quality undergraduate education.

Recommendation 12: Augment available sources of funding, optimise allocation and provide greater flexibility towards utilisation

Issues: Funding remains a key issue in facilitating quality research in most universities. The low quantum of funds, the cumbersome process of acquiring them and the lack of fund raising capabilities in the university/faculty members have severely hampered growth of research.

Concerted efforts are needed in funding research. Various sources of funding should thus be explored.

- Large scale public funding is necessary for nationally relevant research projects.
- Recruiting companies should contribute towards university research funds. Industries should be encouraged to sponsor and collaborate on research projects. Laboratories named after sponsoring companies can be established. Also, Sponsored Chairs by industry can increase the number of faculty and researchers without any additional cost to the university.
- Universities should formulate strategies to convert research findings into commercial applications, thus generating funds. Alternate means like consultancy, online courses, etc., should be explored. Universities should also establish and leverage alumni network.
- Government funding agencies should proactively encourage and guide faculty members from universities to submit research proposals. A system of open competition for research grants should be developed.
- Collaborative funding between countries and universities should be encouraged.

To increase research funding in the longer term, alumni/corporate fellowships should be looked at. For instance, NASSCOM has developed a public-private partnership framework under which fellowships could be provided to students. Collaboration with foreign universities in which students and co-guides get a chance to attend foreign universities has been worked out as part of the initiative. Academia should evolve strategies to increase such funding avenues substantially. Such initiatives also have the merit of wider industry academia interaction.

Primarily however, professional financial management is needed at universities. There should be in-built flexibility and lenient guidelines for utilisation of funds. It is also important that faculty in research institutes and universities are trained in the utilisation of funds.

Recommendation 13: Encourage private participation in research activities by fostering industry-academia interaction

Issues: The two worlds, academy and industry, are viewed as divergent because of perceived vested interests which often leads to mistrust.

It is important that there is a change in this mindset and that new ways of establishing and institutionalising permanent linkages are explored. The value of domain knowledge expertise is bound to increase as the economy matures and knowledge gets integrated as an important component of the economy. Industry should take cognizance of this and should support doctoral programmes in both basic and applied research disciplines. Further, social sciences can contribute to innovation in business processes, and in the overall understanding and progress of the society. Industry can participate in academic research activities by.

- Investing in infrastructure building.
- Inviting students to spend a semester in industry.
- Allowing people from industry to take special lectures in universities.
- Getting involved in monitoring and updating curriculum.
- Offering research projects to people in academia either alone or by collaborating with other industries.
- Conducting or participating in science fairs, seminars, workshops and popularisation programmes etc.
- Sponsoring research in universities directly. As an example, TCS sponsors research projects in various colleges instead of giving one time infrastructure grant. This ensures more than just monetary support and leads to healthier interaction.

At the same time, academia should open its doors to industry. Lateral entry provision should be facilitated for those interested in academics with a background in industry. It should also facilitate continuing education of industry employees by designing and delivering short courses. Appropriate methodologies should be developed to carry out all collaborative efforts. It is essential to clarify issues such as sharing of intellectual property rights. Industry associations must facilitate interaction and collaborations between industry and academia.

A culture of research in the private sector is essential to develop more prospects for doctorates and increase efficiency and diversity in the system. To encourage Indian as well as foreign industries to carry out research activities in the country,

- Industry should be incentivised to use indigenous technology.
- New science and technology parks in the private sector should provide research and development facilities at subsidised rates for all companies.
- Knowledge hubs should be created in each state, which should provide space and other facilities like patent cell, entrepreneurship cell. Multinational companies which aim at creating large research centres in India can pilot launch their operations in the knowledge hubs. Knowledge hubs will facilitate market driven research and product development.

Part D: Fostering a global outlook in research

Research as an activity requires exchange of ideas and sharing of knowledge at a broader level. In today's globalising world, there is a pressing need for India to provide its students and faculty with international and multicultural exposure.

Recommendation 14: Attract NRI/PIO scientists by providing attractive opportunities in the country

Issues: Researchers often leave India for a better environment that offers variety of choices, opportunities and intellectual freedom. Such researchers find it difficult to return back because of the absence of an enabling and nurturing system in the country.

Provide flexibility in the system: Currently, the rigidity of entry in the university system repels the scientists who might otherwise consider coming back to India.

- The system should be made more flexible to encourage talent at all levels. Respect for talent rather than "seniority" should be built into the system. To attract the best people, it becomes important to offer them positions that are professionally better than what they currently have in their country of residence.
- Positions of Research Professors with advancement capability based on research excellence and not age should be created. Young scientists should get equal independence as their senior counterparts.
- Adjunct positions in industry and research laboratories should be created for inviting NRIs.

- Institutional mechanisms should be created to allow scholars to go back and forth and to freely invite other researchers and collaborators. In case, the scientist returns back, he/she should be encouraged to continue to maintain contact with the researchers in the lab and guide them.
- The system should also enable appointment at the level of Director, Dean, Vice-Chancellors and Technical/Scientific advisors to Union and/or state government. At the same time, there should be effective monitoring mechanisms to ensure accountability and to prevent misuse of such positions.

Offer more resources and create nurturing environment: Creating a challenging and excellence-oriented environment with appropriate resources is vital.

- Substantial amounts of "start-up funds" for setting up labs and hiring post-doctoral students should be made available to the researchers. The researchers should also be given freedom to generate their own funds.
- A congenial environment to foster independent thinking and working is a must. This requires providing facilitating administration as well as maintaining best standards in research.

Recommendation 15: Formalise collaboration with foreign institutions and researchers

Issues: Failure to attract foreign students and collaborate with foreign universities and researchers has led to an absence of multicultural and international exposure for both Indian students and faculty.

Collaborative programmes with foreign universities and research institutions will encourage faculty and students to learn and exchange ideas and practices on latest developments.

- Indian scientists should be given generous travel grants to attend international conferences. Further, they should be given adequate and comprehensive support to organise international meetings.
- Visa procedures for research exchanges should be simplified. Just as credible business travellers are granted multiple entry visas valid over a longer period, similar facilities for scientific visas can be looked into. The post of Academic Attachés in various consulates should be created and filled. They can play an important role in facilitating scientific exchanges between countries. In addition, this will also provide an alternative employment avenue for people with a research background. Multiple entry provision for foreign researchers would also benefit frequent collaboration by considerable reduction in the hassles of obtaining visas.
- Joint supervision of doctoral thesis is one area where cooperation should be promoted. Length and type of exchange programmes should be so designed that our faculty as well as research students gain adequate benefits.
- Other forms of collaboration which could be looked at are joint degree programmes with foreign universities.
- Initiatives should be taken to invite faculty from abroad to not only give special guest lectures but also teach partial or full courses.
- A public/private non-profit corporation like Carnegie, Ford and Rhodes Scholarships of high brand value can be created to pay for faculty exchanges from both industry and research institutes. Individuals who are capable of mobilising funding for such corporations could be chosen to head such institutions.
- Indian institutions should tap the benefits of multi-institution networks by participating in the good ones that already exist or by creating such platforms themselves. The McDonnell International Scholars Academy and McDonnell Academy Global Energy and Environmental Partnership at Washington University in St. Louis are examples of such networks. The two academies collaborate with select universities from across the world. They provide opportunities to the partners to interact, discuss and learn from each other by working on collaborative projects.

Many funding agencies from the developed countries are conscious of the demographic advantage that India has and are keen to participate in joint initiatives in research, training, etc. Funding and collaborative opportunities for the younger people should be widely publicised and national funding agencies should play a proactive role in directly linking up scientists and such diverse international funding agencies. Collaborations should be based on win-win models and should facilitate a need-based, two-way flow of knowledge. One must also ensure the following:

- Intellectual property is well protected.
- Collaborations are based on synergy and not brand name alone.
- Students are not just made to do repetitive work without any meaningful exchange of knowledge.
- Students spend considerable amount of time in the home institutions.

To conclude, excellent infrastructure, favourable research environment, reforms in Higher Education—especially university reforms—and increased funding with sustained investment are all needed to attract students to doctoral programmes. In this context, there is an urgent need to give special attention to the dire situation of the lack of qualified faculty, and to overall spark national interest and attention towards academics. Any initiative or investment in this direction may not produce tangible results in the short term. However, given the enormity of the problem, further procrastination will only lead to greater damage of the system which will render future repairs vastly more expensive, both financially and academically. Hence it is imperative that the Government acts with a sense of urgency and embarks on the remedial path immediately.

III

Creation

19 National Science and Social Science Foundation

Indian scientists made significant contributions to the advancement of science and technology in the 1950s and 60s. This was possible because of the support successive governments extended to science education and research. Numerous research and development institutions were established across the country. However, over the years, in spite of continuing government support, both the quality and quantity of the research output from India has been on the decline. It is necessary to examine the reasons for this decline and implement remedial measures.

One widening realisation of the last few decades has been that knowledge is a continuum and the boundaries between disciplines are increasingly becoming blurred, tenuous and indefinable.

The following major causes for the current crisis in Indian research deserve attention:

- **Lack of interaction:** There is very rigid compartmentalisation of natural and social sciences; as a result, there is little or no interaction between researchers in natural sciences and social sciences.
- **Lack of long-term vision:** Research topics of long-term relevance and importance are not taken up as support tends to be for the duration of three to five years because of our planning process.
- **Lack of differential remuneration:** The principle of differential remuneration based on performance and output is not followed to reward those who perform well and chastise those who do not.
- **Lack of scientific methods:** Current teaching methodologies at school, college and university levels do not inculcate a scientific temper in the students.

NKC is aware that the Science Advisory Council has recently suggested the establishment of a National Science Foundation to address some of these and other issues confronting research. It supports this suggestion, with some modifications that will make the solution more comprehensive and practicable.

NKC feels that in view of the disappearing boundaries between various disciplines of knowledge and knowledge emerging as a continuum, India should set up a National Science and Social Science Foundation (NSSSF) which will look at all knowledge as one seamless entity. We will be the first country to set up such an avant garde organisation—and rightfully so, given our 5,000-year-old tradition of broad-based knowledge.

The objectives of the proposed NSSSF will be to:

a) Suggest policy initiatives to make India a leader in the creation and use of new knowledge in all areas of natural, physical, agricultural, health and social sciences, with emphasis on those areas which cut across traditional disciplines;

b) Ensure that science and technology are maximally used for betterment of the lives of our people;

c) Develop a scientific temper.

The governing board of the Foundation should have a chairman, a vice-chairman and 8-10 members. The chairmanship and vice-chairmanship of the NSSSF should rotate between the sciences and the social sciences, ensuring that if the chairperson is a scientist, the vice-chairperson should be a social scientist and vice-versa.

The chairman, vice-chairman and members of the governing board should be appointed by the Prime Minister and should satisfy the following criteria:

- High level of professional competence.
- High national and international reputation.
- Professional and personal integrity and honesty that are beyond reproach.
- Evidence of absence of any bias or prejudice.
- A strong social commitment, loyalty to the country and concern for others.
- Commitment to social, professional and financial accountability.
- Someone who combines erudition with articulation.
- Courage of convictions.
- Ability to listen to other people's views and modify one's own if reason demands that.

The budget of the NSSSF should be Rs. 1,250 crore a year; which will allow it to fund between 200 and 400 outstanding, long-term (5-10 years), extremely carefully selected projects that have the potential of making India a leader. We should expect at least a 20 per cent success rate. The NSSSF should work towards having at least three to four Indian scientists and/or social scientists produce work in six years which should be worthy of a Nobel Prize. The NSSSF will set up a worldwide review system involving some of the best known scholars around the world for approval of the projects that it supports. The project-funding activity will, however, be only one (though a major one) of the activities of the NSSSF. Some of the major activities and responsibilities of the NSSSF will be to:

- Identify major unsolved problems in various areas of science and social sciences and individuals, groups and/or institutions who can work on them to provide India leadership.
- Identify and set up studies on: (a) relationships of science with other areas of human concern such as economics, sociology, politics, art and literature and vice versa, and (b) social, economic, political, legal, moral and ethical implications of advances in science and technology.
- Identify and set up studies on futuristic interdisciplinary areas in real time.
- Recommend steps that would help inculcate a scientific temper amongst the people of the country as envisioned in the Constitution.
- Help the Government to set up systems that would remove bureaucratic hurdles, increase professional, social and financial accountability; and recognise that creativity in science and social sciences like in all creative endeavours is non-hierarchical.
- Identify and set up studies to find solutions to the problems of the poor and the underprivileged by translating the advances in science and technology.
- Recommend strategies (scientific, technological and social) that would provide additional employment in the rural sector and help set up mechanisms for their implementation with the cooperation of government, industry and NGOs.
- Recommend steps for optimising the use of our natural resources (including marine resources).
- Help set up systems for documentation, standardisation where necessary, validation and use of our traditional knowledge. Ensure that the custodians and providers of such knowledge and wisdom are identified, are involved in the process and share benefits accruing from the use of such knowledge.
- Set up policies for international cooperation in science and social sciences.
- Serve as a platform for the coming together of various departments, organisations and agencies of the Government that are concerned with scientific and social science research and related developmental work, to optimally utilise their collective knowledge and capabilities.

- Set up a mechanism for close interaction between state-funded scientific and social science organisations, private sector and responsible and effective NGOs.
- Set up a system that would ensure that appropriate credit comes to India, the Indian institutions and the Indian scientists and social scientists for their work, and that their work is duly publicised in and outside India (e.g., through our embassies and missions).
- Formulate ethical guidelines for administration of science, doing science, communicating science, and using science; and a system of punishment when those guidelines are compromised. Set up similar guidelines for social sciences.
- Recommend setting up of new organisations or institutions that would help advance these objectives and close down existing institutions which have outlived their utility or are not functioning satisfactorily.
- Prepare and present to the Government of India, periodic reports on the state of science and social sciences in India in the global context, and suggest steps that may be taken to improve it.

20 Legal Framework for Public Funded Research

The National Knowledge Commission (NKC) while deliberating on issues related to the creation and application of knowledge recognises the need to provide impetus to government-funded research and to translate this knowledge into relevant and useful applications to benefit the widest cross-section of people. NKC's consultation with diverse stakeholders has revealed that there is a need to provide incentives to increase innovations, collaborations, licencing and commercialisation.

It is therefore, recommended to enact legislation that creates a uniform legal framework for the government-funded research and gives universities and research institutions ownership and patent rights. This will create an enabling environment for them to commercialise such inventions through licencing arrangements where inventors would also be allowed to receive a share of the royalty. Conferring ownership rights on universities and linking such ownership with the patent system and the market, will make research more attractive and in the process bring about a radical change in the research landscape in India. The proposed enactment could also incorporate important safeguards for exceptional circumstances where the government could be given 'march in rights' to protect the public good.

Uniformity of policy for inventions generated out of government-funded research will provide incentives to various stakeholders as follows:

- Government: The government could retain the right to a non-exclusive, non-transferable, irrevocable paid-up licence to practice the invention throughout the world. It could also have the responsibility and power to monitor the implementation of the act by a provision that requires concerned parties to report to the government on an annual basis on matters pertaining to utilisation of the invention. Since the patent applications would be filed and owned by the relevant institutions, the government would be spared from bearing the costs of filing applications. The government could also be given the right to own the invention where the party decides not to retain title or fails to file the requisite patent application. Finally, 'march in rights' accorded to the government in certain situations involving the public good as well as exceptions for circumstances involving, *inter alia*, national security and defence imperatives would help assuage fears on the same.
- Universities/R&D: For universities and research institutions, revenue generating incentives lie in ownership and control over the fruits of research generated out of government funds. This should encourage filing patents in their own name and entering into commercialisation processes with industry. Further, the inventor, through profit sharing of royalties from licences, would also get rewarded accordingly. The proposed enactment could also provide that the balance of any royalties or income earned after payment of expenses, be ploughed back for scientific research and education.
- Industry: A higher degree of industry participation in university research will result due to clear legal title, a uniform legal regime for all government funded research, commercial gain through collaborative arrangements, opportunities to obtain exclusive licences and new business opportunities for the new inventions.
- People: Finally, the taxpayer, whose resources are used in government funding of research, will also get the benefit of inventions, in the form of products and services once they are commercialised and made available in the market.

Issues that need special attention in drafting the proposed legislation are:

- Calculating exact ratios in which revenues will be divided and the percentage made available to various stakeholders including the actual inventor.

- Understanding national security implications where they arise and carving out exceptions in such situations.
- Identifying specific guidelines, rules and existing provisions of laws that need to be overridden to bring a uniform legislation in place for inventions arising out of government-funded research.
- Establishing the precise nature of various licencing arrangements as well as conditions governing the grant of exclusive licences where applicable.
- Clarifying situations requiring the invocation of 'march in rights' for government intervention and clarification of exceptional situations to the general right of ownership.
- Determining whether plant varieties come under the scope of 'inventions' in light of India's own patent and plant varieties, legislation and analysing the relationships between the proposed act and India's own patent and plant varieties acts.

There are precedents for such legislation such as the American enactment entitled the Patent and Trademark Law Amendments Act, enacted in 1980 and commonly known as the Bayh-Dole Act. It is perhaps significant to note that in the United States, before the Bayh-Dole Act was enacted, the country's federal agencies owned about 28,000 patents, out of which only 5 per cent were licenced to industry to develop commercial products. Subsequent to the enactment of the said act, there has been a massive rise in the number of patents filed by and granted to universities, the number of universities involved in patenting and licencing of inventions, and in the number of new companies that have been set up on the basis of new inventions licenced by universities. There have also been innovative breakthroughs in the form of inventions, technologies and processes, arising from university research. Economic activity of a scale running into billions of dollars has been generated, further creating new jobs in the economy.

In NKC's view, introduction of legislation generally along the lines of the Bayh-Dole Act, while keeping in mind India's specific interests, is necessary to help scientific research develop far-reaching innovations, generate employment and function as a vehicle of significant economic growth.

21 Intellectual Property Rights

A nation's future and its ability to compete in the global market depend greatly on how it generates new ideas and innovates in science and technology. Intellectual property creation and protection are critical issues in global knowledge-based competition. Countries like China, Japan and Korea have improved their respective IPR systems through intense capacity building efforts, with a view to achieving greater innovation. It has become imperative for India to scale up efforts to build a world class IPR infrastructure and ensure that IPR is used in the best national interest for more extensive innovative research, technology transfer, wealth creation and overall benefit of society. NKC's consultations with various stakeholders have helped to identify some key areas that will facilitate such systemic reform. Some of these areas involve the granting of product and process patents, in which both the configuration of the state mechanism for patent examination and the systematisation of a substantive perspective of patent examination, keeping both treaty obligations and national interests in mind are crucial issues. Other critical areas involve alternative non-patent modalities for the creation and sharing of knowledge and inventions. Below, one area, namely, the configuration of the patent examination mechanisms, is discussed, with some reference to allied issues in patent utilisation.

1. Modernisation of IP Offices

The processes in the IP offices need to become more accessible and user-friendly and therefore, the ultimate objective of all efforts to modernise the patent offices must be to facilitate more transparency and procedural ease for the inventor as well as the common man. NKC is aware of the initiatives proposed by the Ministry of Commerce and Industry in this regard, especially those pertaining to modernisation of infrastructure, computerisation, digitisation, e-filing, re-engineering of procedures with information technology integration, human resource development, efficiency, transparency of procedures and creation of an operational environment of global standards. The need to be sensitive to the needs of the everyday citizen is crucial if the IP offices have to transform themselves into service providers, delivering solutions with the greatest efficiency and highest quality standards. In this respect, some suggestions are as follows:

- The patent offices must be adequately e-enabled in real time with adequate search facilities so that all its transactions are transparent and publicly accessible.
- The examination procedures, practices and decisions in the IP offices should be streamlined and consistent
- A new detailed and clear manual of the examination procedure and practice, accompanied by full text versions of all the relevant IP laws of the country, should be created, periodically updated and made available to the public, in soft and hard copy. Interested stakeholders, particularly including civil society as the major stakeholder, must be involved in its preparation. This is particularly important since new Indian patent examination procedures will need to be devised keeping both treaty obligations and national interests in mind, and the creation of an adversarial process of patent examination will be crucial in these procedures.
- There must be an educational section for public awareness on IP (including the current status of IP law on various topics) made available in the public domain in all official languages of the country.
- The patent granting procedure must involve adequate web-based notification of an application with complete details to give sufficient opportunity for any pre-grant objections to be filed. It is particularly essential to provide e-access in real

time to all steps of a patent application, from the detailed patent description, examination reports at each stage and all amendments introduced at various points, in order to maintain complete transparency.

- There is urgent need to develop a comprehensive patent database that provides the latest information on patents, including patent applications and decisions of patent offices. At the same time, the patent offices must have access to relevant international databases and search engines, including databases with prior art literature.
- To achieve the best global standards in quality and access, the IP offices should aim to become International Search Authority (ISA) and International Preliminary Examination Authority (IPEA) under the PCT and to this end, aim to conform to the PCT standards in respect of possession or access to minimum documentation, number of administrative and technically qualified staff and IT support systems.
- Efforts should also be made to develop quantifiable indices for measuring, monitoring and managing quality and efficiency.
- To ensure that the services of the IP offices reach the common people engaged in rural technologies, artisanry, crafts and traditional knowledge, there should be special schemes and establishments in the patent offices to deal with claims involving the creation and protection of traditional knowledge in its various forms. Since ensuring effective and competent legal representation is a critical problem for such groups, mechanisms should be evolved that incentivise such representation by the best patent lawyers in the country.
- For each sector of highly technical patents, it may be necessary to constitute specific empowered committees of experts as part of the patent evaluation process in the patent office to decide on the suitability of granting a patent, in accordance with the provisions of the law. These committees must adhere to strict time-bound procedures of examination and sufficient safeguards must also be maintained to ensure confidentiality and prevent any subversion of the process.

2. Incentive Mechanisms to Attract and Retain Quality Talent

An incentive-driven system of human resources management, including fast track career structures for deserving staff should be developed within the IP offices to attract and retain competent personnel. As the IP offices will be competing with the private industry to attract qualified scientists and engineers, they will need to reach out proactively to institutions of eminence. Candidates applying for the post of a patent examiner must be tested on a combination of skills, such as scientific/technical knowledge, practical experience of such knowledge, critical analysis, written and oral communication skills and problem-solving. Further, to ensure the availability of trained personnel in all technology sectors, the appointment of such personnel should be done periodically in a manner that ensures adequate proportional representation of each sector, by considering as an illustrative benchmark, the volume of applications and grants in the sector.

In order to deal with the existing problem of attrition of trained examiners to scientific/technical institutions and the private sector, the Flexible Complementing Scheme which has been applied to scientific and technical group "A" posts should also be implemented for the technical staff of the IP offices. Furthermore, pay scales of patent examiners should be increased for those who successfully undergo IPR training. Additionally, a fast track career should be provided to examiners who consistently perform exceptionally better than average. To this end, a transparent annual confidential reporting system should be introduced. In this context, it is important that performance in IP offices must be measured on the basis of turnaround time for applications and decisions as well as the sustainability and tenability of the decisions made, and not on the basis of the rate of rejection/ acceptance of applications.

3. Training and Human Resources Development for IP Offices

There is need to intensify IPR training efforts in the IP offices and Intellectual Property Training Institute (IPTI), including induction sessions for new staff, mid-career courses and regular exposure to global best practices in IPR, wherever available, keeping in mind the best national interest. At the same time, there must be relevant safeguard procedures in place to avoid potential conflict of interest issues between trainer and trainee. The overriding aim of IPR training is to ensure legal and technological competence consistent with the best international standards. For training of IP office personnel, an in-house Professional Development Committee (PDC) should also be formed. The PDC should identify training requirements of the IP offices and collaborate with IPTI to impart up-to-date IP training. Steps could also be taken to invite Indian scientists located in India and abroad who have experience in patent examination processes to participate in training initiatives with Indian patent examiners. However, in-country expertise must be urgently developed for training and sensitising IP regulatory staff in the new India-specific treaty-compliant patent examination procedures that will be required for the new IP offices.

The IPTI should, with active involvement from stakeholders, prepare a comprehensive induction-training course for new patent examiners on various IP topics such as patent searches (including international databases), substantive requirements for patentability of an application, examination procedure as well as drafting of objections to the grant of a patent, where a list of standard clauses of objections could be developed. Such a course could be of duration of three/six months. The course material should be standardised and could be made available on the Intranet. Once again, procedures for maintaining the adversarial nature of the new India-specific treaty-compliant patent examination process must form a major component of these programmes.

After the completion of the induction-training programme, a senior patent examiner could be assigned to each examiner as a training officer who would act as a mentor by supervising work, providing further training on a case-by-case basis and eventually reporting on the work of the examiner. Such training could last for a period of about six months. The IPTI should also provide advanced level courses in examination and international IPR issues after about a year to 18 months, including courses on pre-grant and post-grant opposition procedures.

The IPTI should also collaborate with legal associations and organisations to set up specialised certificate and diploma courses in IPR and hold qualifying examinations for a patent attorney to act before the IP offices. This would ensure that highest professional standards are maintained. Appropriate public-private partnerships (PPPs) could also be evolved for this purpose.

4. IPR Education and Development of IPR Cells

Educational efforts on IPR must go beyond the IP offices and reach out to scientists and engineers working in national research institutes, universities, industry, the Bar, as well as to researchers and students, not just in the metropolitan areas but also in the smaller towns and rural areas of the country. Law schools throughout the country must also design specialised up-to-date courses and programmes on IPR and the process of creating faculty chairs on the subject must also be intensified through better incentives for academia. Business schools also need to incorporate IPR dimensions in their curricula.

There is also an urgent need to set up IPR cells in major scientific and educational institutions in the country with trained staff, competent in the legal and technical aspects of relevant disciplines.

5. Establishment of a New Institution for Cutting Edge Policy Expertise

The sheer complexity and scale of IPR capacity building for the 21st century require an independent world-class institute exclusively devoted to the field of IP. Once established, a National Institute of Intellectual Property Management (NIIPM), located in New Delhi, would be responsible for imparting training on a regular basis to various stakeholders, conducting cutting edge research, serving as a think tank to advise the government on IPR issues as well as conducting public awareness on IPR. Crucial parameters to set up the NIIPM include the establishment of an infrastructure of international standards, development of human resource expertise and aspects relating to finance. Initially, the NIIPM could be funded by the Central government. Gradually through public-private partnerships and other innovative financial mechanisms, the revenue generated from training programmes would aim at ensuring self-sufficiency in the long run. The mandate of such an institution must involve policy research on the procedures to be adopted for patent examination so as to yield crucial input for periodic revision of these procedures. Also, this mandate must transcend the limited purview of the patent-oriented process for intellectual property management and must address itself innovatively to systematic exploration of other modalities for social utilisation of knowledge and inventions through structures such as copyrights and commons.

6. IPR Tribunal, Special Rules of Procedure and Judicial Training

Efficient enforcement is an indispensable facet of a strong IPR regime. IPR has emerged as a specialised area within law with urgent demands for speedy and efficient disposal of cases. It has become necessary to create a separate tribunal with jurisdiction over disputes in all aspects of IPR and develop a pool of competent judges who are trained in the legal as well as the technical aspects of IPR. The IPR tribunal should be designed to deal with the appeals arising from the decisions of IP offices. In case of appeals where issues to be decided involve technical considerations, the tribunal should consist of three judges having considerable experience in law, where at least two of them also have technical qualifications.

To avoid undue delays and legal uncertainties, detailed and streamlined procedures with fixed time limits should be chalked out for the IPR tribunal after consultations with stakeholders, including civil society. There should be a strict adherence to these procedures.

Training of the judiciary in IPR needs to be viewed as an essential IPR enforcement issue. The National Judicial Academy is already engaged in training judges on a variety of areas, including IPR. Such training efforts have to be intensified and the establishment of the NIIPM would be a significant step in this regard.

7. Protection of Traditional Knowledge (TK) through Traditional Knowledge Digital Library (TKDL) and Promoting Incentives for Wealth Creation from TK

The creation of the TKDL database is a significant effort to codify and classify traditional knowledge of the country. While there is increasing recognition of the important role of the TKDL to prevent misappropriation and grant of 'wrong patents' as well as to provide incentives for innovation and wealth creation, the key challenge here is to ensure its effective utilisation to achieve these objectives.

The Government of India has also already taken steps to allow access of the TKDL database to some international patent offices under nondisclosure agreements for the purpose of search and examination. Steps need to be taken for the use and incorporation of TKDL into the minimum search documentation lists of International Search Authorities and other patent offices while processing patent applications. Further, to prevent misappropriation and to facilitate more transparency, it is also necessary to disclose and declare all pertinent sources of information relating to TK in patent applications.

To create incentives for commercialisation of TK, companies should be able to access the TKDL upon payment of adequate user fees and subject to the condition that inventions arising out of the TKDL would require royalty sharing with the Government. The Government should also take active steps to encourage investments in TK through collaborative efforts with industry and civil society. Innovative financial mechanisms should be evolved so that the revenue generated by the government from commercialisation of TKDL and other commercially synergistic initiatives is used to create a TK Development Fund. The proceeds of the fund would be used to conserve TK generally, conduct research on TK, expand the TKDL and benefit communities that have contributed to the creation of TK.

8. IP and Small and Medium Enterprises (SMEs)

It is crucial at the governmental level to invest in the IP needs of SMEs. There is need to facilitate better awareness on the strategic aspects of creating, managing, protecting and leveraging IP as a tool to further business opportunities and enable wealth creation. SMEs are emerging as crucial players in the global knowledge economy and unlike larger firms, they may not have the necessary resources to make the best use of IP. In this context, it is essential for special awareness campaigns for SMEs so that they are made fully aware of the various implications of IP and optimally translates such understandings into their everyday business practices.

9. Global Technology Acquisition Fund

The strategic positioning of India as a technology superpower will depend not just on development indigenous technological expertise but also on the ability to make crucial technology acquisitions in the global market. Countries like Japan and Korea have successfully used such acquisitions to expand their IP portfolio and some Indian companies, especially in the pharmaceuticals and biotech sectors, have already been engaged in such acquisitions. However, such examples are sporadic and there is need for a national strategy on technology acquisition, with the aim of leapfrogging our expertise in key areas. A Global Technology Acquisition Fund, created by the Central government, could be a significant step forward in facilitating such acquisitions, especially for the SMEs. The funds could be parked with a financial institution or a special purpose vehicle

(SPV) could be created to manage the fund, with members of industry and S&T invited as board members. Relevant financial instruments, including support in the form of loans and equity, could be evolved, for such technology-intensive acquisition.

10. IPR and New Technologies

It has become imperative for technical institutions, scientists, examiners and other relevant stakeholders to be fully aware of the IPR dimensions of new and rapidly changing technologies, especially in ICT, biotechnology, nano-technology, electronics, engineering, bioinformatics, etc. There is therefore, need for high-powered expert bodies that can help identify IPR issues arising out of each of such areas, with a view to evolving necessary IPR policies that would optimally foster greater global competitiveness for Indian industry as well as ensure faster innovation, wealth creation and overall development.

22 Innovation in India

The National Knowledge Commission identified the role of innovation as one of the key factors in India's economic growth. Innovation is a process to achieve measurable value enhancement in any commercial activity, through introduction of new or improved goods, services, operational and organisational processes. It is a significant factor in facilitating competitiveness, improvement in market share and quality as well as reduction in costs.

NKC conducted a nationwide survey among large firms, as well as small and medium enterprises to explore the role being played by innovation in fuelling India's economic growth. The NKC survey reveals that innovation intensity (i.e., the percentage of revenue derived from products/services which are less than three years old) has increased for large firms as well as small and medium enterprises. The strategic prioritisation of innovation as a factor critical to growth and competitiveness has also achieved significant prominence since the start of economic liberalisation in India. The NKC survey further highlights crucial parameters at the firm level that have enabled some firms to be more innovative than others, including the role of structural frameworks and processes. It is expected that dissemination of the survey results across India's industrial spectrum will highlight best practices in industry and thereby also generate catalytic impact on a wider scale.

However, it is pertinent to point out that the most critical external barrier for both large firms and small and medium enterprises is skill shortage arising out of lack of emphasis on industrial innovation, problem-solving, design, experimentation, etc., in the education curricula. There is also need for more effective collaboration between industry, universities and R&D institutions. Systematic reform of the higher education system (including skill-based marketable vocational education) in India is essential to develop the required intellectual capital as well as generate effective synergies among industry, government, the educational system, the R&D environment and the consumer. Innovation is a complex activity that requires widespread interaction across the entire economy, from the grassroots to the large firm level. We recommend a comprehensive campaign to address these issues and to spur efforts to make India a global leader in innovation.

Executive Summary

Introduction

While literature on innovation has been growing in recent times, the NKC survey on innovation is perhaps the first detailed and in-depth quantitative and qualitative survey on innovation in India (as defined more broadly than R&D) using firm level aggregate statistical data on a nationwide scale, with a sample that includes the top industry leaders as well as a large number of small and medium enterprises (SMEs), and across varied industrial profiles, ranging from manufacturing and services to diversified businesses. It is expected that the survey will provide feedback and information on current innovation trends to firms as well as generate necessary catalysing effects for business innovation to take place in India on an even larger scale, thus ensuring sustained innovation-led economic growth in the coming years.

NKC defines innovation in the following manner for the purposes of this survey:

"Innovation is defined as a process by which varying degrees of measurable value enhancement is planned and achieved, in any commercial activity. This process may be breakthrough or incremental, and it may occur systematically in a company or sporadically; it may be achieved by:

- introducing new or improved goods or services and/or
- implementing new or improved operational processes and/or
- implementing new or improved organisational/managerial processes

in order to improve market share, competitiveness and quality, while reducing costs."

Innovation and competitiveness have a dynamic, mutual relationship. Innovation thrives in a competitive environment and in turn, plays a key role in the achievement of such an environment. Innovation generates economic value, new jobs in the economy and cultures of entrepreneurship. By virtue of its relationship with competitiveness, innovation emerges as a factor in promoting economic growth.

Given the fact that the Indian economy is growing at 6-8 per cent per year while exports are growing at 30 per cent Cumulative Annual Growth Rate (CAGR), and many Indian firms are successfully competing against international firms and brands, it can be concluded that this has been made possible by a combination of factors, including enabling environment, rising capital and labour productivity as well as improved quality of goods and services at lower costs.

In the growth of the Indian economy, innovation is emerging as a key driver, although this may neither be apparent nor readily visible. In this respect, one of the aims of this study by NKC is to understand the role played by innovation in India as a driver of such growth.

Key Results

1. Increase in Growth and Innovation

a. 'Innovation intensity' (i.e., the percentage of revenue derived from products/services which are less than three years old) has increased for large firms and SMEs, with SMEs registering a greater increase in innovation intensity than large firms. 42 per cent of the large firms and 17 per cent of the SMEs are also 'highly innovative' firms (i.e., firms who have introduced 'new to world' innovations during the course of business in the last five years).

b. Nearly half of the large firms and SMEs attribute more than 25 per cent of change in the following factors to innovation: increase in competitiveness, increase in profitability, reduction in costs and increase in market share. For large firms,

Innovation and competitiveness have a dynamic, mutual relationship. Innovation thrives in a competitive environment and in turn, plays a key role in the achievement of such an environment. Innovation generates economic value, new jobs in the economy and cultures of entrepreneurship.

innovation has the most significant impact on competitiveness, while for SMEs, innovation has the most significant impact on increase in market share.

c. Seventeen per cent of the large firms rank innovation as the top strategic priority and 75 per cent rank it among the top 3 priorities. All the large firms in our sample agree (of which 81 per cent strongly agree) that innovation has gained importance as being critical to growth and competitiveness since the start of economic liberalisation in India. All the large firms agree (of which nearly half strongly agree) that they cannot survive and grow without investment in innovation. An overwhelming 96 per cent of large firms in our sample see innovation spending increasing over the next 3-5 years.

2. *Innovation Strategy*

a. Area of business: For large firms, innovation is most highly concentrated in operations and sales and marketing.

b. Factors influencing innovation: More than half of the increase in market share, competitiveness, profitability and reduction in costs due to innovation has occurred in SMEs due to three types of innovation—new products, new processes and new services. At the same time, the customer is the primary external factor that leads more than half of the large firms to innovate.

c. Breakthrough and incremental: 37.3 per cent of large firms have introduced breakthrough innovation, while 76.4 per cent have introduced incremental innovation, which may be an indication that large firms in India are still in the mindset of incremental innovation as compared with breakthrough innovation.

d. Timeframe: The average timeframe (from idea generation to market) of innovation projects for half of the large firms is 1-3 years. Innovation projects in manufacturing firms have longer gestation period than in services.

3. *Which Firms are Innovative?*

- SMEs have greater innovation intensity than large firms.
- Innovation intensity for privately and publicly owned firms is significantly higher than that of government owned firms.
- Firms with majority foreign ownership have greater innovation intensity than those with majority Indian ownership.
- Innovation intensity for MNCs is significantly higher than for non-MNCs while there is little difference in the percentage of 'highly innovative' firms among MNCs and non-MNCs.
- Internal processes for innovation such as maintaining a specific innovation department, allocating funds, rewarding innovative employees, forecasting probabilities of success, formalising processes and systematic attempts, maintaining physical locations for innovation and constituting cross-functional teams, all lead to firms being more innovative. Further, firms with greater R&D spending, innovation spending and strategic prioritisation for innovation are also more likely to be more innovative.
- Firms with their primary market in India have higher innovation intensity than those with primary markets abroad. On the other hand, a greater proportion of firms with their primary market abroad are highly innovative (i.e., have introduced more 'new to world' innovations) as compared with firms with their primary market in India.
- Firms in industries where innovations are patented, with more patent filings and use of IPR consultants are more innovative.
- Firms partnering with government agencies, collaborating with universities and R&D labs also tend to be more innovative.

'Innovation Intensity' (i.e. the percentage of revenue derived from products/services which are less than three years old) has increased for large firms and SMEs, with SMEs registering a greater increase in innovation intensity than large firms.

4. Barriers

a. External

- The most important external barrier to innovation, as perceived by both large firms and SMEs, is skill shortage due to the lack of emphasis on industrial innovation, problem-solving, design, experimentation, etc., in the education curricula.
- Other prominent external barriers are lack of effective collaboration with research in universities and R&D institutions, excessive government regulation as well as insufficient pricing power to derive value from innovations.

b. Internal

- The most important internal barriers as perceived by large firms are lack of organisational focus on innovation as a strategy for growth and competitiveness, inefficient knowledge management systems within the company and poor understanding of customer needs and market dynamics.
- For SMEs, prominent internal barriers are skill shortages due to lack of effective in-house training programmes, inability to move beyond the first successful innovation and develop a sustainable model for continuous innovation, as well as poor understanding of customer needs and market dynamics.

5. Manufacturing versus Services

While innovation intensity is higher for manufacturing than services (for large firms and SMEs), innovation intensity has grown faster from 2001-02 to 2005-06 for services than manufacturing. Further, services firms are more likely to be highly innovative, i.e., they have a greater propensity to introduce 'new to world' innovations.

For all the firms in our sample (large firms and SMEs), innovation has had roughly the same level impact for manufacturing and services firms, in respect of increase in market share and increase in competitiveness. However, innovation has led to a greater increase in profitability for manufacturing firms and a greater reduction in costs for services firms.

Services firms are more likely to partner with government agencies with innovation being the specific purpose. In large firms, the average R&D spend, as a percentage of annual revenue, is lower for the services sector as compared to the manufacturing sector but innovation spending is higher. For SMEs, both R&D and innovation spend are higher in the case of services than manufacturing.

Conclusion

The NKC survey confirms the rising innovation activity and awareness in India as well as the need to continuously and publicly encourage this trend as a key enabler in India's economic growth and competitiveness. However, there is need for further effort along a range of parameters in order to fully realise India's innovation potential. Some of the important steps are:

- Systematic reform of the higher education system (including skill-based marketable vocational education) in India, which would act as an enabler for developing the required intellectual capital as well as lay the foundation for effective collaboration between industry, educational institutions and the government. Therefore, the mandate of the NKC, which is to guide policy and direct reforms to allow India to effectively use and create knowledge capital, is critical and extremely relevant in furthering the cause of innovation and entrepreneurship in the Indian economy.

Internal processes for innovation such as maintaining a specific innovation department, allocating funds, rewarding innovative employees, forecasting probabilities of success, formalising processes and systematic attempts, maintaining physical locations for innovation and constituting cross-functional teams, all lead to firms being more innovative.

- The synergistic use of cumulative energies of the industry, the government, the educational system, the R&D environment and the consumer. The innovation ecosystem is a complex environment that requires the coordinated functioning of a number of diverse factors in order to function effectively.
- Innovation also needs to become as wide spread as possible, spreading across the entire economy, from the grassroots to the large firm level. It is felt that a comprehensive effort to address these issues would act as a critical enabling factor for India to be amongst the global leaders in innovation.

The NKC survey confirms the rising innovation activity and awareness in India as well as the need to continuously and publicly encourage this trend as a key enabler in India's economic growth and competitiveness.

I. Introduction

1. Understanding Innovation in India

1.1 Defining Innovation

1.1.1 There is a widely held view that innovation is primarily driven by high-end technology and R&D. However, high-end technology and R&D are only two of several sources of innovation. The reach and impact of innovation is seen across the value chain to also include other sources of innovation such as various processes and services, marketing, branding, trade, entrepreneurship, market research, customer surveys, etc. The National Knowledge Commission (NKC) therefore defines innovation in a more comprehensive sense, where along with products and services, processes and economic value enhancement are also paramount.

1.1.2 NKC defines innovation in the following manner for the purposes of this countrywide survey: "Innovation is defined as a process by which varying degrees of measurable value enhancement is planned and achieved, in any commercial activity. This process may be breakthrough or incremental, and it may occur systematically in a company or sporadically; it may be achieved by:

- introducing new or improved goods or services and/or
- implementing new or improved operational processes and/or
- implementing new or improved organisational/managerial processes

in order to improve market share, competitiveness and quality, while reducing costs."

1.1.3 Nearly 90 per cent of the firms that were part of this survey have agreed with the aforesaid definition. Other illustrative definitions of innovation, as provided by some of the firms surveyed, are as follows:

"Innovation occurs at the intersection of invention and insight. It is about the application of invention—the fusion of new developments and new approaches to solve problems."[1]

"Innovation is a creative idea focused on a customer touch point that: (1) creates unique and compelling solutions valued by our customers, (2) creates real and substantial competitive advantage, and (3) creates extraordinary value for our company."[2]

"Innovation is not limited to commercial activity. It encompasses immeasurable value enhancement to customers, talent search and retention, employee satisfaction through opportunity to innovate and also value addition at industry level leading to brand enhancement."[3]

"Innovation lies at the interface between 'invention' and 'the customer' and results in enhanced value to the customer."[4]

"Innovation is about identifying and executing: a) newer opportunities and b) newer geographies."[5]

1.2 Innovation and Global Competitiveness

1.2.1 Innovation and competitiveness have a dynamic, mutual relationship. Innovation thrives in a competitive environment and in turn, plays a key role in the achievement of such an environment. Innovation generates economic value, new

> *"Innovation is defined as a process by which varying degrees of measurable value enhancement is planned and achieved, in any commercial activity by the introduction of new or improved goods, services and processes."*

---

1. Definition proposed by IBM India Limited.
2. Definition proposed by Whirlpool India Limited.
3. Definition proposed by Kotak Mahindra Private Limited.
4. Definition proposed by Phillips Electronics India Limited.
5. Definition proposed by Reliance Industries Limited.

"Innovation is the 'necessary core competence' to remain competitive in this new landscape."

jobs in the economy and cultures of entrepreneurship. By virtue of its relationship with competitiveness, innovation emerges as a factor in promoting economic growth.[6] A recent World Bank study on innovation notes that 'Innovation can be a critical driver of increased productivity and competitiveness and ultimately poverty alleviation...Innovation is not an end in itself but a means to productivity growth and higher living standards."[7]

1.2.2 Globalisation provides opportunities as well as challenges for nations to use innovation as a strategic lever to generate knowledge flows. It provides unprecedented potential for innovation to be used as a tool for revenue generation, so that nations with a strong knowledge base, can once and for all, escape "the stranglehold of poverty".[8] At the same time, globalisation creates challenges for firms to either innovate or perish. "In the race to the top slot, the only way ahead for companies is to innovate...the only way to stay ahead is to innovate."[9] As such, Innovation is the "necessary core competence" to remain competitive in the new landscape."[10]

1.2.3 In understanding the significance of innovation, the possibilities offered by complex and interconnected global networks become relevant. The ability to "adapt to changing market conditions and anticipate future technologies and economic trends"[11] and leverage innovation across a large number of markets provides "opportunities for exploiting economies of scale as well as scope."[12] Innovation is therefore also emerging as a global activity "dependent on international networks of knowledge sharing...requiring the combination of various disciplines."[13] In short, in this globalised landscape, comparative knowledge advantage and the availability of cutting edge innovation at lower costs are becoming critical factors in the race to achieve economic competitiveness.

1.3 Innovation and India

1.3.1 Given the fact that the Indian economy is growing at 6-8 per cent per year while exports are growing at 30 per cent CAGR[14], and many Indian firms are successfully competing against international firms and brands, it can be concluded that this has been made possible by a combination of factors, including enabling environment, rising capital and labour productivity as well as improved quality of goods and services at lower costs. The efforts of Indian companies to improve performance are also being supplemented by foreign investments in areas ranging from R&D to manufacture

In the growth of the Indian economy, innovation is emerging as a key driver, although this may neither be apparent nor readily visible.

---

6. Some of the significant findings on innovation and competitiveness from this survey are illustrated with greater detail in the pages to follow. See, for example sub-section 2.1.3 of this report for an understanding of how innovation and firm behaviour relate to competitiveness.

7. World Bank (2007). *Unleashing India's Innovation: Towards Sustainable and Inclusive Growth*. p. 1, 12.

8. Joseph Schumpeter was one of the first economists to link innovation with economic growth. See, Bowonder, Kelkar, N.G. Satish, J.K. Racheria (2006). "Innovation in India: Recent Trends", TTMC *Research paper*, March 31.

9. Govindarajan, Vijay (2007). *Outlook Business*, May 5, p. 86.

10. Hamel, G. and C.K. Prahalad (1990). "The Core competence of the Corporation", *Harvard Business Review* 68 (3): 79-91; also see Bowonder *et al.*, supra note 8 as above; See also, Krishnan, Rishikesha (2004). "In the global economy, firms have to derive competence through Innovation...nations and organizations need to innovate to survive." *Economic Times*, July 19.

11. See Bowonder *et al.*, supra note 8 as above; also Haque, I. (1995). *Trade, Development and International Competitiveness*, World Bank.

12. See Bowonder *et al.*, supra note 8 as above, p.2.

13. See Bound, Kirsten (2007). "India: The Uneven Innovator: The Atlas of Ideas: Mapping the New Geography of Science", Demos, p.8.

14. Cumulative Annual Growth Rate.

of consumer durables, electronics, automobiles, textiles, services, etc.[15] In the post-liberalisation scenario, with the introduction of "economic policies aimed at eliminating industrial licensing, reducing protection for internal products, allowing foreign direct investment and minimising government controls and unleashing competition"[16], Indian firms have been exposed to market forces where innovation will increasingly play a key role in ensuring economic survival and achievement. In the growth of the Indian economy, innovation is emerging as a key driver, although this may neither be apparent nor readily visible. In this respect, one of the aims of this study by NKC is to understand the role played by innovation in India as a driver of such growth.

1.3.2 Statistics are already emerging on the increasing significance of innovation and scale and scope of such innovation occurring among the country's firms today. This NKC study reveals that 42 per cent of large firms[17] and 17 per cent of SMEs have introduced 'new to the world' innovations during the course of their business. Seventeen per cent of the large firms rank innovation as the top strategic priority and 75 per cent rank it among the top 3 priorities. All the large firms in our sample agree (of which 81 per cent strongly agree) that innovation has gained importance as being critical to growth and competitiveness since the start of economic liberalisation in India. Further, according to a recent study on 'Innovation and Manufacturing in India', a staggering 89 per cent of the respondents said that the importance of innovation has increased significantly over the last 10 years and 39 per cent felt that innovation has become "critical to their operations."[18]

1.3.3 India is emerging as a global hub of innovation-low cost as well as high value products and services.[19] Recent acquisitions by Indian companies in the global market also signify an increasing trend by Indian companies to leverage the various possibilities of innovation that the global market offers. In addition, there has been recent commentary on India's 'inherent reasons' for innovative activity such as the existence of an open society, a technology base, democracy, diversity, an environment that allows experimentation, a vibrant capital market, availability of young populations necessary as human capital to fully reap the demographic dividend, full and free competition in the private sector, opportunities for technological leapfrogging as well as the availability of necessary infrastructure.[20]

1.3.4 In this increasingly skill-driven knowledge economy, necessary investments in education, including enterprise-based vocational education and training and market-based knowledge and skills in higher education, are going to be crucial to maintain India's innovation-driven growth and its cutting edge in knowledge-based industries.[21] India has to

In this increasingly skill-driven knowledge economy, necessary investments in education, including enterprise-based vocational education and training and market-based knowledge and skills in higher education, are going to be crucial to maintain India's innovation-driven growth and its cutting edge in knowledge-based industries.

15. See for example, the recent World Bank study on innovation (as noted in supra note 7 as above) that states that, "more than 8 per cent a year growth has been driven by a jump in export-oriented, skill-intensive manufacturing (pharma, petrochemicals, auto parts and assembly) and services (IT, business services, finance)...these have been accompanied by a jump in innovative activities....higher productivity and economic growth have raised living standards and reduced the number of poor people" at pages 1-2. The World Bank quotes Planning Commission of India statistics that the consumption-poverty head count ratio has fallen from 36 per cent in 1993-94 to 27.8 per cent in 2004-2005. It notes that "while there is no established causal link between Innovation and poverty alleviation, it is plausible to presume that Innovation can have a longer-term impact on poverty by increasing growth as well as a more direct impact through pro-poor Innovation efforts." Also see, the recent Goldman Sachs study quoted in Bound (supra note 13 as above) which states that "India has the potential to grow faster than China in the long term...in just a few years India has been transformed from an aid recipient to a global competitor."

16. See Bowonder *et al.* (as noted in supra note 8 as above), p.2.

17. Large enterprises are those having annual turnover of more than Rs. 100 crore, Medium enterprises have annual turnover between Rs. 10 and Rs. 100 crore and small enterprises have annual turnover less than Rs. 10 crore.

18. CII-BCG Executive Survey, "Innovation in Indian Manufacturing", 2007, p.8.

19. See for example, Bowonder *et al* pp.133-134 (as noted in supra note 8 as above), which states that global firms have used three options for sourcing innovations from India, namely, locating centres of innovations in India through fully owned subsidiaries; outsourcing innovations to Indian firms or research centres and acquiring innovative entrepreneurial firms or start-ups. Bowonder *et al.* also refers to "a recent workshop at Harvard Business School' where 'India was ranked as the most preferred destination for locating Innovation centres." Bowonder *et al* further note that this is an indication of India soon becoming a global innovation hub. Further, Bowonder *et al* note that 'Emerging markets like India, China, the Philippines, Thailand etc., are becoming the testing grounds for innovative products. Also, as these are likely to experience faster growth Innovations targeted towards the bottom of the pyramid are likely to be the order of the day. Indian innovators face the challenge of identifying such windows of opportunity and also realising them in a sustainable manner." See also, World Bank study on innovation (as noted in supra note 7 as above), which states that "India is increasingly becoming a top global innovator for high tech products and services", p.i; See also Michael Candon-Brookes, IBM-India, in *Mint*, May 8, 2007 stating that "India is the hub for high value global innovation".

20. See Prof. Vijay Govindarajan (as noted in supra note 9 as above).

21. See for example, chapter V of the World Bank study on innovation (as noted in supra note 7 as above).

develop ways and means to translate its immense innovation potential into high value commercial products and services.

1.4 Innovation and the National Knowledge Commission

1.4.1 Innovation forms part of NKC's objective of recommending ways and means to promote the use of knowledge in order to advance India's economic growth and competitiveness. Apart from a host of areas related to knowledge at all levels, NKC is also currently engaged in consultations on issues directly related to innovation such as entrepreneurship and intellectual property rights. It has already made recommendations on other related areas such as higher education, vocational education and on enacting a uniform legal framework for public funded research.[22]

1.4.2 While literature on innovation has been growing in recent times, this survey is perhaps the first detailed and in-depth quantitative and qualitative survey on innovation in India (as defined more broadly than R&D) using firm level aggregate statistical data on a nationwide scale, with a sample that includes the top industry leaders as well as a large number of small and medium enterprises, and across varied industrial profiles, ranging from manufacturing and services to diversified businesses.[23] It is expected that the survey will provide feedback and information on current innovation trends to firms as well as generate necessary catalysing effects for business innovation to take place in India on an even larger scale, thus ensuring sustained innovation-led economic growth in the coming years.

1.4.3 Chapter I highlights the relevance of innovation in today's globalised and interdependent market space, and its role as a driver for growth and competitiveness. It studies the unique opportunities and challenges that India is faced with in its effort to fully realise its innovation potential, and become a global innovation hub.

Chapter II analyses macroeconomic trends in innovation observed by the firms in our sample. The emerging trends indicate that innovation intensity is increasing, firms are introducing innovations that are new to local as well as global markets, and innovation is driving growth in the economy to a significant extent. We see that firms increasingly realise the importance of innovation as being critical to growth and competitiveness. Innovation seems to have surpassed its status as being merely a buzzword, and is now firmly established as an integral part of firms' business practices.

In Chapter III, we study strategic issues pertaining to innovation. We observe the departure from the conventional notion that innovation is a measure of R&D through the high concentration of innovation activities in firm operations. The manner in which innovation takes place in SMEs is analysed in detail, as well as the average timeframe of innovation projects. Lastly, we explore four conceptual types of innovation as experienced by firms, i.e. systematic, sporadic, incremental and breakthrough.

In Chapter IV, we examine the factors that lead some firms to be more innovative than others. The firms' structure, internal and external processes are all analysed in detail—along with their impact on innovation in a firm. Firm structure includes aspects of firm ownership, size and operation; internal processes include setting up special departments or officers for innovation, specifically allocating funds for innovation projects in annual budgets, setting up physical centres for innovation, etc; and external processes which include collaboration with government agencies set up specifically for the purpose of innovation, collaboration with universities and R&D labs, using the services of IPR consultants, etc.

Firms increasingly realise the importance of innovation as being critical to growth and competitiveness. Innovation seems to have surpassed its status as being merely a buzzword, and is now firmly established as an integral part of firms' business practices.

22. See National Knowledge Commission, "Report to the Nation, 2006" for recommendations already submitted for the year 2006 and *www.knowledgecommission.gov.in* for recommendations submitted after January 12, 2007 and for information on other consultative processes as well as NKC's work generally.

23. See for example, the World Bank study (as noted in supra note 7 as above) that focuses on macro level policies of innovation; see also Bowonder *et al* (as noted in supra note 8 as above) that lays particular emphasis on R&D and case studies; see also the CII-BCG survey (as noted in supra note 18 as above) on manufacturing and the Demos Report (as noted in supra note 13 as above) that stresses on science and innovation.

Chapter V outlines the internal as well as external barriers to innovation faced by firms, i.e., the factors that hold back firms from reaching their innovation potential.

Chapter VI compares the experiences of firms in the manufacturing and services sectors with innovation. Since the growth of the services sector is a critical driver in India's economic growth, we expect innovation to play an increasingly significant role.

Chapter VII concludes and sums up the NKC findings.

Highlights of the NKC Study on Innovation

- The first detailed and in-depth quantitative and qualitative survey on innovation in India (as defined more broadly than R&D) at this scale.
- 137 firms interviewed, out of which 58 are large firms and 79 are SMEs.
- Firms represent a wide range of sectors from manufacturing and services including mining, automotives, home appliances, paper, steel, energy, pharmaceuticals, textiles, IT/ITeS, banking and financial, health care, aviation, retail, shipping, biotechnology, media, diversified, etc. See Section VI: Consultation for a list of the firms that participated in the NKC survey, along with a sectoral breakdown.
- The first platform that has brought together industry leaders in various sectors including the CEOs of Reliance, Infosys, Tata Group, IBM, ICICI Bank, CRISIL, Biocon, Kotak Mahindra Bank, ONGC, SAIL, BSNL, Nuclear Power Corporation of India, etc., as well as industry chambers CII (Confederation of Indian Industry), PHDCCI (Punjab, Haryana and Delhi Chambers of Commerce and Industry), MCCIA (Maratha Chambers of Commerce, Industry and Agriculture) and academics from the Indian Institutes of Management, Bangalore, Lucknow and Ahmedabad.
- Methodology: Separate questionnaires on innovation for large firms and SMEs.
- Reports to Prime Minister on the topic and seeks to generate and facilitate policies that would accelerate innovation-led economic growth in India.
- Provides feedback to firms so that they can use this information to improve processes.
- Expected outcome: Add to innovation literature and generate catalytic impact on a large scale to embed the spirit of innovation.

Results from NKC Survey

II. General Trends in Innovation

We also use the term 'highly innovative' to refer to firms that have introduced a 'new to world' innovation during the course of their business in the last five years.

2.1 Measure of Innovation in the Economy and Impact on Economic Growth

This section highlights the prevalence of innovation in the economy and studies its impact on economic growth. The NKC hypothesis is that innovation is increasing, driving growth and increasing competitiveness in various sectors of the Indian economy. This section presents evidence from the NKC survey database to support the NKC hypothesis.

We use 'innovation intensity' to measure the prevalence of innovation in a firm—where innovation intensity is defined to be "the percentage of revenue derived from products/services which are less than three years old", consistent with the NKC definition of innovation as already stated in Chapter I. Sub-section 2.1.1 presents results regarding innovation intensity for large firms and SMEs.

Innovation intensity measures the percentage of revenue derived from products/services that are new to the firm. However, focusing only on innovation intensity is not comprehensive enough, especially when the question is whether a particular product, process or service is truly 'innovative', i.e., whether such an innovation is new to the market itself (i.e., local, national or global). As such, there could be a situation where a firm is constantly introducing imitation products, which leads to a high value of innovation intensity, but is not necessarily 'innovative' enough to introduce a new product/service to the market. Therefore, for the sake of clarity in this study, innovation intensity is not considered in isolation but in conjunction with the introduction of innovations that are 'new to the industry', 'new to the Indian market' or 'new to the global market'. In this context, we also use the term 'highly innovative' to refer to firms that have introduced a 'new to world' innovation during the course of their business in the last five years. Sub-section 2.1.2 of this chapter presents further details on these aspects.

Since our sample consists of the largest firms in the Indian economy as well as a large base of SMEs[24], firm-level growth indicators are used as a proxy for overall growth in economy. Sub-section 2.1.3 studies the improvement in these indicators over the last five years, and measures the impact attributable to innovation.

2.1.1 Innovation intensity has increased: It can be seen from Figure 22.1 below that innovation intensity has significantly increased for large firms in our sample from 2001-02 to 2005-06. The average value of innovation intensity has increased from 6.49 per cent in 2001-02 to 11.15 per cent in 2005-06, and the median value increased from 2.27 per cent in 2001-02 to 5.88 per cent in 2005-06.[25]

Innovation intensity values are expected to be higher for SMEs, and this is seen from Figure 22.2. More than 60 per cent of the SMEs in our sample have innovation intensity greater than 20 per cent, as compared to less than 25 per cent of the large firms in our sample. This could perhaps be due to a number of reasons, including the fact that small enterprises can pioneer revolutionary technologies and are relatively free from the inertia that can act as a restraint on larger firms.[26] In addition, large firms are also likely to have a larger portfolio of established products and services, and therefore the revenue derived from new products/services would account for a lower proportion in the overall revenue figures than in the case of SMEs.

More than 60 per cent of the SMEs in our sample have innovation intensity greater than 20 per cent, as compared to less than 25 per cent of the large firms in our sample.

24. See Section VI: Consultation for the list of firms that participated in the NKC survey.

25. The average and the median have a difference in their values when the distribution is skewed, which is the case for the distribution of innovation intensity. The average represents the expected value of innovation intensity, and is more sensitive to extreme values. The median represents the value that splits the distribution into half and is less affected by extreme values. For the purposes of this report, we quote both the average and the median, since they capture different aspects of the innovation intensity distribution.

26. Shell Springboard and Vivid Economics (2006). "Opportunities for Innovation: The business opportunities for SMEs in tackling the causes of climate change", October.

Figure 22.1: Innovation Intensity for Large Firms

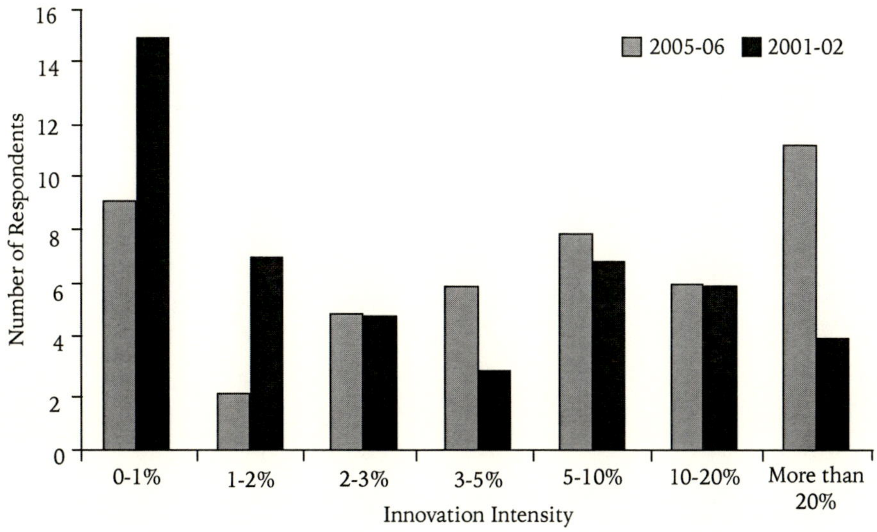

Figure 22.2: Innovation Intensity for SMEs

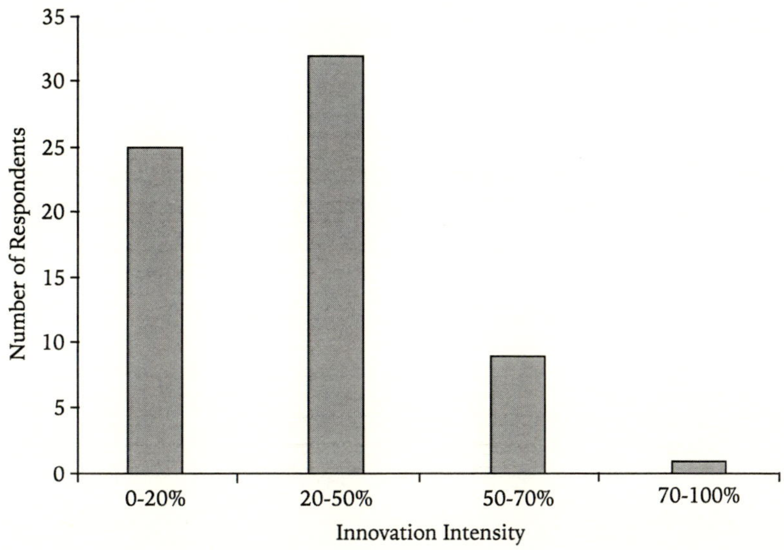

2.1.2 Innovation intensity measures the revenue derived from products/processes/services that are new to the firm. However, over the course of the last five years, a large number of firms in our sample have introduced innovations that are not only new to the company but also new to the industry, new to the Indian market and new to the global market.

Figure 22.3 shows the proportion of large firms and SMEs in our sample that has succeeded in pushing forward the innovation frontier. More than 90 per cent of the large firms in our sample have introduced innovations that are new to the company, industry and the Indian market and 42 per cent have introduced innovations that are new to the global market as well, i.e., 42 per cent of large firms are 'highly innovative' as defined by NKC for the purposes of this survey. This indicates a high level of international competitiveness in India's innovation activities.

More than 90 per cent of the large firms in our sample have introduced innovations that are new to the company, industry and the Indian market and 42 per cent have introduced innovations that are new to the global market as well.

Figure 22.3: In the Last Five years, Have You Introduced Innovations that are

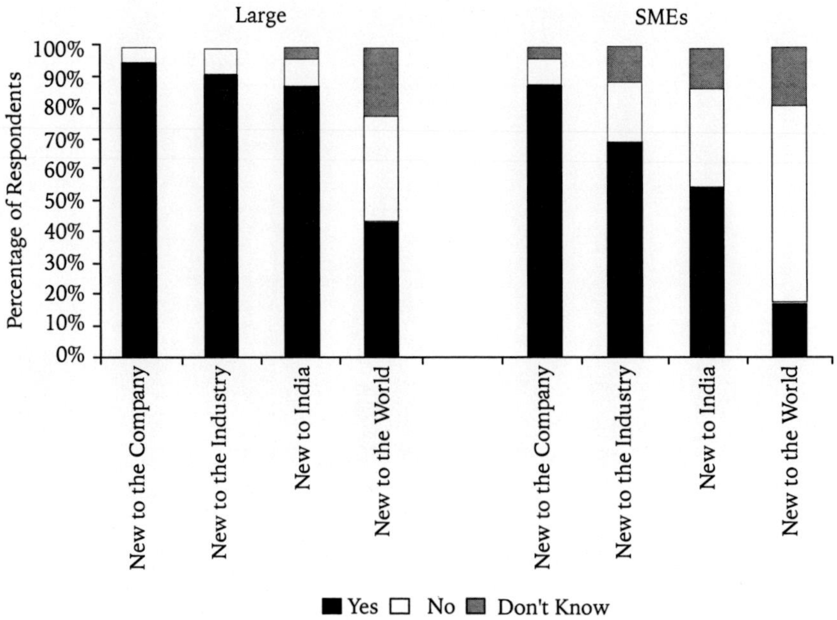

In comparison, 70 per cent, 56 per cent and 17 per cent of SMEs have introduced innovation that is new to the industry, new to India and new to the world, respectively. Therefore, 17 per cent of the SMEs are 'highly innovative', as defined by NKC for the purposes of this survey. This indicates that SMEs are not as successful as large firms in pushing forward the innovation frontier though the introduction of new innovations are novel to national and global markets. This could be due to a lower awareness of SMEs of the uniqueness of their products, a reporting bias on the part of large firms, or it could genuinely imply that while SMEs are able to capture advantages or meet unmet demand in local markets, they are less able to do the same at a national or international level.

2.1.3 Firms in various sectors in the Indian economy are driving growth and competitiveness, as can be seen from the NKC survey database. Over the last five years, of the large firms in our sample,

(a) 77 per cent have experienced an increase in market share;

(b) 94 per cent have experienced an increase in competitiveness;

(c) 92 per cent have experienced an increase in profitability; and

(d) 84 per cent have experienced a reduction in costs.

Similarly, over the last five years, of the SMEs in our sample,

(a) 76 per cent have experienced an increase in market share;

(b) 84 per cent have experienced an increase in competitiveness;

(c) 69 per cent have experienced an increase in profitability; and

(d) 55 per cent have experienced a reduction in costs.

Figure 22.4 shows the degree of impact that innovation has had on each of these indicators in the case of large firms. To illustrate, 17 per cent of large firms claim that innovation has led to greater than 50 per cent increase in competitiveness; 31 per cent claim it has led to 25-50 per cent increase in competitiveness; 43 per cent claim it has led to 0-25 per cent increase in competitiveness and the remaining 6 per cent claim it has had no impact.

Seventeen per cent of large firms claim that innovation has led to greater than 50 per cent increase in competitiveness.

It can be observed from Figure 22.4 that:

- the proportion of firms that attribute no change to innovation is extremely low (less than 20 per cent) in each case, and
- nearly half of the firms attribute more than 25 per cent of the change in each indicator to innovation.

Figure 22.4: Per cent Change in Firm Level Indicators Attributable to Innovation for Large Firms

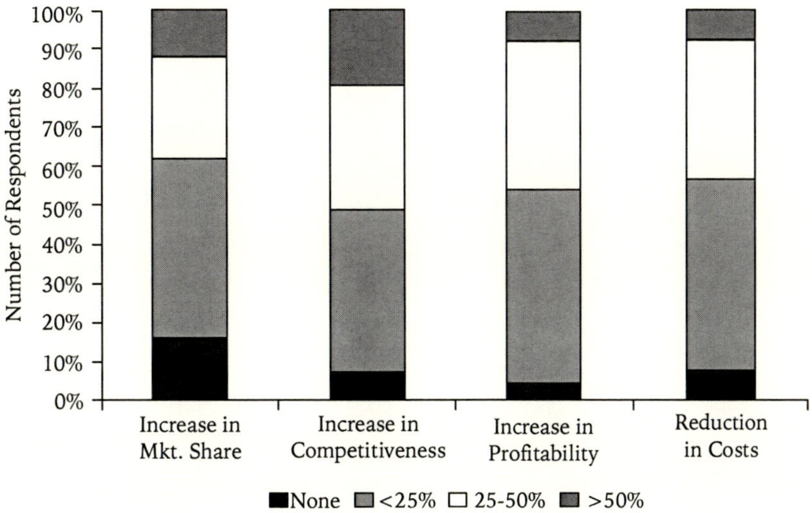

This implies that innovation has a significant impact on these indicators of firm growth.

Also, the proportion of firms that attributes, 25-50 per cent and >50 per cent of the change in an indicator to innovation is the highest in the case of competitiveness. It can be inferred that for large firms, innovation has the most significant impact on competitiveness. Similarly, the remaining indicators are, in decreasing order of impact of innovation: increase in profitability, reduction in costs and increase in market share.

The previous results of large firms can be compared with the experience of SMEs, as seen from Figure 22.5 below:

Figure 22.5: Per cent Change in Firm Level Indicators Attributable to Innovation for SMEs

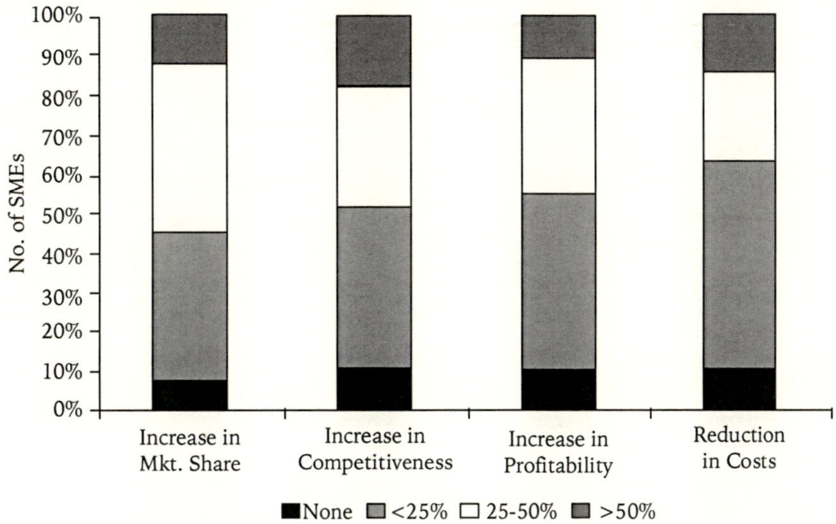

For large firms, innovation has the most significant impact on competitiveness.

To illustrate, 19 per cent of SMEs claim that innovation has led to greater than 50 per cent increase in competitiveness; 30 per cent claim it has led to 25-50 per cent increase in competitiveness; 41 per cent claim it has led to 0-25 per cent increase in competitiveness and the remaining 10 per cent claim it has had no impact.

Further, it can be observed from Figure 22.5 as above that:

- the proportion of firms that attribute no change to innovation is extremely low (less than 10 per cent) in each case, and
- nearly half of the firms attribute more than 25 per cent of the change in each indicator to innovation.

This implies that innovation has a significant impact on these indicators of firm growth in the case of SMEs as well.

Also, in the case of SMEs, the proportion of firms that attribute 25-50 per cent and >50 per cent of the change in an indicator to innovation is the highest in the case of increase in market share. It can be inferred that for SMEs, innovation has the most significant impact on increase in market share. Similarly, the remaining indicators can be listed as follows, in decreasing order of impact of innovation: increase in competitiveness, increase in profitability and reduction in costs.

It could be inferred from the observations stated above that in the case of SMEs, innovation by and large leads to greater increase in market share, competitiveness and profitability rather than reduction in costs. Unlike large firms where nearly half of the large firms have attributed significantly positive results on each of the four indicators due to innovation, in the case of SMEs, only 35 per cent of the SMEs attribute a significant reduction of costs due to innovation. Scaling up of large scale innovation efforts in the case of SMEs, therefore may not find sufficient traction unless top leadership within SMEs perceive cost reduction as a necessary corollary to innovation efforts.

2.2 Approach to Innovation

The increased understanding of the role of innovation in driving growth and improving competitiveness in the Indian economy has led to greater interest and visibility of innovation in the Indian media and public attention.[27] This section attempts to quantify how firms view innovation and the strategic importance placed on innovation.

2.2.1 Strategic Approach

The growing strategic importance placed by firms on innovation is evident from the following points:

- All the large firms in our sample rank innovation as being amongst the top 10 strategic priorities, with 17 per cent ranking it as the top strategic priority and 75 per cent ranking it as being amongst the top 3 priorities.[28]
- All the firms in our sample—large firms and SMEs—agree (of which more than 70 per cent strongly agree) that innovation is good for business, even if it does not always result in higher market share or better competitiveness.
- All the large firms agree (of which nearly half strongly agree) that they cannot survive and grow without investment in Innovation.
- 65 per cent of large firms (and 59 per cent of SMEs) disagree that innovation is a high-risk activity.

The increased understanding of the role of innovation in driving growth and improving competitiveness in the Indian economy has led to greater interest and visibility of innovation in the Indian media and public attention.

27. For instance, several conferences have been organised by industry chambers specifically on innovation. In the last two years, there has been a dramatic increase in the number of studies on innovation in India and the number of cover stories in business magazines; innovation awards have been instituted by government, private and media agencies; a successful innovation consultancy has existed in India for the past 7 years, etc.

28. This observation could be subject to respondent bias, where applicable. See also, the CII-BCG report "Innovation in Indian Manufacturing, 2007" also concludes that innovation is a top priority for Indian companies, with 91 per cent of firms naming innovation as a top 3 priority.

2.2.2 *Operational Approach*

In addition to recognising the strategic importance of innovation, firms are taking concrete steps to incorporate innovation as a business practice that is essential for the firm's survival and success. This is evident from the increasing innovation spending and the increasing attempt by firms to encourage innovation across the board, by not restricting it to top and middle management.

- Innovation has taken place largely in response to specific problems or challenges thrown up by the market or competitors, as observed by 65 per cent of large firms and 83 per cent of SMEs in our sample.
- Almost 70 per cent of large firms are satisfied with their returns on investment in innovation.
- An overwhelming 96 per cent of large firms in our sample see innovation spending increasing over the next 3-5 years.
- Half the large firms claim that the motivation to innovate is driven by the entire firm, whereas less than half claim that it is primarily driven by top and middle management. In fact, all the large firms in our sample reward employees for successfully demonstrating their capabilities as innovators.
- The reverse is true in the case of SMEs—less than 30 per cent of the SMEs in our sample claim that the motivation to innovate is driven by the entire firm, whereas more than 60 per cent claim that it is primarily driven by top and middle management.
- Although innovation may be driven primarily by top management in the case of SMEs, there is an effort to mainstream innovation as a business process—more than 70 per cent of SMEs discuss innovation at their annual board meetings and more than half discuss it at their shareholder meetings.

2.2.3 *Change Since Liberalisation*

It is evident that the economic liberalisation of 1991 led to a significant increase in competitiveness in the Indian economy, and therefore, to an increase in the importance of innovation. This is supported by the experience of firms in our sample:

- As expected, all the large firms in our sample agree (of which 81 per cent strongly agree) that innovation has gained importance as being critical to growth and competitiveness since the start of economic liberalisation in India.
- However, prior to the 1990s, 77 per cent of large firms in our sample had introduced new or improved products/services/ processes based on innovation.

2.3 Chapter Summary

'Innovation intensity' (i.e., the percentage of revenue derived from products/services which are less than three years old) has increased for large firms and SMEs, with SMEs registering a greater increase in innovation intensity than large firms. Forty-two per cent of the large firms and 17 per cent of the SMEs are also 'highly innovative' firms (i.e., firms who have introduced 'new to world' innovations during the course of business in the last five years). Nearly half of the large firms and SMEs attribute more than 25 per cent of change in the following factors to innovation: increase in competitiveness, increase in profitability, reduction in costs and increase in market share. For large firms, innovation has the most significant impact on competitiveness, while for SMEs, Innovation has the most significant impact on increase in market share. Seventeen per cent of the large firms rank innovation as the top strategic priority and 75 per cent rank it among the top 3 priorities. All the large firms in our sample agree (of which 81 per cent strongly agree) that innovation has gained importance as being critical to growth and competitiveness since the start of economic liberalisation in India. All the large firms agree (of which nearly half strongly agree) that they cannot survive and grow without investment in innovation. An overwhelming 96 per cent of large

Although innovation may be driven primarily by top management in the case of SMEs, there is an effort to mainstream innovation as a business process—more than 70 per cent of SMEs discuss innovation at their annual board meetings and more than half discuss it at their shareholder meetings.

firms in our sample see innovation spending increasing over the next 3-5 years.

III. Innovation Strategy

This chapter analyses key strategic issues pertaining to innovation, particularly in respect of firm operations, factors influencing innovation, general conceptual types of innovation and the average timeframes of innovation projects from idea generation to the market.

3.1 Area of Business

Large firms in our sample were asked to pick the area of business where innovation is most highly concentrated. The results are shown in Figure 22.6 below. It is clear that the activity where innovation is most highly concentrated continues to be operations,[29] with sales and marketing being the next most important. Interestingly, the only firms that named R&D as the most important area of focus were pharmaceuticals firms. This emphasis on process is a sharp departure from traditional R&D and manufacture-centric notions of innovation.

Figure 22.6: Innovation for Large Firms, Area of Business

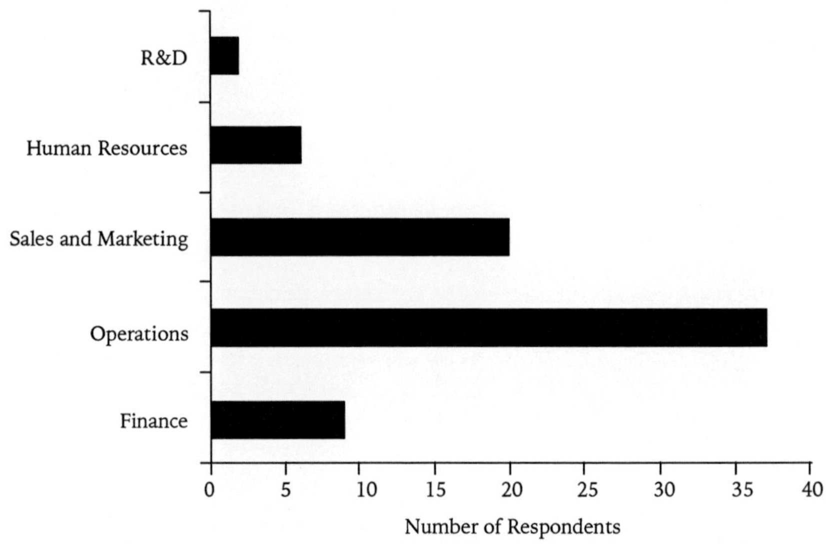

3.2 Factors Influencing Innovation in SMEs

We have seen in Section 2.1.3 that innovation has had a significant impact on firm-level indicators of growth. This section studies how that impact has come about i.e., through new products, new processes, new services, new methods of production, new sources of raw materials, new ways of organising administration, new ways of managing finance or opening up of new markets. The SMEs in our sample were asked to report which of the above measures resulted in an increase in market share, increase in competitiveness, increase in profitability and reduction in costs.

It can be seen from Figure 22.7 below that more than half of the increase in market share, competitiveness, profitability and reduction in costs due to innovation has occurred due to only three types of innovation—new products, new processes and

The activity where innovation is most highly concentrated continues to be operations, with sales and marketing being the next most important.

29. This finding is in direct contrast with that of the CII-BCG report "Innovation in Indian Manufacturing", where respondents stated that innovation covered all the stated areas of business. Our findings could be different because unlike the BCG-CII report, respondents in this survey were forced to prioritise between the above focused areas.

new services. Other types of innovation such as new methods of production and new ways of organising administration have had a significant impact on cost reduction. Opening up of new markets has had an impact on the increase in competitiveness.

Figure 22.7: What would You Attribute the Change to?

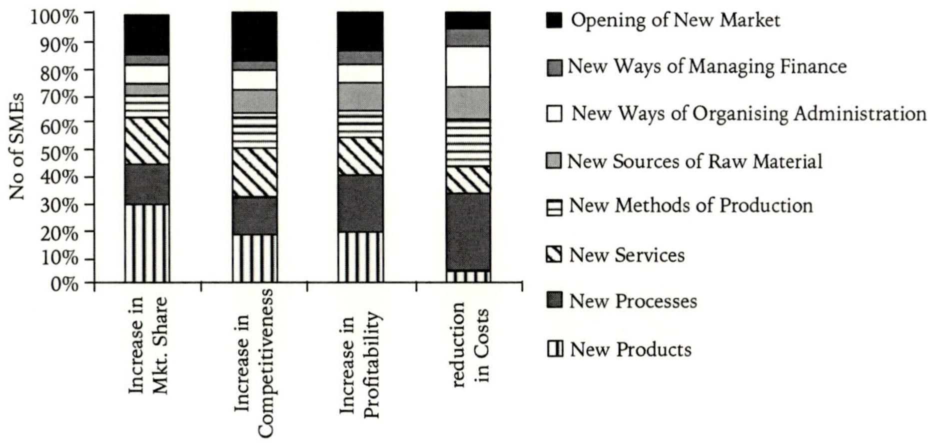

3.3 Conceptual Types of Innovation

Figure 22.8 below demonstrates the manner in which innovation takes place in large firms—systematic *vs.* sporadic, incremental *vs.* breakthrough. The numbers in each quadrant represent the proportion of large firms, for instance, 27.5 per cent of firms have experienced systematic breakthrough innovation, whereas 5 per cent have experienced sporadic breakthrough innovation. Therefore, 32.5 per cent of the large firms in our sample have experienced breakthrough innovation.

Figure 22.8:

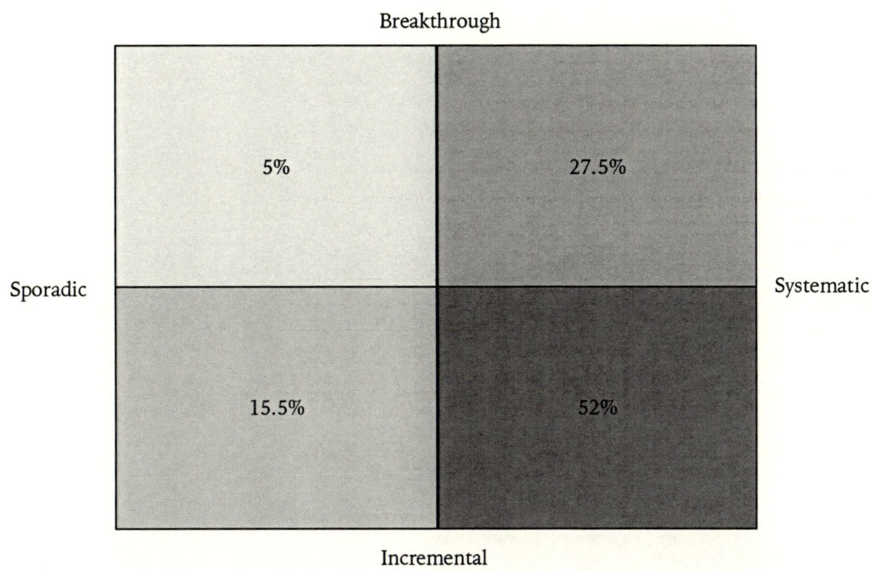

Figure 22.8 above shows that all the four conceptual types of innovation—systematic, sporadic, breakthrough and incremental—are occurring simultaneously at varying degrees in India's economy today. The largest proportion (more than half) of large

The largest proportion of large firms lies in the systematic incremental quadrant, which may be an indication that large firms in India are still in the mindset of incremental innovation as compared with breakthrough innovation.

firms lies in the systematic incremental quadrant, as can be seen from Figure 22.8, which may be an indication that large firms in India are still in the mindset of incremental innovation as compared with breakthrough innovation. This finding is reinforced by Figure 22.9 below, which shows the proportion of firms that have introduced breakthrough or incremental innovation.

In addition, only 2 (out of 22) highly innovative firms in our sample lie in the sporadic half of our sample, with the remaining 20 lying in the systematic half. This may indicate that a significant bulk of 'new to world' innovation is very much a planned and systematic activity, and only occurs as a result of concrete steps taken by firms to innovate.

From Figure 22.9 below, we see that 37.3 per cent of firms have introduced breakthrough innovation, while 76.4 per cent have introduced incremental innovation. Of the firms that have introduced breakthrough innovation, 63 per cent is 'new to world'; and of the firms that have introduced incremental innovation, 39.5 per cent is 'new to world'.

At the same time, from our survey database, we can infer that highly innovative firms have introduced 'new to world' innovations that are not just breakthrough but also incremental in nature. Figure 22.10 below shows the proportion of highly innovative firms that have introduced breakthrough or incremental innovation.

Figure 22.9: The Proportion of Firms that have Introduced Breakthrough, Incremental or Both Types of Innovation

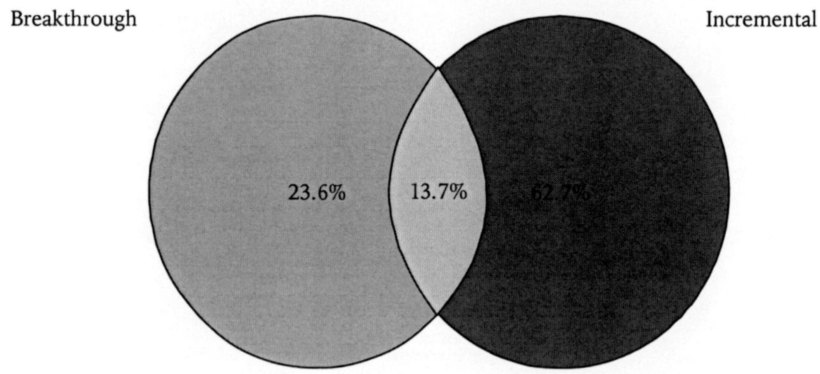

Figure 22.10: Highly Innovative Firms

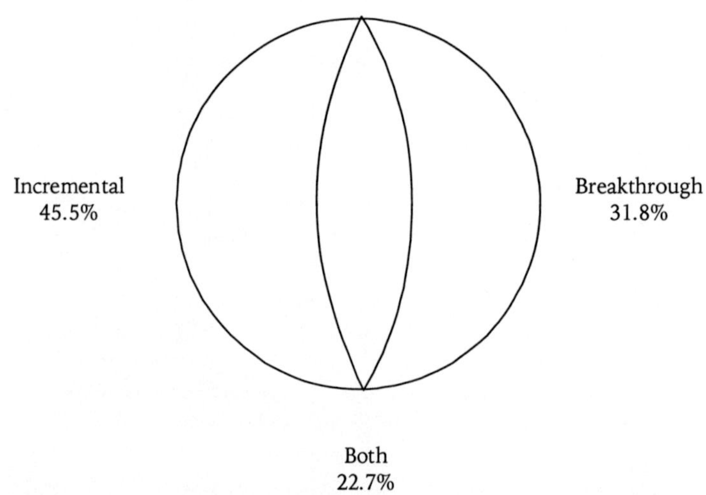

This shows that more than half of the 'new to world' innovation introduced by large firms has been incremental in nature.

3.4 Timeframe for Innovation Projects

The average timeframe (from idea generation to market) of innovation projects for the large firms in our sample is displayed in Figure 22.11 below. For half the large firms in our sample, the average timeframe of innovation projects is 1–3 years. It is also evident from the figure that innovation projects in manufacturing firms have longer gestation period than in services. Interestingly, we also observe that not a single services sector firm undertakes innovation projects that take more than three years from idea generation to market, on average.

Figure 22.11: **Average Timeframe of Innovation Projects for Large Firms**

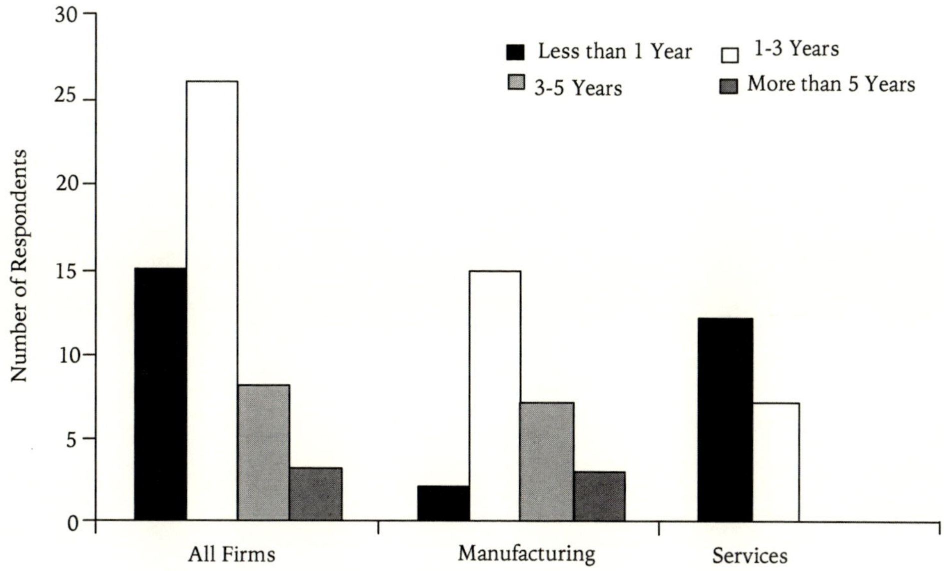

3.5 Chapter Summary

For large firms, innovation is most highly concentrated in operations and sales and marketing. More than half of the increase in market share, competitiveness, profitability and reduction in costs due to innovation has occurred in SMEs due to three types of innovation—new products, new processes and new services.

37.3 per cent of large firms have introduced breakthrough innovation, while 76.4 per cent have introduced incremental innovation, which may be an indication that large firms in India are still in the mindset of incremental innovation as compared with breakthrough innovation. The average timeframe (from idea generation to market) of innovation projects for half of the large firms is 1-3 years. Innovation projects in manufacturing firms have longer gestation period than in services.

IV. Firm Structure and Processes

4.1 Impact of Firm Structure on Innovativeness

This sub-section studies the impact of factors such as firm ownership and structure on innovativeness.[30] Table 22.1 correlates innovation intensity with factors such as size of firm, age of firm, etc., for large firms.

4.1.1 *Size of Firm:* Table 22.1 indicates that innovation intensity has an inverse relationship with the size of the firm—as measured both by the number of employees and the annual revenue. Consistent with this inverse relationship within large firms, we have also observed that SMEs have higher innovation intensity than large firms (sub-section 2.1.1).

Table 22.1: Relationship between Firm Structure and Innovation Intensity for Large Firms[31]

Factor	Correlation with Innovation Intensity
Age of firm	– 0.081
Size of firm (no. of employees)*	– 0.311*
Size of firm (annual revenue)*	– 0.268*
Profits	0.046
R&D spending*	0.298*
Spending on other innovation*	0.353*
Ranking of innovation as a strategic priority*	0.280*

Note: * These correlations are significant at the 5 per cent level.

Table 22.2: Relationship between Firm Structure and Innovativeness

Indicator	Indicator Value	Number of Firms	Average Innovation Intensity	Median Innovation Intensity	Number of Highly Innovative Firms
Entire sample		52	11.15%	5.88%	22
Majority stakeholder	Public	27	12.78%	8.13%	15
	Private	13	13.36%	8.89%	3
	Government	10	2.61%	1.55%	4
Majority stakeholder	Indian	39	10.92%	5.88%	17
	Foreign	10	14.94%	10%	5
Are you an MNC?	Yes	21	14%	10%	9
	No	31	9.38%	3.62%	13

4.1.2 *Majority Stakeholder (Public/Private/Government).* Innovation intensity for privately and publicly owned firms is significantly higher than that of government-owned firms (refer to Table 22.2).

Innovation intensity has an inverse relationship with the size of the firm—as measured both by the number of employees and the annual revenue.

30. As explained in Chapter II, section 1, innovativeness is measured by innovation intensity as well as by 'new to world' innovation. We define firms that have introduced innovation that is new to the world in the last five years as 'highly innovative' firms. For a detailed explanation of the methodology followed in this section, refer to a note on methodology at the end of the chapter.

31. In this test, the null hypothesis states that no relationship exists between innovation intensity and each of the above factors. Based on the size of our sample, we can reject the null hypothesis in the rows that are marked with a *. In other words, a relationship does exist between innovation intensity and the factors marked with a *.

Foreign ownership does not lead to a significantly higher propensity to be highly innovative, i.e., in respect of introduction of 'new to world' innovations. This indicates that Indian firms have the potential to compete globally in their innovation efforts.

Comparing private and public ownership, it is interesting to note that innovation intensity is higher in the case of privately-owned firms.

However, more than half of the publicly-owned firms are highly innovative (as defined by NKC for the purposes of this survey) whereas less than a quarter of the privately-owned firms are highly innovative.

4.1.3 *Majority Stakeholder (Indian/Foreign)*. Firms with majority foreign ownership have greater innovation intensity than those with majority Indian ownership (refer to Table 22.2). In addition, 50 per cent of the former and 43.5 per cent of the latter are highly innovative.

This suggests that although average innovation intensity is significantly different (10.9 per cent for Indian-owned firms as compared with 14.9 per cent for foreign-owned firms), there is a high degree of 'new to world' type innovativeness in both categories. In other words, foreign-owned firms generate greater revenue through the introduction of new products/services—this may be due to the introduction of existing global product lines to the Indian market, bringing best global practices to conducting business in India and other similar factors. However, foreign ownership does not lead to a significantly higher propensity to be highly innovative, i.e., in respect of introduction of 'new to world' innovations. This indicates that Indian firms have the potential to compete globally in their innovation efforts.

4.1.4 *MNC (Yes/No)*. Innovation intensity for MNCs is significantly higher than for non-MNCs (average innovation intensity is 14 per cent for MNCs, as compared to 9.38 per cent for non-MNCs, refer to Table 22.2). However, 42 per cent of non-MNCs are highly innovative, and 43 per cent of MNCs are highly innovative. This is similar to the conclusions arrived at for Indian-owned/foreign-owned firms.

4.2 Impact of Internal Firm Processes on Innovativeness

This section establishes the impact of deliberate efforts made by firms, such as allocating funds and other resources specifically for innovation, systematising and formalising processes related to innovation, etc., on innovativeness, as seen from Table 22.3 below.

Table 22.3[32]: Relationship between Internal Processes and Innovativeness

Indicator	Indicator Value	No. of Firms	Average Innovation Intensity	Median Innovation Intensity	Number of Highly Innovative Firms
Entire sample		52	11.15%	5.88%	22
Do you have a special department/officer for innovation?	Yes[33]	34	10.16%	4.38%[34]	16
	No	18	13.27%	9.25%	6
Do you allocate funds specifically for innovation?	Yes	36	10.68%	5.67%[35]	16
	No	16	12.25%	6.67%	6

contd...

32. The results from Table 22.3 could be subject to respondent bias, where applicable.

33. The firms who have a special department/officer for innovation that are 'highly innovative' include Biocon, CRISIL, Infosys, etc.

34. All PSUs in our sample lie in this category. Removing PSUs, the average innovation intensity for firms having a dedicated department or officer for innovation rises to 13.1 per cent and the median rises to 7.7 per cent.

35. As before, nearly all PSUs lie in this category. Removing PSUs, the average innovation intensity for firms allocating funds specifically for innovation rises to 13.04 per cent and the median rises to 9 per cent.

...contd...

Indicator	Indicator Value	No. of Firms	Average Innovation Intensity	Median Innovation Intensity	Number of Highly Innovative Firms
Do you formally forecast the probability of success for innovation projects?	Yes	37	12.71%	7.22%	16
	No	14	7.73%	2.85%	5
Do you reward employees who are successful innovators?	Yes	50	10.74%	5.59%	21
	No[36]	1	-	-	-
Do you have formal processes to analyse the causes of success/failure of innovation projects?	Yes	32	12.18%	10%	15
	No	19	9.33%	6.36%	6
Do you make systematic attempts to track innovations that are taking place in your industry or related areas?	Yes	46	11.61%	5.56%	19
	No	5	8.1%	7.5%	2
How many, if any, physical locations for innovation does your company have?	None	7	8.9%	4%	0
	1 – 5	26	11.26%	4.88%	10
	5 – 10	6	7.8%	0.83%	5
	More than 10	12	11.73%	6.39%	7
Do you constitute cross-functional teams to tackle and deliver mega innovation projects?	Yes	42	12.72%	7.5%	20
	No	8	4.56%	2.48%	1
How many patents have you filed in the last 5 years?	0 – 10	26	9.44%	4.6%	13
	10 – 20	0	-	-	-
	More than 20	16	13.34%	10%	9

4.2.1 Table 22.1 indicates that firms with higher a) R&D spending; b) Innovation spending; and c) greater strategic priority placed on innovation; all have higher values of innovation intensity.[37]

4.2.2 A significant observation that arises from Table 22.3 is the increasing awareness of the need to establish processes for innovation. This can be seen by the fact that in each case, 60 per cent or more of the large firms in our sample are already institutionalising systems to manage innovation.

4.2.3 *Special Department or Officer Dedicated to Innovation*: Unexpectedly, we find that innovation intensity is lower for firms which have a special department or officer dedicated to innovation. We also find that all the PSUs in our sample[38] have a special department or officer dedicated to innovation. When we remove the PSUs from the sample, the average innovation intensity for firms having a dedicated department or officer for innovation rises to 13.1 per cent, and the median rises to 7.7 per cent (compared with the values 10.16 per cent and 4.38 per cent in Table 22.3, which have been calculated for all firms having a dedicated department or officer for innovation).

These figures imply that though PSUs have created dedicated departments for innovation, they have not been effective in increasing innovation intensity.

However, at the same time, we find that for firms other than PSUs, having a special department or officer for Innovation has led to an increase in innovation intensity. This is further supported by the fact that firms having a special department or officer for innovation are also more likely to be highly innovative (see Table 22.3).

4.2.4 *Allocate Funds Specifically for Innovation in Annual Budgets:* Similar to the previous case, we observe a counter-intuitive decrease in innovation intensity for firms that allocate funds specifically for innovation in annual

36. The only firm responding 'No' is Shoppers Stop.

37. This can be seen by the positive and significant value of correlation in each of these cases.

38. With the exclusion of Rural Electrification Corporation.

budgets. Again, all the PSUs in our sample[39] claim that they allocate funds specifically for innovation in annual budgets. However, when we remove the PSUs from this sample, we find that the average innovation intensity for firms allocating funds specifically for Innovation rises to 13.04 per cent and the median rises to 9 per cent (compared with the values 10.68 per cent and 5.67 per cent in Table 22.3). This implies that in the case of PSUs, allocation of funds specifically for Innovation in annual budgets has not perhaps been effective in increasing innovation intensity.

At the same time, firms (other than PSUs) that allocate funds specifically to innovation have higher innovation intensity. They are also more likely to be highly innovative (refer to Table 22.3).

4.2.5 *Impact of Other Processes:* In all the other cases, both innovation intensity and the proportion of highly innovative firms is higher for firms who undertake particular processes, such as the following: formally forecasting probability of success; rewarding employees who have successfully demonstrated their capabilities as innovators; formal processes to analyse the causes of success/failure of innovation projects; systematic attempts to track innovations in industry or related areas, setting up physical locations for innovation; and constituting cross-functional teams to deliver mega innovation projects (refer to Table 22.3).

4.2.6 From the data sample, we are unable to analyse the impact of firm structure and internal processes on innovation in the case of SMEs because of insignificant results.[40]

4.2.7 *Patenting Behaviour and Innovation:* There appears to be a segment within large firms (i.e., 40 per cent of large firms) who have filed greater than 20 patents and have achieved much higher degrees of innovation intensity and highly innovative percentages. At the same time, there is still a substantial segment of large firms (i.e., 60 per cent) who have filed only between 0–10 patents in the last 5 years. Further, there are no firms in our sample that have filed between 10 and 20 patents in the last 5 years.

Firms that have filed for more than 20 patents have higher innovation intensity and are more highly innovative than firms which have filed 0-10 patents in the last 5 years. (Refer to Table 22.3, which indicates that average innovation intensity for firms that have filed for more than 20 patents in the last 5 years is 13.34 per cent, compared with 9.44 per cent for firms that filed for less than 10 patents in the last 5 years. Also, 57 per cent of the former are highly innovative, while 50 per cent of the latter are highly innovative.) Certain large firms therefore, are becoming increasingly aware of IP as a means of increasing innovativeness and are assuming positions of leadership in this regard.[41] At the same time, it appears that there is need for large firms to enter, at least the intermediate bracket, i.e., 10-20 patent filings in order to be competitive with the leaders, who would, with experience of success, try for further innovation in the coming years.

Further, the relationship between innovation and IP protection in the perception of large firms is evident from our sample. When asked how firms perceive the value of IP, nearly 80 per cent respond that they view it as a valuable

In the case of PSUs, allocation of funds specifically for innovation in annual budgets has not perhaps been effective in increasing innovation intensity. At the same time, firms (other than PSUs) that allocate funds specifically to innovation have higher innovation intensity. They are also more likely to be highly innovative.

39. With the exception of Punjab National Bank, Central Bank of India and Rural Electrification Corporation.

40. In case of firm structure, this is because the number of firms that have foreign ownership, public ownership or primary markets abroad is too low to give significant results. All the correlations are also insignificant. In the case of internal processes, we find that discussing innovation at annual board meetings and holding annual audits to study the success/failure of innovation projects has an insignificant impact on innovation intensity. The number of SMEs that have shareholder meetings is too low to give significant results. This might be due to the fact that SMEs are unable to properly implement these processes, or there could be flaws in our data.

41. Note that 74 per cent of the large firms in our sample have access to a patenting process.

corporate asset *per se*, 17 per cent view it as a measure of R&D and only 4 per cent view it as an employee reward mechanism.

This means that within large firms, there is significant agreement on the role of IP in revenue generation, while we notice a disparity between such perception and actual translation into results in terms of patent filings.

The situation is quite different for the SMEs in our sample—only three per cent of SMEs have filed more than five patents in the last five years, and therefore we do not have enough evidence to study the impact on innovation for SMEs.

Firms that have filed for more than 20 patents have higher innovation intensity and are more highly innovative than firms which have filed 0-10 patents in the last five years.

4.3 Impact of External Processes on Innovativeness

This section analyses efforts made by firms for external collaboration, seeking external information, using consultants, etc., and establishes the impact of these efforts on innovativeness.

4.3.1 *Primary Market (India/Abroad)*. It is extremely interesting to observe that firms with their primary market in India have higher innovation intensity than those with primary markets abroad (refer to Table 22.4). It was expected that firms with their primary market abroad would be more innovative because of exposure to global competition. However, it could be the case that Indian firms with their primary market abroad are more focused on catching up with the local competition.

On the other hand, a greater proportion of firms with their primary market abroad are highly innovative as compared with firms with their primary market in India. This implies that exposure to global competition may not lead to an increase in innovation intensity (i.e., in proportion of revenue earned from innovation in the last three years) but does lead to an increase in the likelihood of becoming highly innovative (i.e., in the propensity of firms to introduce 'new to world' innovations).

4.3.2 *Partnerships with Government Agencies*. Several government programmes have been established with the explicit purpose of driving innovation in the Indian economy—notable amongst these are the NMITLI (New Millennium Indian Technology Leadership Initiative), TePP (Technopreneurs Promotion Programme), NIF (National Innovation Foundation), TDB (Technology Development Board), HGT (Home Grown Technology Program), etc.

We find a small proportion of firms (roughly 30 per cent of large firms and 10 per cent of SMEs) in our sample partnering with government agencies for the purpose of innovation. These firms have a significantly higher innovation intensity (refer to Table 22.4—the average innovation intensity is 14.14 per cent for large firms[42] that partner with government agencies, as compared with 9.88 per cent for firms that do not) as well as a significantly higher likelihood to be highly innovative (refer to Table 22.4, which indicates that 59 per cent of these firms are highly innovative, whereas only 36 per cent of firms that do not partner with government agencies are highly innovative).

It is extremely interesting to observe that firms with their primary market in India have higher innovation intensity than those with primary markets abroad.

42. The number of SMEs who engage in partnerships with government agencies is too low to get significant results on the impact on innovation intensity.

Table 22.4: Relationship between External Processes and Innovativeness

Indicator	Value	No. of Firms	Average Innovation Intensity	Median Innovation Intensity	Number of highly innovative Firms
Entire sample		52	11.15%	5.88%	22
Primary market	India	38	11.66%	7%	14
	Abroad	14	9.81%	4.65%	8
Do you partner with government agencies for the purpose of innovation?	Yes	17	14.14%	8.33%	10
	No	33	9.88%	4.83%	12
Do you collaborate with universities?	Yes	33	12.05%	6.79%	17
	No	16	8.6%	4.7%	6
Do you collaborate with R&D labs?	Yes	35	12.02%	5.77%	17
	No	14	9.71%	6.21%	5
Are innovations patented in your industry?	Yes	30	12.2%	7.73%	16
	No	22	9.73%	5%	6
Do you use IPR consultants in India?	Yes	27	11.75%	3%	12
	No	24	10.52%	6.35%	10
Do you use IPR consultants abroad?	Yes	19	16.28%	14.61%	11
	No	26	7.7%	4.75%	10

From the above, we can conclude that further investigation is required into the strengths and weaknesses of these government support programmes for innovation. There may be a case for extending and scaling up these programsme. There has also been discussion in recent times on setting up of a National Innovation Programme, under the aegis of the Government. In order to develop norms conducive to collaboration between industry and R&D labs or universities, such a plan could help facilitate the following: enable researchers to set up commercial entities while in professional employment with their research organisations; enable research organisations to invest knowledge including inventions and Innovations as equity in the new enterprises; as well as facilitate mobility of researchers and encourage setting up incubation centres.[43] Public-private-partnerships (PPP) have also emerged as a tool for effecting innovation and it is expected that this trend will continue in future.

4.3.3 *Collaboration with Universities and R&D Labs.* There is a clear indication that collaboration with universities and R&D labs enhances firm innovativeness. Table 22.4 indicates that innovation intensity is higher for firms that collaborate and that the proportion of highly innovative firms is also higher. In fact, more than half of the large firms and SMEs in our sample claim that the lack of cooperation with universities and R&D labs is an important barrier to innovation (see Chapter V on Barriers). It could be argued here that the Indian industry-R&D relationship has yet to achieve critical mass. In the case of Indian industries, this could be a powerful competitive tool, which could also perhaps require some facilitating institutional mechanisms.

Innovation intensity is higher for firms that collaborate and that the proportion of highly innovative firms is also higher. In fact, more than half of the large firms and SMEs in our sample claim that the lack of cooperation with universities and R&D labs is an important barrier to innovation.

43. See also for example, the draft proposal from CSIR entitled "Encouraging Development and Commercialisation of Inventions and Innovations: A new Impetus" dated April 10, 2007.

4.3.4 *IP Regime.* Of the large firms in our sample, 57 per cent claim that innovations are patented in their industry.[44] Of these firms, more than half are highly innovative, whereas of the firms that claim that innovations are not patented, roughly one quarter are highly innovative. Innovation intensity is also higher in the case of firms that have protection for their intellectual property (refer to Table 22.4, which indicates that the average innovation intensity increases from 9.73 per cent to 12.2 per cent in the case of firms that claim innovations are patented in their industry).

Comparing this with the experience of SMEs, only 33 per cent claim that innovations are patented in their industry. This could perhaps explain the very low percentage of patent filings by SMEs as seen in sub-section 4.2.7. At the same time, we find that SMEs have higher innovation intensity and a higher proportion of highly innovative firms if innovations are patented in their industry. (The average innovation intensity for SMEs if innovations are patented in their industry is 36 per cent, as compared with 26 per cent for SMEs if innovations are not patented in their industry. The proportion of highly innovative firms is 12.5 per cent for the former, as compared with 10 per cent for the latter.)

It also appears therefore, that there is still scope for enhanced patentability within industrial sectors and such opportunities have not yet been fully exploited.

4.3.5 *Royalties from IP.* In terms of royalties earned and costs incurred from IP licencing, both revenue earned from IP royalties and costs incurred are in the 0-5 per cent bracket for 95 per cent of large firms in our sample. This indicates that revenue generation from IP licenses as well as IP licencing for innovation generally may still be at a somewhat nascent stage in India today. In an interdependent globalised space, where science is complex, the scope for licencing of IP at various stages of the manufacturing process, may increasingly become pertinent, for reasons of cost as well as comparative advantage.

4.3.6 *Use IPR Consultants.* More than half the large firms in our sample use the services of IPR consultants in India and 36 per cent use the services of IPR consultants abroad. Innovation intensity is slightly higher for firms using the services of IPR consultants in India but it is significantly higher for firms using IPR consultants abroad (refer to Table 22.4, which indicates that average innovation intensity for firms using IPR consultants in India is 11.75 per cent, as compared with 10.52 per cent for firms that don't; whereas it is 16.28 per cent for firms that use IPR consultants abroad, as compared with 7.7 per cent for firms that don't). The proportion of highly innovative firms is also the highest for firms using IPR consultants abroad (Table 22.4 indicates that 44 per cent of firms using IPR consultants in India are highly innovative, as compared with 42 per cent of firms that do not use IPR consultants in India; while the corresponding figures are 58 per cent and 38 per cent respectively for firms that use the services of IPR consultants abroad). This also signifies the necessity for extensive IPR capacity building within the country.

External Collaboration

While partnering with government agencies and collaborating with universities and R&D labs both lead to greater innovation, it can be seen from Table 22.4 that the former has a greater impact. This might be due to the fact that the government schemes are specifically targeted, which in turn could lead to higher levels of innovation for a firm.

At the same time, we find that SMEs have higher innovation intensity and a higher proportion of highly innovative firms if innovations are patented in their industry.

44. Interestingly, of the firms who claim that innovations are not patented in their industry, more than half foresee patentable innovations in the next 10 years. This is reflective of the evolving IPR regime in India.

4.3.7 *Seek Information from Customer, Suppliers and Distributors*. All the large firms in our sample seek information from customers, suppliers and distributors and use this information to improve their products and services.

4.3.8 *Source of Funding for Innovation Activities*. Nearly all the firms in our sample use internal funds to fund their innovation activities, rather than venture capital, bank loans or government grants. A small proportion (roughly 10 per cent) of SMEs uses bank loans as an additional source of funding for innovation.

4.3.9 *Primary External factor to Innovate*. The customer is the primary external factor that leads firms to innovate, according to more than half of the large firms in our sample. The market is the next most important external factor, and the industry and the economy are relatively less important.

4.4 Chapter Summary

SMEs have greater innovation intensity than large firms. Innovation intensity for privately- and publicly-owned firms is significantly higher than that of government-owned firms. Firms with majority foreign ownership have greater innovation intensity than those with majority Indian ownership. Innovation intensity for MNCs is significantly higher than for non-MNCs while there is little difference in the percentage of 'highly innovative' firms among MNCs and non-MNCs.

Internal processes for innovation such as maintaining a specific innovation department, allocating funds, rewarding innovative employees, forecasting probabilities of success, formalising processes and systematic attempts, maintaining physical locations for innovation and constituting cross-functional teams, all lead to firms being more innovative. Further, firms with greater R&D spending, Innovation spending and strategic prioritisation for innovation are also more likely to be more innovative.

Firms with their primary market in India have higher innovation intensity than those with primary markets abroad. On the other hand, a greater proportion of firms with their primary market abroad are highly innovative (i.e., have introduced more 'new to world' innovations) as compared with firms with their primary market in India. Firms in industries where innovations are patented, with more patent filings and use of IPR consultants are more innovative. Firms partnering with government agencies, collaborating with universities and R&D labs also tend to be more innovative.

Intellectual Property Rights and Innovation

From sub-sections 4.2.7, 4.3.4 and 4.3.6, it is evident that innovation is positively impacted by protection for firms' intellectual property in the case of large firms and to some extent, also in the case of SMEs.

This can be seen by the fact that

1. Firms in industries where innovations are patented have higher innovation intensity and are more likely to be highly innovative (sub-section 4.3.4).
2. Firms that have filed more than 20 patents have higher innovation intensity than those with less than 10 filings and are more likely to be highly innovative (sub-section 4.2.7).
3. Firms that use IPR consultants have higher innovation intensity and are more likely to be highly innovative (sub-section 4.3.6).

The customer is the primary external factor that leads more than half of the large firms to innovate.

V. Barriers to Innovation

5.1 External and Internal Barriers

5.1.1 This section analyses the barriers to innovation perceived by large firms and SMEs. The barriers have been classified into (1) external – those that could arise due to the regulatory environment, the market, the intellectual property rights (IPR) regime, etc., and (2) internal – those that could arise due to internal firm processes such as internal resistance to change, inefficient systems and processes to manage innovation, etc. The figures below display firms' ranking of importance for barriers to innovation.

It is interesting to note that in most cases, more firms considered a particular barrier to be 'Not Important' rather than 'Important'. This signifies a positive attitude towards innovation at a general level. Also, on average, firms perceive external barriers more important than internal barriers.

Figure 22.12: External Barriers to Innovation: Ranking of Importance for Large Firms

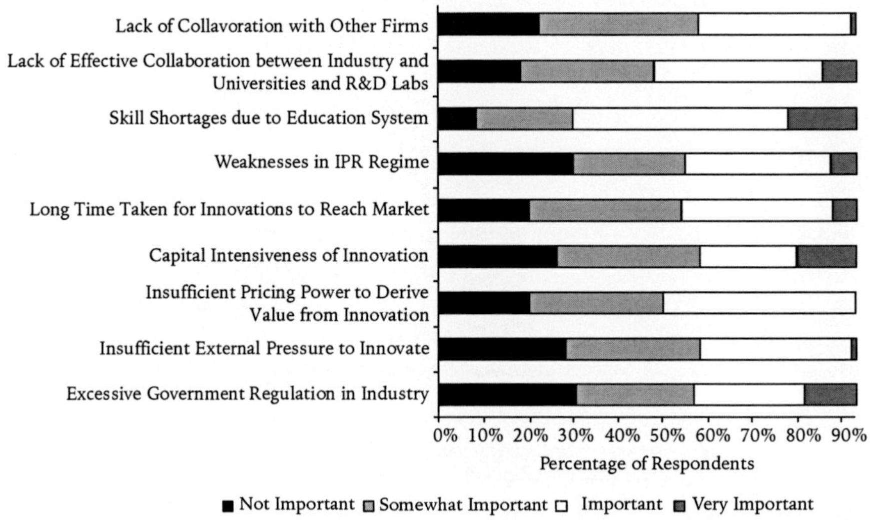

5.1.2 *External Barriers:* We observe that only 43 per cent of large firms think that excessive government regulation in their industry is an important barrier to innovation. In addition, only 42 per cent of large firms perceive insufficient external pressure to innovate as an important barrier to innovation. This could be a reflection of the existence of competitiveness as a spur to innovation efforts in the current economy.

The most important external barrier to innovation, as perceived by both large firms and SMEs, is skill shortages due to the lack of emphasis on industrial innovation, problem-solving, design, experimentation, etc., in the education curricula. It is critical to focus on policy reform in the higher and vocational educational curricula in order for India to achieve its Innovation potential.

The next most important external barriers as perceived by large firms are, in decreasing order of importance as follows: the lack of effective collaboration between industry and research conducted in universities and R&D institutions; insufficient pricing power to derive value from Innovations.

For SMEs, the most important external barriers are: excessive government regulation; the lack of effective collaboration between industry and research conducted in universities and R&D institutions.

5.1.3 *Internal Barriers:* The most important internal barriers as perceived by large firms, in decreasing order of importance are: lack of organisational focus on innovation as a strategy for growth and competitiveness; inefficient knowledge management systems within the company; and poor understanding of customer needs and market dynamics.

Figure 22.13: External Barriers to Innovation: Ranking of Importance for SMEs

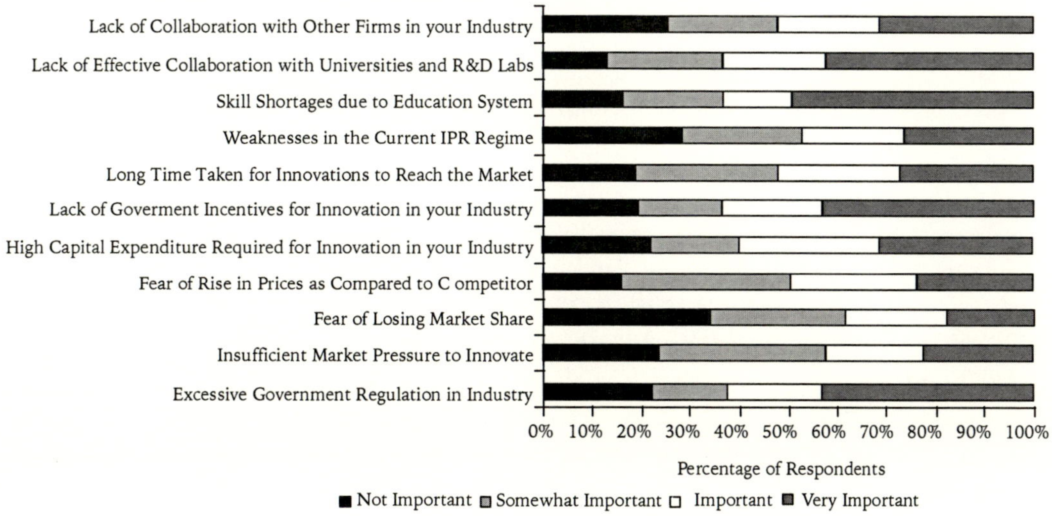

Figure 22.14: Internal Barriers to Innovation: Ranking of Importance for Large Firms

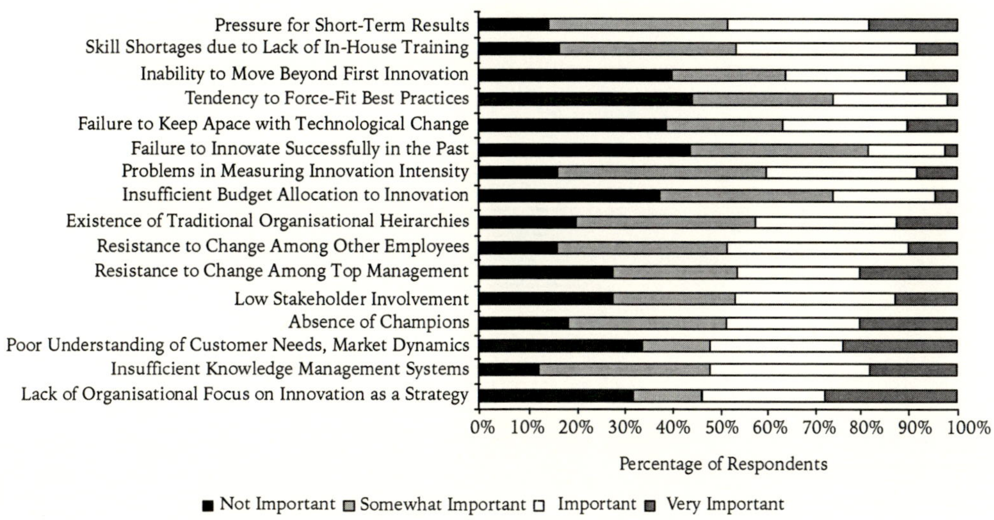

Figure 22.15: Internal Barriers to Innovation: Ranking of Importance for SMEs

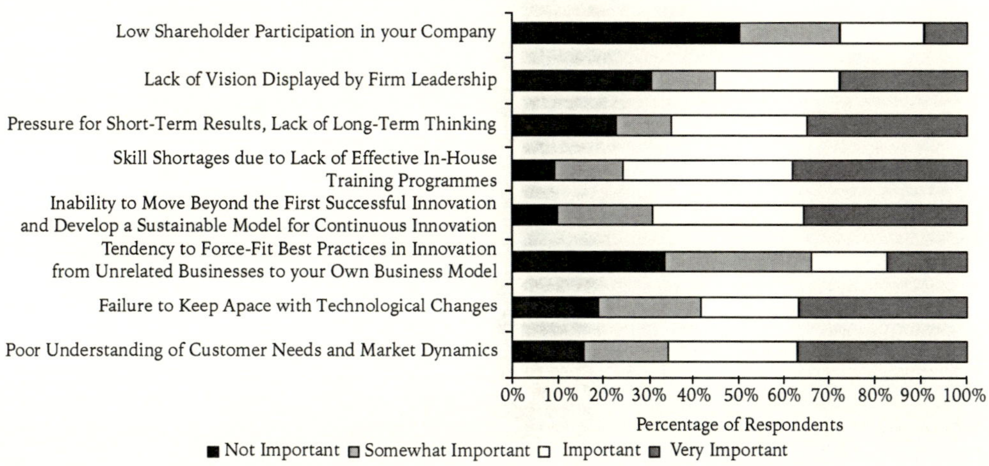

The most important internal barriers as perceived by SMEs, in decreasing order of importance are: skill shortages due to lack of effective in-house training programmes; inability to move beyond the first successful innovation and develop a sustainable model for continuous innovation; and poor understanding of customer needs and market dynamics.

Therefore, while SMEs are able to target small and emerging markets, are open to radical innovation and can try new business models, they have issues in scaling up and gaining a deeper understanding of the market.

5.2 Chapter Summary

The most important external barrier to innovation, as perceived by both large firms and SMEs, is skill shortages due to the lack of emphasis on industrial innovation, problem-solving, design, experimentation, etc., in the education curricula. Other prominent external barriers are lack of effective collaboration with research in universities and R&D institutions, excessive government regulation as well as insufficient pricing power to derive value from innovations.

The most important internal barriers as perceived by large firms are lack of organisational focus on innovation as a strategy for growth and competitiveness; inefficient knowledge management systems within the company; and poor understanding of customer needs and market dynamics. For SMEs, prominent internal barriers are skill shortages due to lack of effective in-house training programmes; inability to move beyond the first successful innovation and develop a sustainable model for continuous innovation; as well as poor understanding of customer needs and market dynamics.

The most important internal barriers as perceived by large firms are lack of organisational focus on innovation as a strategy for growth and competitiveness; inefficient knowledge management systems within the company; and poor understanding of customer needs and market dynamics.

VI. Innovation in Manufacturing and Services Firms

The literature on innovation in India has largely been silent on the specific experiences of the services sector with innovation. With the changing composition of Indian economic growth to be increasingly services-led, NKC sees innovation playing a crucial role in this growth. Services contributed as much as 68.6 per cent of the overall average growth in GDP in the last five years between 2002-03 and 2006-07.[45]

6.1 Innovation Intensity

From the results of our survey, we observe that innovation intensity is higher for manufacturing than for services (for both large firms and SMEs, refer to Table 22.5 below). However, we do see that innovation intensity has grown faster from 2001-02 to 2005-06 for services than for manufacturing (the rate of growth over this four-year period was 62.8 per cent for manufacturing and 80.5 per cent for services). This finding reflects the overall trend in the economy as well—that the services sector is smaller but growing more rapidly than the manufacturing sector.

6.2 Highly Innovative Firms

Although services sector firms have lower innovation intensity, they are more likely to be highly innovative (both in the case of large firms and SMEs—while 37 per cent and 7 per cent of large and SME firms in the manufacturing sector are highly innovative respectively, 42 per cent and 17 per cent of large and SME firms in the services sector are highly innovative respectively, refer to Table 22.5).

The above findings as highlighted in 6.1 and 6.2 could indicate that firms in the services sector do not innovate as consistently as manufacturing firms, and therefore have a smaller percentage of revenue from new products or services. It could also be possible that the innovations in the services sector may themselves be of lower revenue value than the ones in the manufacturing sector. However, services firms have experienced a higher degree of success as measured by 'new to world' innovation, which could also perhaps be a reflection of increasing services-led efforts leading to economic growth in recent times.

Table 22.5:

	Manufacturing		Services	
	Large Firms	SMEs	Large Firms	SMEs
Average innovation intensity, 2005-06	12%	33%	9%	27%
Average innovation intensity, 2001-02	7.4%	-	5%	-
Proportion of highly innovative firms	37%	7%	42%	17%
Average R&D expenditure, as a per cent of revenue	2.04%	5%	1.06%	7%
Average innovation expenditure, as a per cent of revenue	1.25%	4%	1.91%	7%
Percentage of firms that collaborate with government agencies for the purpose of innovation	22%	9%	31.5%	12%
Percentage of firms that collaborate with universities	67%	26.5%	52.5%	44%
Percentage of firms that collaborate with R&D labs	78%	30%	42%	21%

The services sector is smaller but growing more rapidly than the manufacturing sector.

45. Source: India Economic Survey, 2006-07. See *http://indiabudget.nic.in*

6.3 Impact of Innovation on Firm Growth

For all the firms in our sample (large firms and SMEs), innovation has had roughly the same level impact for manufacturing and services firms, in respect of increase in market share and increase in competitiveness. However, innovation has led to a greater increase in profitability for manufacturing firms and a greater reduction in costs for services firms. Cost reduction in the global services market could be a significant aim for the services firms' competitiveness. This can be seen from Figure 22.16, by observing the proportion of firms that attribute more than 25 per cent of the change in any indicator to innovation.

It can also be seen from Figure 22.16 that the proportion of firms that attribute no change to innovation is slightly higher in the case of services sector firms. This indicates that innovation has had a greater degree of impact on growth in the manufacturing sector so far. It would be interesting to note how this aspect changes in India's transition to becoming an increasingly services-based economy.

6.4 Partnerships with Government Agencies

We find that 22 per cent and 8 per cent of large and SME manufacturing sector firms, respectively partner with government agencies, as compared with 31.5 per cent and 12 per cent, respectively for services sector firms. Therefore, services firms are more likely to partner with government agencies with innovation being the specific purpose.

Figure 22.16: Change Attributable to Innovation, All Firms

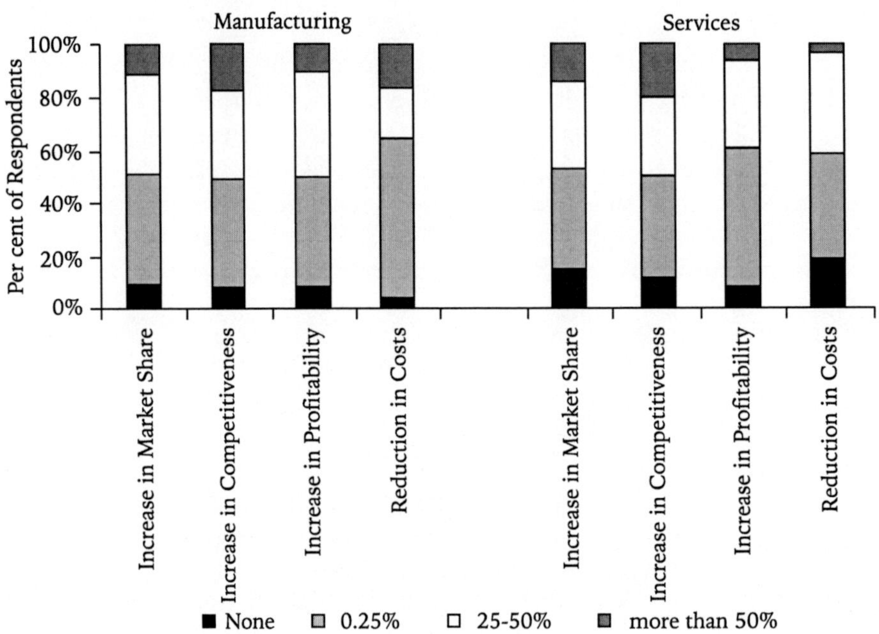

6.5 Collaboration with Universities and R&D Labs

- Large firms: More firms in the manufacturing sector collaborate with universities and R&D labs, as compared with the services sector;
- SMEs: More firms in the services sector collaborate with universities than in the manufacturing sector, and the reverse is true for collaboration with R&D labs.

Innovation has led to a greater increase in profitability for manufacturing firms and a greater reduction in costs for services firms.

6.6 Spending on R&D and Innovation

- Large firms: The average R&D spend, as a percentage of annual revenue, is lower for the services sector as compared to the manufacturing sector but innovation spending is higher.
- SMEs: Both R&D and innovation spend are higher in the case of services than manufacturing.

6.7 Further Remarks

From the above, it seems that large firms in the services sector are more specifically focused towards innovation generally, as is clear from a higher spend on innovation and collaboration with government agencies/schemes specifically for the purpose of innovation; and lower R&D spend and lower collaboration with universities and R&D labs. As we have seen in Chapter IV, collaboration with government schemes has a higher impact on innovation than collaboration with universities and R&D labs.

Similarly, SMEs in the services sector spend more on innovation and R&D as well as collaborate with government agencies/ schemes for the purpose of innovation. They also have higher collaboration with universities but lower collaboration with R&D labs.

6.8 Chapter Summary

While innovation intensity is higher for manufacturing than services (for large firms and SMEs), innovation intensity has grown faster from 2001-02 to 2005-06 for services than manufacturing. Further, services firms are more likely to be highly innovative, i.e. they have a greater propensity to introduce 'new to world' innovations. For all the firms in our sample (large firms and SMEs), innovation has had roughly the same level impact for manufacturing and services firms, in respect of increase in market share and increase in competitiveness. However, innovation has led to a greater increase in profitability for manufacturing firms and a greater reduction in costs for services firms.

Services firms are more likely to partner with government agencies with innovation being the specific purpose. In large firms, the average R&D spend, as a percentage of annual revenue, is lower for the services sector as compared to the manufacturing sector but innovation spending is higher. For SMEs, both R&D and innovation spend are higher in the case of services than manufacturing.

Services firms are more likely to partner with government agencies with innovation being the specific purpose. In large firms, the average R&D spend, as a percentage of annual revenue, is lower for the services sector as compared to the manufacturing sector but innovation spending is higher.

VII. Concluding Observations

The NKC survey confirms the rising innovation activity and awareness in India as well as the need to continuously and publicly encourage this trend as a key enabler in India's economic growth and competitiveness. It reinforces the fact that innovation is growing in the Indian economy significantly. However, there is need for further effort along a range of parameters in order to fully realise India's innovation potential. The spread and impact of innovation depends on several factors which must relate to each other in order to achieve optimal results.

7.1 Innovation Impact

We have seen from the previous chapters that innovation intensity has increased for large firms as well as SMEs. SMEs have experienced faster rates of increase as compared to large firms whereas large firms have a greater percentage of 'new to world' innovations, i.e., they are more 'highly innovative' than SMEs. We also find that more than 80 per cent of both large firms and SMEs have achieved greater competitiveness, profitability, market share and reduction of costs due to innovation. Nearly half of the large firms and SMEs attribute a change of greater than 25 per cent in each of those four factors to innovation. Increase in competitiveness and increase in market share are the most significant changes due to innovation in large firms and SMEs respectively. Eighty-one per cent of the large firms strongly agree that innovation has gained importance as being critical to growth and competitiveness since the start of economic liberalisation in India. Further, 37.3 per cent of firms have introduced breakthrough innovation, while 76.4 per cent have introduced incremental innovation. Of the firms that have introduced breakthrough innovation, 63 per cent is 'new to world'; and of the firms that have introduced incremental innovation, 39.5 per cent is 'new to world'. This indicates a significant rise in innovation-led efforts for economic growth in the country.

7.2 Processes and Services

Innovation is occurring in process (i.e., not just in product development) as well as in the services sector (i.e., not just manufacturing). Although services sector firms have lower innovation intensity, they are more likely to be highly innovative. Innovation is most highly concentrated in operations, with sales and marketing being the next most important. This emphasis on process is a departure from traditional R&D and manufacture-centric notions of innovation. Interestingly, we also observe that in our sample not a single services sector firm undertakes innovation projects that take more than three years from idea generation to market, on average. Firm processes (internal and external) are observed to have a positive impact on Innovation. There is increasing awareness of the need to establish processes for innovation. This can be seen by the fact that in each case, 60 per cent or more of the large firms in our sample are already institutionalising systems to manage innovation.

7.3 Intellectual Property

Firms in industries where innovations are patented have higher innovation intensity and are also more likely to be highly innovative. Firms that have filed more than 20 patents in the last five years have higher innovation intensity than those with less than 10 filings and are also more likely to be highly innovative. Further, firms that use IPR consultants have higher innovation intensity and are more likely to be highly innovative. At the same time, there is potential for increased scope of patentability, use of licencing as well as a greater translation of IP awareness into concrete revenue generation and asset creation.

7.4 Education

The most important external barrier to innovation, as perceived by both large firms and SMEs is skill shortage, due to the lack of emphasis on creativity, problem-solving, design, experimentation, etc., in the education curricula. In order to unleash India's innovation potential, an essential step is systematic reform of the higher education system in India, which would act as an enabler for developing the required intellectual capital as well as in laying the foundation for effective collaboration

> *Innovation is most highly concentrated in operations, with sales and marketing being the next most important. This emphasis on process is a departure from traditional R&D and manufacture-centric notions of innovation.*

The most important external barrier to innovation, as perceived by both large firms and SMEs is skill shortage, due to the lack of emphasis on creativity, problem-solving, design, experimentation, etc., in the education curricula.

between industry and educational institutions. It could be argued that innovation, education (including vocational education) and entrepreneurship are three ends of a triangle, each of which is related to the other. NKC has already made recommendations to the Prime Minister for reform in the higher education system, focusing on expansion, excellence and inclusion. In addition, NKC has also made recommendations to overhaul the system of vocational education and training (VET), with a focus on increasing industry participation in VET, which would correct the imbalance of supply and demand in VET and act as a more effective tool to address the skill shortages faced by industry. Through VET, emphasis is to be laid on skill development and inculcating a culture of entrepreneurship. Public-private-partnerships (PPP) between industry-government-academia also need to be explored. To incentivise R&D, NKC has also recommended the enactment of uniform legislation for public funded research, which is discussed under sub-section 7.5 below. Educational reforms are crucial in enabling innovation-led economic growth in the country.

7.5 R&D Collaboration

The second most important external barrier as perceived by large firms is the lack of effective collaboration between industry with research conducted in universities and R&D institutions. In fact, more than half of the large firms and SMEs claim that the lack of cooperation with universities and R&D labs is an important barrier to innovation. Conversely, there is a clear indication that collaboration with universities and R&D labs does enhance firm innovativeness. Innovation intensity is higher for firms that collaborate and the proportion of highly innovative firms is also higher. In order to create more incentives for R&D, NKC has recommended the enactment of legislation for government-funded research in the country, that would enable the following: give universities and research institutions ownership and patent rights over inventions arising out of government-funded research; create an enabling environment for universities and research institutions to commercialise such inventions through licencing arrangements/partnerships where inventors would also be allowed to receive a share of the royalty; and also thereby generally facilitate more collaborative efforts with industry.[46] There are precedents for such legislation such as the American enactment entitled the Patent and Trademark Law Amendments Act, enacted in 1980 and commonly known as the Bayh-Dole Act. Introduction of legislation generally along the lines of the Bayh-Dole Act, while keeping in mind India's specific interests, is necessary to help scientific research develop far-reaching innovations, generate employment and function as a vehicle of significant economic growth.

7.6 Government Partnerships

The study finds a small proportion of firms (roughly 30 per cent of large firms and 10 per cent of SMEs) partnering with government agencies for the purpose of innovation. These firms have a significantly higher innovation intensity as well as a significantly higher likelihood to be highly innovative. Several government programmes have been established with the explicit purpose of driving innovation in the Indian economy—notable amongst these are the NMITLI (New Millennium Indian Technology Leadership Initiative), TePP (Technopreneurs Promotion Programme), NIF (National Innovation Foundation), TDB (Technology Development Board), HGT (Home Grown Technology Program), etc. There has also been discussion in recent times on setting up of a National Innovation Programme, under the aegis of the Government. Public-private partnerships (PPP) have emerged as a tool for effecting innovation and it is expected that this trend will continue in future.

Several government programmes have been established with the explicit purpose of driving innovation in the Indian economy—notable amongst these are the NMITLI (New Millennium Indian Technology Leadership Initiative), TePP (Technopreneurs Promotion Programme), NIF (National Innovation Foundation), TDB (Technology Development Board), HGT (Home Grown Technology Program), etc.

46. For a full text of the said recommendation, refer to *http://knowledgecommission.gov.in/recommendations/legal.asp*

7.7 Other Barriers to Overcome

However, large firms have noted other barriers such as: insufficient pricing power to derive value from innovations; lack of organisational focus on innovation as a strategy for growth and competitiveness; inefficient knowledge management systems within the company; and poor understanding of customer needs and market dynamics. Similarly, SMEs also express the inability to move beyond the first successful innovation and develop a sustainable model for continuous innovation; as well as a poor understanding of customer needs and market dynamics. This is an indication of the need to achieve economies of scale in new to market, new to country and new to world' innovations. Further, innovation needs to be pursued as a strategy in itself, with benchmarking and clear organisational targets. At the same time, it appears that there is need to also address information asymmetries arising from the markets.

7.8 Systemic Reforms

Innovation is an effort that requires the synergistic use of cumulative energies of the industry, the government, the educational system, the R&D environment and the consumer. The innovation ecosystem, as seen from Figure 22.17 below, is a complex environment that requires the coordinated functioning of a number of diverse factors in order to function effectively. Innovation also needs to become as widespread as possible, spreading across the entire economy, from the grassroots to the large firm level.[47] As already noted above, crucial to the goal of increasing innovation-led growth is the need to bring about reforms in the education system, especially in respect of higher education and skill-based marketable vocational education. Therefore, the mandate of the NKC, which is to guide policy and direct reforms to allow India to effectively use and create knowledge capital, is critical and extremely relevant to furthering the cause of innovation and entrepreneurship in the Indian economy. It is felt that a comprehensive effort to address these issues would act as a critical enabling factor for India to be amongst the global leaders in innovation.

Figure 22.17: The Innovation Ecosystem

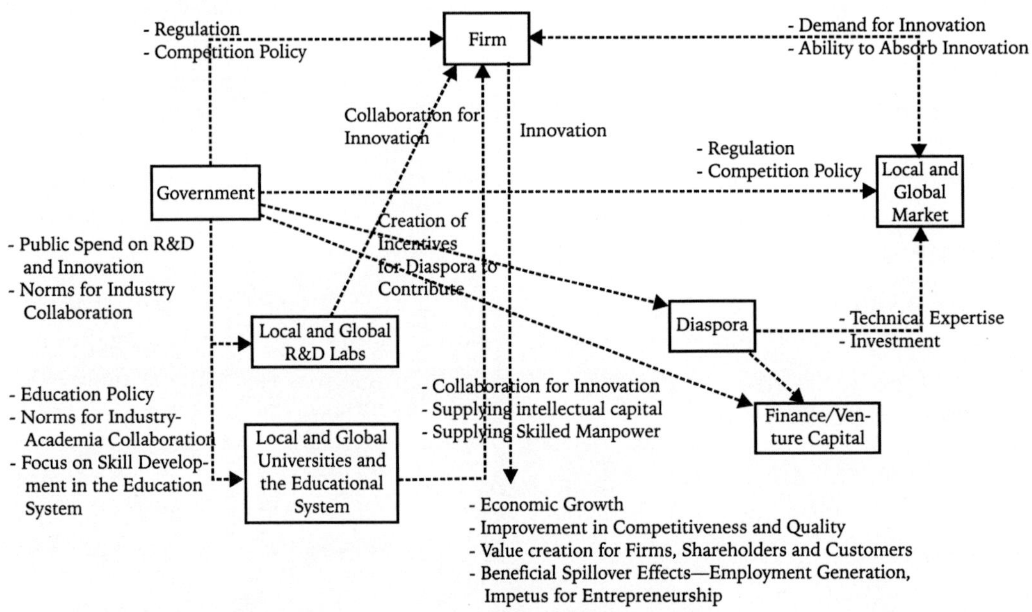

---

47. See, for example, the World Bank study on innovation (as noted in supra note 7 as above) which states that, "to unleash its Innovation potential, India needs to develop a strategy that: focuses on increasing competition as part of improving its investment climate, supported by stronger skills, better information infrastructure, and more finance—public and private; strengthens its efforts to create and commercialize knowledge, as well as better diffuse existing global and local knowledge and increase the capacity of smaller enterprises to absorb it—if all enterprises could costlessly achieve national best practice based on knowledge already used in India, the output of the economy could increase more than five-fold; fosters more inclusive Innovation—by promoting more formal R&D efforts for poor people and more creative grassroots efforts by them, and by improving the ability of informal enterprises to exploit existing knowledge", in the Executive Summary. See also, the notable work carried out by the National Innovation Foundation in respect of grassroots innovation.

A Note on Methodology

Chapter IV studies the impact of firm structure and processes on innovation by studying the following:

1. Impact on Innovation Intensity

The factors that we take up in Chapter IV may have a continuous distribution (that is, one which may have infinitely many possible outcomes, such as age of firm, size of firm, etc.) or a discrete distribution (one which has a finite number of possible outcomes, such as nature of ownership—public/private/government). In the former case, we correlate the factor in question with innovation intensity. In the latter case, we split the sample and compare the average and median innovation intensity for the different values of the discrete variable (for instance, in the case of nature of ownership, we compare the average and median innovation intensity for privately-owned firms, publicly-held firms and government-owned firms i.e., PSUs).

2. Impact on Propensity to be 'Highly Innovative'

In addition to using innovation intensity as a measure of innovative capability of a firm, we introduce an additional measure of innovativeness. We have seen in Figure 22.3 in Chapter II that 42 per cent of the large firms and 17 per cent of the SMEs in our sample have introduced innovation that is new to the global market in the last five years. From this point on, we define such firms to be 'highly innovative', and study whether efforts made by firms to establish processes to manage innovation do in fact result in firms becoming 'highly innovative'.

To check how this definition relates with innovation intensity, see the table below. It can be seen that highly innovative firms have higher innovation intensity as compared to the entire sample. (Note that since the distribution of innovation intensity is skewed, the median is a better measure to consider in this case.)

	Average Innovation Intensity	Median Innovation Intensity
Entire sample	11.15%	5.88%
Highly innovative firms	11.38%	8%

23 Entrepreneurship in India

The National Knowledge Commission recognises the growing significance and visible impact of entrepreneurship on wealth-creation and employment-generation in India. Considering its importance, NKC has undertaken a study on entrepreneurship to explore factors that have promoted entrepreneurship in India as well as others which could further encourage and facilitate even greater growth of entrepreneurship in the country. This report compliments earlier NKC studies and recommendations on Innovation and Vocational Education and Training. The NKC study has found that entrepreneurship flourishes as a result of a combined input of some key 'triggers', such as a helpful business environment, access to early-stage finance, education, individual motivation and some socio-cultural factors. To accelerate the growth of entrepreneurship in the country would require the support of multiple stakeholders such as the government, the financial institutions, educational institutions, incubator providers, chambers of commerce, entrepreneurial networks and associations as well as family and the larger community.

Based on the NKC study, some policy recommendations to further enhance entrepreneurship are as follows:

1. **Supportive Business Environment:** Make it easier to conduct business by consolidating and simplifying processes, improving delivery time and curbing corrupt practices. In particular, prioritise the MCA-21 project and ensure the following:
    - Make Single Window Clearance meaningful.
    - Introduce a Single Composite Application Form for all clearances.
    - Introduce a Single Unique Company Number for company, tax and social security registrations.
2. **New Institutional Mechanisms:**
    - Set up commercial courts to deal with commercial disputes and to speed up contract enforcement.
    - Introduce Limited Liability Partnerships (LLPs) in order to ensure flexibility and low cost of operation while limiting personal liability.
    - Establish a Global Technology Acquisition Fund for Intellectual Property (IP).
3. **Facilitate Information Flows:**

- Create 'one stop shops', web based portals and information handbooks for entrepreneurs. (NKC proposes to set up an all encompassing website on Entrepreneurship as a one-stop portal.)
- Widely publicise risk management tools such as the SME Rating Agency (SMERA), Credit Appraisal and Rating Tool (CART), Risk Assessment Model (RAM) and improving information flows through the Credit Information Bureau India Limited (CIBIL).
- Increase awareness of the Credit Guarantee Fund Trust Scheme (CGTSI). Ensure visibility and access of the 'Central Plan Scheme Monitoring System' (CPSMS), which has been proposed in the annual budget for the year 2008-09.

4. **Access to Early Stage Finance:** Banks, Venture Capitalists, Angel Investors etc., need to be more proactive in assessing the business opportunities generated by Indian entrepreneurs.

5. **Incentives for Seed Capital Funding:**

   - Establish a secondary market for smaller companies, which provides exit options to the seed stage investor and value addition for the entrepreneur.
   - Create new instruments and institutions for start-up funding, involving multiple stakeholders (public and private).

6. **Business Incubation for Entrepreneurs (BIE):** Develop and put in place a comprehensive BIE policy to increase quantity, enhance quality and increase access to financing.

7. **Industry-Academia Synergies:**

   - Enact a uniform legislation for publicly funded research which would grant IP rights for successful results of research to universities/research centres and also entitle the inventor to a share of the royalties from commercialisation.
   - Enable PhDs/researchers to set up commercial entities while engaged in universities or professional employment, as well as encourage universities/research organisations to establish commercial enterprises based on their new inventions.

8. **Entrepreneurship Education:** Make entrepreneurship a core subject in business schools and explore possibilities of setting up specialised entrepreneurship schools at the under-graduate and postgraduate levels.

9. **Vocational Educational Training (VET)/Skill Development (See NKC Report to the Nation 2006)**: Modernise VET by formalising:

   - Performance based training and assessment
   - Innovative delivery models
   - Incentives to states
   - Skills in spoken and written English as a priority
   - A transparent industry based certification system
   - A transparent rating system for VET institutions

10. **Promoting Entrepreneurial Culture:**

    - Reward and recognise successful entrepreneurs ranging from the local to the national level and formally recognise entrepreneurial networks and associations.

The Report on Entrepreneurship has concluded that the aforesaid recommendations are critical to significantly enhance entrepreneurship in the country and the NKC looks forward to being involved in their implementation, as may be appropriate.

Executive Summary

Why Entrepreneurship: Given the increasing significance and visible impact of entrepreneurship in wealth-creation and employment-generation, NKC considers it critical to India's growth and development. It has undertaken this study to explore factors that have advanced entrepreneurship in India as also various other factors that could further encourage and facilitate even greater growth.

Definition: For the purposes of this study and keeping in mind its key role in creating value, NKC defines entrepreneurship as follows:

> Entrepreneurship is the professional application of knowledge, skills and competencies and/or of monetizing a new idea, by an individual or a set of people by launching an enterprise *de novo* or diversifying from an existing one (distinct from seeking self employment as in a profession or trade), thus to pursue growth while generating wealth, employment and social good.

Methodology: The methodology adopted in preparing this report is based on one-on-one interviews with one hundred and fifty five entrepreneurs from diverse backgrounds, in selected cities across India, as well as collecting information from consultations with other relevant stakeholders in the entrepreneurial ecosystem (such as educational institutions, incubation centres, the financial community, chambers of commerce, entrepreneurial associations etc.) across the country.

Key Findings

- A successful entrepreneurship ecosystem is the function of a number of factors working in tandem. Key 'Entrepreneurial Triggers' are: individual motivations, socio-cultural factors, access to early-stage finance education and business environment.
- Prominent 'Motivation Triggers' are 'independence', 'market opportunity', 'family background', 'new idea', 'challenge', and 'dream desire'. Motivation triggers vary according to parameters such as region, gender, age, family background and work experience. 'Challenge' is the principal 'motivation driver'. 99.4 per cent of the entrepreneurs interviewed did not want to be in a routine job. Seventy-four per cent of the entrepreneurs interviewed received family support, underscoring its crucial significance.
- Sixty-three per cent of the entrepreneurs interviewed were self-financed, while other sources included banks, venture capital (VC), angel investors and state finance corporations. Among those financed by banks, a majority who approached banks (61 per cent) did receive bank finance. Yet there is a widely held perception among entrepreneurs that it is very difficult to get bank loans at the start-up stage while becoming comparatively easier at the growth stage. Perceptions regarding bank finance have not improved in case of entrepreneurs who started ventures after 2000 and are mainly in knowledge-intensive sectors.
- Ninety-five per cent of entrepreneurs believe education is a critical success factor. Education is a key trigger to evoke entrepreneurial inclinations. Ninety-eight per cent of the entrepreneurs are graduates. However, only 16 per cent chose a specific sector as a result of their educational background.
- Nearly one in two entrepreneurs considered skill shortages in recruitment to be a problem of average importance, while nearly one in three considered it 'somewhat difficult' or 'very difficult' to find candidates with the right skills. More than a third of the entrepreneurs faced problems in accessing as well as retaining employees generally.
- Fifty per cent of the entrepreneurs experienced difficulties while seeking statutory clearances and licences. Two-thirds faced hassles while filing taxes and 60 per cent claimed to have encountered corruption. Another hurdle was in accessing reliable information on registration procedures, finance and other schemes. Fifty-six per cent claimed that the paucity of quality infrastructure—especially transport, power and telecommunications—was a critical barrier.

Key Recommendations

- There is a need to demystify perceptions of risk and failure by facilitating dissemination of best practices as well as documentation of unsuccessful ideas in the entrepreneurial space. Recognition and rewards right from the local up to the national level will energise and encourage new entrepreneurs. Involving entrepreneurial networks and associations will also help in giving visibility and encouragement to entrepreneurship.

- An imaginative combination of assessing debt and equity would require positive efforts on the part of banks, financial institutions, VCs, angel investors and private equity (PE) funds. In India, financiers need to be more proactive in assessing the business opportunities generated by Indian entrepreneurs. Innovations in risk management will also reduce information asymmetry and make funding more accessible.

- Angel investors, VCs and PE funds are beginning to become more active, particularly in knowledge-intensive sectors, and need incentives for greater involvement. To create incentives for seed capital funding, some steps include the following: establishing a secondary market for smaller companies, creating new instruments for start-up funding and providing financial literacy to start-ups.

- Synergies between education (including modern vocational education training/skill development), innovation (converting ideas into wealth and employment) and entrepreneurship should be encouraged. NKC has already recommended the need to enact a uniform legislation for publicly funded research that would grant IP rights for successful results of research to universities/research centres and also entitle the inventor to a share of the royalties from commercialisation, as a source of innovation and entrepreneurial advancement. India's innovation intensity could also improve significantly if more Ph.D. and other research scholars are encouraged by providing a supportive environment for entrepreneurship. There is also a need to significantly increase Business Incubation for Entrepreneurship (BIE) by comprehensively exploring policy options to improve access to financing. While valuable work is being done by Indian incubators, there is huge scope for them to become entrepreneurial themselves by providing services such as market data, helping in preparing business models, recruiting skilled employees, etc.

- Growing the pool of skilled people is a key priority. This entirely depends upon access to quality education. The key challenges in higher education relate to ensuring access, inclusiveness and excellence. In Vocational Education and Training (VET) there is need to completely overhaul and modernise current institutions and practices. Reforms in VET require innovative delivery models, providing incentives for states, ensuring performance-based training and assessment, re-branding, certification, encouraging learning-by-doing, incentivising English speaking skills, ensuring flexibility of VET alongside the higher education stream, for easier crossover and choice, as critical success factors.

- Economic liberalisation has been a key catalyst to encourage entrepreneurship. There are a number of initiatives at the central and state levels which aim to improve the ease of doing business. In fact, the *Doing Business Report 2008* (published by the World Bank-IFC) states that India can jump 55 places from its current rank of 120th if some of the local best practices are adopted nationwide. Priority should be given to the *MCA-21* project (initiated by the Ministry of Company Affairs) to fully automate processes of enforcement and compliance. Other suggestions to enhance entrepreneurship include the following: meaningful implementation of the Single Window System; introducing a Single Composite Application Form as already done in a few states; introducing a 'Single Unique Company Number' (for company, tax and social security registrations); reducing the frequency of tax payments for entrepreneurs from monthly to quarterly; creating specialised commercial courts; introducing Limited Liability Partnerships (LLPs); and creating 'one-stop shops' to provide all relevant information needed to start an entrepreneurial activity. There are a number of websites relating to entrepreneurship in India. In this regard, NKC proposes to explore the possibility of having an all encompassing website on entrepreneurship as a one-stop information portal for current and aspiring entrepreneurs. In addition, entrepreneurship in India will also grow significantly with the spread of e-governance and quality infrastructure development.

I. Introduction: Why Entrepreneurship

1.1 Defining Entrepreneurship

1.1.1 Entrepreneurship means different things to different people.[1] Conceptually and in practice, the term hints of no stereotypical model. Yet its very etymology—derived from the French '*entreprendre* which literally means, 'to undertake'[2]—indicates the minimum characteristics of an entrepreneur.

1.1.2 From the perspective of economic functions, three crucial characteristics of entrepreneurial activity are: risk taking, innovation and venturing into new business activities for profit.[3]

1.1.3 For the purposes of this study and keeping in mind its key role in creating value, NKC defines entrepreneurship as follows:

> Entrepreneurship is the professional application of knowledge, skills and competencies and/or of monetizing a new idea, by an individual or a set of people by launching an enterprise *de novo* or diversifying from an existing one (distinct from seeking self employment as in a profession or trade), thus to pursue growth while generating wealth, employment and social good.

1.2 Role of Entrepreneurship in the Economy: Creating Value

1.2.1 The entrepreneur who implements "new combinations of means of production" plays a crucial role in disturbing the *status quo* through innovation—or "creative destruction"—and thereby becomes an agent of change.[4] As such, the 'dynamic equilibrium' achieved by a constantly innovating entrepreneur could generate the conditions for:

a. increasing opportunities for employment (comprising various competitive skill sets);

b. additional wealth creation;

Entrepreneurship is the professional application of knowledge, skills and competencies and/or of monetizing a new idea, by an individual or a set of people by launching an enterprise de novo or diversifying from an existing one (distinct from seeking self employment as in a profession or trade), thus to pursue growth while generating wealth, employment and social good.

---

1. Entrepreneurship has been understood to mean, among other things: "the ability to create and build something from practically nothing" (Timmons, J.A. (1989). *The Entrepreneurial Mind*); "the creation of new economic opportunities" (Wennekers and Thurik, (1999). *Linking Entrepreneurship and Economic Growth*); "creating and managing vision and demonstrating leadership" (Wickham (1998). *Strategic Entrepreneurship: A Decision Making Approach to New Venture Creation and Management*, page 34); "the ability to see and evaluate business opportunities" (Meredith (1982). *The Practice of Entrepreneurship*, page 3; see also the GEM studies that distinguish between 'need based' and 'opportunity based' entrepreneurship); 'a practice with a knowledge base' (Drucker, Peter, *Innovation and Entrepreneurship*, page viii); "an ability to assemble or reassemble from what is available into a new kind of activity" (Marris, Peter (1968). "The Social Barriers to African Entrepreneurship", *Journal of Developing Societies*, October, as quoted in Thomas A. Timberg (1978). *The Marwaris: From Traders to Industrialists*, page 19); "the shifting of economic resources out of an area of lower productivity into one of higher productivity and yield" (*The Economist*, October 13, 2007, page 18 of the special section on Innovation, quoting Jean Baptiste Say) as well as "an activity characterised by the goals of profitability, growth and innovative practices" (see Joseph Schumpeter's works generally, quoted in Kirby, supra note 1 as above, page 10).

2. David Kirby (2003). *Entrepreneurship*, McGraw Hill, page 13; see also "Entrepreneurial Management: In Pursuit of Opportunity", *The Intellectual Venture Capitalist*: John H. McArthur and the work of the Harvard Business School, 1980-1995 (Ed. Thomas K. McCraw and Jeffrey L. Cruikshank (1999). Harvard Business School Press); insight provided by Mohit Malik, Innova Consulting, New Delhi; coinage of the term is also attributed to the economist Jean Baptiste Say.

3. See McCraw *et al.* in supra note 2 as above; see also Davidson, Per (2004). *Researching Entrepreneurship*, Springer, page 1-3, who succinctly states that "researching Entrepreneurship is fun, fascinating and frustrating...one of the fascinations is the richness of the phenomenon, which leads to one of its greatest frustrations, namely the lack of a common understanding of what precisely Entrepreneurship is". See also Goel, Abhishek Neharika Vohra, Liyan Zhang, Bhupinder Arora' "Attitudes of the Youth towards Entrepreneurs and Entrepreneurship: A Cross Cultural Comparison of India and China", Indian Institute of Management (IIM) Ahmedabad paper; Goel *et al.* summarise some of the existing approaches as follows: "leader manager" (Mill, 1848; Brockhaus and Horwitz, 1986; McClelland, 1961); "innovator" (Schumpeter, 1934); "risk taker" (Brockhaus and Horwitz, 1986); "with internal locus of control" (Rotter, 1966; as in B & H, 1986); and 'different from managers' (Penrose); quoting Cunnigham and Lischeron (1991), who understood the term from the following perspectives: "psychological", "opportunity", leadership and intrapreneurship (within organisations)

4. David Kirby, supra note 2 as above on page 15 quoting Joseph Schumpeter.

c. introduction and dissemination of new methods and technology; and

d. overall economic growth.[5]

It is in the creation of more wealth, and in the constant innovation from prevailing to the next best practices, that the significance and importance of entrepreneurship lies.

1.2.2 As such, the development of entrepreneurship in a particular milieu depends not on a single overriding factor but rather on "a constellation of factors" at the individual, societal and national levels.[6] Entrepreneurship depends on individual motivations, individual experiences, socio-cultural (including family) traditions, educational opportunities, availability of relevant skills and attitudes, supporting financial institutions and access to credit, existence of commercial trading centres, supporting infrastructure including trade routes with efficient transport and communication facilities, macroeconomic environment and overall political stability.[7] It has also been argued that innovation and entrepreneurship flourish best in decentralised systems by empowered people, who are willing to explore new ideas as well as willing to deal with exogenous influences.[8]

1.3 Entrepreneurship in India

1.3.1 Entrepreneurship has been "embedded in the Indian genius and is a part of its tradition."[9] To quote the renowned economist, T.N. Srinivasan, "India has been an entrepreneurial society...we had the entrepreneurial skill but suppressed it for too long a time... and now it is thriving."[10] The entrepreneurial spirit is an ongoing characteristic of India's history, particularly visible in a number of communities engaged primarily in trading.[11] Traditionally, the entrepreneurship of such communities is facilitated principally by the successful use of informal "entrepreneurial ecosystems" and interdependent business networks.[12] Further, there is also a rich tradition within the Indian diaspora, spanning the past several hundred years, whose spirit of enterprise is legion.[13]

It is in the creation of more wealth, and in the constant innovation from prevailing to the next best practices, that the significance and importance of entrepreneurship lies.

5. See, for example Drucker, Peter *Innovation and Entrepreneurship*, supra note 1 as above, pages 1-7, who attributes the surge of employment figures between 1965 and 1985 and the creation of 40 million jobs in USA to entrepreneurship. In his words, "Where did all the new jobs come from? The answer is everywhere and nowhere; in other words, from no one single source." See also, the results of the SEAF study, 2004, "The Development Impact of Small and Medium Enterprises: Lessons Learnt from SEAF Investments", Report, Small Enterprise Development Funds, which stated that for every dollar invested on average, ten additional dollars were generated in the local economy, accompanied by the creation of new jobs, introduction of new business methods and integration into supply chains. See also Dossani Rafiq and Asawari Desai (2006). *Accessing Early Stage Risk Capital in India*, Stanford-TiE Study, page 16; see also, Report of the Symposium on the Small Business Innovation Research Program, National Research Council, USA, 2007. See also, "What it takes to be an Entrepreneur", speech by C.K. Prahalad to GLIM Chennai, *Hindu Business Line* dated February 25, 2008, as quoted in *http://www.ibef.org*; according to the provisional data of the Fifth Economic Census (2005) there are 42.12 million 'enterprises' in India engaged in different economic activities (other than crop production and plantation.) An enterprise is defined in the Fifth Economic Census as "an undertaking engaged in production and/or distribution of goods and/or services not for the sole purpose of own consumption". Five states—Andhra Pradesh, Maharashtra, Tamil Nadu, Uttar Pradesh and West Bengal together account for about 50 per cent of the total enterprises in the country. The total number of persons working in all the enterprises is about 98.97 million. The overall average annual growth rate in enterprises per year during the period 1998 to 2005 was 4.80 per cent and the average annual growth rate in total employment during over the same period was 2.49 per cent.
6. Tripathy Dwijendra (ed.) (1984). *Business Communities of India: A Historical Perspective*, page 18.
7. See Tripathy supra note 6 as above, page 18- 19; Timberg supra note 1 as above, page 15 quoting Gadgil, D.R. (1958). *Origins of the Modern Indian Business Class*, page 1-16; see also, Gopalakrishnan, R. (2007). "Prosperity Beyond Our Cities by Spreading Enterprise", A.D. Shroff Memorial Lecture, October 17, page 8.
8. R. Gopalakrishnan, supra note 7 as above, page 3, 6.
9. R. Gopalakrishnan, supra note 7 as above, page 8.
10. Srinivasan, T.N. (2007). in an interview to *The Hindu Business Line*, April 23.
11. See Tripathy, supra note 6 as above, for an overview of business communities in India at different epochs; see also, Timberg, supra note 1 as above on the Marwari business community; see also Markovits, Claude *The Global World of Indian Merchants, 1750-1947: Traders of Sind from Bukhara to Panama*; see also Rutten, Mario *Farms and Factories: Social Profiles of Large Farmers and Rural Industrialists in Western India*.
12. This topic is explained in detail in the following chapter. Examples include community credit networks, forms of reciprocal social support, apprenticeships, business networks, the availability of markets as well as the influence of factors such as migration, in part influenced by geography. A web of social interdependence along with "contact with other professionals, sharing a particular body of values...a sense of belonging and by the very nature of the alliances, sharing a community of interests" (Melvin Weber) are a part of such informal ecosystems that have already existed in the country.
13. R. Gopalakrishnan, supra note 7 as above, page 7; see also, Markovits, supra note 11 as above.

1.3.2 Entrepreneurship in India occurs in "far more encompassing and far reaching ways than in developed countries", and could therefore, be far more complex, "for there is so much more that needs to be done."[14] Commentators today celebrate the ubiquitous Indian attitude of *'Jugaad'* (a Hindi word roughly translated as "creative improvisation...a tool to somehow find a solution based on a refusal to accept defeat, and calling on initiative, quick thinking, cunning and resolve...to quickly fulfill market demands at the lowest possible prices"[15]) as an entrepreneurial trait that has been as much a part of everyday Indian living as its rich tradition of philosophy and speculation.

1.3.3 The salience of entrepreneurship in India has intensified in recent times, particularly with the rise in knowledge-intensive services. New entrepreneurs who do not belong to traditional business communities have begun to emerge in large numbers. Entrepreneurship has grown rapidly, visibly so, creating wealth and generating employment, especially in the past 20 years. Crucial efforts initiated after economic liberalisation—including systematic attempts to reduce the 'licence raj', greater efforts to make finance more easily accessible to entrepreneurs and other institutional support to 'techno-preneurs'—have helped improve the climate for entrepreneurship.[16]

The software industry, in particular, its initial growth arising largely out of the "interstices inadvertently left untouched by the State", has today taken giant strides, with the top companies working "within the market and with a fuller understanding of the rules of international commerce."[17]

Thus, the opportunities created by today's global knowledge economy coupled with the "unshackling of indigenous enterprise", have contributed to making India a "fertile ground" for entrepreneurship.[18]

1.3.4 Statistics on the growth of India's technology driven entrepreneurship are telling. In a recent survey by the Deloitte group, India ranks 2nd globally as home to the fastest growing technology firms. Eighty-two Indian companies entered the Deloitte Technology Fast 500 list of Asia-Pacific Companies in 2007 and the companies that have made it to the Technology Fast 50 of India have an average three-year revenue growth of 489 per cent.[19] In this respect, particularly in high skill innovation driven entrepreneurship, the opportunities offered by complex and interconnected global networks are also relevant. The ability to "adapt to changing market conditions and anticipate future technologies and economic trends"[20] and leverage across a large number of markets provides "opportunities for exploiting economies of scale."[21] As such, comparative knowledge leverage at lower costs would play a key role in the race to achieve economic competitiveness.

Entrepreneurship in India occurs in "far more encompassing and far reaching ways than in developed countries", and could therefore be far more complex, "for there is so much more that needs to be done."

14. Khanna, Tarun (2007). *Billions of Entrepreneurs: How China and India are Reshaping their Future and Yours*, page 20; see also C.K. Prahalad speech to GLIN Chennai, supra note 5 as above at *www.ibef.org*

15. See Verma, Pawan K. *Being Indian*; see also Rai, Vinay (2007). *Think India*, pages 29-31; also, Nath, Kamal (2007). *India's Century: The Age of Entrepreneurship in the World's Biggest Democracy*,page 3-5 where he extols *Jugaad* as "innovation...a survival tool for Indians, where every obstacle became an opportunity"; also for a general overview of India's historical tradition of dialogue on matters beyond the speculative, see Sen, Amartya (2005). *The Argumentative Indian*.

16. See Abhishek Goel *et al.*, supra note 3 as above.

17. Tarun Khanna, supra note 14 as above, page 24, 130; see also, *The Economist*, October 13, 2007, page 21 of the special section on Innovation, which also quotes Curtis Carlson, Head of California's Stanford Research Institute, stating, "China and India are a tsunami about to overwhelm us."

18. See Tarun Khanna, supra note 14 as above, page 121, 126 ; see also references to recent acquisitions by Indian companies in the global market, especially Tata acquisition of Corus and Mittal Steel acquisition of Arcelor recently; also Gupta, Rajat (2001). "Creating Indian Entrepreneurs", McKinsey and Company; see also Kamal Nath, supra note 15 as above, where he states that "the sinews of the new Indian industry are respect for knowledge, knowledge systems and knowledge protection" at page 128; see also Abhishek Goel *et al.*, supra note 3 as above, to quote, "entrepreneurial activity has been identified as one resource that needs to be tapped by developing countries to enable them to compete in a globalizing market economy."

19. *The Economic Times*, November 25, 2007.

20. See Bowonder, Kelkat, N.G. Satish, J.K. Racheria, (2006). "Innovation in India: Recent Trends", TTMC *Research Paper*, March 31; also Haque, I. (1995). *Trade, Development and International Competitiveness*, World Bank.

21. See Bowonder *et al.*, supra note 20 as above, page 2. See also "Innovation in India", report of the National Knowledge Commission, 2007, which surveys large firms as well as SMEs across India and confirms the rise in innovation activity.

The opportunities created by today's global knowledge economy coupled with the "unshackling of indigenous enterprise", have contributed to making India a "fertile ground" for entrepreneurship.

1.3.5 Recent surveys, such as those undertaken by Goldman Sachs and PricewaterhouseCoopers, have estimated that India has the potential to be among the world's leading economies by 2050.[22] Further, India's economy can potentially gain significantly from the country's characteristic features—a democratic open society, a strong technology base (with capacity for leapfrogging), unparalleled diversity, vibrant capital markets (including growing private equity and venture capital markets), an increasingly youthful population (50 per cent of India is 25 years and younger), a sizeable market of a large number of customers with vast unmet needs as well as an environment of full and free competition in the private sector.[23]

1.3.6 In this situation, India enjoys enormous potential for the creation of wealth through knowledge. Entrepreneurship and Innovation are the key drivers for generating wealth from knowledge, supported principally by the availability of skilled human resources, access to finance and the ability of the State to create an enabling environment.

1.3.7 The entrepreneurship 'Pyramid' in India (in terms of sectors and numbers of people engaged) is made up of the following:[24]

- *Level 1:* Agriculture and other activities: Crop production, plantation, forestry, livestock, fishing, mining and quarrying.
- *Level 2:* Trading services: Wholesale and retail trade; hotels and restaurants.
- *Level 3:* Old economy or traditional sectors: Manufacturing, electricity, gas and water supply.
- *Level 4:* Emerging sectors (including knowledge-intensive sectors): IT, finance, insurance and business services, construction, community, social and personal services, supply chain, transport-storage-communications, etc.

1.3.8 Levels 2 and 3 (Trading and Manufacturing) of the above pyramid comprise the traditional areas of entrepreneurship. Level 4, on the other hand, is an emerging/modern sector of entrepreneurship with high growth rates. In future we may expect a broadening of Levels 3 and 4 with the activities from Levels 1 and 2 migrating to the other levels.[25] Such trends are already being seen upon analysing time series data regarding registration of new companies according to sectors (See Figure 23.2). The number of new companies registered (a proportion of which relate to entrepreneurship) has in general been increasing over the past years. The figure below clearly shows that the number of new companies in Level 4 has been growing at a much faster rate compared to those in the other levels. At the same time, it must be noted that most entrepreneurial ventures in Levels 1 and 2 do not register themselves as companies and instead function largely as self-employed entities.

Entrepreneurship and innovation are the key drivers for generating wealth from knowledge, supported principally by the availability of skilled human resources, access to finance and the ability of the State to create an enabling environment.

---

22. See *Outlook Business*, May 5, 2007; Goldman Sachs' BRIC report states that by 2050, India could have a GDP of $37.66 trillion, just marginally less than USA's estimated $38.51 trillion. The PricewaterhouseCoopers report, *The World in 2050* states that India could be the fastest growing economy by 2050.

23. Govindarajan, Vijay (2007). *Outlook Business*, May 5.

24. This 'pyramid' is illustrative and provides an understanding of the type of sectors in which entrepreneurship takes place in India. Some statistics from the the 4th CSO Economic Census (1998) were useful in this regard. While the said census does not cover enterprises engaged in crop production and plantation, we include them in our understanding of Level 1 of the Pyramid. As per the census, 41 per cent of all existing enterprises in India (excluding those engaged in crop production and plantation) are engaged in activities falling under Level 2 and 18 per cent are engaged in activities falling under Level 3. Further, Level 4 in this pyramid represents emerging/modern sectors of entrepreneurship with high growth rates.

25. In the NKC sample, among the entrepreneurs interviewed who started ventures before 1990, 77 per cent of them belonged to the manufacturing sector, 11 per cent were in the 'knowledge-intensive services' sector, and 13 per cent were in the 'other services' sector. On the other hand, of the entrepreneurs interviewed who started their business after 1990, 57 per cent were involved in 'knowledge intensive services', 23 per cent in 'manufacturing', and 20 per cent in 'other services'. This could indicate a shift from entrepreneurship in traditional sectors into emerging and high-tech areas. See also Tarun Khanna, supra note 14 as above at page 207. Further, according to the annual budget for 2008-2009, estimated growth rates in services and manufacturing are 10.7 per cent and 9.4 per cent respectively.

Figure 23.1: Entrepreneurship Pyramid

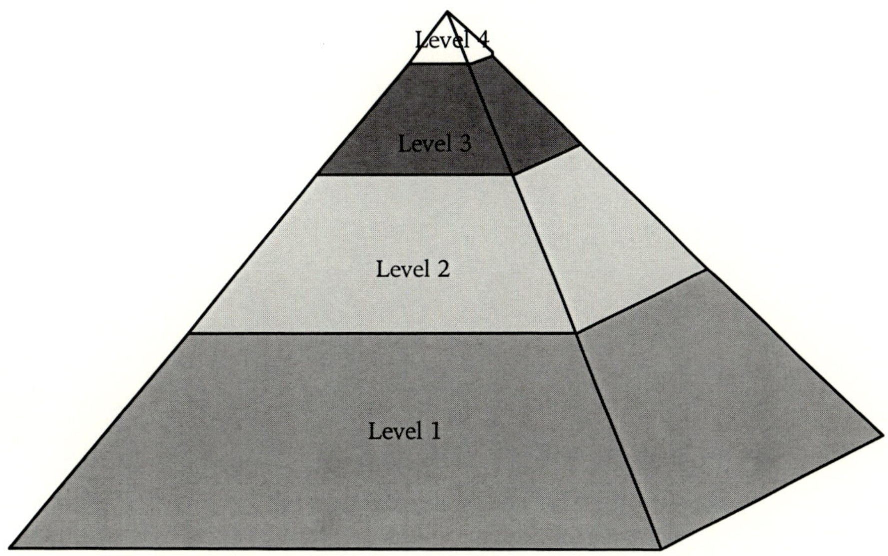

Figure 23.2: Registration of New Companies According to Nature of Economic Activity

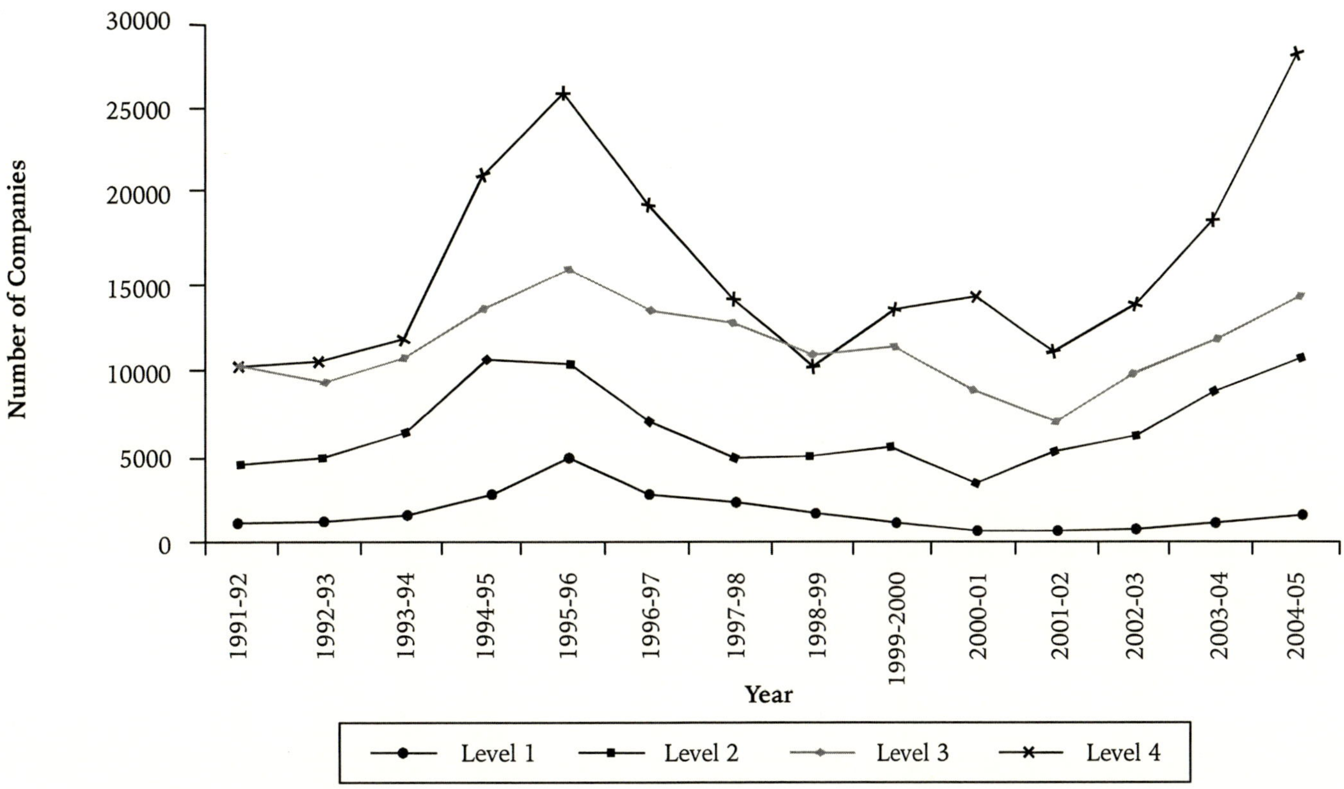

Note: Data for 2001-02 was not available.

Source: Based on data received from Ministry of Company Affairs.

Entrepreneurship and Innovation are the key drivers for generating wealth from knowledge, supported principally by the availability of skilled human resources, access to finance and the ability of the State to create an enabling environment.

This study explores factors that have advanced entrepreneurship in India as also various others that could further encourage and facilitate even greater growth.

1.3.9 *Design of NKC Study:* Given the increasing significance and visible impact of entrepreneurship in wealth creation and employment-generation, NKC considered the subject to be of immense importance in India's growth and development. This study explores factors that have advanced entrepreneurship in India as also various others that could further encourage and facilitate even greater growth. The methodology adopted for this exploration includes structured one-on-one interviews with entrepreneurs and other stakeholders in the entrepreneurial ecosystem (such as educational institutions, incubation centres, the banking and financial sector, including angel investors and venture capitalists, as well as chambers of commerce, entrepreneurial associations, etc.) across the country. For the list of 155 entrepreneurs interviewed along with a brief background (see Consultations). For details on Methodology. Most of the entrepreneurs interviewed are from Ahmedabad, Pune, Bangalore, Chennai, Hyderabad and Kolkata.[26]

Overall, responses from more than 200 stakeholders were collected. This study also refers to relevant literature on the topic, both at the academic and policy levels.

1.3.10 A classification of the entrepreneurs interviewed in terms of some key parameters such as sectors, turnover, employment, age, family background, gender and time period are as follows:

- **Sector:** The bulk of the entrepreneurs interviewed belong to the 'manufacturing' and 'knowledge-intensive services' sectors. (See Levels 3 and 4 of the pyramid above); in addition, an ancillary segment of 'other services' is also covered.[27]
- **Turnover:** While entrepreneurs revealed a wide range in annual turnover (from less than Rs. 1 crore to more than Rs. 500 crore), the majority in the sample report a turnover of less than Rs. 100 crore (< Rs. 1 crore: 22 per cent; Rs. 1-10 crore: 35 per cent; Rs. 10-100 crore: 30 per cent). The median turnover was Rs. 5 crore.
- **Employment:** About 81 per cent of the entrepreneurs interviewed have less than 250 employees each (<10 employees: 17 per cent; 10-50 employees: 33 per cent; 50-250 employees: 31 per cent; >250 employees: 19 per cent). The median number of employees is 44.
- **Age:** While entrepreneurs across a range of age groups (from 21 to 70) were interviewed, the median age of the sample of entrepreneurs is 43. In fact, one-fourth of the entrepreneurs are under 35, which enabled us to get valuable insights from younger entrepreneurs. The median age at which individuals in the sample became entrepreneurs was 27.
- **Family Background:** The sample comprises three types of entrepreneurs: first generation entrepreneurs, second generation entrepreneurs in the same business and second generation entrepreneurs in a different business. In fact, 63 per cent of the entrepreneurs interviewed were first generation entrepreneurs, 22 per cent were second generation entrepreneurs who started their own businesses and 15 per cent were second generation entrepreneurs running their family businesses. Since the growth in scale and scope of entrepreneurship is intimately connected to the increasing numbers of first generation entrepreneurs, most of the entrepreneurs interviewed belong to this segment.

While entrepreneurs across a range of age groups (from 21 to 70) were interviewed, the median age of the sample of entrepreneurs is 43. In fact, one-fourth of the entrepreneurs are under 35, which enabled us to get valuable insights from younger entrepreneurs. The median age at which individuals in the sample became entrepreneurs was 27.

26. A few entrepreneurs from National Capital Region (NCR) and Mumbai were also interviewed.

27. 'Manufacturing' includes auto components, steel, textiles, leather, ceramics, etc; 'Knowledge-intensive services' include IT/ITeS, animation, business services, finance, health care, etc; 'Other services' includes services such as travel and tours, event management, catering, retail, etc. This focus does not take away from the importance of the other sectors, where very interesting developments are taking place and are subjects of very rich and detailed analytical study.

- **Gender:** About 16 per cent of the entrepreneurs interviewed were women.
- **Time Period:** To explore factors across various time periods, the sample is spread as follows. Forty-one per cent of the sample entrepreneurs started their ventures before 1991; 25 per cent started during the 1990s and 34 per cent after 2000.

1.3.11 Based on the interviews, this study concludes that a successful entrepreneurship ecosystem is the function of a number of factors working in tandem. These are classified as 'Entrepreneurial Triggers'.[28] Each of these triggers is discussed in the subsequent chapters. These are as follows:

- Individual Motivations for Entrepreneurship.
- Socio-Cultural Factors.
- Access to Early Stage Finance.
- Education and Incubation.
- Business Environment for Entrepreneurship.

These are dynamic issues and are continuously evolving and need to be periodically monitored.

1.4 Chapter Summary

While there are various definitions of entrepreneurship, there are some common themes. Entrepreneurship involves risk taking, being innovative as well as using knowledge and skills to set up new ventures or diversify from existing ones. Entrepreneurship adds significant value to the economy by creating wealth and generating employment. India has a rich tradition of entrepreneurship, practised in diverse ways. Entrepreneurship is embedded in the Indian mindset. After economic liberalisation, there has been increased salience of entrepreneurship in India, particularly in the high growth and knowledge-intensive sectors. The NKC study examines entrepreneurship across a range of parameters to identify and understand the principal enabling and hindering factors. Entrepreneurship flourishes as a combined result of a number of key triggers such as individual motivations, socio-cultural attitudes, access to early stage finance, education and incubation as well as the overall business environment. These are specifically referred to in this study.

Based on the interviews, this study concludes that a successful entrepreneurship ecosystem is the function of a number of factors working in tandem. These are classified as 'Entrepreneurial Triggers'.

28. Conversely, when we asked entrepreneurs about the most significant obstacles in scaling up (from small to medium, or medium to large), the three main responses pertained to finance, human resources/skills and infrastructure. Newer entrepreneurs also have to deal with issues relating to obtaining clients, acquiring office space, getting a good team and marketing their product or service. As such, some of the key challenges facing the 'small and medium' sector in India today include the following: inadequate access to finance (including lack of financial information, access to private equity, venture capital and very limited access to secondary market instruments), fragmented markets, lack of easy access to national and international markets, lack of awareness of global best practices and innovations, delays in settlement of dues by larger buyers, inadequacy of quality infrastructure and of opportunities for marketing of products and services etc. See in particular, the 'Policy Package for Stepping Up Credit to SMEs', announced by the Finance Minister, as quoted in Annexure IV of the RBI Master Circular on Lending to SME sector, dated July 2, 2007.

II. What Motivates Entrepreneurship

2.1 What are some of the Motivations?

2.1.1 There are varied approaches to understanding why some individuals decide to venture into entrepreneurship and, thereby, "break through traditional ways of doing things."[29] Notwithstanding numerous studies on "entrepreneurial traits", there are no "well-defined psychological attitudes or profiles that describe all entrepreneurs or characteristics to which entrepreneurs generally conform."[30] As Amar Bhide put it, "There is no ideal profile. Entrepreneurs can be gregarious or taciturn, analytical or intuitive, cautious or daring."[31] Some theoretical explanations of what motivates entrepreneurs include the following:

- The 'Achievement Orientation' or the desire to achieve purely for the sake of achievement alone.[32]
- The interrelation between religion, norms, values, behaviour and the economy in a particular epoch.[33]
- The ability to comprehend opportunity, i.e., "to reinterpret the meaning of things, fit them together in new ways" and "see what others may have missed, such as an unsatisfied demand."[34]
- The capacity to sustain a high degree of interest in the advancement and technological development of the industrial process and in the improvement in the scale of industrial operations.[35]
- The ability to make the best of what one has, in order to get what one needs, i.e., the capacity to innovate in figuring out the best ways to reach the market with minimum expenditure of time, effort and money.[36]

2.1.2 The NKC Study confirms that there is no single motivating factor that triggers the decision to become an entrepreneur. As seen from the figure below, the significant 'Motivation Triggers' are: 'Independence' (stemming from the freedom to do 'one's own thing'), 'Market Opportunity', 'Family Background' in entrepreneurship, a 'New Idea' (with business potential), the prospect of 'Challenge' offered by entrepreneurship as well as a long cherished 'Dream Desire' to become an entrepreneur.

2.1.3 'Internal' factors (such as Independence, Challenge and Dream Desire, i.e., the idea that 'by nature, man cannot but be an entrepreneur') cumulatively account for the bulk of the total motivating triggers (42 per cent). This lends credence to the argument that the entrepreneurs are driven more by their own inner drive rather than by external conditions. At the same time, as elaborated in the paragraphs that follow, 'market opportunity' as an additional motivating factor has also shown a steady rise over the last two decades. This fact gives rise to the argument that macro environment plays a crucial role in influencing the initial decision of an individual to become an entrepreneur.

According to Amar Bhide, "there is no ideal profile. Entrepreneurs can be gregarious or taciturn, analytical or intuitive, cautious or daring."

---

29. Rutten, Mario *Farms and Factories: Social Profiles of Large Farmers and Rural Industrialists in Western India*, page 23; see also paras 1.1 and 1.2; read with relevant footnotes in Chapter 1.
30. See, for example, *Entrepreneurial Management: In Pursuit of Opportunity*, The Intellectual Venture Capitalist: John H. McArthur and the work of the Harvard Business School, 1980-1995 (Ed. Thomas K. McCraw and Jeffrey L. Cruikshank. Harvard Business School Press, 1999) who discusses various studies; to quote, "Although this individually and psychologically oriented research has pointed to some interesting correlations, unfortunate consequences too easily result from such a focus. It implicitly suggests that, if one could only discern the psychological profile of an entrepreneur and then hold an individual up against that profile, one could predict whether that individual has the potential to become an entrepreneur, or is one already. Yet none of the proposed "profiles" applies to all entrepreneurs, and many entrepreneurs refuse to conform to any of these profiles."
31. Bhide, Amar (1994). *How Entrepreneurs Craft*, Harvard Business Review, March-April.
32. Attributed to David McClelland, see Mario Rutten, supra note 16 as above, at page 23; See also , Gopalakrishnan, R. (2007). "Prosperity Beyond Our Cities by Spreading Enterprise", AD Shroff Memorial Lecture, October 17; see generally, David Kirby, supra note 1 as above.
33. Attributed to the sociologist Max Weber, see Mario Rutten, supra note 16 as above at page 23.
34. Marris, Peter (1968). "The Social Barriers of African Entrepreneurship", *Journal of Developing Societies* (October), as quoted in Thomas A. Timberg (1978). *The Marwaris: From Traders to Industrialists*, page 19; see also, the GEM studies on entrepreneurship that distinguish between 'need based' and 'opportunity based' entrepreneurship.
35. Mario Rutten, supra note 16 as above at page 24.
36. See the work of Saras D. Sarasvathy generally on the 'affordable loss principle', at the University of Virginia, Darden School Foundation.

2.1.4 To illustrate the many reasons for becoming an entrepreneur, here are some direct quotes from entrepreneurs interviewed for the NKC study:

- "Entrepreneurship offers the opportunity to create something of one's own."
- "Entrepreneurs get the opportunity to make the road as well as walk on it."
- "Entrepreneurship allows people to think outside the box and make thoughts work."
- "Entrepreneurs are not confined to a particular area of business; they need to know everything about how business runs."
- "Entrepreneurship allows possibilities for constant self-actualisation."
- "Entrepreneurship is about the ability to survive long enough till one succeeds."
- "Entrepreneurship is about the sheer joy of taking an idea and making it work."
- "Entrepreneurs are like lotuses—born out of dirt—and all they need is a flourishing environment."
- "Entrepreneurs like to do it their way—they are virtually unemployable."
- "Entrepreneurship brings pride, passion and self-respect, from doing things on one's own."
- "Entrepreneurship gives the freedom to try something new and break stereotypes."
- "Entrepreneurship provides a constant learning experience and a continuous process of growth."
- "Entrepreneurship brings a sense of belongingness derived from doing one's own thing and providing employment to many."
- "Entrepreneurship provides the opportunity to create wealth and make the best of the economic environment."

Figure 23.3: Motivation to become an Entrepreneur

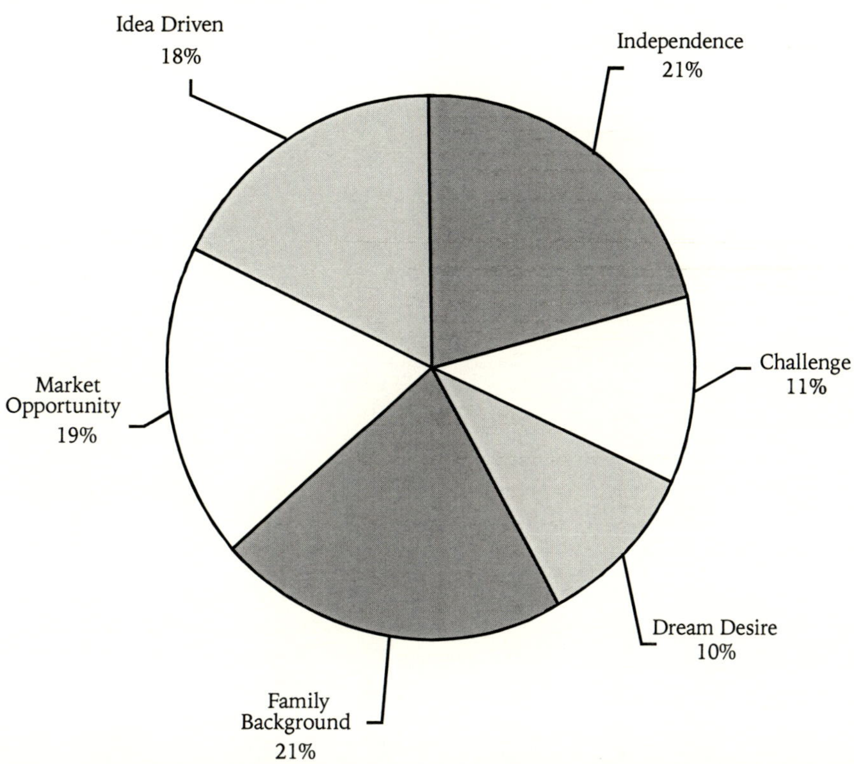

The entrepreneurs are driven more by their own inner drive rather than by external conditions. At the same time, 'market opportunity' as an additional motivating factor has also shown a steady rise over the last two decades.

2.2 Variations in Motivation Triggers

The NKC Study also reveals interesting variations across region, gender, age, family background, time period and levels of work experience.

2.2.1 *Variations According to Region:* The most significant motivating trigger for entrepreneurship was found to be wide ranging across regions—from 'family background' being the prime trigger in Ahmedabad and Kolkata to 'market opportunity' serving as the most important motivator in Bangalore. Gujarat has been a traditional trading and business hub that may explain greater influence of family background as a prime trigger. In West Bengal, the seeds of entrepreneurship were sown by migrants belonging to traditional business communities from Rajasthan. On the other hand, Bangalore, an IT hub and a centre of educational excellence, has emerged as an attractive centre for knowledge entrepreneurship, driven by increasing market opportunity. Chennai and Pune have also been educational centres of repute, which may explain the pre-eminence of idea-driven entrepreneurship in these cities. Interestingly, entrepreneurs from Hyderabad valued 'independence' as a trigger more than other factors.

Figure 23.4: Highest Motivation—Variations According to Region

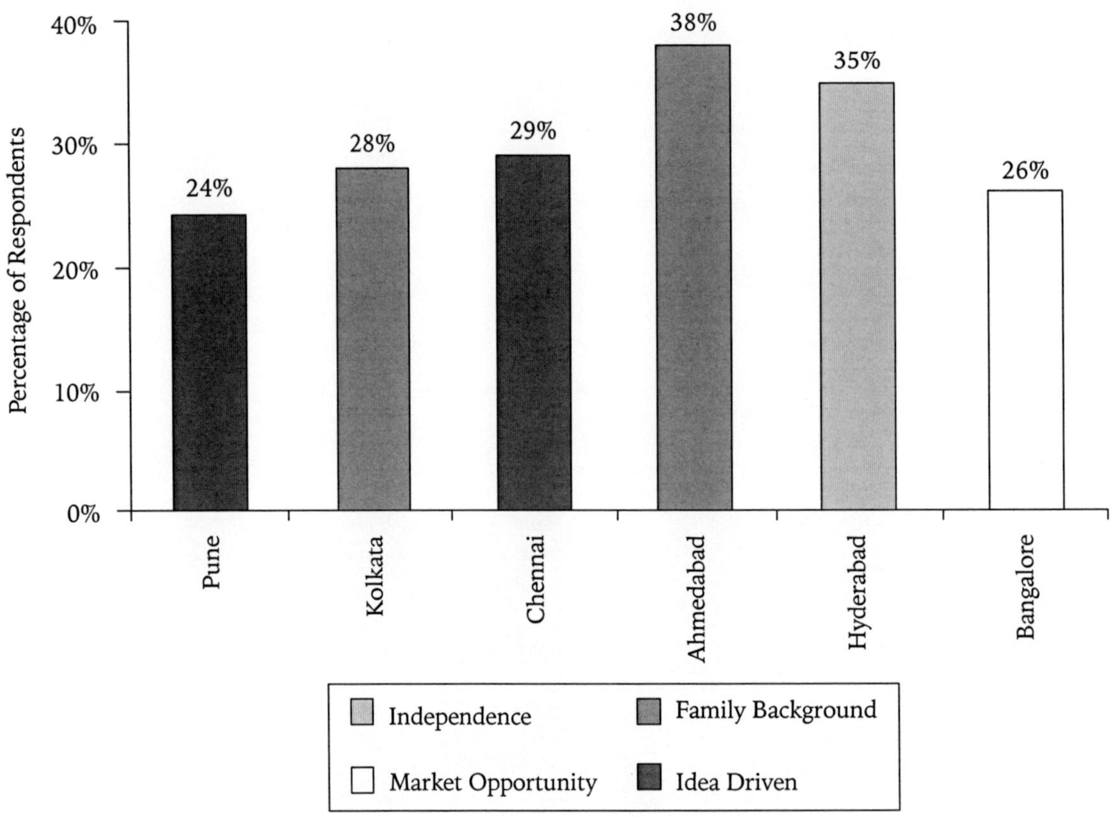

2.2.2 *Variations According to Gender:* For female entrepreneurs, the independence derived from entrepreneurship, as well as the identification of a marketable idea are the most important motivators (25 per cent each). Male entrepreneurs on the other hand, were found to be most significantly influenced by 'family background' (24 per cent) with 'independence' (21 per cent) coming a close second as a motivating trigger.

The most significant motivating trigger for entrepreneurship was found to be wide ranging across regions—from 'family background' being the prime trigger in Ahmedabad and Kolkata to 'market opportunity' serving as the most important motivator in Bangalore.

Figure 23.5: Motivation—Variations According to Gender

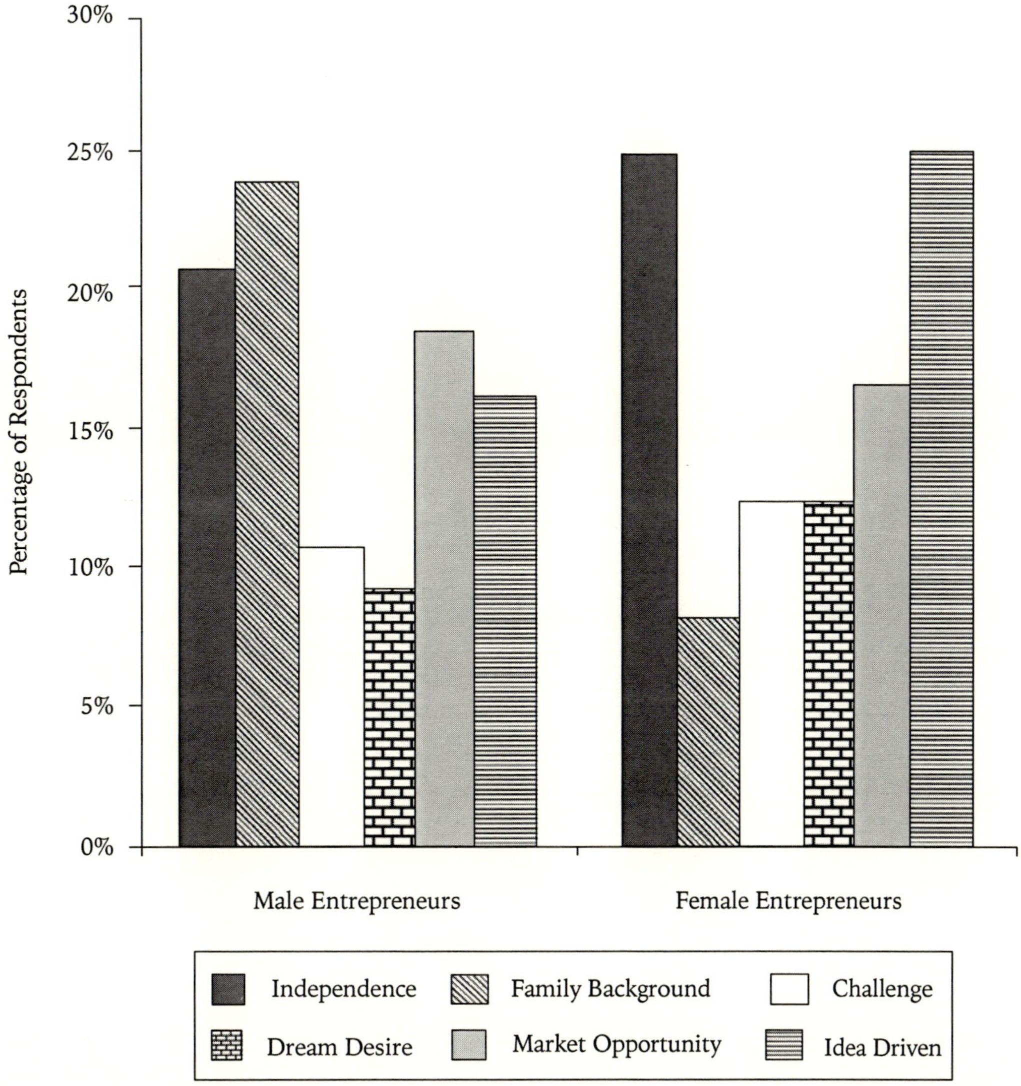

2.2.3 *Variations According to Age:* 'Idea-driven' motivators are more significant for entrepreneurs above the age of 35 and exert a minimal influence on those below 35. Further, 'market opportunity' is a far significant motivating factor for the below-35 age-group compared to those above that age.

2.2.4 *Variations According to Family Background:* The study found that 'independence' is the most powerful motivator for the first-generation entrepreneur (33 per cent), while it has almost no significance in motivating second generation entrepreneurs (only 4 per cent among those second generation entrepreneurs in the same business and only 3 per cent for the second generation entrepreneurs in a different business).

Predictably, 'family background' is the prime motivating factor among the second generation, whether in the same family business (74 per cent) or in a different one (34 per cent), though the extent to which it serves as a motivation trigger varies significantly. Further, 'family background' is a more significant motivator for the second generation compared with the first generation. This may be because the second generation entrepreneur is more likely to be influenced by a family environment that extols entrepreneurship,

The study found that 'independence' is the most powerful motivator for the first generation entrepreneur.

Figure 23.6: Motivation – Variations according to Age

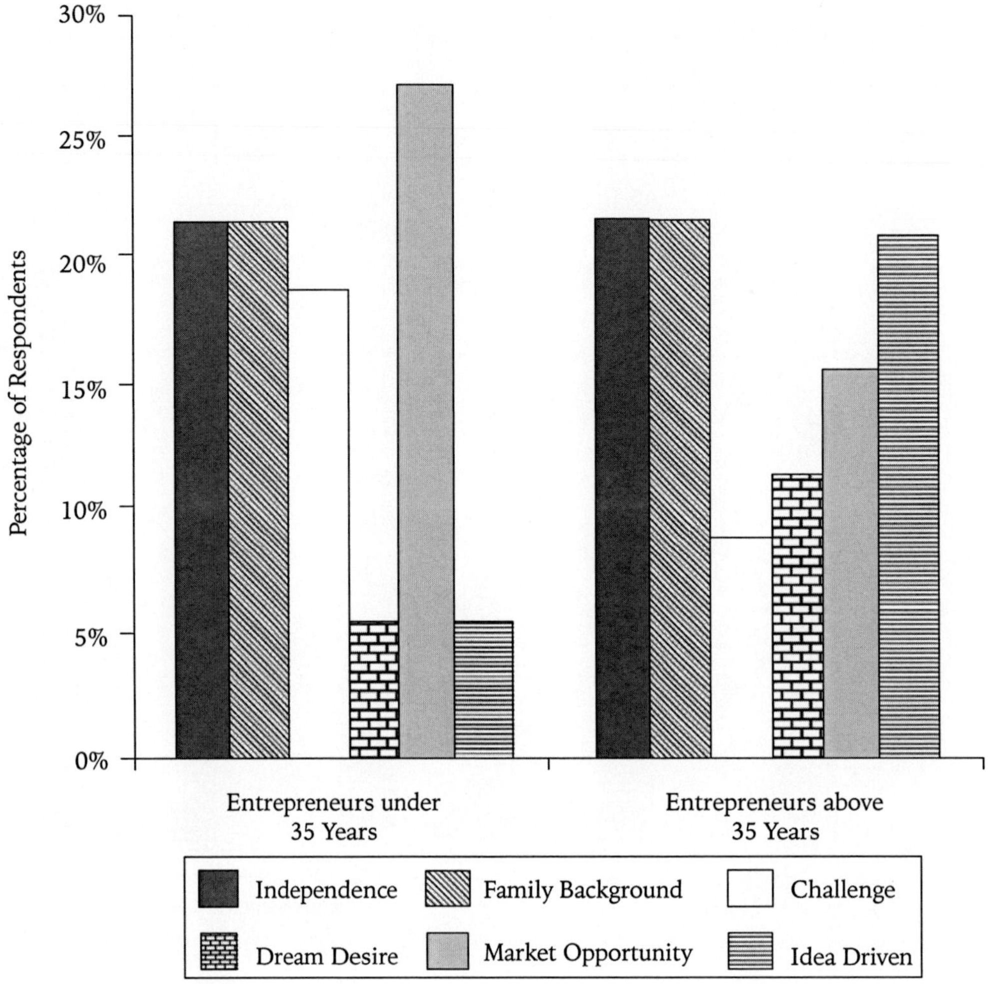

2.2.5 *Variations According to Time Periods:* The NKC study found that 'market opportunity' has become an increasingly significant motivating trigger since the economic liberalisation gathered momentum. Twenty-eight per cent of those in the sample who started enterprises during 1991-1999 and 22 per cent of those starting after 2000 cited 'market opportunity' as the main motivating factor, compared to 11 per cent of those starting enterprises before 1991. Simultaneously, 'independence' has increasingly become a significant motivating factor since the turn of the century—primarily motivating 12 per cent of those starting new enterprises before 1991; 19 per cent of those doing so during 1991-1999 and 35 per cent of those starting out after 2000. The study also noticed that 'family background' has served less as a motivating factor after the launch of economic reforms—from primarily motivating 31 per cent before 1991 to influencing 14 per cent during 1991-1999 and 12 per cent after 2000. (See Figure 23.8.)

2.2.6 *Variations According to Levels of Work Experience:* The study found that levels of work experience significantly influenced motivational triggers.

The NKC study found that 'market opportunity' has become an increasingly significant motivating trigger since the economic liberalisation gathered momentum.

Figure 23.7: **Motivation—Variations according to Family Background**

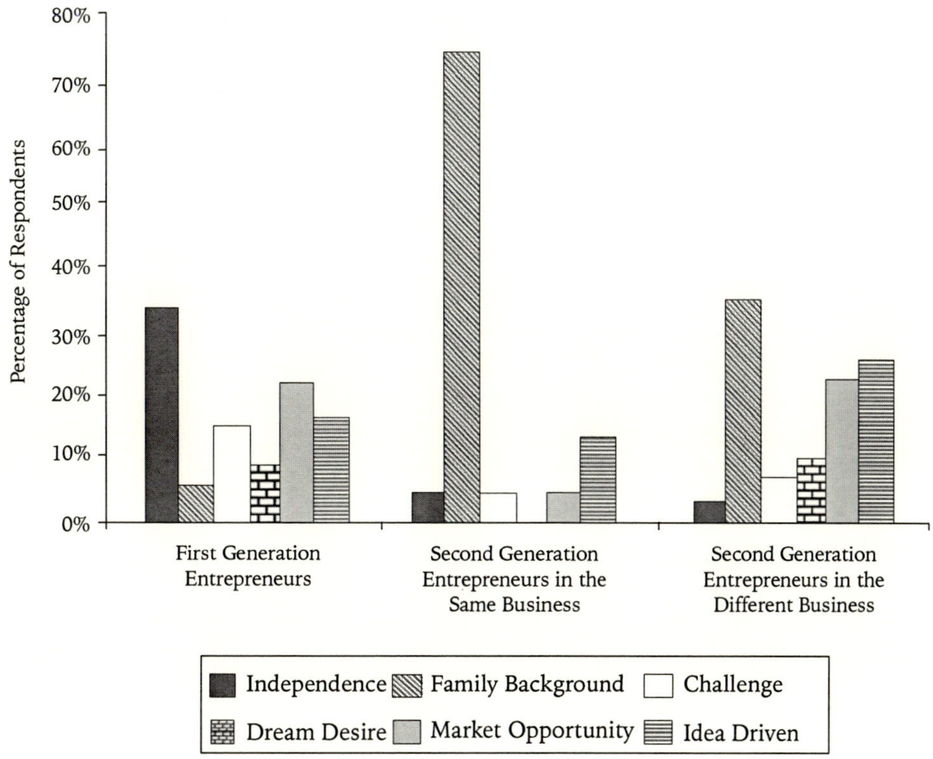

Figure 23.8: **Motivation—Variations according to Time Periods**

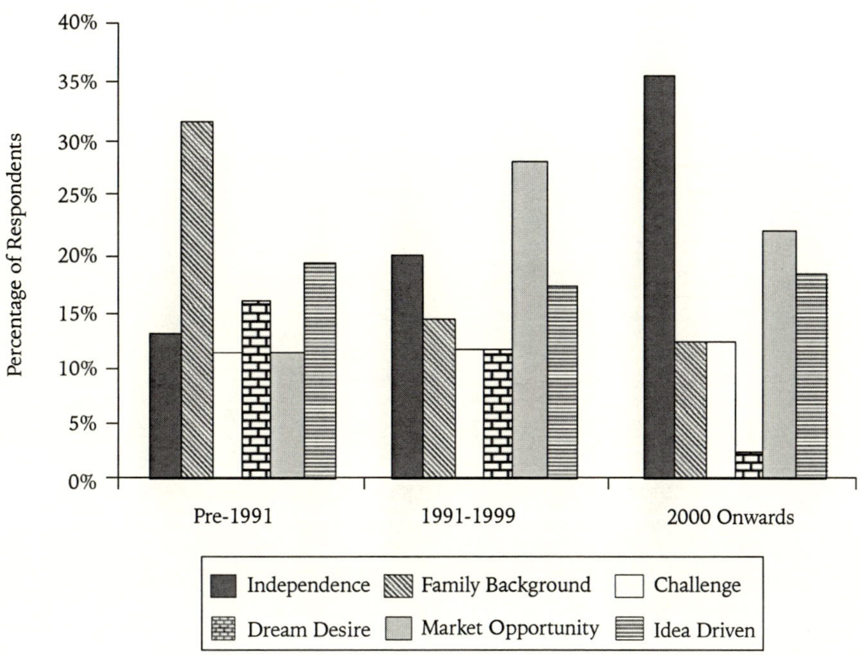

'Independence' was the least important trigger for those entrepreneurs who started out without work experience and the most important factor for those with 5-10 years of work experience before starting out as entrepreneurs.

- It found that 'family background' became less significant with increasing levels of work experience. While this was the most significant trigger for those entrepreneurs who started out without work experience, it was the least important motivational factor for those with more than 10 years' experience, for whom other factors such as 'market opportunity' and 'challenge' were more significant.
- 'Independence' was the least important trigger for those entrepreneurs who started out without work experience and the most important factor for those with 5-10 years of work experience before starting out as entrepreneurs; it was also a significant trigger for those with at least some work experience.
- The study found that 'market opportunity' did not act as a significant trigger for those who started out without any work experience but became, by far, the most important trigger for those with more than 10 years' work experience. The study also found that there was a strong correlation between previous work experience and 'business idea origin', thereby impacting the nature of enterprise. Among those who had work experience, 53 per cent started enterprises in fields related to those in which they had previously worked (as distinct from merely replicating the business idea of their former employers). Thus, the study found instances of a person employed in an IT company starting one's own IT venture, a person with experience in the media launching his/her own event management company, and so on. While working as employees, these entrepreneurs identified market gaps and designed innovative products or services, which enabled them to become entrepreneurs.[37]
- 'Idea driven' triggers are very important, but they were found to be of greater significance for those who start out without any work experience (21 per cent) than for those with substantial work experience (13 per cent).

Figure 23.9: Motivation – Variations According to Level of Work Experience

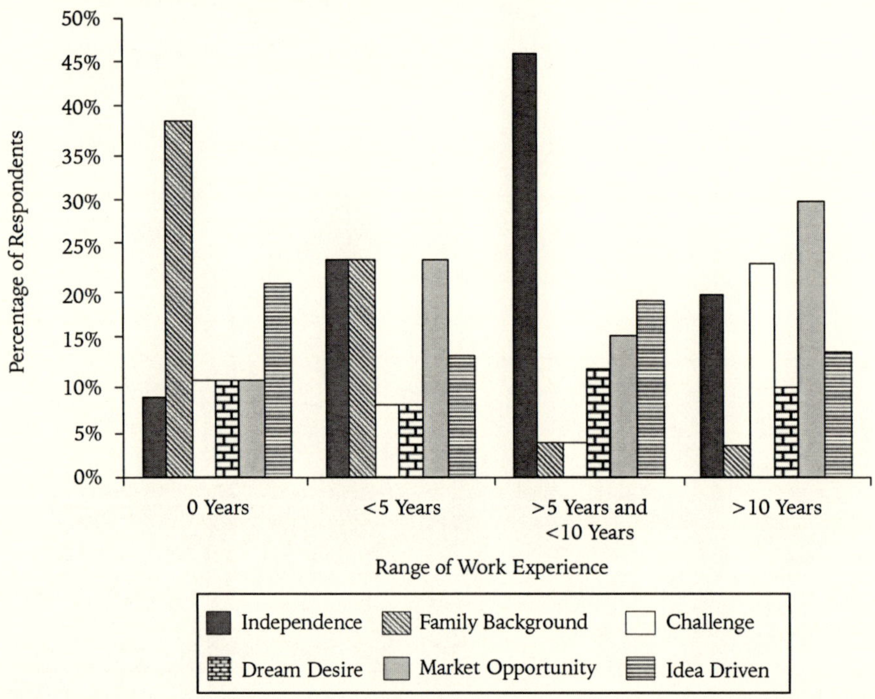

'Idea-driven' triggers are very important, but they were found to be of greater significance for those who start out without any work experience (21 per cent) than for those with substantial work experience (13 per cent).

37. For instance, we interviewed an entrepreneur who was initially a doctor and teaching at medical colleges, who then got an offer to build and manage hospitals. Now as an entrepreneur he is building his own hospitals and pharmacy stores. Clearly, apart from being influenced by his education, his prior work experience also influenced his first business venture.

2.3 Positive Factors: What Excites Entrepreneurs?

2.3.1 When entrepreneurs were asked: "Where do you see yourself five years from now?", it was discovered that most entrepreneurs envision the future of their business in terms of the nature and quality of work (and other intangibles) rather than only in terms of turnover and growth rates. While some entrepreneurs spoke about getting more clients or venturing into the international market, others spoke about being leaders in their respective markets. Some said they see the future in terms of diversifying into newer areas, while others elaborated on dreams of building their current ventures into world-class enterprises. The vision of growth was found to vary according to both the age of the entrepreneur as well as the age of the enterprise. This clearly shows that entrepreneurs are intensely involved with the work they engage in and view future possibilities through their work, rather than in financial terms alone.

2.3.2 To understand the degree of ambition among entrepreneurs regarding their own growth, the study calculated the Compound Annual Growth Rate (CAGR) based on each enterprise's current turnover and the turnover that the entrepreneurs themselves expected to generate in five years time. The median 'expected' CAGR of the sample was found to be 38 per cent, ranging widely from 5 per cent to almost 200 per cent. Further examination showed that 76 per cent of the companies with above-median CAGR (identified as high growth companies, based on five-year turnover estimates provided by the entrepreneurs themselves) belong to the knowledge-intensive services sector, 14 per cent to the manufacturing sector, and only 10 per cent to the 'other services' sector. Among those enterprises forecasting above 100 per cent CAGR, 88 per cent are from the knowledge-intensive services sector. Therefore, entrepreneurs in the knowledge-intensive services clearly see higher growth potential compared to entrepreneurs engaged in other sectors. The high ambition levels displayed by entrepreneurs interviewed seem to contradict findings of some other studies on the subject.[38]

2.3.3 The study found that 51 per cent of the entrepreneurs interviewed had already diversified or were planning to diversify in the near future. Among the entrepreneurs who had diversified, some had more than one business in the same or related field. For example, one entrepreneur began by building and managing hospitals and then promoted a pharmacy chain. Another who was engaged in manufacturing sanitary wares, also started a pottery unit. In many instances, entrepreneurs had also diversified into areas unrelated to their original business. For instance, one entrepreneur who started with managing franchise NIIT centres, went on to set up institutes for hotel management and nursing, and is now foraying into unrelated fields of biotechnology and renewable energy. Another started off with manufacturing auto components, and then diversified into agro industry and the BPO services. The study found varied reasons for diversifying—some entrepreneurs diversified to utilise a natural advantage arising from the nature of their current business, while others tried to avail of opportunities in new sectors.

2.3.4 In this respect, it is relevant to look at some of the critical 'drivers' of entrepreneurship, which reveal the positive factors that motivate entrepreneurs during their journey. Some observations are as follows:

- **Challenge**: Challenge is the principal 'Motivation Driver', though not the main trigger, for entrepreneurship. While only 11 per cent of those interviewed cited 'challenge' as the main motivating factor for starting a business, as many as 38 per cent said they consider the challenge in entrepreneurship to be the main driver for the excitement and satisfaction of doing business.

- **Independence**: Independence is important, both as a trigger and as a driver. It is a crucial trigger (as 22 per cent of those interviewed said) as well as a significant driver (32 per cent).

The study found that 51 per cent of the entrepreneurs interviewed had already diversified or were planning to diversify in the near future. Among the entrepreneurs who had diversified, some had more than one business in the same or related field.

---

38. See here, for example, the GEM India report 2002 that states that very few firms anticipated growth or offered new products or used new technologies. See also, Bhide, Amar (2004). "What Role for Entrepreneurship in India" (in *http://www.bhide.net/publications.html*). Bhide concluded that in Bangalore, "less than a quarter of entrepreneurs are expected to grow significantly in the next five years.' He instead found that 'entrepreneurs preferred to diversify into new businesses rather than expand". See also, GEM 2007 Executive Report which concludes that "India's high-growth expectation earlystage Entrepreneurship (HEA) 2000-06 rate is one-fifth that of China".

- **Money**: Money is a secondary factor during the business development (12 per cent) and is considered less significant as an excitement factor than either challenge or independence.

2.3.5 *Overall Satisfaction:* An overwhelming 99.4 per cent of the entrepreneurs said they do not want to be in a routine job, signifying that they are satisfied with their vocation and do not regret their initial decision to become entrepreneurs.

2.3.6 *Variations in Motivation Drivers Across Gender and Age:* The fact that entrepreneurship 'creates employment opportunities' exerts a more significant impact as an excitement factor for female entrepreneurs than males. The study found that entrepreneurs above the age of 35 also feel the same compared to those below 35 years.

2.3.7 *Change in Mindset:* The study also found that there has been a gradual change in mindset towards ownership among entrepreneurs. While older businesses were traditionally run as family concerns, newer entrepreneurs are found to be inclined to decouple ownership from management. The latter are more comfortable with the idea of a professional manager, from outside the family, taking control of their business. Younger entrepreneurs, particularly in the knowledge-intensive sectors, are also open to the idea of selling off a business and starting new ventures ('Serial Entrepreneurs'). Unlike older counterparts, new generation entrepreneurs are not averse to selling off (or handing over the day-to-day management of) their business, once it becomes mature. As a result, there are instances of entrepreneurs in their 30s who are already on their third or fourth venture, after having established successful businesses earlier.

Figure 23.10: Positive Factors

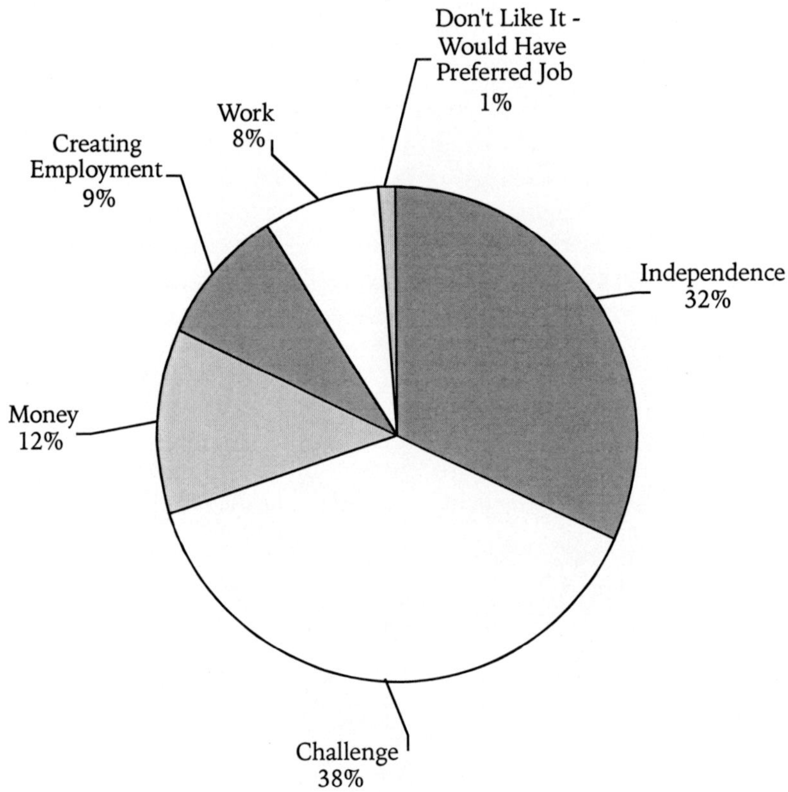

An overwhelming 99.4 per cent of the entrepreneurs said they do not want to be in a routine job, signifying that they are satisfied with their vocation and do not regret their initial decision to become entrepreneurs.

Figure 23.11: Positive Factors – Variations According to Gender

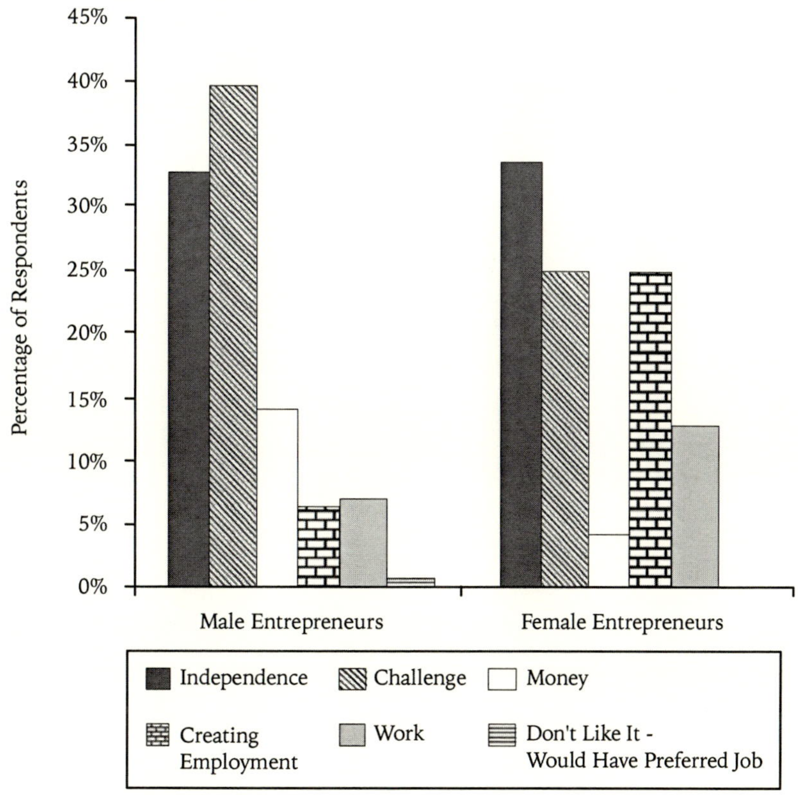

Figure 23.12: Positive Factors – Variations According to Age

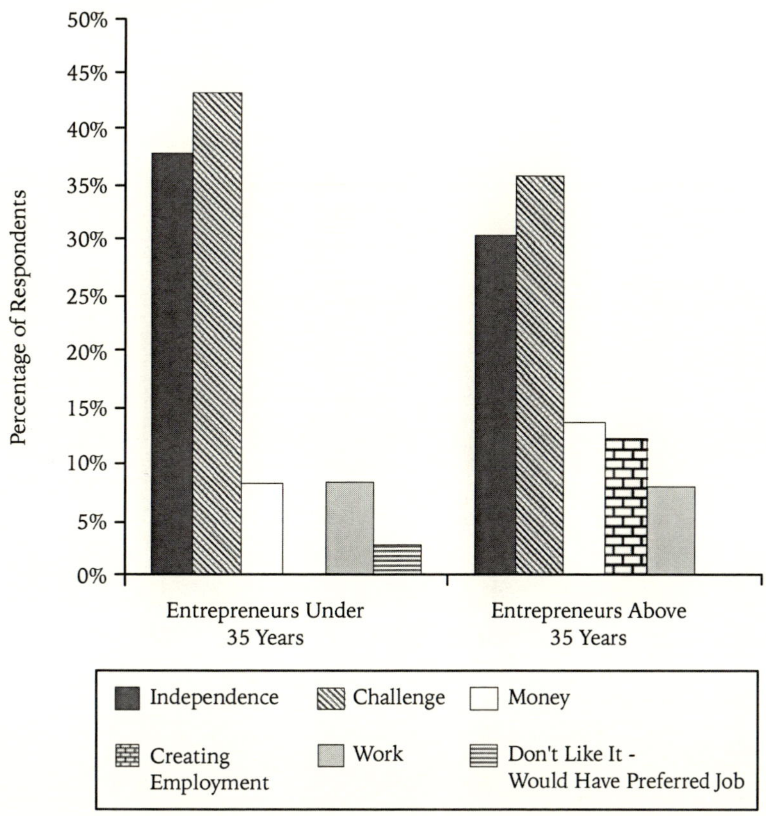

2.4 Chapter Summary

There is no common set of traits, psychological attitudes or profiles that apply to all entrepreneurs alike or to which all entrepreneurs generally conform. Significant motivating factors are: 'Independence' (stemming from the freedom to do 'one's own thing'), 'Market Opportunity', 'Family Background', a 'New Idea' (with business potential), the prospect of 'Challenge', as well as a long cherished 'Dream Desire' to become an entrepreneur. Internal triggers are the primary motivators, while external factors such as market opportunity are also growing in importance. There are variations in motivation triggers on parameters such as region, gender, age, family background, time period and levels of work experience. 'Challenge' is the principal motivation driver or positive factor, even if not the most important trigger. Entrepreneurs view the future in terms of the nature and quality of work as well as turnover increase. By their very nature, entrepreneurs tend to be ambitious. Monetary gain is not as significant as either challenge or independence. There are also variations in the excitement factors based on gender and age. Almost all entrepreneurs do not want to be in a routine job and are generally satisfied with their experience in entrepreneurship. An emerging trend is to welcome professional management of their enterprises and seek new opportunities, which is described as 'Serial Entrepreneurship'. This is particularly evident amongst entrepreneurs in the knowledge-intensive sectors.

III. Socio-Cultural Factors

3.1 General Importance

3.1.1 Socio-cultural factors such as social norms, family values, networks and social value of entrepreneurship, play a key role in nurturing the entrepreneurial ecosystem.[39] A historical and sociological understanding of certain communities in India, which have been traditionally engaged in business, confirms the role of social factors that encourage entrepreneurship.[40] Important success factors include the pragmatic use of social and family networks as well as 'webs of interdependence' that continuously facilitate the development of entrepreneurial ecosystems at the community level. In Melvin M. Weber's words, "specialized professionals maintain webs of intimate contact with other professionals, wherever they may be. They share a particular body of values; their roles are defined by the organized structure of their groups; they undoubtedly have a sense of belonging to the groups; and by the nature of the alliances, all share a community of interests."[41]

3.1.2 To illustrate, the "constellation of socio-cultural forces"[42] that has been responsible for the development of business enterprise in certain communities comprises the following:

- Credit facilities: The existence of community banks and credit networks (including profit-sharing schemes) has traditionally ensured availability of liquidity. While describing the Sarafi System used by Marwaris in Benaras, Alan R. Cohen remarked as follows: "Firms in the system borrowed from each other whenever short of cash, loans were payable on demand, "even at midnight" and interest was tallied and settled once a year, with total borrowing offset by total lending."[43]
- Infrastructural support: Traditional networks assure infrastructural support such as access to storage facilities for goods along trade routes, remittance facilities and arrangements for accommodation.[44] Thomas Timberg, for example, cites how G.D. Birla's grandfather, Shiv Narain, stayed in a cooperative '*basa*' (collective mess) in then Bombay (now Mumbai) when he first arrived from his village of Pilani in the 1860s.[45]
- Socialisation: The community encourages socialisation into entrepreneurship, the inculcation of commercial morality (respecting the contract, making ethical profits etc), notions of thrift as well as training opportunities, such as apprenticeships to learn techniques of business. Mechanisms for 'cushioning of conflict' and division of labour and authority also develop through the joint family system and social networks.

Socio-cultural factors such as social norms, family values, networks and social value of entrepreneurship, play a key role in nurturing the entrepreneurial ecosystem. A historical and sociological understanding of certain communities in India, which have been traditionally engaged in business, confirms the role of social factors that encourage entrepreneurship.

---

39. See for example, Jackson and Rodkey (1994), quoted in Abhishek Goel *et al.*, that "socialization had an impact on an individual's attitude towards entrepreneurship...this socialization took place at home, at the place of education and other spheres of interaction." Status and social value attached to entrepreneurship also influence motivations, supra note 2 as above.

40. For an overview on various business communities in India in various time periods, see for example, Tripathy, Dwijendra (ed.) (1984). *Business Communities of India: A Historical Perspective*, supra note 13 as above; see also, Timberg, Thomas A. (1978). *The Marwaris: From Traders to Industrialists*, supra note 8 as above on the Marwari business community; Markovits, Claude *The Global World of Indian Merchants, 1750-1947: Traders of Sind from Bukhara to Panama*, Rutten, Mario *Farms and Factories: Social Profiles of Large Farmers and Rural Industrialists in Western India*; the role of various communities such as the Parsis, Jain merchants, Mahajans, Gujaratis, business communities in Punjab, Jews, Chettiyars etc., is a fascinating subject of study; see also Harish Damodaran (forthcoming), 'India's New Capitalists' on the sociology and history of some of India's business communities since Independence. The use of the term community is in its generic sociological sense, to refer to a social group, typically endogamous, to which are connected certain "stereotypes, traditions, occupational directions, attitudes and social positions...a community may be separated internally by caste, ritual, regional or economic differences", see for example Timberg at page 5; see also Chapter 1 of this report.

41. Weber, Melvin M. "Towards a Definition of Interest Community", in P. Worsley (ed.) (1972). *Modern Sociology: Introductory Readings*, quoted in Timberg at page 11.

42. See Tripathy, supra note 13 as above, at page 18.

43. Cohen, Alan " Tradition, Values and Inter-role Conflict in Indian Family Business", quoted in Timberg at page 6.

44. See Timberg, supra note 8 as above, at page 5.

45. Timberg, supra note 8 as above, at page 17.

The community encourages socialisation into entrepreneurship, the inculcation of commercial morality, notions of thrift, as well as training opportunities such as apprenticeships.

- Market development: In certain geographical locations, the presence of entrepreneurial communities led to the development of futures markets. Further, migration of the community (e.g. the Marwaris) to commercial centres such as ports and trading hubs encouraged entrepreneurship in these places.[46]

3.1.3 The role of intra-caste networks in furthering entrepreneurship, especially among marginalised groups, deserves to be studied in greater detail. Generally, among the four *varnas* in Hinduism, Vaishyas have been traditionally involved in trade. However, the influence of notions of pollution and purity, if any, on entrepreneurial behaviour, among so-called 'high' and 'low' caste population, remains to be explored. It remains to be analysed whether other castes are less inhibited in undertaking manual entrepreneurial activities, compared to upper castes. Another topic worth exploring is the role of entrepreneurship as a means of expressing aspirations among marginalised groups, who otherwise have limited access to opportunities in the formal sectors.[47]

3.2 Degree of Family Support as a Factor

3.2.1 The NKC study explores the degree of family support (a socio-cultural factor, particularly in India) that the entrepreneurs received at the time of starting their venture. Overall, as many as 74 per cent of the entrepreneurs were supported by their families (as seen from the figure below, 51 per cent were 'very supportive' and 23 per cent were 'supportive'), which further underscores the importance of social institutions for entrepreneurs in India.

3.2.2 At the same time, the study also reveals interesting variations in family support across regions, family backgrounds, gender, age and levels of work experience.[48] Some of these are described below:

a. **Variations according to region:** Ahmedabad (home to traditional entrepreneurial communities) shows a higher degree of family support for entrepreneurship (88 per cent) compared to the national average (74 per cent). This shows that traditional commercial areas have a greater confidence in supporting entrepreneurship. Such favourable social perceptions regarding entrepreneurship, in turn, influence the degree of family support that entrepreneurs receive.

b. **Variations according to family background:** Second generation entrepreneurs in the same business enjoy a much higher degree of family support (96 per cent) than second generation entrepreneurs in a different business (88 per cent) or first generation entrepreneurs (67 per cent). Families of second generation entrepreneurs, already familiar with the practice of entrepreneurship have less fear of risk and failure and therefore, provide greater support. Further, second generation entrepreneurs in a different business have to deal with families that are less familiar with the new area of business. This often results in reduced levels of support for such entrepreneurs, when compared to those entering into or expanding the same business.

The NKC study explores the degree of family support (a socio-cultural factor, particularly in India) that the entrepreneurs received at the time of starting their venture.

---

46. Some examples of such centres being Calcutta (now Kolkata), Bombay (now Mumbai), Ahmedabad and Kanpur; see Timberg chapter 1.

47. Generalisations on caste and entrepreneurship are difficult to arrive at, just as there are ethnographic studies on certain communities. See Tripathy at page 17-19, where NR Sheth in his article, "Theoretical Framework for the Study of Indian Business Communities" cites the work of Saberwal on entrepreneurship among Ramgarhias in Punjab and Owens' work among the low caste peasant community of Mahishyas in Howrah for understanding of how marginalised communities may use entrepreneurship to rise in the social hierarchy. However, Sheth also cites Barnett's work on the Kontaikatti Velalars, where strict caste rules prohibiting association with lower castes, deterred upper castes from entering entrepreneurship. At the same time, among upper castes, we observe the existence of the Iyenger family in Chennai whose TVS Group, founded by TV Sundaram Iyenger in 1911, are among India's leaders in the auto sector; further, it is also argued that the precise lack of opportunities in the formal sector may act as a spur for marginalised groups to rise as entrepreneurs, as long as the intra and inter-caste business networks allow sufficient openness and mobility. See also, Harish Damodaran (forthcoming), *India's New Capitalists*.

48. See, for example, Abhishek Goel *et al.*, supra note 2 as above on attitudes towards entrepreneurship among youth from various regions in India.

Figure 23.13: **Family Support to Entrepreneurs**

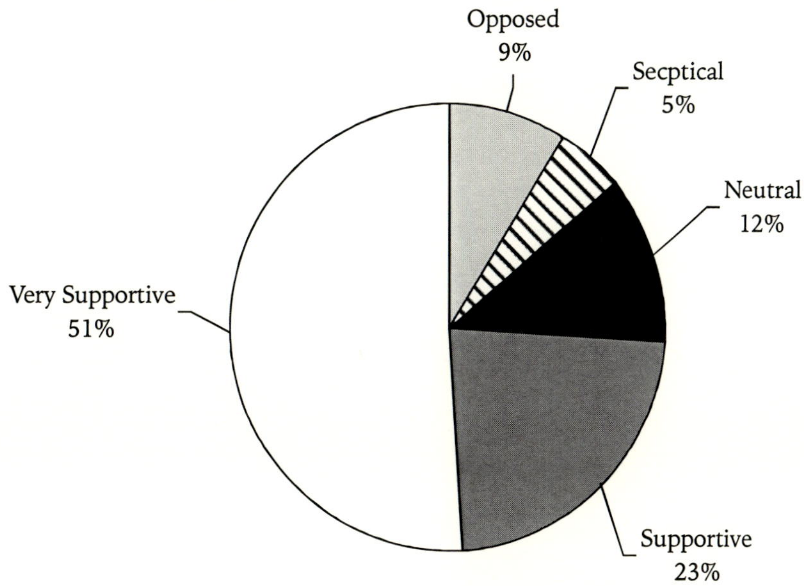

Figure 23.14: **Family Support—Variations According to Region**

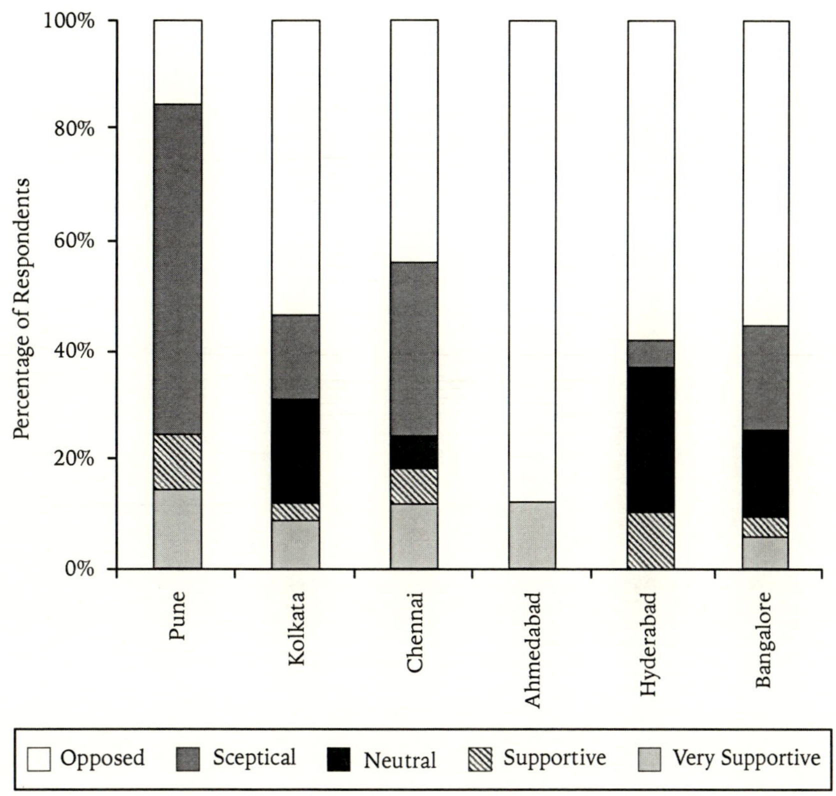

Entrepreneurs with more than ten years' work experience receive marginally greater family support at the time of starting up (78 per cent), compared to those with less than ten years' experience (71 per cent).

c. **Variations according to work experience:** Entrepreneurs with more than 10 years' work experience receive marginally greater family support at the time of starting up (78 per cent), compared to those with less than 10 years' experience (71 per cent).

Once a person is employed, the perceived opportunity costs (in terms of leaving a remunerative position in order to start a new venture) could be higher, which could explain why entrepreneurs with less than 10 years' work experience receive relatively less support. Moreover, those with more than 10 years' prior experience would have acquired the professional expertise, financial security and social capital required to become successful entrepreneurs, as a result of which their perceived risks could be lower. This could explain the relatively higher levels of family support among such entrepreneurs.

Figure 23.15: Family Support—Variations According to Family Background

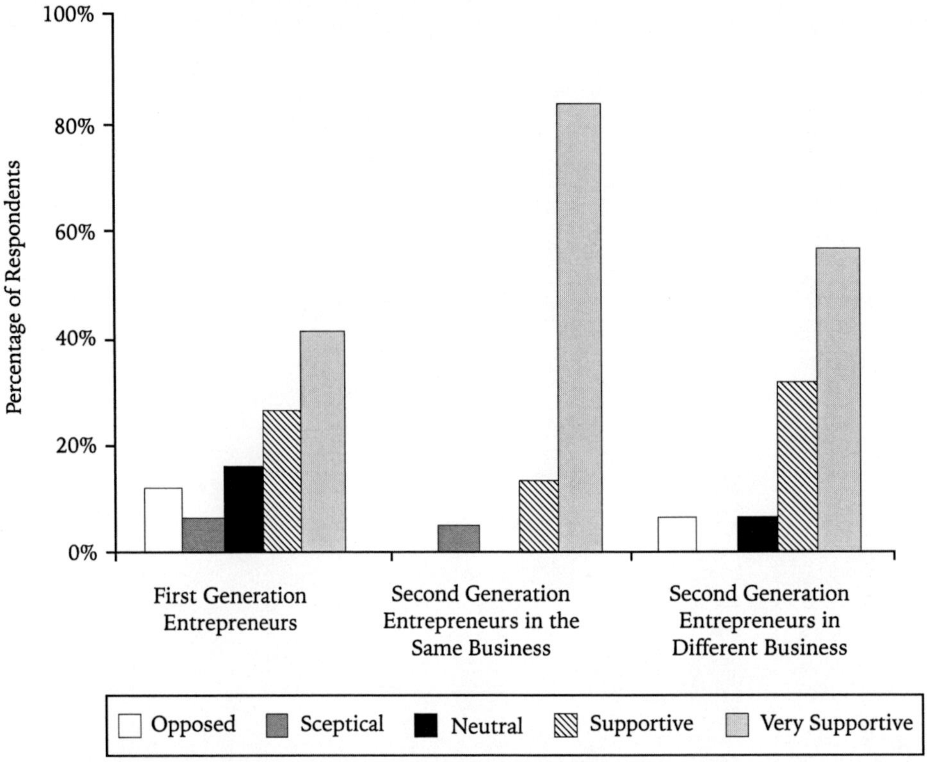

3.3 Gender as a Factor in Entrepreneurship

3.3.1 *Gender as a Factor in Entrepreneurship:* Of the 24 female entrepreneurs interviewed, two-thirds said that their gender did not make any difference to their entrepreneurial ventures. More than one-fifth considered their gender to be an advantage rather than a disadvantage as an entrepreneur. Only 13 per cent of the female entrepreneurs interviewed said that their gender had hindered them on their way to becoming successful entrepreneurs.

Figure 23.16: **Family Support to First Generation Entrepreneurs—Variations According to Work Experience**

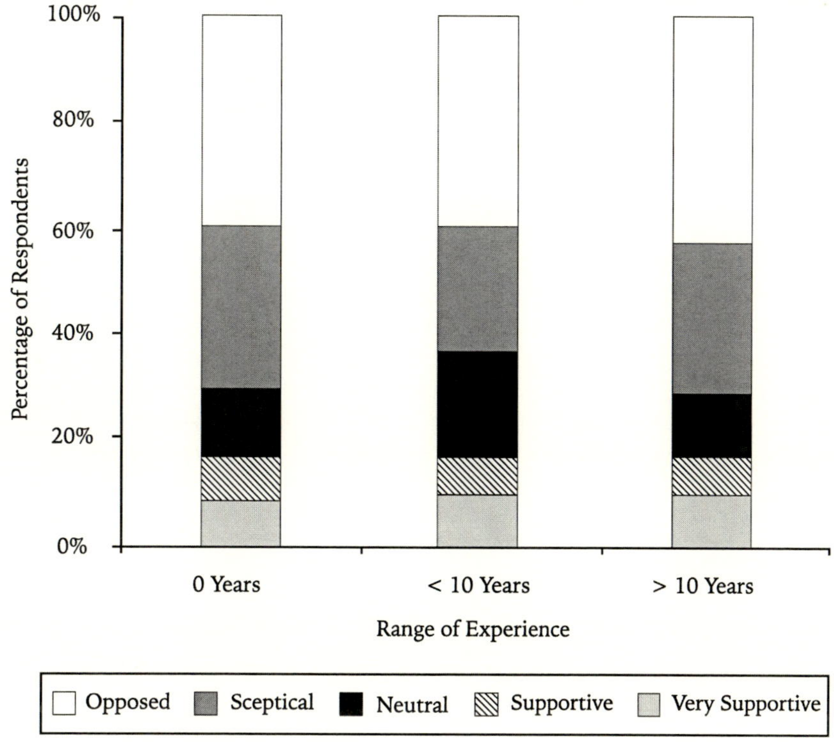

Figure 2.17: **Gender as a Factor in Entrepreneurship**

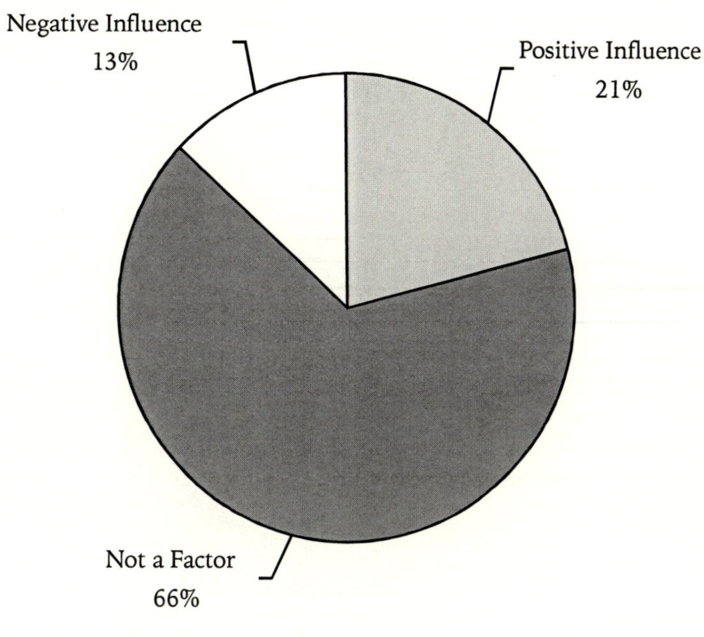

Two-thirds of the female entrepreneurs interviewed said their gender did not make any difference to their entrepreneurial ventures.

3.3.2 *Some More Illustrative Points on Gender:* A female entrepreneur from Kolkata mentioned that gender becomes an issue only because people have preconceived notions, and hence, as a woman entrepreneur, she had to continuously 'over-prove' herself. Another entrepreneur said that while women are able to deal with the details of business, they face problems because their family life suffers. At the same time, exactly the opposite sentiment was expressed by a female entrepreneur from Hyderabad who said that running her own business gave her the flexibility (in terms of timings) so that she could manage her family life and run her business as and when it best suited her. A female entrepreneur from Bangalore said that women make better entrepreneurs than men because of their inherent ability to multitask, a crucial skill for an entrepreneur who has to handle many jobs simultaneously.

3.3.3 *Key Challenges:* At the same time, a number of female entrepreneurs also said that they would benefit from programmes that could provide assistance in obtaining finance, marketing support, counselling and other core support (such as functional day care centres, crèches etc). As examples, organisations such as the Association of Lady Entrepreneurs of Andhra Pradesh (ALEAP), the Association of Women Entrepreneurs of Karnataka (AWAKE)[49] and the Federation of Indian Women Entrepreneurs (FIWE) etc., focus exclusively on the development of entrepreneurship among women. ALEAP assists women in identifying projects, in marketing their products as well as in conducting training programmes. It also assists in providing finance to its members through an innovative Mutual Credit Guarantee Scheme (MCGS) and currently also has two industrial estates exclusively for women.

3.4 Encouraging and Celebrating Entrepreneurship

3.4.1 Institutional and informal associations as well as networks of entrepreneurs can play a significant role in encouraging entrepreneurship. Some of the major industry associations in India include CII, FICCI and ASSOCHAM. Our consultations with local chambers of commerce such as Mahratta Chambers of Commerce, Industries and Agriculture (MCCIA) in Pune, Bengal Chambers of Commerce and Industry (BCCI) in Kolkata, Gujarat Chambers of Commerce and Industry (GCCI) in Ahmedabad, Federation of Andhra Pradesh Chamber of Commerce and Industry (FAPCCI) in Hyderabad and Federation of Karnataka Chambers of Commerce and Industry (FKCCI)[50] in Bangalore revealed that chambers of commerce can and do play institutional roles in nurturing young entrepreneurs, through their established networks as well as by providing platforms for discussing entrepreneurial best practices and experiences. For these organisations, the challenge would be to go beyond the traditional role of catering to mid-size and large companies and take active steps to reach out more to young entrepreneurs. Some illustrations of associations involved with entrepreneurial initiatives and encouraging entrepreneurship are described below.

3.4.2 An interesting initiative is that of the Bharatiya Yuva Shakti Trust (BYST, also known as 'Business and Youth Starting Together'), that provides key support in finance and training. BYST primarily caters to underprivileged groups (with per capita family income less than Rs. 5000) between 18 and 35 years. BYST leverages financial assistance through the Credit Guarantee Scheme of the Government of India and also provides active mentoring assistance through an active network of established entrepreneurs.[51]

3.4.3 Other groups such as the National Entrepreneurship Network (NEN)[52] and The Indus Entrepreneurs (TiE[53]) are also very active in providing mentoring and networking in the entrepreneurial ecosystem, especially in the knowledge-

Institutional and informal associations as well as networks of entrepreneurs can play a significant role in encouraging Entrepreneurship.

---

49. The NKC Entrepreneurship team had the opportunity of interacting with the founders of ALEAP and AWAKE.

50. These institutions have historically played an active role in development of Indian commerce and industry. Apart from representing industry at various governmental and industrial fora, such institutions also conduct seminars and conferences and publish reports on key issues in Indian industry.

51. From consultations with BYST, it is understood that BYST has tied up with Indian Bank and leverages the credit guarantee scheme to make available loans of up to Rs. 5 lakh. BYST selects entrepreneurs and has a mentor network of about 3000 (80 per cent of whom are entrepreneurs from SME sectors). BYST also has a mentor development programme, where mentors are supposed to undergo online training and get a certificate. On an average, mentors are said to spend 15-20 hours a month on upcoming entrepreneurs.

52. Founded in 2002, NEN is a not-for-profit initiative of the Wadhwani Foundation, working to "inspire, educate and support the next generation of high-growth entrepreneurs in India... NEN works with academic institutions to help build and ramp-up entrepreneurship programmes and create a constant flow of high-impact, world-class activities designed to facilitate success in the real world". See *www.nenonline.org*

53. Successful entrepreneurs and professionals founded The Indus Entrepreneurs, also known as Talent, Ideas and Enterprises in Silicon Valley in 1992, with roots in the Indus region. There are over 12,000 members and more than 1600 'charter members', including successful entrepreneurs, venture capitalists, private equity players, Angels, law firms and technology and management professionals. See *www.tie.org*

driven and high growth sectors in key metropolitan cities. NEN, for example, also supports 'entrepreneurship cell' workshops in educational institutions and organises a national 'Entrepreneurship Week' every year, which brings together a large number of educational institutions and supporting networks. TiE also organises networking events among entrepreneurs and investors. A recent initiative is the 'Pan-IIT Entrepreneurship Movement' involving alumni of all the seven IITs, to evolve a brand that would provide strong fraternity links among IIT alumni and entrepreneurs.

3.4.4 The task of ensuring greater social affinity for entrepreneurship requires dissemination of best practices as well as documenting unsuccessful ideas, as part of raising awareness about entrepreneurial experiences at all levels. A key socio-cultural factor also pertains to social attitudes towards risk and failure. To better understand and manage risk as well as create a supportive social environment for entrepreneurs, it is essential to remove the stigma associated with failure. This is possible by acknowledging the value of experience gained, "being smart enough to recognize mistakes and change strategies" and being quick in "adopting the successful approaches that work."[54] In this respect, it is imperative to launch entrepreneurship outreach events (not just in schools and colleges, but also through the media) where entrepreneurial experiences (including unsuccessful experiences) can be shared widely. Social networks at the informal level also play their part in helping entrepreneurs to share experiences and best practices. Recognition and reward systems, at the local, state as well as national and global levels, will also help in encouraging entrepreneurial behaviour and celebrating the spirit of entrepreneurship.

3.5 Chapter Summary

Socio-cultural factors such as norms, values, social networks, social perceptions and the degree of cultural acceptance of, and support for entrepreneurship are important for entrepreneurs. Communities traditionally associated with business and trade have leveraged networks and natural webs of interdependence, in building informal ecosystems that provide credit support, infrastructure, socialisation and risk management. The role of caste requires separate analysis. The NKC study reveals that most of the entrepreneurs received family support, thereby underscoring its importance in India. Variations in the degree of family support are seen across region, based on family background, work experience and gender. Encouraging entrepreneurship involves widening the social base of capital, which in turn also means enlarging networks and including access to new entrepreneurs from communities not traditionally associated with business. Two-thirds of female entrepreneurs interviewed said that gender did not make any difference to their entrepreneurial ventures. Formal and informal associations play a key role in nurturing entrepreneurship. The task of ensuring greater social acceptability for entrepreneurship also requires dissemination of best practices, documenting unsuccessful ideas as well as other entrepreneurial experiences at all levels. Reward and recognition at various levels, from local to global, also help in promoting entrepreneurship.

To better understand and manage risk as well as create a supportive social environment for entrepreneurs, it is essential to remove the stigma associated with failure.

54. Bhide, Amar (1994). *How Entrepreneurs Craft*, Harvard Business Review, March-April. The stigma associated with failure is relative to cultures. For example, it is said that VCs in Silicon Valley would also consider the entrepreneurs previous ventures, even if unsuccessful, in order to value the entrepreneur's experience and incorporate such into investment decisions. It is also pertinent here to relate an interesting apocryphal anecdote, attributed to Thomas Alva Edison. When asked once on the number of experiments that failed to generate any substantial results, he had apparently replied that, far from failing in any, he had instead discovered the many ways that would not work for that particular experiment.

IV. Access to Early Stage Finance

4.1 General Importance

4.1.1 Ready access to early-stage finance, especially seed capital, is a critical factor in a favourable entrepreneurial ecosystem. It is a key factor in deciding whether to become an entrepreneur as well as in deciding the nature of the enterprise to promote. This is especially important for younger and first generation entrepreneurs. There are two basic types of early stage finance: debt (largely from banks and financial institutions) and equity (from sources such as angels, venture capital funds and private equity funds). While traditional bank financing largely relies on the criteria of adequate collateral and established track record to judge credit worthiness before disbursement of funds, the equity-based sources are less risk averse and restrictive in financing start-ups. However, as of now, traditional debt-based models cover a wider range of entrepreneurial sectors, compared to venture capitalists (VCs) and private equity (PE) funds. Since VCs and PE funds, by and large, are more visible in the knowledge-intensive sectors, it is expected that a combination of novel debt and equity models will spur early stage finance for first generation entrepreneurs in the foreseeable future.

4.2 Statistics on Early Stage Finance from the NKC Study

4.2.1 *Self-financed:* The NKC Study found that a majority of the entrepreneurs interviewed (63 per cent) had actually been self-financed at the start-up stage. In the NKC sample, bank loans accounted for start-up finance for 22 per cent of the entrepreneurs while 9 per cent received loans from state finance corporations. VCs and angels account for the early-stage capital needs of 6 per cent of the entrepreneurs interviewed. Of the entrepreneurs who approached banks, 61 per cent did actually receive bank finance.

Figure 23.18: Sources of Start-up Phase Funding

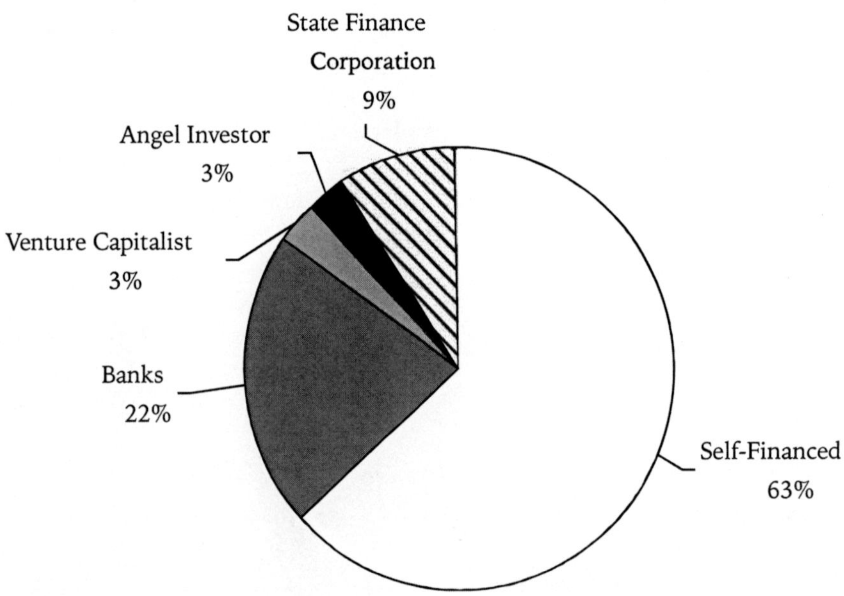

It is expected that a combination of novel debt and equity models will spur early stage finance for first generation entrepreneurs in the forseeable future.

4.2.2 On a closer examination of the sources of self-financing, the study found that nearly half of the self-financed entrepreneurs borrowed start-up money from family or friends. Nearly a third of these entrepreneurs invested their own savings into the start-up, while money from an existing family business helped only about one-fifth of the self-financed entrepreneurs. This could be a reflection of greater confidence among new entrepreneurs in their own abilities as well as the crucial significance of the socio-cultural support systems of family and friends discussed in the previous chapter.

4.2.3 Further, the study found that among the self-financed entrepreneurs, there was little variation according to gender. Compared to their male counterparts, women received marginally more borrowings from family and friends, and slightly less investments from other family businesses. Overall, the general trends among self-financed entrepreneurs do not show significant variation according to gender.

Figure 23.19: Sources of Self-Financing

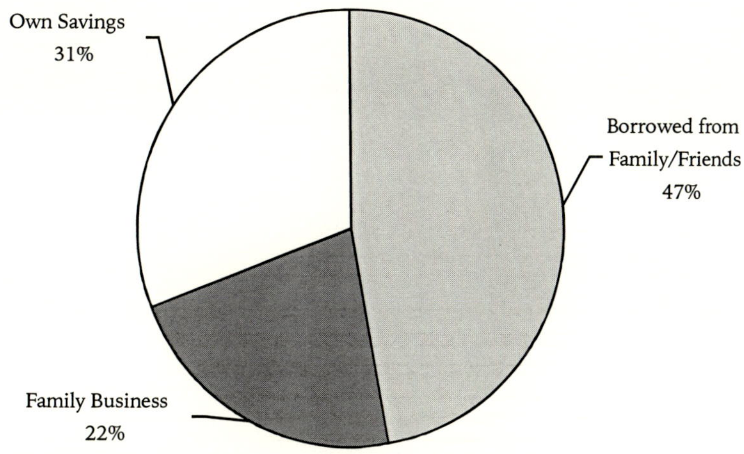

Figure 23.20: Sources of Self-Financing—Variations According to Gender

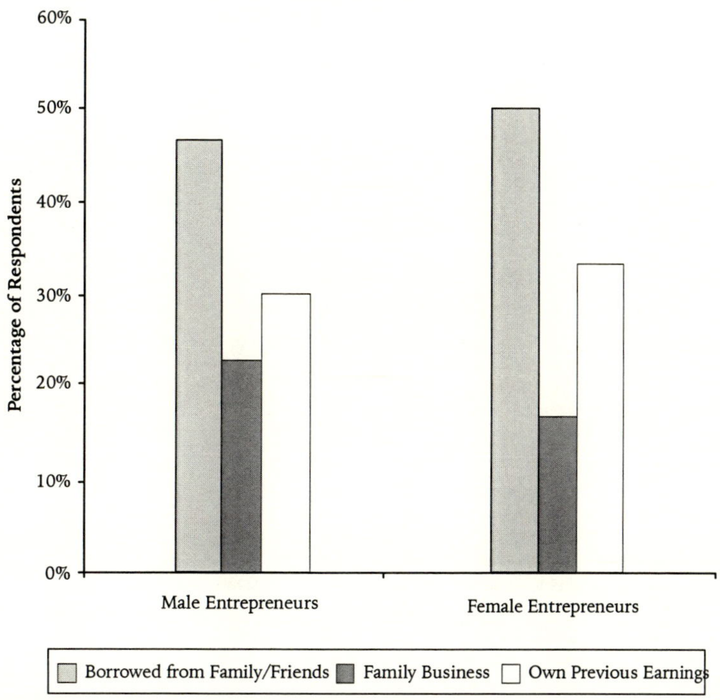

The study found that nearly half of the self-financed entrepreneurs borrowed start-up money from family or friends.

4.2.4 *Bank Finance:* It was earlier noted that of the entrepreneurs who actually approached banks, 61 per cent did receive some funds from banks. Since most of the entrepreneurs were self-financed (for various reasons), NKC asked the entrepreneurs—in order to understand what they think of bank financing—to rate their perceptions on access to bank loans at the start-up stage and then at the growth stage (on a scale of 'difficult', 'average' and 'easy'). From the responses, it is observed that access to early stage finance from banks is perceived to be very difficult at the start-up stage but becomes comparatively easy at the growth stage. Of the entrepreneurs interviewed, 42 per cent said that it was difficult to obtain finance at the start-up stage, 20 per cent said that it was easy and 38 per cent scored the ease or difficulty of access as 'average'. However, at the growth stage, it was almost reverse. While the average stayed the same at 38 per cent, 49 per cent found it easy and only 13 per cent found it difficult to access finance at the growth stage.

Thus, entrepreneurs believe that the stage of a business influences perceptions of risk on the part of the banks and that a successful track record makes it easier to access bank credit. They said that it is most difficult to access credit from banks for their ventures precisely when they need it the most.

4.2.5 Interestingly, on perceptions regarding credit from banks, the study noticed little variation between first generation and second generation entrepreneurs. There was almost no difference in accessibility to bank credit for second generation entrepreneurs starting a different business from first generation entrepreneurs as for practical purposes, both were starting afresh. This suggests that even a successful history of family business does not *per se* make any significant difference in obtaining bank loans other than when there is sufficient collateral and a clear business plan that banks would examine and approve according to their own guidelines.

Figure 23.21: Access to Finance from Banks at Different Phases

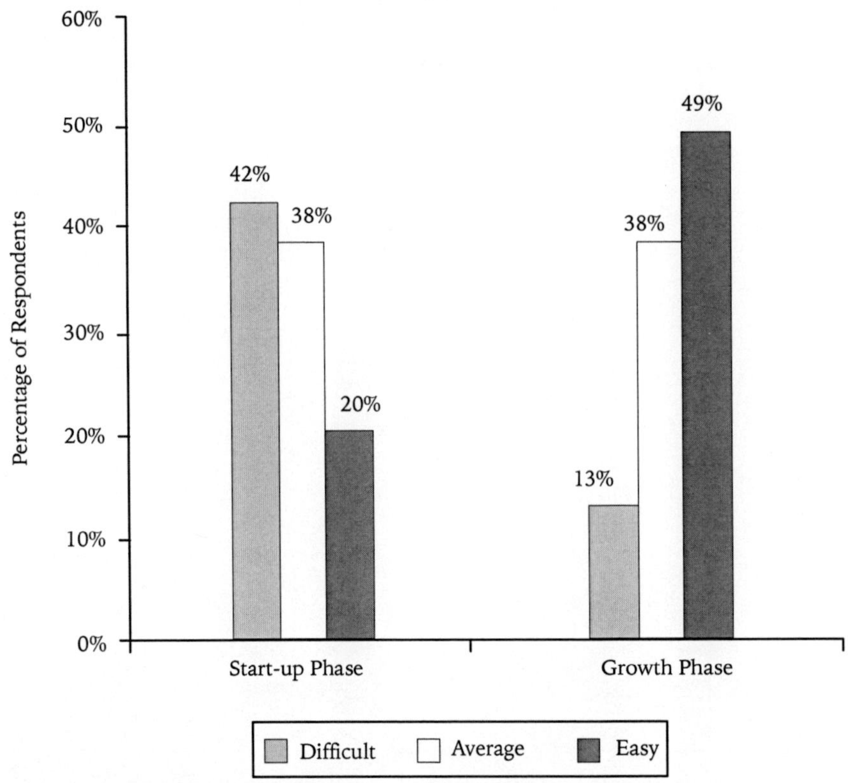

It is observed that access to early stage finance from banks is perceived to be very difficult at the start-up stage but becomes comparatively easy at the growth stage.

Figure 23.22: **Access to Finance from Banks—Variations According to Family Background**

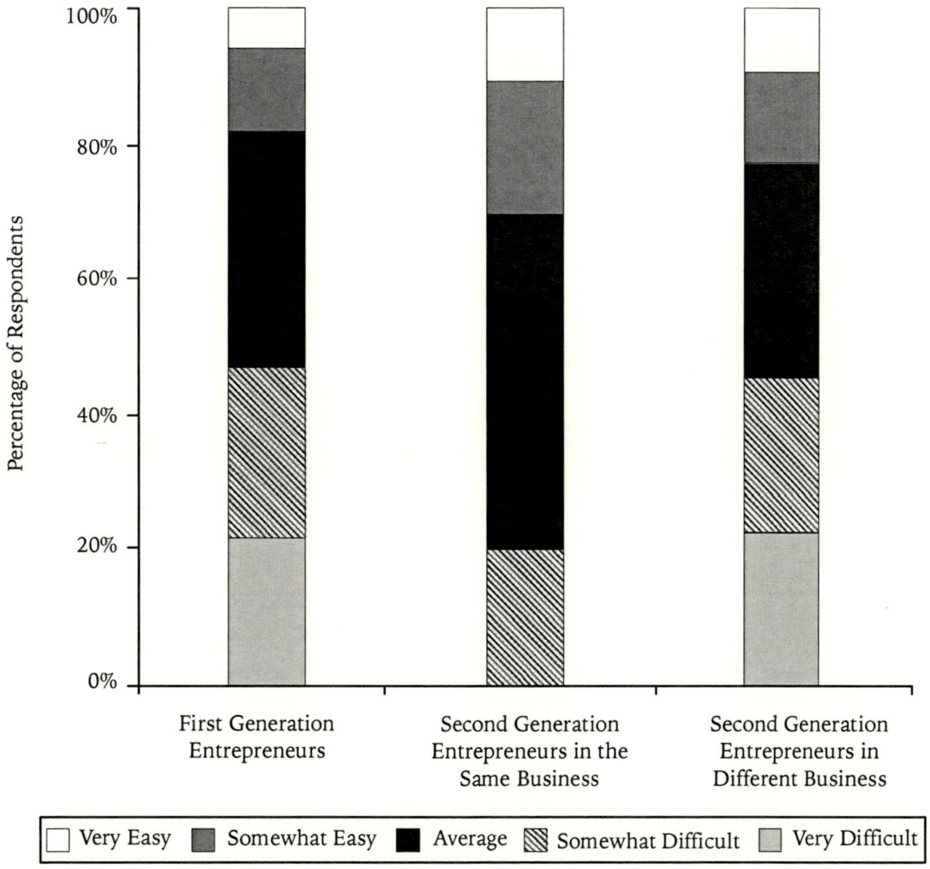

4.2.6 *Changes Over a Period of Time:* An analysis of entrepreneurial responses indicates that the availability of bank finance is less favourable for enterprises started after year 2000 compared to those that were established in the 1990s or earlier. Of the entrepreneurs who started business after year 2000, a much larger percentage found it 'somewhat difficult' or 'very difficult' to access bank funding. Many of the enterprises which commenced business after 2000 are in the knowledge-intensive sectors, where information asymmetry and perceived higher levels of risks may have inhibited bank credit availability. It is in these sectors that angel investors and VCs are slowly beginning to fill a crucial market gap. Yet, even among VCs and angels, there is scope for improvement. While 41 per cent of entrepreneurs said they find VCs 'satisfactory' or 'very satisfactory', 32 per cent still find them 'unsatisfactory' and as many as 27 per cent expressed themselves as largely 'indifferent' to VCs in the financial space. Overall the role of banks, VCs and angel investors continues to be highly underexploited for the advancement of entrepreneurial activities in India. Access to finance is one of the biggest limiting factors in achieving significantly higher levels of entrepreneurial growth in India.

Of the entrepreneurs who started business after year 2000, a much larger percentage found it 'somewhat difficult' or 'very difficult' to access bank funding.

Figure 23.23: Access to Finance from Banks—Variations According to Time Periods

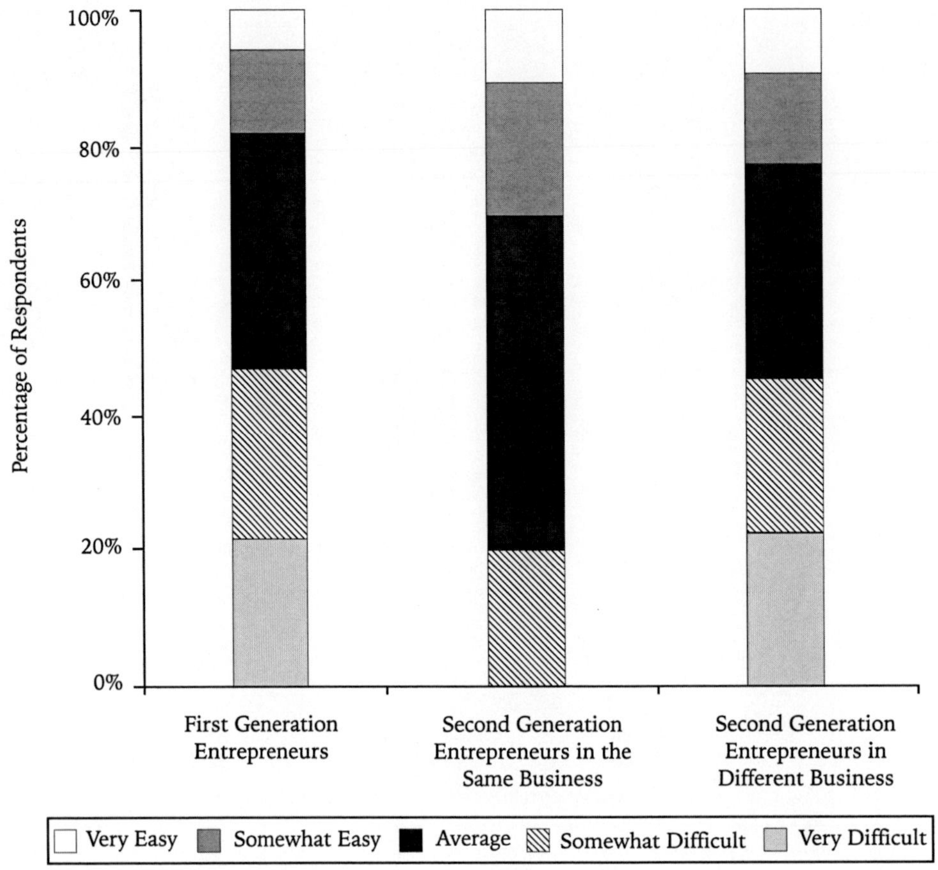

Figure 23.24: Perceptions on Venture Capital

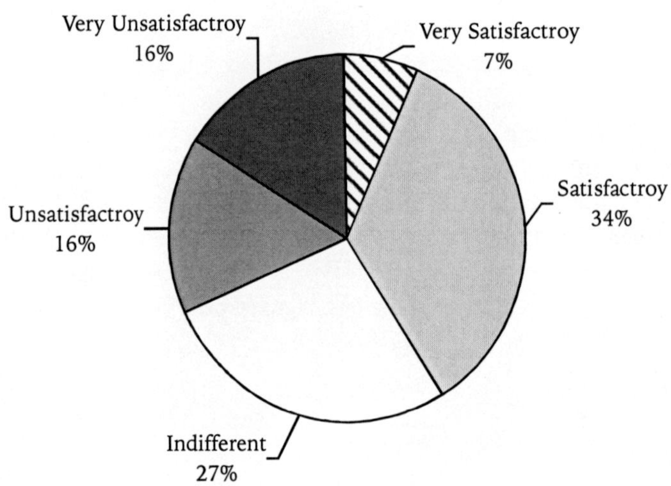

Overall the role of banks, VCs and angel investors continues to be highly underexploited for the advancement of entrepreneurial activities in India.

4.3 Entrepreneurship and the Banking Sector

4.3.1 It may, therefore, be useful to highlight some key financial packages developed for the SME sector in recent years.[55] Some of the key interventions include recommendations from the numerous committees set up by the Reserve Bank of India (RBI)[56], the Union Finance Minister's 'Policy Package for Stepping up Credit to SMEs as well as the enactment of the Micro, Small and Medium Enterprises Development Act (MSME Act) in 2006. The key aim is to facilitate access to finance and incentivise efficient use of funds by entrepreneurs, to bring about greater growth in numbers and overall competitiveness. Some of the significant financial policies are as follows:

a. **Risk Management:** A transparent rating system for SMEs, where the cost of credit is linked to the credit rating of the enterprise, thereby incentivising SMEs to get credit rated; availability of a Credit Appraisal and Rating Tool (CART) and a comprehensive Risk Assessment Model (RAM), which public sector banks could best use.[57]

   In this regard, Credit Information Bureau (India) Limited (CIBIL), Dun & Bradstreet Information Services India Private Limited (D&B), SIDBI, and a few other banks have together set up SMERA (SME Rating Agency)—the first rating agency in India focusing primarily on the SME segment. Since its inception in September 2005, SMERA has rated over 1400 SMEs. Initial signs appear to be encouraging. According to SMERA reports, "the rated companies have reported varied experience in terms of interest rate reduction, larger loan size, faster turnaround in processing of loan applications, bigger export orders, and better internal assessment. Specifically, thanks to SMERA rating, a particular unit benefited not just with 450 basis points reduction in interest on its loan, but also managed to obtain a bigger loan from its bank. Banks have also reported reduction in interest rate by 25 to 100 basis points for 'SMERA rated companies.'[58] SMERA rating as a driving force for encouraging entrepreneurship needs for greater publicity and marketing across the country.

b. **Credit Guarantee:** To encourage collateral free loans, the Credit Guarantee Cover offers to 'Member Lending Institutions'[59] (MLIs), up to 75 per cent of amount of default under the Credit Guarantee Fund Trust Scheme for Small Industries (CGTSI).[60] The figure below shows an increase in the approved guarantee amounts as well as in the number of MLIs over the last few years.

c. **Other Policies:** Some other policies pertain to the following: (i) increasing credit flow[61]; (ii) widening credit spread[62]; (iii) use of cluster approaches[63] (including corporate clusters); (iv) debt restructuring[64]; (v) fixing time

SMERA rating as a driving force for encouraging entrepreneurship needs far greater publicity and marketing across the country.

---

55. It is pertinent here to refer to the Small Industries Development Bank of India (SIDBI) set up by an Act of the Parliament in 1990, to promote financing and development of small scale industries and to function as the nodal agency for execution of SME programmes of the Government of India; see also the RBI Master Circular on lending to SME sector dated July 2, 2007; *http://www.reservebank.com/scripts/BS_ViewMasterCirculars*

56. See particularly, the noteworthy work in this regard by the Nayak Committee, Kapur Committee and Ganguly Committee, each set up by the RBI.

57. See the Policy Package for Stepping up Credit to SMEs, announced by the Union Finance Minister, quoted in the RBI Master Circular dated July 2, 2007.

58. See in particular, an interview with Mr. Rajesh Dubey, CEO, SMERA; *http://smera.in/media/Emerging%20SME%20Nov%20Issue.pdf.*

59. Member Lending Institutions (MLIs) include banks and financial institutions.

60. The said scheme covers term loans and grant of working capital facilities up to Rs. 25 lakh to new and existing SSIs without collateral security and third party guarantee. See the Finance Minister's policy package, Annexure IV, RBI Master Circular dated July 2, 2007; also reduction of one time guarantee fee from 1.5 per cent to 1 per cent and annual service fee from 0.75 per cent to 0.5 per cent for SIDBI loans up to Rs. 5 lakh has been announced in the annual budget for 2008-09. For details on the credit guarantee scheme, see also *http://www.laghu-udyog.com/schemes/sccrguarn.htm*

61. See generally, Annexure IV of the RBI Master Circular dated July 2, 2007. Public sector banks have been advised to achieve at least a minimum of 20 per cent on year growth in credit to SMEs, with the objective of doubling the flow of credit to SMEs from Rs. 67, 600 crore in 2004-05 to 135,200 crore in 2009-10.

62. See Section IV, read with Annexure IV, RBI Master Circular dated July 2, 2007. Advice to increase credit cover to include an addition of at least five new tiny, small and medium enterprises at each semi-urban/urban branch of a commercial bank per year; public sector banks have been advised by RBI to open at least one specialised SSI/SME branch in each district.

63. Use of cluster-based financing for SMEs (in places with relative homogeneity and critical mass) that offer possibilities of reduction of transaction costs and mitigation of risk, through holistic views of credit risk, opportunities to deal with recognised groups, availability of information for risk assessment and adequate monitoring arrangements. Corporate linked cluster models which encourage new entrepreneurs to link as suppliers or manufacturers with successful large industries, who could also provide guarantee covers etc. See RBI Master Circular dated July 2, 2007; also report of the working group on the flow of credit to the SSI sector (Ganguly Committee) as quoted in the said master circular.

64. See Section IV of the RBI Master Circular, dated July 2, 2007 along with the Policy Package for SMEs for more liberal policies relating to restructuring of debt, debt restructuring mechanism by RBI and fixing of guidelines on rehabilitation of sick SSIs (based on the Kohli working group recommendations).

limits for disposal of applications[65]; and (vi) fixing stringent penalties for delayed payments. While such schemes underline the increasing recognition of entrepreneurship, there is need for independent monitoring and evaluation of their impact. It is relevant to highlight here the government plan to put in place a 'Central Plan Schemes Monitoring System' (CPSMS), as mentioned in the Budget for 2008-09. Within the CPSMS, monitoring for the SME segment should receive visibility and priority.

Table 23.1: Credit Guarantee Scheme in India

Period	Active MLIs	Number of Proposals Approved	Credit Amount Approved	Cumulative Guarantees Approved (Rs. in lakh)
FY 2000-01	9	951	606	606
FY 2001-02	16	2296	2952	3558
FY 2002-03	22	4955	5867	9425
FY 2003-04	29	6603	11760	21185
FY 2004-05	32	9516	32677	53862
FY 2005-06	36	16284	46191	100053
FY 2006-07	40	27457	70453	170506
FY 2007-08*	44	13283	44714	215220

Note: *Up to 30 September 2007.

Source: Ministry of Micro, Small and Medium Enterprises (MSME); *http://www.laghu-udyog.com/schemes/sccrguarn.htm*

4.3.2 *Micro Small and Medium Enterprises Development Act (MSME Act):* Further, the enactment of a specialised legislation targeted at meeting specific needs of the micro, small and medium enterprises, is another noteworthy step. Section 10 of the MSME Act states expressly that "the policies and practices in respect of credit to the micro, small and medium enterprises shall be progressive" ...and that the RBI would issue guidelines from time to time, "to ensure timely and smooth flow of credit to such enterprises, minimize the incidence of sickness and enhance the competitiveness of such enterprises." Section 12 of the Act also calls for the constitution of one or more funds for the sector, to which the government would provide grants. Since the MSME Act was enacted only in 2006, it may be too early to assess its impact on entrepreneurship.

4.3.3 *Need for More Information Flows:* While recognising the improvements in policies that seek to facilitate easy access to early stage finance, there is need for more effective implementation on the part of banks as well as for removal of information asymmetries at various levels. Commentators have criticised 'skewed incentives' that exist for Indian bankers, as a result of which 'banks display inertia' and are 'characteristically risk averse'.[66] Banks too are beginning to recognise entrepreneurship. For example, State Bank of India (SBI) has introduced special consultancy cells to address functional inadequacies and develop multidimensional skills for entrepreneurship.[67] From the perspective of banks, the crucial need is to encourage entrepreneurs to achieve greater scale of operations and develop multidimensional expertise.[68] Increased awareness of financial schemes backed by efficient credit information and rating systems is expected to ensure greater ease of access to traditional sources of finance.

Within the Central Plan Schemes Monitoring System (CPSMS), monitoring for the SME segment should receive visibility and priority.

65. See Section IV of the RBI Master Circular for an overview of guidelines for disposal of applications for SSIs and stringent provisions (including penal provisions) for delayed payments to entrepreneurs; see also MSME Act 2006.
66. Khanna, Tarun "Billions of Entrepreneurs", page 92, quoting Abhijit Banerjee, Shawn Cole and Esther Duflo, "Banking Reforms in India", working paper, Massachusetts Institute of Technology, June 2004.
67. Mr. R. Kuppanna of SBI, Chennai provided valuable insights in this regard.
68. See also Sabharwal, Manish (2007). "Babies or Dwarfs?" *Business India*, October 21; see also John Hamm, "Why Entrepreneurs don't Scale", *Harvard Business Review*, 2002 where the author states that the very qualities that help entrepreneurs in launching businesses (i.e., task orientation, single mindedness, working in isolation) can inhibit scaling up.

A key development relating to flow of credit information has been the establishment of CIBIL (see 4.3.1.a). Credit reporting helps remove information asymmetries—reducing problems of adverse selection and moral hazard. According to CIBIL, "aggregate bank credit to the private sector is higher in countries where information sharing is more developed. Analyses of firm level data show that access to bank credit is easier in countries where credit bureaus exist." According to recent estimates, CIBIL currently has 146 members including 77 banks, 16 housing finance companies (HFCs), 10 financial institutions (FIs), 2 credit card companies, 6 state financial corporations (SFCs) and 35 major non-banking financial companies (NBFCs). CIBIL's 'Commercial Bureau' has a database of over 15.6 lakh accounts contributed by 65 members while its 'Consumer Bureau' has a database of over 100 million accounts contributed by 83 members.[69] It is expected that greater information availability will create the necessary transparency that will, in turn, make funding decisions easier.

In addition, India's corporate laws have elaborate rules of disclosure, particularly for public listed companies. Further, private institutions such as the Centre for Monitoring Indian Economy (CMIE) also provide clearing-house facilities for publicly traded as well as some private companies in India.[70]

While there are a few websites containing information on entrepreneurial needs, NKC proposes to explore the possibility of an all encompassing website on entrepreneurship as a one-stop information portal for current and aspiring entrepreneurs.

4.3.4 *Other Innovations:* While this study has not examined rural and informal sector entrepreneurship, there are interesting financial innovations such as micro-finance, micro-equity, mutual guarantee associations and various other guarantee models that are also evolving in those spaces in India today. It is important to encourage win-win solutions that involve multiple stakeholders and provide various incentives. Two illustrations of innovative initiatives, namely Mutual Credit Guarantee and the Network Enterprises Fund are highlighted in the following boxes:

Box 23.1: Mutual Credit Guarantee

A Mutual Guarantee Association (MGA) is an association comprising entrepreneurs who together create an organisation which establishes a dialogue with banks. The association thus plays the role of an intermediary between entrepreneurs and banks, facilitating access to bank and other credit. Each member is required to make a certain contribution to the common fund, which is then used as a guarantee to help members access credit from traditional banks. MGAs thus constitute an effective tool for smaller entrepreneurs to overcome the challenge of gaining access to credit from traditional sources of finance such as banks. Traditional financial institutions also benefit from MGAs, which can help them reduce administrative costs and level of risk. In the MGA scheme, part of the analysis of the loan application is undertaken by the association itself, which has an intimate knowledge of the SME sector. The MGA and the bank share risk.

The first MGAs appeared in Europe in the 1940s and, since then, they have expanded considerably, both in number and in size. At the end of 2000, in the 15 EU countries, over 1.4 million SMEs were members of MGAs, benefiting from 14,173,907 guarantees. Italy, with a strong presence of SMEs, currently has 800 *Confidi* (mutual guarantee schemes). One of the impressive achievements of the mutual guarantee schemes in Italy has been to keep the average default rate of the guarantee loans far lower than the average in corresponding banking operations; it is reported that the average national insolvency is about 9 per cent-10 per cent, while the insolvency on *Confidi* counter-guaranteed loans is around 1.5 per cent-2 per cent.

In India, the Indian Institute of Rural Development (IIRD), with support from UNIDO, launched the Mutual Credit Guarantee Fund Scheme (MCGFS) in 2000. The project was designed to help hand block printing textile clusters (at Sanganer and Bagru near Jaipur) overcome the difficulty in accessing credit arising from their inability to offer traditional forms of collateral. Among industry associations, the ALEAP Credit Guarantee Association (ACGA) has entered into a tripartite agreement with Andhra Bank and CGTSI for implementation of MCGS in the state of Andhra Pradesh wherein member SSI (small-scale) units can avail of collateral-free bank finance.

Source: "Making Social Capital Work: Mutual Guarantee Associations for Artisans", September 2002, Social Finance Programme, Employment Sector, ILO; *http://www.nmcc-vikas.gov.in/ComptitivenessManagement/SMEFinanceCredit/Pages/MutualCreaditGuaranteeFinanceSchemes.aspx*

It is expected that greater information availability will create the necessary transparency that will, in turn, make funding decisions easier.

69. *http://www.cibil.com/newsletter.htm*

70. Tarun Khanna, "Billions of Entrepreneurs", page 61; see also *www.cmie.com*

Box 23.2: Network Enterprises Fund

Network Enterprises Fund (NEF) was created by IFMR (Institute for Financial Management and Research) Trust in January 2008 as an equity fund that invests in commercially viable, sustainable enterprises in sectors impacting low income households. It aims to go beyond solely providing micro-finance to the entrepreneur by ensuring participation in economic activities on a sustainable basis. The equity fund created under NEF seeks to create a network of enterprises (NEs) to provide the economically disadvantaged a platform to engage with the markets, as producers and consumers of goods and services. NEs are expected to act as intermediaries between the formal markets and low-income groups, to demonstrate and implement market-based solutions. They will help in aggregation of primary producers, facilitating 'backward and forward linkages', providing technical and managerial support and delivering basic services. They are also expected to work in partnership with grassroots organisations. Each NE will complement the work of the other, and yet specialise in what it can do best. The key value proposition that networking offers is that it preserves the competitive advantage of disaggregated low cost of production and yet manages to take advantage of standardisation and scaled economies through networks created. NEF will be exploring the potential for supporting industries such as dairy, rural BPO, food, crafts, village tourism and rural infrastructure such as drinking water, education, skill development, low cost housing, waste recycling, health care and rural energy. This is a very recent initiative and it will be interesting to watch its impact on rural entrepreneurship in the years to come.

Source: Information received from Network Enterprises Fund

4.4 New Sources of Finance—Angel Investors, VCs and PE Funds

4.4.1 Unlike traditional banking finance, which is largely debt-based, the relatively newer sources of finance—such as angel investors, VCs and PE funds—invest equity with the expectation of much higher returns. The lending decisions of banks are governed by the ability of businesses to service the loan and the availability of collateral. On the other hand, equity investors make capital investments (with a different emphasis and understanding of collateral) in return for significantly larger returns within a defined exit horizon. Further, the level of mentoring and guidance for running the business is more intense in the case of early stage investors, unlike traditional banking financiers. While banks expect repayment on fixed interest rates within particular time horizons, there is variation among different types of early stage investors on crucial investment decisions, return expectations and strategies for exit. The emergence of angel investors, VCs and PE funds (including cross-border investment) and their active involvement in the equity market in India (especially in the knowledge-based industries) over the last few years is one of the most significant financial developments that could impact the growth of entrepreneurship in India. For recent figures on such investment, see Figures 23.25, 23.26, 23.27, 23.28 and Tables 23.3 and 23.4.

4.4.2 Angel Investors: Angel investors are typically high-net-worth individuals (HNIs) who have often been successful entrepreneurs themselves. They re-deploy their wealth in next generation businesses. They invest in new idea enterprises (that do not yet have external validation), help bring these ideas to market, take significant risks and invest a lot of time and energy in mentoring, management guidance and networking. Angel investors are also governed by considerations other than finance alone, such as belief in entrepreneurship itself. Their time horizons are limited and aimed at ensuring the availability of larger institutional funding, mainly from VCs. In recent years, institutional seed funds that perform the roles of sophisticated angel investors have also emerged in India. Where access to early stage capital is a serious issue, angel investors have the potential to become one of the most important catalysts for increasing the number of new entrepreneurial ventures in India.

The lending decisions of banks are governed by the ability of businesses to service the loan and the availability of collateral. On the other hand, equity investors make capital investments (with a different emphasis and understanding of collateral) in return for significantly larger returns within a defined exit horizon.

Box 23.3: Angel Investment - Illustrations

One recent innovative deal that deserves mention is the seed fund investment of about Rs. 4 crore (US$ 1 million) in TRI-Thinklabs in December 2007. TRIThinklabs is the brainchild of two IIT Mumbai graduates, Gagan Goyal and Abhishek Biswal, who were incubated in SINE, IIT Mumbai. The company is working on 'Career Oriented Embedded Systems Training' using robotics as a practical learning tool. It has already trained over 10,000 students in an 'In-Campus Workshop Model' over the last 12 months, in a hands-on environment to enable maximum exposure to actual shop-floor conditions. Over the next few years, it aims to train over 10,000 students per year, working with engineering and science colleges in about seven cities in India. The broad goal of the company is to help provide trained skilled resources in the critical area of manufacturing, especially in hardware, automation and power sectors. The seed fund worked closely with the entrepreneurs before investing, on issues such as developing the idea, positioning it in the market, evolving strategy, obtaining feedback from industry, financial modelling, etc. In return, it has taken a stake of less than 30 per cent in equity.[71]

4.4.3 *Venture Capital:* Venture capital funding provides funds for early-stage companies once they have passed the seed stage and report some returns. VC investments are traditionally made for scaling up operations (i.e., developing, launching and expanding new products or services). VCs take lesser degrees of risk and invest more money than angel investors. However, a VC is about more than financial support alone.[72] VCs provide entrepreneurial support and partnership-based value-addition, often in the form of providing financial advice, human resources, IP issues, establishing networks with customers and overall guidance in company strategy. In return, VCs also retain a degree of control over decisions governing the company's functioning (e.g., through board seats and legal covenants[73]), and usually look at fixed time horizons for predetermined exit, usually via a private equity fund. As illustrations, two recent VC investments by Helion Ventures Limited provide insights on the type of new, high value added, wealth generating ideas that are evolving in India today.[74]

Box 23.4: Venture Capital Deals - Illustrations

Jigrahak Mobile Solutions, which received an investment of US$2.2 million in 2006, offers technology solutions in the mobile-commerce space. It has developed a mobile platform that allows end-customers to choose from a variety of products and services from a range of service providers like MakeMyTrip, cinema halls, flower merchants, banks, etc. Customers can also make payments using mobile phones in a quick and secure manner. It was founded by Sourabh Jain who invested his own savings for a year before receiving VC funding. A combination of factors ensured funding for Jigrahak: it is in the mobile space with a growing number of subscribers in India; it has a ready number of interested service providers and it does not charge end-customers for completing transactions. Helion also played an active mentoring role and has two of its directors on Jigrahak's board. Another example of VC investment in the knowledge-intensive sector is the US$6.5 million funding received by Anantara Solutions Private Limited in 2007 from a combination of investors led by Helion. Anantara is in the 'Second Generation Outsourcing' space that shifts the focus from cost arbitrage alone to generating high value through offshore business consulting and IT services frequently delivered through a set of partner companies that Anantara recruits and manages. It was founded by G.B. Prabhat (who had substantial prior experience with Satyam) and his management team of eight partners. Within months, Anantara has enlisted new clients from India as well as the UK, Germany, France and Hong Kong. It was also short listed for the NASSCOM '100 IT Innovators' register in 2007.

4.4.4 *Private Equity:* Private Equity (PE) funds are among the largest sources of funding for enterprises that are relatively secure with an established track record, requiring significantly large funds for expansion and growth. PEs make

Angel investors are typically high-net-worth individuals (HNIs) who have often been successful entrepreneurs themselves. They re-deploy their wealth in next-generation businesses.

71. Anand Lunia of Seed fund provided valuable inputs in this regard.
72. See Varshney, Vishnu *Venture Financing in India*, GVFL, for a historical overview of VC investment in India. In particular, see page 37 for key advice on VC funding.
73. Examples of VC control provisions typically include board seats, control over Reserved Matters (such as sales, acquisitions, budgets, executive appointment/removal and strategic business change) as well as legal rights over the company (such as right of first refusal over sale of shares, tag along rights, drag along rights, liquidation preference, non-compete clauses, rights of further participation and anti-dilution protection)
74. Ashish Gupta of Helion Ventures provided valuable inputs in this regard.

Private Equity (PE) funds are among the largest sources of funding for enterprises that are relatively secure with an established track record, requiring significantly large funds for expansion and growth.

capital investments in companies not yet quoted on a stock exchange in exchange for equity and management participation. As such, they take reasonably well-defined risks and their exit strategy is usually up to the stage when the company goes public or gets acquired at high value.

4.4.5 Some significant features of angel investors, VCs and PE funds are illustrated in the Table 4.2.[75]

Table 23.2: New Sources of Finance

Type of Investor	Stage of Enterprise	Risk & Return	Amount Invested	Equity	Mentoring Involvement	Monetary Source	Challenges	Exit Horizon
Angel	Seed; "SeriesA"	Very high risk; also Return on Investment (ROI) > 25%	Less; equity (preferred, convertible) usually $100,00 -200,000; typically 5-10 lakh and up to Rs. 4 crore	1-5%; also varies	Very high; personal	Largely individual; also fund	Prove business model, idea to market, validate product	Short; flexible
VC	Early; after start-up	Medium risk; ROI> 25%	High; equity up to $5million	20%	High; less personal	Typically other financial institutions; also individuals	Scale, team, accountability, sustainability	5-7 yrs; till next round of financing/ acquisition
PE funds	Late-pre IPO	Less risk, high ROI	Large; equity; $15m estimates	>20%	Low	Other financial institutions, market	Mergers, divestment, leadership restructuring	Short-till IPO/ acquisition

4.4.6 Recent studies show a gradual increase in the volume of VC and PE investments in high growth sectors over the last few years.[76] Principally, investments have targeted the IT/ITeS, health care and life sciences, media and entertainment, telecom, banking, financial and insurance services as well as engineering and construction sectors. Mumbai, Delhi/ NCR and Bangalore are key investment destinations,[77] while some other key regions for such investments are Chennai, Hyderabad, Ahmedabad, Pune and Kolkata. The bulk of investments are driven to the late stage. However, according to a recent survey, there has also been a rise in seed and early stage investments in 2007.[78] Some recent figures from the Indian Venture Capital Association[79] are as follows:

Recent studies show a gradual increase in the volume of VC and PE investments in high growth sectors over the last few years.

75. Also refer to Seed fund's work in this regard, see *www.seedfund.in*; see also *www.nenonline.org*; further, Ashish Gupta (Helion) and Anand Lunia (SeedFund) provided valuable inputs in this regard.

76. See for example, the figures of the Indian Venture Capital Association; also a study conducted by Venture Intelligence and US-India Venture Capital Association, as reported in *The Times of India* dated January 31, 2008.

77. According to the said survey (supra note 76 as above), companies in south India received 37 per cent of all VC investments and those in western India received 36 per cent of investments in 2007.

78. According to the said survey (supra note 76 as above), over 50 per cent of the VC investments during 2007 were below $5 million, out of which 23 per cent was below $ 2 million.

79. See *http://www.indiavca.org/IVCA%20Presentation_February%202008.pdf*

Figure 23.25: Investments by Sector—Number of Deals

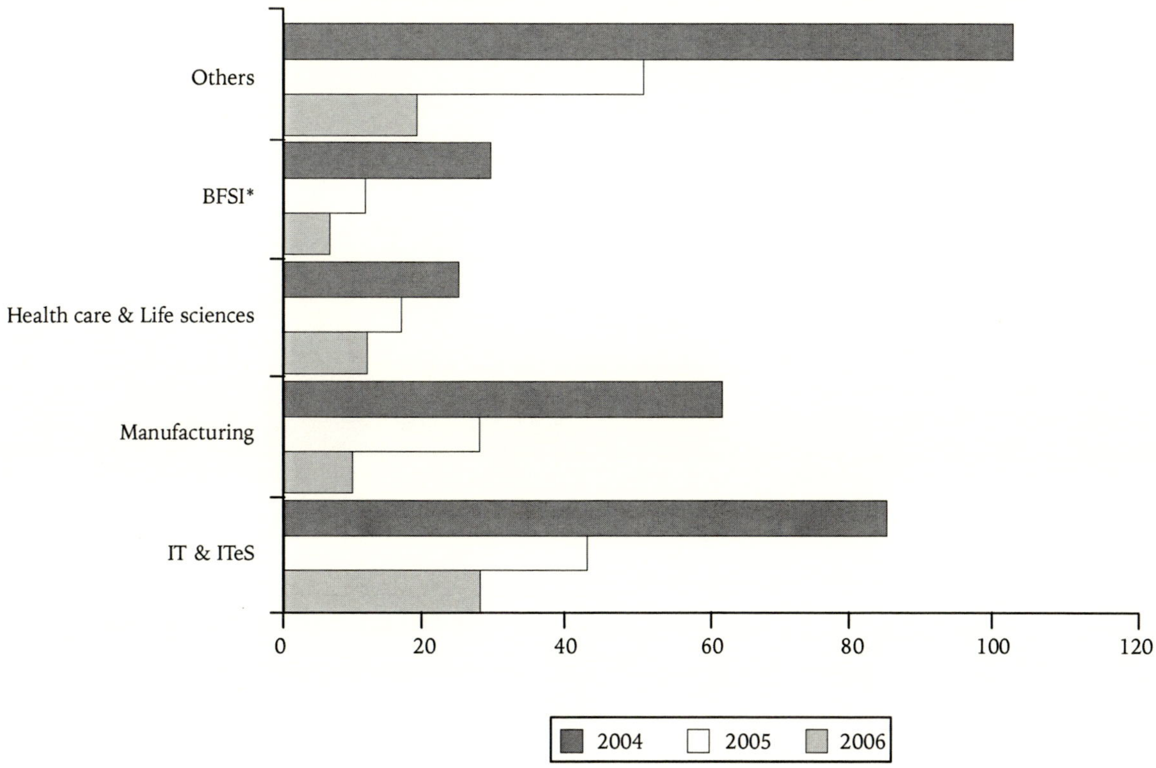

Note: * Banking Financial Services and Insurance 2006: Others: textile, garments, media & entertainment, retail, engineering/construction, food & beverage, real estate.

Source: TSJ Venture Intelligence.

Figure 23.26: Investments by Sector—Number of Deals PE/VC Investments by Industry in 2007 (Total US$ 14.2 Bn)

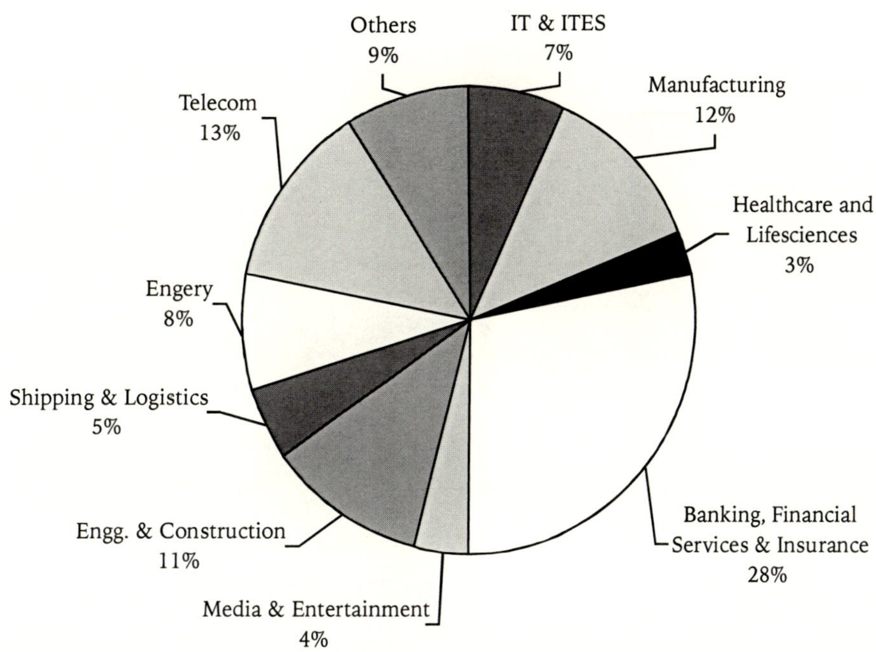

Source: TSJ Venture Intelligence.

Figure 23.27: Growth of Venture Capital and Private Equity in India, 2000–2007

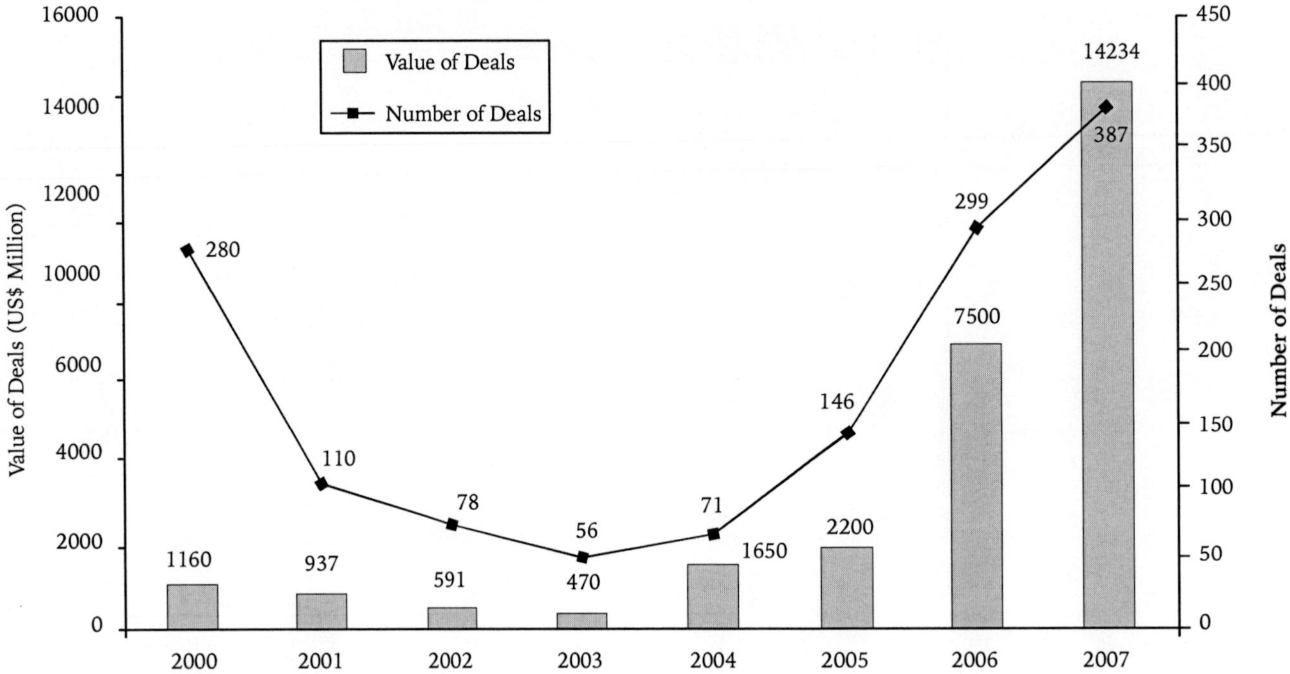

Source: TSJ Venture Intelligence.

Figure 23.28: Investments by Stage—Number of Deals

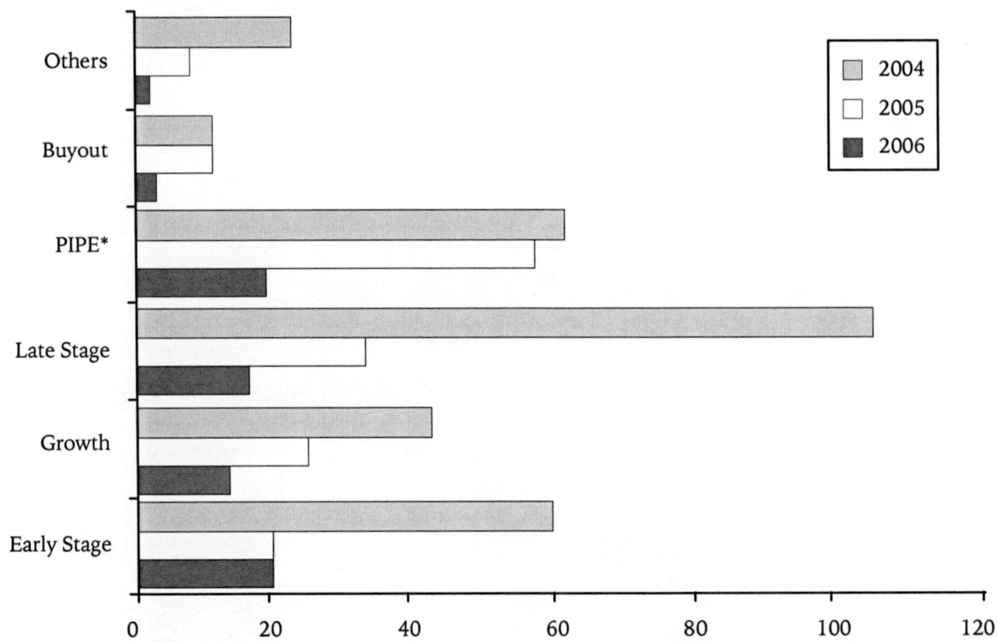

Note: PIPE* — Private investment in public equity

Source: TSJ Venture intelligence

Table 23.3: PE Investments by Stage (2007)

Stage of Company Development	No. of Deals	Amount (US$ million)
Venture capital	98	542
Growth PE	32	1321
Late	136	5070
Pre IPO	14	434
Private investment in public equity	80	4210
Buyout	7	173
Buyout – Large	3	474
Other (Includes infrastructure investment)	17	2010
Total	387	14234

Source: TSJ Venture Intelligence.

Table 23.4: Top Cities Attracting PE Investments (2007)

City	No. of Deals	Value (US$ million)
Mumbai	103	5995
Delhi/ NCR	63	2688
Bangalore	49	685
Hyderabad	41	1380
Chennai	32	824
Ahmedabad	14	492
Kolkata	12	339

Source: TSJ Venture Intelligence.

4.5 Some Critical Issues in Financing

4.5.1 *Ensuring Ready Availability of Seed Capital:* Ensuring a ready supply of seed capital and a wider source of capital across geographies is a critical financial issue for entrepreneurs in India. It is essential to move beyond a few informal angel investors and promote more incentive schemes to encourage seed capital funding in India. While there has been growing foreign investment in India in recent years, a 2006 study states that over 90 per cent of such funds are invested in late stage initiatives by mature firms.[80] VCs and PE funds generally invest in reasonably established enterprises. Since investments in SMEs typically generate returns and add value in various ways, it is important to examine the issue of incentivising start-up capital with greater rigour.[81] With the rise of entrepreneurial activity in India, it is also expected that a number of innovative finance models will emerge in the coming years.[82]

It is essential to move beyond a few informal angel investors and promote more incentive schemes to encourage seed capital funding in India.

80. See also Rafiq Dossani and Asawari Desai, *Accessing Early Stage Risk Capital in India*, Stanford-Ti E Study, 2006, page 16; for policy options, see also report of the Committee on Technology Innovation and Venture Capital submitted to the Planning Commission in July 2006.

81. See also, the results of the SEAF study, 2004, "The Development Impact of Small and Medium Enterprises: lessons learnt from SEAF Investments"; report on Small Enterprise Development Funds, which stated that for every dollar invested on average, ten additional dollars were generated in the local economy, accompanied by the creation of new jobs, introduction of new business methods and integration into supply chains, quoted in Dossani and Desai, supra note 80 as above.

82. For an overview of policy options, see also report of the Committee on Technology Innovation and Venture Capital submitted to the Planning Commission in July 2006.

4.5.2 *Lack of Relevant Secondary Markets:* The absence of equity markets for listing and trading of small-cap companies means that the options for raising capital are limited. The lack of such an exchange also means that the options before a seed investor, in terms of finding a market and for exit, remain obscure. Further, the relative lack of capital flow from big corporate players to start-up entrepreneurs at the seed stage (and the absence of incentives for doing so) makes it difficult to sustain a critical mass of seed funding in the entrepreneurial sector.

4.5.3 *Relative Lack of Market Understanding among Start-ups:* Start-up funders who actively mentor through a company's initial days, often have to face serious challenges in communicating the product or service as a marketable proposition. Start-ups also need guidance regarding scaling-up, including decisions involving professionalising, teamwork, corporate structuring etc. Angels and VCs consider these issues as well as scaling up questions to be extremely significant. In this respect, it is useful to point out that one-third of the entrepreneurs interviewed took to entrepreneurship on their own. However, the trend of starting with a core team has become more marked in the recent years. New entrepreneurs feel that it does help to work in teams, ideally with varying skill sets.

Regarding market research before starting up, less than half of the entrepreneurs interviewed had either prepared a business plan or undertaken market research before starting their business venture. While the financial community looks for clear business plans and scaling up particulars, entrepreneurs often decide to test the waters based on a variety of other factors, without necessarily going into traditional details. The efficacy of such risk-taking behaviour does merit further analysis.[83]

4.6 Key Suggestions to Incentivise Seed Stage and Early Stage Funding in India

4.6.1 Some of the key suggestions to provide more incentives for greater seed capital funding as well as involvement of angel investors and VCs are as follows:

a. **Explore innovative models:** To help knowledge-based start-ups, Venture Debt is a novel idea that is worth exploring. Venture Debt combines traditional debt options with venture capital. To help knowledge-based start-ups move from idea to market in the least possible time, angels and seed investors prefer their investments to be utilised in activities that lead to substantial value addition (such as R&D, building of teams, developing products and marketing networks, knowledge investments, etc.) rather than on brick and mortar costs (such as leasing of infrastructure, hardware, fixed and working capital, etc.) Venture Debt is an option that could be used here for traditional brick and mortar costs. Such debt could be serviced by banks such as SIDBI and/or by private players who could bear the risks to which traditional banking mechanisms may otherwise be averse. While Venture Debt is prevalent in USA, it has not yet become current in India. It will be interesting to examine the feasibility, especially for knowledge-based start-ups.[84]

   Alternatively, other models could involve a blend of traditional debt and equity. The lender could have the option of converting debt into equity over a period of time. This gives an incentive to the lender to fund start-ups as well as participate in their growth.[85] Further, greater availability of soft loans (i.e., loans at below-market rates of interest and on easier terms) at the start-up stage from banks will also supplement the efforts of angel investors.

> *It is useful to point out that one-third of the entrepreneurs interviewed took to entrepreneurship on their own. However, the trend of starting with a core team has become more marked in the recent years.*

83. See the work of Saras D Sarasvathy generally on the 'affordable loss principle', at the University of Virginia, Darden School Foundation.

84. See for example, SIDBI's recent efforts to provide equity financing in selected areas; see *http://economictimes.indiatimes.com/News/Economy/Finance/SIDBI_to_focus_on_direct_equity_support_to_SMEs_of_north_/rssarticleshow/2628546.cms*; also on SIDBI's proposed initiative on creating a Rs. 2000 crore worth risk capital fund to support new entrepreneurs and encourage angel investors, see, *http://www.financialexpress.com/news/SIDBI-beginswork- on-Rs-2-000cr-risk-capital-fund/281567/*; see also annual budget speech 2008-09 of the Union Finance Minister, P. Chidambaram on achieving greater financial inclusion through facilitative efforts. It is relevant here to point out that SIDBI has already earmarked a sum of Rs. 11 crore for equity financing to select SMEs (with a typical stake of about 30 per cent) in north India. See *The Economic Times* dated December 18, 2007. Further, it has set up funds in the IT sector, grassroots innovation and knowledge based industries.

85. See also for example, mezzanine financing as another relevant financial instrument. See *www. iciciventure.com/mezzanine_practice.html*

The lender could have the option of converting debt into equity over a period of time. This gives an incentive to the lender to fund start-ups as well as participate in their growth.

Some initiatives are already underway in India. For example, the National Association of Software and Service Companies (NASSCOM) and ICICI Knowledge Park are planning to set up a US $25 million VC fund to help start-ups with Intellectual Property (IP). The fund, to be registered with the SEBI, will look after the brick-and-mortar costs of start-ups.[86]

b. **Set up a public fund for start-up entrepreneurs using innovative PPP mechanisms:** A variant of ideas mentioned in 4.6.1 (a) is to establish a public fund that typically provides start-up capital.[87] In this respect, suitable PPPs could be promoted. In the USA, for example, the Small Business Investment Company (SBIC) scheme allows private seed and VC fund investors to borrow funds at favourable terms[88] from the government. These loans are then invested as equity in start-ups, where the seed investor also provides crucial mentoring skills and contacts with business networks. Such a scheme allows the government to share some of the high risks involved in start-ups and, at the same time, encourages more seed investors and VCs to enter start-up and early stage financing. Further, under the SBIC scheme, there are special benefits for investing in less developed sectors of the economy as well as for disadvantaged sections of the population. In India, areas such as rural entrepreneurship and efforts to develop a more inclusive entrepreneurial environment could receive a fillip from such a scheme. Further, special incentives such as tax benefits on capital gains arising out of such seed stage investment could also be considered as ways of increasing big corporate appetite to invest in start-ups.

The NKC, for example, has already recommended an SME Fund in its recommendations on Intellectual Property Rights (IPR), which may enable crucial technology acquisition abroad.[89] In his Annual Budget 2008-09 speech, the Union Finance Minister also proposed to create a Rs. 2000 crore risk capital fund for the SME sector within SIDBI.[90] The Economic Survey 2008 also discusses a proposal to set up a Small Enterprises Development Fund under SIDBI.[91] The involvement of various stakeholders in this fund could signify a major and positive departure from past practices.

c. **Create a secondary market for smaller companies:** A stock exchange that is specifically designed for smaller companies will provide significant advantages. From the company's point of view, it will ensure visibility, help in accessing additional capital, create a market with a public value for its shares and also help to broaden the shareholder base. From the seed stage investor's point of view, the prime advantage lies in the creation of a market that is small enough for the company to attract the attention of other shareholders (including bigger companies and VCs), and thereby also provide appropriate exit options. Such an exchange will also help generate significant 'network' with the wider business community. The exchange would need to incorporate distinctive regulations tailored to the needs of the smaller companies and investors, with appropriate monitoring and quality checks, ensuring public trading of shares of small companies within a well-supervised, yet simplified, regulatory environment.[92]

A stock exchange that is specifically designed for smaller companies will provide significant advantages.

---

86. *The Economic Times,* dated January 13, 2008; see also *http://www.vccircle.com/2008/01/12/nasscom-icici-knowledge-parks-25-million-early-stagefund-kicks-off/*

87. See for example, the recommendation of the Ganguly Committee Working Group set up by RBI, on SME Development Fund. See also section 12, 13 of the MSME Act, 2006; in this respect, see also the proposed venture capital fund to be set up by NASSCOM and ICICI Knowledge Park.

88. Typically, these loans are availed by VCs and seed funds at low interest rates, with clauses that allow deferment of interest and capital repayment till the enterprise earns profits. See, *http://www.sba.gov/aboutsba/sbaprograms/inv/index.html*

89. See NKC's recommendations on IPR at *http://knowledgecommission.gov.in/recommendations/intellectual.asp*

90. In addition, there is also a proposal to create a fund of Rs. 2000 crore in SIDBI for enhancing refinance capability of the MSME sector.

91. Incidentally, SIDBI has already embarked on equity financing in targeted areas of the country. It has earmarked Rs. 11 crore for equity financing to select SMEs in north India. *http://sify.com/finance/fullstory.php?id=14576864*

92. In this context, see recent statements by senior SEBI officials on establishing a new stock exchange for small companies. *The Hindu*, February 1, 2008. See also for example, the recent study on the AIM entitled, 'From Local to Global–The Rise of AIM as a Stock Market for Growing Companies', London School of Economics and Political Science (LSE), September 2007; see *http://www.londonstockexchange.com/NR/rdonlyres/4B0DF62A-BE1E-44F5-8616-EA2891873F1D/0/AIMshortreport.pdf*. The AIM in the London Stock Exchange was established in 1995 and has a membership of over 2100 companies from over 22 countries, in over 30 business sectors, together raising over 2.2 billion pounds and providing a vibrant environment of new entrepreneurial energies and innovation.

There are examples of similar exchanges set up in other parts of the world, most notably the Alternative Investment Market (AIM) in London, which has raised about £49 billion since its inception in 1995.[93] Some examples of stock exchanges for smaller companies around the world (as of December 2006) are:[94]

Table 23.5 Stock Exchanges for Smaller Companies

Location	Exchange	Domestic	Foreign	Total
London	AIM	1328	306	1634
Germany	Entry Standard	70	6	76
Euronext-Paris	Alternext	73	2	75
Spain	Nuevo Mercado	10	1	11
Italy	Mercato Expandi	26	0	26
Ireland	Irish Enterprise	19	4	23
OMX	Investor & NM List	34	0	34
Toronto	TSX Ventures	2,244	0	2,244
Hong Kong	Growth Enterprise	198	0	198
Korea	KOSDAQ	962	0	962
Singapore	SESDAQ	129	40	169
Tokyo	Mothers	185	2	187

d. **Make incubators responsive to market needs:** Making incubators into entrepreneurial services, with active involvement from industry, to promote products and services that meet market needs, requires significant scaling up in the quantity and quality of incubation services. This topic is discussed in greater detail in the following chapter. While not yet seen in India, the methodology followed by Y Combinator, a US venture firm specialising in early stage start-ups (seed funding), could provide interesting insights. Y Combinator's core competence lies in working with the start-ups in transitioning from idea to company. Some of their value additions include the following: assisting in initial issues such as incorporation, intellectual property and creating the team; securing network connections, especially with lawyers and other professionals; and assisting start-ups in dealing with investors and acquirers, once the company becomes relatively mature.[95]

e. **Encourage enabling business environment:** Ensuring simplified regulatory processes, improving delivery time, eliminating corruption, meeting information needs and improving corporate governance norms for entrepreneurial start-ups, are some of the overall enablers to create a better business and regulatory environment.

Making incubators into entrepreneurial services, with active involvement from industry, requires significant scaling up in the quantity and quality of incubation services.

93. See for example, the LSE study, supra note 92 as above, stating that AIM has raised more 15.7 billion pounds in 2006.

94. World Federation of Exchanges, quoted in the LSE study, supra note 92 as above at page 18.

95. *www.ycombinator.com*; It invests mostly in software and web services. It makes small investments (rarely more than $20,000) in return for small stakes in the companies it funds (usually 2-10 per cent).

4.7 Chapter Summary

A combination of debt and equity models will spur early stage finance for entrepreneurship in the foreseeable future. Most of the entrepreneurs interviewed were self-financed; at the same time, a majority of those who approached banks did receive loans. Yet, there is a widely held perception that it is very diff cult to get bank loans at the start-up stage while becoming comparatively easy at the growth stage. While there are new initiatives and schemes, perceptions on bank finance have not improved for entrepreneurs who have started ventures after 2000, most of which are in the knowledge-intensive sectors. It is in these sectors, where the information asymmetries and perceived risk levels are considered higher, that Angels, VCs and PE funds are beginning to fill a crucial market gap and need incentives for more involvement.

Improving risk management by developing transparent rating systems and devising information tools are expected to address information asymmetries. Recent financial schemes reflect greater recognition being given to entrepreneurship. In addition, interesting financial innovations are occurring in the rural and informal entrepreneurial spaces. Seed capital funding needs incentives for greater involvement. Some ideas worth exploring include establishing a secondary market for newer companies; creating new mechanisms for start-up funding, enhancing understanding of the financial aspects of entrepreneurship among start-ups and improving the business environment for entrepreneurship. A secondary market for smaller companies will, in particular, provide exit options to the seed stage investor as well as value-addition to the entrepreneur by ensuring visibility, access to additional capital, broadening the shareholder base and generating networks with the wider business community.

V. Education, Innovation and Entrepreneurship

5.1 Interlinking Education, Innovation and Entrepreneurship

5.1.1 Generating a critical mass of entrepreneurs oriented to high levels of growth depends on the quality of education provided and the presence of an environment that encourages innovation. Three interconnected areas provide possibilities for mutually beneficial synergies through the flow of ideas and wealth, which could generate high level of dynamism. These are: education (especially, quality vocational training and skill development), innovation[96] (generating commercial value through new and improved ideas) and entrepreneurship. Together, these are the cornerstones of inclusive and sustainable growth. See Figure 23.29.

- Education is indispensable for skill development and fundamental to entrepreneurship and innovation. The ability to innovate and generate commercially valuable new products and processes can only take place in environments that encourage experimentation and value addition.
- Innovation catalyses entrepreneurship by providing ideas that can be converted into wealth (through goods and services). Innovation helps reveal market opportunities for entrepreneurship to develop and flourish. Innovations are not limited to those involving high-end technology alone. Any new idea that generates commercial value is by itself the spur for a new entrepreneur to plan a venture. To quote the economist, T.N. Srinivasan, "Innovation and entrepreneurship is a two-way relationship. In one sense, in innovation, someone finds something but that somebody may not be equipped to translate that something into a commercial proposition. That is where entrepreneurship comes in."[97]
- An entrepreneurial culture drives creation of wealth from knowledge and generates impetus for further innovation. Entrepreneurship, in turn, helps generate new jobs in the economy and creates a culture of independence, risk-taking and confidence, more so amongst the two as a generator of new ideas and opportunities.

5.2 Significance of Education

5.2.1 The importance of education for social progress and economic development is undisputed.[98] In this respect, the nature and role of education in catalysing entrepreneurship, especially in the highly skilled and knowledge-driven sectors is a topic requiring special attention. One major determinant for growth of entrepreneurship is the availability of adequate number of skilled human resources, people who can take advantage of the opportunities provided by a growing economy at the local, national and global levels. To quote T. N. Srinivasan again: "If the future demand for labour is going to be in activities which require much more skills, much more education, much more specific training and so on, are we providing them?... We are not anticipating future growth in labour demand of specific categories and providing the facilities to train them."[99]

5.2.2 At a general level, the multi-dimensional nature of the required entrepreneurial skills originates in education and involves a combination of critical (objective, analytical and logical) as well as creative and empathetic (lateral, imaginative and emotional)[100] thinking. Imparting such skills is a process, which starts right from the school stage. However,

The ability to innovate and generate commercially valuable new products and processes can only take place in environments that encourage experimentation and value addition.

96. For the purposes of its innovation study, NKC has defined innovation as "a process by which varying degrees of measurable value enhancement is planned and achieved, in any commercial activity. This process may be breakthrough or incremental, and it may occur systematically in a company or sporadically; it may be achieved by: a) introducing new/improved goods/services; and/or b) implementing new/improved operational processes; and/or c) implementing new/improved organizational/ managerial processes, in order to improve market share, competitiveness and quality, while reducing costs." See NKC Innovation Report, 2007 at *http://knowledgecommission.gov.in/downloads/documents/NKC_Innovation.pdf*
97. Srinivasan, T.N. (2007). "Create a Framework that helps Entrepreneurs", interview to *The Hindu, Business Line*, April 23.
98. NKC, Letter to the Prime Minister on Higher Education; see *http://knowledgecommission.gov.in/downloads/recommendations/HigherEducationLetterPM.pdf*
99. Srinivasan, T.N. (2007). "Create a Framework that helps Entrepreneurs", interview to *The Hindu Business Line*, April 23.
100. Kirby, David (2003). *Entrepreneurship*, McGraw Hill. p.145; see also, Sarasvathy, Saras "Entrepreneurial Thinking *versus* Managerial Thinking" quoted in *www.businessgyan.com*

critical aspects of higher education include professional education, vocational education and training (VET) and skill development.

Figure 23.29: Building Synergies

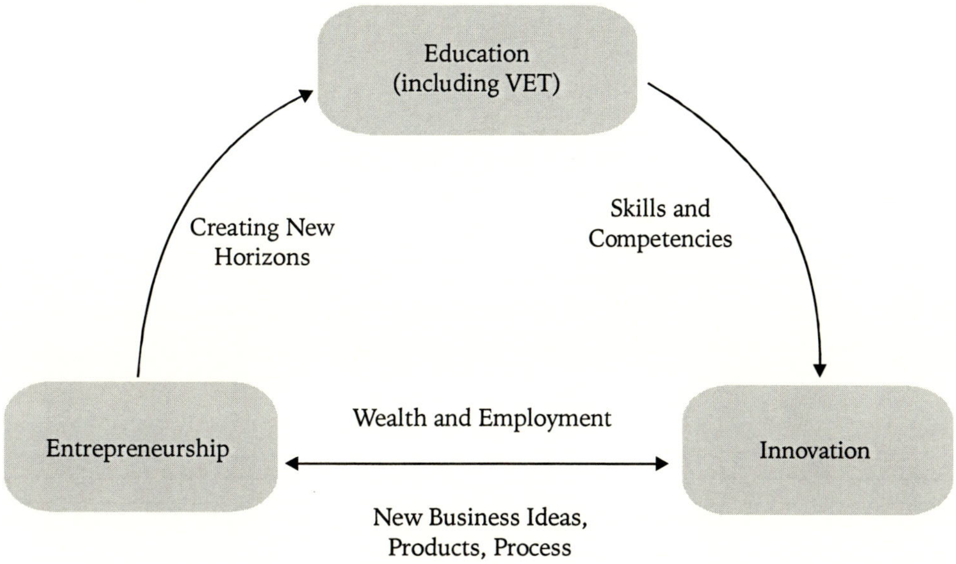

5.3 Key Issues

5.3.1 *Higher and Professional Education:* In its earlier recommendations to the Prime Minister, NKC has expressly stated that the crucial challenge is to find ways of ensuring expansion, excellence and inclusiveness in higher education.[101] This mammoth task calls for systemic reforms such as bringing about regulatory changes, diversifying sources of funding and ensuring qualitative improvements in infrastructure and curricula. In addition, NKC has also emphasised the need to make large-scale improvements in related areas including:

a. Intensifying the quality and scale of industry interaction with academia.

b. Providing commercial and legal incentive structures that promote such collaboration (such as granting IP rights to universities and research centres for inventions developed from publicly funded research and encouraging commercialisation, where the inventor also has a stake in the royalties).[102]

c. Interconnecting the knowledge institutions in the country (through digital broadband network with gigabit capabilities).[103]

d. Finding sustainable and workable models for continuous innovation-driven entrepreneurship.

Implementation of recommendations in these areas is essential to further facilitate the growth of knowledge-driven entrepreneurship on a very large scale throughout the country. In this respect, it is pertinent to point out that there is

One major determinant for growth of entrepreneurship is the availability of adequate number of skilled human resources, people who can take advantage of the opportunities provided by a growing economy at the local, national and global levels.

101. For details of the NKC's recommendations on higher education, VET and professional education, refer to *www.knowledgecommission.gov.in*

102. For details of the NKC's recommendations on legal framework on public funded research and IPR, see *www.knowledgecommission.gov.in*

103. See *http://knowledgecommission.gov.in/downloads/recommendations/KnowledgeNetworkLetterPM.pdf*

Democratisation of innovation is releasing 'untapped energies of people everywhere that could solve the world's weightiest problems'.

already an increase in budgetary allocations for education. The annual budget for the year 2008-09 has proposed increasing the total allocation for the education sector by 20 per cent from Rs. 28,674 crore in 2007-08 to Rs. 34,400 crore.

5.3.2 *Vocational Education & Training - Skill Development:* It is pertinent here to note that only 5 per cent of India's existing workforce has received skill training as against 96 per cent in Korea, 75 per cent in Germany, 80 per cent in Japan and 68 per cent in United Kingdom.[104] VET needs to be given high priority in India. Skill development is crucial to reap the demographic dividend in India, where the size of the working age population, as per the annual budget 2008-09, is estimated to increase from 77.5 crore in 2008 to 95 crore in 2026. NKC has earlier recommended the need for grassroots reforms in this area, such as innovative delivery models, re-branding, improving certification and monitoring as well as increasing flexibility of VET with the school and higher education streams.[105] Currently, there is stigma associated with VET as a result of various systemic flaws, such as the following:

a. Returns from VET are low and the quality of training does not meet the needs of industry.[106]

b. There is little incentive to pursue VET courses since most of these do not lead to a job.

c. Facilities in most VET institutes are old and outdated.

d. Different aspects of VET are in the hands of different ministries and therefore, VET has become a 'policy orphan'.

e. There is lack of any assessment of skills and requirements at the entry stage itself.

f. There is need to provide incentives for training in spoken and written English.

g. Performance outcomes in VET institutions are not measured with industry participation and there is no incentive for better performance.

h. Current certification systems are inadequate and in need of overhaul. The emphasis should be on designing institutional systems that are 'accreditation-light' and 'certification-heavy', focusing more on empowering the student for a variety of industry needs.

5.3.3 *Innovation:* Globalisation has spurred the phenomenon of 'mass innovation', triggering rapid and disruptive change in companies. This democratisation of innovation is releasing 'untapped energies of people everywhere that could solve the world's weightiest problems'.[107] Younger and smaller companies are leveraging on innovative breakthroughs, carrying out the classic Schumpeterian 'creative destruction' to create wealth and find newer solutions. As such, "large returns to national economic capability can result from relatively small national investments in transitioning new technologies to the market" and with "appropriate policy support, promising innovations can become commercial propositions that drive growth".[108] In the global race today, "the only way ahead for companies is to innovate".[109]

VET needs to be given high priority in India. Skill development is crucial to reap the demographic dividend in India, where the size of the working age population, as per the annual budget 2008-09, is estimated to increase.

---

104. XI Five Year Plan document, Chapter 5, page 3.

105. See *www.knowledgecommission.gov.in* for NKC's recommendations on VET. In India, skill acquisition takes place through two basic structural streams—a small formal one and a large informal one. The formal structure includes: (a) higher technical education imparted through professional colleges; (b) vocational education in schools at the post-secondary stage; (c) technical training in specialised institutions; and (d) apprenticeship training. The unorganised sector which constitutes about 93 per cent of the workforce is not supported by any structural system of acquiring or upgrading skills. By and large, skill formation takes place through informal channels like family occupations, on-the-job training under master craftsmen with no linkages to the formal education training and certification. Training needs in this sector are highly diverse and multi-skill oriented.

106. Unlike other areas of education, VET outcomes are easier to measure because they are 'binary', largely in terms of employability and the capacity to sustain productive employment.

107. Vaitheeswaran, Vijay (2007). "Something New under the Sun" and "The Age of Mass Innovation", in *The Economist*, dated October 13, where he also quotes Vinod Khosla saying, "A crisis is a terrible thing to waste".

108. Attributed to Charles Wessner, National Research Council, USA in "Small Business Innovation Research Program", Report of Symposium, 2007, page 33.

109. Prof. Vijay Govindarajan, *Outlook Business*, May 5, 2007.

Innovation has emerged as one of the drivers of India's economic growth, and is a factor in increasing competitiveness, profitability and market share as well as reduced costs. NKC conducted a survey in 2006-07 on innovation occurring in large firms and SMEs across the country. According to its report, "Innovation in India", the "innovation intensity" (i.e., the percentage of revenue derived from products or services which are less than three years old) has increased for large firms as well as SMEs in India. The strategic prioritisation of innovation has also intensified since economic liberalisation. Moreover, an interesting finding is that SMEs register a greater increase in 'innovation intensity' than large firms. This could also indicate that smaller, decentralised, creative and experimentation-oriented organisations could be the torchbearers of large-scale 'disruptive innovation' in the country.

However, in order to fully realise India's potential for innovation—from grassroots to the large firms – certain key actions such as reforms in higher education, investment in research and building formal and informal academia-industry linkages have become imperative. According to the NKC survey, the most significant external barrier to innovation for large firms and SMEs continues to be "skills-shortages, arising out of lack of emphasis on creativity, problem-solving, design and experimentation etc., in the education curricula." As such the report noted that "it is critical to focus on policy reform in the higher and vocational educational curricula in order for India to achieve its innovation potential".

5.4 Key Statistics from NKC Study

5.4.1 *Importance of Education for Entrepreneurship:* As seen from Figure 23.30, there is universal acknowledgement regarding the importance of education. As many as 95 per cent of entrepreneurs think education is a critical success factor for every individual, generally; this is not surprising since 98 per cent of the entrepreneurs interviewed have at least an undergraduate degree. Of the 95 per cent who value education generally, 53 per cent (i.e., 50 per cent of the overall sample) consider education a key trigger to evoke entrepreneurial inclinations. (i.e., they feel their education has helped them to be successful entrepreneurs). Further, 32 per cent of this 53 per cent (i.e., 16 per cent overall) got into their respective business sectors as a result of their particular educational background.

Figure 23.30: Importance of Education

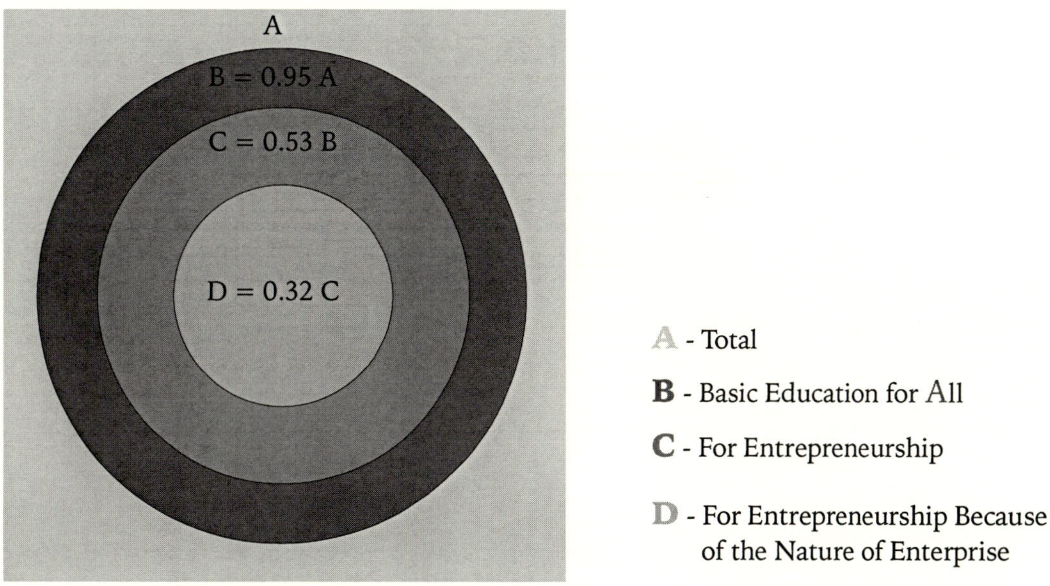

In order to fully realise India's potential for innovation—from grassroots to the large firms—certain key actions such as reforms in higher education, investment in research and building formal and informal academia-industry linkages have become imperative.

5.4.2 *Qualifications of Entrepreneurs:* Some observations regarding the qualifications of the entrepreneurs are as follows:

- Only 2 per cent of the entrepreneurs interviewed have a Ph.D. degree. This may lead one to conclude that many more doctorate degree holders (Ph.Ds) could be potential entrepreneurs provided an enabling environment is created. Indian academia is yet to appreciate the kind of flexibility that prevails in campuses abroad, especially in the Silicon Valley where many Ph.D. students and academics are also very successful entrepreneurs. In this respect, Indian institutions could encourage entrepreneurship through promotional policies such as the following: enabling Ph.Ds/ researchers to set up commercial entities while engaged in universities or professional employment; allowing institutional mobility and flexibility; encouraging universities/research organisations to establish commercial enterprises based on their new inventions and enabling industry and other research organisations to invest in new inventions, enterprises and innovations as equity, etc.[110]
- While nearly 80 per cent of the entrepreneurs interviewed have a science/engineering background, only 16 per cent of the overall sample said that they consider their education relevant for their particular entrepreneurial venture. This leads one to wonder how much more entrepreneurs might gain if their curricula paid more attention to post-education business opportunities.
- Seventy per cent of the entrepreneurs interviewed do not have an MBA qualification. This may suggest that an MBA degree is not a *sine qua non* to become an entrepreneur, though perceptions may be changing. There is potential even in those who may not have a background in business and science education to become entrepreneurs.

Figure 23.31: Qualification of Entrepreneurs

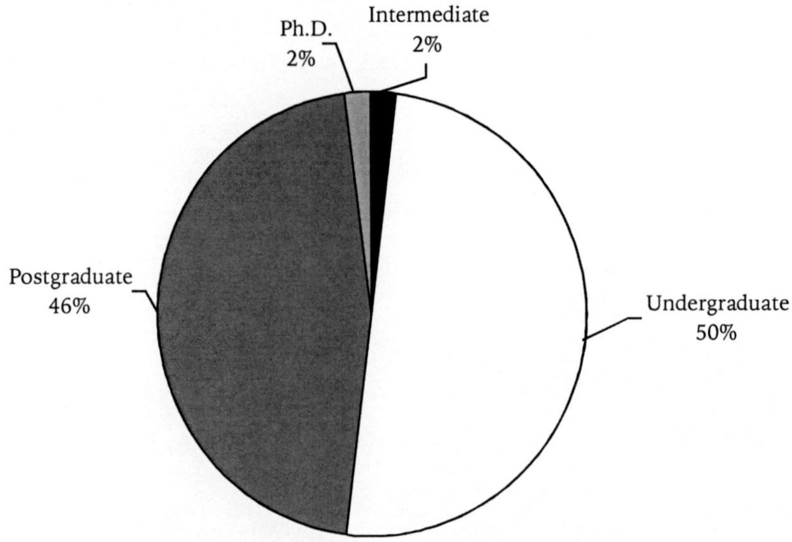

Indian academia is yet to appreciate the kind of flexibility that prevails in campuses abroad, especially in the Silicon Valley where many Ph.D. students and academics are also very successful entrepreneurs.

110. See also, for example, the draft proposal from CSIR entitled, "Encouraging Development and Commercialization of Inventions and Innovation: A New Impetus", dated April 10, 2007.

- One in every five entrepreneurs interviewed have a liberal arts degree, which would suggest that entrepreneurship is as much about technical skills as about acquiring a holistic understanding of the social and business environment and opportunities.

5.4.3 *Qualifications – The Changing Scenario:* The NKC study found that for entrepreneurial ventures, established since the beginning of this decade, the ratio of MBAs and postgraduate entrepreneurs has steadily increased, while the number of undergraduate entrepreneurs has decreased. This indicates a growing importance of higher and professional education among the new generation of entrepreneurs.

Further, since the year 2000, a larger proportion of entrepreneurs with MBA degrees were also found to have prior work experience, compared to the pre-2000 figures. This may be a trend among knowledge entrepreneurs for gaining formal experience through employment prior to starting their own enterprises. While a large number of the entrepreneurs interviewed (39 per cent) became entrepreneurs right after completing their education and without any prior work experience, for the remaining 61 per cent, the median number of years they had worked as an employee in another organisation was seven years.

5.4.4 *Availability of Skilled Employees:* When entrepreneurs were asked to rate on the availability of skilled employees (along a scale ranging from 'very easy', 'somewhat easy', 'average', 'somewhat difficult' and 'very difficult'), only 25 per cent of the entrepreneurs rated it 'very easy' or 'somewhat easy' to find skilled employees. Nearly one in two entrepreneurs (45 per cent) said they consider skills-shortage to be a problem of 'average' importance, while nearly one in three entrepreneurs considered it 'somewhat difficult' or 'very difficult' to find employees with the right skills. The lack of skilled resources is going to be one of the most significant rate-limiters for entrepreneurial growth in India.

Figure 23.32: Qualification of Entrepreneurs—Variations According to Time Period

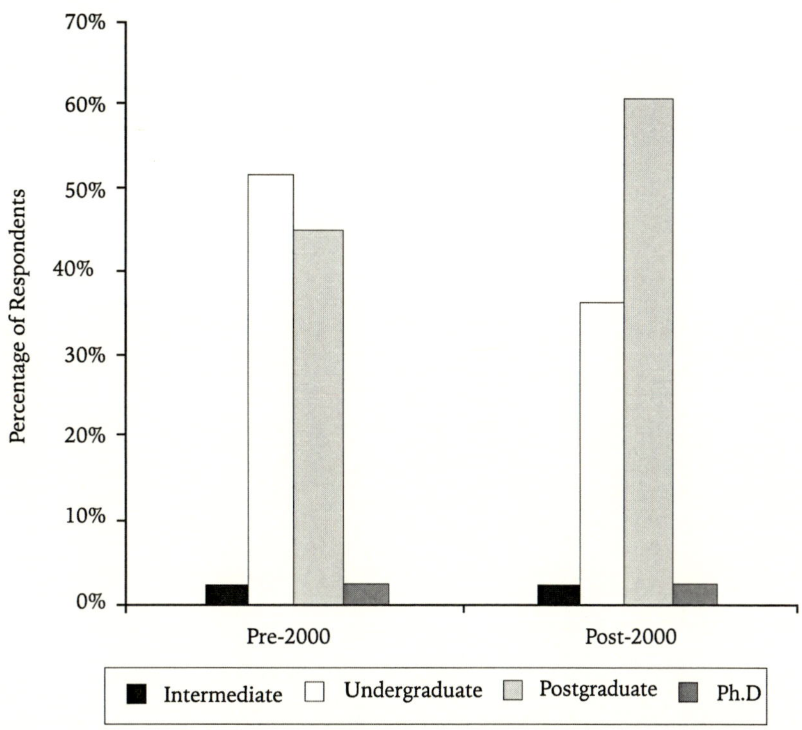

Entrepreneurship is as much about technical skills as it is about acquiring a holistic understanding of the social and business environment.

Figure 23.33: MBA and Entrepreneurship—Variations According to Time Period

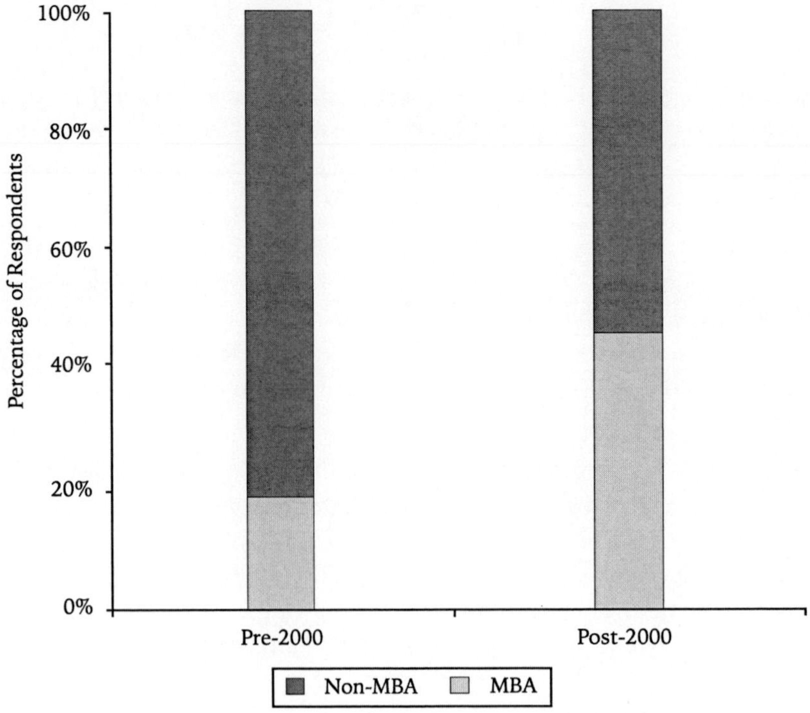

Figure 23.34: Profile of MBA Graduates in Different Time Periods—Variations According to Work Experience

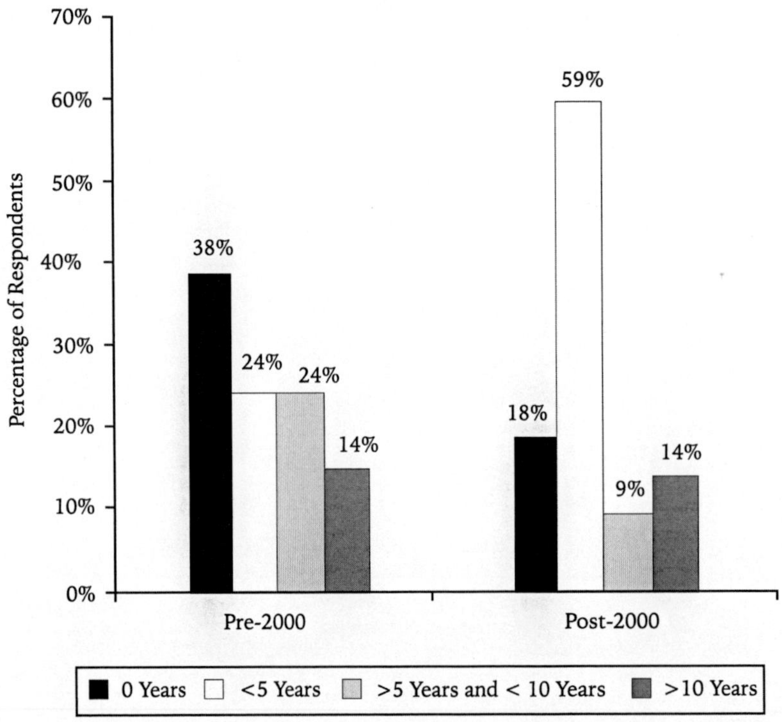

The lack of skilled resources is going to be one of the most significant rate-limiters for entrepreneurial growth in India.

This observation is similar to a recent survey, which states that 33 per cent of Indian CEOs are worried about the poor availability of skilled employees.[111] According to another recent survey, manpower and infrastructure are seen as among the most important barriers for entrepreneurship in India.[112] A recent McKinsey study reveals the critical nature of challenge regarding shortage of talent faced by executives worldwide.[113] According to this survey conducted in 2006, finding talented people is likely to be "the single most important managerial preoccupation" for companies. Another McKinsey survey conducted in 2007 revealed that nearly half of the respondents expect 'intensifying competition for talent' and 'the increasingly global nature of that competition' would have a major impact on their companies over the next five years.

According to the 2007 McKinsey study, three external factors are at work—demographic change (people born after 1980, empowered by information, have a 'different outlook' and see their career as a series of two-to-three year jobs and readily switch); globalisation (requiring talented people, with an international mindset, who are also willing to work abroad) and the rise of the knowledge worker (who would generate up to 'three times more profit' than other employees). In addition, the company's internal factors (HR policies) are responsible for the talent crunch.

In a similar vein, another recent report states that "investments in human capital and businesses are low when compared to rising economic needs" which, in turn could adversely impact growth rates.[114]

5.4.4.1 The Nature of Skills-Related Issues: Entrepreneurs face problems in both recruiting and retaining skilled employees. More than a third of the entrepreneurs interviewed face this problem. While retention remains an issue, entrepreneurs do not consider the problem of retaining employees as acute as the problem in recruiting them.

Figure 23.35: Availability of Skills

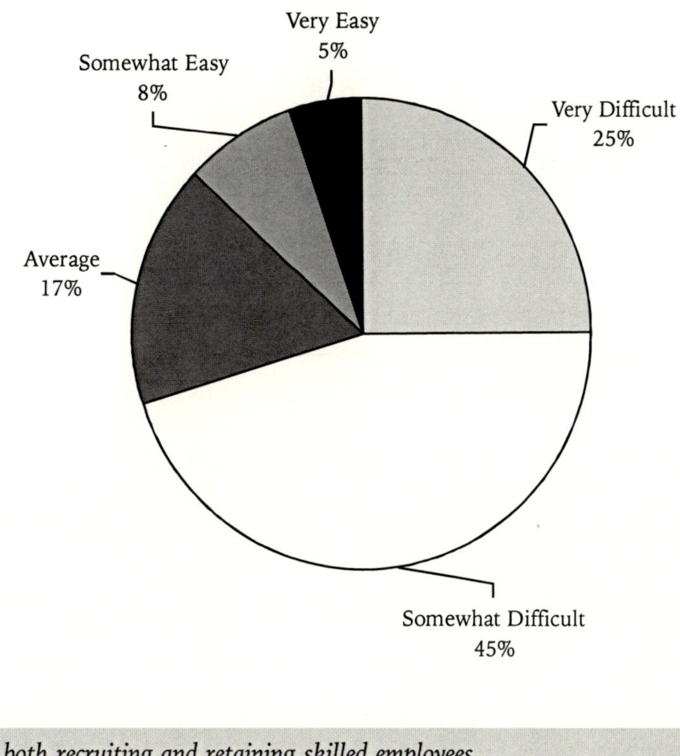

Entrepreneurs face problems in both recruiting and retaining skilled employees.

111. *The Times of India* dated January 28, 2008, page 19, quoting a recent PWC Global CEO survey.

112. See KPMG TiE Study, "Entrepreneurial India", 2008.

113. *The McKinsey Quarterly* (2008). "Making Talent a Strategic Priority", January.

114. Global Economic Outlook 2008/Deloitte Research, quoted in *Hindustan Times Business* dated February 18, 2008.

Figure 23.36: Issues of Skills

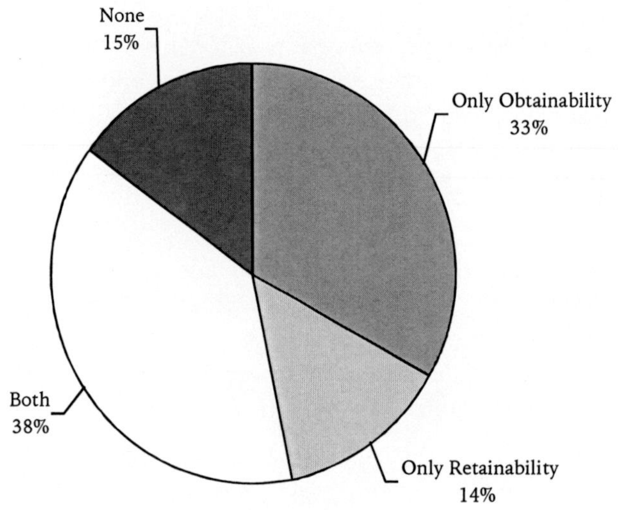

5.4.4.2 Variations According to Skill Types: In general, entrepreneurs face problems in recruiting high-skilled as well as low-skilled employees. This implies that there is a need for an increase in supply of both categories of employees. Therefore, vocational education is as critical as higher education. Within this, recruiting and retaining high-skilled employees is more difficult compared to low-skilled employees. This may suggest that low-skilled employees do not gain the necessary higher market value and mobility with work experience, compared to their highly skilled counterparts. In other words, lack of skills reduces options for individuals. For entrepreneurs, retaining low-skilled employees may not be as significant a problem perhaps because wages for low-skilled workers are more or less the same across sectors and companies. Conversely, this also means that modernisation and improved quality of vocational training could increase value and lead to increased mobility of this group. Periodic upgrading of skills may also increase growth opportunities for employees.

Figure 23.37: Issues with Skills—Variations According to Type of Skills

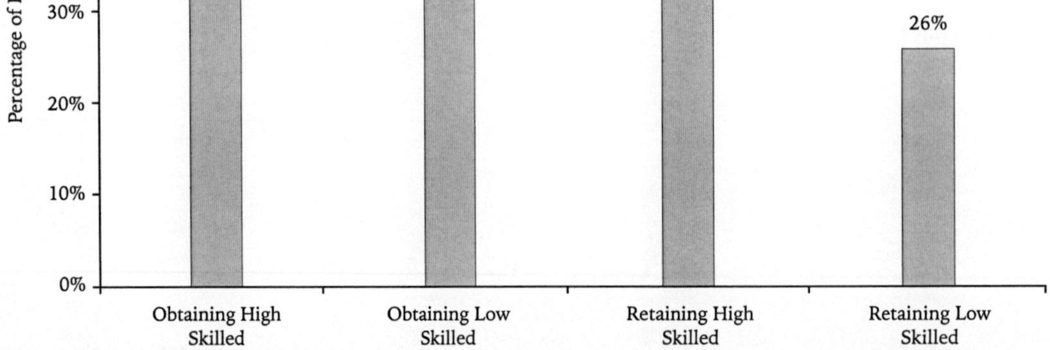

There is a need for increase in supply of high-skilled as well as low-skilled employees.

Figure 23.38: Issues of Skills—Variations According to Age of Enterprise

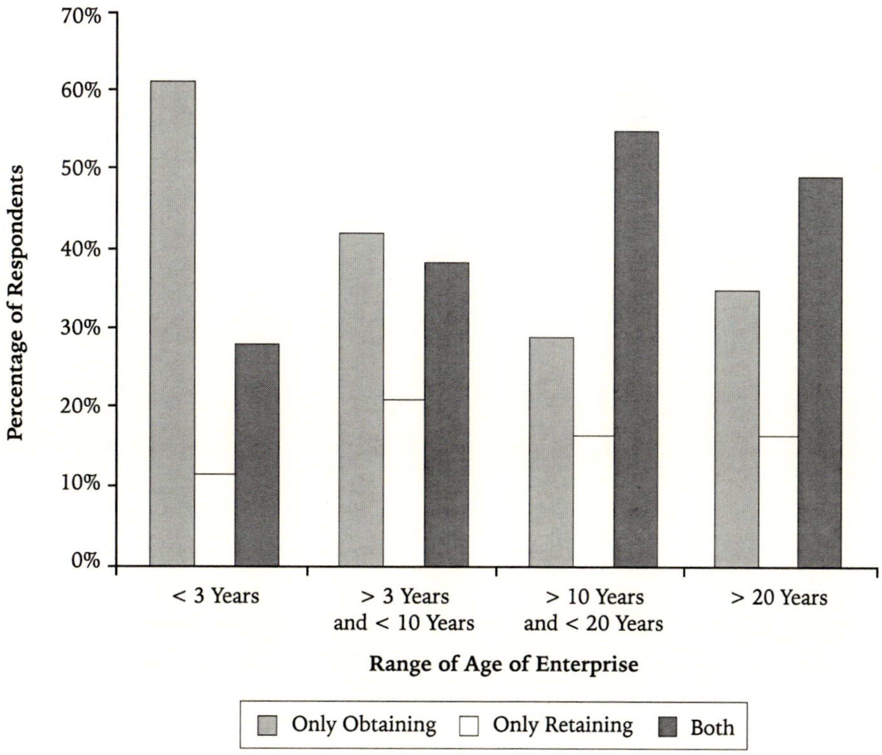

5.4.4.3 Variations According to Age of Enterprise: Enterprises that are under three years old find it more difficult to hire skilled employees, as compared to those that have been operational for a longer time. The relative lack of brand value of new firms makes it difficult for them to attract talent. Refer to Figure 23.38.

5.4.4.4 A more detailed analysis is necessary to understand the relationship between attrition and incentives (such as appropriate HR policies, stake in enterprise, long-term incentives, learning opportunities, autonomy of decision-making and professionalisation of functions). Some of the entrepreneurs interviewed already have such mechanisms in place.

5.5 Eleventh Five Year Plan Initiatives in School Education, Higher Education and Development of VET

5.5.1 It is relevant here to highlight some of the key initiatives recently undertaken by the Government of India in order to expand quantity, improve quality and achieve inclusiveness, via significant increase in allocation for education in the Eleventh Five Year Plan. There is an increase in the resource allocation for education from 7.68 per cent in the Tenth Five Year Plan to 19.29 per cent in the Eleventh Five Year Plan.[115] It has stipulated five targets areas for monitoring:[116] (i) drop out rates of children which are targeted to be reduced at the elementary level from 52.2 per cent in 2003-04 to 20 per cent by 2011-12; (ii) minimum standards of educational attainment in elementary schools; (iii) increased literacy rate, which is targeted to be increased (for persons of age 7 years or more) to 85 per cent by 2011-12; (iv)

There is an increase in the resource allocation for education from 7.68 per cent in the Tenth Five Year Plan to 19.29 per cent in the Eleventh Five Year Plan.

115. Eleventh Five Year Plan (2007-2012), 54th NDC Meeting, December 2007, Volume 1, Chapter 3, page 13, Table 3.13.

116. Eleventh Five Year Plan (2007-2012), 54th NDC Meeting, Volume 1, Chapter 1, page 26. Twenty-seven targets at the national level fall in six major categories. The six categories are: (a) Income and Poverty, (b) Education, (c) Health; (d) Women and Children, (e) Infrastructure, and (f) Environment.

gender gap in literacy, which is targeted to be reduced to 10 percentage points by 2011-12; and (v) increasing the percentage of each cohort entering higher education from the present 10 per cent to 15 per cent by 2011-12.[117] The Plan also emphasises upgrading quality in primary education,[118] expansion of secondary education,[119] upgrading higher education (including technical education) and the use of ICT throughout the education system.

5.5.2 In addition, the current Plan has targeted setting up 30 new Central universities, 8 new Indian Institutes of Technology (IITs), 7 new Indian Institutes of Management (IIMs), 10 new National Institutes of Technology (NITs), 3 Indian Institutes of Science Education and Research (IISERs), 20 Indian Institutes of Information Technology (IIITs) and 2 new Schools of Planning and Architecture (SPA) and a number of new degree colleges.[120] For upgrading science education and research infrastructure in the universities, it is envisaged that the existing Science and Engineering Research Council (SERC) mechanism of the Department of Science and Technology should be restructured to constitute a National Science and Engineering Research Board (NSERB). The NSERB would aim at expanding and strengthening the S&T base in the universities, building research capabilities in the academic sector and ensuring funding for undertaking internationally competitive research programmes.[121]

5.5.3 The Eleventh Plan also aims to launch a National Skill Development Mission (NSDM) and has proposed to allocate Rs. 31,200 crore for this. In the annual budget for 2008-09, the Government of India has proposed the establishment of a non-profit corporation, to fulfil the NSDM goals, with about Rs. 15,000 crore as capital from various sources, public and private, and an initial government equity of Rs. 1000 crore. During the Plan period, the mission is expected to spearhead efforts to increase the number of trained personnel from 2.5 million to 10 million. It is expected to coordinate the relevant VET work of 17 different ministries and departments of the Government of India, involve the private sector and facilitate a collaborative process. The public-private partnership (PPP) mode is expected to restructure and reposition existing infrastructure, with coordination from concerned ministries. Further, in 20 identified high growth sectors, private initiatives with government support are also planned. Respective industry associations in each sector are expected to outline their vision for the 'Sectoral Skill Development Initiative' (SSDI). The NSDM would engage with each of these sectors to work out appropriate deliverables and strategies in the respective 'Sectoral Skill Development Plans'. It would then prescribe a national framework for domain-specific standards and common principles to create an enabling environment for private investment in skill training.

5.5.4 In this respect, the NSDM's objectives include the following:

a. 'Skills Mapping'.

b. Expanding and modernising the existing 'Public Sector Skill Development' infrastructure and its utilisation by a factor of five.

c. Enlarging the coverage of skills from 150 to 1000 trades.

In the annual budget for 2008-09, the Government of India has proposed the establishment of a non-profit corporation, to ful-fill the NSDM goals.

117. Eleventh Five Year Plan (2007-2012), 54th NDC Meeting, Volume 1, Chapter 1, page 26.

118. Eleventh Five Year Plan, 54th NDC Meeting, Volume 2, Chapter 1, page 9; other plans include providing universal enrolment of 6-14 age group children including the 'hard to reach' segment; substantial improvement in quality and standards with the ultimate objective to achieve standards of Kendriya Vidyalayas under the CBSE pattern; all gender, social and regional gaps in enrolments to be eliminated by 2011-12; one year pre-school education for children entering primary school; dropout at primary level to be eliminated and the dropout rate at the elementary level to be reduced from over 50 per cent to 20 per cent by 2011-12; all States/UTs to adopt NCERT Quality Monitoring Tools.

119. Eleventh Five Year Plan, Volume 2, Chapter 1, page 16. The Eleventh Plan aims to: (i) raise the minimum level of education to class X level and accordingly universalise access to secondary education; (ii) ensure good quality secondary education with focus on Science, Mathematics and English; and (iii) major reduction in gender, social and regional gaps in enrolments, dropouts and schools retention. The norm will be to provide a secondary school within 5 km and a higher secondary school within 7-8 km of every habitation. The GER in secondary education is targeted to increase from 52 per cent in 2004-05 to 75 per cent by 2011-12 and the combined secondary and senior secondary GER from 40 per cent to 65 per cent in the same period.

120. Eleventh Five Year Plan, Volume 2, Chapter 1, page 28.

121. Eleventh Five Year Plan, Volume 2, Chapter 1, page 29.

The public-private partnership (PPP) mode is expected to restructure and reposition existing infrastructure, with coordination from concerned ministries.

d. Setting up 50,000 skill development web-based learning centres through the PPP mode.

e. Facilitating the repositioning of employment exchanges as outreach points of the NSDM.

f. Establishing a national qualifications framework (with 'equivalence' and horizontal mobility between various VET, technical and academic streams at more than one career point).

g. Establishing a 'credible accreditation system', a 'guidance framework' (for all accrediting agencies), a 'national skill inventory' and a 'national database for skill deficiency mapping' on a national web portal as well as a 'trainee placement and tracking system'.

5.5.5 Further, the NSDM has an action plan for the Ministry of Rural Development under which 600 new RUDISETIs (Rural Development and Self Employment Training Institutes) would be set up. These RUDISETIs are expected to focus on developing entrepreneurship by collaborating with the Entrepreneurship Development Institute (EDI), which is an autonomous non-profit organisation set up to promote entrepreneurship through education, research and training.[122]

5.6 Other Suggestions to Enhance Entrepreneurship

5.6.1 *Content and Learning Methods:* The NKC consultations with entrepreneurs reveal that it is important to develop pedagogic methods, examination systems and curricula that encourage critical and lateral thinking. The ability to promote entrepreneurship requires an enquiring mind that is able to make connections between theory and practice. Entrepreneurs feel that there is a need to recreate real-life situations in the classroom with the help of examples and illustrations so that students are able to get a 'concrete feel' of various aspects of the outside world. At the same time, many entrepreneurs also feel that the starting point for reforming teaching methods and encouraging variety in career options, must be at the school stage itself, where the pressure to learn by rote and to join typically stereotypical career paths are huge. Right from the school stage, pedagogy should encourage original thinking and not rote learning. One specific suggestion from several entrepreneurs is to introduce manuals in school curricula on 'How Things Work', on various practical aspects of everyday living.

5.6.2 *Teaching and Entrepreneurship:* While entrepreneurship has been introduced as a course in a number of business school curricula, there needs to be a greater thrust in making entrepreneurship a priority subject. Other aspects of entrepreneurship such as business ethics, early enterprise management, aspects of scaling up, Indian corporate law and relevant international laws, should also be a part of such curricula.[123] A noteworthy development is the recent proposal to set up a School of Entrepreneurship offering undergraduate and postgraduate degrees in IIT Kharagpur.[124] Such initiatives need to be encouraged for widespread adaptation in other educational institutions, including institutions located outside metropolitan areas. The involvement of the burgeoning NRI community and alumni networks in funding such schools must be encouraged.

5.6.3 *Encourage Student-led Entrepreneurial Activities on Campus:* Entrepreneurship cannot be learnt only by 'chalk and talk'.[125] Shared activities outside the confines of the textbook are imperative to develop leadership and team building skills that are necessary for entrepreneurship.[126] It is necessary to encourage activities within educational institutions, where

Right from the school stage, pedagogy should encourage original thinking and not rote learning.

---

122. See *www.ediindia.org*

123. The Indian School of Business (ISB) in Hyderabad, a pioneer in actively encouraging entrepreneurship, has introduced Entrepreneurship as a compulsory subject.

124. *http://www.indiaedunews.net/IIT/IIT-Kgp_to_set_up_%27entrepreneurship_school%27_2986/*; here, alumni involvement for funding, especially NRI involvement will be a key factor.

125. Laura Parkin, Executive Director, NEN, provided valuable insights in this regard. See also, *http://economictimes.indiatimes.com/Interview/Laura_Parkin_Executive_Director_NEN/articleshow/2681558.cms*

126. Kirby, David (2003). *Entrepreneurship*, p.1. Research on entrepreneurship undertaken by the UK Small Business Trust (1988) indicates that only 13 per cent of the surveyed sample believed that entrepreneurial skills could not be acquired by a process of learning.

entrepreneurial abilities find opportunities and fertile ground to grow. In several educational institutions, student-led and faculty-supported activities have been able to create awareness and prepare necessary mindsets about entrepreneurship. Examples include the Entrepreneurship and Innovation Cell at IIM Bangalore and the Entrepreneurship Cell at IIT Bombay, which engage in activities such as business plan contests, assisting start-ups and incubation centres. Initiatives such as 'business plan contests' (with angel/VC/private sector assistance, which could directly become entrepreneurial ventures with rewards in terms of seed funding), instructional programmes that deal with the basic practicalities of entrepreneurship and platforms to interact with other entrepreneurs and the financial community (especially VCs and angels) need to be intensified and encouraged.

5.6.4 *Performance-Oriented VET Skill Development:* While the NSDM is a significant and landmark initiative, special care needs to be taken to ensure that NSDM outlays are utilised to actually transform VET. This issue is significant since it relates to the concept of equality of opportunity itself. At the basic structural level, the VET policy needs performance-based models that link incentives to outcomes. Further, decentralised approaches in governance and accountability, being rooted in local realties, may be more useful in implementation of VET plans. This could be done through the State Councils for Vocational Training (SCVT) in each state.

Fresh thought is needed in understanding the entry-stage requirements of each trainee, according to which tailored supportive courses can be developed. English language skills as well as a transparent industry-backed certification system for each trainee should be made compulsory. Learning by doing or earning needs to be encouraged with renewed vigour, which may require a fresh look into relevant issues enshrined in relevant laws.

Further, the process of connecting financing to performance-based outcomes in VET needs to be given thrust through nationwide publication and dissemination of learning outcomes in the form of a Vocational Skill Primer that measures each VET institution. Publication of performance-based outcomes is therefore, the first step in developing a transparent and independent rating agency and system in VET. Bringing about systemic changes in the way the VET policy is executed is the only way to enable the country to take advantage of its democratic dividend and realise its human resource potential. This is a task where the State must perform its role, and where the industry must also play an increasingly valuable role.

5.6.5 *Enterprise Centres in Major Educational and Research Institutions:* Special enterprise centres focused on translating innovation-driven ideas into viable businesses would greatly enhance entrepreneurship. Currently, incubation centres provide assistance to selected start-ups. Enterprise centres in major educational and research institutions can provide institutional support for entrepreneurship, on a larger scale, and on a more systematic basis. The institutions could also provide extensive industry linkages on different aspects of business, law and finance. Elaborate models of profit-sharing and advisory assistance can also be provided. NKC has already recommended the establishment of IPR Cells in major scientific and educational institutions with competent staff, trained in law and technical aspects of various disciplines in order to capture the value and exclusivity of new ideas and innovations.[127] Further, as already mentioned, NKC has recommended the enactment of legislation that creates a legal framework for public funded research and provides universities and research institutions ownership and patent rights. This will create an enabling environment for the institutions to commercialise such inventions through licencing arrangements where the inventors would also receive a share of royalties.[128]

In several educational institutions, student-led and faculty-supported activities have been able to create awareness and prepare necessary mindsets about entrepreneurship.

127. See NKC's recommendations on IPR at *http://www.knowledgecommission.gov.in/downloads/recommendations/IPRPM.pdf*

128. See NKC's recommendations on legal framework for public funded research at *http://www.knowledgecommission.gov.in/downloads/recommendations/ LegislationPM.pdf*

NKC has recommended the enactment of legislation that creates a legal framework for public funded research and provides universities and research institutions ownership and patent rights.

5.7 Business Incubation for Entrepreneurship (BIE)

5.7.1 The process of Business Incubation for Entrepreneurship (BIE) is a critical organisational support mechanism for fledgling entrepreneurs at the initial stage. The quality and scale of BIE could become one of the most important tools to enhance the entrepreneurial ecosystem in the country. A typical high quality business incubator provides the following services to a budding entrepreneur: physical infrastructure, administrative support, management guidance/ mentoring, help in formulation of a business plan, technical support, intellectual property (IP) advice where applicable, facilitating access to finance and encouraging networking with the greater and relevant business community.[129] At the start-up stage, the entrepreneur is beset with significant challenges of marketability and resources (financial and otherwise), which successful incubation can help address. In this respect, the transformation of a business idea into a revenue-generating product requires the need to be familiar with not just technology but also key market indicators such as risk, business space, scaling-up challenges, cash flows, corporate governance, human resources as well as ethics. Some illustrations of Business Incubation for Entrepreneurship in India are listed in Table 23.6.

5.7.2 Globally, the concept of business incubation has evolved to meet changing demands.[130] The 'first generation' incubators (in the 1980s) focused on infrastructural needs such as affordable space and shared facilities. The 'second generation' incubators (from the 1990s onwards) have tried to respond to needs of counseling, networking, skill enhancement, professional support and seed capital. To meet newer demands of globalisation, widening scope and scale of business and rapidly changing technology, it is expected that business incubation will further develop. Shifts from the purely non-profit models to PPPs and for-profit models could also be seen in future. In this respect, some of the private ventures already in operation are The Life Science Incubator at ICICI Knowledge Park located in Hyderabad, the International Biotech Park in Hinjawadi and Nirma Labs in Ahmedabad.

5.7.3 In India, in order to develop technopreneurship, the Ministry of Science and Technology (MoST) initiated the Science and Technology Entrepreneurship Park (STEP) programme under the National Science and Technology Entrepreneurship Development Board (NSTEDB) in 1984 in collaboration with financial institutions such as IDBI, IFCI and ICICI. STEP has tried to foster linkages between academia, industry and R&D institutions to inculcate a culture of Entrepreneurship.[131] Other ministries today supplement MoST's pioneering efforts and the private sector is also entering the incubation space.[132] Another initiative envisaged is the Technology Incubation Development of Entrepreneurs (TIDE) under the Department of Information Technology (DIT).[133] A fund worth Rs. 25 crore is proposed to be set up, from which selected start-ups will receive a funding of Rs. 25 lakh to Rs. 50 lakh per start-up for a two-year period. This initiative will also be promoted through premier institutions such as the Indian Institute of Science (IISC), the Indian Institutes of Technology (IITs) and the Indian Institutes of Management (IIMs). Further, the ISBA (The Indian STEP and Business Incubator Association) was set up in 2004 to serve as a professional apex body to promote business incubation in India.[134]

To meet newer demands of globalisation, widening scope and scale of business and rapidly changing technology, it is expected that business incubation will further develop.

---

129. *http://en.wikipedia.org/wiki/Business_incubator; http://www.nbia.org/resource_center/what_is/index.php*

130. See *http://www.unescap.org/tid/publication/indpub2323_part2ivD.pdf*

131. *http://www.unescap.org/tid/publication/indpub2323_part2ivD.pdf*

132. *http://economictimes.indiatimes.com/Economy/Incubation_biz_set_to_hit_growth/articleshow/2749998.cms*

133. See Mint, dated March 17, 2008; *http://www.livemint.com/2008/03/17231518/At-this-research-institute-qu.html.*

134. *http://www.isba.in/index.php?option=com_content&task=view&id=22&Itemid=46*

5.7.4 During consultations with incubators,[135] and various organisations providing mentoring and networking assistance to entrepreneurs[136] as well as members of the financial community, the NKC study found that incubator support in India is largely in the form of physical infrastructure, technical support (access to libraries, labs and academic resources), management advice and helping in access to finance (largely from government agencies such as the Technology Development Board and the Technopreneur Promotion Programme under DSIR and TIFAC).[137] Typically, 'incubatees' are selected on the basis of a periodic competitive selection process lasting between four and six months, during which the participants also work on their respective business plans and at the end of which, a memorandum of understanding (MoU) is signed between the institution and the selected 'incubatee'. Incubation facilities are located in major institutions of excellence and have contributed much to the development of technopreneurship in India. Given below is a list of the incubation centres that were consulted, along with relevant structural aspects such as type of sectors catered to, eligibility, entry point etc.[138]

Table 23.6: Illustrations of Incubation for Entrepreneurship

	Year of Establishment	Type of Incubation	Eligible Applicants (primarily)	Entry Point for Incubates	Number of Incubates (so far)
CIIE, IIM-A	2001	Hi-Tech	All	Prototype stage	24
NSRCEL, IIM-B	2001	Mixed	All	Idea stage	6
TeNeT, IIT-M[139]		Hi- Tech	All	Pre-idea	20
SINE, IIT-B	2004	Hi-Tech	Faculty/Students/Alumni	Post-idea	26
TBI, IIT-D	2000	Hi-Tech	Faculty/Students/Alumni	Post-idea	19
TREC-STEP	1986	Hi-Tech	All	Pre-idea	182
Nirma Labs	2004	Hi-Tech	All	Pre/Post-ideastage	

5.7.5 It is also relevant here to highlight the role of some organisations and associations involved in mentoring in India. For example, apart from assisting with finance, BYST has an active mentoring programme for start-ups launched by the economically less privileged, with trained entrepreneurs as mentors. NEN is engaged with over 280 institutes, with a student base of over 300,000 and over 500 faculty members from the institutes themselves.[140] It has also assisted in conducting certificate courses for 'Entrepreneurship Educators', along with developing content, thinking and pedagogy. Students in various institutions have also set up 'entrepreneurship cells' which provide a platform for expert mentoring, conduct business plan/idea competitions as well as interact with respective incubation cells. Similarly, TIE is another organisation actively involved with mentoring young entrepreneurs. Through networking events and initiatives such as 'TIE-ISB Connect',[141] it has facilitated the interactions among entrepreneurs as well as members of the financial community (including angels and VCs), with successful entrepreneurs and other professionals as mentors. Another recent mentoring initiative here is the 'Pan-IIT Entrepreneurship Movement' launched in January 2008 that seeks to

Students in various institutions have also set up 'entrepreneurship cells' which provide a platform for expert mentoring, conduct business plan/idea competitions as well as interact with respective incubation cells.

135. During the course of our study, we had the opportunity to interact with the following incubators: TeNeT (IIT Chennai); Center for Innovation, Incubation and Entrepreneurship (IIM Ahmedabad); NSRCEL (IIM Bangalore); Society for Innovation and Entrepreneurship (SINE, IIT Mumbai); FITT (IIT Delhi); Nirma Labs (Ahmedabad) and TREC-STEP (REC Trichy).

136. Examples include KASSIA, ALEAP, AWAKE, T I E, NEN and the various chambers of commerce.

137. Relevant government programmes here are NMITLI, TePP, TDB, Home Grown Technology Programme etc.

138. These figures are based on consultations conducted with the respective incubators in 2007.

139. While not a formal incubator, TENET is an established research group, which broadly aims at 'providing world class technology at an affordable price'. See, *www.tenet.res.in*

140. See *www.nenonline.org*. NEN also conducts e-cell workshops, a national 'entrepreneurship week' every year and connects institutions on best practices.

141. *http://www.tie-isbconnect.com/index.html*

provide a platform for interactions among IIT alumni.[142] While these are valuable initiatives, there is need for far greater scale and scope, for mentoring to take off on a wider and more sustainable institutional basis throughout the country. In this respect, chambers of commerce with their large institutional and networking leverage, also have the potential to play a much more active mentoring role. However, this is yet to take off.

5.7.6 Consultations with members of the financial community (including angels and VCs) reveal that incubation in India requires greater thrust on the business and financial aspects of entrepreneurship. This is very significant for the growth of entrepreneurship in India that "virtually hinges on its ability to bridge the time gap for an idea to be taken from the laboratory to commercial utilization."[143] While the incubation facilities in educational institutions are indeed playing an important role in translating ideas to commercial ventures, there is a need for explosive growth, both in the structural framework of incubation itself as well as intensifying rigour in the type of services that can be provided by such facilities. Compared to countries such as the USA, China and Korea, India's business incubation environment still lags behind and is in need of qualitative and quantitative transformation.

5.7.7 According to a recent report by the Expert Committee on 'Technology Innovation and Venture Capital',[144] submitted to the Planning Commission in 2006, incubation efforts in universities and research institutions have not always succeeded for a number of reasons. First, the consulting staff of the institution does not always have relevant complementary skills in business development and marketing. Second, the incubator managers do not always have effective networks with angel investors and risk capital providers, a point that becomes even more pertinent because incubators are not themselves venture funds. The first issue can be addressed through better networking with the local business services community and venture funds. The second problem requires direct investments from high net worth individuals to such enterprises emerging from the incubators. IP issues also require special attention. While leading institutions such as the IITs have developed IPR policies, there is need for far greater awareness on the role of IPR in converting ideas into commercial propositions.

5.7.8 Here are some key suggestions to improve the process of Business Incubation for Entrepreneurship (BIE) in India. The three relevant areas pertain to quantity, quality and financing:

- **Quantity**: There is a need to massively increase the number of incubators in the country. The USA has about 1400 incubators while China and Korea have about 800 and 400 respectively.[145] According to 'The Indian STEPS (Science and Technology Entrepreneurs' Parks) and Business Incubation Association (ISBA), the apex professional body supporting business incubation', India has only about 100 incubators.[146] Scaling up the numbers also means widening the reach beyond centres of excellence in metropolitan cities (i.e., beyond IITs and the top-grade engineering and business schools), going beyond alumni entrepreneurs and exploring areas beyond high tech. Further, there is a need to widen the incubation horizon beyond the idea-stage to accommodate issues relating to scaling up. There are initiatives already being proposed. For example, there are plans in Gujarat to set up a number of incubation centres with possible venture capital infusion in certain selected regions.[147] Expansion of incubation centres on a globally competitive scale will necessitate much greater involvement of private players as well as PPPs to supplement the current governmental initiatives.

Compared to countries such as the USA, China and Korea, India's business incubation environment still lags behind and is in need of qualitative and quantitative transformation.

142. *www.iit.org/paniit.php*

143. *http://economictimes.indiatimes.com/Economy/Incubation_biz_set_to_hit_growth/articleshow/2749998.cms*

144. Report of the Committee on Technology Innovation and Venture Capital submitted to the Planning Commission in July 2006, page 15.

145. See, supra note 40 as above; also check, *http://www.nbia.org/resource_center/bus_inc_facts/index.php* which states that there are 5000 incubators worldwide, with North America accounting for about 1400 and China about 500.

146. *The Economic Times* dated February 3, 2008; see also *http://economictimes.indiatimes.com/articleshow/msid-2749998,prtpage-1.cms*

147. See *Business Standard* dated February 25, 2008; see *http://www.businessstandard.com/common/news_article.php?autono=314844&leftnm=3&sub Left=0&chkFlg*

Workshops on best practices will also help spread the knowledge base and to build sustainable incubation models throughout the country.

- **Quality**: There is a need to develop greater marketability of ideas to industry (especially on aspects relating to marketability, ability to understand cash flows, issues in scaling up, monetising potential of an idea, financial advice on risk mitigation-management-measurement, analysis of unsuccessful ventures, business ethics, outcome measurement, sustainability, etc). This will require incubation centres to be entrepreneurial themselves, in terms of ready and organic adaptability to the market, development of business processes and infusion of greater business dynamism. Workshops on best practices will also help spread the knowledge base and to build sustainable incubation models throughout the country. It is also essential here to develop formal and informal systems of active, regular mentoring with successful entrepreneurs as well as platforms for networking and peer recognition and honour of successful emerging entrepreneurs at regular intervals.[148]

- **Finance**: Access to finance and its timely disbursal is one of the biggest barriers to entrepreneurship. Given the need for scale and globally competitive quality, it is imperative to look beyond the limited grants that are available from the MoST. While MoST grants have served a useful purpose and will continue to do so, what is required is a large-scale infusion of capital in this service sector, along with viable business models that could be replicated. This requires intensifying and encouraging the role of angel investors and VCs in the incubation and mentoring programmes. The active involvement of industry (including successful entrepreneurs, banks, VCs, angels, chambers of commerce, associations, etc.) as part of the social networks for mentoring, will supplement the efforts of academics within the educational institutions. Viable PPPs and business models need to be worked out to enhance the range of finance options in incubation. Above all, there is immediate need to create awareness in the banking sector on the huge competitive advantage and business opportunities of entrepreneurship in India.

5.7.9 To bring about a qualitative and quantitative transformation in BIE, there is need to develop a comprehensive Incubation Policy at the national level which would *inter alia,* explore the following:

- Crucial incentive structures such as special enterprise zones (given the level of infrastructural problems that start-ups face), tax sops, banking policies, micro-funds, innovative financial schemes, outcome measurement and delivery mechanisms.

- Practical business models for incubators that align incentive structures towards measurable performance outcomes and provide stake in the outcomes and fund allocations.

- The structure of delivery mechanisms (including PPP and for profit models), the diversification of financial options and ways of building sustainable synergies with industry.

To bring about a qualitative and quantitative transformation in BIE, there is need to develop a comprehensive incubation policy.

148. There is a separate ministry *on MSMEs (www.msme.gov.in)* which is entrusted with the task of looking into the specific needs of the micro, small and medium enterprise sector and has, *inter alia,* also instituted special entrepreneur awards in various categories.

5.8 Chapter Summary

Entrepreneurship requires ample number of productive human resources with multiple skills for a sustained period of time that can transform opportunities, provided by the economy, at the local, national and global levels. Three interconnected areas provide possibilities for mutually beneficial synergies through the flow of ideas and wealth, which could generate high level of dynamism. These are: education (including quality vocational training-skill development), innovation (generating commercial value through new and improved ideas) and entrepreneurship. Entrepreneurs generally agree on the utility of education. However, there is potential to improve the relevance of subjects of study. High-tech innovations translating into wealth generating ideas could also improve if more Ph.Ds and research scholars are provided a flexible supportive environment for entrepreneurship in their institutions. There are major problems of availability of skilled employees. More than a third of the entrepreneurs face problems in both recruiting and retaining employees. As such, VET and skill development is going to be critical for entrepreneurship and employment generation in India.

While recognising recent government initiatives to significantly raise allocation for education, some suggestions on improving the educational space for entrepreneurship include the following: improve content and learning methods; introduce entrepreneurship as a compulsory subject in business schools (also consider prospects for NRI and alumni networks' involvement in funding new entrepreneurship schools); encourage student-led entrepreneurial activities on campus with active stakeholder participation; and introduce performance-based VET (linking performance to outcomes, incentivising states, introducing English speaking skills, learning by doing, etc). Further, there is a need to significantly increase Business Incubation for Entrepreneurship (BIE) by comprehensively exploring policy issues pertaining to increasing quantity, improving quality and enhancing financing. While valuable work has been done by incubators, there is huge scope for them to become entrepreneurial themselves in terms of ready and organic adaptability to the market, development of business processes and infusion of greater dynamism.

VI. Business Environment and Entrepreneurship

6.1 General Significance

6.1.1 A prerequisite for nurturing entrepreneurship is the creation of a favourable business environment. This goal is at the heart of India's economic liberalisation initiatives. The key parameters of a conducive business environment include smooth flow of information; ease of starting a business and obtaining various clearances and permits; ease of filing taxes; an efficient legal system; enabling legislations and regulations; absence of corruption; and world-class infrastructure facilities. The entrepreneurs interviewed highlighted some of the critical bottlenecks in this regard, as shown in Figure 23.29 below.

Figure 23.29: Problems Faced by Entrepreneurs

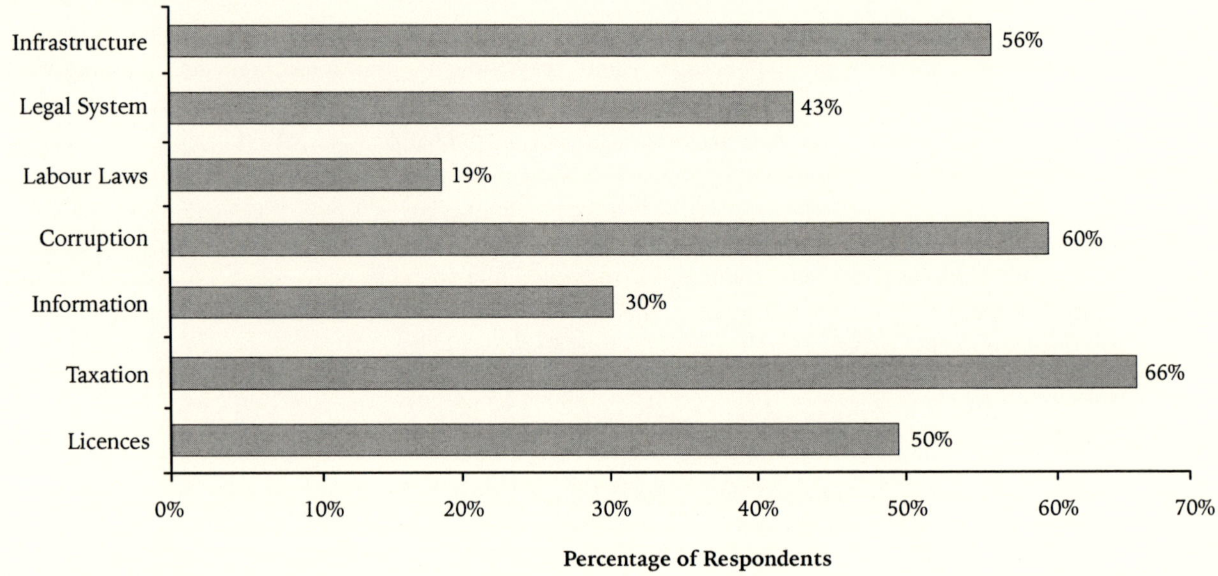

6.1.2 Various comparative studies on business regulations in India, as well as in other countries are also quite revealing.[149] While these studies recognise India's comparative advantage in human resources, skills, demographic profile and growing domestic demand, India fares poorly *vis-à-vis* its business environment. For instance, in the *'Doing Business 2008'* report (See Box 23.5), which is published by World Bank and the International Finance Corporation, India ranks 120th out of 178 countries—even behind countries such as the Maldives (60th), Pakistan (76th), Sri Lanka (101st), Bangladesh (107th) and Nepal (111th). The OECD draft report on regulatory framework in market for goods and services places India behind various countries, including Chile and Brazil.[150] The *Global Competitiveness Report 2007-08* of the World Economic Forum places India in the 48th position among 131 countries.[151] Clearly, there appears to be need for qualitative improvement in the business facilitation environment.

> *A prerequisite for nurturing entrepreneurship is the creation of a favourable business environment. This goal is at the heart of India's economic liberalisation initiatives.*

---

149. See for instance, *Doing Business* by World Bank 2007, 2008; *Global Competitiveness Report 2007* by World Economic Forum and GEM *Global Report 2007* and GEM *India Report 2002*.

150. "Improving Business Climate" (PPT Presentation) *http://darpg.nic.in/arpgwebsite/Conference/ChiefSecyConf-PPTs/dipp200407.ppt*

151. *http://www.gcr.weforum.org/*

Box 23.5: Doing Business in India Indicators

- Starting a business: 13 procedures; 33 days.
- Dealing with licenses: 20 procedures; 224 days.
- Registering property: 6 procedures; 62 days.
- Paying taxes: 60 payments per year; 271 hours per year.
- Enforcing contracts: 46 procedures; 1420 days.
- Closing a business: 10 years; recovery rate 11.6 per cent.

6.2 Access to Relevant Information

6.2.1 An entrepreneur starting a business requires access to reliable information on various aspects of business such as regulatory issues, statutory compliances, registration processes, available sources of finance, infrastructure and so on. However in India, this information is largely diffused and dispersed. The lack of readily available information compels new entrepreneurs to employ intermediaries to advise them on essential aspects of starting a business, thereby incurring additional costs. Over one-third of the entrepreneurs interviewed said they had faced problems because of lack of information at the start-up stage. While most entrepreneurs highlighted this problem, it was found to be the most severe for entrepreneurs under the age of 35, with 42 per cent of such entrepreneurs highlighting information deficit as a major hurdle (see Figure 23.40).

Figure 23.40: Information deficit as a hurdle

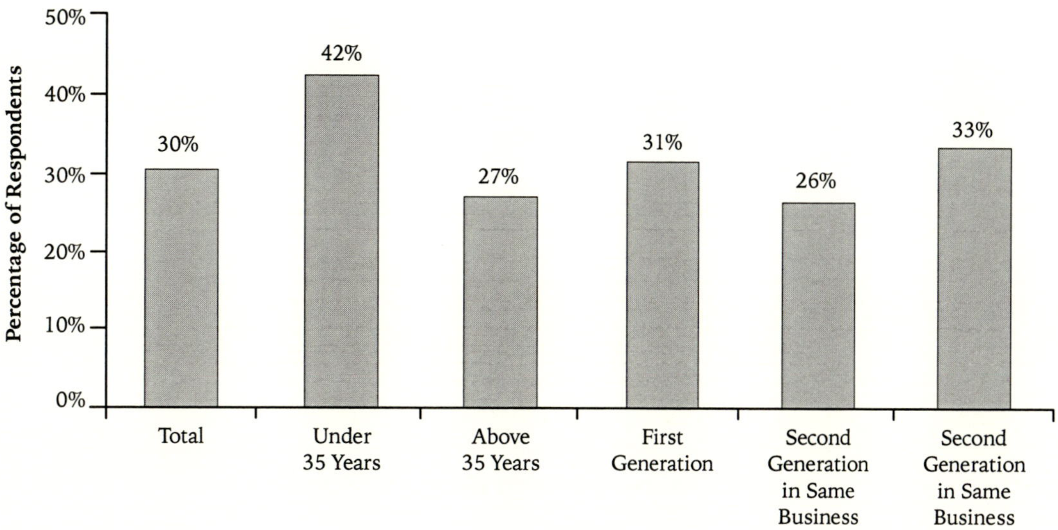

6.2.2 Suggestions to Ease Information Access: Develop comprehensive sources of information through the following:

a. Entrepreneur information handbooks (by public and/or private sources) on aspects such as starting and operating a trading business, a manufacturing business, a technology business, a service business and other sectors. Such handbooks should also contain all relevant statutory requirements and procedures, fee structures, government subsidies (if any), tax procedures and funding sources. In addition, there could be ways of incorporating case studies of successful start-

The lack of readily available information compels new entrepreneurs to employ intermediaries to advise them on essential aspects of starting a business, thereby incurring additional costs.

In a spirit of free and fair competition to provide optimal information services, the proposed 'one stop shops' would also have the potential of becoming a business enterprise on their own.

ups in different categories. Where the government undertakes this task, the official version should be readily available, in hard and soft copy and also advertised by the government regularly in national newspapers rather than on obscure notice boards.[152]

b. **One Stop Shops:** There is need for 'one stop shops' that could provide comprehensive information on entrepreneurship, such as the 'One Stop Capital Shops' in the USA, the UK's 'Direct Access Government Online Resource' and Singapore's online government resource, 'EnterpriseOne.'[153] Relevant ministries in India (Ministry of Company Affairs, MSME, Commerce and Industry, etc.) could explore the feasibility of such one stop shops. In a spirit of free and fair competition to provide optimal information services, the proposed 'one stop shops' would also have the potential of becoming a business enterprise on their own.

c. **Web Sources in India:** In India, a few attempts have been made to create online information resources for entrepreneurs. Some examples include a web portal developed jointly by the National Science and Technology Entrepreneurship Development Board (NSTEDB), Department of Science and Technology and FICCI,[154] the website of the Ministry of Micro, Small and Medium Enterprises, Government of India[155] and the business segment of the National Portal of India.[156] Another interesting private initiative is the online resource called 'SME Toolkit' started jointly by ICICI Bank, IBM and IFC.[157] In this regard, NKC proposes to explore the possibility of having an all encompassing website on entrepreneurship as a one-stop information portal for current and aspiring entrepreneurs.

6.3 Ease of Starting and Operating Business

6.3.1 Difficulty and delays in meeting various government requirements such as registration of company, obtaining licences and registering property still confront entrepreneurs. The World Bank report, *Doing Business in South Asia 2007* says that, it takes 35 days (in Mumbai) to 52 days (in New Delhi) to start a business in India. The official costs of starting a business are high and the process quite complex, involving no less than 13 procedures.[158] A large number of separate registrations—Tax Account Number (TAN), Permanent Account Number (PAN), Value Added Tax (VAT), Employees Provident Fund Organization (EPFO), Employees State Insurance Corporation (ESIC), among others are required for any business to start operations. Registering property itself requires six procedures and an average of 62 days.[159] Different rates of stamp duty and transfer charges exist across states. Apart from these initial procedural hurdles, an entrepreneur also has to obtain other permits and clearances, both at the Central and state levels. These include land use approvals, building permits, power connections, water and sewerage connections and so on. Even in states where the single window system has been put in place, most entrepreneurs do not find them satisfactory; "There is a single window but many ventilators", as an entrepreneur from Hyderabad aptly put it.[160] About 50 per cent of the entrepreneurs

The official costs of starting a business are high and the process quite complex, involving no less than 13 procedures.

152. Mr. Subramani Ramachandrappa of Richcore Lifesciences provided valuable insights in this regard.

153. See *http://www.direct.gov.uk/en/index.htm* for UK's Direct Access Online Resource; for Singapore's online resource, EnterpriseOne, see *http://www.business.gov.sg/*. See also "China and the Knowledge Economy, 2002", p.61, World Bank Institute.

154. *www.techno-preneur.net.in*

155. *www.laghu-udyog.com*

156. *www.india.gov.in/business.php*

157. *http://www.smetoolkit.org/smetoolkit/en*

158. *Doing Business 2008*, World Bank-IFC, *http://www.doingbusiness.org/documents/FullReport/2008/DB08_Full_Report.pdf*

159. *Doing Business 2008*, World Bank-IFC.

160. For example, entrepreneurs state that single window clearance in Andhra Pradesh is supposed to ensure clearances from Inspectorate of Factories, Inspectorate of Boilers, Electrical Inspectorate, *Panchayat*/Municipality/HUDA, Fire Services, Chief Controller of Explosives, Pollution Control Board, etc. In practice, however, entrepreneurs state that they still need to obtain separate clearances from the Pollution Control Board and the Chief Controller of Explosives. The latter is a Central government institution.

interviewed claimed to have problems while applying for and obtaining various clearances and licences. However, the perception regarding licences has gradually improved over the years. (See Figure 23.41)

Figure 23.41: Obtaining Licences as a Hurdle—Variations According to Time Period

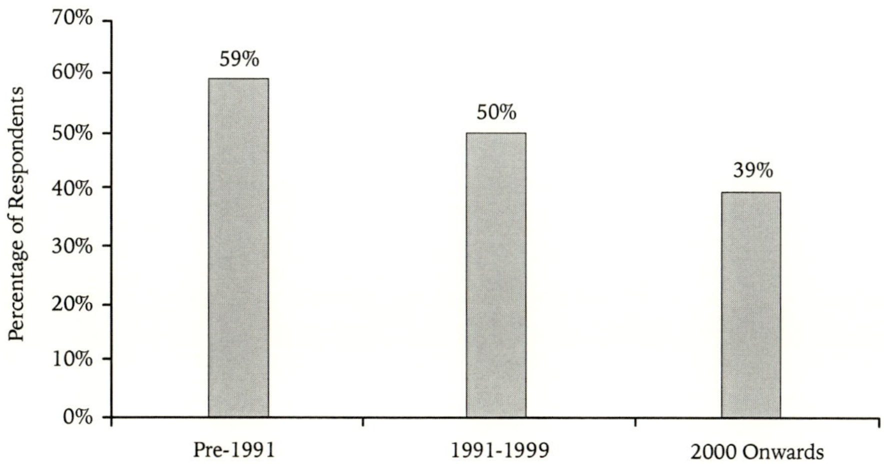

6.3.2 *Corruption:* Almost 60 per cent of the entrepreneurs interviewed said they faced corruption at some time during their entrepreneurial journey while dealing with governmental procedures and officials. That is a very disturbing statistic.

6.3.3 *Initiatives Already Underway-MCA-21:* One of the key reforms undertaken to ease the process of starting a business in India includes MCA-21, the e-Governance project of the Ministry of Company Affairs which aims to fully automate processes of compliance and enforcement. The objective of this initiative is to make services such as registration of companies transparent. The key benefits of this project are expected to include online incorporation of companies; simplifying the processes of filing of forms and returns; registration as well as verification of charges from any location; inspection of public documents of companies; and establishing a centralised database repository of companies.[161]

6.3.4 *Single Unique Company Number:* Another idea that needs to be explored is the proposal of a Single Unique Company Number that a new business can use for company, tax and social security registrations. This has also been suggested by the World Bank Report, *Doing Business in South Asia 2007.* Once such a number is adopted, the relevant registration information could be forwarded directly by the registry of companies to the tax administration offices, the EPFO and the ESIC.[162]

6.3.5 *Single Window System:* In order to facilitate the process of obtaining clearances, many states have introduced the 'single window clearance' procedure. However, the power to accord approvals is still vested with various departments and agencies under their separate statutes and notifications. The existing legal framework does not allow one consolidated department or agency to accord all requisite clearances. Nevertheless, some state governments have taken initiatives to overcome this problem. For instance, in Rajasthan, the rules of business have been amended for specially empowered bodies to accord approvals for subjects under different departments; significantly, the amendments disallow any department to review the decisions of these empowered bodies. Other similar legislations include the Andhra Pradesh Infrastructure Development Enabling Act, 2001, the Chhattisgarh Audyogik Nivesh Protsahan Adhiniyam, 2002 and the Orissa Industries Facilitation Act, 2004.[163]

MCA-21, the e-Governance project of the Ministry of Company Affairs aims to fully automate processes of compliance and enforcement.

161. *http://www.mca.gov.in/MinistryWebsite/dca/help/ProcessHandbook.pdf*

162. *Doing Business in South Asia, 2007*, World Bank-IFC; *http://www.doingbusiness.org/Documents/SouthAsia07/Full_report.pdf*

163. For details on respective state measures, see *Single Window System in States/ UTs*, 2002, published by the Department of Industrial Policy and Promotion (DIPP).

Other simplifying actions include the introduction of a Single Composite Application Form (SCAF) which allows an entrepreneur to submit a single application form for obtaining various clearances and approvals.

6.3.6 *Single Composite Application Form:* Other simplifying actions include the introduction of a Single Composite Application Form (SCAF) which allows an entrepreneur to submit a single application form for obtaining different clearances and approvals from various departments and government authorities. States that have introduced this initiative include Andhra Pradesh, Gujarat, Karnataka, Kerala, Orissa, Punjab, Rajasthan, Tamil Nadu and Uttar Pradesh.

6.3.7 *Illustrative International Best Practices:* Mexico, Thailand and Latvia have succeeded in limiting inspections to 10 per cent, 15 per cent and 20 per cent of shipments respectively, by following a risk assessment policy that calculates the probability of inspections based on profiles of businesses.[164] With the introduction of electronic filing of documents for trading (import, export and trans-shipment permit applications), the time for cargo clearances in Singapore fell from four days to 30 minutes; the number of shipments processed rose three-fold and cost to businesses of handling trade documents fell by a third.[165] Mauritius has launched a virtual one stop shop linking the commercial registry and tax, and local authorities through a central electronic database.[166]

6.3.8 *Illustrative National Best Practices:* The World Bank-IFC Report, *Doing Business in South Asia 2007*, mentions some Indian cities known for their respective best practices (see Box 23.6). Examples include Jaipur (for starting business), Bhubaneswar (for obtaining construction clearances), Bangalore (for obtaining building permits) and Hyderabad (for obtaining land use approvals and registering property). Maharashtra and Karnataka have taken steps to ease the process of registering property. While Maharashtra has taken steps to lower stamp duties, Karnataka has reduced the time taken in the mutation and execution of sale deeds. Further, regarding mode of payment of stamp duty, Karnataka has discontinued the use of stamp paper and enabled payment through bank draft. Chennai has a 24-hour online container tracking system while Bangalore has an e-payment gateway for custom duties. The Mumbai Port Trust has also started an Online Port Community System.[167] In fact, the *Doing Business in South Asia 2007* report states that India can jump 55 places from its current rank if some of the local best practices are adopted nationwide.

Box 23.6: Best Practices in India

Starting a business: Jaipur

Dealing with licences: Bhubaneswar

Registering property: Hyderabad

Paying taxes: Bhubaneswar, Chandigarh

Trading across borders: Chennai

Enforcing contracts: Bhubaneswar

Closing a business: Bangalore

Source: Doing Business Report, 2007

The Doing Business in South Asia 2007 report states that India can jump 55 places from its current rank if some of the local best practices are adopted nationwide.

164. "Improving Business Climate" (PPT Presentation) *http://darpg.nic.in/arpgwebsite/Conference/ChiefSecyConf-PPTs/dipp200407.ppt*; further, such a policy not only led to reduction of delays, but also increased the detection of smuggled goods.

165. "Improving Business Climate" (PPT Presentation) *http://darpg.nic.in/arpgwebsite/Conference/ChiefSecyConf-PPTs/dipp200407.ppt*

166. *Doing Business 2008*, World Bank-IFC.

167. *Doing Business 2008*, World Bank-IFC.

6.4 Taxation

6.4.1 Entrepreneurs also faced problems relating to cumbersome tax procedures as well as multiplicity of taxes. According to the World Bank-IFC Report, *Doing Business 2008*, India's tax regime requires 60 separate payments every year.[168] Collection of taxes through different government agencies also increases the problems of complying with tax regulation. There also exists a multiplicity of taxes. In addition to service tax, CENVAT and custom duties that are imposed by the central government, state and local levels of governments levy respective state VAT/sales tax, entertainment tax and entry tax.[169] As seen in Figure 23.42 below, 27 per cent of entrepreneurs interviewed said they had faced problems because of multiplicity of taxes alone; 13 per cent faced a problem with complexity of procedures alone and 26 per cent faced problems with both. In other words, 66 per cent of the entrepreneurs interviewed, i.e., two out of every three entrepreneurs, faced difficulties with regard to some aspect of taxation—the multiplicity of taxes or the complexity of filing procedures, or both.

Figure 23.42: Problems Relating to Taxation

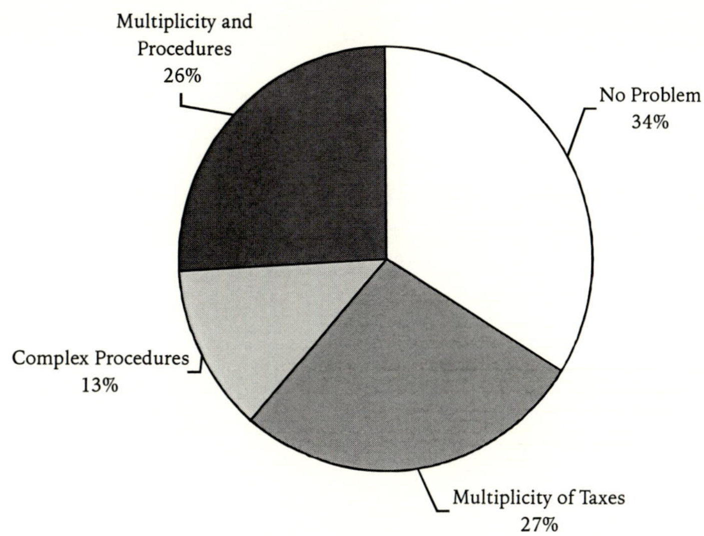

6.4.2 *Process Re-engineering in e-Governance:* Entrepreneurs were also of the opinion that while online filing of taxes had been introduced, tax compliance was still not easy since forms and procedures are still complicated. For instance, an entrepreneur from Kolkata said that almost one-third of his time was spent in doing paperwork and complying with multiple tax requirements. This confirms NKC's earlier recommendations that e-governance initiatives should be more about re-engineering government processes rather than only about front-end computerisation.[170]

6.4.3 *Key Initiatives in Taxation:* The introduction of Value Added Tax (VAT) in April 2005 was a significant measure. With the VAT system in operation, it has also been recently reported that Indian states have, in principle, agreed to move towards a common classification of all merchandise sold within the country—the 'Harmonised System of Nomenclature' (HSN).[171] Currently, the same product can be taxed at different rates across states leading to problems of cost uncertainty

e-Governance initiatives should be more about re-engineering government processes rather than only about front-end computerisation.

---

168. See "Soon, 24x7 paperless port transactions", *The Indian Express*, dated October 22, 2007.

169. *Doing Business 2008*, World Bank-IFC.

170. See, *http://knowledgecommission.gov.in/recommendations/egovernance.asp*

171. See "States agree to uniform classification of goods", *Mint*, dated December 6, 2007; India being a signatory of ITA (International Trade Agreement) has to comply with the tariff guidelines of the World Customs Organization (WCO). The WCO has a standard classification called the Harmonised System of Nomenclature (HSN) that classifies various products and also decides on the tax structure for each category. The HSN code classifies products and services in 5,019 different categories, which are revised on a regular basis to incorporate technological changes.

for entrepreneurs. A common classification of all merchandise sold throughout the country, coupled with fixation of tax rates for all classifications, is a move towards greater uniformity and thereby, less cost uncertainty for entrepreneurs.[172] A single HSN code for all the products under VAT across the country could also help states in making operational the Tax Information Network (TINXYS), an online network intended to bring transparency to inter-state transactions.[173]

There are also state-level initiatives to help entrepreneurs. Maharashtra has, for instance, computerised registration procedures for sales tax/VAT, which drastically reduces the time taken in filing tax returns. Another reform measure whose feasibility needs to be explored is reducing the frequency of payments by entrepreneurs from monthly to a quarterly basis.[174] The issue of consolidation of tax forms also needs to be examined in detail. For example, an entrepreneur in Sweden can file multiple taxes—corporate income tax, value added tax, labour contributions as well as property tax—in a single form.[175]

6.5 Legal System

6.5.1 Of the entrepreneurs interviewed, 43 per cent said they find the current legal procedures and requirements to be either 'extremely unsatisfactory' or 'somewhat unsatisfactory' (see Figure 23.43). Their complaints largely relate to procedures of law such as the slow pace of enforcing contracts as well as the current bankruptcy and labour law procedures. Nineteen per cent of the entrepreneurs interviewed said they feel constrained by labour laws (see Figure 23.39). According to the World Bank-IFC's *Doing Business 2008* report, it takes on an average, 10 years to complete bankruptcy proceedings in India. Further, claimants can expect to recover an average of less than 11.6 cents on the dollar. While official liquidators are appointed to carry out liquidations, the procedures are often long drawn. Another legal issue is that of unlimited liability for promoters in partnership concerns and proprietorship businesses due to the absence of Limited Liability Partnerships (LLPs) as a legal entity in India.

Figure 6.5: Helpfulness of Legal System

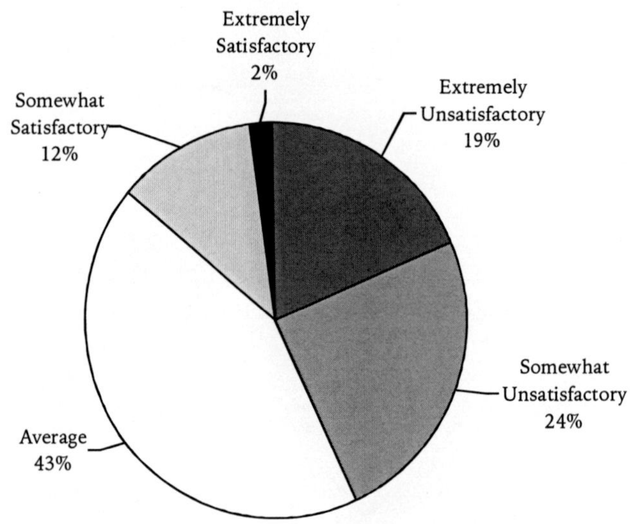

According to the World Bank-IFC's Doing Business 2008 report, it takes on an average, 10 years to complete bankruptcy proceedings in India.

172. HSN is also expected to assist in India's smooth transition to the goods and service tax system (GST).

173. *http://www.rediff.com/money/2006/aug/07vat.htm*

174. See *Doing Business in South Asia 2007; http://www.doingbusiness.org/Documents/SouthAsia07/Full_report.pdf*

175. *Doing Business 2008*, World Bank-IFC.

6.5.2 *Suggested Improvements:* Some of the legal reforms that would facilitate a better environment for entrepreneurship are as follows:

a. **Specialised Commercial Courts:** Since the debt recovery tribunals in India have jurisdiction to entertain only debt related issues, a possible reform for speedy enforcement of contracts would be the establishment of separate specialised commercial courts, which would deal with all types of commercial disputes.[176]

b. **Undertake Reforms in Bankruptcy Laws:** Discussions are also underway to change India's bankruptcy laws. The draft Companies Bill 2007 is expected to simplify rules and procedures. Establishment of institutions such as the National Company Law Tribunal (NCLT) and National Company Law Appellate Tribunal (NCALT) are also expected to bring about improvements in dealing with cases relating to insolvency, rehabilitation and liquidation and winding up proceedings. RBI's Advisory Group on Bankruptcy Laws has also recommended the enactment of a new bankruptcy code to deal more quickly with liquidations.[177]

c. **One Person Company/LLPs:** The draft Companies Bill 2007 is also expected to propose a new entity called a one person company (OPC) that would provide individual entrepreneurs the flexibility and low cost of forming a proprietorship/partnership concern while restricting their personal liabilities to that of a private limited company.[178] Similarly, the government is also expected to enact a law on limited liability partnerships soon.[179]

6.6 Infrastructure

6.6.1 The reliability and availability of world-class infrastructure services is critical for the growth of entrepreneurship. India's physical infrastructure—roads/highways, railways, ports, airports, power, telecom—is seen as a bottleneck to the smooth operation of all economic activity. The high transport and supply-chain costs that poor infrastructure entails are significant, particularly for a small entrepreneur. Enterprises surveyed in the *Global Competitiveness Report 2007-08*, rated inadequate infrastructure as "the most problematic factor" for doing business in India.[180] In this report, while India scores well on 'soft' parameters such as higher education, the rule of law and political legislation, it loses out on the adequacy of infrastructure facilities. According to another recent survey, 40 per cent of Indian CEOs are worried about the quality of infrastructure in the country.[181]

6.6.2 Of the entrepreneurs interviewed, 56 per cent found the current infrastructure in India to be unfavourable, rating it as 'extremely unsatisfactory' or 'somewhat unsatisfactory' (see Figure 23.44). However, perceptions have improved—while 67 per cent of the pre-1990 entrepreneurs rated infrastructure as unfavourable, among the post-2000 entrepreneurs, only 36 per cent felt the same. This could be due to improvements in the country's infrastructure and/or there being a higher proportion of service-based enterprises among the post-2000 enterprises which have lower dependence on infrastructure.

6.6.3 *Availability of Work Space:* Another crucial infrastructure issue for a new entrepreneur is the availability of adequate work space. There are interesting differences based on family backgrounds as seen in Figure 23.45 below. Among first generation entrepreneurs, only 15 per cent reported already having work space at the start-up stage. A majority of second generation entrepreneurs in the same business (69 per cent) already had work space to start operations. However, this figure dips significantly for second generation entrepreneurs, who pursue a different business (33 per cent).

The high transport and supply-chain costs that poor infrastructure entails are significant, particularly for a small entrepreneur.

176. "Improving Business Climate" (PPT Presentation) *http://darpg.nic.in/arpgwebsite/Conference/ChiefSecyConf-PPTs/dipp200407.ppt*; such courts have been established in Tanzania and Peru.

177. See RBI (2002). Report of the Standing Committee on International Financial Standards and Codes.

178. See "One-person companies", *The Economic Times*, dated December 3, 2007.

179. See the reports of 'Naresh Chandra Committee on Regulation of Private Companies and Partnership Concerns' and the 'Expert Committee on Company Law (Dr.J.J. Irani Committee)'.

180. *http://www.gcr.weforum.org*

181. *The Times of India*, dated January 19, 2008, quoting a recent PWC Global CEO Survey.

Figure 23.44: **Availabilty of Infrastructure**

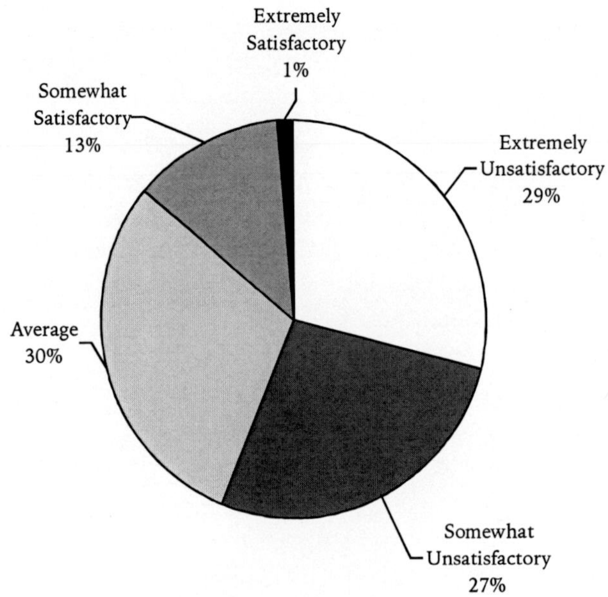

Another pattern observed is that leasing of work space is more prevalent among first generation and second generation entrepreneurs pursuing a business different from that of their family. Of the first generation entrepreneurs, 29 per cent leased work space compared to 17 per cent among second generation entrepreneurs in a different business.

Figure 23.45: **Office Space with Entrepreneurs—Variation According to Family Background**

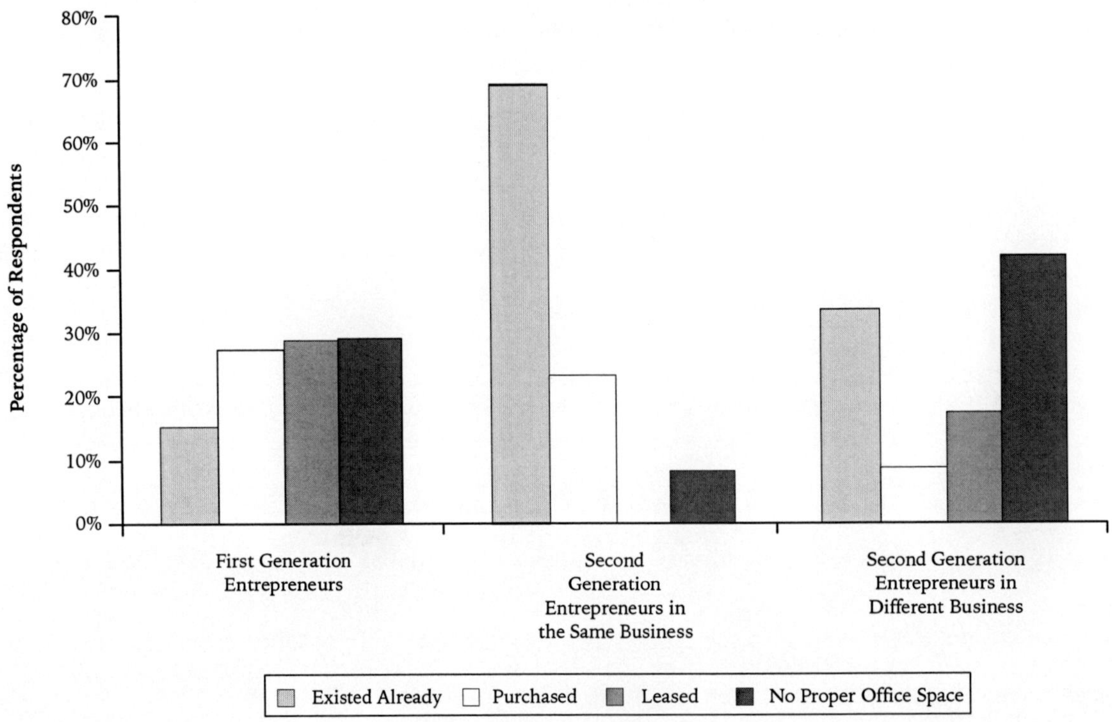

Leasing of work space is more prevalent among first generation and second generation entrepreneurs pursuing a business different from that of their family.

6.6.4 *Some Illustrative Examples of Infrastructural Issues:* Interestingly, an entrepreneur from Bangalore operated from a makeshift office inside a PCO booth in his early days in the service industry. Another entrepreneur, also from Bangalore, stated that power failures, poor bandwidth and insufficient public transport led her to incur high unplanned costs. In order to ensure the smooth operation of her business, she had to purchase generators, fix additional Internet lines and even provide housing for her employees near her office premises. Another problem that manufacturing entrepreneurs in Hyderabad and Bangalore, in particular, face is the shortage of industrial land. A sudden spurt of growth in these cities has led to an increase in the demand for land, resulting in shortage of industrial estates as well as rapid escalation in land prices. Without basic infrastructure, entrepreneurs cannot envisage shifting to alternative places outside the main city, as feasible. Entrepreneurs also mentioned difficulties in transportation of physical goods. An entrepreneur from Hyderabad said that while it takes 60 days for a consignment from Hyderabad to reach USA, it would take only 21 days from China. Complaints relating to power varied across regions. While the interviewees in Kolkata complained about inferior quality of power supply, entrepreneurs in Ahmedabad had issues with the high cost of power.[182]

6.6.5 *Some Recent Initiatives:* Since inadequate infrastructure is seen as a critical bottleneck to economic growth, the government has given high priority to quality infrastructure development, incorporating various delivery mechanisms such as PPPs (see Box 23.7). The total investment in infrastructure in 2006-07 is estimated to be around 5 per cent of GDP. The total investment in infrastructure in the Eleventh Five Year Plan is projected at Rs. 20, 60, 193 crore or 7.65 per cent of GDP.[183] Among the key infrastructure development projects are the National Highways Development Project (NHDP), Pradhan Mantri Gram Sadak Yojana (PMGSY), National Maritime Development Programme, Bharat Nirman for rural infrastructure, Jawaharlal Nehru National Urban Renewal Mission (JNNURM) and Integrated Development of Small and Medium Towns (IDSMT). At the same time, the private sector's share for investment in infrastructure is expected to increase from 20 per cent to 30 per cent during the current Plan period. (see Table 23.7)

Table 23.7: Infrastructure: Deficit and Eleventh Plan Targets

Sector	Target	XI Plan Targets
Roads/Highways	65,569 km of NH comprise only 2% of network & carry 40% of traffic; 12% 4-laned; 50% 2-laned; and 38% single-laned	6-lane 6,500 km in GQ; 4-lane 6,736 km NS-EW; 4-lane 12,109 km; 2-lane 20,000 km; 1,000 km Expressway
Ports	Inadequate berths and rail/road connectivity	New capacity: 485 mn. MT in major ports; 345 mn. MT in minor ports
Airports	Inadequate runways, aircraft handling capacity, parking space and terminal buildings	Modernise 4 metro and 35 non-metro airports; 3 greenfield in NE; 7 other greenfield airports
Railways	Old technology; saturated routes: slow speeds (freight: 22 kmph; passengers: 50 kmph); low payload to fare ratio (2.5)	10,300 km new rail; 10,000 km gauge conversion; modernise 21 stations; dedicated freight corridors
Power	11% peaking deficit; 7% energy shortage; 40% transmission and distribution losses; absence of competition	Add 78,000 MW; access to all rural households
Irrigation	1123 BCM utilisable water resources; yet near crisis in per capita availability and storage; only 43% of net sown area irrigated	Develop 16 mha major and minor works; 10.25 mha CAD; 2.18 mha flood control
Telecom/IT	Only 18% of market accessed; obsolete hardware; acute human resources' shortages	Reach 600 mn subscribers – 200 mn in rural areas; 20 mn broadband; 40 mn Internet

Source: Chapter 12, Development of Infrastructure, Eleventh Five Year Plan, 54th NDC Meeting

A sudden spurt of growth in these cities has led to an increase in the demand for land, resulting in shortage of industrial estates as well as rapid escalation in land prices.

182. In Gujarat, the rate of electricity is Rs. 516 P/KWh for domestic users and Rs. 501 P/KWh for industrial users. (according to the Economic Survey 2006-07).

183. Chapter 12, Development of Infrastructure, Eleventh Five Year Plan, 54th NDC Meeting.

Box 23.7: PPP in India

Public-private partnership (PPP) in infrastructure refers to a project based on a contract or concession agreement, between a government or statutory entity on the one side and a private sector company on the other, for delivering an infrastructure service upon payment of user charges. The Government of India has established a Cabinet Committee on Infrastructure (CoI) and a high-level Committee of Secretaries (CoS), in addition to sector-wise task forces to streamline rapid decision-making and operationalise PPPs in highways, airports, sea ports, power generation, railways, etc. It has initiated the Viability Gap Funding (VGF) scheme and established the India Infrastructure Finance Company Limited (IIFCL) to provide long-term debt finance to PPP projects, and has intensified its efforts on strengthening public sector capacity and enabling environment for attracting private sector participation in infrastructure. Overall, the government sees PPPs as an important tool for producing an accelerated and larger pipeline of infrastructure investments and catching up with the infrastructure deficit in the country.

While 86 PPP projects have been contracted, there are an estimated 500 PPP projects that exist in India, together valued at about Rs. 340 billion, in 12 states and 3 central agencies. The roads and port sectors constitute a major portion of the number and size of PPPs. Till October 2006, 12 proposals have been given in-principle approval under the VGF. (See: 'Facilitating Public Private Partnership for Accelerated Infrastructure Development in India,' Regional Workshop of Chief Secretaries on PPP, December 2006)

PPPs contribute private capital and managerial efficiencies to enhance public services. Some of the PPPs may provide entrepreneurial opportunities where none existed before. For example, the task of modernising airports in various cities in India has received a fillip due to the involvement of private players such as the GMR Group who had themselves started as entrepreneurs.

6.7 Does the State facilitate Entrepreneurship?

6.7.1 *General Government Facilitation:* The NKC study found a significant majority of entrepreneurs saying that the government is generally 'not helpful'. In the interviews, 61 per cent of the entrepreneurs rated 'helpfulness of government' as 'extremely unsatisfactory' or 'somewhat unsatisfactory' (see Figure 23.46). Some entrepreneurs said that while the government has some very significant policies to help entrepreneurs, the implementation of these policies is extremely poor. Some were of the view that government schemes and initiatives are not publicised adequately. Others said that corruption and red-tapism result in the schemes not reaching the targeted people. Currently, there are a number of policies and schemes in place to promote and assist entrepreneurs in India, at Central and state levels.[184] The Ministry of Micro, Small and Medium Enterprises also provides a package of incentives and subsidies for the promotion of micro and small enterprises (See Box 23.8). The challenge is to make the policies into catalysts for driving entrepreneurship in India.

Box 23.8: Package for Promotion of Small and Medium Entrepreneurs, 2007

1. **Legislation:** The Micro, Small and Medium Enterprises Development Bill, 2006 has been enacted for the promotion and development of micro, small and medium enterprises. The Government is also expected to enact relevant law on limited liability partnerships.
2. **Credit Support:** RBI has issued guidelines to the public sector banks to ensure 20 per cent year-on-year growth in credit to the SME sector. The State Industrial Development Bank of India (SIDBI) is expected to upscale its credit operations for micro enterprises and cover 50 lakh additional beneficiaries over five years beginning 2006-07. The Union government to provide grants to SIDBI to augment its portfolio risk fund and enable it to create a risk capital fund. To strengthen the

184. Some examples include the Food Processing Policy, Auto Policy, Information Technology Act and National Jute Policy.

credit guarantee fund, the corpus of the fund is expected to be raised from Rs. 1189 crore as of 01 April 2006 to Rs. 2500 crore over a period of 5 years.

3. **Fiscal Support:** The Government is expected to examine the feasibility of increase in the General Excise Exemption (GEE) limit and the existing eligibility limit for GEE; also consider extending the time limit for payment of excise duty by micro and small enterprises and extending the GEE benefits to small enterprises on their graduation to medium enterprises for a limited period.
4. **Support for Cluster Based Development:** Accelerate the holistic development of clusters, including provision of common facility centres, developed sites for new enterprises, upgradation of existing industrial infrastructure and provision of exhibition grounds/halls and also for creation and management of infrastructure-related assets in the public-private partnership mode. The ceiling on project cost is expected to be raised to Rs. 10 crore.
5. **Technologies and Quality Upgradation Support:** Four Training-cum-Product Development Centres (TPDCs) for agro and food processing industries to be set up. A Technology Mission to be set up to assist MSMEs in technology upgradation, energy conservation and pollution mitigation.
6. **Support for Entrepreneurial and Managerial Development:** Fifty thousand entrepreneurs to be trained in information technology, catering, agro and food processing, pharmaceuticals, biotechnology, etc., during the Eleventh Plan; a new scheme to be formulated to provide financial assistance to select management/business schools and technical institutes, to conduct tailor-made courses for new as well as existing micro and small entrepreneurs; a new scheme to be also be formulated to provide financial assistance to five select universities/colleges to run 1200 entrepreneurial clubs.

Source: http://www.laghu-udyog.com/publications/circulars/GazNot/promotion_package_english.pdf

Figure 23.46: Helpfulness of Government

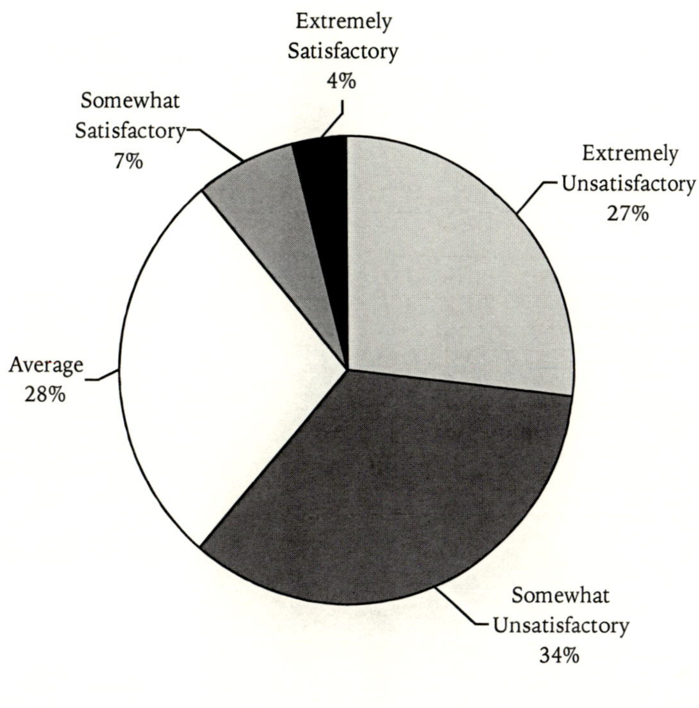

6.8 Chapter Summary

A critical prerequisite for nurturing entrepreneurship is the creation of a favourable business environment. The key parameters of a conducive business environment include the smooth flow of information, ease of starting a business and obtaining various clearances and permits, ease of filing taxes, an efficient legal system, enabling legislations and regulations, absence of corruption and world class infrastructure facilities. Half of the entrepreneurs interviewed have encountered problems relating to obtaining clearances and licences. Two-thirds have faced hassles while fi ling taxes. About 60 per cent of the entrepreneurs interviewed have encountered corruption at some point during their entrepreneurial journey. Entrepreneurs have also emphasized the lack of information, as well as poor implementation of government schemes, as significant impediments. About 56 per cent of entrepreneurs stressed that the lack of availability of quality infrastructure—transport, power and telecommunications—is a critical problem restricting entrepreneurship.

While India has the potential to derive comparative advantage in human resources, skills, demographic profile and growing domestic demand, recent studies such as the World Bank report *Doing Business 2008*, rate India poorly on indicators of the business environment. According to the *Doing Business* report, India ranks 120th out of 178 countries on conducive business environment. There are a number of initiatives at the Central and state levels, which aim at improving the ease of doing business. In fact, the World Bank-IFC report says that India can jump 55 places from its current rank if some of its own local best practices are adopted nationwide. For example, the Ministry of Company Affairs has initiated the MCA-21 project designed to fully automate all processes related to the proactive enforcement and compliance of the legal requirements under the Companies Act, 1956. Other suggestions to improve the business environment for Entrepreneurship include the following: meaningful implementation of the Single Window System; Single Composite Application Form; PPPs in infrastructure, specialised commercial courts; relevant amendments in company laws to introduce LLPs; setting up 'one stop shops' for information needs; and improving tax processes and process re-engineering in e-governance. NKC also proposes to explore the possibility of having an all encompassing website on entrepreneurship as a one stop information portal for current and aspiring entrepreneurs.

VII. Conclusion: Encouraging Entrepreneurship

7.1 Comprehensive Campaign

7.1.1 A comprehensive campaign to raise the tempo of entrepreneurship in India will necessarily need the concerted efforts of a number of agencies. Based on the narrative in the previous chapters and interviews with stakeholders, there are a few key action points that will encourage and enhance entrepreneurship in the country. As seen in previous chapters, enhancing entrepreneurship involves the community, family, academia, financial players, government, industry and potential entrepreneurs themselves. Promoting entrepreneurship means encouraging people to be self-reliant in taking economic decisions and creating wealth and employment. NKC believes that entrepreneurship has enormous scope in India's growth story.

7.1.2 Advice to Entrepreneurs: During the interviews, entrepreneurs were asked what advice they would like to offer to upcoming entrepreneurs. Below is a list of illustrative responses:

- Increase networks with other entrepreneurs to encourage sharing of ideas and experiences, and to mentor upcoming entrepreneurs.
- Document failures as much as successes and learn from each experience.
- Invest in people and build teams that follow inclusive approaches (address the needs of talent at all levels), develop incentives and bolster human resources—'translate business strategy into talent strategy'.
- Understand the product and markets well.
- Conduct extensive background research, especially on marketing and financial aspects.
- Focus on quality—'Cost is forgotten, quality never'.
- Match the skills, mindsets and beliefs with the business venture—focus on core strength and excel.
- Do not cling on to the venture—especially in up-scaling—hire individuals who are better than you; if you are responsible, give autonomy and divest authority.
- Be open to ideas. Take informed risks.
- Hard work, persistence, perseverance, confidence—these are the 'must qualities' for every entrepreneur.
- Be honest—never compromise on ethics or offer bribes.
- Build strong foundations and then grow; take incremental steps.
- A history of paying taxes and having a decent balance sheet helps when you approach lending institutions.
- Possess 'ferocious ambition' and believe that the 'sky is the limit'.
- Develop clear business plans and targets for growth.
- Undertake information disclosures and participate in the development of the rating processes of banks, to enable better risk management for finance.

7.1.3 What the Government Can Do: Encourage a conducive business environment; ensure simplified start-up processes; improve the delivery time; reduce corruption; collate informational needs of start-ups; improve corporate governance norms; create an environment that will reduce risk; and encourage more seed funds and corporate players to provide start-up funding. In particular:

- Create up-to-date information source for start-up entrepreneurs in the form of source books, web portals and one stop shops, and widen dissemination of all relevant information.
- Introduce a single unique company number to be used by new businesses for company, social security and tax registrations.

- Improve the current single window system of getting clearances and introduce a single composite application form.
- Ease the process of filing taxes by reducing the frequency of tax payments and multiplicity of procedures.
- Create specialised commercial courts for speedy enforcement of contracts.
- Reform bankruptcy laws to ease the process of closing down businesses.
- Speed up development of world-class infrastructure.
- Ensure proper publicity and implementation of various promotional schemes and policies.
- Set up a public fund for new entrepreneurs using innovative PPP mechanisms.
- Explore venture debt instruments with the help of innovative PPP mechanisms, through SIDBI and similar institutions.
- Establish a secondary market for trade in stocks of smaller companies.
- Develop a comprehensive incubation policy at the national level, which would increase quantity, enhance quality and increase access to financing.
- Explore crucial incentive structures in incubation such as land schemes (given the level of infrastructure problems that start-ups face), tax sops, banking policies, micro funds, innovative financial schemes, outcome measurement and delivery mechanisms.
- Explore possibilities of PPP as well as private incubation centres as a way to increase the number of incubation centres in the country and thereby providing wider access to incubation opportunity for new entrepreneurs.
- NKC has already recommended that the Government should set up a global technology acquisition fund in intellectual property (IP), which can enable crucial technology acquisition across the world, especially for SMEs. Funds could be placed with a financial institution or a special purpose vehicle (SPV) could be created to manage the fund, with members of industry and government invited on the board. Relevant financial instruments, including support in the form of loans and equity could be evolved for such technology intensive acquisition.
- NKC has also suggested the need to enact legislation that creates a legal framework for public funded research. Such legislation would give universities and research institutions ownership and patent rights and create an enabling environment for them to commercialise such inventions through licencing arrangements where the inventors would also receive a share of royalties.
- Frame appropriate polices to encourage innovation among smaller institutions and companies and encourage transition among R&D/educational institutions.
- Give high priority to VET policy and bring about a transformation in the sector through innovative delivery models, re-branding, improving certification and monitoring as well as increasing flexibility of VET with the higher education stream.
- Explore performance-based models in VET policy that links incentives to outcomes. Incentivise SCVTs and states; assess the entry stage requirements of each trainee; align financial incentives to teaching of requisite English language skills as well as to a transparent industry-backed certification system for each trainee. Encourage learning by doing earning; connect financing to performance-based outcomes through nationwide publication and dissemination of learning outcomes in the form of a Vocational Skill Primer, that measures each VET institution; publication of performance-based outcomes becomes therefore, the first step in developing a transparent, independent rating system in VET.
- Develop recognition and reward systems for entrepreneurship, at the local, state as well as national levels (such as those instituted by MSME at the national level).
- Implement far-reaching changes in higher education policy to enhance quality, quantity and inclusiveness.
- Modernise and make transparent and accessible IPR infrastructure.
- Explore the possibility of innovative social security for entrepreneurs to encourage ability to take risks.

7.1.4 How can Chambers of Commerce/Industrial Associations/Other Networks Help:

- Chambers need to take active steps to give prominence to regular entrepreneurial meetings, discussions and networking.
- Chambers need to go beyond mid-size and large companies to reach out to young entrepreneurs.
- Scale up current initiatives on entrepreneurship; coordinate across associations and networks, and beyond metropolitan cities and top educational institutions.
- Create networks of entrepreneurship initiatives that are being undertaken across the country.
- Strengthen mentoring programmes for upcoming entrepreneurs and actively leverage networks with successful entrepreneurs.
- Provide platforms for discussing entrepreneurial best practices and experiences by holding nationwide workshops.
- Create forums for partnerships with and mentoring by financial institutions.

7.1.5 Role of Educational Institutions/R&D Centres:

- Develop content, learning methods, pedagogy, examination systems and curricula that encourage critical and lateral thinking; incorporate case studies of real life situations in the curriculum so that students are able to get a 'concrete feel' of the outside world; introduce manuals in school curricula on 'how things work' on various practical aspects of everyday living; explore ideas for flexibility of vocational education with mainstream education for greater linkages between theory and practice.
- Make Entrepreneurship a core subject in business schools, including topics relating to business ethics, early enterprise management, relevant aspects of scaling-up, Indian corporate law and relevant international laws in curricula, explore possibilities of establishing entrepreneurship schools at the undergraduate and postgraduate levels such as the one envisaged at IIT Kharagpur, with possible alumni and NRI involvement.
- Encourage student-led entrepreneurial activities in campus with active stakeholder participation; encourage initiatives such as business plan contests with angel/VC/private sector assistance by holding 'enterprise *melas*'. Encourage activities that deal with the basic practicalities of entrepreneurship and platforms to interact with various entrepreneurs, the financial community (especially VCs and angels) and relevant networks.
- Set up enterprise centres in major educational and research centres, with industry linkages, partnerships and supporting incubation activities.
- Create greater linkages with industry; provide flexible options and supporting environment for those with Ph.D. degrees to translate high tech innovations into wealth generating ideas and entrepreneurial ventures; enable researchers to set up commercial entities while in professional employment with research organisations; facilitate mobility and flexibility; encourage universities/research organisations to establish commercial enterprises based on their new inventions.
- Enable research organisations to invest through knowledge, positioning inventions and innovations as equity in the new enterprises.

7.1.6 Business Incubation Centres:

- Make incubation a core business proposition to trigger entrepreneurship.
- Develop feasible business models at the incubation stage which align incentive structures towards measurable performance outcomes and provide stake in the outcomes (through knowledge equity, etc.).
- Emphasise the financial and commercialisation aspects of incubation (i.e., on the feasibility of taking an idea to market, understanding risk mitigation-measurement-strategy, cash flows, analysis of business failures, ethics, etc., and not only technical feasibility) where the financial community can play a significant role.

- Actively involve industry (other successful entrepreneurs, angels, VCs, banks, chambers of commerce, associations, etc.) as part of the social networks for mentoring, thereby supplementing the efforts of academics within the educational institutions.
- Develop formal and informal systems of active, regular mentoring by successful entrepreneurs, platforms for networking and peer recognition, and honour successful emerging entrepreneurs at regular intervals.
- Widen incubation and mentoring beyond technology related ventures, alumni and centres of excellence in metropolitan centres.
- Widen the incubation horizon beyond the start-up stage to also include scaling up.
- Hold national and state level incubation seminars and workshops.

7.1.7 Role of the Financial Community:

- Banks must consider entrepreneurship as a major business opportunity.
- Explore innovative options such as venture debt, soft loans etc., for start-ups.
- Encourage current efforts on development of systematic risk management systems (SMERA-credit ratings, CIBIL-information disclosures, CART-credit appraisal tools, RAM-risk assessment models, etc.,) as ways to increase risk appetite.
- Incentivise entrepreneurs to undertake ratings and information disclosures by linking cost of credit to ratings (where more holistic ideas of risk can be evolved).
- Encourage the setting up of special industrial and management consultancy departments in banks to address functional inadequacies and market gaps, as well as develop multi-dimensional skills and increased information flows to encourage entrepreneurial funding.
- Actively assist entrepreneurs to develop multiple skills necessary for scaling up.
- Implement significant policy initiatives, including relevant RBI recommendations which facilitate ease of credit flow to small entrepreneurs.
- Banks need to reduce information asymmetries at various levels and disseminate information on various relevant issues (ratings, policies, schemes, consultancies, etc.,).
- Banks could explore ways to monetise aspects of the knowledge industry (including intellectual property in the form of licences etc., as assets) with a view to better finance for such sectors.
- Realise the enormous potential for greater involvement of angels and VCs at the seed stage, especially in the newer, high growth sectors of the economy.
- Increase awareness on the activities of angel/VC financing through greater involvement with educational and research institutions, incubation centres, etc.
- Scale up and publicise best practices in financial innovations for entrepreneurship.

7.1.8 At the National Level:

- Encourage and celebrate entrepreneurship—reward and acknowledge its role in wealth creation and employment generation.
- Widen the social base of capital, including access to new entrepreneurs from communities not traditionally associated with business, especially from marginalised groups.
- Launch entrepreneurship outreach events (not just in schools and colleges but also through the media).
- Improve general perceptions regarding entrepreneurship to influence family and community support for first generation entrepreneurs.

Figure 23.47: The Entrepreneurial Ecosystem

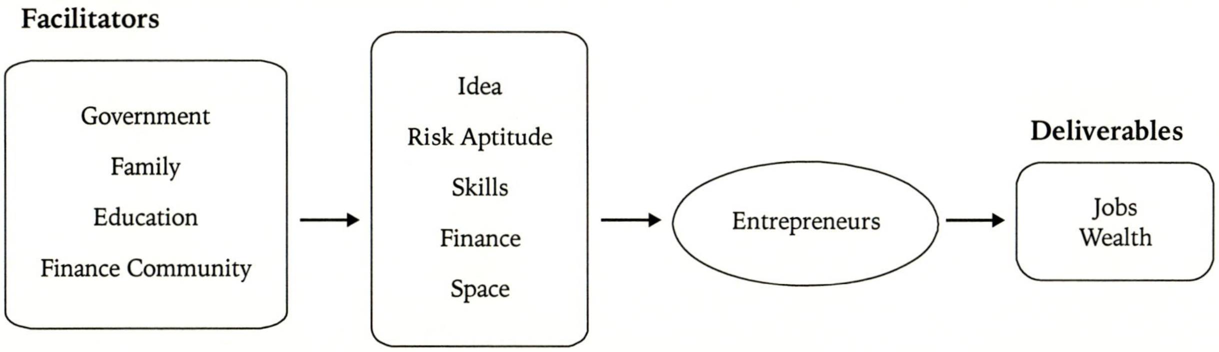

Methodology

This study is based on formal one-on-one interviews with entrepreneurs and other stakeholders of the entrepreneurial ecosystem, along with review of policy literature by NKC researchers. The interviews were conducted across six cities of India—Pune, Kolkata, Chennai, Ahmedabad, Hyderabad and Bangalore, while a few responses are also included from the National Capital Region (NCR) and Mumbai. Without exception, all entrepreneurs were forthcoming with their responses and displayed significant interest and involvement. Interviews with entrepreneurs were based on a flexible framework of questions while keeping core issues as a priority: background, entrepreneurial turning points, views on facilitative triggers and the nature of roadblocks. We also conducted interviews with other stakeholders such as the financial community (bankers, angel investors, venture capitalists, state finance corporations, etc.), educational institutions, incubation centres, incubatees, chambers of commerce, industry associations, institutional networks and associations of entrepreneurs. Finally, we also requested and received profiles of some entrepreneurial icons whose personal narratives provide rich insight and direction.

Besides qualitative data on some key issues (such as availability of human resources, helpfulness of government, infrastructure, etc.), we also asked entrepreneurs to rate their perceptions along numerical scales. Based on both quantitative parameters (such as gender, age of entrepreneur, sector, year of starting, educational qualifications, turnover of enterprise, number of employees, etc.) and qualitative parameters (such as family support, importance of education, financial assistance, taxation policies, corruption, regulatory issues, problems in scaling up, etc.), statistical measures were computed. Further based on consultations with other stakeholders, we received additional suggestions to enhance entrepreneurship in the country. These have been duly acknowledged.

This study explores some of the most significant entrepreneurial issues in India with a view to recommending broad policies that would further enhance the spread of entrepreneurship. While highlighting broad issues, the study has not made detailed empirical investigations on micro issues based on rigorous econometric techniques.

List of Resources

This section contains a list of resources, relevant for entrepreneurs and other stakeholders in the entrepreneurial ecosystem.

List of Resources

1. *http://msme.gov.in/ and http://www.laghu-udyog.com/* - The Ministry of Micro, Small And Medium Enterprises lists various government schemes for entrepreneurs.
2. *http://www.techno-preneur.net/* - The Technology Innovation Management and Entrepreneurship Information Service assists technopreneurs in finding technologies, projects, funding options and information on policy environment, incentive schemes and industrial infrastructure available in the country, covering Central and state governments.
3. *http://www.sidbi.in/* - The Small Industrial Development Bank of India works towards empowering micro, small and medium enterprises.
4. *http://dst.gov.in/scientific-programme/t-d-tdb.htm* - The Technology Development Board aims at accelerating the development and commercialisation of indigenous technology or adapting imported technology to wider domestic application. The board provides financial assistance in the form of equity, soft loans or grants.
5. *http://www.dsir.nic.in/tpdup/tepp/tepp.htm* - The Technopreneur Promotion Programme is run by Department of Scientific & Industrial Research.
6. *http://www.numsum.com/spreadsheet/show/48465* - This lists VCs based in India and/or making investments in Indian companies.
7. *http://www.indiavca.org/* - The Indian Venture Capital and Private Equity Association (IVCA) is a member based national organisation that represents venture capital and private equity firms.
8. *http://www.indianangelnetwork.com/* - The Indian Angel Network (IAN) is India's first and largest angel network with successful entrepreneurs and high profile CEOs interested in investing in early stage businesses across India, which have the potential to create disproportionate value. IAN has invested in multiple sectors like information technology, intellectual property, hospitality, mobile, education, Internet, etc.
9. *http://ycombinator.com/* - Y Combinator is a US venture firm specialising in early stage start-ups (seed funding). It helps start-ups through what is for many the hardest step, from idea to company, and invests mostly in software and web services. It makes small investments (rarely more than $20,000) in return for small stakes in the companies it funds (usually industry 2-10 per cent).
10. *http://www.thenetworkenterprisesfund.in/* - The Network Enterprises Fund is an equity fund that invests in commercially viable, sustainable enterprises in sectors impacting low-income households.
11. *http://www.gvfl.com/home.htm* - Gujarat Venture Finance Limited is a pioneer of venture capital in India. It is an independent, board-managed, autonomous venture finance company based at Ahmedabad.
12. *http://www.theseedfund.com/* - The Seed Fund, based in Mumbai, is a partnership and network of experienced investors, entrepreneurs and executives with a mission to find and invest in unique, high potential, early-stage IT companies.
13. *http://www.ventureintelligence.in/* - Venture Intelligence is the leading provider of information and networking services to the private equity and venture capital ecosystem.
14. *http://www.nenonline.org/* - The National Entrepreneurship Network (NEN) is a network of over 280 top academic institutions across India encompassing a 300,000+ strong student base and over 500 faculty members leading entrepreneurship programmes at various institutes.
15. *http://www.tie.org/* - The Indus Entrepreneurs, also known as Talent Ideas and Enterprise is spread across 11 countries, fostering entrepreneurship globally through mentoring, networking and education.
16. *http://www.aleap.org* – The Association of Lady Entrepreneurs of Andhra Pradesh (ALEAP) provides a platform to female entrepreneurs who help each other and work in collaboration for welfare maximisation.
17. *http://www.bystonline.org/* - The Bharat Yuva Shakti Trust works with young people in the age group of 18-35, who are either unemployed or underemployed, providing financial and mentoring support to establish their own ventures.
18. *www.ediindia.org/* - The Entrepreneurship Development Institute of India (EDI), set-up in 1983 fosters entrepreneurship through various programmes and courses.
19. *http://barcamp.org/* - BarCamp is an international network of technopreneurs who meet from time to time to share ideas and sell products.

20. *http://www.businessgyan.com/* - This is a Karnataka-based business magazine on entrepreneurship.

21. *http://www.kassia.com/* - Kassia is a premier voluntary state level non-government institution of small-scale industries in Karnataka.

22. *http://maccia.org.in/* - The Mahratta Chamber of Commerce, Industry & Agriculture (MACCIA) is the local chamber of commerce in Pune serving the Maharashtra region.

23. *http://www.gujaratchamber.org/* - The Gujarat Chamber of Commerce and Industry is a local chamber of commerce in Ahmedabad.

24. *http://www.biztradeshows.com/cii-chennai/* - The Chennai wing of Confederation of Indian industry.

25. *http://www.bengalchamber.com/* - The Bengal Chamber of Commerce and Industry, located in Kolkata, is an important chamber of commerce especially for the eastern region.

26. *http://www.fapcci.in/* - The Federation of Andhra Pradesh Chambers of Commerce is a local chamber of commerce.

27. *http://www.fkcci.org/Site/index.php* - The Federation of Karnataka Chambers of Commerce & Industry is a local chamber of commerce largely catering to entrepreneurs in Bangalore.

Glossary

AIM	Alternative Investment Market
ALEAP	Association of Lady Entrepreneurs of Andhra Pradesh
ASSOCHAM	Association of Chambers of Commerce
AWAKE	Association of Women Entrepreneurs of Karnataka
BCCI	Bengal Chamber of Commerce and Industry
BIE	Business Incubation for Entrepreneurship
BPO	Business Process Outsourcing
BYST	Bharatiya Yuva Shakti Trust
CAGR	Compound Annual Growth Rate
CART	Credit Appraisal and Rating Tool
CENVAT	Central Value Added Tax
CIBIL	Credit Information Bureau (India) Limited
CII	Confederation of Indian Industry
CIIE	Centre for Innovation, Incubation and Entrepreneurship
CMIE	Centre for Monitoring Indian Economy
CSO	Central Statistical Organization
DIT	Department of Information Technology
DSB	Dun and Bradstreet
EDI	Entrepreneurship Development Institute
EPFO	Employees Providend Fund Organization
ESIC	Employees State Insurance Organization
FAPCII	Federation of Andhra Pradesh Chambers of Commerce and Industry
FICCI	Federation of Indian Chambers of Commerce and Industry
FITT	Foundation for Innovation and Technology Transfer
FIWE	Federation of Indian Women Entrepreneurs
FKCCI	Federation of Karnataka Chambers of Commerce and Industry
GCCI	Gujarat Chamber of Commerce and Industry
GEM	Global Entrepreneurship Monitor
HSN	Harmonised System of Nomenclature
IDSMT	Integrated Development of Small and Medium Towns
IIIT	Indian Institute of Information Technology
IIM	Indian Institute of Management
IISc	Indian Institute of Science
IISER	Indian Institute of Science Education and Research
IIT	Indian Institute of Technology
IP	Intellectual Property

IPR	Intellectual Property Rights
IPO	Initial Public Offer
ISB	Indian School of Business
ISBA	Indian STEP and Business Incubator Association
IT	Information Technology
ITeS	Information Technology enabled Services
JNNURM	Jawaharlal Nehru National Urban Renewal Mission
KASSIA	Karnataka Small-Scale Industries' Association
LLP	Limited Liability Partnership
MCA	Ministry of Company Affairs
MCCIA	Mahratta Chamber of Commerce, Industry and Agriculture
MCGS	Mutual Credit Guarantee Scheme
MGA	Mutual Guarantee Association
MLI	Member Lending Institutions
MOST	Ministry of Science and Technology
MSME	Micro Small and Medium Enterprises
NASSCOM	National Association of Software and Service Companies
NCALT	National Company Law Appellate Tribunal
NCLT	National Company Law Tribunal
NEF	Network Enterprises Fund
NEN	National Entrepreneurship Network
NHDP	National Highways Development Project
NIT	National Institute of Technology
NKC	National Knowledge Commission
NSDM	National Skill Development Mission
NSERB	National Science and Engineering Research Board
NSRCEL	N. S. Raghavan Centre for Entrepreneurial Learning
NSTEDB	National Science and Technology Entrepreneurship Development Board
OPC	One Person Company
PAN	Permanent Account Number
PE	Private Equity
PMGSY	Pradhan Mantri Gram Sadak Yojana
PPP	Public-Private Partnership
RAM	Risk Assessment Model
R&D	Research and Development
RBI	Reserve Bank of India
RUDISETIs	Rural Development and Self Employment Training Institutes

SBI	State Bank of India
SBIC	Small Business Investment Company
SCAF	Single Composite Application Form
SCVT	State Councils for Vocational Training
SIDBI	Small Industries Development Bank of India
SEBI	Securities and Exchange Board of India
SERC	Science and Engineering Research Council
SINE	Society for Innovation and Entrepreneurship
SME	Small and Medium Enterprises
SMERA	SME Rating Agency
SPA	School of Planning and Architecture
SPV	Special Purpose Vehicle
STEP	Science and Technology Entrepreneurship Park
TAN	Tax Account Number
TDB	Technology Development Board
TeNeT	The Telecommunications and Computer Networking Group
TePP	Technopreneur Promotion Programme
TIDE	Technology Incubation Development of Entrepreneurs
TiE	The Indus Entrepreneurs
VAT	Value Added Tax
VC	Venture Capital
VET	Vocational Education and Training

IV

Applications

24 Traditional Health Systems

The current global health sector trends suggest that medical pluralism, to which Indian traditional medical systems can contribute critical components, will shape the future of health care. This shift from singularity to plurality is taking place because it is becoming increasingly evident that no single source of health science has the capacity to contribute solutions to all of society's health needs. India has a comparative advantage and can be a world leader in the era of medical pluralism because it has strong foundations in evidence-based biomedical sciences as well as an immensely rich and complex indigenous medical heritage of its own. The Government has already undertaken and encouraged several initiatives in the area of traditional medicine within the country including establishment of the Department of AYUSH in the Ministry of Health and creating support programmes in S&T agencies like CSIR, ICMR, DBT and DST. To accelerate this momentum, the National Knowledge Commission (NKC) consulted extensively with diverse stakeholders within the related fields and also constituted a Working Group of researchers, private sector representatives and policy makers. NKC recommendations on strategies to promote the knowledge systems of traditional medicine are as follows:

1. *Transform traditional medicine education:* The quality of and access to education in traditional medicine in the country needs urgent improvement. There are currently 450 poorly endowed colleges (undergraduate and postgraduate) admitting around 25,000 students in the country. These colleges are not training students to play leadership roles in the emerging era of medical pluralism. The major reason for this lacuna is that education in traditional medicine fails to provide the transformational catalysis necessary to link traditional medical system sources to evidence-based approaches. This has led to isolation of such education and lack of its pluralistic integration into mainstream evidence-based medicine education, which is essential if India's traditional medical heritage is to find its rightful place in global medical pluralism.

   It is recommended that efforts be made to introduce evidence-based approaches into the current educational framework, possibly through institutions of the standard of IISc, IITs and AIIMS with commensurate financial outlays.

2. *Strengthen research on traditional health systems:* Investments in research and development of traditional medicine have been sub-critical and fragmented resulting in scarcity of evidence about the efficacy of Traditional Health System (THS). In addition, these efforts have also been frequently characterised by a lack of rigorous evidence-based approaches. There has also been little appreciation of the role that social science research must play in comprehending the variety of societal perceptions and responses so critical to ideas of medical pluralism. There is a need to urgently establish a network of world-class research programmes in different parts of the country to address these lacunae, with appropriate institutional and incentive structures. It is essential for India to make original, rigorously evidence-based contributions to the world of medicine in fields such as pharmacogenomics, immunology, drug discovery and cardiology via imaginative examination of traditional ideas such as *prakriti*, *rasayana* or *rasa*.

3. *Strengthen pharmacopoeial standards:* Despite extensive documentation of medicinal plants, there is a strong need for creating internationally acceptable pharmacopoeias for herbal medications, as well as eco-system specific, regional pharmacopoeias for various bio-geographic regions of India.

4. *Increase quality and quantity of clinical trials and certification:* Promotion of traditional medicine goes hand-in-hand with increase in the quality of rigorous, yet sensitively designed clinical trials to support or refute traditional medical claims of efficacy. Also, lack of information on toxicological data/safety studies makes it difficult to evaluate the risk profile of

traditional medications. There is a need for greater institutional enabling of such evaluations and trials. These should be accompanied by a world-class certification process, which will assist the achievement of internationally acceptable standards for good manufacturing, laboratory, clinical, agricultural and collection practices. The pre-clinical and clinical efficacy validation and standardisation of 10 best THS products for global market should be supported as a flagship project. Similarly, technological upgradation of the manufacturing units involved in manufacture of these successful products to international standards must be carried out.

5. *Digitise traditional knowledge:* The work underway for creating a comprehensive Traditional Knowledge Digital Library (TKDL) should be diversified and expanded. A major programme should be established for digitisation of India's medical manuscripts (located both within India and abroad) and for making this digital library accessible to teaching and research institutions in India. To modernise data-mining from the vast corpus of traditional medical literature, an all-India coordinated 'Traditional Knowledge Informatics Programme' should be constructed to create a comprehensive list of available plant material-medica (2,000 species), their products (40,000 formulations) and clinical applications (5,000 conditions).

6. *Create suitable framework of intellectual property rights*: Emphasis should be put on creating suitable intellectual property rights framework in the country for protection of the sources of traditional medical knowledge. At the same time sufficient incentives should be created for commercialisation of traditional medications. Steps should be taken for the use and incorporation of TKDL, with all pertinent sources of information, into the minimum search documentation lists of International Search Authorities and other patent offices while processing patent applications. Lack of clarity regarding the 'ownership' issue for traditional knowledge must be addressed in the TKDL. This is especially pressing since underprivileged communities are commonly the primary sources of such knowledge. The need is to create IPR systems that ensure that such knowledge remains in the public domain and is "protected" for the communities of origin through mechanisms such as Geographical Indicators (GIs). An approach to the commercial dissemination of traditional medications will be to allow companies to access TKDL upon payment of adequate user fees and subject to the condition that invention arising out of the TKDL would require royalty sharing. Both user fees and royalty must be shared between government and the communities identified as the sources of the knowledge, and innovative modalities will need to be found to administer such distribution. The revenue generated by the government from commercialisation of TKDL and other commercially synergistic initiatives should be used to create a 'Traditional Knowledge Development Fund' and its proceeds should be used for conservation, evidence-based analysis and research on traditional knowledge and for the benefit of communities that have contributed to the creation of traditional knowledge.

7. *Establish goals for conservation of natural resources:* Natural populations of around 12 per cent of the 6000 species of potentially medicinal plants are currently estimated to be under threat due to degradation and loss of habitats alongside unsustainable ways of harvesting and lack of cultivation. The problem of growing scarcity also leads to the danger of more counterfeit material being marketed. It is therefore necessary to support conservation and sustainable harvesting efforts in the forestry sector and cultivation in the agricultural sector. Direct support for conservation and cultivation as well as indirect methods through incentive policies should be pursued for nurturing these plant resources. The wild gene pool of India's medicinal plants should be secured, via establishment of a nationwide network of 300 "Forest Gene Banks" across the 10 bio-geographic regions of the country.

8. *Support non-government and corporate initiatives for promotion of THS:* The non-government and private sector have played an important role in building the public image of traditional health sciences. Non-governmental research and education institutions, NGOs and corporates with a global vision must be strategically supported in the interest of enhancing national and international awareness of India's rich health system heritage.

9. *Promote international cooperation:* International cooperation in exploration of traditional health systems must be given a big boost through substantial initiatives like strategic research collaborations with reputed research centres and establishing wellness centres in countries that offer promising market opportunities. EXIM bank of India must be supported to work with industry to open world markets for these products and services.

10. *Support primary health care in rural areas:* With 70 per cent of the Indian population relying on traditional medicine for primary health care in the absence of adequate state primary health care, it becomes necessary to establish evidence-based guidelines for this informal-sector usage. A nationwide network of Home Herbal Garden and Community Herbal Gardens

(CHG) can be created to support the primary health care needs of rural communities for those plants and medications established as efficacious by evidence-based research.

11. *Create a major re-branding exercise of Indian traditional medicine:* Better branding of Indian traditional medicines proven to be effective in well-designed clinical trials can increase safe and effective health care options. Such proven medications should be integrated with the national health care system. Such evidence-based, well-validated and uniquely Indian holistic health care system combinations must be marketed extensively globally.

    In order to achieve these goals as rapidly and efficiently as possible, the Government of India may consider establishing a National Mission on Traditional Health Knowledge (NMTHK), which would take up these tasks in an organised way. It should be a relatively small body in terms of its own infrastructure with powers to enable it to recommend targeted funding in identified areas. It should support initiatives at many different levels, including state and local levels, and coordinate with Ministries of Health, Science & Technology, Forestry, Agriculture and Commerce as well as with the NGOs and private sector. The Mission leader must be a person with high public credibility, have extensive knowledge and experience in the field with established managerial capabilities and experience of dealing with all the concerned stakeholders.

25 Agriculture

The National Knowledge Commission is seriously concerned about deep crisis in Indian agriculture which has been in the making for some time. There are several dimensions of this problem. The proportion of the population employed in agriculture is as much as 52 per cent, yet agriculture contributes just 18.5 per cent to the national GDP. Thus, per capita GDP and average living standards in agriculture are significantly lower than in the non-agriculture sector. Growth in terms of yield per hectare and employment creation has also slowed down in the sector and per capita availability of food grains has shown no discernible increase for more than three decades. The recent suicides of farmers are symptoms of a much deeper malaise. Thus, in order to transform India into a knowledge economy, it is imperative that we focus on agriculture on a priority basis. In this regard NKC believes that appropriate application of knowledge in agriculture can play a major role in boosting the agrarian economy and giving the Indian farmer a competitive edge in the global market.

We note that various commissions and working groups set up by the Government of India at different times have made a number of important and extremely useful recommendations. Yet it is a matter of concern that most of these recommendations have not been implemented. We urge you to consider these recommendations for speedy implementation. In addition, we would like to make some further recommendations, based on discussions with a variety of stakeholders representing agricultural scientists, managers of extension services, independent analysts and representatives of farmers' organisations and of companies linked with commercial farming. We recommend the following concrete steps for the revitalisation of knowledge generation and application in agriculture:

A. Knowledge Generation

1. Modernise and stimulate agricultural research institutions, coordinate research and make research support more flexible.
   - Each State Agricultural University (SAU) and Indian Council of Agricultural Research (ICAR) institute should create a research policy unit comprising core faculty and also including other issue-based stakeholders.
   - Based on the research policy and programmes, expected research output and linkages to extension and other stakeholders, each SAU and ICAR institute must put forward a set of valuation indicators, to be used for periodic assessment and public scrutiny.
   - Both the ICAR and SAU should assign about 50 per cent of their total research resources (largely Plan funds) to support a competitive grants system, with its deployment focused on priority multi-disciplinary and regional research areas.
   - Priority problem-oriented research in a competitive funding mode should be promoted, for example by identifying a group of scientists reputed for excellence in an area and encouraging them to form a coalition to work on specific problems in mission mode, with required funding support.
   - Regional coordination units should be initiated under the umbrella of the SAUs, and should include representatives of ICAR, relevant line departments, Agricultural Technology Management Agency (ATMA), rural credit agencies, cooperatives, private sector, farmers' organisations and key civil society organisations falling within the particular region.

- Decentralisation of research management and authority and distribution of accountability at different levels in the ICAR and SAUs are required. Scientists and research teams should be empowered to function in this decentralised system, with administrative and financial support. This will require the amendment of the Model Act (1966) and University Acts binding all SAUs, and a change in the legal status of the ICAR to grant full administrative and financial autonomy with enhanced funding.
- There should be emphasis on ensuring research relevant to farmers' needs, by encouraging and institutionalising greater interaction between research and extension personnel and providing feedback mechanisms for farmers.

2. Improve the organisation of agricultural research.
   - The Research Project File (RPF) system in ICAR institutes has fossilised and does not assist the conduct or management of relevant research. The lab/project file must be made mandatory in SAUs and ICAR institutes and computerised on a priority basis, preferably by 2009-10. This will enable the creation of a research database within the organisation and at the national level.
   - Based on this lab/project file system, there should be an annual scientific audit of each programme/project.
3. Direct more research to neglected areas.
   - Much more research activity is required for enhancing productivity in rain-fed agriculture and the cultivation of traditional staples.
   - Research into improvements in post-harvest technology and storage patterns should be promoted with special funds allocation.
   - The possibilities and problems associated with *jhum* cultivation must be addressed.
   - Agriculture and rural livelihoods in the northeastern region deserve very special attention, including with the establishment of a sub-cadre of agricultural graduates well trained to meet local R&D needs.
   - While water management has been and remains a major area of agricultural research, there is need for more locally specific result-oriented research to develop techniques that can be easily applied by farmers.
   - More research is also required to address the mitigation of, and adaptation to, climate change.
4. Provide more effective incentives for researchers.
   - Agricultural research should be made attractive as a career option for young scientists through appropriate recruitment and personnel policies, incorporating a flexible system of incentives in career advancement and remuneration.
   - The ICAR and SAUs should promote and recognise quality and relevant scientific output by promoting research publication, establishment and working of patents, technology development and transfer. These should be accompanied by strong disincentives for unethical and fraudulent professional practices.
   - In order to promote team-based research, a system of equitable incentives for the leader and the members of the team should be devised.
   - As in the ICAR, the SAUs should introduce sabbatical leave, giving scientists the freedom to choose any laboratory or relevant institution within or outside the country for advanced studies during the sabbatical period with full pay. In addition, lien may be given to those scientists who have developed a technology area (including a patent) with high public interest value, to work on such development in their own capacity, in case the technology is not being developed by other parties.
5. Change the curricula in agricultural universities to ensure greater relevance.
   - Curricula should be changed with a bottom-up approach to prepare students for careers in agri-businesses and agri-clinics, and to give them new skills in entrepreneurship development, communication skills, computer knowledge, agribusiness, environment science and biotechnology. This requires both the introduction of new courses and major reforms in the examination system.

- With the increasing feminisation of agriculture, it is very important that agricultural curriculum should be engendered by introducing basic courses on gender concerns in agricultural development.
- The system should be able to provide periodic (and more frequent) refresher training for extension workers to upgrade their technical efficiency.
- Non-formal education programmes should be initiated in need-based vocational modules to generate para-professionals for technological and economic empowerment of the rural youth.

6. Exploit the opportunities and meet the challenges of intellectual property rights.
   - Any licencing of IPR enabled technology by public research must be done without in any manner excluding its access by resource-poor farmers.
   - As the holder of thousands of farmers' varieties of plants and animal genetic stocks, the ICAR must immediately enunciate the policy and guidelines on the access to these materials by the private sector and the IPR-related regulations applicable on the genetic material being accessed by these parties.
   - There should be total transparency on all transfer or exchange of genetic material, and clear regulation to prevent private appropriation of farmers' varieties and animal stocks by misusing IPRs within or outside country.
   - The ICAR and SAUs must enunciated must lay down clear guidelines to ensure benefit sharing with farmers who have preserved genetic resources, with respect to themselves and also other commercial parties.
7. Encourage and regulate private agricultural research.
   - While private sector presence is rapidly increasing in biotechnology, critical input services and related areas, the thrust of private activity is on market-driven knowledge and services. Public-private partnerships should be leveraged to benefit resource poor farmers, who tend to have less access and to ensure that private research meets social needs.
   - In the case of biotechnology and its application to crop plants and animals, particularly those in the food and feed chain, research on bio-safety aspects and processes leading to the release of such plant varieties in the environment should assume the highest priority, with transparency and civil society participation.
   - Systems need to be developed to monitor the results of private research so as to avoid the problems associated with conflict of interest.

B. Knowledge Applications

The current system of agricultural extension in the country is based on a linear transfer of technology model, which needs to be made more responsive to local situations and community needs. To improve the scope and efficiency of extension, the focus should shift to providing an integrated range of services, making grass root workers devote more time to location-specific problems and be more accountable to the community.

8. Make knowledge applications in agriculture community-driven and farmer-led.
   - Both *panchayats* and community-based organisations should be treated as platforms for delivery of an integrated range of services from production to post-harvest storage to marketing.
   - New methods of collaboration between scientists and farmers must be institutionalised in order to identity their needs, set priorities in work programmes, test and refine the technologies and evaluate the final results.
9. Redesign the existing support systems.
   - Support systems should move from input-centric model to output-centric models. This requires redesigning the support systems and incentives in the existing centrally sponsored schemes like Rastriya Krishi Vikas Yojana (RKVY), National Rural Employment Guarantee Scheme (NREGS), National Horticulture Mission, National Food Security Mission and National Watershed Programme.

- The scope of the NREGS should be expanded to support small and marginal farmers in the production of food crops like traditional staples such as millets, organic soil management, natural pest management, system of rice intensification (SRI), etc.

10. Document and disseminate successful experiences and good practices.
    - The current extension system is based on technologies generated in the formal research institutions. This completely ignores the successful technologies generated by farmers and civil society organisations, which are based on local knowledge and may be more locally adaptable and with stronger ecological principles.
    - Therefore, special initiatives are required to find and document the successful experiences of farmers in particular areas and encourage their dissemination by the formal institutions and support systems.
11. Improve the capacities and expertise of extension workers.
    - Extension workers must be provided with the necessary resources and facilities to carry out their work effectively, including transport and communication facilities such as two-wheelers and mobile phones where necessary.
    - The present extension staff must be retrained to be able to provide information and assistance not only for agriculture and animal husbandry, fisheries and horticulture but also with respect to methods of storage, transport, market access, value addition, credit, etc.
    - The syllabi in agricultural colleges and agricultural polytechnics must be restructured to prepare a cadre of extension workers who can broaden extension delivery.
    - Institutional arrangements need to be developed to ensure continuing education of those involved in agricultural extension, whether in public institutions or in private capacity.
12. Restructure Agricultural Technology Management Agency (ATMA) to make it more decentralised, participatory and locally responsive.
    - The staff of the various line departments connected with agricultural development (agriculture, horticulture, animal husbandry, dairying, fisheries) should be placed under the control of ATMA at the district level, with technical support, monitoring and quality control provided by the respective departments at the state level.
    - This calls for restructuring the line departments at various levels and the recruitment of a competent and experienced Project Director in each district, with the exclusive function of management of the ATMA.
    - The district level agricultural sector management programmes and plans for ATMA need to be prepared with a bottom-up participatory approach emphasising convergence and based on consultations with all stakeholders at the village level, which can then be consolidated at block and district level.
    - The Department of Marketing, Department of Credit, agricultural universities, KVKs, NGOs, etc., should be partners in the planning process and provide support to the ATMA, in addition to implementing collaborative activities and programmes. The District Collector as the chairperson of the governing board of ATMA can play an important role in ensuring the participation of these partners.
    - The implementation of the district level plans should be through Result Oriented Management (ROM) rather than the target-oriented management approach which is followed at present in ATMA. This process requires that short term management training be provided to all categories of staff and stakeholders engaged in implementation issues.
13. Enhance and regulate the role of private players in agricultural extension delivery.
    - The already large involvement of private agencies in agricultural extension should be recognised and encouraged, and most importantly, integrated with the public provision through some institutionalised mechanisms.
    - At the same time, problems of conflict of interest in private provision must be minimised by appropriate regulation, with broad guidelines and a clear code of conduct.

- The existing multi-agency and multi-media extension strategies need to be coordinated, with some integration and interaction on content between various extension providers such as farm schools, information kiosks, web-based providers, *kisan* call centres, agri-clinics, mass media, etc.
- Contract farming has the potential to benefit small farmers when practiced appropriately, by providing larger scales of operation and assured market and price for the produce. To ensure the positive effects while preventing exploitation of farmers, legislative benchmarking of minimal standards in the conduct and practices of such contracts should be defined by the Central government, leaving flexibility to states for enacting state-specific laws, which could be either *at par* or above the central benchmark.

14. Create a web-enabled knowledge bank on all aspects of agriculture.

    - Such a knowledge bank should strive to include all traditional knowledge that is credible *prima facie* or validated, all modern knowledge generated by research over the years with location-specific features highlighted, and appropriate information on post harvest and value addition aspects.
    - It must also include dynamic data on marketing and market price movements, seasonal agricultural advisories, regional meteorological information, etc.

We believe that these changes are both necessary and desirable in order to encourage the creation and dissemination of useful and relevant knowledge in agriculture.

26 Enhancing Quality of Life

A. Setting up Panchayat Gyan Kendras

The National Knowledge Commission considers it imperative to ensure that the applications of knowledge are used for the well-being of common people, especially in rural areas. Our consultations with a working group of experts involved with grassroots organisations helped identify some workable ideas and existing projects that have potential for scaling up. One of the projects identified for implementation after discussions focused on the need to set up Panchayat Gyan Kendras (PGKs) throughout the country. The findings from this project form the basis for our policy suggestions in this letter.

We believe that it is essential to build capacity in *panchayats* to ensure participatory decision-making and a healthier democracy. Building a system that can tap and develop locally available knowledge resources through *panchayats* is crucial for the efficient implementation of initiatives such as NREGA. Such a system also provides creative outlets for harnessing local knowledge to meet a variety of needs in diverse areas such as health, education, agriculture, forestry, water, etc. On a short term basis, NKC, along with the Mazdoor Kisan Shakti Sangathan (MKSS) and the School for Democracy, Rajasthan, helped set up a PGK in Rajsamand district in Rajasthan to efficiently implement the NREGA and use the systems developed to create a more participatory, transparent and accountable *gram panchayat*. We believe that eventually, if a network of such PGKs is set up across the country, it will help identify, harness and replicate the tremendous human resource and knowledge pool that exists, to improve the quality of life of India's people.

Panchayat Gyan Kendra in Every Block

We recommend that every block in the country should have at least one PGK. The PGK can become a resource centre to demonstrate best practices, evolve local solutions and serve as a training institution. It can also offer an opportunity to bring together elected representatives (including *panchayat* representatives), policy makers and civil society in a creative endeavour of local self-government for efficient delivery of basic services. This system of PGKs can be initiated through the broader platform of a Panchayat Knowledge Mission, for maximum scale, commitment and effect. While it is envisaged that the PGK will eventually develop into a comprehensive resource, it could initially concentrate on areas related to the NREGA. As such, the PGK can immediately address the following issues in the NREGA by building demonstrable systems of people-based implementation:

1. People's Planning: Institutionalisation of proper planning mechanisms requires area-specific processes, evolved after concentrated effort at the local level. The PGK could be required to carry out:
    - An initial review of existing plans and initiation of the peoples planning process.
    - A tentative revised plan for the first year of NREGA works to be prepared in three months.
    - Institutionalising a long-term planning process in a year's time.
2. Worksite Management: The NREGA can work well if there is decentralised accountability at every one of the hundreds of worksites in each district. An efficient worksite management system will change the work culture, involve a new set of educated unemployed youth and bring about skill upgradation in an organised manner. The PGK can serve as the platform for implementation of the following:

- Initial training of NREGA worksite managers ('upgraded mates') in three months.
- Facilitating adequate training and competencies of all worksite managers in the block in one year.
- Institutionalising worksite management systems including systems for training women masons, appropriate worksite facilities, improved tools and certified worksite managers. This would require a period of two years.

3. Computerisation of the *Panchayat* Office: To address efficiency and accountability issues, the PGK can assist in computerising the *panchayat* office. This would involve:
   - Computerisation of NREGA documents in six months.
   - A fully computerised and organised *panchayat* office in 12 months.
   - Institutionalising this process with innovations such as information kiosks at the *panchayat* level, over a period of two years.
4. Use of ICT: Use of ICT innovations for better governance would involve proper record maintenance, enhanced transparency and proactive disclosure, efficient and timely wage payments and facilities for financial inclusion at the *gram panchayat* level. This could also include innovations to reduce the digital gap, by making the PGK a public Internet point of the *panchayat*. To ensure transparency, ICT should also be employed in bank transactions for wages as well as to create bank accounts for NREGA workers. This would provide an important system of checks and balances.

   One such initiative is a live pilot jointly launched by NIC and India Post in the state of Orissa in December 2008. In this pilot, postal agents in villages have been equipped with mobile phones enhanced with unique secure transaction technology, and supported by smart card readers and finger-print sensors, to interact with NREGA workers and securely deliver payments. Near real-time data entry from these terminals to the block level system using mobile data connection ensures minimal latency and enhanced transparency in servicing worker requests. While the first phase of the live pilot is focused on secure delivery of payments to the workers, the larger goal of this exercise is to create "pseudo-bank accounts" for all the participants, which will be hosted by India Post (and any other treasury authorised by the Government of India). A similar pilot project for enabling wage payments through ICT is also under consideration in Rajsamand district in Rajasthan.
5. Disclosure Processes: To ensure transparency in *panchayats*, due mechanisms need to be incorporated including an open office, open inspection and an institutionalised system of proactive disclosure for NREGA, as well as other *panchayat* programmes and functions. For all *panchayat* offices, this would require a year.
6. Social Audit: To further ensure a system of accountability and monitoring, a full social audit of all NREGA works in the *panchayat* needs to be conducted twice a year. This would aim to cover neighbouring *panchayats* and eventually the block within one year.
7. Programmes for Skill Upgradation: Such programmes for NREGA workers in the *gram panchayat* could be evolved based on local skills and local employment opportunities. These could then be institutionalised in a phased manner in the block and district. Locally appropriate and useful labour intensive works could be proposed and tried out, so that they can be included in the list of permissible works under NREGA.
8. Effective Local Designs for Labour Intensive Works to Build Rural Infrastructure: The NREGA is an employment generation programme which requires the use of labour resources on a priority basis. NREGA allows various types of labour intensive works to be carried out—such as water harvesting structures, forestry, roads, etc. To increase efficiency and reduce drudgery, relevant designs have to take into account locally available material, geo-climatic conditions and social factors, including the need to optimally use human resources of the area. This task requires a local centre for innovation and design, which could be facilitated by the PGK. Further, the productive value of these works could be enhanced with appropriate scientific and technical inputs. In a related letter, we have discussed the need for ergonomic tools, especially among workers involved in manual labour tasks.
9. Design of Appropriate Worksite Facilities: The NREGA mandates that all workers be provided with clean drinking water, shade, crèche facilities for small children and first-aid facilities at the worksite. This is crucial to ensure dignity of labour

and to make the worksite a safe working environment. This task also requires an appropriate set of local designs for management as well as the means of delivering these facilities.

10. Convergence of Different Social Sector Programmes: Finally, the NREGA offers huge potential for facilitating convergence of different social sector programmes as it brings together rural labour at one place. This can enable a number of empowerment and awareness generating efforts in health, education, workers rights and understanding of democratic processes. The PGK could function as a platform for organising *melas*, workshops and training, which not only deal with the NREGA but also enhance participatory processes in all social sector programmes in the *panchayat*. The PGK could thus play a critical role in creating a well-informed citizenry.

11. Establishing a Panchayat Knowledge Mission: The knowledge gathered and generated, and the lessons learnt in different parts of the country in the PGKs need to be brought together on one platform so that a cross fertilisation of ideas can take place. Also, there is a need for national resource centres, to provide technical and appropriate support to help PGKs carry out their objectives and overcome challenges through creativity and innovation. Such an effort would require flexibility and support best provided through a mission approach. The Panchayat Knowledge Mission and its special resource units can enlist technical help and expertise to meet demands for such support from any part of the country.

We believe that building a network of PGKs, backed by ICT and transparency mechanisms will create a wealth of innovative, scalable best practices and qualitatively improve democratic governance in the country.

B. Designing Ergonomic Tools

The National Knowledge Commission considers it imperative to ensure that the applications of knowledge are used for the well-being of common people, especially in rural areas. Our consultations with a working group of experts involved with grassroots organisations helped identify some workable ideas and existing projects that have potential for scaling up. One of the pilot projects selected for implementation after discussions focused on the urgent requirement for ergonomic tools, especially among NREGA workers. This project recognises the enormous skills involved in manual work and aims to give workers tools that will help them carry out their task in a more specific and less physically taxing manner. The findings from this project form the basis for our policy suggestions. In this section, key issues discussed pertain to designing ergonomic tools as a means of improving dignity of labour, encouraging energy efficiency, reducing workloads for women, reducing drudgery, increasing skillful engagement and improving productivity.

MAEER MIT Institute of Design (MITID), Pune in collaboration with Mazdoor Kisan Shakti Sangathan (MKSS), Rajasthan were identified by NKC as 'host institutions' to conceptualise fresh perspectives in tool design. Based on consultations and feedback received, we suggest the following steps to enable a qualitative improvement in general working conditions in occupations involving manual labour:

1. Improve Dignity of Labour: Creating a people-based development process is essential to improve working conditions and ensure dignity of labour. Large-scale government schemes which generate employment opportunities for those involved in manual labour should incorporate necessary processes and incentives for providing appropriate work environment, facilities and ergonomic tools to workers. Dignity of labour will be enhanced if basic facilities for water, shade, first-aid and child-care are also provided at the worksite. Also pertinent here is the need to define appropriate work hours, productivity norms and mechanisms for grievance redressal to address issues of harassment and exploitation.
2. Modernise Tools and Technology: Redesigning low-cost tools for greater efficiency and modernising tool kits needs to take into account India-specific factors such as the geographical and cultural diversity of the country. These factors include land, terrain, clothing, social conditions, traditional practices in tool-use and significantly, specific problems faced by women workers. There is also an urgent need to recognise that the tools currently used are of a very basic nature and involve low appropriate technology, minimum production complexity and local production. Also, these tools are often multi-purpose in nature and therefore unable to deliver efficiency in specialised tasks. For example, it is recognised that digging trenches for irrigation and digging for road development have become very specialised tasks, requiring special energy efficient tools. While traditionally single tools have served the purpose of multiple tasks, there is increasing realisation now on the need to design a variety of specialised tools. The following suggestions will help address such issues:
   - Explore co-creation and a participatory design approach and process;
   - Involve the beneficiaries during testing and validation;
   - Engage social mobilisation mechanisms extensively;
   - Carry out strategic grouping of tools based on functionality and tasks;
   - Articulate strategies and norms for maintenance and up-keep of tools;
   - Identify and analyse areas of mechanised and semi-mechanised tools/equipments, keeping in mind efficiency and employment opportunities;
   - Identify and partner with manufacturing clusters and manufacturers, including small and medium enterprises;
   - Alter the weight of tools keeping needs of women workers in mind. Weight reduction of tools makes the task easier and less intense;
   - To optimise the weight of the tool, bring about changes in the profile as well as the angle of the blade used, specific to the type of operation (e.g., 'angular digging edge' to dig better, 'multiple digging edge', 'dimensioned digging edge' etc.);

- By optimising on materials (e.g., use of medium carbon steel) weight can be reduced while keeping the digging quality unchanged;
- Use mechanical traction devices to enable load carrying from one point to the other (both vertically and horizontally) to overcome drudgery and ensure dignity of labour;
- Provide necessary tools in the form of a 'tool kit' to the beneficiaries as another means of upgrading skills. The tool kits must be available at worksites and carrying them from home to the work place should be discouraged. Such modern tool kits must be evolved for not just field labour but other works such as plumbing, masonry, carpentry and electrification; and
- Aid heavy labour intensive tasks by semi-mechanised or mechanical traction devices to overcome drudgery and increase efficiency. This would also ensure that labour displacing machines do not take away the livelihood of workers.

3. Funding Mechanisms for Development of Tool Kits and Provisions for Loans: To ensure financial and operational sustainability as well as to achieve scale, it is necessary to create appropriate funding mechanisms that catalyse the task of creating relevant R&D. This will also encourage various industrial, academic and research institutions and engage young minds in a critical, if often overlooked part of the development process. From the point of view of the beneficiaries, the incorporation of redesigned tools and related R&D within the structure of an employment scheme (such as NREGA), would facilitate easy access and also encourage R&D providers. Within a programme like the NREGA, there is a need for appropriate designs of tools for women, as well as for those who are physically weak and caught in a vicious cycle of low nutrition and reduced physical efficiency. The proposed Skill Development Mission could also create mechanisms to encourage the redesigning of such tools. Further, in this respect, it is necessary to incentivise private sector producers and importers of low-cost cutting-edge, human dignity-enhancing tools and implements. Incentives such as tax and duty policies favourable to local production as well as low-cost loans for buying such tools should also be considered.
4. Training and Upskilling Manpower: In order to harness the true potential of India's demographic dividend, we have highlighted the urgent need to produce skilled manpower and upgrade human resources. In this respect, as a means of encouraging the use of ergonomic tools and skill development, schemes for lifelong skill upgradation through training programmes must also be available for workers engaged in manual labour. Further, such training must be available locally to enhance access, taking into account context-based technical and planning specifics.
5. Portals and Guilds for Workers: Creating portals and guilds for workers will enable easy access of information on the availability of jobs and also facilitate transactions such as purchase of relevant material and ergonomic tools. In this respect, a key objective of the proposed Skill Development Mission is to develop employment exchanges as outreach points for storing and providing information on employment and skill development as well as enabling them to function as career counselling centres. At the local level, institutions such as the *panchayats* should be involved to manage such portals or kiosks.

We believe that implementation of these suggestions will better the working conditions of people engaged in manual and other tasks in the country. This will also help in heralding a change in mind sets, which is essential to improve human capital and dignity.

V

Services

27 E-governance

After a series of discussions and reviews of various E-governance efforts at the Centre and state levels, NKC formed a special group, under the chairmanship of Nandan Nilekani, to study E-governance. The report of this group was discussed at the Planning Commission and presented to the Minister for Communications and Information Technology. Thereafter, several discussions were held with other stakeholders including the Administrative Reforms Commission. Based on these discussions, NKC is convinced that E-governance is more about an opportunity for administrative reforms than merely about electronics and information technology and infrastructure. NKC's recommendations on E-governance which broadly relate to processes and standards, infrastructure and organisation are as follows:

1. *Government process re-engineering before any computerisation:* At present the E-governance efforts are primarily based on computerising age-old processes left behind by British Raj and compounded by a plethora of new layers and silos by Indian bureaucracy, each working within departmental boundaries and pet priorities. As a result, we are computerising cumbersome processes and hence not commensurately benefiting from it. Simply digitising the existing government processes merely adds an additional layer of expense, complexity, delay and confusion. NKC feels that there is now a unique opportunity in the history of India to leave behind the British Raj and re-engineer and modernise government processes to build a new India of the 21st century. Hence, it is essential to first redesign the government processes keeping the citizen at the centre, providing for the enablement of citizens, businesses, producers and consumers, replacing the old mistrust and control regime of the colonial past. This redesigning of government processes will drastically reduce the numbers and duration of successive steps required to obtain services. It will also provide traceable records, enable enforcement of individual performance, accountability, efficiency and productivity, as well as transparency of policies and processes.
2. *Ten to twenty important processes and services:* To make an immediate impact on citizens, it is critical to identify and simplify important processes and services, say 10 to 20 to begin with, which are currently cumbersome, bureaucratic and prone to unnecessary delays and even corruption. These processes can be simplified and made available as web-based services. Initially, these services could include birth certificate, death certificate, proof of residence and ration/ID cards. Other processes can be added over a period of time. This approach will require each state to implement these processes in concert and learn from each other.
3. *Common standards:* At present, various state governments are choosing their own ways of selectively computerising their processes and provide E-governance. Many of these programmes are vendor-driven and not scalable. It is critical to develop and enforce citizen/business entitlement standards uniformly over all states and central ministries and functions, spanning from voting, taxes, certificates, financial products, law enforcement and welfare for individuals, properties of land, institutions, businesses, etc. These standards should not be hardware-centric and vendor-dependent but should enable easy participation by any state, *panchayat* institution, business, NGO or citizen, whenever they decide. These standards, templates and data formats must be designed carefully by teams of experts drawn from government, IT companies, academia, R&D institutions and users or stakeholders who understand latest trends, technology, software, user interfaces and interoperability requirements. NKC recommends that all state governments follow these standards. At the same time, it is also conscious of the need to incorporate some of the standards followed by state governments.
4. *Best practices and lessons from the past:* A great deal of work has already been done in various central ministries and in state governments. The key is to learn from these and design best practices that are affordable and applicable nationwide to

ensure ease of use and interoperability. NKC notes that the Government's own offices, laboratories and directorates have an immense amount of useful and relevant data (e.g. the seven centres of the National Bureau of Soil Science and Land Use Planning - NBSSLUP), which needs to be digitised and made publicly accessible for use and analysis. Data collected by one agency should be made available across all agencies as well as to the public, subject to national security considerations.

5. *National infrastructure:* It is important to provide secure broadband infrastructure and associated hardware, software and hosting facilities nationwide with easy access at all levels. This infrastructure should be based on a 'user pays' principle, public-private partnership in investments and mutual accountability and efficiency. This infrastructure creation should be led by the Central government to enforce a high level of security, uniformity and standards at every interface, regardless of state language, culture, legacy and financial health.

6. *Web-based services:* To enforce standards and to keep the governance uniformly responsive and transparent, it is recommended that state governments use templates created by the Central government to offer localised data and services in Indian languages. In this model, the private sector can invest in creation of access-infrastructure and building relevant business models for user-fee collection and its sharing across all stakeholders, to ensure sustainability and adaptation for future needs. This also implies that all public institutions will make sure that all public data is available on the web.

7. *Open source software:* Because of the enormous size and scope of the E-governance effort in India and because of the availability of globally recognised software talent of Indians, we must actively encourage open source software implementations and open standards wherever possible. This will allow us to have cost-effective solutions and help develop open software products and standards. It will also help improve scaling up and minimise delays caused by repeat tendering.

8. *Specialist CITO (chief information technology officer):* Each state and major Central government departments must create an empowered chief information technology officer, with relevant expertise and skills in the domain subject and IT usage. These posts must be filled on open recruitment and draw the best and the brightest from India's technologically qualified talent. These officers should be paid market salaries and have a three-year contract with the Government, which can be renewed depending on performance.

9. *New national programmes:* As government plans to spend hundreds of thousands of crores on Bharat Nirman, Rural Employment Guarantee Scheme and urban development initiatives, it is recommended that we mandate that each of these programmes begin with well engineered E-governance implementation and web-interface that ensures speedy delivery, productivity and efficiency. It is recommended to invest one to two per cent of the national programme budget in establishing new processes and associated E-governance infrastructure to improve delivery and reduce leakages.

10. *Focused organisation:* For national E-governance to succeed, it is critical to create an appropriate central organisation with structures that can operate in a mission mode, with full autonomy and accountability. NKC recommends creation of an organisation with a chief executive officer (CEO), with board members drawn from the IT industry and government to redesign processes and procedures, to represent a multiplicity of stakeholders and diversity in domain expertise, and to drive the national E-governance plan with facilitation from the CIT Ministry.

    The task of this organisation shall include but not be limited to:

    a) administrative reforms related to process re-engineering;

    b) providing and maintaining common national ICT infrastructure for E-governance;

    c) providing leadership and framework for implementation, with immediate focus on selected mission mode projects; and

    d) providing a neutral consulting framework and standards for E-governance with the help of CITOs.

There is a need to re-engineer our processes first to change our basic governance pattern for simplicity, transparency, productivity and efficiency, to select 10 to 20 important services that make a critical difference, to offer web-based services, develop common standards and deploy a common platform or infrastructure for E-governance to make it citizen-centric.

As a next step, NKC recommends focusing on the organisational issues related to re-engineering government processes with strong committed leadership, autonomy, flexibility, clarity of purpose, predefined deliverables, measurable milestones and periodic monitoring in order to implement the national E-governance programme within three to five years.

VI

Consultations

Consultations

Members of NKC Working Group on Libraries

Smt. Kalpana Dasgupta (Chairperson)
Former Director, Central Secretariat Library, New Delhi

Dr. S. Arunachalam
Distinguished Fellow, M.S. Swaminathan Research Foundation, Chennai

Mr. K.K. Banerjee
Director, Raja Rammohan Roy Library Foundation, Kolkata

Mr. K. Jayakumar
Joint Secretary, Ministry of Culture, New Delhi

Dr. H.K. Kaul
Founding Director, DELNET, New Delhi

Mr. K.K. Kochukoshy
Librarian, Central Reference Library, Kolkata

Mr. Manoj Kumar K.
Acting Director, INFLIBNET, Ahmedabad

Prof. S. Mandal
Director, National Library, Kolkata

Prof. P.B. Mangla
Former Head of Dept. of Library and Information Science, University of Delhi

Dr. T.A.V. Murthy
Librarian, CIEFL, Hyderabad

Dr. Harsha Parekh
Former Head of Dept. of Library Science and University Librarian, SNDT Women's University, Mumbai

Dr. A.R.D. Prasad
Associate Professor, Documentation Research and Training Centre, Indian Statistical Institute, Bangalore

List of People Consulted by the NKC in relation to Translation and the National Translation Mission

1. Mr. K.P.R. Nair
   Konark Publishers
2. Mr. Keshav Desairaju
   Joint Secretary
   Department of Secondary and Higher Education
   Ministry of HRD
3. Dr. M. Sridhar
   Dept. of English, University of Hyderabad
4. Prof. Alok Bhalla
   Dept. of English
   Central Institute of English and Foreign Languages (C.I.E.F.L)
5. Dr. D.S. Navin
   National Book Trust
6. Prof. G. Uma Maheshwar Rao
   Centre for Applied Linguistics & Translation Studies, CALTS, University of Hyderabad
7. Prof. Vanamala Viswanath
   Dept. of English
   Jnanabharathi
   Bangalore University
8. Dr. Neeti Badwe
   Professor of German
   Department of Foreign Languages
   University of Poona
9. Prof. Harish Trivedi
   Department of English
   Delhi University

10. Prof. Pushpak Bhattacharya,
Professor of Computer Science
Department of Computer Science & Engineering
Indian Institute of Technology, Mumbai

11. Mr. Benny Kurian
National Book Trust

12. Ms. Kamini Mahadevan
Pearson Education India

13. Dr. Sujata Roy
Joint Director
Hindi Medium Implementation Committee
University of Delhi

14. Mr. Abhijit Dutta
Globalisation Specialist
IBM Global Services India Pvt. Ltd.

15. Ms. Geeta Dharmarajan
KATHA

16. Ms. Mini Krishnan
Oxford University Press

17. Prof. Udaya Narayana Singh
Director, Central Institute of Indian Languages

18. Ms. Radhika Menon
Tulika

19. Dr. S.N. Ojha
Visva-Bharati Computer Centre
Santiniketan

20. Mr. Rubin D'Cruz
National Book Trust

21. Prof. Bijay Kumar,
Chairman
CSTT (Commission for Scientific and
Technical Terminology)

22. Mr. N.V. Sathyanarayana
Chairman and Managing Director
Informatics (India) Ltd

23. Dr. Shalini R.Urs
Executive Director
iSIM - International School of Information
Management, University of Mysore

24. Dr. Sukrita P. Kumar

25. Dr. Apoorvanand

26. Dr. Sanjay Sharma
Dept. of History, Delhi University

27. Abhay Dube
Editor, English Language Programme
Centre for the Study of Developing Societies

28. Ravi Kant
Editor, Deevan-E-Sarai, Sarai Programme
Centre for the Study of Developing Societies

29. Arvind Mohan
Ex-Associate Editor
Hindustan Times

30. Dr. Hemant Darbari
Centre for Development of Advanced Computing

31. Mahmood Farooqui
Centre for the Study of Developing Societies

List of People Consulted by the NKC in Relation to National Knowledge Network

1. Mr. Pankaj Agrawala
Joint Secretary, Director of Grievances & Nodal Officer
(RTI), E-Infrastructure/E-Learning, Ministry of
Communication & Information Technology (C&IT)
Government of India

2. Mr. Shailendra Agarwal
Data Networks Circle, Bharat Sanchar Nigam Ltd.
(BSNL)

3. Dr. Alhad G. Apte
Head, Computer Division, Bhabha Atomic Research
Centre (BARC)

4. Mr. N. Arjun
CEO, Bharti Airtel Limited

5. Prof. N. Balakrishnan
Professor, Multimedia, Computational
Electromagnetics, Computer and Network Security,
Natural Language Processing, Indian Institute of
Science, IISc.

6. Mr. Subhash Bhargava
Chairman, VSNL Broadband Ltd.

7. Mr. R. Chandrashekhar
Additional Secretary, Ministry of C& IT
Government of India

8. Dr. R. Chidambaram
Principal Scientific Advisor to the
Government of India

9. Mr. Vipin Dhaundiyal
Head, Government and PSU Business Reliance Infocomm Ltd.

10. Prof. P.S. Dhekney
Visiting Professor and Head Computer Division
Bhabha Atomic Research Centre (BARC)

11. Dr. B.K. Gairola
Director General, National Informatics Centre (NIC)
Government of India

12. Mr. J.R. Gupta
Director (O)
Bharat Sanchar Nigam Limited (BSNL)

13. Mr. Lav Gupta
Corporate Office, Bharat Sanchar Nigam Limited (BSNL)

14. Prof. B.N. Jain
Professor, Computer Networking, Multimedia, Communication Systems
IIT Delhi

15. Mr. Puneet Jhingan
Head, Business Development
Reliance Infocomm Limited

16. Mr. Ashok Jhunjhunwala
Professor, IIT Chennai

17. Dr. H.K. Kaul
Director, DELNET

18. Mr. A. Krishnan
General Manager & Head Business Solutions Group
Bharti Tele-Ventures Limited

19. Mr. Pradeep Kumar
RailTel Corporation of India Ltd.

20. Dr S.N. Ragu Kumar
All India Institute of Medical Sciences (AIIMS)

21. Mr. Sandeep Mathur
President, Tata Indicom Enterprise Business Unit
Videsh Sanchar Nigam Ltd. (VSNL)

22. Dr. K. Madhu Murthy
Advisor, All India Council for Technical Education (AICTE)

23. Mr. Sri Nath
Executive Director
Videsh Sanchar Nigam Ltd. (VSNL)

24. Mr. V. Ponraj
ICT Adviser to President of India, President's Secretariat, Government of India

25. Mr. C.R. Prasad
CMD, Gas Authority of India (GAIL)

26. Mr. Rajshri Purkayastha
Solution Architect, TATA Indicom Enterprise Business Unit

27. Prof. S.V. Raghavan
Professor, Department of Computer Science and Engineering, IIT Chennai

28. Dr. Gulshan Rai
Executive Director, ERNET India, Ministry of Communication and Information Technology(C&IT)
Government of India.

29. Dr. S. Ramakrishnan
Director General, Centre for Development of Advanced Computing (C-DAC)

30. Dr. D.P.S. Seth
Former member, Telecom Regulatory Authority of India (TRAI)

31. Mr. Devinder Singh
Reliance Infocomm Ltd.

32. Dr. Neeraj Sinha
Scientist 'E'
Office of the Principal Scientific Adviser to the Government of India

33. Mr. Rajiv Sinha
Executive Director, RailTel Corporation of India Ltd.

34. Dr. Sitaram
Distinguished Scientist, CC R&D (ECS), DRDO, Ministry of Defence, Government of India

35. Mr. Anil Srivastava
Chief Strategy Advisor, Capital Technology Information Services, Inc U.S.A.

36. Dr. N. Subramanian
Centre for Development of Advanced Computing (C-DAC)

37. Dr. M.S. Swaminathan
Chairman, M.S. Swaminathan Research Foundation

38. Mr. Shilesh Tiwari
RailTel Corporation of India Ltd.

39. Mr. Sharad Trivedi
DGM, Data Networks, BSNL

40. Dr. R.S. Tyagi
Deputy Director, Head Computer Faculty
All India Institute of Medical Sciences, (AIIMS)

41. Mr. T.K. Wali
    GM (Telecom, LD&C)
    M/S Power Grid Authority of India Ltd.

Health Information Network

The following were the members of the Working Group on Health Information Network:

1. Prof. N.K. Ganguly
   Chairman, Indian Council of Medical Research
2. Dr. B.S. Bedi
   Adviser, CDAC & Media Lab Asia,
   Former Senior Director & Head Med. Electronics and Telemedicine
   Dept. of IT, Govt. of India
3. Mr. Partha Chattopadhya
   CD(DRS), Ministry of Health and Family Welfare
4. Dr. Shiban Ganju
   Convener, I HIND
5. Dr. Shiva Kumar
   Member, National Advisory Council
6. Dr. Ramakrishnan
   Director General, C-DAC
7. Prof. K. Srinath Reddy
   President, Public Health Foundation of India
8. Mr. Rajdeep Sahrawat
   Vice President, NASSCOM
9. Mr. Raj Shah
   CEO, Capital Technology Information Services (CTIS)
10. Dr. Y.K. Sharma
    Deputy Director General, NIC

Quality of Life

1. Mr. Bunker Roy
   Barefoot College, Tilonia, Convenor
2. Ms. Renana Jhabwala
   Coordinator and Member, Executive Committee
   Self-Employed Women's Association (SEWA)
   Ahmedabad
3. Mr. Vijay Mahajan
   Basix, Hyderabad
4. Mr. Nikhil Dey
   Mazdoor Kisan Shakti Sangathan
   Rajasthan
5. Mr. Joe Madiath
   Executive Director, Gram Vikas, Orissa
6. Mr. Ashok Khosla
   President, Development Alternatives, Delhi
7. Dr. Mira Shiva
   Coordinator, Initiative for Health Equity & Society
8. Mr. Ashok Chatterjee
   Former Director, National Institute of Design
   Ahmedabad

Members of the Working Group on Legal Education

1. Justice M. Jagannadha Rao
   Chairperson
   Former Judge, Supreme Court of India
   Former Chairperson, Law Commission of India
2. Justice Leila Seth
   Member
   Former Judge, Delhi High Court
   Former Chief Justice, High Court of Himachal Pradesh
3. Prof. N. R. Madhava Menon
   Member
   Former Vice Chancellor, National Law School of India University (NLSIU), Bangalore
   Former Vice Chancellor, West Bengal National University of Juridical Sciences (NUJS) Kolkata
   Former Director, National Judicial Academy, Bhopal
4. Mr. P.P. Rao
   Member
   Senior Advocate, Supreme Court of India
5. Prof. B.S. Chimni
   Member
   Former Vice Chancellor, NUJS, Kolkata
   Professor, Jawaharlal Nehru University, New Delhi
6. Mr. Nishith Desai
   Member
   Managing Partner, Nishith Desai Associates, Mumbai
7. Dr. Mohan Gopal
   Member
   Former Vice Chancellor, NLSIU, Bangalore
   Director, National Judicial Academy, Bhopal

Members of the Working Group on Management Education

The following are the members of the Working Group:

1. Mr. P.M. Sinha (Chairperson)
   Former CEO, Pepsi India
2. Prof. Amitava Bose
   Former Director, IIM Calcutta
3. Prof. Jahar Saha
   Former Director, IIM Ahmedabad
4. Prof. K.R.S. Murthy
   Former Director, IIM Bangalore
5. Dr. Nachiket Mor
   Dy. Managing Director, ICICI Bank, Mumbai
6. Mr. R. Gopalkrishnan
   Executive Director, Tata Sons, Mumbai

Members of the NKC Working Group on Engineering Education

1. Professor M.S. Ananth (Chairman)
   Director, Indian Institute of Technology, Madras
2. Professor Anil Marathe
   Indian Institute of Technology, Bombay
3. Professor Ashok Thakur
   Vice Chancellor, West Bengal Technical University
4. Professor Gokhale
   Director, National Institute of Technology, Nagpur
5. Professor S.N. Maheshwari
   Indian Institute of Technology, Delhi
6. Professor N. Satyamurthy
   Indian Institute of Technology, Kanpur
7. Professor Vijay Gupta
   Vice-Chancellor, Lovely Professional University
8. Dr. M.P. Ravindra
   Vice President, Education, Infosys, Bangalore
9. Dr. Y.S. Rajan
   Principal Adviser, Confederation of Indian Industries
10. Dr. Sandhya Chintala representing Dr. Kiran Karnik
    Chairman, NASSCOM
11. Mr. Baba Kalyani
    Chairman and MD, Bharat Forge

Special Invitees:

1. Prof. M.V. Krishnamurthy
   Director (Academic Research), VIT University
2. Prof. H.P. Khincha
   Vice-Chancellor, Visvesarya Technology University

Members of the Working Group on Open and Distance Education

1. Prof. Ram Takwale(Chairman)
   Former Vice-Chancellor, Indira Gandhi National Open University, Yashwantrao Chavan Maharashtra Open University
2. Prof Badrinath Koul
   Former Pro-Vice-Chancellor, IGNOU
3. Prof. Salil Mishra
   Reader of History, School of Social Sciences, IGNOU
4. Prof. Parvin Sinclair
   Director, School of Sciences, IGNOU
5. Dr. Vijay Kumar
   Assistant Provost and Director of Academic Computing, MIT
6. Prof. V.S. Prasad
   Director, National Assessment and Accreditation Council (NAAC), Bangalore, Former Vice-Chancellor, Dr. B.R. Ambedkar Open University, Hyderabad
7. Dr. B.S. Bhatia
   Former Director, Development and Education Computing Unit (DECU) Space Applications Centre (SAC), Ahmedabad
8. Mr. Rajendra Pawar
   Chairman, NIIT
9. Dr. Surabhi Banerjee
   Vice Chancellor, Netaji Subhas Open University (NSOU), Kolkata

NKC Consultations on School Education

National Workshops

National Seminar on School Education at NKC, New Delhi 29th July 2006

1. Prof. R Govinda
   Head, School and Non-formal Education Unit, National Institute of Educational Planning and Administration (NIEPA)

2. Dr. Vimla Ramachandran
3. Mr. Vinod Raina
   Hoshangabad Science Teaching Program
4. Parth Shah
   Centre for Civil Society
5. Dr. Madan M. Jha
   Secretary, Dept. of Human Resource Development
6. Dr. Vasanthi V. Devi
   Kalvi Alliance for Education, Tamil Nadu
7. Dr. V.P. Niranjanaradhya
   Senior Research Officer, Centre for Child and the Law
   National Law School of India University
8. Ms. Madhu Prasad
   Reader, Dept. of Philosophy, Zakir Husain College
   Delhi University
9. Ambarish Rai
   People's Campaign for Common School System
10. Dinesh Abrol
    NISTADS, India
11. Subhash Kuntia
    Joint Secretary, Dept. of School Education and Literacy
    MHRD
12. Champak Chaterjee
    JT Secretary, MHRD
13. Manju Bharatram
    Principal, Shri Ram School
14. Anita Rampal
    Department of Education, Delhi University
15. Vrinda Swaroop
    Joint Secretary, MHRD

National Seminar on School Education at NKC, New Delhi 20th November 2007

1. Ms. Shikha Pal
   Deepalaya Foundation
2. Ms. Monideepa Ray Choudhary
   Deepalaya Foundation
3. Mr. Mani
   Education Officer, CBSE
4. Sh. Sandeep Pandey
   Co- Founder, ASHA for Education
5. Prof. R. Govinda
   NUEPA
6. Ms. Puja Sondhi
   Teach for America
7. Ms. Mamta Saihia
   Bharti Foundation
8. Prof. James Tooley
   President, The Education Fund
9. Smt. Kumud Bansal
   Secretary (retd.), Elementary Education and Literacy
   Govt. of India
10. Prof. Shyam Menon
    Delhi University
11. Ms. Annie Koshi
    Principal, St Mary's School
12. Smt. Lata Vaidyanathan
    Principal, Modern School, BK
13. Mr. Dhir Jhingran
    Room to Read
14. Prof. Pratap Bhanu Mehta
    Centre for Policy Research
15. Mr. K. B. Kain
    Principal, Delhi Public School, Jaipur
16. Dr. Madhav Chavan
    PRATHAM
17. Prof. Krishna Kumar
    Director, NCERT

Regional Workshops

Southern Region at National Institute of Advances Studies, Bangalore, 17th-18th July 2007

1. Prof. A.R. Vasavi (Nodal Convener),
   National Institute of Advanced Studies (NIAS)
2. Sh. D.R. Garg, IAS
   Secretary, Sarva Shiksha Abhiyan, Andhra Pradesh
3. Mr. Rao
   Rishi Valley Rural Schools
4. Sh. Vijay Bhaskar
   Secretary, Primary and Secondary Education, Karnataka
5. Prof. P.R. Panchamukhi
   Founder-Director, Centre for Multi-Disciplinary
   Development Research, Dharwad
6. Ms. Benazir Baig
   Raza Education and Social Welfare Society

7. Mr. Samiullah
   Raza Education and Social Welfare Society and General Secretary, Federation of Karnataka Muslims' Association
8. Father Claude D'Souza
   St. Joseph's College of Arts and Science
9. Dr. Padma Sarangapani
   DQEP, NIAS
10. Dr. Sonali Nag
    The Promise Foundation
11. Ms. Mythili Ramachandra
    Rishi Valley Foundation
12. Kamal Peter
    Oracle Education Initiative
13. Sister Cecilia D' Souza
    Maria Krupa, Provincial Head, Mysore
14. Ms. Mamatha M.R.
    Swami Vivekananda Youth Movement (SVYM)
15. Ms. Malathi
    SVYM
16. Mr. M.P. Vijayakumar
    State project Director, Sarva Shiksha Abhiyan
17. Ms. Lakshmi
    Principal, Olcott Memorial High School
18. Mr. Muralidharan
    Founder-President, Sevalaya
19. Dr. Aruna Ratnam
    Project Officer, Education, UNICEF
20. Mr. Balaji Sampath
    Tamil Nadu Science Forum
21. Mr. S.M. Arasu
    Prime Educational and Social Trust
22. Mr. Desigan
23. Mr. K.T. Radhakrishna
    Kerala Sahitya Shastra Parishad
24. Dr. Ajit Kumar
    Director, Centre for Socio-Economic and Environmental Studies (CSES)
25. Dr. K.M. Unnikrishnan
    Senior Lecturer, DIET Kasaragod
26. Mr. C. Madhusudhanan
27. Ms. K. Latha
    NIAS

Central Region at IIM Lucknow, 3rd and 4th August 2007

1. Dr. M.M. Jha (Nodal Convener)
   Principal Secretary, Department of Education
   Govt. of Bihar
2. Sh. Raghuvansh Kumar
   Director, Bihar School Education Board
3. Sh. Ajit Kumar,
   Deputy Director, Secondary Education, HRD Bihar
4. Dr. P.P. Ghosh
   Director, Asian Development Research Institute (ADRI), Patna
5. Smt Abha Rani,
   Bihar Education Project Council
6. Sh. Mahendra Sahni,
   General Secretary, Teachers Association, Bihar
7. Sh. Kedar Nath Pandey,
   General Secretary, Bihar State Secondary Teachers Association
8. Smt. Bilkas Jahan,
   Principal, Govt. Secondary School, Bankipur, Patna
9. Sh. Bisheshwar Yadav,
   Principal, Govt. Secondary School, Gardhanibagh Patna
10. Sh. Satrughan Pd. Singh,
    Chairman, Bihar State Secondary Teachers Association
11. Sh. Jagdish Pandey (Thakurai),
    Chairman, Uttar Pradesh Secondary Teachers Association
12. Job Zachariah
    Education Specialist, UNICEF, Patna
13. Mr. Bhushan Kumar
    PRATHAM, Nawada, Bihar
14. Sr. Sudha Vargheese
    NariGunjan, Patna
15. Mr. Vinay Kanth
    East and West Foundation
16. Mr. Sanjib Kundu
    PRATHAM
17. J.B. Tubid
    Secretary, HRD, Jharkhand

18. Sh. Rabindra Singh
General Secretary, Jharkhand Secondary Teachers Association, Ranchi
19. Smt. Poonam Kumari,
Principal, DIET, Ratu, Ranchi
20. Sh. S.S. Pradhan
Asst. Programme Officer
Jharkhand Education Project, Ranchi
21. Sh. S.B. Kundu,
Teacher, Middle School, Ghaghra Khunti, Ranchi
22. Sh. Kritwas Kumar
Teacher, E.L.T.I. Ratu DIET Campus, Ranchi
23. Mr. H.K. Jaiswal
PRATHAM, Jharkhand
24. Dr. Yoginder Sikand
Professor, Jamia Milia Islamia University
25. Mr. Manoj Kumar
Principal Secretary Primary Education, Jharkhand
26. Ms. Shruti Nag
PRATHAM
27. Sh. Abhimanyu Tewari
President, Uttar Pradesh Prathmik Shikshak Sangh
28. Dr. Veena Gupta
Moradabad, UP
29. Mr. Vinobha
UNICEF, Project Director
30. Ms. Mira Kumari
PRATHAM
31. Mr. Smitin Brid
PRATHAM
32. Mr. Amit Bajpai
PRATHAM
33. Dr. Mishra
Directorate of Education, M.P.
34. Dr. Manohar
Commissioner, Rajeev Gandhi Shiksha Mission, M.P.
35. Dr. Vinod Raina
Eklavya Foundation
36. Sh. S.S. Pachpor
Director, MP Open School
37. Smt. Uma Sri
UNICEF
38. Mr. K.L. Shejwar
Block Resource Coordinator, Gohad Block
39. Mr. Sajaan Singh Shekhawat
PRATHAM
40. Mr. Shutanshu Shukla
Rajya Shiksha Kendra, Madhya Pradhesh

Eastern Region at Indian Council of Social Science Research Kolkata, 25th and 26th August 2007

1. Ms. Nandita Chatterjee, IAS
Principal Secretary, School Education, West Bengal
2. Mr. Dibyen Mukherjee
Director, School Education, West Bengal
3. Mr. Manik Chandra Dolui
Joint Director, Department of School Education, School Education, West Bengal
4. Dr. Rathindranath De
Director, SCERT, West Bengal
5. Mr. Tushyant Nariala
State Project Director, Sarva Shiksha Abhiyan, District Primary Education Program, West Bengal
6. Ms. Sampa Basu
Department of Development and Planning, West Bengal
7. Mr. Tapas Kumar Layek
West Bengal Board of Madrassa Education
8. Mr. M. Fazlur Raldai
Secretary, Board of Madrassa Education, West Bengal
9. Mr. Udayan Bhowmik
District Inspector, Department of Secondary Education, Howrah
10. Dr. R.C. Chattopadhya
Professor, IIM Kolkata
11. Ms. Preeti Mondol
School Teacher (Retd.), Barasat District
North 24 Pargana
12. Ms. Bhupali Ray
Headmistress, Suniti Academy, Cooch Behar
13. Mr. Gopa Dutta
President, West Bengal Council of Higher Secondary Education
14. Mr. Ujjwal Basu
President, West Bengal Board of Secondary Education
15. Mr. Kumar Rana
Senior Research Associate, Pratichi Research Trust
Kolkata

16. Dr. Manabi Majumdar
    Professor, Centre for Studies in Social Sciences, Kolkata
17. Dr. Achin Chakravarty
    Professor, Institute of Development Studies, Kolkata
18. Dr. Malini Bhattacharya
    Professor, Institute of Development Studies, Kolkata
19. Ms. Sandhya Das
    Principal, DIET Joynagar, 24 Parganas (South)
    West Bengal
20. Mr. Somnath Roy
    Principal, DIET Baraguli, Nadia District
    West Bengal
21. Mr. Shiv Prasad Mukhopadhyay
    General Secretary, All Bengal Teacher's Association
22. Mr. Ranju Gopal Mukherjee
    Vice-Chancellor, (Retd.) North Bengal University
23. Mr. Bhabesh Moitra
    Principal, Teacher's Education College, Kolkata
24. Mr. J.B. Dutta
    Consultant, Shishu Shiksha Kendra, Kolkata
25. Mr. Pranab Chanda
    Principal, College for Teacher Education, Siliguri
26. Mr. Pranab.K. Chaudhary
    David Hare Training College, Kolkata
27. Mr. Debashis Maiti
    Secretary, West Bengal Council of Rabindra Open
    Schooling, Kolkata
28. Mr. Dev Kumar Chakrabarty
    Shishu Shiksha Mission, Sidhu-Kanu Bhawan, Kolkata
29. Mr. Sujit Sinha
    Swanirbhar, NGO, West Bengal
30. Dr. Arijit Chaudhry
    Honourary Visiting Professor, Indian Statistical
    Institute
31. Mr. Baidynath Mukherjee
    President, All Bengal Teachers' Association
32. Dr. S. Bhattacharya
    President, West Bengal Board of Primary Education
33. Dr. P. Bhattacharya
    Professor, Center for Studies in Social Sciences, Kolkata
34. Dr. Sudipta Bhattacharyya
    Reader, Department of Economics and Politics
    Visva Bharati Univerisity
35. Dr. Parthapritam Pal
    Professor, IIM Calcutta
36. Dr. Niladri Saha
    Senior Lecturer, Barisat College
    24 Parganas, West Bengal
37. Dr. Samir Guha Roy
    (Ex) Professor, Indian Statistical Institute
38. Mr. Suresh Patnaik
    Secretary, School Education, Orissa
39. Mr. D.C. Mishra
    Director, Secondary Education, Orissa
40. Mr. Sebak Tripathy
    Director, State Institute of Education and Training and
    SCERT, Orissa.
41. Dr. P.K. Acharya
    Reader, Department of Social Anthropology, NKC
    Centre for Development Studies, Bhubaneswar
42. Mr. D.K. Singh
    State Project Director, Sarva Shiksha Abhiyan, Orissa
43. Dr. M.K. Pathy
    Principal, P.M. Institute of Advanced Studies in
    Education, Sambalpur, Orissa
44. Dr. U.C. Khadanga
    Dr. P.M. Institute of Advanced Studies in Education,
    Sambalpur, Orissa
45. Mr. Anil Pradhan
    Member-Secretary, Sikshasandhan, Bhubaneswar
46. Dr. Uddhab C. Nayak
    Agragamee, District Rayagada, Bhubaneswar
47. Mr. Akhileswar Mishra
    Headmaster, D.M. School, Bhubaneswar
48. Dr. Madan Mohan Jha
    Principal Secretary, Education, Govt. of Bihar
49. Dr. A.R. Vasavi
    Professor, National Institute of Advanced Studies
50. Mr. A.K. Behara
    Joint Director, OPEPA
51. Dr. G.C. Nanda
    Additional Directory (Pedagogy), Orissa Primary
    Education Programme Authority (OPEPA)
52. Dr. M.K. Mishra
    State Tribal Coordinator, OPEPA

53. Mr. G.C. Mishra
DI of schools, Jeypore, Koratput, Orissa

54. Mr. B.K. Ghosh
DI of schools, Birapada, Mayurbhanj, Orissa

55. Dr. Adikanda Mahanta
SI of schools, Chitrada, Baripada, Orissa

56. Dr. Minakshi Panda
Teacher Educator, DIET, Khurda, Orissa

57. Dr. Susandhya Mag
Teacher Educator, DIET, Dhenkanal, Orissa

58. Dr. P.P. Mahato
Chairman, Anthropology Research Committee
Bhubaneswar

North-East Region at Indian Institute of Technology, Guwahati
10th and 11th September 2007

1. Prof. J.B. Baruah
Nodal Convener, Dept. of Chemistry, IIT Guwahati

2. Mr. Prateek Hajela
Mission Director, Sarva Shiksha Abhiyan (SSA), Assam

3. Mr. Abdul Wahab
Lecturer, District Institute of Educational Training (DIET), Kamrup

4. Mr. Ashok Mutum
PRATHAM, Assam

5. Smt. Juriti Borgohain
Banikanta College of Teacher Education, Assam

6. Mr. Ramen Sharma
G.U. Model H.E. School, Assam

7. Mr. Ajit K. Choudhury
SSA, Assam

8. Mr. Kandarpa Kalita
SSA, Assam

9. Ms. R. Laskar
SSA, Assam

10. Ms. Shahnaz Deka
GBN Academy

11. Fr. V.M. Thomas
Don Bosco Institute (DBI), Guwahati

12. Sr. Elizabeth George
DBI, Guwahati

13. Dr. A. Basu
HSS, Guwahati

14. Mr. C. Sonowal
Teacher, Kendriya Vidyalaya, Khanapara

15. Prof. N. Bhagwati

16. Ms. L. Sangma
Secretary, Education, Meghalaya

17. Sh. P.K. Hajong
Inspector of Schools, South Garo and West Garo Hills, Meghalaya

18. Ms. A Kynjing
Senior Lecturer, DERT, Shillong

19. Mr. K.J. Lohe
Joint Director, School Education, Nagaland

20. Mr. K.Z. Mero
Chairperson, Village Education Committee, Chizami

21. Dr. Benjongkumba
Lecturer, Zunheboto Govt. College

22. Ms. Seno Tsuhah
Govt, Primary School and North East Network Coordinator

23. Mr. J.H. Biakmawia
Principal, KM H/SS, Mizoram

24. Ms. H. Zirkungi
SCERT, Mizoram

25. Mr. Lalhmachhunana
Young Mizo Association

26. Mr. H. Lalsawmliana
Young Mizo Association

27. Prof. Lianzela
Mizoram University

28. Mr. C. Laremruata
Mizoram Educational Foundation

29. Mr. R.K. Sukumar
State project Director, SSA, Manipur

30. Mr. M. Harekrishna
Director, Education (Schools), Manipur

31. Mr. V. Tonsing
High School Principal, Manipur

32. Ms. Grace Jajo
Fraternal Green Cross Volunteers for Village Development (FGCVVD), Manipur

33. Mr. N. Dhiren Singh
Principal, Jawahar Navodaya Vidyalaya, Imphal

34. Mr. P.D. Rai
Educational Development Trust of Sikkim

35. Fr. George A. D'Souza
Principal, Namchi Public School, Sikkim

36. Mr. K.N. Subudhi
Deputy Director, VE (Coord.), Human Resource Development Department (HRDD), Sikkim

37. Mr. B. Bagdas
Joint Director, PME, HRDD, Sikkim

38. Ms. Anamika Debarma
Headmistress, Higher Secondary, Jirania, Tripura

39. Mr. N. Sinha
Lecturer, SCERT, Tripura

40. Mr. L.C. Das
Headmaster, Higher Secondary, Udaypur, Tripura

41. Ms. A. Deb Burman
Tripura Adibashi Mahila Samiti

42. Mr. M. Rina
Deputy Director, School Education, Arunachal Pradesh

43. Mr. B.P. Sinha
Principal, DIET, Roing, Arunachal Pradesh

44. Ms. Labi Lombi
Arunachal Citizens' Rights (ACR)

45. Mr. Ashok Tajo
Deputy Director, SSA, Arunachal Pradesh

46. Mr. Binoy Boruah
Teacher, Govt. School University Campus, Rono Hills Arunachal Pradesh

47. Mr. G. Tachang
Block Resource Centre Coordinator, Mengio Arunachal Pradesh

Northern Region at India Habitat Centre, Delhi
20th November 2007

1. Mr. Mohammad Rafi
Director of Education, Srinagar

2. Prof. Neeraj Sharma
Pratham, Jammu Education Movement

3. Dr. Renu Nanda
Assistant Director, Centre for Adult and Continuing Education, Jammu University

4. Prof. Bashir Ahmed Dar
Srinagar

5. Mr. Ramzan
Teacher and Teacher Trainer, Jammu

6. Prof. Jagdish Sharma
Jammu

7. Prof. G.N. Masoodi
Srinagar

8. Dr. M.K. Bhandary
Deputy Commissioner, Leh

9. Sh. Krishna Kumar, IAS
State Project Director, SSA, Punjab

10. Dr. Malviner Ahuja
Reader, Punjab University

11. Mr. Kulwarn Singh
DIET Ajjowal, Punjab

12. Sh. Ramesh Dutt
Lecturer in English, Govt. Girls Senior Secondary School, Khanna

13. Sh. Devinderpal Singh Dhillon
DEO, Amritsar

14. Ms. Kalpna Rashmi
SSA, Haryana

15. Mr. Vivek Sharma
PRATHAM

16. Dr. Dinesh Sharma
Block Education Officer, Haryana

17. Smt. Kalpna Singh
Principal, Govt. Senior Secondary, Haryana

18. Sh. Rajpal
Headmaster, Govt. High School, Haryana

19. Sh. Suraj Prakash
Teacher, Primary School, Haryana

20. Sh. Satya Dev Prakash
DIET Palwal, Haryana

21. Dr. Yogesh Vasistha
SCERT, Gurgaon, Haryana

22. Sh. Rajedev Singh
DIET Mattarsham, Hissar, Haryana

23. Sh. Harshvardhan Joshi
DIET Solan, Himachal Pradesh

24. Sh. Ramesh Verma
SCERT, Solan

25. Sh. Pardeep Thakur
Himachal Gyan Vigyan Samiti (HGVS)

26. Dr. O.P. Bhuraita
HGVS

27. Sh. Joginder Singh Rao
Principal, Govt. Senior Secondary, Bilaspur
Himachal Pradesh

28. Sh. R.K. Duggal
District Project Director

29. Sh. Paramjeet Singh
Deputy Director, Higher Education
Higher Education

30. Sh. Surjeet Singh Rao
Principal, Govt. Senior Secondary, Moorang
Himachal Pradesh

31. Sh. Sanjeev Atri
Principal, Govt. Senior Secondary, Kaffota
Himachal Pradesh

32. Dr. Harendra S. Adhikari
SCERT Uttarakhand

33. Sh. V. Rama Rao
Education Advisor, Dehradun

34. Sh. B.S. Negi
Principal, Govt. Intercollege, Miyanwala, Dehradun

35. Dr. Anita Chauhan
DIET, Baghpat, Uttar Pradesh

36. Sh. Rajesh Kumar
Lokmitra, Uttar Pradesh

37. Sh. Ajay Kumar Singh
Mandaliya Sahayak Shiksha Nideshak

38. Sh. Kader Ahmed
Coordinator, Nayi Panchayat Resource Coordinator
Rae Bareli

39. Sh. Jeetendra Kumar
N.I.O.S., Noida

40. Mr. Kamlesh Bhartiya
GGIE Meerut

41. Mr. O.P. Arya
GGIE, Meerut

42. Mr. Sanjay Yadav
Deputy Director, School Education, Meerut

43. Sh. S.K. Sethia
State Project Director, SSA and DPI Schools
Chandigarh (U.T.)

44. Dr. S. Dahiya
Director, SIE, Chandigarh (U.T.)

45. Ms. Harsh Batra
Principal, Govt. college of Education, Chandigarh

46. Ms. Jasvir Chahal
Senior Lecturer, Govt. College of Education
Chandigarh

47. Mr. Shailendra Sharma
PRATHAM, Delhi

48. Mr. Anil Kumar
S.I., In Service Teacher Training, Delhi

49. Ms. Neelam Katara
Education Officer, Kendriya Vidyala Sangathan
(Delhi region)

50. Mr. N. S. Mehra
ADE (School)

51. Mr. S.D. Sharma
Principal, Govt. Boys Senior Secondary School
Shakti Nagar, Delhi

52. Mr. Dinesh Kumar
Govt. Boys Senior Secondary School, Gokulpuri

Western Region, Indian Institute of Education, Pune
23rd November 2007

1. Mr. Begde
Director, SCERT, Maharashtra

2. Dr. Gajanand Patil
Principal, DIET Yavatmal

3. Smt. Mruguja Prakash Kulkarni
Asst. Teacher, Modern High School, Pune

4. Mr. Rangnath Jayram Thorat
Sri Bhairavnath High School, Sinnar, Nasik

5. Sh. S.G. Patil
Sriram Vidyalaya, Panchvati, Nasik

6. Ms. Asha Sundararajan
MOEMS India, Mumbai

7. Prof. Ram Takwale
Ex Vice-Chancellor, IGNOU, YCMOU and Pune University

8. Mr. Ramesh Panse
Maharashtra Knowledge Corporation Limited (MKCL)
Grammangal

9. Ms. Aditi Natu
MKCL

10. Mr. Alok Sharma
Assisstant Professor, SIEMAT, Raipur

11. Mr. Yogesh Shivhare
District Project Coordinator, Rajiv Gandhi Shiksha Mission, Durg, Chhattisgarh

12. Mr. Hemant Upadhyaya
Deputy Director, DPI, Raipur

13. Mr. O.P. Birthare
Principal, Basic Training Institute, Bilaspur Chhattisgarh

14. Mr. Yogesh Agarwal
President, Mitra Jan Kalankari Samiti, Rajnanadgaon Chhattisgarh

15. Mr. Lakshmi Nath
Pathak Principal, Shishu Mandir Higher Senior Secondary, Naila, Chhattisgarh

16. Ms. Deepa Dass
SIEMAT, Raipur

17. Mr. S.K. Verma
Assistant Professor, SCERT, Raipur

18. Mr. V.P. Chandra
Lecturer, DIET, Nagri, Chhattisgarh

19. Ms. Gayatri Vijay
Deputy Director, School Education, Kota

20. Ms. Snehlata Chaddha
Principal, Srinathpuram, Kota

21. Mr. Shailendra Rajawat
Academic Officer, Secondary Education, Ajmer

22. Mr. Radheyshyam
Principal, Jaipur Primary School

23. Mr. Anil Gupta
Sandhan, Jaipur

24. Mr. Arvind Ojha
Urmul Trust, Bikaner

25. Mr. Dushyant Agarwal
Project Officer, SIERT, Udaipur

26. Ms. Riddhi Shah
Seva Mandir, Udaipur

27. Ms. Megha Jain
Seva Mandir, Udaipur

28. Ms. Meena Bhatt
State Project Director, SSA, Gujarat

29. Mr. H.N. Chavda
Gujarat Secondary and Higher Secondary Board

30. Mr. H.N. Hingu
Joint CEO, SCOPE, Gujarat

31. Mr. Rajabhai Pathak
Principal, Swastik Secondary School, Gujarat

32. Mr. Architt Bhatt
Principal, Tripada International School

33. Dr. V.B. Bhensdadia
Deputy Director, Commissioner of Schools, Gujarat

34. Mr. Ketan Thaker
CRCC, Rampura, Dist. Ahmedabad, Gujarat

35. Dr. B.P. Choudhury
DIET, Patan, Gujarat

36. Ms. Roda Billimoria
Sir Shapurji Billimoria Foundation

Members of the NKC Working Group on Open Access and Open Courseware

1. Dr. V. Balaji
Head, KMS (Knowledge Management and Sharing) Group, ICRISAT (International Crops Research Institute for the Semi-Arid Tropics)

2. Dr. K. Mangala Sunder
Webcourses Coordinator
NPTEL (National Programme on Technology Enhanced Learning), IIT (Indian Institute of Technology) Madras

3. Dr. Rajan Welukar
Vice-Chancellor
Yashwantrao Chavan Maharashtra Open University

4. Dr. H.P. Dikshit
NBHM Professor
PDPM- Indian Institute of Information Technology

5. Anand Patwardhan
Executive Director
TIFAC (Technology Information Forecasting and Assessment Council)

6. Dr. Subbiah Arunachalam
MS Swaminathan Foundation

7. Dr. Vijay Kumar
Co-convener, Asst. Provost and Director of Academic Computing, MIT

8. Dr. A.S. Kolaskar
   Convener, Advisor, National Knowledge Commission

Consultations

I. Workshops on Maths and Science were held at:

1. Tata Institute of Fundamental Research
   Mumbai, 16 August 2007
2. Indian Institute of Science,
   Bangalore, 23 August 2007
3. South Campus, Delhi University
   Delhi, 10 September 2007
4. SN Bose Centre for Basic Sciences
   Kolkata, 5 October 2007

II. The following is the List of Experts who were Interviewed in their Individual Capacity:

1. Prof. Manindra Agarwal
   Department of Computer Science, IIT Kanpur
2. Prof. K.R. Parthasarthy
   Theoretical Statistics and Mathematics Unit, ISI Delhi
3. Prof. S. Ramaswamy
   Director, Ramanujan Research Center for Higher Mathematics, Alagappa University
4. Prof. V. Vinay
   Chief Technology Officer, Geodesic Information Limited
5. Prof. T.V. Ramakrishnan
   Department of Physics, BHU
6. Prof. Shiva Prasad
   Director, IndoFrench Centre and Department of Physics, IIT Bombay
7. Prof. N. Mukunda
   Former President, IAS and Centre for High Energy Physics, IISc
8. Prof. Alladi Sitaram
   Statistics and Mathematics Unit, ISI Bangalore
9. Prof. C.S. Yogananda
   Sri Jayachamarajendra College of Engineering
10. Prof. S.G. Dani
    School of Mathematics, TIFR
11. Prof. Rajendra Bhatia
    Theoretical Statistics and Mathematics Unit, ISI Delhi
12. Dr. Rajesh Gopakumar
    Harish-Chandra Research Institute, Allahabad
13. Prof. Dinesh Singh
    Director, South Campus, Delhi University
14. Prof. P. Banerjee
    Director, NISTADS, CSIR
15. Prof. Suman Kapur
    School of Life Sciences, BITS Pilani
16. Prof. K.R. Sreenivasan
    Director, ICTP, Trieste
17. Dr. Challa Suguna
    Scientist, Centre for Cellular Biology, Hyderabad
18. Prof. M.S. Raghunathan
    School of Mathematics, TIFR
19. Dr. Somdatta Sinha
    Scientist, Centre for Cellular Biology, Hyderabad
20. Dr. Pramod Kumar Yadav
    Dean, School of Life Sciences, JNU
21. Mr. Kiran Karnik
    Former President, NASSCOM
22. Prof. Sanjay Puri
    Dean, School of Physical Sciences, JNU
23. Dr. S.K. Sikka
    Scientific Secretary, Office of Principal Scientific Adviser
24. Prof. C.S. Seshadri
    Director, Chennai Mathematical Institute
25. Prof. N. Satyamurthy
    Director, IISER, Mohali
26. Mr. Ramesh Panse
    Member, MKCL
27. Dr. M.K. Mishra
    Orissa Sahitya Academy, Bhubaneswar
28. Mr. Venkatesh Valluri
    Agilent Technologies
29. Mr. P. S. Deodhar
    Executive Chairman, APLAB Limited
30. Dr. Achyutananda Samanta
    Vice-Chancellor, KIIT University

Consultations

We did an extensive survey and received opinions from more than 250 diverse stakeholders (from academia, research institutions, industry, etc.) on the subject. Later, we organised a workshop inviting partcipants to delve on the issues of fostering industry academia relationships and improving the research environment in universities. Following is the list of experts who took part in the workshop:

1. Dr. K.V. Subramaniam, Director, Reliance Life Sciences
2. Mr. Venkatesh Vallury, Managing Director, Agilent Technologies
3. Dr. Shilpa Vora, Principal Research Scientist, HLRC
4. Ms. Valsa Williams, Intel Technology India Pvt. Ltd.
5. Dr. Sandhya Chintala, Director, Education Initiative, NASSCOM
6. Dr. Vidyasagar, Executive Vice-President, TCS
7. Dr. Meenu Singh, Additional Professor of Pediatrics, PGIMER, Chandigarh
8. Dr. Bala Subramanian, Director, LVPEI
9. Dr. Y.S. Rajan, Principal Advisor, CII
10. Dr. R.B. Grover, Director, Knowledge Management Group, BARC
11. Dr. Gyan Arora, Tata Motors
12. Prof. G.D. Yadav, UICT
13. Dr. Sushma Gupta, Ranbaxy Laboratories
14. Prof. B.D. Singh, Dean Sciences, Banaras Hindu University
15. Prof. E. Haribabu, Dean Social Sciences, University of Hyderabad
16. Dr. A.N. Desai, The Bombay Textile Research Association
17. Prof. Balaji Parthsarthy, IIIT Bangalore
18. Prof. Pankaj Jalote, IIT Delhi
19. Prof. Shashiprabha, Jawahar Lal Nehru University
20. Dr. J.K. Bhasin, NEERI
21. Dr. Ajit Ranade, Chief Economist, Aditya Birla Group
22. Dr. Rajendra Singh, CMIR Dhanbad
23. Prof. Varyam Singh, Dean Languages, JNU
24. Dr. Ashok Ganguly, Member, National Knowledge Commission
25. Dr. Sujatha Ramdorai, Member, National Knowledge Commission

List of Respondents

The following is the list of large firms that responded to the questionnaire, in alphabetical order:

1. Arvind Mills Ltd.
2. Ashok Leyland Ltd.
3. Aurobindo Pharma Ltd.
4. Ballarpur Industries Ltd.[48]
5. Bharat Forge Ltd.
6. Bharat Heavy Electricals Ltd.
7. Bharat Sanchar Nigam Ltd.[49]
8. Biocon Ltd.
9. Cadila Healthcare Ltd.
10. Central Bank of India
11. Citigroup Global Services Ltd.
12. CRISIL Ltd.
13. Essel Group of Companies – Zee Group
14. Fortis Healthcare Ltd.
15. Glenmark Pharmaceuticals Ltd.
16. Great Eastern Shipping Co. Ltd.
17. Gujarat Co-operative Milk Marketing Federation Ltd.
18. HCL Infosytems Ltd.
19. IBM India Ltd.
20. ICICI Bank Ltd.
21. Indian Airlines Ltd.[50]
22. Infosys Technologies Ltd.
23. Jagran Prakashan Ltd.
24. Jet Airways (India) Ltd.
25. Jindal Stainless Ltd.
26. Kirloskar Brothers Ltd.
27. Kotak Mahindra Bank Ltd.
28. Kudremukh Iron Ore Company Ltd.[51]
29. Mahindra & Mahindra (Mahindra Group)

48. The response of Ballarpur Industries Ltd. is not part of the findings of this report, since it was received after 20th April 2007.

49. BSNL's response is not part of the findings of this report, since it was received after 20th April 2007.

50. Indian Airlines' response is not part of the findings of this report, since it was received after 20th April 2007.

51. Kudremukh Iron Ore Company Ltd. responded to NKC by sending material on their innovation activities. They did not fill up the questionnaire.

30. MSPL Ltd.
31. National Bank for Agriculture and Rural Development (NABARD)
32. National Mineral Dev. Corp. Ltd.
33. NTPC Ltd.
34. Nuclear Power Corporation of India Ltd.
35. Oil and Natural Gas Corporation Ltd.
36. Oil India Ltd.
37. Pantaloon Retail
38. Philips Electronics India Ltd.
39. Power Grid Corporation of India Ltd.[52]
40. Punjab National Bank
41. Reliance Industries Ltd.
42. RPG Enterprises
43. Rural Electrification Corpn.
44. Sesa Goa Ltd.
45. Shopper's Stop Ltd.
46. SICPA India Ltd.
47. Singareni Collieries Co. Ltd.
48. Star Group India
49. Steel Authority of India Ltd.
50. Sun Pharmaceuticals Industries Ltd.
51. Syndicate Bank
52. Tata Consultancy Services Ltd.
53. Tata Group[53]
54. Tata Motors Ltd.
55. Tata Steel Ltd.
56. Thermax Ltd.
57. West Coast Paper Mills Ltd.
58. Whirlpool India Ltd.

Categories of Large Firms

1. Manufacturing	
a. Mining	4
b. Automotive	3
c. Home appliances	2
d. Paper	1
e. Steel	3
f. Energy, electricity, power, oil and gas	6
g. Energy and environment	1
h. Pharmaceuticals	4
i. Textiles	1
2. Services	
j. IT/ ITeS	5
k. Banking and financial services	8
l. Health care delivery	2
m. Aviation	1
n. Retail	3
o. Shipping	1
3. Both	
p. Biotechnology	1
q. Media	3
r. Diversified	3
TOTAL	52

The Small and Medium Enterprises (SMEs) as well as other organisations that participated in the NKC study on Innovation, in alphabetical order, are as follows:

1. Abhinav Enterprises
2. Accurate
3. Affair
4. Agricultural & Processed Food Products Export Development Authority (APEDA)
5. Ajay Windecor Products
6. Ajinkya Enterprises
7. Artzone
8. Asha Chemicals
9. Athitya

52. Power Grid Corporation of India Ltd. responded to NKC by sending material on their innovation activities. They did not fill up the questionnaire.

53. Ratan Tata responded to NKC by sending material on Tata Group's innovation strategy. He did not fill up the questionnaire. Therefore, there are 58 respondents on this list, of which 55 have filled up the questionnaire. The analysis in this document is based on 52 responses.

10. Atul Electro Formers Pvt. Ltd.
11. Auto Cluster Development & Research Institute Ltd.
12. Beed Cyber Infotech
13. CADLine India
14. Cartoprint
15. Clean Foods Ltd.
16. Dayal Fertilizers Group
17. Digital Empowerment Foundation
18. Dnyaneshwar Vidyapeeth
19. Electronica Machine Tools Ltd.
20. Engg Tools & Equipment
21. Feelings
22. Golopore IMS
23. GreenGarden
24. Hoyt Engineering Solutions Pvt. Ltd.
25. Ideal Computer Education
26. Ideal Diamond Products Pvt. Ltd
27. Indian Academy of Foreign Trade & Development
28. Innova Rubbers Pvt. Ltd.
29. Innovative Technomics Pvt. Ltd.
30. Intelux Electronics Pvt. Ltd.
31. International Institute of Corporate Management
32. International Institute of Information Technology
33. KNOW-IT34KPMG
35. Lakshmi Embroidery
36. Logus Business Systems
37. Macintel
38. Maharashtra Knowledge Corporation Ltd.
39. Mana Pet Clinic Labs
40. Manjushri Extrusions Ltd
41. Mavin Adhesives Pvt. Ltd.
42. Medsynaptic Pvt. Ltd.
43. Melk Services
44. Membrane Filters Pvt. Ltd.
45. Mutha Founders Pvt. Ltd.
46. N V Electronics Pvt. Ltd.
47. Neelesh Engineers
48. Nichrome India Ltd.
49. Nirmiti Electronics Pvt. Ltd.
50. Paranjape Metal Shapes Pvt. Ltd.
51. Pragati Leadership Institute Pvt. Ltd.
52. Praj Industries Ltd.
53. Prajakta Computer Education
54. Prescient Technologies Pvt. Ltd.
55. Rezonant Design
56. Rohini Industries
57. Ronak Associates
58. SAI Test Plat Pvt. Ltd.
59. SEMCO ELECTRIC Pvt. Ltd.
60. Serum Institute
61. Shree Systems
62. Simply Delicious
63. Smile Automation Pvt. Ltd.
64. Sumanya HMX Systems Ltd.
65. Symtronics Automation Pvt. Ltd.
66. System India Computer and Management Services
67. Tact Global Services
68. Teamfill
69. Tecel Magnetics
70. Technical Associates Ltd.
71. Tony Travels Pvt. Ltd.
72. Unite Industries
73. Virane Engineers
74. Voicetech Solutions
75. Weaver Computer Embroidery System
76. Yenkey Instruments & Controls Pvt. Ltd.
77. Zarekar Computers
78. Zephyr Industries/Zephyrs Systems

List of Stakeholders and Details of Entrepreneurs Surveyed

This section contains a list of entrepreneurs (city-wise) and other stakeholders in the ecosystem whom we interviewed for the purpose of this study.

Entrepreneurs

Pune

1. Mr. Vishwas Joshi and Subhada Joshi, Girikand Travels Pvt. Ltd.

2. Mr. M.D. Adoni, Certified Management Consultant
3. Mr. Milind Pandit, Akshay Urja Pvt. Ltd.
4. Ms. Gayatri & Mr. Gopal Tambe, FRP Toilets
5. Mr. N.S. Rao, Intelux Electronics
6. Ms. Rajashree Jhangle, Simply Delicious
7. Mr. Ravi Bhagwat, Symtronics Automation Private Limited
8. Dr. Sunita Chaudhari, Consulting Ayurvedacharya
9. Mr. Vincent D'Souza, V.R. Coatings Pvt. Ltd.
10. Mr. Linesh Thakur, Aishwarya Enterprises
11. Mr. Subhash Devi, Membrane Filters
12. Ms. Mrunal Gokhale, Feelings Flowers
13. Mr. Ravindra Bam, Ajay Windecor
14. Mr. Vivek Sawant, Maharashtra Knowledge Corporation Ltd.
15. Mr. Pravin Dhole, Technofour
16. Mr. Sunil Bhandari, Food Grade Products
17. Mr. Raj Pathak, Akshay Urja Pvt. Limited
18. Mr. H.M. Bakshi, Innova Group
19. Mr. Firoz Poonawalla, Fila Rozil Exporters Pvt. Ltd.
20. Dr. Ashish Dhawad, Medsynaptic Pvt. Ltd.
21. Dr. Prashant Lahane, Medsynaptic Pvt. Ltd.
22. Mr. Anil Deshpande, Atul Electroformers Private Limited

Kolkata

1. Mr. Partha Das, Partha Das and Associates
2. Dr. Aloke Roy, Medica Synergie
3. Mr. Amit Dastidar and Mr. Subhajit Bhattacharya, The Event Managers
4. Mr. Sourav Chakraborty, Aunwesha Knowledge Technologies Pvt. Ltd.
5. Mr. Siddharth Pansari, Pansari Group of Enterprises
6. Mr. Anjan Ghosh, Kol Web
7. Mr. Jhelum Chowdhry, Crystal Research and Consulting Pvt. Ltd.
8. Ms. Sunira Chamaria, Sunira Foods
9. Mr. Arun Lohia, Alliance Mills (Lessees) Ltd.
10. Mr. Rajiv Poddar, Smartpower Computer Center
11. Mr. Namit Shah, Harley Group
12. Mr. Sidharth Kaul, NICCO Engineering
13. Mr. Aditya Chamaria, Indian Ropeways & Engg Co. Ltd.
14. Dr. Mousmi Ghosh, Future Business School
15. Mr. Vijay Kumar Shroff, Vijay Kumar & Co. (Jute) Pvt. Ltd.
16. Mr. Cecil Anthony, Synergy Group
17. Mr. S. Bhattacharya, Midland Packers
18. Mr. Shoummo Acharya, VI eTrans Pvt. Ltd.
19. Mr. S. Daspal, Info Horizon
20. Mr. Manish Chandani & Mr. Talat Ahmed, Ajanta Leather Fashions Pvt. Ltd.
21. Mr. Pradip Poddar, Shanta Colibri (India) Pvt. Ltd.
22. Mr. Nitin Himatsingka, Car Showroom
23. Mr. Indraneil Bose, Futuretech Solutions
24. Mr. Kumar Shivam, ALB Consultancy
25. Ms. Roopa Mehta, SASHA
26. Mr. P.K. Saha, P.K. Saha & Associates
27. Dr. Partha Ray, R.M. Clinical Laboratoies Pvt. Ltd.
28. Mr. Ashish Mitra, Exterior-Interiors Ltd.
29. Mr. Prateek Surekha, Brainwave Live
30. Mr. Ankur Gattani, Lifelines
31. Mr. Sundeep Tibrewal, *ResolveQuery.com*

Chennai

1. Mr. Ramachandran N. & Mr. T. Srinivasan, MEL Systems & Services Ltd.
2. Mr. Ramachandran A., Ganga Chemicals
3. Mr. Sanjeevi V, eLogistics Pvt. Ltd.
4. Mr. G.R. Ravi, Medik India Phytoceuticals
5. Mr. L. Ashok, Futurenet Technologies
6. Mr. Govindachari P.S, Rajsriya Group of Industries
7. Mr. K Shivaram Alva, Allva Plast
8. Mr. V.P.N. Rahman, Nadeem Leatherware Exports
9. Mr. Vara Prasad Raju P, Sigma Solid Strips Pvt. Ltd.
10. Mr. Amit Vaishnav, Megafoods Products Madras (P)
11. Mr. D.S. Balachandra Babu, Fram Implements Pvt. Ltd.
12. Mr. Naveen Velagapalli, Vitalife Clinic
13. Mr. Suhas Gopinath, Globals ITeS Pvt. Ltd.

14. Mr. B.A. Srinivasa, Vivek Ltd.
15. Ms. Rajeshwari, Akshya
16. Mr. A Benedict, Mercy Hygiene Healthcare Products
17. Mr. Anoop Mehandale, Latent View Analytics

Ahmedabad

1. Mr. Rupesh Shah, Sonya Ceramics
2. Dr. Nita Goswami, Rucha Pharmaceuticals
3. Mr. Indrajit Simlai, SSBI Exports
4. Mr. Jasvinder Singh, ACTUNIV
5. Mr. Sajjan Kejriwal, Acme International Ltd.
6. Mr. Samir N Patel, Amos Enterprise Ltd.
7. Mr. Malay Kantharia, Team Spirits India Pvt. Ltd.
8. Mr. E. Sarath Babu, Foodking
9. Ms. Kala Amin, Kanisha
10. Mr. Samir Shah, JBS Group of Companies
11. Ms. Seema Mehta, Sparkle Granites
12. Ms. Jayshree Mehta, Infinium Toyota
13. Mr. Amit Khaitan, *Gujaratgifts.com*
14. Mr. Abhay Panjiyar, CEON Solutions Pvt. Ltd.
15. Mr. Aniket Nagri, Nagri Group
16. Mr. Bhakti Vohra, Vastrapur Times
17. Mr. Deepak Vakil, Yeti Leather Products
18. Mr. Rajiv Gandhi, Hester Pharmaceuticals Ltd.
19. Mr. S.V. Modi, S.V. Modi Export Import
20. Mr. Sushil Handa, Claris Lifesciences Ltd.
21. Mr. Sheshgiri Bekal, Incubatee at Nirma Labs

Hyderabad

1. Mr. V. Venkata Raju, VEM Technology Pvt. Ltd.
2. Mr. N.K. Malani, Sri Venkateswara Coir Products Pvt. Ltd.
3. Mr. Nitin Vyakaranam, Arthayantra
4. Ms. Devika Vardarajan, Polaris Management Services Pvt. Ltd.
5. Mr. Narne Prabhakar, Hyderabad Tulaman Ltd.
6. Mr. Jayadev Meela, Sudhakar Polymers Ltd.
7. Mr. V. Anil Reddy, Nayastrap Ltd.
8. Mr. Devendra Surana, Bhagyanagar India Ltd.
9. Mr. Ravindra Modi, Surya Masale
10. Mr. D. Nagarjuna Sarma, Imprint Travels
11. Mr. Sriram Yalamati, Matrix Equipment Pvt. Ltd.
12. Mr. Sreeram M.M, S & U MEK Engineers Pvt. Ltd.
13. Mr. Ramesh Datla, Elico Ltd.
14. Ms. Aartee Patil, Icon Accessories Pvt. Ltd.
15. Mr. A.N. Gupta, Premier Explosives Ltd.
16. Ms. Durga Rani, Hyma Industries
17. Ms. Vijay Lakshmi, Anu Group
18. Mr. Rajeev Puri, Sukhjit Starch and Chemicals Ltd.
19. Mr. Ram Prasad, Sri Sarada Industries

Bangalore

1. Mr. J. Crasta, CM Envirosystems Pvt. Ltd.
2. Mr. Subramani Ramachandra, Richcore Lifesciences Pvt. Ltd.
3. Mr. J.R. Bangera, Premiers Starch Products Pvt. Ltd.
4. Ms. Madhura Chatrapathy, Food Associates; AWAKE; ASCENT
5. Mr. Srikumar Narayan, Winfoware Technologies Pvt. Ltd.
6. Mr. D.R. Srikantaiah, Associated Trading Corporation
7. Ms. Raj Bhasin, Bhasinsoft India Ltd.
8. Mr. M.S. Sidhu, Apara Enterprise solutions Pvt. Ltd.
9. Ms Uma Reddy, Hitech Magnetics
10. Mr. Shivakumar, Indigo Edge
11. Mr. Ravi Venkatesan, OnTrac
12. Dr. Krishnaswamy, Animal Biotech (Bangalore) Pvt. Ltd.
13. Mr. Tallam Venkatesh, Press Tools & Elements Pvt. Ltd.
14. Mr. Mansoor Ahmed, Tiger Tail Studios, BrewHaHa
15. Mr. Balakrishna M.R., Mediateck
16. Mr. Satyanarayana, Informatics India
17. Dr. Sunita Maheshwari, Teleradiology Solutions
18. Mr. Srinath Shetty, Gift Wrapped
19. Mr. S. Babu, Ashwin Precision Products Pvt. Ltd.
20. Mr. M.C.R. Shetty, Porlu Packers

21. Mr. Philip Lewis, Electro Mech Corporation
22. Mr. K. Ganesh, Tutor Vista
23. Mr. M.K. Panduranga Setty, Mysore Snack Foods Ltd.
24. Dr. Rajeshwari, Manu Pet Clinic
25. Mr. K.N. Jayalingappa, Transphone Corporation I.T.I. Ancilliary Industries Association
26. Mr. R.S.H. Raju, Bluechip Solutions
27. Mr. V.C. Karthic, Buzzworks Business Services Pvt. Ltd.
28. Ms. Suma Krishnaswamy, Global Greens
29. Ms. Padma Seshadri, Atithya Hotels
30. Mr. Muralidhar, Innova Security Investments Ltd.
31. Mr. R.C. Purohit, Bhoruka Steel and Services Ltd.
32. Mr. K. Shiva Shanmugam, Sivasakhti Engineering Company
33. Ms. Usha Nagaraj, Srimati Mahila Co-operative Bank, FKCCI
34. Mr. Babu Sathian, Process Pumps Pvt. Ltd.
35. Mr. Veerendra Shivhare, mGinger
36. Mr. Balaji Pasumarthy, Business Gyan
37. Mr. Divye Tela, Cheesecare Corporate Services

Others

1. Mr. Priyankar Baid, P.B. Tech Impact Solutions, New Delhi
2. Mr. Atul Nigam, i2k Solutions, Mumbai
3. Mr. Nalin Agrawal, INREA Research, Mumbai
4. Mr. Abhishek Biswal, TRI India, Mumbai
5. Mr. Sanjay Labroo, Asahi India Glass Ltd., New Delhi
6. Mr. Pratap S. Mungi, Mungi Brothers, Mumbai
7. Mr. Ramesh Suri, Subros Ltd., New Delhi
8. Mr. Arvind Kapur, Rico Auto Industries Ltd., Gurgaon

Other Stakeholders in the Ecosystem

1. Ms. Lalita Gupte, ICICI Venture
2. Ms. Bala Deshpande, ICICI Venture
3. Mr. Kanwaljit Singh, Helion Venture Partners
4. Mr. Ashish Gupta, Helion Venture Partners
5. Mr. Anand Lunia, The Seed Fund
6. Mr. Pravin Gandhi, The Seed Fund
7. Mr. Vishnu Varshney, Gujarat Venture Finance Ltd (GVFL)
8. Mr. R. Kuppanna, SBI Chennai
9. Mr. Puneet Gupta, NEF
10. Ms. Laxmi Venkatraman, BYST
11. Ms. Laura Parkin, NEN
12. Mr. Manak Singh, TIE
13. Mr. Paul Murphy, Microsoft India
14. Dr. Subhashish Gangopadhya, IDF
15. Mr. Mohit Malik, Anoova Consulting
16. Mr. Krishnan Iyer, Sequoia Capital India
17. Mr. Harish Damodran, *The Hindu Business Line*
18. Mr. Manish Sabharwal, TeamLease Services Ltd.
19. Prof. Suresh Bhagavatula, NSRCEL, IIM Bangalore
20. Mr. R.M.P. Jawahar, TREC-STEP
21. Ms. Poyni Bhatt, SINE, IIT Bombay
22. Dr. Madhu Mehta, NIRMA Labs
23. Dr. A. Wali, FITT, IIT Delhi
24. Mr. Nitin Kundra, Entrepreneurship and Innovation Cell, IIM Bangalore
25. Prof. Ashok Jhunjhunwala, TeNeT, IIT Madras
26. Centre for Innovation, Incubation & Entrepreneurship (CIIE), IIM Ahmedabad
27. Prof. Subramonia Sarma, Indian School of Business (ISB)
28. Mr. Brahmananda Rao & Mr. Rajeswara Prasad, Andhra Pradesh State Finance Corporation (APSFC)
29. Ms. Ramadevi Kanneganti, ALEAP
30. Mr. S. Subba Rao, Andhra Pradesh Industrial Development Corporation (APIDC)
31. Mr. Khokon Mukhopadhyaya, Bengal Chambers of Commerce
32. Mr. Kaushik Shah, Gujarat Chambers of Commerce and Industry
33. Mr. Sampat Raman, Federation of Karnataka Chamber of Commerce & Industry (FKCCI)
34. Representatives of Tamil Nadu Adi Dravidar Housing Development Corporation (TAHDCO)

35. Mr. Mritunjoy Bandyopadhya, Agastya Associates
36. Dr R.C. Rane Intas Pharmaceuticals
37. Mr. V.V. Sanyasi Rao, Anakapalle Merchants Association
38. Mr. Uday Bhaskar, Zen Technologies
39. Mr. Y. Rambabu, Ushodaya Enterprise
40. Dr. Pulastya Vora, CSM Services
41. Mr. K.M. Pai, Bell Ceramics Ltd.
42. Dr. Shrikant Joshi, International Advanced Research Centre for Powder Metallurgy
43. Prof. M.G.K. Murty, Centre for Environmental Adaptation
44. Mr. M. Raja Reddy, Srinivasa Industries
45. Mr. Arun Kumar D, AGI Glaspac

Classification of Entrepreneurs Interviewed

(i) Based on the Sector of their Operations

Figure A.1: Categorisation by Sector

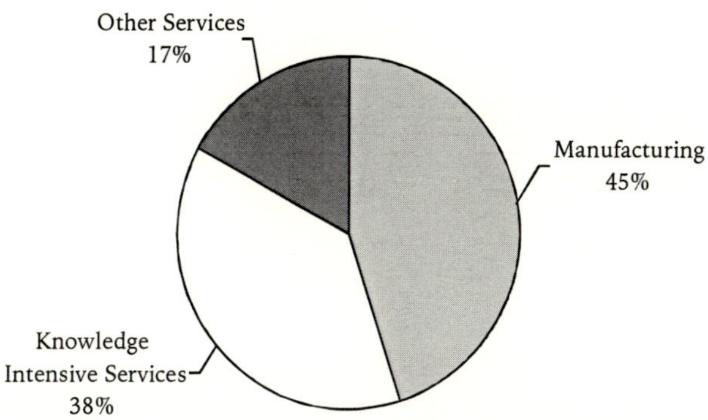

(ii) Based on the Time Period of Venturing into Entrepreneurship

Figure A.2: Categorisation by Time Period

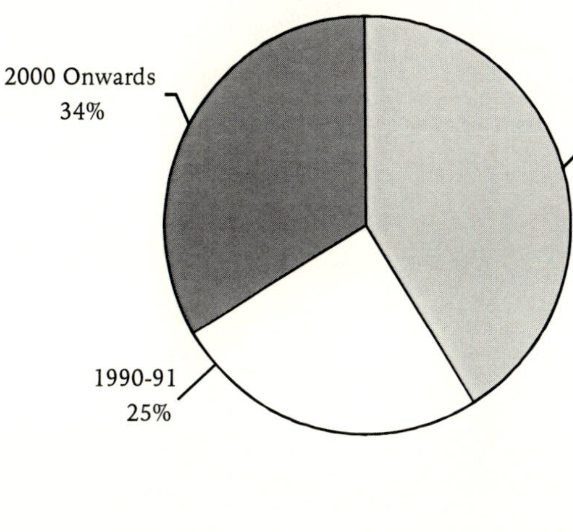

(iii) Based on the Company's Turnover

Figure A.3: Categorisation by Turnover

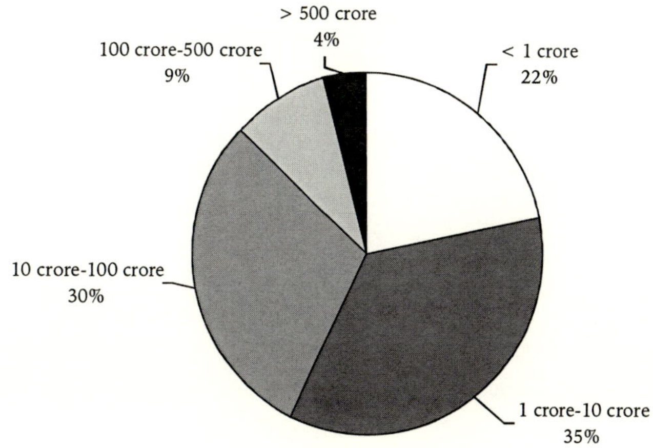

(iv) Based on the Number of People they Employ

Figure A.4: Categorisation by number of employees

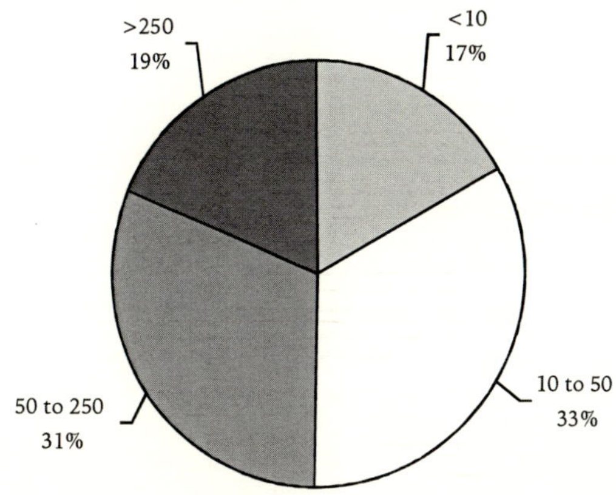

(v) Based on the Fmily Background

Figure A.5: Categorisation by family background

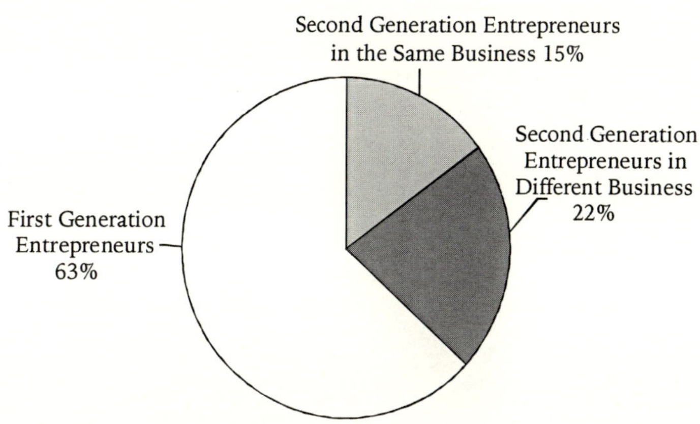

Consultations

Working Groups

A. Language

1. Prof. Meenakshi Mukherjee
   Hyderabad University
2. Dr. Partha Ghosh
   S.N. Bose National Centre for Basic Sciences, Kolkata
3. Dr. M.P. Parameswaran
   KSSP Kerala
4. Mr. K.K. Krishnakumar
   BGVS Kerala
5. Mrs. Shesha Prasad
   Kendriya Vidyalaya Picket, Secunderabad
6. Prof. U.N. Singh
   Central Institute of Indian Languages, Mysore
7. Prof. Jacob Tharu
   CIEFL

B. Undergraduate Education

1. Dr. Kiran Datar
   Delhi University
2. Dr. S.K. Garg
   Deen Dayal Upadhyaya College, Delhi
3. Dr. Meenakshi Gopinath
   Lady Sri Ram College, Delhi
4. Dr. Fraser Mascarenhas
   St. Xavier's College, Mumbai
5. Dr. B.K. Mishra
   Science College, Patna
6. Prof. Prasanta Ray
   Presidency College, Kolkata
7. Dr. Anil Wilson
   St. Stephen's College, New Delhi

C. Medical Education

1. Dr. Sneh Bhargava
   AIIMS, New Delhi
2. Dr. N.G. Desai
   IHBAS, Delhi
3. Dr. N.K. Ganguly
   ICMR, New Delhi
4. Dr. V.I. Mathan
   CMC, Vellore
5. Dr. G.N. Rao
   LVP Eye Institute, Hyderabad
6. Dr. S.K. Reddy
   AIIMS, New Delhi
7. Dr. S.K. Sarin
   G.B. Pant Hospital, New Delhi
8. Dr. D. Shetty
   Narayana Hrudayalaya, Bangalore
9. Dr. K.K. Talwar
   PGIMER, Chandigarh
10. Dr. P.N. Tandon
    National Brain Research Centre, Haryana
11. Dr. M.S. Valiathan
    INSA

Workshops

A. Literacy

1. Prof. U.R. Ananthamurthy
2. Shri Champak Chatterjee
   Department of Elementary Education & Literacy, Govt. of India
3. Dr. Uma Bisht
   State Resource Centre, Lucknow
4. Prof. S.K. Gandhe
   Indian Institute of Education, Pune
5. Dr. Shaibal Gupta
   ADRI, Bihar
6. Mr. Subrata Gupta
   District Magistrate, Burdwan, West Bengal
7. Mr. Amba Jamir
   The Missing Link- Society for Environment & Communication, Assam
8. Mrs. Vandana K. Jena
   NLM, Govt. of India
9. Dr. Ashok Khosla
   Development Alternatives, New Delhi
10. Prof. Saidul Haque
    District Primary School Council, Burdwan
    West Bengal
11. Dr. Brij Kothari
    IIM, Ahmedabad

12. Dr. R.V.G. Menon
    KSSP, Kerala
13. Prof. K.C. Nori
    TCS, Hyderabad
14. Dr. M.P. Parmeswaran
    KSSP, Kerala
15. Mrs. Usha Bafna
    Deputy Director Literacy & Continuing Education
    Govt. of Rajasthan
16. Prof. Vinod Raina
    Hoshangabad Science Teaching Programme
17. Prof. Anita Rampal
    Department of Education, University of Delhi
18. Mr. Vivek Sharma
    PRATHAM, New Delhi
19. Dr. P.M. Bhargava
    NKC
20. Dr. Jayati Ghosh
    NKC
21. Dr. Ashok Kolaskar
    NKC

B. Translation

1. Mr. K.P.R.Nair
   Konark Publishers
2. Mr. Keshav Desairaju
   Ministry of HRD
3. Dr. M. Sridhar
   University of Hyderabad
4. Prof. Alok Bhalla
   Central Institute of English and Foreign Languages (CIEFL)
5. Dr. D.S. Navin
   National Book Trust
6. Prof. G. Uma Maheshwar Rao
   Centre for Applied Linguistics & Translation Studies
7. Prof. Vanamala Viswanath
   Jnanabharathi, Bangalore University
8. Dr. Neeti Badwe
   Department of Foreign Languages, University of Poona
9. Prof. Harish Trivedi
   University of Delhi
10. Prof. Pushpak Bhattacharya
    Department of Computer Science & Engineering, IIT
11. Mr. Benny Kurian
    National Book Trust
12. Ms. Kamini Mahadevan
    Pearson Education India
13. Dr. Apoorvanand
14. Dr. Sujata Roy
    Hindi Medium Implementation Committee, University of Delhi
15. Mr. Abhijit Dutta
    IBM Global Services India Pvt. Ltd.
16. Ms. Geeta Dharmarajan
    KATHA
17. Ms. Mini Krishnan
    Oxford University Press
18. Prof. Udaya Narayana Singh
    Central Institute of Indian Languages
19. Ms. Radhika Menon
    Tulika
20. Dr. S.N. Ojha
    Santiniketan
21. Mr. Rubin D'Cruz
    National Book Trust
22. Prof. Bijay Kumar
    Commission for Scientific and Technical Terminology
23. Mr. N.V. Sathyanarayana
    Informatics (India) Ltd.
24. Dr. Shalini R.Urs
    ISIM - International School of Information Management, University of Mysore
25. Dr. Sukrita P. Kumar
26. Dr. Jayati Ghosh
    NKC

C. Knowledge Network

1. Mr. Pankaj Agarwal
   DIT
2. Mr. Shailendra Agarwal
   BSNL
3. Dr. Alhad G. Apte
   BARC

4. Mr. N. Arjun
Bharti Airtel Limited
5. Prof. N. Balakrishnan
Indian Institute of Science, IISc.
6. Mr. Subhash Bhargava
VSNL Broadband Ltd.
7. Mr. R. Chandrashekhar
DIT
8. Dr. R. Chidambaram
Principal Scientific Adviser to GoI
9. Mr. Vipin Dhaundiyal
Reliance Infocomm Ltd.
10. Prof. P.S. Dhekney
BARC
11. Dr. B.K. Gairola
NIC
12. Mr. J.R. Gupta
BSNL
13. Mr. Lav Gupta
BSNL
14. Prof B.N. Jain
IIT, Delhi
15. Mr. Puneet Jhingan
Reliance Infocomm Limited
16. Mr. Ashok Jhunjhunwala
IIT Chennai
17. Dr. H.K. Kaul
DelNet
18. Mr. A. Krishnan
Bharti Tele-Ventures Limited
19. Mr. Pradeep Kumar
RailTel Corporation of India Ltd.
20. Dr. S.N. Ragu Kumar
AIIMS
21. Mr. Sandeep Mathur
VSNL
22. Dr. K. Madhu Murthy
AICTE
23. Mr. Sri Nath
VSNL
24. Mr. V. Ponraj
ICT Adviser to President of India
25. Mr. C.R. Prasad
GAIL
26. Mr. Rajshri Purkayastha
TATA Indicom Enterprise Business Unit
27. Prof. S.V. Raghavan
IIT, Chennai
28. Dr. Gulshan Rai
ERNET
29. Dr. S. Ramakrishnan
C-DAC
30. Dr. D.P.S. Seth
Former Member, TRAI
31. Mr. Devinder Singh
Reliance Infocomm Ltd.
32. Dr. Neeraj Sinha
Office of the Principal Scientific Adviser to GoI
33. Mr. Rajiv Sinha
RailTel Corporation of India Ltd.
34. Dr. Sitaram
DRDO
35. Mr. Anil Srivastava
Capital Technology Information Services, Inc.
36. Dr. N. Subramanian
C-DAC
37. Dr. M.S. Swaminathan
M.S. Swaminathan Research Foundation
38. Mr. Shilesh Tiwari
RailTel Corporation of India Ltd
39. Mr. Sharad Trivedi
BSNL
40. Dr. R.S. Tyagi
AIIMS

D. School Education

1. Prof. R. Govinda
NIEPA
2. Dr. Vimla Ramachandran
3. Mr. Vinod Raina
Hoshangabad Science Teaching Program
4. Mr. Parth Shah
Centre for Civil Society
5. Dr. Madan M. Jha
Deptt. of Human Resource Development, Bihar

6. Dr. Vasanthi V. Devi
   Kalvi Alliance for Education, Tamil Nadu
7. Dr. V.P. Niranjanaradhya
   National Law School of India University
8. Ms. Madhu Prasad
   Zakir Husain College, Delhi University
9. Mr. Ambarish Rai
   People's Campaign for Common School System
10. Mr. Dinesh Abrol
    NISTADS, India
11. Mr. Subhash Kuntia
    Dept of School Education and Literacy, MHRD
12. Mr. Champak Chatterjee
    MHRD
13. Ms. Manju Bharatram
    Shri Ram School
14. Ms. Anita Rampal
    Department of Education, Delhi University
15. Ms. Vrinda Swaroop
    MHRD
16. Dr. P.M. Bhargava
    NKC
17. Dr. Jayati Ghosh
    NKC

E. Open Education

1. Prof. H.P. Dikshit
   IGNOU
2. Dr. Gulshan Rai
   ERNET
3. Prof. Mangala Sunder
   NPTEL, IIT Madras
4. Prof. S. Sadagopan
   IIT Bangalore
5. Prof. D.B. Pathak
   KRESIT, IIT-Bombay
6. Prof. Ashok Jhunjhunwallah
   IIT Madras
7. Dr. S Arunachalam
   MS Swaminathan Foundation
8. Prof. Welukar
   YCMOU
9. Dr. Prasad
   NAAC
10. Ms. Swati Chaudhuri
    Education Committee, FICCI
11. Mr. Vivek Sawant
    Maharashtra Knowledge Corp. Ltd.
12. Dr. Uma Ganesh
    Kalzoom Technologies
13. Dr. S. Ramani
    HP Labs
14. Dr. B.K. Gairola
    NIC
15. Mr. V. Ponraj
    ICT Adviser to President of India
16. Dr. Kalpana Dasgupta
    Libraries Working Group, NKC
17. Prof. Krithivasan
    KRESIT, IIT-Bombay
18. Prof. Y.S. Rajan
    CII
19. Prof. Ashish Rajadhyaksha
    Centre for the Study of Culture and Society
20. Dr. Ravindra
    Infosys
21. Dr. Sridhar Iyer
    KRESIT, IIT B
22. Ms. Vidya Natampally
    Microsoft
23. Dr. V. Balaji
    ICRISAT
24. Prof. Ram Takwale
    IGNOU
25. Dr. K.C. Green
    Campus Computing Project
26. Dr. Gerald Hanley
    MERLOT
27. Dr. Phil Long
    MIT
28. Mr. Jeff Merriman
    MIT
29. Dr. Mark Schulz
    School of ITEE, Australia

30. Prof. David Wiley
    Utah State University
31. Dr. Vijay Kumar
    MIT
32. Prof. Ashok Kolaskar
    NKC
33. Dr. N. Sarat Chandra Babu
    C-DAC
34. Dr. Madhav Pulipati
    IEG, Govt. of AP
35. Mr. Ashish Khushu
    Sun Microsystems
36. Dr. Deepak Bhatnagar
    TIFAC
37. Dr. Neeraj Saxena
    TIFAC
38. Mr. Mahendran
    TIFAC
39. Dr. Abhishek
    TIFAC
40. Prof. Krithi Ramamritham
    IIT Bombay
41. Dr. A.K. Parate
    UGC
42. Dr. Mukesh Aghi
    Universitas 21 Global
43. Dr. Fun Den Wang
    CORE, China
44. Mr. Manoj Kumar
    INFLIBNET
45. Mr. Amarnath Reddy
    IEG
46. Dr. Srinivasan Reddy
    IEG
47. Mr. K. Sriram
    VA Technologies
48. Dr. S. Ramakrishnan
    CDAC
49. Mr. Kiran Karnik
    NASSCOM
50. Dr. C.R. Mitra
    Former Director, BITS Pilani

F. Science And Technology

1. Dr. U.R. Rao
   Former Director, ISRO
2. Prof. R. Ramaswamy
   Jawaharlal Nehru University
3. Prof. Senthil Todadri
4. Dr. B.M. Hegde
   Postgraduate Medical Education Board, Govt. of India
5. Prof. C.S. Seshadri
   Chennai Mathematical Institute, Chennai
6. Dr. Mangala Rai
   ICAR
7. Prof. Sabyasachi Bhattacharya
   TIFR
8. Dr. A.V. Rama Rao
   AVRA Laboratories
9. Prof. Ajit Kembhavi
   IUCAA, Pune
10. Prof. S. Umapathy
    IISc, Bangalore
11. Prof. S.M. Chitre
    University of Mumbai
12. Prof. Sanjeev Galande
    National Center for Cell Science, Pune
13. Dr. N.K. Ganguly ICMR
14. Dr. V. Rao Aiyagari
    SERC, Department of Science and Technology
15. P.M. Bhargava
    NKC
16. Ashok Ganguly
    NKC
17. Deepak Nayyar
    NKC
18. Ashok Kolaskar
    NKC

G. Intellectual Property Rights

1. Dr. R.A. Mashelkar
   CSIR
2. Dr. P.M. Bhargava
   NKC

3. Dr. Prabuddha Ganguli
IIT Mumbai

4. Mr. Anjan Das
CII

5. Dr. Malathi Lakshmikumaran
Lakshmikumaran and Sridharan

6. Dr. Krishna Ravi Srinivas
IIM Bangalore

7. Mr. Akash Taneja
FICCI

8. Dr. Ramesh Shukla
Board of Appeal, European Patent Court

9. Dr. Somesh Kr. Mathur
RIS

10. Mr. Anand Grover
Lawyers Collective

11. Mr. V.K. Gupta
NISCAIR

12. Mr. Naresh Nandan Prasad
DIPP, Ministry of Commerce and Industry

13. Mr. R.K. Gupta
CSIR

14. Mr. Anand Wali
IIT Delhi

15. Mr. T.C. James
DIPP, Ministry of Commerce and Industry

16. Dr. B.K. Keayla
National Working Group on Patent Laws

17. Mr. Rakesh Prasad
ALG Associates

H. Vocational Education

1. Gen. S.S. Mehta
CII

2. Dr. Pankaj Chandra
IIM A

3. Dr. Partha Mukhopadhyay
CPR

4. Mr. K.P. Murthy
MICO-BOSCH

5. Dr. P.M. Bhargava
NKC

6. Mr. Vivek Singhal
India Development Coalition of America

I. Muslim Education

1. Dr. M. Saleemuddin
Aligarh Muslim University

2. Dr. Azra Razzack
Delhi University

3. Prof. Zoya Hasan
JNU

4. Dr. Farida Khan
Delhi University

5. Dr. Nasreen Fazalbhoy
University of Mumbai

6. Begam Nusrat Shervani
Bharat Sewa Trust

7. Mr. Ahmad Shervani
Bharat Sewa Trust

8. Ms. Sahiba Farooqui
All India Democratic Women's Association

9. Dr. Sughra Mehdi
Muslim Women's Forum

10. Dr. Safia Mehdi
Muslim Women's Forum

11. Dr. Abu Saleh Shariff
NCAER

12. Prof. Akhtarul Wasey
Jamia Millia Islamia

13. Mr. Raziuddin Aquil
Centre for Studies in Social Sciences

14. Mr. Adil Siddiqui
Darul Uloom Deoband

15. Mr. Yoginder Sikand
Centre for Jawaharlal Nehru Studies

16. Dr. Syed Iqbal Hasnain
Calicut University

17. Mr. Dayaram
Aga Khan Foundation

18. Dr. Arshad Alam
Jamia Milia University

19. Mr. Arshad Amanullah
SARAI

20. Mr. Tanweer Fazal

21. Jayati Ghosh
    NKC

NKC Consultations

Stakeholders' Inputs

Literacy

National Seminar, New Delhi, 30 July 2006

Translation

1. Workshop on Translation, New Delhi
   11th February 2006
2. Translation in the Sciences and Social Sciences
   New Delhi, 8 July 2006
3. Workshop on National Translation Mission
   Mysore, 12-13 April 2007

National Knowledge Network

Stakeholders Workshop on Research and Educational Network for India, New Delhi, 10 October 2006

Portal

1. Stakeholders Workshop on India Energy Portal, New Delhi, 25 June 2007
2. Stakeholders Workshop on India Biodiversity Portal, New Delhi, 16 October 2007

School Education

1. National Workshop, New Delhi, 29 July 2006
2. Listening forum with school children and NKC Chairman, Mr. Sam Pitroda, New Delhi, 13 January 2007
3. Regional Level Workshops
   i. Regional Workshop on School Education for the Southern Region (Karnataka, Andhra Pradesh, Tamil Nadu, Puducherry, Kerala), National Institute of Advances Studies (NIAS), Bangalore, 17-18 July 2007
   ii. Regional Workshop on School Education for the Central Region (Uttar Pradesh, Bihar, Jharkhand, Madhya Pradesh), Indian Institute of Management, Lucknow, 3-4 August 2007
   iii. Regional Workshop on School Education for the Eastern Region (West Bengal and Orissa), Indian Council of Social Science Research (Eastern Branch), Kolkata, 25-26 August 2007
   iv. Regional Workshop on School Education for the North-East Region (Arunachal Pradesh, Assam, Manipur, Meghalaya, Mizoram, Nagaland, Sikkim and Tripura), Indian Institute of Technology, Guwahati 11-12 September 2007
   v. Regional Workshop on School Education for the Northern Region (Jammu and Kashmir, Punjab, Haryana, Himachal Pradesh, Uttarakhand, Uttar Pradesh, Chandigarh (UT), Delhi), India Habitat Centre, Delhi, 20 November 2007
   vi. Regional Workshop on School Education for the Western Region (Maharashtra, Chhattisgarh, Rajasthan, Gujarat), Indian Institute of Education, Pune, 23 November 2007
4. National Seminar involving educationists, academics, representatives from the government, private schools and civil society organisations, New Delhi, 10 December 2007

Muslim Education

National Workshop, New Delhi, 23 September 2006.

Vocational Education

National Workshop, New Delhi, 11 April 2006

Open and Distance Education

Symposium on Open Educational Resources, New Delhi, 31 July 2006

Intellectual Property Rights

Symposium on Intellectual Property Rights (IPR) Protection and Management in India, New Delhi, 10 October 2006

Science and Technology

1. Brainstorming Session for the identification of High Impact Areas in Science and Technology, New Delhi, 31 July 2006
2. Meeting with Dr. Bement, Director, National Science Foundation (NSF), USA, New Delhi, 17-18 October 2006

More Talented Students in Maths and Science

Workshops on attracting more talented students in Maths and Science held at:

1. Tata Institute of Fundamental Research, Mumbai, 16 August 2007
2. IISc, Bangalore, 23 August 2007
3. South Campus, Delhi University, 10 September 2007
4. SN Bose Centre for Basic Sciences, Kolkata, 5 October 2007

Innovation

NKC-PHDCCI Workshop on Innovation in Small and Medium Enterprises

1. Taj Residency, Lucknow 6 November 2006
2. PHD Chamber of Commerce and Industry New Delhi, 18 December 2006
3. Indian Institute of Management Bangalore, 5 January 2007

Entrepreneurship

1. Entrepreneurship Pilot Discussion, New Delhi, 23 December 2006
2. Interviews for Entrepreneurship Study
   - i. Pune, Mahratta Chambers of Commerce, Industries and Agriculture (MCCIA) 13-15 February 2007
   - ii. Kolkata, Bengal Chambers of Commerce and Industry (BCCI), 18-20 July 2007
   - iii. Chennai, Confederation of Indian Industries (CII), Chennai, 22-24 August 2007
   - iv. Ahmedabad, Gujarat Chambers of Commerce and Industry (GCCI), 10-12 September 2007
   - v. Hyderabad, Federation of Andhra Pradesh Chambers of Commerce and Industry (FAPCCI), 18-20 September 2007
   - vi. Bengaluru, Federation of Karnataka Chambers of Commerce and Industry (FKCCI), 24-26 October 2007

Agriculture

Workshop on Agricultural Research and Extension, New Delhi, 15 January 2007

Public Outreach

Libraries

1. Library Outreach Workshop, Indian Institute of Technology, New Delhi, 19 May 2007
2. Library Outreach Programme for the Northeastern States, Mizoram University, Aizawl, 5 June 2007
3. Library Outreach Programme for the Eastern Region National Library, Kolkata, 7 June 2007
4. Library Outreach Programme for Libraries in the Social Science sector, NASSDOC, New Delhi, 2 July 2007
5. Library Outreach Programme for School Libraries NCERT, New Delhi, 20 July 2007

Higher Education

1. Discussion on NKC Recommendations
   - i. Select College Principals, New Delhi, 12 September 2007
   - ii. National Seminar: Vice-Chancellors, Academicians, Teacher Associations, Bangalore University, Centre for Educational and Social Studies, Bangalore, 19-20 September 2007
   - iii. Select College Principals St. Xavier's College Mumbai, 28 September 2007
   - iv. Vice-Chancellors, Head of departments, North Eastern Hill University (NEHU) Shillong, Meghalaya, 22 November 2007
   - v. Select College Principals Patna, 10 December 2007
   - vi. Select College Principals Pune, 8 December 2007
2. Higher Education Summit, FICCI, 2-3 November 2007
3. Consultative meeting on Perspectives on Higher Education, USEFI, 15 November 2007
4. Right to Education-Actions Now Aspen Institute and CII 19 December 2007

Presentations to State Governments

1. Bihar Secretariat, Patna Bihar, 8 January 2008

2. Uttar Pradesh Secretariat, Lucknow
Uttar Pradesh, 3 January 2008

3. Karnataka Secretariat, Bangalore
Karnataka, 4 December 2007

4. Orissa Secretariat, Bhubaneswar
Orissa, 27 November 2007

5. Himachal Pradesh Secretariat, Shimla
Himachal Pradesh, 21 November 2007

6. Jharkhand Secretariat, Ranchi
Jharkhand, 13 November 2007

7. Assam Secretariat, Guwahati
Assam, 29 October 2007

8. Madhya Pradesh Secretariat, Bhopal
Madhya Pradesh, 18 October 2007

9. Chhattisgarh Secretariat, Raipur
Chhattisgarh, 27 September 2007

10. Maharashtra Secretariat, Mumbai
Maharashtra, 24 September 2007

11. Punjab Secretariat, Chandigarh
Punjab, 27 August 2007

12. West Bengal Secretariat, Kolkata
West Bengal, 10 August 2007

13. Uttarakhand Secretariat, Dehradun
Uttarakhand, 6 August 2007

14. Rajasthan Secretariat, Jaipur
Rajasthan, 4 August 2007

15. Tamil Nadu Secretariat, Chennai
Tamil Nadu, 14 July 2007

16. Puducherry Secretariat, Puducherry
Puducherry, 13 July 2007

17. MCRHRD, Hyderabad
Andhra Pradesh, 25 June 2007

18. Delhi Secretariat, Delhi
Delhi, 5 June 2007

Members of Working Groups 2007

Health Information Network

1. Prof. N.K. Ganguly
Chairman, Indian Council of Medical Research

2. Dr. B.S. Bedi
Adviser, CDAC & Media Lab Asia
Former Senior Director & Head Med.
Electronics and Telemedicine Dept. of IT
Govt. of India (GoI)

3. Mr. Partha Chattopadhya
CD (DRS), Ministry of Health and Family
Welfare, (GoI)

4. Dr. Shiban Ganju
Convener, I HIND

5. Dr. Shiva Kumar
Member, National Advisory Council

6. Dr. Ramakrishnan
Director General, C-DAC

7. Prof. K. Srinath Reddy
President, Public Health Foundation of India

8. Mr. Rajdeep Sahrawat
Vice President, NASSCOM

9. Mr. Raj Shah
CEO, Capital Technology Information Services (CTIS)

10. Dr. Y.K. Sharma
Deputy Director General, NIC

Legal Education

1. Justice M. Jagannadha Rao, Chairperson
Former Judge, Supreme Court of India Former
Chairperson, Law Commission of India

2. Justice Leila Seth, Member
Former Judge, Delhi High Court
Former Chief Justice, High Court of Himachal Pradesh

3. Prof. N.R. Madhava Menon, Member
Former Vice-Chancellor, National Law School of India
University (NLSIU), Bangalore
Former Vice-Chancellor, West Bengal National
University of Juridical Sciences (NUJS) Kolkata
Former Director, National Judicial Academy, Bhopal

4. Mr. P.P. Rao, Member
Senior Advocate, Supreme Court of India

5. Prof. B.S. Chimni, Member
Former Vice-Chancellor, NUJS, Kolkata
Professor, Jawaharlal Nehru University
New Delhi

6. Mr. Nishith Desai, Member
   Managing Partner, Nishith Desai Associates
   Mumbai

7. Dr. Mohan Gopal, Member
   Former Vice-Chancellor, NLSIU, Bangalore
   Director, National Judicial Academy, Bhopal

Medical Education

1. Dr. Sneh Bhargava
   AIIMS, New Delhi

2. Dr. N.G. Desai
   IHBAS, Delhi

3. Dr. N.K. Ganguly
   ICMR, New Delhi

4. Dr. V.I. Mathan
   CMC, Vellore

5. Dr. G.N. Rao
   LVP Eye Institute, Hyderabad

6. Dr. S.K. Reddy
   AIIMS, New Delhi

7. Dr. S.K. Sarin
   G.B. Pant Hospital, New Delhi

8. Dr. D. Shetty
   Narayana Hrudayalaya, Bangalore

9. Dr. K.K. Talwar
   PGIMER, Chandigarh

10. Dr. P.N. Tandon
    National Brain Research Centre, Haryana

11. Dr. M.S. Valiathan
    INSA

Management Education

1. Mr. P.M. Sinha
   Pepsi India

2. Prof. Amitava Bose
   IIM, Kolkata

3. Prof. Jahar Saha
   IIM, Ahmedabad

4. Prof. K.R.S. Murthy
   IIM, Bangalore

5. Dr. Nachiket Mor
   Dy. Managing Director, ICICI Bank, Mumbai

6. Mr. R. Gopalkrishnan
   Executive Director, Tata Sons, Mumbai

Open and Distance Education

1. Prof. Ram Takwale (Chairman)
   Former Vice-Chancellor, Indira Gandhi National Open University, Yashwantrao Chavan Maharashtra Open University

2. Prof. Badrinath Koul
   Former Pro-Vice-Chancellor, IGNOU

3. Prof. Salil Mishra,
   Reader of History, School of Social Sciences, IGNOU

4. Prof. Parvin Sinclair
   Director, School of Sciences, IGNOU

5. Dr. Vijay Kumar
   Assistant Provost and Director of Academic Computing, MIT

6. Prof. V.S. Prasad
   Director, National Assessment and Accreditation Council (NAAC), Bangalore
   Former Vice-Chancellor, Dr. B.R. Ambedkar Open University, Hyderabad

7. Dr. B.S. Bhatia
   Former Director, Development and Education Computing Unit (DECU) Space Applications Centre (SAC), Ahmedabad

8. Mr. Rajendra Pawar
   Chairman, NIIT

9. Dr. Surabhi Banerjee
   Vice Chancellor, Netaji Subhas Open University (NSOU), Kolkata

Open Educational Resources

1. Dr. V. Balaji
   Head, KMS (Knowledge Management and Sharing) Group, ICRISAT (International Crops Research Institute for the Semi-Arid Tropics)

2. Dr. K. Mangala Sunder
   Webcourses Coordinator, NPTEL (National Programme on Technology Enhanced Learning), Indian Institute of Technology (IIT) Madras

3. Dr. Rajan Welukar
   Vice-Chancellor, Yashwantrao Chavan Maharashtra Open University

4. Dr. H.P. Dikshit
   NBHM Professor, PDPM, Indian Institute of Information Technology
5. Anand Patwardhan
   Executive Director, Technology Information Forecasting and Assessment Council (TIFAC)
6. Dr. Subbiah Arunachalam
   MS Swaminathan Foundation
7. Dr. Vijay Kumar
   Co-convener Asst. Provost and Director of Academic Computing, MIT
8. Dr. A.S. Kolaskar
   Convener Advisor, National Knowledge Commission

Traditional Health Systems

1. Mr. Ravi Prasad
   CEO, Himalaya Drugs
2. Mr. Amit Agarwal,
   Director R&D, Natural Remedies, Bangalore
3. Mr. S.R. Rao
   Head (HR), EXIM Bank, Mumbai
4. Dr. B.G. Krishnaswamy
   Representative, Arya Vaidya Pharmacy, Coimbatore
5. Dr. Narendra Bhatt
   CEO, The ZANDU Pharmaceutical Works Ltd. Mumbai
6. Dr. Bhushan Patwardhan
   Professor & Director, Interdisciplinary School of Health Sciences, University of Pune
7. Dr. G.G. Gangadharan
   Joint Director, FRLHT, Bangalore
8. Dr. Padma Venkat
   Joint Director, FRLHT, Bangalore Vaidya Vilas Nanal Pune
9. Dr. Urmila Thatte
   M.D., D.N.B., Ph.D., Dept., of Clinical Pharmacology, TN Medical College & BYL Nair Hospital, Mumbai
10. Mr. B.S. Sajwan
    CEO, NMPB, GoI, New Delhi
11. Dr. Vasantha Muthuswamy
    Sr. Deputy Director General & Chief, ICMR, New Delhi
12. Mr. Verghese Samuel
    JS, AYUSH
13. Dr. P.M. Bhargava
    Former Vice-Chairman, KC, GoI
14. Darshan Shankar
    FRLHT

Agriculture

1. Dr. Bala Ravi (Chairman)
   Advisor
   M.S. Swaminathan Research Foundation
2. Dr. Suman Sahai
   Convener, Gene Campaign
3. Dr. Rajeswari Raina
   Senior Research Fellow
   Centre for Policy Research
4. Dr. Rasheed Sulaiman V
   Director, Centre for Research on Innovation and Science Policy
5. Dr. Ramanjaneyulu G.V.
   Executive Director, Centre for Sustainable Agriculture
6. Mr. Debashish Mitra
   Founder and Managing Director
   Calypso Foods
7. Dr. Vijay Jawandhia
   Shetkari Sanghatana Paik
8. Dr. P. Geethakutty
   Head, Centre for Gender Studies
   National Institute of Rural Development
9. Prof. S. Venku Reddy
   Executive Director, Participatory Rural Development Initiatives
10. Dr. N.K. Sanghi
    Adviser, Watershed Support Services and Activities Network (WASSAN)
11. Mr. R. Kevichusa (retd.)
    Former Official Department of Agriculture
    Government of Nagaland

More Students in Maths and Science

1. Prof. J. Sashidhara Prasad
   Ex Vice-Chancellor, University of Mysore
2. Mr. Ramji Raghavan
   Chairman, Agastya International Foundation

3. Prof. Dipankar Chatterji
   Convener, KVPY Program, IISc
4. Dr. Savithri Singh
   Principal, Acharya Narendra Dev College
5. Prof. L.K. Maheshwari
   Director, Birla Institute of Technology and Science
6. Dr. M. Vidyasagar
   Executive Vice President
   Tata Consultancy Services
7. Prof. S.C. Lakhotia
   Banaras Hindu University

Members of the National Knowledge Commission

Sam Pitroda (Chairman)

Ashok Ganguly

P. Balaram

Jayati Ghosh

Deepak Nayyar

Nandan Nilekani

Sujatha Ramdorai

Amitabh Mattoo

Advisors and Staff

S. Regunathan (Advisor)

Kiran Datar (Advisor)

C.N.S. Nair (Advisor)

Kumud Bansal (Advisor)

Amlanjyoti Goswami (Research Associate)

Sukhman Randhawa (Research Associate)

Namita Dalmia (Research Associate)

Megha Pradhan (Research Associate)

Vikas Bagri (Research Associate)

Deepti Ayyanki (Research Assistant)

Bindeshwary Rai (Research Assistant)

Aashima Seth (Executive Assistant)

Former Members, Advisors and Staff

Andre Beteille (Member)

P.M. Bhargava (Member)

Pratap Bhanu Mehta (Member)

Ashok Kolaskar (Advisor)

Kalpana Dasgupta (Advisor)

Razia Sultan Ismail Abbasi (Advisor)

Sunil Bahri (Executive Director)

Mitakshara Kumari (Research Associate)

Rohan Mukherjee (Research Associate)

Shriya Anand (Research Associate)

Shomikho Raha (Research Associate)

Kaushik Barua (Research Associate)

Aditi Saraf (Research Associate)

Pallavi Raghavan (Research Associate)

Pratibha Bajaj (Research Associate)

Kanan Dhru (Research Associate)